W9-ASG-157

READINGS
FROM BRITISH DRAMA

READINGS FROM BRITISH DRAMA

EXTRACTS FROM BRITISH AND IRISH PLAYS

BY

ALLARDYCE NICOLL M.A.

PROFESSOR OF ENGLISH LANGUAGE AND LITERATURE IN THE
UNIVERSITY OF LONDON (EAST LONDON COLLEGE)
AUTHOR OF "BRITISH DRAMA" "AN INTRODUCTION TO
DRAMATIC THEORY" "THE DEVELOPMENT OF THE THEATRE" ETC.

NEW YORK
THOMAS Y. CROWELL COMPANY
PUBLISHERS

1929

Printed in Great Britain at THE BALLANTYNE PRESS *by*
SPOTTISWOODE, BALLANTYNE & CO. LTD.
Colchester, London & Eton

PREFACE

THIS collection of representative passages from British and Irish plays is intended to be a companion volume to *British Drama*; it provides, as it were, the illustrative quotations which could not be included within the pages of that general history of the drama. On the other hand, this volume is not merely a dependent or supplementary one. It has been designed to stand by itself if need be, presenting by quotation and comment a broad outline of the main movements in the world of the theatre from medieval times to the present day. I have emphasized in the Introduction my belief that a play should be studied not by scenes, but as a whole; yet something may be said in favour of the extraction of scenes or passages when an endeavour is being made to follow the development of dramatic style and the larger tendencies of a period. In the selection of passages I have made no attempt to choose the most beautiful, and in this respect the plan of my work differs completely from that of the famous *Specimens of English Dramatic Poets*. There the aim was to take the finest and most effective scenes, and to present æsthetic criticism upon their loveliness. My aim is purely historical, and I have inserted several passages weak or ridiculous in themselves because these seemed to be symbolic or representative of general movements in the age. Moreover, I have frequently descended to spheres of dramatic writing—such as eighteenth-century opera and nineteenth-century melodrama—which are usually neglected entirely by the critics, because productive of no real literary worth. Specimens of these are included here, for, although intrinsically of no value, the spheres themselves had a very considerable influence on the later developments in the theatre. The result is that this book contains extracts from a large number of lesser-known plays which have either never been reprinted

5

or have been reprinted only in limited and 'scholarly' editions. Some of these extracts seem to me worthy of praise, others are almost below the scope of serious æsthetic criticism ; but all, I believe, are representative, and are accordingly calculated to give the student of our English stage a clearer perspective and a deeper appreciation of those general and larger developments which must be taken into account along with the particular manifestations of dramatic artistry. Many of the plays included here could not be obtained in any but the major (or in a very few specialized) libraries ; the majority could not be easily reprinted in full in an ordinary student's edition—indeed, would be of little use if thus reprinted in full ; so that an endeavour has been made in planning this collection to serve as far as possible the purposes of the student who has a certain knowledge of the greater masterpieces of our stage, but who desires to round off that knowledge by gaining some appreciation of the literary movements as a whole. It will be understood, however, that as 'representative quality' was taken as the aim of this volume there had to be included here many well-known plays in order that a true perspective might be gained. Some of these well-known plays are readily obtainable in complete texts, but I hope that I have been able to extract from them such scenes as are valuable for the general study of the drama of their times, and to indicate points of interest connecting those scenes with others from plays of different authorship.

As far as possible the passages given here reproduce the original texts. Old spellings and capitalization have been retained, save for the expansion of contractions and the correction of one or two obvious printers' errors. Where the original punctuation does not confuse the sense it has been retained, and the necessary alterations or additions have been as conservative as possible. For the sake of uniformity speech-headings in early plays have been standardized, and stage directions have been italicized throughout. A very few stage directions, mostly marking 'asides,' have been added, and in some instances short introductory stage directions have been inserted in order to make the passages readily comprehensible. In general, my aim has been,

6

PREFACE

where confusion could not arise, to leave the texts as these appeared in the first or in standard corrected editions.

I have to thank many modern dramatists for their assistance in the preparation of the materials for this book ; and likewise many publishers of copyright texts. I have, I trust, indicated my full indebtedness to each in the notes to the separate extracts.

A. N.

August 1928

CONTENTS

9

EXTRACTS FROM BRITISH & IRISH PLAYS

III. LATE SIXTEENTH CENTURY

IV. EARLY SEVENTEENTH CENTURY

CONTENTS

V. RESTORATION

VI. EIGHTEENTH CENTURY

EXTRACTS FROM BRITISH & IRISH PLAYS

VII. NINETEENTH CENTURY (TO 1870)

CONTENTS

VIII. THE MODERN PERIOD

EXTRACTS FROM BRITISH & IRISH PLAYS

READINGS
FROM BRITISH DRAMA

INTRODUCTION

IT may seem somewhat strange to introduce this book of
selections from the works of our dramatists by stating,
and stating categorically, that drama is not to be studied
by mere scenes alone. Unquestionably Lamb's *Specimens
of English Dramatic Poets* had an evil effect in the early
nineteenth century, because that volume led budding playwrights—and even older playwrights who ought to have
known better—into the belief that a tragedy or a comedy
could be built up out of a series of individual scenes, or that
the presence of two or three poetically effective passages
could entitle a drama to almost unqualified praise. The
truth is—and this must never be forgotten—that a play is
a play, a complete unity to be considered as a whole, and
ultimately dependent for its success upon its theatrical
qualities. Poetry may enter in as it does in Shakespeare's
tragedies, but only as an element subordinate to the rest,
as a beauty perhaps, but a beauty which is ornamental
rather than structural. When we study the history of our
drama, therefore, it behoves us to read entire plays, endeavouring with an inner eye to visualize these plays, giving
material form to the spirit characters imprisoned in paper
and print, seeing these characters move before us as the
lines they speak are carried to our brains. Only thus can
we come to an appreciation either of the worth of individual
dramas or of the main tendencies in the development of our
dramatic literature. This volume, then, is not intended as
a substitute for the complete texts of the authors here
represented.

While this is so, it is, on the other hand, true that few
readers or students of the stage can devote sufficient time to
peruse, far less to see represented, as many plays as might

serve to give them a conception of the larger developments in dramatic literature, and it is also true that many highly representative plays have never been reprinted and are to be seen only in the greater libraries such as the British Museum. It is not that these plays are necessarily rare. It may be difficult to obtain copies of some earlier dramas because of their excessive rarity or high commercial value ; but what ordinary library or what ordinary reader possesses copies of eighteenth-century sentimental comedies or nine-teenth-century melodramas ? Perhaps a few shillings will secure them when they are found in a bookseller's stock, but the finding is precisely the difficulty. Nor can these minor dramas be entirely ignored ; if we are to have any general idea of dramatic development they must be taken into account both for the taste of the times and for the reactions to which they gave rise. This book, therefore, is intended to provide, alongside extracts from greater dramas, at least short specimens of the work of many authors who might otherwise remain for the majority nothing but names in a text-book.

Because of this, the aim in selecting has been to choose rather representative than beautiful passages. This is no volume of elegant extracts from the drama ; it is designed to show scenes typical both of the work of separate authors and of the tendencies of a period. Attempts have been made to include, besides the selections from the plays of greater dramatists, passages culled from plays popular in their own time, but now forgotten. Shakespeare, for obvious reasons, finds no place here ; it is assumed that he, at least, is known to every reader. At the same time, several sections in this book have been inserted largely because comparison with Shakespeare's plays will help toward an understanding of his greatness and of the greatness of the Elizabethan age.

While the primary object of this book is to provide first material for a study of British drama, it has also another purpose. The qualities which make a play great are, perhaps, in the first instance, treatment of plot (in other words, constructive power) and character-drawing. The re-fashioning of Cinthio's story and the individualizing of

16

INTRODUCTION

Othello, Desdemona, and Iago are those things which made *Othello* a great play. Obviously such dramatic qualities can be studied only when we read plays in their entirety ; but in addition to these there is one other element which must go to the making of a great drama, and this, it seems, has not been sufficiently analysed from the theatrical point of view. A dramatist, just as any other literary man, has to express himself by means of words, words which the actor in his turn interprets on the stage, giving passion and tone to what is provided for him in cold print. We have had many studies on the subject of Shakespeare's poetry ; the language itself of Shakespeare's contemporaries has been closely analysed ; but there have been few attempts made to consider this language from the point of view of the theatre. In other words, the medium of the dramatist—language applied to the requirements of the theatre—has been largely neglected by critics. A gloriously poetic passage, magnificent in its utterance when read in the study, may well be a blemish in a play, although an equally beautiful poetic passage may be given a definite theatrical value by an able playwright.[1]

This question of the medium of the dramatist is an all-important one. It has been said above that constructive power and the ability to draw character are the chief qualities which make the great dramatist ; but both of these qualities will be useless unless the author has formed for himself, or has been given by others, a medium through which he can explain his conceptions to his auditors. In many ways a study of dramatic glory and decline is a study of adequate and inadequate media. In the Middle Ages drama is fettered by rime, and the traditions of rime are carried on in the sixteenth-century ' fourteeners.' Then, just at the time when the great Elizabethan revival is about to burst forth, there come pioneers who express themselves in blank verse and in prose. Greene and Marlowe in the one medium and Gascoigne and Lyly in the other tentatively try the possibilities of each ; almost at once the triumph of a

---

[1] Any reader who is interested in this subject is confidently recommended to study carefully the dialogue-essay entitled *Histriophone* (1925) by Mr Bonamy Dobrée, as well as the subtle analysis by the same writer of Congreve's style (in the " World's Classics " Congreve).

Shakespeare is assured. It is not too much to say that, had Shakespeare been born in 1544 instead of 1564, he could never have given us *Hamlet* or *Othello*. His mind would have been so deeply occupied in the finding of a medium for himself that construction and character would have been neglected. His greatness is largely dependent upon the fact that he found already fashioned both a blank verse and a prose medium suited for his efforts. Shakespeare's prose, or rather the reconstructed prose of Greene and Lyly, with its imprisoned poetic flavour, was excellently suited for his romantic comedy, just as the stalwart prose of Ben Jonson, itself too with a slightly passionate colouring, was suited for the comedy of humours. When an age had passed new desires were attained, and this older prose style was no longer adequate. The history of the Restoration comedy of manners, therefore, is in one way a history of a new prose style which eventually found its master in Congreve. Dryden's able but rougher efforts, Etherege's aristocratically careless attempts, Wycherley's cynical strength—these led gradually to the flower which was *The Way of the World*. Again came a decline. Eighteenth-century drama is full of good scenes and of good characters, but the adequate medium is lost. Save for a few individual authors, the dramatists blunder along in the chillness of pseudo-classic blank verse or in the artificialities of sentimental prose. Nowhere more clearly is the difference between dramatic and non-dramatic prose seen than in this Augustan age. Many are the playwrights who pen passages which might have come from an Addison, a Steele, or a Richardson ; yet what was suitable for a *Spectator* essay or for a *Clarissa* letter loses all worth when translated to terms of the theatre. The same weakness is seen in nineteenth-century poetic tragedy. It is not to be denied that there are many passages in these plays of a distinctly beautiful character, but we search in vain from 1800 to 1850 for any play which will show verse dialogue which is essentially dramatic. Again, one may say that the failure of the romantic poets in the theatre was largely a failure to find a fitting medium for the expression of their ideas. It is my belief that in our modern period we have a dramatic development comparable

18

INTRODUCTION

with that of any preceding age, and once more it is seen that this modern movement springs from the discovery of an adequate medium. Nothing new or great could arise so long as the playwrights had only an undramatic blank verse, an artificial comedy prose, and a no less artificial melodramatic prose. Once Robertson had developed (however faultily) a new language the success of the future was certain. Translations of Ibsen showed the same style in variant forms, and by 1900 the fresh medium was established.

It is impossible here to attempt any detailed analysis of the qualities of a truly dramatic medium, whether in prose or in verse, for I wish the passages quoted to take first place and to speak for themselves. It would, however, be well worth the while of any student of the drama to consider carefully the qualities of a number of these passages, comparing, for example, a selection from an eighteenth-century sentimentalized play with, on the one hand, a Restoration comedy and, on the other, with some modern drama ; or else placing side by side a scene from Heywood or another Elizabethan with a scene from a romantic dramatist. One thing such a comparison will teach. While within a single period one dramatist may learn from another, while a Shakespeare may borrow from a Lyly or a Marlowe, the slavish imitation by writers of one period of the writers of another is doomed to failure. Much of the dismal distress of the romantic theatre came from weak copying of Elizabethan models. At the same time, while wholesale imitation is fatal, modern writers may learn much from the past. The modern comedy of manners goes back in more respects than one to the Restoration style, and Congrevian periods are echoed in our own times. The essential is that in imitation the thing imitated should have some qualities which bring it into touch with the later period. In copying Elizabethan blank verse Shelley and his companions were at fault ; in copying Restoration manners Mr Somerset Maugham and his companions are right.

This study of dramatic media may also be extended to other kindred spheres. Since very early times entertainers have known the value of dialect for the purpose of arousing laughter. The trick was used by mimic actors of Roman days; it appears in some of our early moralities; it was a part of the stock-in-trade of Italian *commedia dell' arte* companies; and in modern comedy the Irishman, the Scot, the Welshman, and the foreigner with his broken English have become familiar figures. Alongside the development of standard speech designed for the expression of comic material there has been evolved the use of non-standard speech, intended because of its variant from the norm to create merriment. Not only dialect, of course, has been called in here to aid the dramatist. The language of pedantry—indeed, the peculiar language of any specialized profession—when intruded into daily life provides the same contrast as does that of a peasant conversing with a peer. The old Dottore of Italian improvised comedy is cousin-german to Holofernes in *Love's Labour's Lost*, and Pistol has his elder brother in Capitano Rinoceronte. So, too, the affectations, either of high Society or of those who would ape high Society, have been freely utilized. Malapropisms on the one hand and the artificial oaths of a Lord Foppington on the other have caused many a laugh in the theatre. The comic writer has more than one instrument at his command, and in those periods when comedy flourished we see that the instruments are most brilliantly polished and most carefully tended. The adage that a good workman never quarrels with his tools may be true; but it is also true that a good workman will usually keep his tools in better trim and will have a surer sense of those tools which will best serve his purpose than the mere journeyman or the vapid amateur. The tools of drama are its media of expression; its materials are man and his ways.

The opportunities of the dramatist for evolving, if not fresh media, at least fresh uses for media already in existence, are well shown by the development in our own days of new types of dialect drama. Dialect originally intruded only for a particular character or a particular group of characters, the playwright endeavouring to throw these figures into relief against the surrounding world of normal persons. Teg or Teague in Howard's *The Committee* is an instance in point. It was only in later times that men came to realize that a completely dialectal comedy could be successful. *The Play-*

boy of the Western World is the triumph of the new conception, where the dialect (expressing a certain sphere of life removed by certain peculiarities from 'normal' city existence) is used, not to form a contrast with something else, but in and for itself. The whole success of the Irish school depends upon the realization that in this use of dialect unrelieved lies a veritable treasure-trove for the dramatist, and similar attempts are being made in the realm of Lowland Scots. Still further, it has been found in recent years that dialect has powers beyond the mere expression of the comic. In the eighteenth century, when the Irish brogue (or what passed theatrically as such) was heard on the stage, the audience knew that the cue had come for laughter ; to-day the Irish brogue may as easily be the cue for tears or for that emotion of tragedy which, because of its profundity and terror, brings with it thoughts and passions beyond the reach of tears. *Riders to the Sea* stands in relation to tragedy in the same position as *The Playboy of the Western World* stands in relation to comedy, and, once more, it is not alone. The Southern Irish has been utilized for serious plays by a whole group of dramatists ; Mr St John Ervine has shown the potentialities of Belfast speech ; in Scotland *Campbell of Kilmhor* has given at least the suggestion of an independent but kindred development. In each of these groups it has to be noted that the medium of expression is inextricably welded with the material of the drama. Synge's tragedy could not convey the impression it does had he not worked out for himself that peculiar speech, half literary and half naturalistic, which provided for the Irish dialects the equivalent of Dante's cardinal and aulic Italian tongue. If we turn the dialogue of *Riders to the Sea* into standard English and read it without a trace of Irish inflection, the whole drama becomes meaningless.

This leads to a consideration of the relations subsisting between the form of expression and the material employed. In the following series of extracts I have given a number of 'ghostly' passages, and again these might well be compared one with another, and each in turn brought alongside the introduction of the supernatural in Shakespeare's plays. Shakespeare succeeds in evoking the impression of the immaterial in *Hamlet* largely through his language. In other words, the basis is laid by the language for the acceptance of the ghostly apparition. The short nervous words of the watch indicate suspense ; the darkness, the chill—all called forth by the use of words—contribute to the general impression ; so that when eventually Hamlet's father appears on the stage we are prepared to accept him for what he purports to be—a vision from another world. We may contrast these scenes with the corresponding scenes in Dryden's *The Conquest of Granada*. Here no preparation is made, and as a consequence the mind is not ready to accept the ghost as a ghost. Moreover, the language all moves on the material plane ; its images are concrete ; and we are never lifted, as we are by Shakespeare, to a level where the spiritual and the substantial seem to meet. This study of the introduction of the supernatural might lead toward a study of what may be called language in crisis. Dryden's ghost is too prolix, and many dramatists have forgotten that words in themselves are of no use in a play. When they approach a scene of cardinal importance they are inclined to let loose upon their auditors a wealth of words which, beautiful though they may be, are not suited to the calling forth of that impression at which they aim. In Shakespeare's hands a Lear is dying, a Cordelia dead, a whole world in ruin and torment, and at the very height of the tragic emotion come those famous lines when the aged King, uttering his

> " Never, never, never, never, never !
> Pray you, undo this button,"

would seem to, yet does not, descend from a higher to a bathetic plane. The simplicity of the lines, their directness, their concrete substance, have a strength which otherwise would have been unattainable. Another dramatist would have immersed Lear in a flood of rich and poetic words ; Shakespeare knew that, when the highest passions are stirred, external beauty fades to insignificance. Helen of Troy has no part in the grief of Andromache.

Even in these short passages this welding of language and substance (or this failure to harmonize the two) may be studied, comparisons may be made, and estimates formed of the respective powers of varying periods and of different dramatists. Again, I should insist that such a study is in no way a substitute for the reading of whole plays, but the analysis and comparison of the shorter passages may perhaps serve to call attention to certain features which might be lost in more widely extended reading, and may lead toward the closer and detailed examination of other scenes not represented here.

I. MEDIEVAL

THERE is no possibility of discovering a homogeneous entity in medieval drama. A score of diverse elements, no doubt, went to the building up of the great mystery cycles ; material records of many of these elements have now vanished beyond recall ; so that all we may do is to endeavour, by the exercise of the historical imagination, to picture the general conditions amid which the drama during the thirteenth, fourteenth, and fifteenth centuries once more rose to a position of social importance.

The mystery cycle forms the centre of our study. Clearly it would be impossible to represent here more than a mere fragment of these vast compilations, but an attempt has been made, by taking the Shrewsbury fragment as illustrative of the liturgical stage, the Towneley passage as illustrative of a certain realism, and the York passage as illustrative of the more bombastic elements, to indicate at least some of the main features of this special form of drama.

From the mystery play springs the morality with its allegorical characters in place of the Biblical figures shown in the earlier type. In spite of the use of personifications, however, the morality marks a distinct advance, both because it encouraged inventiveness and because it permitted the introduction of more realistic scenes than are to be discovered in the mystery sphere. *Wealth and Health* presents a Dutch Hance or Hans alongside of Ill-will and Shrewd-wit, and Bale's *Kynge Johan* points forward toward the Elizabethan chronicle-history play.

With the *Interludium de Clerico et Puella* we turn back —chronologically. It seems to be undeniable that the Middle Ages—and the Dark Ages before them—knew of a certain form of secular drama. This secular drama is traceable back to the Roman mime, which outwardly died a slow and lingering death when the barbaric hordes swept down upon the Imperial city. One readily realizes that records

24

of this mimic entertainment would be difficult to find in an age when religion coloured the whole of social life, especially so when much of this entertainment must have been of an improvised character. It would be of a farcical nature, and might very well be—in all probability always was—vulgar and obscene. The *Interludium* shows its impress on English drama, while there are cognate French texts which point toward the existence of the same species abroad. Heywood's early sixteenth-century work is based partly on French examples of this type, and this, forming a link between the new and the old, has to be brought into connexion with the earlier medieval forms.

All of this medieval drama is in verse, sometimes highly complicated, as in the verse of the mysteries, sometimes reduced to couplets in morality plays. It is used flexibly enough by some anonymous writers (particularly by that unknown comic genius who created the famous "Mak" playlet of the shepherds), but it forms a fetter to free expression. It was not until the sixteenth century that man discovered other media.

1. SHREWSBURY FRAGMENT

Officium Pastorum

The so-called "Shrewsbury fragments" were first discovered in the year 1890; they are preserved in a manuscript at the library attached to Shrewsbury School, and are of particular interest because they represent a stage of drama between the pure elaboration of the liturgy and the later secular treatment of Biblical themes. Particular notice should be taken of the 'narrative' portions in Latin, followed by the dramatic representation of the narrative, the little play as yet remaining dependent upon the service which it was intended to embellish. Beyond this point of interest the Shrewsbury fragments are important because they are among the earliest actors' 'parts' which time has vouchsafed to us. This *Officium Pastorum* gives the text of the play as prepared for the actor impersonating the Third Shepherd, only the cues of the others being inserted.

(The text was first given by Professor Skeat in *The Academy* (1890); it has since been presented by J. M. Manly in *Specimens of Pre-Shakespearean Drama* (1897), and by O. Waterhouse in *The Non-Cycle Mystery Plays* (Early English Text Society, 1909), from the latter of which this extract is taken.)

The Shepherds see the Star and welcome Christ

Pastores erant in regione eadem uigilantes et custodientes gregem suum. Et ecce angelus Domini astitit iuxta illos et timuerunt timore magno.[1]

[II Pastor.]	We, Tib !
III Pastor.	Telle on !
[II Pastor.]	. . . . þe [2] nyght.
III Pastor.	Brether, what may þis be, Þus bright to man & best ? [3]
[II Pastor.]	. . . . at hand.
III Pastor.	Whi say ȝe [4] so ?
[II Pastor.]	. . . . warand.

III Pastor.	Suche siȝt was neuer sene
	  Before in oure Iewery ;
	Sum merueles wil hit mene
	  Þat mun [5] be here in hy.[6]

[II Pastor.]	. . . . a sang.

III Pastor.	Ȝe lye, bothe, by þis liȝt,
	  And raues as recheles royes ! [7]
	Hit was an angel briȝt
	  Þat made þis nobulle noyes.[8]

[II Pastor.]	. . . . of prophecy.

III Pastor.	He said a barn schuld be
	  In þe burgh of Bedlem born ;
	And of þis, mynnes me,[9]
	  Oure fadres fond beforn.

[II Pastor.]	. . . . Iewus kyng.

III Pastor.	Now may we se þe same
	  Euen in oure pase puruayed ;
	Þe angel nemed his name——
	  " Crist, Saueour," he saied.

[II Pastor.]	. . . . not raue.

III Pastor.	Ȝone brightnes wil vs bring
	  Vnto þat blisful boure ; [10]
	For solace schal we syng
	  To seke oure Saueour.

Transeamus usque Bethelem et uideamus hoc verbum quod factum est, quod fecit Dominus et ostendit nobis.[11]

[II Pastor.]	. . . . to knawe.
III Pastor.	For no-þing thar vs drede, But thank God of all gode ;

---

[1] Presumably this passage, set to music, was sung or intoned by choir or priest. [2] þ = th. [3] beast. [4] ye (ȝ = y or gh). [5] must. [6] high.
[7] royes = rois or kings ; probably a reference to an early Herod.
[8] noise. [9] I remember. [10] bower.
[11] Likewise sung or chanted.

MEDIEVAL

Þis light euer wil vs lede
    To fynde þat frely fode.[1]
[II PASTOR.] . . . . . . I mene.
III PASTOR. A! loke to me, my Lord dere,
    All if I put me noght in prese![2]
    To suche a prince without pere
    Haue I no presand[3] þat may plese.
    But lo! a horn-spone haue I here
    Þat may herbar[4] an hundrith pese:[5]
    Þis gift I gif þe with gode chere,
    Suche dayntese wil do no disease.
    Fare-wele now, swete swayn,
    God graunt þe lifyng lang!

2. TOWNELEY CYCLE

The Killing of Abel

The mystery cycle which is usually called the Towneley derives its name from the fact that it was preserved in manuscript at Towneley Hall in Lancashire. Various attempts have been made to discover its original home, but without definite success. The plays in the cycle are marked by an interesting realism of touch, particularly in the presentation of lower-class characters. The passage given below has been chosen from *The Killing of Abel*, and well shows how the medieval dramatists were able to introduce individuality even within the bounds of the Biblical story. Cain is a work-worn ploughman, and is approached by his sanctimonious brother Abel in the midst of his toil; the pair might have been found in any English village.

(The Towneley plays have been edited for the Early English Text Society by George England, with an introduction by A. W. Pollard (1897). From this the following extract is taken.)

CAIN IS IRRITATED BY ABEL'S SERMONIZING

ABELL. Broder, ther is none here aboute
    That wold the any grefe;[6]
    Bot, leif[7] brother, here my sawe[8]——
    It is the custom of oure law,
    All that wyrk as the wise
    Shall worship god with sacrifice.
    Oure fader vs bad, oure fader vs kend,[9]
    That oure tend[10] shuld be brend.[11]
    Com furth, brothere, and let vs gang
    To worship god; we dwell[12] full lang;

[1] lovely creature. [2] Even if I do not push myself forward. [3] present.
[4] harbour (= hold).   [5] peas.   [6] Who desires thee any harm.
[7] dear. [8] advice. [9] taught. [10] tenth or tithe. [11] burnt. [12] delay.

27

Gif we hym [1] parte of oure fee,
Corne or catall, wheder it be.[2]
And therfor, brother, let vs weynd,[3]
And first clens vs from the feynd [4]
Or [5] we make sacrifice;
Then blis withoutten end
Get we for oure seruyce,
Of hym that is oure saulis leche.[6]

    CAYN. How! let furth youre geyse,[7] the foxe
      will preche;
How long wilt thou me appech [8]
    With thi sermonyng?
Hold thi tong, yit I say,
Euen ther [9] the good wife strokid the hay;
Or sit downe in the dwill [10] way,
    With thi vayn carpyng.
Shuld I leife [11] my plogh & all thyng [12]
And go with the to make offeryng?
Nay! thou fyndys me not so mad!
Go to the dwill, and say I bad!
What gifys god the to rose [13] hym so?
Me gifys he noght bot soro and wo.[14]

    ABELL. Caym,[15] leife this vayn carpyng,
For god giffys the all thi lifyng.

    CAYN. Yit boroed I neuer a farthyng
Of hym, here my hend.[16]

    ABELL. Brother, as elders haue vs kend,
First shuld we tend with oure hend,
And to his lofyng [17] sithen [18] be brend.

    CAYN. My farthyng is in the preest [19] hand
Syn last tym I offyrd.

    ABELL. Leif brother, let vs be walkand; [20]
I wold oure tend were profyrd . . . .

    DEUS [*who suddenly appears*]. Cam, whi art thou
      so rebell
Agans thi brother abell?
Thar thou nowther flyte ne chyde, [21]
If thou tend right thou gettis thi mede; [22]
And be thou sekir,[23] if thou teynd fals,
Thou bese alowed ther after als.[24]

---

[1] Let us give him.   [2] whichever it be.
[3] wend, go.   [4] fiend.   [5] Ere.   [6] souls' leech.
[7] geese.   [8] accuse.   [9] where.   [10] devil's.
[11] leave.   [12] things.   [13] glorify.   [14] sorrow and woe.
[15] Caym and Cam are variants of Cayn or Cain.   [16] here is my hand.
[17] praise.   [18] afterward.   [19] priest's.   [20] walking.
[21] Thou must neither quarrel nor chide.
[22] If you give the tithes duly you will get your reward.
[23] sure.   [24] It is appointed to you accordingly.

MEDIEVAL

CAYN [*not seeing God*]. Whi, who is that hob-ouer-
the-wall?
We! who was that piped so small?
Come go we hens, for perels all;
    God is out of hys wit.
Com furth, abell, & let vs weynd;
Me thynk that god is not my freynd,
    On land then will I flyt.
  ABELL. A, Caym, brother, that is ill done.
  CAYN. No, but go we hens sone;
And if I may, I shall be
Ther as god shall not me see.
  ABELL. Dere brother, I will fayre
On feld ther [1] oure bestis ar,
To looke if thay be holgh [2] or full.
  CAYN. Na, na, abide, we haue a craw to pull;
Hark, speke with me or [3] thou go;
What! wenys thou to skape so? [4]
We! na! I aght the a fowll dispyte,[5]
And now is tyme that I hit qwite.
  ABELL. Brother, whi art thou so to me in ire?
  CAYN. We! theyf, whi brend thi tend so shyre? [6]
Ther myne did bot smoked
Right as it wold vs both haue choked.
  ABELL. Godis will I trow it were
That myn brened so clere;
If thyne smoked am I to wite? [7]
  CAYN. We! Yei! that shalt thou sore abite; [8]
With cheke bon,[9] or that I blyn,[10]
Shal I the & thy life twyn; [11]
So lig [12] down ther and take thi rest,
Thus shall shrewes be chastysed best.

3. YORK CYCLE

The Coming of the Three Kings to Herod

The York cycle is preserved in a single manuscript of the
first half of the fifteenth century, with a few additions of later
date. Most of the component 'pageants' or scenes must come
from at least a century earlier. In all forty-eight playlets and
one fragment are here preserved. The York cycle has neither
the comic depth shown in some sections of the Towneley series
nor the poetic power seen in some individual scenes elsewhere;

[1] where.   [2] hollow, empty.   [3] ere.
[4] do you think to escape me thus?   [5] I owe you a foul injury.
[6] clear.   [7] to blame.   [8] you'll pay for it sorely.
[9] cheekbone.   [10] before I stop.   [11] separate.   [12] lie.

EXTRACTS FROM BRITISH & IRISH PLAYS

but it is thoroughly representative in its treatment of the Biblical material, and displays a very interesting realism in its dialogue. The passage chosen is from the Goldsmiths' play of the *Adoration* ; it has been selected for the purpose of presenting Herod's ranting, which, with the exploits of the devils, seems to have had a constant attraction for medieval audiences. It may be noted that in all the cycles there is a tendency to make Herod (and other boastful monarchs) speak in rimed alliterative verse.

(The York cycle has been excellently edited by Lucy Toulmin Smith (Oxford, 1885). From this edition the extracts given below are taken.)

THE THREE KINGS COME TO HEROD'S COURT

I Rex. A! lorde, þat lenys þis lastand light,[1]
Whilke [2] has vs ledde oute of oure lande,
Kepe þe, sir kyng, and comly knyght,
And all þi folke þat we here fande.
    HEROD. Mahounde,[3] my god and most of myght,
Þat has myn hele [4] all in his hande,
He saffe you sirs! [5] semely in sight;
And telle vs now som new tythande.[6]
    II Rex. Sum shall we saie ȝou [7] sirs,
A sterne stud vs by-forne,[8].
That makis vs speak and spir [9]
Of ane þat is nowe borne.
    HEROD. Nowe borne! þat birthe halde I badde.
And certis, vn-witty [10] men ȝe werre
To lepe ouere lande to late [11] a ladde.
Say when lost ȝe hym? ought lange be-fore?
All wyse men will wene ȝe madde,
And therfore moffis it neuere more.[12]
    III Rex. Ȝis certis, such hartyng [13] haue we hadde,
We schall noȝt seys or we come thore.[14]
    HEROD. This were a wondir thyng!
Say, what barne shulde þat be?
    I Rex. Sir, he shall be kyng
Of Jewes and of Jude.
    HEROD. Kyng! in þe deuyl way, dogges, Fy!

---

[1] that grants this steady light (þ = th; *y* and *i* are interchangeable, as are *u* and *v*).　　[2] Which (= who).
[3] Herod in the mysteries regularly swears by Mahounde or Mohammed.
[4] health (= safety).　　[5] May he keep you safe, sirs !
[6] tidings (= news).　　[7] you (ȝ = y).
[8] A star stood before us.　　[9] inquire.　　[10] foolish.
[11] seek.　　[12] say no more about it.
[13] admonition.　　[14] cease ere we come there.

30

MEDIEVAL

Now I se wele ȝe roþe [1] and raue.
Be ony skymeryng of the skye
Wheu ȝe shulde knawe owthir kyng or knave?
Nay, I am kyng and non but I,
That shall ȝe kenne yff þat ȝe craue,
And I am juge of all Jury
To speke or spille,[2] to saie or saffe.
Swilke gawdes [3] may gretely greue,
To wittenesse þat neuere was.
    [I] REX. Nowe Lorde, we aske but leue,
Be youre poure to passe.
    HEROD. Whedir? in þe deuyls name.
To late a ladde here in my lande?
Fals harlottis, but [4] ȝe hye you hame,
Ȝe shall be bette [5] and boune in bande.
    II CONSUL. My lorde, to felle þis foule deffame,
Lattis all such wondir folle on hande,
And speres þaim sadly [6] of þe same,
So shall ȝe stabely [7] vndirstande
Þer mynde and þer menyng,
And takis gud tente [8] þam too.
    HEROD. I thanke þe of þis thyng,
And certis, so will I do.

HEROD HEARS NEWS OF THE THREE KINGS

    NUNTIUS. Mahounde with-outen pere
My lorde! ȝou saue! and see.
    HEROD. Messenger, come nere,
And, bewcher! [9] wele ye be.
What tydyngis telles þou, any? . . .
    NUNTIUS. I mette tow townes betwene
Thre kyngis with crounes clene,
Rydand full ryally.
    HEROD. A! my blys! boy, þon burdis to brode! [10] . . .
O we! by sonne and mone,
Þan tydis vs talis [11] to nyght.
Hopes þou þei will come sone
Hedir, as þei haue hight,[12]
For to telle me tythande?
    NUNTIUS. Nay, lorde, þat daunce is done.
    HEROD. Why, whedir are þei gone?
    NUNTIUS. Ilkone [13] in-to ther owne lande.

---

[1] boast.   [2] slay.   [3] Such tricks.   [4] unless.
[5] beaten.   [6] inquire of them seriously.   [7] truly.
[8] heed.   [9] beausire.   [10] You talk too broadly !
[11] tales.   [12] promised.   [13] Every one.

HEROD. What, forthe away fro me?
NUNTIUS. 3a, lord, in faitht ful faste.
For I herde and toke hede
How þat þei wente, all thre,
In to ther awne contre.
HEROD. A! dogges, þe deuell 3ou spede.
NUNTIUS. Sir, more of þer menyng
3itt well I vndirstode
How þei hadde made offering
Unto þat frely foode [1]
Þat now of newe is borne.
Þai saie he schulde be kyng,
And welde all erthely thyng.
HEROD. Allas! þan am I lorne.[2]
Fy on þayme! faytours,[3] fy!
Wille þei be-gylle me þus.
NUNTIUS. Lorde, by ther prophicy,
Þei named his name Jesus.
HEROD. Fy! on þe, ladde, þou lyes!
II CONSUL. Hense! tyte,[4] but þou þe hye,
With doulle her schall þou dye,[5]
That wreyes hym on this wise.[6]
NUNTIUS. 3e wyte me all with wrang,[7]
Itt is þus and wele warre.
HEROD. Thou lyes! false traytoure strange,
Looke neuere þou negh me nere.[8]
Vppon liffe and lyme [9]
May I þat faitour fange,[10]
Full high I schall gar hym hange,[11]
Both þe harlott and hym.

4. UNKNOWN AUTHOR

Wealth and Health

The morality play, representing a regular dramatic development from the cyclical mystery, is of special importance because of the freedom it gave to the dramatist. Instead of being fettered by the Biblical story, he could now invent his own themes and characters, and, although the former might be professedly didactic in aim and the latter mere personifications, he came distinctly nearer to the creation of a type of drama which aimed at entertainment alone and to a depiction of

[1] noble creature. [2] lost. [3] deceivers. [4] quickly.
[5] Unless you get off, you'll die miserably.
[6] Who anger him in this wise. [7] You blame me wrongfully.
[8] See that you never come near me. [9] limb.
[10] seize. [11] I'll get him hanged.

32

ordinary real-life characters. In this *enterlude of Welth, and Helth, very mery and full of Pastyme*, it may be that a moral purpose is designed, but alongside of the characters Welth and Helth we meet with gay Shrewd wyt, presumptuous Ilwyll, and the Dutchman Hance, all of whom provide ample " Pastyme." Note should be taken of the Dutch-English spoken by Hance, introduced for the purpose of comedy. The morality is of importance, too, in that it introduces us to dramatic performances no longer amateur, but professional. " Foure may easely play this Playe " we are told on the title-page, an indication that the playwright had in mind, not the teeming multitude of artisans who interpreted the mysteries, but one of those small groups of vagrant players who were the forerunners of the great Elizabethan companies.

(*Wealth and Health* was entered in the Stationers' Register in 1557. The unique copy of the original quarto, discovered in 1906, is in the British Museum ; from this an edition was prepared by W. W. Greg and Percy Simpson.)

A Rascal Crew

ILWYLL. Wyl ye go hence. I thanke ye masters with al my hert.
I wyl seke you out, I warrant you; feare not.
Now they be gone, I am glad by saint mary.
A lyttel while heare I purpose to tary:
How to deceyue welth, helth, and libertie
Now must I deuyse.
For I am a chylde that is pas grace,
Ilwyll I am called that in euery place
Doth much mischiefe: this is a playne case.
Vertue I doo vtterly dispise,
But if they wyst what I were
Then of my purpose I should be neuer ye nere.
I wyl kepe my tonge leste that I mar
My whole intent and wyll.
But now I meruayle by this day
Where shrewd wit is gone a stray:
Some crafty touche is in his way.
I here him, peace, stand styll.
                          [*Entreth* SHREWD WYT *with a songe.*
    SHREWD WYT. Dieu vous garde playsaunce.
On seuen or no mumchaunce, what yonkers dare auaunce,
To playe a grote or twaine.
Loe heare I haue in store
Two or three grotes and no more;
I take great thought therfore.
For to kepe it, it is much payne.
I come now out of a place

C   33

Where is a company of small grace,
Theues and hores that spendes a pace:
They were dronken all the sorte.
One of their purces I did aspy
Out of his sleue where it dyd lye
And one wynked on me with his eye,
But ther began the sporte.
Their false falsehode, and I crafty wyt
Got the purse: loe, heare I haue it.
I ran my way and let hym syt. . . ,
And yf that I had yll wyll here
With this money we wolde make good chere.
Gentle brother wyll, I pray the apeare
For thou art in some corner.
    [ILWYLL.] I woulde come in but I am a fearde
Least that I be taken by the bearde
Wyth some catchepol; I haue heard
How thou haste stollen a purse.
    SHREWD WYT. Thou horson, art thou mad?   Cum in I say;
This is not the fyrste hazard that I haue scaped.
Yf I make an hand to decke my selfe gay
What am I the worse?
    ILWYLL. From thy company I cannot abyde;
I must nedes holde vpon thy side.
Yllwyll and shrewdwit who can hyde
For they will be together.
    SHREWD WYT. Now welcome wyll, and what cheare?
By god I thought for thee a thousand yere.
Peace for gods body who cummeth there?
Hance bere pot Ascon router.
                            [Entreth HANCE with a dutche songe.
    HANCE. Gut nynen scone rutters by the moder got
It heist õwne schon, for staue ye nete
De questeker mau iche bie do do
Vau the groate bombarde well ic wete
Dartyck dowsant van enheb it mete
Ic best de mauikin van de Koining dangliler
De grot Keyser kind ic bene his busketer.
    ILWYLL. Here ye not dronken hance how he be gins to prate?
The malowperte fleminge is a little to cheke mate.
    SHREWD WYT. Let the knaue alone, for his name is war.
Such dronken flemminges your company wil mar.
    HANCE. Ic best nen emond, ic best in soche
Ye secte nete vell ic forstaue ye in doche.
    ILWYLL. Cumpt hore leyf; with your gound stand nere;
Yt becummes you better to handle a potte of beare.
    HANCE. Dat maght icvell dan, ic can skynke frelyck
        Tab bers frow, ic bringes brore, begotts nemerick.

SHREWD WYT. The horsen knaue by the masse is dronke.
A winking for depe his eyen be cleane lonck.
    HANCE. Ic foraue ye vell ye seg dac ic flope
Nenike, nenike, ic compte hore for an andor cope.
    ILWYLL. Wel coppin I pray the hartly tell vs trew
Wherfore comest thou hether for any thing to sew? . . .
Is he gone? Forewel, hanykin bowse,
I pray god giue him a hounded drouse,
For I trow a knaue brought hym to house.
But now brother wyt,
We must deuose how that we may
Be in seruice with welth alwaye.
Let me here what thou canst do or say
To helpe for to contryue it.
    SHREWD WYT. For thy pleasure that I shall.
This wyll I doo first of all—
Flatter and lye, and euermore call
Them my good maysters styll.
Then with swering, lying and powlinge
Brybry, theft, and preuy pyking
Thus I shred wet, wyll euer be doinge
I warrant ther yll wyll.
    ILWYLL. I cun thee thanke, this is well deuysed.
And I, yll wil, wolde haue euery man dispised.
But now another thing must be contriued
Or els al wilbe nought.
There is one they call good remedy
In this realme, he hath great actority;
He is a noble man and much worthy.
Many things he hath wrought.
He is called lust, discreete and indifference
Willing to fulfil his soueraines commaundement.
He is not fraide to do right punishment
Therfore of him I am afrayde.
    SHREWD WYT. So am I to; this maketh me very sadde,
Yet oftentimes I haue bene harde bestadde;
Now yt I am warned of him I am very glad.
Sum crafty wyle for him shalbe hade.

5. JOHN BALE (1495–1563)

Kynge Johan

    As the morality developed the secular and realistic scenes
came to have more and more domination over the original
didactic and abstract elements. Called still by allegorical
names, many of the characters were depicted with a lifelikeness
which stamped them as English citizens, evil and virtuous.

This movement led naturally toward the establishment within the morality framework of figures who, even in name, were intended to be real persons, the primal impulse no doubt coming from the evident appropriateness of choosing the reign of some king as a kind of concrete example of the general truth inculcated in the play. John Bale's *Kynge Johan* is the prime example of this most fully developed morality type or of this primitive chronicle history. John, Pandulph, Simon of Swinsett, and the Pope enter in person, yet they are companioned not by courtiers and clerics, but by Ynglond (England), Sedycyon (Sedition), Commynalte (Commons), Nobylyte (Nobles), Dissimulacyon, and half a score of similar characters. As a dramatic document, therefore, as a typical transition text, *Kynge Johan* has a value far beyond its intrinsic worth.

(The play has been preserved in manuscript. It was edited by J. P. Collier for the Camden Society in 1838; and, in a revised text, it appears in Manly's *Specimens of Pre-Shakespearean Drama*.)

PANDULPH ACCUSES JOHN AND HIS ASSOCIATES

PANDULPHUS. What, Commynalte, ys this the counaunt kepyng?
Thou toldyst me thee woldest take hym no more for thi Kyng.

COMMYNALTE. *Peccavi, mea culpa* : I submyt me to yowr holynes.

PANDULPHUS. Gett the hence than shortly, and go about thi besynes.
Wayet on thy capttaynes, Nobelyte and the Clargy,
With cyvyll order, and the other company.
Blow owt your tromppettes and sett forth manfully,
The Frenche kyng Phelype by sea doth hether apply
With the power of Fraunce to subdew this herytyke.

JOHAN. I defy both hym and the, lewde scysmatyke.
Why wylt thu forsake thy prince or thy prince leve the?

COMMYNALTE. I must nedes obbay whan holy chirch commandyth me.   [*Go owt* COMMYNALTE.

YNGLOND. Yf thou leve thy kyng take me never for thy mother.

PANDULPHUS. Tush, care not thu for that, I shall provyd the another.
Yt ware fytter for you to be in another place.

YNGLOND. Yt shall becum me to wayte upon his grace,
And do hym seruyce where as he ys resydente,
For I was gevyn hym of the Lord omnypotente.

[PANDULPHUS.] Thow mayest not abyde here, for whye we have hym curssyd.

YNGLOND. I beshrow yowr hartes, so have ye me on pursed.
Yf he be acurssed than are we a mete cuppell,
For I am interdyct; no salve that sore can suppell.

[PANDULPHUS.] I say gett the hence, and make me no more pratyng.

YNGLOND. I wyll not a-waye from myn owne lawfull Kyng,
Appoynted of God, tyll deth shall us departe.

MEDIEVAL

[PANDULPHUS.] Wyll ye not, indede? Well than, ye are lyke to
   smarte.

YNGLOND. I smarte all redy throw your most suttell practyse,
And am clene ondone by your false merchandyce,
Your pardons, your bulles, your purgatory pyckepurse,
Your lent fastes, your schryftes, that I pray god geve you his
   cursse.

PANDULPHUS. Thu shalt smart better or we have done with the,
For we have this howr great nauyes upon the see
In every quarter with this loller here to fyght,
And to conquarre hym for the holy chyrchis ryght.
We have on the northe Alexander, the kyng of Scotts,
With an armye of men that for their townnes cast lottes.
On the sowthe syde we have the french kyng with his power,
Which wyll sle and burne tyll he cum to London tower.
In the west parts we have Kyng Alphonso with the spanyards,
With sheppes full of gonepowder now cummyng hether towards,
And on the est syde we have esterlynges, Danes and Norways,
With such power landynge as can be resystyd nowayes.

JOHAN. All that is not true that you have here expressed.

PANDULPHUS. By the masse, so true as I have now confessed.

JOHAN. And what do ye meane by such an hurly-burlye?

PANDULPHUS. For the churches ryght to subdue ye manfullye.

SEDYCYON. To all that wyll fyght I proclame a Jubyle
Of cleane remyssyon, thys tyrant here to slee,
Destroye hys people, burne up both cytie and towne
That the Pope of Rome maye have hys scepture and crowne.
In the churches cawse to dye thys daye be bolde;
Your sowles shall to heaven ere your fleshe and bones be colde.

JOHAN. Most mercyfull god, as my trust is in the
So comforte me now in this extremyte;
As thou helpyst David in his most hevynes,
So helpe me this hour of thy grace mercye and goodnes.

PANDULPHUS. This outward remorse that ye show here evydent
Ys a grett lykelyhod and token of amendment.
How say ye, Kyng Johan, can ye fynd now in your hart
To obaye holy chyrch and geve ower your froward part?

JOHAN. Were yt so possyble to hold thes enmyes backe
That my swete Ynglond perysh not in this sheppewracke?

PANDULPHUS. Possyble, quoth he; yea they shuld go bake indede
And ther grett armyse to some other quarters leade
Or elles they have not so many good blyssyngs now
But as many cursyngs they shall have I make god avowe.
I promyse you sur ye shall have specyall faver
Yf ye wyll submyt your-sylfe to holy chyrch here.

JOHAN. I trust than ye wyll graunt some delyberacyon,
To have an answere of thys your protestacyon.

SEDYCYON. Tush, gyve upp the crowne, and make no more a-do.

JOHAN. Your spirytuall charyte wyll be better to me than so.
The crowne of a realme is a matter of great wayght;
In gyvynge it upp we maye not be to slayght.
SEDYCYON. I saye gyve it up; let us have no more a-do.
PANDULPHUS. Yea, and in our warres we wyll no farder go.
JOHAN. Ye wyll gyve me leave to talke first with my clergye.
SEDYCYON. With them ye nede not; they are at a point alreadye.
JOHAN. Than with my lawers to heare what they wyll tell.
SEDYCYON. Ye shall ever have them as the clergye gyve them
   counsell.
JOHAN. Then wyll I commen with my nobylyte.
SEDYCYON. We have hym so jugled he wyll not to you agree.
JOHAN. Yet shall I be content to do as he counsell me.
PANDULPHUS. Than be not to long from hence I wyll advyse ye.
                    [*Exeunt* JOHAN *and* YNGLOND.
SEDYCYON. Is not thys a sport? By the messe it is. I trowe
What welthe and pleasure wyll now to our kyngedom growe.
England is our owne whych is the most plesaunte grounde
In all the rounde worlde. Now may we realms confounde.
Our Holy Father maye now lyve at hys pleasure
And have habundaunce of wenches wynes and treasure.
He is now able to kepe downe Christe and his gospell,
True fayth to exyle and all vertues to expell.
Now shall we ruffle it in velvetts, gold and sylke,
With shaven crownes, syde gownes and rochettes whyte as mylke.
By the messe Pandulphus now may we synge cantate
And crowe confitebor with a joyfull jubilate.
Holde me or els for laughynge I must burste.

6. UNKNOWN AUTHOR

Interludium de Clerico et Puella

Practically nothing exists of medieval secular farce in English,
although France can show some examples of a rude entertainment which seems to have affinities with the *mimus* of classical
Rome. The nearest approach we can make to this type of
drama is the *Interludium de Clerico et Puella,* written on a
familiar *Dame Siriz* theme, and preserved in a manuscript of
the fourteenth century. This little playlet is incomplete, but
it shows three well-developed characters and at least the rudi-
ments of a simple plot. No one can say how far it is representative of a regular species of medieval entertainment, but,
putting it alongside of similar French texts, we may safely assert
that it was by no means a unique experiment in its age. No
doubt we have here something closely approaching the primitive
dialogue carried by wandering *mimi* not only throughout
England, but throughout the whole of Europe.

38

MEDIEVAL

(This *Interludium* is in the Northumbrian dialect, and has been conjecturally dated in the late thirteenth century. It was printed from the original manuscript (British Museum MS. Add. 23,986) by Wright and Halliwell in *Reliquiæ Antiquæ* (1841). An edited text is given in Cook's *Middle English Reader*.)

THE CLERK SUES THE GIRL

CLERICUS. Damishel, reste wel.
PUELLA. Sir, welcum, by Saynt Michel.
CLERICUS. Wer esty sire? Wer esty dame? [1]
PUELLA. By Gode, es noþer her at hame. [2]
CLERICUS. Wel won suilc a man to life,
Þat suilc a may mithe have to wyfe. [3]
PUELLA. Do way, [4] by Crist and Leonard,
No wil Y lufe [5] na clerc fayllard, [6]
Na kepi herbherg [7] clerc in huse no y flore [8]
Bot his hers ly wit-uten dore. [9]
Go forth þi way, god sire, [10]
For her hastu losyt al þi wile. [11]
CLERICUS. Nu, nu, [12] by Crist and by sant Jhon,
In al þis land ne wist I none. [13]
Mayden, that hi luf mor þan þe, [14]
Hif me micht ever þe bether be. [15]
For þe hy sory nicht and day, [16]
Y may say, hay wayle uay!
Y luf þe mar [17] þan mi lif,
Þu hates me mar þan gayt dos cnif. [18]
Þat es nought for mys-gilt, [19]
Certhes, for þi luf ham hi spilt. [20]
A, suythe [21] mayden, reu of me [22]
Þat es ty luf, hand ay salbe. [23]
For þe luf of þy mod[er] of efne, [24]
Þu mend þi mode, [25] and her my stevene. [26]

[1] Where is your father? Where is your mother?
[2] neither is at home here. [3] That such a maiden might have as wife.
[4] Go away. [5] I will not love.
[6] deceiving. [7] Nor do I care to harbour.
[8] in house or on floor (a conventional phrase).
[9] Unless his rump lie out of doors.
[10] good sir. [11] For here you have lost all your wile.
[12] Now, now. [13] I know none.
[14] that I love more than thee. [15] If I might ever the better be (an oath).
[16] For thee I sorrow night and day. [17] more.
[18] You hate me more than goat (?; MS. "yayt") does knife (?; MS. "chuief").
[19] crime. [20] am I ruined, undone.
[21] sweet. [22] take pity on me.
[23] and aye shall be. [24] For the love of the Mother of Heaven.
[25] change your mind. [26] hear my story (voice).

PUELLA. By Crist of hevene and sant Jone,
Clerc of scole ne kepi non,[1]
For many god wymman haf þai don scam.[2]
By Crist, þu michtis haf be at hame.[3]
    CLERICUS. Synt it nothir gat may be,[4]
Jhesu Crist, by-tech y þe,[5]
And send neulit bot tharinne,[6]
Þat yi be lesit of al my pine[7]
    PUELLA. Go nu, truan,[8] go nu, go,
For mikel þu canstu of sory and wo.[9]

THE CLERK GOES TO SEEK AID OF MOME HELWIS

CLERICUS. God te blis,[10] Mome [11] Helwis.
MOME HELWIS. Son, welcum, by san Dinis!
CLERICUS. Hic [12] am comin to þe, Mome,
Þu hel me noth, þu say me sone.[13]
Hic am a clerc þat hauntes scole,
Y lidy [14] my lif wyt mikel dole;[15]
Me wor lever to be dedh,[16]
Þan led the lif þat hyc ledh,
For ay mayden with and schen,[17]
Fayrer hoo lond hawy non syen.[18]
Yo hat mayden Malkyn, y wene;[19]
Nu þu wost quam y mene,[20]
Yo wonys [21] at the tounes ende,
Þat suyt [22] lif, so fayr and hende.[23]
Bot if ȝo wit hir mod amende,[24]
Neuly Crist my ded me send.[25]
Men send me hyder, vyt-uten fayle,
To haf þi help an ty cunsayle.[26]
Þar for amy [27] cummen here,
Þat þu salt be my herand-bere,[28]

[1] I care for no school-clerk.
[2] For they have shamed many a good woman.
[3] you might (as well) have been at home.
[4] Since it may not be any other way.
[5] To Jesus Christ I commend thee (MS. " by-tethy ").
[6] May he send help soon.   [7] That I be freed from all my misery.
[8] vagabond (truant).   [9] For much you can (do) of sorrow and woe.
[10] God bless thee.   [11] Mome = Mone = Aunt.   [12] I.
[13] conceal naught from me, tell me quickly.   [14] I lead.
[15] with much grief.   [16] I had rather be dead.
[17] For a maid white and bright.   [18] A fairer one on land have I not seen.
[19] She is called Maid Malkyn, I ween.
[20] Now you know whom I mean.   [21] She dwells.   [22] sweet.
[23] dainty.   [24] Unless you change her mood.
[25] Quickly Christ may send me my death.
[26] I was sent hither, without fail, to have thy help and counsel.
[27] Therefore am I.   [28] Message-bearer.

To mac me and þat mayden sayct,[1]
And hi sal gef þe of myn ayct,[2]
So þat hever [3] al þi lyf
Saltu be þe better wyf.
So help me Crist! and hy may spede,[4]
Riche saltu haf þi mede.[5]
    MOME HELWIS. A, son, wat saystu? [6] benedicite,
Lift hup þi hand, and blis þe.
For it es boyt syn and scam,[7]
That þu on me hafs layt thys blam.[8]
For hic am an ald quyne [9] and a lam.[10]
Y led my lyf wit Godis love.
Wit my roc y me fede,[11]
Cani do non othir dede,[12]
Bot my pater noster and my crede,
To say Crist for missedede,[13]
And myn avy Mary.[14]
For my scynnes [15] hic am sory,
And my de profundis,
For al that yn sin lys.[16]
For cani me non oþir þink,
Þat wot Crist,[17] of hevene kync.[18]
Jhesu Crist, of hevene hey,[19]
Gef that þay may hang hey,[20]
And gef þat hy may se,
Þat þay be heng on a tre,[21]
That þis ley as leyit onne me.[22]
For aly wymam ami on.[23]

7. JOHN HEYWOOD (1497–c. 1580)

Johan Johan

With John Heywood a new spirit seems to come into English drama, the interlude freeing itself of the abstractions of the morality play and depending upon laughter and merriment alone. Yet in many ways Heywood's work may be regarded as a culmination rather than as a beginning, for in it are to be traced the features of the old mime-drama. It seems highly probable that rude secular farces, often introducing as a main

[1] together.
[2] And I shall give thee of my goods.
[3] ever. [4] prosper.
[5] You shall have your rich reward.
[6] what sayest thou? [7] It is but sin and shame.
[8] laid this blame. [9] old quean. [10] lame.
[11] With my distaff I feed myself. [12] I can't do anything else.
[13] To say it to Christ for my sins. [14] *Ave Maria.* [15] Sins.
[16] lies. [17] Christ knows that. [18] King. [19] of high heaven.
[20] Grant that they may hang high. [21] That they be hanged on a tree.
[22] Who have lied this lie on me. [23] For a holy woman am I one.

theme the cheating of a witless husband, provided rude amusement throughout the Middle Ages, and that Heywood's work is to a large extent a development of already existing forms. *Johan Johan* has been selected for quotation here because of its excellent scene where Johan Johan, the husband, has to do the menial jobs while his wife, Tyb, and Syr Jhan, the priest, consume the pie he longs for.

(*A mery play Betwene Johan Johan the husbande, Tyb his wyfe, & syr Jhãn the preest* was printed in 1534; a reprint was issued between 1819 and 1830, and another appeared, under the editorship of A. W. Pollard, in C. M. Gayley's *Representative English Comedies* (1907), vol. i.)

JOHAN JOHAN IS SET TO WORK BY HIS WIFE

TYB.   What, art come so sone?
Gyue vs water to wasshe nowe—haue done.
                    [*Than he bryngeth the payle empty.*
JOHAN. By kockes soule, it was euen nowe full to ye brynk
But it was out agayne or I coude thynke:
Wherof I marueled, by god almyght
And than I loked betwene me and the lyght
And I spyed a clyfte, both large and wyde.
Lo wyfe, here it is on the tone [1] syde.
    TYB. Why dost not stop it?
    JOHAN.   Why howe shall I do it?
    TYB. Take a lytle wax.
    JOHAN.   Howe shal I come to it?
    SYR JHAN. Mary here be ii wax candyls I say
Whiche my gossyp margery gaue me yesterday.
    TYB. Tusshe let hym alone, for by the rode
It is pyte to helpe hym or do hym good.
    SIR JHAN. What Jhãn Jhãn, canst thou make no shyfte?
Take this waxe and stop therewith the clyfte.
    JOHAN. This waxe is as harde as any wyre.
    TYB. Thou must chafe it a lytle at the fyre.
    JOHAN. She yt broughte the [2] these waxe candelles twayne
She is a good companyon certayn.
    TYB. What was it not my gossyp margery?
    SIR JHAN. Yes she is a blessed woman surely.
    TYB. Nowe wolde god I were as good as she
For she is vertuous and full of charyte.
    JOHAN. Nowe so God help me, and by my holydome,
She is the erranst baud betwene this and Rome.
    TYB. What sayst?
    JOHAN.   Mary I chafe the wax,
And I chafe it so hard, that my fyngers krakks

----

[1] the one.   [2] thee.

MEDIEVAL

But take vp this py,[1] that I here torne;
And [2] it stand long, ywys it wyll borne.[3]

TYB. Ye but thou must chafe the wax I say.

JOHAN. Byd hym syt down I the [4] pray.
Syt down good syr Johan, I you requyre.

TYB. Go I say and chafe the wax by the fyre
Whyle that we sup, syr Jhãn and I.

JOHAN. And how now, what wyll ye do with the py?
Shall I not ete thereof, a morsell?

TYB. Go and chafe the wax, whyle thou art well
And let vs haue no more pratyng thus.

SIR JHAN. Benedicite.

JOHAN.   Dominus.

TYB. Now go chafe the wax with a myschyfe.

JOHAN. What, I come to blysse the bord [5] swete wyfe
It is my custome now and than.
Mych good do it you, master syr Jhãn.

TYB. Go chafe the wax, and here no lenger tary.

JOHAN. And is not this a very purgatory
To se folkes ete, and may not ete a byt?
By kokkes soule, I am a very wodcok.
This payle here, now a vengaunce take it
Now my wyfe gyueth me a proud mok.

TYB. What dost?

JOHAN.   Mary I chafe the wax here
And I ymagyn to make you good chere
That a vengaunce take you both as ye syt
For I know well, I shall not ete a byt.
But yet in feyth, yf I myght ete one morsell
I wold thynk the matter went very well.

SYR JHAN. Gossyp Jhãn Jhãn, now mych good do it you.
What chere make you, there by the fyre?

JOHAN. Master parson, I thank yow now
I fare well inow, after myne own desyre.

SYR JHAN. What dost Jhãn Jhãn, I the requyre?

JOHAN. I chafe the wax here by the fyre.

TYB. Here is good drynk, and here is a good py.

SIR JHAN. We fare very well, thankyd be our lady.

TYB. Loke how the kokold chafyth the wax that is hard
And for his lyfe, daryth not loke hetherward.

SYR JHAN. What doth my gossyp?

JOHAN.   I chafe the wax
And I chafe it so hard, that my fyngers krakkes
And eke the smoke puttyth out my eyes two
I burne my face, and ray my clothys also,
And yet I dare not say one word
And they syt laughyng, yender at the bord.

[1] pie.   [2] If.   [3] burn.   [4] thee.   [5] board.

TYB. Now by my trouth, it is a prety jape
For a wyfe, to make her husband her ape.
Loke of Jhãn Jhãn, which maketh hard shyft
To chafe the wax, to stop therwith the clyft.

JOHAN. Ye that a vengeaunce take ye both two
Both hym and the, and the and hym also;
And that ye may choke, with the same mete
At the furst mursell, that ye do ete.

TYB. Of what thyng now dost thou clatter
Jhãn Jhãn? or wherof dost thou patter?

JOHAN. I chafe the wax, and make hard shyft
To stop herwith of the payll the ryft.

SYR JHAN. So must he do Jhãn Jhãn, by my father kyn
That is bound of wedlok in the yoke.

JOHAN. Loke how the pyld preest crammyth in
That wold to god he myght therwith choke.

TYB. Now master parson, pleasyth your goodnes
To tell vs some tale, of myrth or sadnes
For our pastyme, in way of communycacyon.

SYR JHAN. I am content to do it, for our recreacyon
And of iii myracles I shall to you say.

JOHAN. What, must I chafe the wax all day
And stand here, rostyng by the fyre? . . .

TYB [*after the pie is consumed*]. And had ye no meate
  Johan Johan no had?

JOHAN. No Tyb my wyfe, I had not a whyt.

TYB. What not a morsell?

JOHAN.   No not one byt
For honger I trowe I shall fall in a sowne.[1]

SIR JHAN. O, that were pyte, I swere by my crowne.

----

[1] swoon.

II. EARLY SIXTEENTH CENTURY

WHEN we enter the sixteenth century we leave the sphere of the amateur and approach toward the glories of the professional theatre. Amateurism still rules in the universities and the Inns of Court, but now we begin to trace the wanderings of little bands of actors who naturally demanded a new technique and a more exact attention to theatrical possibility. Mr W. J. Lawrence in his recent brilliant book, *Pre-Restoration Stage Studies* (1927), has analysed the influence of these small groups of players on some extant dramas. Four men and a boy seems to have been a familiar number for the composition of a troupe, and the influence of this limited number is to be seen in those early plays which advertise the fact that " Four may easily " perform them. In this connexion there is an exceedingly interesting scene in that drama of *Sir Thomas More* (*c.* 1593–94), which, preserved in manuscript, is thought by many to contain three pages in Shakespeare's handwriting. In this play More is approached by just such a theatrical company. " Welcome good freend," he cries. " What is your will with me ? "

> PLAYER. My Lord, my fellowes and my selfe,
> Are come to tender ye our willing seruice,
> So please you to commaund vs.
> MOORE. What, for a play, you meane?
> Whom doo ye serue?
> PLAYER. My Lord Cardinalles grace.
> MOORE. My Lord Cardinalls players? now trust me, welcome...
> I prethee tell me, what playes haue ye?
> PLAYER. Diuers my Lord: the Cradle of Securitie,
> Hit nayle o'th head, impacient pouertie,
> The play of foure Pees, diues and Lazarus,
> Lustie Iuuentus, and the mariage of witt and wisedome.[1]
> MOORE. The mariage of witt and wisedome? that my Lads,
> Ile none but that, the theame is very good,

---

[1] As several of these plays have been preserved, this seems to be a record of real dramas and may be taken as a typical early repertory.

And many maintaine a liberall argument.
To marie wit to wisedome, asks some cunning,
Many haue witt, that may come short of wisedome.
Weele see how Mr Poet playes his part,
And whether witt or wisedome grace his arte.
Goe, make him drinke, and all his fellowes too,
How manie are ye?
    PLAYER. Foure men and a boy Sir.
    MOORE. But one boy? then I see
Ther's but fewe women in the play.
    PLAYER. Three my Lord: dame Science, Lady vanitie,
And wisedome she her selfe.
    MOORE. And one boy play them all? bir Lady, hees loden.

Arrangements are then made for the performance of *The Marriage of Wit and Wisdom* in More's house, and, just as the spectators have seated themselves, one of the players, habited for the part he is to interpret, "*Inclination* the vise," enters to make an apology to the patron.

INCLINATION. We would desire your honor but to stay a little, one of my fellowes is but run to Oagles, for a long beard for young witt, and heele be heere presently.
MOORE. A long beard for young witt? why man, he may be with out a beard till he come to mariage, for witt goes not all by the hayre: when comes witt in?
INCLINATION. In the second Scene, next to the Prologue my Lord.
MOORE. Why play on till that Sceane come, and by that time witts beard will be growne, or else the fellowe returned with it.

The little play goes on, but Luggins, the actor, returns not with his beard, and More, indulging himself in his gay humour, takes his part for the nonce and allows the performance to go forward.

This passage has been quoted because it provides for us a truly excellent picture of a typical early sixteenth-century performance, and allows us to get behind the scenes at a morality show. These moralities remained popular until Shakespeare's time, but alongside of them were developing other forms of dramatic art which were destined to become popular in later years. Heywood polished and vivified the older farce (see p. 41), and other authors introduced a kind of tragi-comedy which was to form one of the chief types of English drama for centuries to come. In *Fulgens and Lucres* and in *Apius and Virginia* we can see examples of

46

this tragi-comedy, either introducing comic scenes alongside of tragic or presenting an atmosphere which, seriously inclined, did not prepare the way for an unhappy conclusion. These early tragi-comedies are still bound to the morality—*Apius and Virginia* has its Vice in Haphazard as well as a series of allegorical characters—but gradually the outward morality traditions were cast off, until the purely secular drama stood independent.

From abroad, too, came other forces which were to have a deep influence on the formation of the Elizabethan theatre. New knowledge of Terence and Seneca taught the secrets of form, while the neo-classic plays of Renascence Italy were eagerly studied. Out of these influences grew regular tragedy and comedy, but the English audiences would not accept the frigid decorum taught on the Continent. The typical Elizabethan drama takes its rise from a combination of the various elements—the classics giving form and sometimes characterization, the interludes giving farcical fun, and the tragi-comedies giving that freedom from restraint which later so offended Continental critics of our stage. The chronicle history, the play neither tragedy nor comedy, formed the representative dramatic fare of this epoch.

I. UNKNOWN AUTHOR.[1]

Apius and Virginia

Apius and Virginia belongs to, and is thoroughly representative of, a group of tragi-comedies which helps to bridge the gulf between the medieval drama and the Elizabethan. These plays, which include *Horestes* and *Cambises*, deal with matter which is presumably 'classical,' but all bring in alongside the serious characters figures who are either designated by the term Vice or have connexions with that rascal of the moralities. Each of these dramas, also, is thoroughly moral in aim, so that we may almost define them as later morality plays using classical legend or history for didactic end and mingling together the technique of medieval times and the newer style borrowed from a study of Seneca and Plautus. *Apius and Virginia* has been chosen to represent this group partly because of the engaging character of Haphazard the Vice, and partly because, even more than the others, it is typical of the transition stage. Among

[1] The play was written by one whose initials were R. B., but who has not been identified.

its characters are numbered no less than seven personifications, and these take an active part in the development of the plot. In *Apius and Virginia*, therefore, we get a play which holds to romantic tragedy and tragi-comedy the same position as Bale's *Kinge Johan* does to Elizabethan chronicle histories.

(There is no certainty as to the date of this drama ; all that can be said is that, whenever it was written, it belongs in spirit to an early period.   It was printed in 1575.)

JUSTICE IS METED OUT TO THE VICE

IUSTICE. Oh gorgan Iudge, what lawles life thou most wicked led?
Thy soking sinne hath sonke thy soule, thy vertues all are fled:
Thou chast and vndefiled life didest seeke for to have spotted,
And thy Reward is ready here, by Iustice now alotted.

REWARDE. Thy iust *Reward*, is deadly death, wherfore come
    wend away,
To death I straight will do thy corps, then lust shall haue his pray:
Virginius thou wofull knight, come neare and take thy foe,
In prison thou make him fast, no more let him do so:
Let Claudius for tirrany be hanged on a tree.

VIRGINIUS. Ah right *Reward*, the Gods be blist, This day I chaunce
    to see.

HAPHAZARD. Why how now my Lord *Apius*, what cheare?
Why where is my Reward for this geare?
Why dyd I ride run and reuell,
And for all my iaunting now am made a Iauell?
Why run sir knaue call me *Claudius*?
Then run with a vengeaunce watch *Virginius*,
Then ride sirra, is *Virginia* at Church,
Then gallope to see where her father doth lurche,
Then vp sirra, now what counsell?
Of Dame bewty what newes canst thou tell?
Thus in hurly burly from piller to poste,
Poore *Haphazard* daily was toste,
And now with *Virginius* he goes sadly walking,
And nothing at all will listen my talking,
But shall I be so vsed at his hands,
As leue I were neare in Limbo bands,
That Dronel, that drowsy Drakenosed driuill,
He never learned his manners in Siuill:
A Iudge may cause a gentleman, a gentleman nay a iack hearinge,
As honest as he that caries his hose on his neck for feare of wering,
A Caitife, a Cutthrote, a churle worthy blame,
I wyll serue him no longer; the Deuill geue him shame:
Yet by the Mouse foote, I am not content,
I will haue a reward sure, els will I repent.
To master reward I straight waies will go,

48

The worst that can hap is but a noo:
But sure I know his honesty is such,
That he will recompence me, with litle or much:
And well this prouerb commeth in my head,
Birlady halfe a loafe is better then nere a whit of bread,
Therfore hap, and be happely, hap that hap may,
I wyll put it in hazard, I geue it assay:
Alhayle, maister *Reward* and rightuous Iustice,
I beseech you let me be recompenced to, according to my seruice,
For why all this long time I haue liued in hope.

REWARDE. Then for thy reward, then here is a rope.

HAPHAZARD. Nay softe my maisters by saincte Thomas of trunions,
I am not disposed to by of your onions:
A rope (quoth you) away with that showing,
It would greue a man hauing two plowes goyng,
Nay stay I pray you, and let the Cat winke,
It is naught in dry sommer, for letting my drinke.

IUSTICE. Let or let not, there is no remedy, hanging shalbe thy
    reward verely.

HAPHAZARD. Is there nothing but hanging to my lot doth fall,
Then take you my rewarde much good doo it you withall.
I am not so hasty although I be clayming,
But that I can aford you, the most of my gayning:
I wyll set, let, graunt, yelde, permit and promise,
All the reuenewes to you of my seruice:
I am friendly, I am kindly, I proffer you faire,
You shall be my ful executor and heyre.

REWARDE. Nay make you ready first to dye by the roode,
Then we will dispose it as we think it good:
Then those that with you to this dyd consent,
[Th]e lyke reward shall cause them repent.

IUSTICE. Nay stay a while; *Virginius* is comming.
Nay soft *Haphazard* you are not so cunning,
Thus to escape without punishment,

REWARDE. No certis it is not so expedient,

                    [*Here entreth* VIRGINIUS.

VIRGINIUS. Oh noble *Iustice* duty done, behold I come againe,
To shew you that *Apius* he him selfe hath lewdly slaine,
As soon as he in prison was enclosed out of sight
He desperate for bluddy deede, did slea him selfe out right,
And *Claudius* doth mercy craue who did the deede for feare,
Voutchsafe oh Iudge to saue his life, though countrie he forbeare.

IUSTICE. We graunt him grace at thy request, but bannish him
    the lande.
And see that death be done out right on him that here doth stand.

HAPHAZARD. Nay M. *Virginius* take him by the hande.
I craue not for seruice; the thing worth ought.
Hanging quoth you, it is the last end of my thought.

D   49

Fye for shame fye, stay by my fathers soule,
Why this is like to Tom turners doule.
Hang one man, and saue all the rest,
Take part one with another, plaine dealing is best.
    REWARDE. This is our dealing, thus deale we with thee,
Take him hence *Virginius* goe trusse him to a tree.
    HAPHAZARD. Ye shall in a ropes name, whether away with me.
    VIRGINIUS. Come wend thou in haste, thy death for to take,
To the hangman I will leade thee, a quick dispatch to make.
    HAPHAZARD. Must I needes hange, by the gods it doth spight me,
To thinke how crabbedly this silke lase will bite me:
Then come cosin cutpurs, come runne haste and folowe me,
Haphazard must hange, come folow the lyuerie.

2. HENRY MEDWALL (*fl.* 1480–1500)

Fulgens and Lucres

Among recent literary discoveries none has a greater value than the finding in the Mostyn Library of a copy of the play known as *Fulgens and Lucres*. This was in 1919 when, although the drama had been known to exist, all hopes of unearthing it had perished. It is now among the treasures of the Henry E. Huntington Library in California. The value of *Fulgens* lies in the fact that it is by far the earliest secular drama which has come down to us. Presumably written about 1490, it places the development of the regular theatre many years earlier than other records would allow. Moreover, it shows the use of certain dramatic devices which were later to be made use of by Elizabethan dramatists. For the interest of the passage, there has been chosen for quotation here the opening lines of the play. These form a kind of introduction, or prelude, characters A and B discussing the performance in anticipation.

(*Fulgens and Lucres* was reprinted in facsimile with an introduction by Seymour de Ricci in 1920. More recently an edited text has been prepared by Professor A. W. Reed and Dr F. S. Boas (1926).)

A PRELUDE TO A PLAY

Intrat A [1] *dicens.*

    A. For goddis will
What meane ye syrs to stond so still?
Haue not ye etyn & your full
And payd no thinge therfore?
I wys syrs thus dare I say,
He that shall for the shott pay

---

[1] A of course stands for one of the unnamed characters in this introductory interlude.

Vouchsaueth that ye largely assay
Suche mete as he hath in store.
I trowe your disshes be not bare
Nor yet ye do the wyne spare,
Therfore be mery as ye fare;
Ye ar welcom eche oon
Unto this house with oute faynynge.
But I meruayle moche of one thinge:
That after this mery drynkynge
And good recreacyon
There is no wordes amonge this presse—
Non sunt loquele neque sermones—
But as it were men in sadnes
Here ye stonde musynge,
Where aboute I can not tell—
Or some els praty damesell
For to daunce and sprynge.
Tell me what calt is it not so?
I am sure here shalbe some what a do
And I wis I will know it or I go
With oute I be dryuyn hens.   [*Intrat* B.
    B. Nay nay hardely man I vndertake
No man wyll suche mastryes make
And it were but for the maner sake
Thou mast tary by licence
Among other men and see the play.
I warand no man wyll say the nay.
    A. I thinke it well euyn as ye say
That no man wyll me greue.
But I pray you tell me that agayn,
Shall here be a play?
    B. Ye for certeyn.
    A. By my trouth therof am I glad and fayn.
And ye will me beleue
Of all the worlde I loue suche sport;
It dothe me so myche plesure and comfort
And that causith me euer to resort
Wher suche thing is to do.
I trowe your owyn selfe be oon
Of them that shall play.
    B. Nay I am none.
I trowe thou spekyst in derision
To lyke me therto.
    A. Nay I mok not, wot ye well;
For I thought verely by your apparell
That ye had bene a player.
    B. Nay never a dell.
    A. Than I cry you mercy.

I was to blame. Lo therefore I say
Ther is somyche nyce aray
Amonges these galandis now aday
That a man shall not lightly
Know a player from a nother man.
But now to the purpose wher I began
I see well here shalbe a play than.
    B. Ye that ther shall doutles
And I trow ye shall like it well.
    A. It semeth than that ye can tell
Sumwhat of the mater?
    B. Ye I am of counsell;
One tolde me all the processe.
    A. And I pray you what shall it be?
               [B *tells* A *the story of the play.*
    A. Yes be ye sure whan thei haue all done
I wyll not spare to shew you my mynd—
Praise who wyll or dis praise I will not be behynd.
I wyll gest ther on what so euer shal befall
If I can fynd any man to gest withall.
    B. Pees, no moo wordes for now they come.
The plears bene euyn here at hand.
    A. So thei be so selp me god & halydome.
I pray you tell me where I shall stand.
    B. Mary stand euyn here by me I warand.
Geue rome there syrs for god avowe
Thei wold cum in if thei myght for you.
    A. Ye but I pray the what canst [1] tell me this—
Who is he that now comyth yn?
    B. Mary it is fulgence the senatour.
    A. Ye is : what the father of the forseide virgyn?
    B. Ye forseth he shall this matere begyn.
    A. And wher is feyr doughter lucrece?
    B. She comyth Anon. I say hold thy pece.

3. NICHOLAS UDALL (1505–56)

Roister Doister

    The date of composition of *Roister Doister* is not known for
a certainty ; it was written probably in the forties of the
sixteenth century, and takes rank as the earliest extant English
comedy (as distinct from the farcical interlude such as *Johan
Johan*). In penning it, the author has clearly had in mind his
Terence, so that native fun and Latin model are fused into the
one play. The comedy is not, perhaps, a great one, but it has
definite form, attempts at least toward genuine delineation of·

    [1] The original reads " calt," which may be a colloquial expression.

EARLY SIXTEENTH CENTURY

character, a series of excellent stage tricks, and a dialogue which is moderately easy in spite of the fettering rime. Roister Doister is, of course, the *miles gloriosus* of Plautan and Terentian comedy, but his companion, Merygreeke, savours of the old English Vice, and the manners depicted are, for the most part, native.

(The play was first printed between 1560 and 1589, but there may be an edition of earlier date. Various later reprints have appeared, among which the Arber (1869) and the Gayley (1907) deserve special notice. The following extracts are based on the Arber edition.)

A Love-letter misread

The point of the following scene lies in the fact that the letter which Roister Doister has caused to be sent to Custance is badly punctuated, so that the original sense is entirely distorted.

CUSTANCE. What gaudyng and foolyng is this afore my doore?

MERYGREEKE. May not folks be honest, pray you, though they be pore?

CUSTANCE. As that thing may be true, so rich folks may be fooles.

ROYSTER. Hir talke is as fine as she had learned in schooles.

MERYGREEKE. Looke partly towarde hir, and drawe a little nere.

CUSTANCE. Get ye home idle folkes.

MERYGREEKE. Why may not we be here?
Nay and ye will haze,[1] haze: otherwise I tell you plaine,
And ye will not haze, then give us our geare againe.

CUSTANCE. In deede I have of yours much gay things God save all.

ROYSTER. Speake gently unto hir, and let hir take all.

MERYGREEKE. Ye are to tender hearted: shall she make us dawes?
Nay dame, I will be plaine with you in my friends cause.

ROYSTER. Let all this passe sweete heart and accept my service.

CUSTANCE. I will not be served with a foole in no wise,
When I choose an husbande I hope to take a man.

MERYGREEKE. And where will ye finde one which can doe that he can?
Now thys man towarde you being so kinde,
You not to make him an answere somewhat to his minde.

CUSTANCE. I sent him a full answere by you dyd I not?

MERYGREEKE. And I reported it.

CUSTANCE. Nay I must speake it againe.

ROYSTER. No, no, he tolde it all.

MERYGREEKE. Was I not metely plaine?

ROYSTER. Yes.

---

[1] Presumably ha'us = have us.

MERYGREEKE. But I would not tell all, for faith if I had
With you dame Custance ere this houre it had been bad,
And not without cause: for this goodly personage,
Ment no lesse than to joyne with you in mariage.

CUSTANCE. Let him wast no more labour nor sute about me.

MERYGREEKE. Ye know not where your preferment lieth I see,
He sending you such a token, ring and letter.

CUSTANCE. Mary here it is, ye never sawe a better.

MERYGREEKE. Let us see your letter.

CUSTANCE.   Holde, reade it if ye can.
And see what letter it is to winne a woman.

MERYGREEKE. " To mine owne deare coney, birde, swete heart,
    and pigsny,
Good Mistresse Custance present these by and by "—
Of this superscription do ye blame the stile?

CUSTANCE. With the rest as good stuffe as ye redde a great
    while.

MERYGREEKE. " Sweete mistresse where as I love you nothing
    at all,
Regarding your substance and richesse chiefe of all,
For your personage, beautie, demeanour and wit,
I commende me unto you never a whit.
Sorie to heare report of your good welfare.
For (as I heare say) suche your conditions are,
That ye be worthie favour of no living man,
To be abhorred of every honest man.
To be taken for a woman enclined to vice.
Nothing at all to Vertue gyving hir due price.
Wherfore concerning mariage, ye are thought
Such a fine Paragon, as nere honest man bought.
And nowe by these presents I do you advertise
That I am minded to marrie you in no wise.
For your goodes and substance, I coulde bee content
To take you as ye are. . . ."

THE SCRIVENER EXPLAINS

ROYSTER. I say the letter thou madest me was not good.

SCRIVENER. Then did ye wrong copy it of likelyhood.

ROYSTER. Yes, out of thy copy worde for worde I wrote.

SCRIVENER. Then was it as ye prayed to have it I wote,
But in reading and pointyng there was made some faulte.

ROYSTER. I wote not, but it made all my matter to haulte.

SCRIVENER. How say you, is this mine originall or no?

ROYSTER. The selfe same that I wrote out of, so mote I go.

SCRIVENER. Loke on your owne fist, and I will looke on this.
And let this man be judge whether I reade amisse.
" To myne own dere coney, birde, sweete heart, and pigsny,

54

Good mistresse Custance, present these by and by."
How now? doth not this superscription agree?

ROYSTER. Reade that is within, and there ye shall the fault see.

SCRIVENER. " Sweete mistress, where as I love you, nothing at all
Regarding your richesse and substance: chiefe of all
For your personage, beautie, demeanour and witte
I commend me unto you: Never a whitte
Sory to heare report of your good welfare.
For (as I heare say) suche your conditions are,
That ye be worthie favour: of no living man
To be abhorred: of every honest man
To be taken for a woman enclined to vice
Nothing at all: to vertue giving hir due price.
Wherefore, concerning mariage, ye are thought
Suche a fine Paragon, as nere honest man bought.
And nowe by these presents I doe you advertise,
That I am minded to marrie you: In no wyse
For your goodes and substance: I can be content
To take you as you are. . . ."
Now, sir, what default can ye find in this letter?

ROYSTER. Of truth, in my mynde there can not be a better.

4. WILLIAM STEVENSON (*fl.* 1550)

Gammer Gurton's Needle

After being attributed to various authors, *A Ryght Pithy,
Pleasaunt and merie Comedie : Intytuled Gammer gurtons Nedle*
has been accepted as the work of William Stevenson. It is
probable that it was acted at Christ's College, Cambridge, in
the session 1553–54. The interest of the play lies in the fact
that it is the only extant specimen of English university comedy,
a form of drama which must have had much to do with later
theatrical developments, and that it is the first extant comedy
of which the theme is entirely English. Obviously the author
has, in structure and style, borrowed from the Roman playwrights, but the story he tells and the characters he introduces
are wholly native. We are presented here not with a *miles
gloriosus* reminiscent of Terence, but with a good Gammer
Gurton, who loses her precious needle, and who, as a result,
sets a whole village in an uproar. The crazy Diccon, the dull-
witted Hodge, Dame Chatte the gossip, Dr Rat the curate, and
Master Baylye are all dragged into the storm, and just as its
height seems nearing the needle is found in the most unexpected
of places. The comedy, perhaps, is a trifle rough ; the scenes
occasionally take on the colouring of mere horseplay ; but there
is a genuine breath of fresh air, a healthy breeziness, in situations

55

and in dialogue which mark out *Gammer Gurton's Needle* as a play not to be forgotten.

(The play was first published in 1575 ; there have been many reprints in modern times. The following extract is taken from the British Museum copy of the original quarto.)

THE NEEDLE, TO HODGE'S DISCOMFITURE, IS RECOVERED

DICCON. Go to, M. Bayly, say on your mind, I know ye are my
    frend.

BAYLY. Then marke ye wel, to recompence this thy former action
Because thou hast offended al, to make them satisfaction,
Before their faces, here kneele downe, & as I shal the teach,
For thou shalt take an othe of hodges leather breache.
First for master Doctor, upon paine of his cursse,
Where he wil pay for al, thou neuer draw thy pursse,
And when ye meete at one pot he shall haue the first pull,
And thou shalt neuer offer him the cup, but it be full.
To good wife chat thou shalt be sworne, euen on the same wyse
If she refuse thy money once, neuer to offer it twise.
Thou shalt be bound by the same here, as thou dost take it
When thou maist drinke of free cost, thou neuer forsake it:
For gammer gurtons sake, againe sworne shalt thou bee
To helpe hir to hir nedle againe if it do lie in thee;
And likewise be bound by the vertue of that
To be of good abering to Gib her great Cat:
Last of al for Hodge, the othe to scanne,
Thou shalt neuer take him, for fine gentleman.

HODGE. Come on fellow Diccon chalbe[1] euen with thee now.

BAYLY. Thou wilt not sticke to do this Diccon I trow.

DICCON. No by my fathers skin, my hand downe I lay it!
Loke as I haue promised, I wil not denay it,
But Hodge take good heede now. . . .   *[He gives him a blow.*

HODGE. Gogs hart thou false villaine dost thou bite me?

BAYLY. What Hodge doth he hurt the or euer he begin?

HODGE. He thrust me into the buttocke, with a bodkin or a pin,
I saie, Gammer, Gammer?

GAMMER.   How now Hodge, how now?

HODGE. Gods malt Gammer gurton.

GAMMER.   Thou art mad ich trow.

HODGE. Will you see the deuil Gammer?

GAMMER.   The deuil sonne god blesse vs.

HODGE. Chould iche were hanged Gammer.

GAMMER.   Mary se ye might dresse vs.

HODGE. Chaue it by the masse Gammer.

GAMMER.   What not my neele Hodge?

[1] Hodge speaks in dialect, where "chal," "cham," and "chave" = "I shall," "I am," and "I have."

HODGE. Your Nedle Gammer, your nedle.

GAMMER. No fie, dost but dodge.

HODGE. Cha found your nedle Gammer, here in my hand be it.

GAMMER. For al the loues on earth Hodge, let me see it.

HODGE. Soft Gammer.

GAMMER. Good Hodge.

HODGE. Soft ich say, tarie a while.

GAMMER. Nay sweete Hodge say truth, and do not me begile.

HODGE. Cham sure on it ich warrant you: it goes no more a stray.

GAMMER. Hodge when I speake so faire: wilt stil say me nay?

HODGE. Go neare the light gammer this wel in faith good lucke.
Chwas almost vndone: twas so far in my buttocke.

GAMMER. Tis mine owne deare nedle Hodge, sykerly I wot.

HODGE. Cham I not a good sonne gammer, cham I not?

GAMMER. Christs blessing light on thee, hast made me for euer.

HODGE. Ich knew that ich must finde it, els choud a had it neuer.

CHAT. By my troth Gossyp gurten, I am euen as glad
As though I mine owne self as good a turne had.

BAYLY. And I by my conscience, to see it so come forth,
Reioyce so much at it, as three nedles be worth.

DR RAT. I am no whit sory to see you so reioyce.

DICCON. Nor I much the gladder for al this noyce:
Yet say gramercy Diccon, for springing of the game.

GAMMER. Gramercy Diccon twenty times, how glad cham,
If that could do so much, your masterdome to come hether,
Master Rat, goodwife Chat, and Diccon together:
Cha but one halfpeny, as far as iche know it,
And chil not rest this night, till ich bestow it.
If euer ye loue me, let vs go in and drinke.

5. GEORGE GASCOIGNE (*c.* 1535–77)

Supposes

The forces which, harmonized and fused, made for the greatness of Elizabethan drama are numerous. The native morality
strain, the medieval farce or interlude, the classical plays of
Terence and of Seneca—all these had to meet before the rise of
a Shakespeare was assured. Among these forces the Italian
comedy was by no means the least important. Performances
of Latin plays had been given in Rome and Ferrara many years
before we learn of similar productions in England, and the
revivals early called forth adapted and original plays in the
vernacular. Many of these must have been known here in
their original forms, and some at least were regularly translated
or paraphrased in an English dress. The earliest of these
translations is *Supposes*, rendered by that great pioneer,
George Gascoigne, from Ariosto's *I Suppositi*. The first prose

version of the latter had been acted at Ferrara in 1509. Printed in 1523, it was succeeded by a recasting of the play in verse, published in 1542. Both of these (the prose and the verse forms) seem to have been before Gascoigne when he was preparing his rendering, but for himself he chose the medium of prose. This choice of medium is not unimportant, for prose, after all, is the most natural form for the expression of comedy, and Gascoigne's experiment was destined to bear rich fruit in succeeding decades. From the stanzaic verse of the mysteries to the rimed couplets of the interludes, and from these on to blank verse, the gradual development of dramatic media is apparent. The last word, so far as innovation is concerned, is being said here by Gascoigne.

(*Supposes* was acted at Gray's Inn in 1566. It was first printed about 1572. The following extract is taken from the second edition, 1575.)

A PLEASANT DEVICE

DULIPO [*really* EROSTRATO, *who has changed places with, and taken the name of, his servant,* DULIPO, *each masquerading as the other*]. I thinke if I had as many eyes as *Argus*, I coulde not haue sought a man more narrowly in euery streete and euery by lane, there are not many Gentlemen, scholers, nor Marchauntes in the Citie of *Ferara*, but I haue mette with them, excepte him: peraduenture hee is come home an other way: but looke where he commeth at the last.

EROSTRATO. In good time haue I spied my good maister.

DULIPO. For the loue of God call me Dulipo (not master,) maintayne the credite that thou haste hitherto kepte, and let me alone.

EROSTRATO. Yet sir let me sometimes do my duetie vnto you, especially where no body heareth.

DULIPO. Yea, but so long the Parat vseth to crie knappe in sporte, that at the last she calleth hir maister knaue in earnest: so long you will vse to call me master, that at the last we shall be heard. What newes?

EROSTRATO. Good.

DULIPO. In deede?

EROSTRATO. Yea excellent, we haue as good as won the wager.

DULIPO. Oh, how happie were I if this were true?

EROSTRATO. Heare you me, yesternight in the euening I walked out, and found *Pasiphilo*, and with small entreating I had him home to supper, where by suche meanes as I vsed, he became my great friend, and tolde me the whole order of our aduersaries determination: yea and what *Damon* doth intend to do also, and hath promised me that fro time to time, what he can espie he will bring me word of it.

DULIPO. I can not tel whether you know him or no, he is not to trust vnto, a very flattering and a lying knaue.

EROSTRATO. I know him very well, he can not deceiue me: and this that he hath told me I know must needes be true.

DULIPO. And what was it in effect?

EROSTRATO. That *Damon* had purposed to giue his daughter in mariage to this doctor, vpon the dower that he hath profered.

DULIPO. Are these your good newes? your excellent newes?

EROSTRATO. Stay a whyle, you will vnderstande me before you heare me.

DULIPO. Well, say on.

EROSTRATO. I answered to that, I was ready to make hir the lyke dower.

DULIPO. Well sayde.

EROSTRATO. Abide, you heare not the worst yet.

DULIPO. O God, is there any worsse behinde?

EROSTRATO. Worsse? why what assurance coulde you suppose that I might make without some speciall consent from *Philogano* my father?

DULIPO. Nay, you can tell, you are better scholer than I.

EROSTRATO. In deede you haue lost your time: for the books that you tosse now a dayes, treate of smal science.

DULIPO. Leaue thy iesting, and proceede.

EROSTRATO. I sayd further, that I receyued letters lately from my father, whereby I vnderstoode that he woulde be heere very shortly to performe all that I had profered: therefore I required him to request *Damon* on my behalf, that he would stay his promise to the doctor for a fourtnight or more.

DULIPO. This is somewhat yet, for by this meanes I shal be sure to linger and liue in hope one fourtnight longer: but, at the fourth-nights ende when *Philogano* commeth not, how shall I then do? yea and though he came, howe may I any way hope of his consent, when he shall see, that to follow this amorous enterprise, I haue set aside all studie, all remembraunce of my duetie, and all dread of shame. Alas, alas, I may go hang myselfe.

EROSTRATO. Comforte your selfe man, and trust in me: there is a salue for euery sore, and doubt you not, to this mischeefe we shall finde a remedie.

DULIPO. O friend reuiue me, that hitherto since I first attempted this matter haue bene continually dying.

EROSTRATO. Well harken a while then: this morning I tooke my horse and rode into the fieldes to solace my self, and as I passed the foorde beyonde *S. Anthonies* gate, I met at the foote of the hill a gentleman riding with two or three men: and as me thought by his habite and his lookes, he should be none of the wisest. He saluted me, and I him: I asked him whence he came, and whither he would? he answered that he had come from *Venice*, then from *Padua*, nowe was going to *Ferrara*, and so his countrey, whiche is

Scienna: As soone as I knewe him to be a *Scenese*, sodenly lifting
vp mine eyes, (as it were with an admiration) I sayd vnto him, are you
a *Scenese*, and come to *Ferrara*? why not, sayde he: quoth I (halfe
and more with a trembling voyce) know you not the daunger that
should ensue if you be knowne in *Ferrara* to be a *Scenese*? he more
than halfe amased, desired me earnestly to tell him what I ment.

DULIPO. I vnderstande not wherto this tendeth.

EROSTRATO. I beleeue you: but harken to me.

DULIPO. Go too then.

EROSTRATO. I answered him in this sorte: Gentleman, bycause
I haue heretofore founde very curteous entertaynement in your
countrey, (beeing a student there,) I accompt my self as it were
bounde to a *Scenese*: and therefore if I knewe of any mishappe
towards any of that countrey, God forbid but I should disclose it:
and I maruell that you knewe not of the iniurie that your countrey-
men offered this other day to the Embassadours of Counte *Hercules*.

DULIPO. What tales he telleth me: what appertayne these to me?

EROSTRATO. If you will harken a whyle, you shall finde them no
tales, but that they appertayne to you more than you thinke for.

DULIPO. Foorth.

EROSTRATO. I tolde him further, these Ambassadoures of Counte
Hercules had dyuers Mules, Waggens, and Charettes, laden with
diuers costly iewels, gorgeous furniture, & other things which they
caried as presents, (passing that way) to the king of *Naples*: the which
were not only stayd in *Sciene* by the officers whom you cal Customers,
but serched, ransacked, tossed & turned, & in the end exacted for
tribute, as if they had bene the goods of a meane marchaunt.

DULIPO. Whither the diuell wil he? is it possible that this geare
appertaine any thing to my cause? I finde neither head nor foote in it.

EROSTRATO. O how impacient you are: I pray you stay a while.

DULIPO. Go to yet a while then.

EROSTRATO. I proceeded, that vpon these causes the Duke sent
his Chauncelor to declare the case vnto the Senate there, of whome
he had the moste vncurteous answere that euer was heard: wher-
vpon he was so enraged with all of that countrey, that for reuenge
he had sworne to spoyle as many of them as euer should come to
Ferara, and to sende them home in their dublet and their hose.

DULIPO. And I pray thee how couldest thou vpon the sudden
deuise or imagine suche a lye? and to what purpose?

EROSTRATO. You shall heare by and by a thing as fitte for our
purpose, as any could haue happened. . . . He, as I say, when he
hard these words, would haue turned the bridle: and I fayning a
countenance as though I were somewhat pensiue and carefull for
him, paused a while, & after with a great sighe saide to him: Gentleman, for the curtesie that (as I said) I haue found in your countrey,
& bicause your affaires shall be the better dispatched, I will finde the
meanes to lodge you in my house, and you shal say to euery man
that you are a *Sicilian* of *Cathanea*, your name *Philogano*, father

60

to me that am in deede of that countrey and citie, called here *Erostrato*. And I (to pleasure you) will (during your abode here) do you reuerence as you were my father.

DULIPO. Out vpon me, what a grosse hedded foole am I? now I perceiue whereto this tale tendeth.

6. ROBERT WILMOT (*fl.* 1566–91) AND OTHERS

Tancred and Gismund

The imitation of Italian academic drama flourished particularly at the Inns of Court, yet always there appeared, even in the midst of the chillest of classical forms, a certain 'romantic' note which showed that there was life-blood coursing beneath the external frigidity of the treatment. In *Tancred and Gismund*, or *Gismond of Salerne*, the horrors at the end are derived from Seneca, but the love-story itself has about it an atmosphere which did not come from neo-classic sources. This story, taken from Boccaccio, tells how Gismund falls in love with Guizard, how Guizard is caught as he comes from her chamber, how his heart is sent to Gismund by her father, and how the heroine finally takes poison and dies. The general working out of the theme is, of course, in the academic style, even to the retention of a chorus, but it was from such plays as this that Kyd and his companions built up their later Elizabethan tragedies. The passage of " stichomythia " should be noted in this extract as well as the formal blank-verse medium which only occasionally seems to tremble back toward the verge of rime.

(The original *Gismond of Salerne* is preserved in two British Museum manuscripts. In this form it was acted at the Inner Temple in 1567. In 1592 Wilmot, one of the authors of the first play, republished it as *Tancred and Gismund*, " Newly reuiued and polished according to the *decorum* of these daies." The following extract is taken from the last-mentioned.)

GUIZARD IS BROUGHT BEFORE TANCRED

IULIO. If it please your highnes, hither haue we broght
This captiue Earl as you commanded vs.
Whom (as we wer fortold) euen there we found
Where by your maiesty we were inioin'd
To watch for him. What more your highnes willes,
This heart and hand shal execute your hest.
TANCRED. Iulio, we thank your paines. Ah Palurin,
Haue we deserued in such traiterous sort
Thou shouldst abuse our kingly courtesies,
Which we too long in fauor haue bestowed
Vpon thy false-dissembling hart with vs?

What grief thou therewithal hast throwen on vs,
What shame vpon our house, what dire distresse
Our soul endures, cannot be vttered.
And durst thou villen dare to vndermine
Our daughters chamber, durst thy shameles face
Be bold to kisse her: th' rest we wil conceale.
Sufficeth that thou knowest I too wel know
All thy proceedings in thy priuat shames.
Herin what hast thou wonne? thine own content,
With the displeasure of thy Lord and king.
The thought whereof if thou hadst had in mind
The least remorce of loue and loyaltie
Might haue restraind thee from so foule a fact.
But Palurin, what may I deem of thee,
Whom neither feare of gods, nor loue of him
(Whose Princely fauor hath been thine vpreare)
Could quench the fewel of thy lewd desires.
Wherfore content thee that we are resolu'd
(And therfore laid to snare thee with this bayt)
That thy iust death, with thine effused blood,
Shal coole the heate and choler of our mood.
   GUIZARD. My Lord the king, neither do I mislike
Your sentence, nor do your smoking sighes
Reacht from the entrals of your boiling heart,
Disturbe the quiet of my calmed thoughts:
For this I feele, and by experience proue,
Such is the force and endlesse might of loue,
As neuer shal the dread of carren death
That hath enuide our ioyes, inuade my breast,
For if it may be found a fault in me
(That euermore haue lou'd your Maiestie)
Likewise to honor and to loue your child,
If loue vnto you both may be a fault,
But vnto her my loue exceedes compare,
Then this hath been my fault, for which I ioy
That in the greatest lust of all my life,
I shall submitte for her sake to endure
The pangues of death. Oh mighty Lord of loue
Strengthen thy vassal, boldlie to receaue
Large wounds into this body for her sake.
Then vse my life or death, my Lord and king,
For your reliefe to ease your grieued soule:
For whether I liue, or els that I must die,
To end your paines I am content to beare:
Knowing by death I shall bewray the trueth
Of that sound heart which liuing was her owne,
And died aliue for her that liued mine.
   TANCRED. Thine, *Palurin*? what, liues my daughter thine?

Traitor thou wrongst me, for she liueth mine.
Rather I wish ten thousand sundrie deaths,
Then I to liue and see my daughter thine.
Thine, that is dearer then my life to me?
Thine, whom I hope to see an Empresse?
Thine, whom I cannot pardon from my sight?
Thine, vnto whom we haue bequeath'd our crown?
Iulio, we wil that thou informe from vs
Renuchio the Capten of our Gard,
That we commaund this traitor be conueyd
Into the dungeon vnderneath our Tower,
There let him rest vntil he be resolu'd
What further we intend, which to vnderstand,
We will *Renuchio* repaire to vs.

   IULIO. O that I might your Maiestie entreate
With clemencie to beutifie your seate,
Toward this Prince distrest by his desires,
Too many, all too strong to captiuate.

   TANCRED. This is the soundest safetie for a king
To cut them off that vex or hinder him.

   IULIO. This haue I found the safetie of a king,
To spare the Subiects that do honor him.

   TANCRED. Haue we been honourd by this leachers lust?

   IULIO. No, but by this deuout submission.

   TANCRED. Our fortune saies we must do what we may.

   IULIO. This is praise-worth, not to do what you may.

   TANCRED. And may the Subiect countermaund the king?

   IULIO. No, but intreat him.

   TANCRED. What he shal decree?

   IULIO. What wisdom shall discern.

   TANCRED. Nay what our word
Shal best determine. We wil not replie.
Thou knowest our mind, our heart cannot be easd,
But with the slaughter of this *Palurin*. . . .

Chorus primus

   CHORUS. Who doth not know the fruits of Paris loue,
Nor vnderstand the end of Helens ioy,
He may behold the fatall ouerthrow
Of Priams house, and of the towne of Troy.
His death at last, and her eternall shame,
For whom so many noble knights were slaine.
So many a Duke, so many a Prince of fame
Bereft his life, and left there in the plaine.
Medeas armed hand, Elizas sword,
Wretched Leander drenched in the floud.
Phillis so long that waited for her Lord
All these too dearly bought their loues with bloud.

7. THOMAS NORTON (1532–84) AND THOMAS SACKVILLE (1536–1608)

Gorboduc

Gorboduc forms a convenient starting-point for the study of English tragedy, for in it we first find a definitely ordered dramatic piece freed from the trappings of the morality play and conscious of foreign (particularly Italian) endeavours along similar lines. *Gorboduc* is not a great play, but it shows us clearly how the serious drama in England was being formed. Seneca and the Italian Senecans are the masters of Norton and Sackville, but the theme is taken from the legendary history of Britain. An effort is being made to depict character, and the dialogue (cast in a blank-verse mould) has a certain dignity which almost atones for its dullness. We are here, of course, in the realm of academic precision, in spite of the fact that Sidney found this tragedy wanting in decorum, but there is just sufficient of freshness in it to place it in a regular line of development which, carried on by the University Wits, finds its culmination in Shakespeare.

(*Gorboduc ; or, Ferrex and Porrex* was acted at the Inner Temple during the Christmas season of 1561. It was published in 1565, and again in 1570. There have been frequent modern reprints.)

FERREX AIRS HIS GRIEVANCES TO HIS COUNSELLORS

FERREX. I meruaile much what reason ledde the king
My Father, thus without all my desert,
To reue me halfe the kingdome, which by course
Of law and nature should remayne to me.
　HERMON. If you with stubborne and vntamed pryde
Had stood against him in rebelling wise,
Or if with grudging minde you had enuied
So slow a slidyng of his aged yeres,
Or sought before your time to haste the course
Of fatall death vpon his royall head,
Or stained your stocke with murder of your kyn :
Some face of reason might perhaps haue seemed,
To yelde some likely cause to spoyle ye thus.
　FERREX. The wrekeful Gods powre on my cursed head,
Eternall plagues and neuer dying woes,
The hellish prince, adiudge my dampned ghost
To *Tantales* thirste, or proude *Ixions* wheele,
Or cruell gripe to gnaw my growing harte,
To during tormentes and vnquenched flames,
If euer I conceyued so foule a thought,
To wisshe his ende of life, or yet of reigne.
　DORDAN. Ne yet your father (O most noble Prince)

Did euer thinke so fowle a thing of you.
For he, with more than fathers tendre loue,
While yet the fates do lende him life to rule,
(Who long might lyue to see your ruling well)
To you my Lorde, and to his other sonne:
Lo he resignes his realme and royaltie:
Which neuer would so wise a Prince haue done,
If he had once misdemed that in your harte
There euer lodged so vnkinde a thought.
But tendre loue (my Lorde) and setled truste
Of your good nature, and your noble minde,
Made him to place you thus in royall throne,
And now to geue you half his realme to guide,
Yea and that halfe which in abounding store
Of things that serue to make a welthy realme,
In stately cities, and in frutefull soyle,
In temperate breathing of the milder heauen,
In thinges of nedeful vse, which frendly sea,
Transportes by traffike from the forreine partes,
In flowing wealth, in honour and in force,
Doth passe the double value of the parte,
That *Porrex* hath allotted to his reigne.
Such is your case, such is your fathers loue.

   FERREX. Ah loue, my frendes? loue wrongs not whom he
    loues.

   DORDAN. Ne yet he wrongeth you, that geueth you
So large a reigne, ere that the course of time
Bring you to kingdome by discended right,
Which time perhaps might end your time before.

   FERREX. Is this no wrong, say you, to reaue from me
My natiue right of halfe so great a realme?
And thus to matche his yonger sonne with me
In egall power, and in as great degree?
Yea and what sonne? the sonne whose swelling pride
Woulde neuer yelde one poinct of reuerence,
Whan I the elder and apparaunt heire
Stoode in the likelihode to possesse the whole,
Yea and that sonne which from his childish age
Enuieth myne honour and doth hate my life.
What will he now do, when his pride, his rage,
The mindefull malice of his grudging harte,
Is armed with force, with wealth, and kingly state?

   HERMON. Was this not wrong, yea yll aduised wrong,
To giue so mad a man so sharpe a sworde,
To so great perill of so great missehappe,
Wide open thus to set so large a waye?

   DORDAN. Alas my Lord, what griefull thing is this,
That of your brother you can thinke so ill?

E

I neuer saw him vtter likelie signe,
Whereby a man might see or once misdeme
Such hate of you, ne such vnyelding pride.
Ill is their counsell, shamefull be their ende,
That raysing such mistrustfull feare in you,
Sowing the seede of such vnkindly hate,
Trauaile by treason to destroy you both.
Wise is your brother, and of noble hope,
Worthie to welde a large and mightie realme
So much a stronger frende haue you therby,
Whose strength is your strength, if you gree in one.

8. UNKNOWN AUTHOR

The Troublesome Reign of John King of England

For comparison with Bale's *Kynge Johan*, parallel passages are given here from that chronicle history which later served as a model for Shakespeare. *The Troublesome Reign* was issued anonymously in 1591, and was reprinted as "by W. Sh." in 1611 and as "by W. Shakespeare" in 1622. These ascriptions are due entirely to the publishers, who no doubt wished the public to confuse this play with the genuine Shakespearian drama. No sure attribution has been made as yet by any modern scholar; at most we can say that *The Troublesome Reign* is in the style of the University Wits. No more illumination could be gained on the development of dramatic characterization and technique than from a careful comparison of the three John plays. With Bale we are still in the realm of theology, with human elements only tentatively appearing; with the author of *The Troublesome Reign* we move in a sphere of crude exposition and vulgar farce; with Shakespeare characterization has emerged triumphant, style is made adequate to its subject, and all unnecessary elements in the plot are deleted or changed.

(The following extracts are based on that of the first edition of 1591.)

THE EXCOMMUNICATION OF KING JOHN

CARDINAL. Then I Pandulph of Pandoa, Legate from the Apostolike Sea, do in the name of Saint Peter and his successor our holy Father Pope Innocent, pronounce thee accursed, discharging euery one of thy subiectes of all dutie and fealtie that they doo owe to thee, and pardon and forgiuenes of sinne to those or them whatsoeuer, which shall carrie armes against thee, or murder thee : This I pronounce, and charge all good men to abhorre thee as an excommunicate person.

JOHN. So sir, the more the Fox is curst the better a fares: if God blesse me and my Land, let the Pope and his shauelings curse and spare not.

CARDINAL. Further more, I charge thee Philip King of France, and al the Kings and Princes of Christendome, to make war vppon this miscreant: and whereas thou hast made a league with him, and confirmed it by oath, I doo in the name of our foresaid father the Pope, acquit thee of that oath, as vnlawful, being made with an heretike; how saist thou Philip, doost thou obey?

JOHN. Brother of Fraunce, what say you to the Cardinall?

PHILIP. I say, I am sorrie for your Majestie, requesting you to submit your selfe to the Church of Rome.

JOHN. And what say you to our league, if I doo not submit?

PHILIP. What should I say? I must obey the Pope.

JOHN. Obey the Pope, and breake your oath to God?

PHILIP. The Legate hath absolu'de me of mine oath:
Then yeeld to Rome, or I defie thee heere.

JOHN. Why Philip, I defie the Pope and thee,
False as thou art, and periured King of Fraunce,
Unworthie man to be accompted King.
Giu'st thou thy sword into a Prelates hands?
Pandulph, where I of Abbots, Monkes, and Friers
Haue taken somewhat to maintaine my warres,
Now will I take no more but all they haue.
Ile rowse the lazie lubbers from their Cells,
And in despight Ile send them to the Pope.
Mother come you with me, and for the rest
That will not follow John in this attempt,
Confusion light vpon their damned soules.
Come Lords, fight for your King, that fighteth for your good.

JOHN SUBMITS TO ROME

PANDULPH. Now John, vnworthie man to breath on earth,
That dost oppugne against thy Mother Church:
Why am I sent for to thy cursed selfe?

JOHN. Thou man of God, Vicegerent for the Pope,
The holy Vicar of S. Peters Church,
Upon my knees, I pardon craue of thee,
And doo submit me to the sea of Rome,
And vow for penaunce of my high offence,
To take on me the holy Crosse of Christ,
And carry Armes in holy Christian warres.

PANDULPH. No John, thy crowching and dissembling thus
Cannot deceiue the Legate of the Pope,
Say what thou wilt, I will not credit thee:
Thy Crowne and Kingdome both are tane away,
And thou art curst without redemption.

JOHN [aside]. Accurst indeed to kneele to such a drudge,
And get no help with thy submission. . . .
No John, submit againe, dissemble yet,

For Priests and Women must be flattered.
[*To* PANDULPH] Yet holy Father thou thy selfe dost know,
No time to late for sinners to repent,
Absolue me then, and John doth sweare to doo
The vttermost what euer thou demaundst.

  PANDULPH. John, now I see thy harty penitence,
I rew and pitty thy distrest estate,
One way is left to reconcile thy selfe,
And only one which I shall shew to thee.
Thou must surrender to the sea of Rome
Thy Crowne and Diademe. . . .

  JOHN. What! shall I giue my Crowne with this right hand?
No: with this hand defend thy Crowne and thee.
What newes with thee?   [*Enter* MESSENGER.

  MESSENGER. Please it your Maiestie, there is discried on the
Coast of Kent an hundred Sayle of Ships, which of all men is thought
to be the French fleete, vnder the conduct of the Dolphin, so that
it puts the cuntrie in a mutinie, so they send to your Grace for
succour.

  JOHN. How now Lord Cardinall, whats your best advise?
These mutinies must be allayd in time,
By pollicy or headstrong rage at least.
O John, these troubles tyre thy wearyed soule,
And like to Luna in a sad Eclipse,
So are thy thoughts and passions for this newes.
Well may it be, when Kings are grieued so,
The vulgar sort worke Princes ouerthrow.

  PANDULPH. K. John, for not effecting of thy plighted vow,
This strange annoyance happens to thy land:
But yet be reconcild vnto the Church,
And nothing shall be grieuous to thy state.

  JOHN. Oh Pandulph, be it as thou hast decreed,
John will not spurne against thy sound aduise,
Come lets away, and with thy helpe I trow,
My Realme shall florish, and my Crowne in peace.

III. LATE SIXTEENTH CENTURY

THE early and mid sixteenth century had prepared the way ; it was left for the last years of Elizabeth's reign to reach fulfilment. This was done partly by perfecting the media of blank verse and prose introduced in *Gorboduc* and *Supposes*, partly by combining and harmonizing the divergent atmospheres which had been brought to the early theatre from sources native and foreign.

The tragi-comedy and the romance still remained among the most popular of dramatic types. *Clyomon and Clamydes* illustrates the most flagrant style in this kind, while the perfection and refinement of the romantic atmosphere can be traced progressively through the comedies of Lyly, Peele, and Greene. Munday's *John a Kent* has also been introduced here in order to show an example of a kindred play-form independent of the school of the University Wits. Tragedy takes several guises in this period. Ranting bombast clothed in lovely verse was made popular by *Tamburlaine*. A subtler psychology was suggested in *Doctor Faustus*, and this play also provided the initial impetus to that dramatic type which seems to have been known contemporaneously as the "infernall." Thrilling incidents and the revenge *motif* made *The Spanish Tragedy* popular and brought many imitators. *The Tragedy of Hoffman* has likewise been illustrated here in order to give an example of a revenge play of capable workmanship apart from Kyd's effort. *The Battle of Alcazar* provides a good specimen of those "noises off" which probably gave as much entertainment to Elizabethan audiences as actual dramatic dialogue.

In the works of the University Wits and of their contemporaries neither tragedy nor comedy has as yet come to realize its high purpose. Poetry tends to be regarded by itself, its dramatic function neglected. Form and construction are still hesitating, and psychological delineation lacks boldness and surety. It was in these years, however,

EXTRACTS FROM BRITISH & IRISH PLAYS

that Shakespeare started to write, and it is his greatest claim to fame that he took what the contemporary stage had to offer him and made that artistically proportioned. Out of Lyly and Greene he fashioned *A Midsummer Night's Dream* and *Twelfth Night*; out of *Tamburlaine* and *Doctor Faustus* and *The Spanish Tragedy* he built up the majesty and the terror of his later tragedies. Had Shakespeare not been, the University Wits would have seemed to do much; with Shakespeare as a touchstone, they seem only pioneers preparing the way and waiting for the master.

1. UNKNOWN AUTHOR

Clyomon and Clamydes

The first and only contemporary edition of this play appeared in 1599—*The Historie of the two valiant Knights, Syr Clyomon Knight of the Golden Sheeld, sonne to the King of Denmarke: And Clamydes the white Knight, sonne to the King of Suauia.* Nothing is known for certain regarding the fortunes of the drama, save that at one time it was acted by the Queen's men. A tentative attribution to Peele on the strength of a lost manuscript note is now thoroughly discredited, and it is generally assumed that, in spite of the late date of publication, *Clyomon* must have been originally written about 1570–80. Its interest lies in the fact that it is one of the very few relics of the once popular 'romance' which apparently dominated the early stage. The titles of many of these are preserved in the Revels' Office accounts, but almost every one has perished. This play gives an excellent idea of the dramatic styles loved by the people immediately before the development of true tragedy and comedy in the hands of the University Wits. The whole drama is written in rimed verse—mostly ' fourteeners '—and tells, in somewhat confusing manner, of the adventures of the two worthies celebrated on the title-page, introducing some crude humour in the figure of " subtill Shift the Vice."

(*Clyomon* was included in the works of Peele as edited by Dyce, and again as edited by Bullen. A facsimile was prepared by J. S. Farmer; and the play was edited separately by W. W. Greg for the Malone Society (1913).)

CLYOMON TALKS TO SHIFT, THE VICE

Here let [SHIFT] *slip vnto the Stage backwards, as though he had puld his leg out of the mire, one boote off, and rise vp to run in againe.*

CLYOMON. Why how now, whither runst thou, art thou foolish in thy mind?

SHIFT. But to fetch one of my legs ant shall please, that I haue
left in the mire behind.

CLYOMON. One of thy legs, why looke man, both thy legs thou
hast,

It is but one of thy bootes thou hast lost, thy labour thou doest
wast.

SHIFT. But one of my bootes, Iesu, I had such a wrench with the
fall,

That I assure, I did thinke one of my legs had gone withall.

CLYOMON. Well let that passe, and tell me what thou art, and
what is thy name?

And from whence thou cam'st, and whither thy iourney thou doest
frame,

That I haue met thee by the way, thus trauelling in this sort?

SHIFT. What you haue requested, ant shall please, I am able to
report,

What I am by my nature each wight shall perceiue

That frequenteth my company, by the learning I haue.

I am the sonne of *Appollo*, and from his high seate I came,

But whither I go, it skils not, for Knowledge is my name:

And who so hath knowledge, what needs he to care

Which way the wind blowe, his way to prepare.

CLYOMON. And art thou Knowledge, of troth I am glad that I
haue met with thee. . . .

Of troth, then for excellencie, I will thee gladly entertaine,

If in case that with me thou wilt promise to remaine.

SHIFT. Nay ant shall please ye, I am like to a woman, say nay
and take it,

When a gentleman profers entertainment, I were a foole to forsake it.

CLYOMON. Well Knowledge, then sith thou art content my seruant
to bee,

And endued with noble qualities, thy personage I see,

Thou hauing perfect knowledge how thy selfe to behaue:

I will send thee of mine arrant, but haste thither I craue:

For here I will stay thy comming againe.

SHIFT. Declare your pleasure sir, and whither I shall go, and then
the case is plain.

CLYOMON. Nay of no great importance, but being here in *Suauia*

And neare vnto the Court, I would haue thee to take thy way

Thither with all speede, because I would heare

If any shewes or triumphs be towards, else would I not come
there,

For onely vpon feates of armes, is all my delight.

SHIFT. If I had knowne so much before, serue that serue will,
I would haue seru'd no martiall Knight.

Well sir, to accomplish your will, to the court I will hy,

And what newes is there stirring, bring word by and by.

EXTRACTS FROM BRITISH & IRISH PLAYS

SHIFT AND BRYAN SANS FOY MAKE A PRISONER OF CLAMYDES

CLAMYDES [*entering with the head of a dragon he has slain*]. Ah
    happy day my deadly foe submitted hath to death,
Lo heere the hand, lo heere the sword that stopt the vitall breath:
Lo heere the head that shall possesse my *Iulianas* deare,
The Knight of the golden Sheeld his force, what neede I now to
    feare:
Since I by force subdued haue this Serpent fierce of might,
Who vanquisht hath as I haue heard, full many a worthie Knight.
Which for to winne my Ladyes loue, their liues haue venterd heere,
Besides that cowardly *Bryan* which the faithlesse shield doth beare:
A number keepes as I haue heard, as captiues in his hold,
Whome he hath by inchantment got, and not through courage bold.
Shall such defamed dastards, dard by Knights, thus beare their
    name?
Shall such as are without all faith, liue to impaire our fame?
Shall valiant harts by cowardly charme, be kept in captiues thrall?
Shall Knights liue subiect to a wretch which hath no hart at all?
Nay first *Clamydes* claime to thee fell *Atrapos* his stroke,
Ere thou doest see such worthy Knights to beare the heauie yoke,
Of cowardly *Bryan* without faith, his charmes let daunt not thee,
And for his force thou needst not feare, the Gods thy shield will be.
Well, to meete the Knight of the golden Shield, yet ten daies space
    I haue,
And to set free these worthy Knights, but rest a while I craue.
Heere in this place neere to this fort, for that I weary am
With trauell, since from killing of the Serpent late I came:
Lo heere a while I mind to rest, and *Bryan* then subdue,
And then to *Alexanders* court, to keepe my promise true.
        [*Heere let him sit downe and rest himselfe.* Enter BRYAN
        SANS FOY, *and* SHIFT.
  BRYAN. Come Knowledge, for here he lyes layd weary on the
    ground:
  SHIFT. Nay, ile not come in his sight, if you would giue me a
    thousand pound.
For he is the terriblest Knight of any you haue heard spoke,
Heele beate a hundreth such as you and I am downe at one stroke.
  BRYAN. Tush, feare thou naught at all, I haue charmed him, and
    he is fast asleepe,
Lying neere vnto the Castle here which I do keepe.
And ten dayes in this sleepe I haue charm'd him to remaine,
Before nature shall ouercome it, that he might wake againe.
In the meane season, lo behold the Serpents head ile take away,
His shield and his apparell, this done, then will I conuay
His body into prison, with other his companions to lye,
Whose strengths, ah Knowledge, I durst neuer attempt to try.

72

LATE SIXTEENTH CENTURY

SHIFT. Ah handle him softly, or else you wil cause him to awake:
BRYAN. Tush, tush, not if all the noyse in the world I were able
to make,
Till ten dayes be expired, the charme will not leaue him,
And then I am sure he will maruell who did thus deceiue him:
So now he is stripped, stay thou here for a season,
And ile go fetch two of my seruants to cary him to prison.   [*Exit.*
SHIFT. Well do so maister *Bryan*, and for your comming ile stay,
Gogs bloud what a villaine am I my master to betray.
Nay sure ile awake him if it be possible ere they carry him to iayle:
Maister, what maister, awake man, what maister, ah it will not
preuaile.
Am not I worthie to be hangd, was euer seene such a deceitfull
knaue?
What villany was in me, when vnto *Bryan* vnderstanding I gaue
Of my maisters being in this forrest, but much I muse indeed
What he meanes to do with my maisters apparell, his shield and the
head?
Well, seeing it is through my villany, my maister is at this drift,
Yet when he is in prison, *Shift* shall not be voide of a shift
To get him away, but if it euer come to his eare
That I was the occasion of it, heele hang me thats cleare.
Well heere comes *Bryan*, ile cloke with him if I may,
To haue the keeping of my maister in prison night and day.
                    [*Enter* BRYAN SANCE FOY, *two seruants.*
BRYAN. Come sirs take vp this body, and cary it into the appointed
place,
And there let it lye, for as yet he shall sleepe ten dayes space.
SHIFT. How say you maister *Bryan*, shall I of him haue the gard?
BRYAN. By my troth policie, thy good will to reward
In hope of thy iust seruice, content I agree   [*Cary him out.*
For to resign the keeping of this same Knight vnto thee.

2. JOHN LYLY (? 1554–1606)

Campaspe

In the eighties of the sixteenth century Euphuism swept like
a wind over London courtly society; the antithesis, the metaphors
and similes, the artificial art which Lyly had shown in his novel
Euphues, captured the attention of all men and marked an
epoch in English prose-writing. Lyly, however, was something
more than a mere stylist, and his plays have a value quite apart
from their adaptation of the new style to the requirements of
dramatic dialogue. Like Greene, he possesses an idyllic fancy
and a certain skill in the depicting of character. He is a student
as Greene was, and he presents us with a romantically coloured
classicism as gracious as that shown in a canvas by Botticelli,

73

EXTRACTS FROM BRITISH & IRISH PLAYS

thus paving a way for the young Shakespeare. For quotation here I have selected some passages from *Campaspe*, probably his earliest play, in which is traced the growing love of Apelles and Campaspe with the imperial magnanimity of Alexander. Campaspe has been sitting for her picture to Apelles, and is introduced as meditating on her changing moods.

(*Campaspe* seems to have been acted in 1584. There are several early quartos, no less than three being dated 1584. The extracts given here are based on the British Museum quarto of that date, which is no doubt the third issue of the play.)

The Awakening of Love

CAMPASPE [*sola*]. *Campaspe*, it is hard to iudge whether thy choice be more vnwise, or thy chaunce vnfortunate. Doest thou preferre, but stay, vtter not that in woordes, which maketh thine eares to glow with thoughts. Tush better thy tongue wagge, then thy heart break. Hath a painter crept further into thy mind then a prince? *Apelles* then *Alexander*? Fond wench, the basenes of thy mind bewraies the meannesse of thy birth. But alas, affection is a fyre which kindleth as well in the bramble as in the oake, & catcheth hold where it first lighteth, not where it may best burne. Larkes that mount aloft in the ayre, build their neastes below in the earth, and women that cast their eyes vpon kinges, may place their hearts vpon vassals. A needle will become thy fingers better then a Lute, and a distaffe is fitter for thy hand then a Scepter. Ants liue safely, til they haue gotten wings, & Iuniper is not blowne vp till it hath gotten an hie top. The meane estate is without care as long as it continueth without pride. But here commeth *Apelles*, in whom I woulde there were the like affection.

APELLES [*entering*]. Gentlewoman, the misfortune I had with your picture, wil put you to some paines to sitte againe to be painted.

CAMPASPE. It is smal paines for me to sit still, but infinit for you to draw stil.

APELLES. No Madame, to painte *Venus* was a pleasure, but to shadowe the sweete face of *Campaspe* it is a heauen.

CAMPASPE. If your tongue were made of the same flesh that your heart is, your wordes would be as your thoughtes are, but such a common thing it is amongst you to commend, that oftentimes for fashion sake you cal them bewtifull, whom you know black.

APELLES. What might men doe to be beleeued?

CAMPASPE. Whet their tongues on their heartes.

APELLES. So they doe, and speake as they think.

CAMPASPE. I would they did.

APELLES. I would they did not.

CAMPASPE. Why, would you haue them dissemble?

APELLES. Not in loue, but their loue. But wil you giue me leaue to aske you a question without offence?

74

CAMPASPE. So that you wil aunswere me an other without excuse.

APELLES. Whom do you loue best in the world?

CAMPASPE. He that made me last in the world.

APELLES. That was a God.

CAMPASPE. I had thought it had beene a man: but whome do you honour most, *Apelles*?

APELLES. The thing that is lykest you, *Campaspe*.

CAMPASPE. My picture?

APELLES. I dare not venture vpon your person. But come, let vs go in: for *Alexander* will thinke it long till we returne.

CAMPASPE CONFESSES HER LOVE

APELLES. I haue now, *Campaspe*, almost made an ende.

CAMPASPE. You tolde me, *Apelles*, you would neuer ende.

APELLES. Neuer end my loue: for it shal be eternal.

CAMPASPE. That is, neither to haue beginning nor ending.

APELLES. You are disposed to mistake, I hope you doe not mistrust.

CAMPASPE. What will you saye, if *Alexander* perceiue your loue?

APELLES. I will say it is no treason to loue.

CAMPASPE. But how if he wil not suffer thee to see my person?

APELLES. Then will I gase continually on thy picture.

CAMPASPE. That will not feede thy heart.

APELLES. Yet shall it fill mine eye: besides the sweete thoughtes, the sure hopes, thy protested faith, will cause me to imbrace thy shadow continually in mine armes, of the which by strong imagination I will make a substaunce.

CAMPASPE. Wel, I must be gon: but this assure your self, that I had rather bee in thy shop grinding colours, then in *Alexanders* court, following higher fortunes.   [*She goes out of the studio.* [*Alone.*] Foolish wench, what hast thou done? that, alas which cannot be vndone, and therfore I feare me vndone. But content is such a life, I care not for aboundance. O *Apelles*, thy loue commeth from the hearte, but *Alexanders* from the mouth. The loue of Kinges is lyke the blowinge of windes, which whistle sometimes gentlye amonge the leaues, and straight waies turne the trees vp by the rootes; or fire which warmeth a farre off, and burneth neere hand; or the sea, which maketh men hoyse their sayles in a flattering calme, and to cut their mastes in a rough storme. They place affection by times, by pollicie, by appointment. if they frowne, who dares cal them vnconstant, if bewray secretes, who will tearme them untrue, if fall to other loues, who trembles not, if he cal them vnfaithfull? In kings there can be no loue, but to Queenes: for as neere must they meete in maiestie, as they doe in affection. It is requisite to stande aloofe from Kinges loue, *Ioue*, and lightening.

THE MAGNANIMITY OF ALEXANDER

ALEXANDER. *Campaspe,* here is newes. *Apelles* is in loue with you.
CAMPASPE. It pleaseth your maiestie to say so. . . .
ALEXANDER. *Apelles,* take *Campaspe,* why moue ye not? *Campaspe,* take *Apelles.* wil it not be? If you be ashamed one of the other, by my consent you shal neuer come togeather. But dissemble not *Campaspe,* do you loue *Apelles?*
CAMPASPE. Pardon my Lord, I loue Apelles.
ALEXANDER. *Apelles,* it were a shame for you, being loued so openly of so faire a virgin, to say the contrary. Doe you loue *Campaspe?*
APELLES. Onely *Campaspe.*
ALEXANDER. Two louing wormes. *Hephestion,*[1] I perceiue *Alexander* cannot subdue the affections of men, though he conquer their countries. Loue falleth like dew aswel vpon the low grasse, as vpon the high Cædar. Sparkes haue their heate, Antes their gall, Flyes their splene. Well, enioy one an other, I giue her thee franckly *Apelles.* Thou shalt see that *Alexander* maketh but a toye of loue, and leadeth affection in fetters, vsing fancy as a foole to make him sport, or a minstrell to make him mery. It is not the amorous glaunce of an eie can settle an idle thought in the heart; no no, it is childrens game, a life for seamsters and scholers; the one pricking in cloutes haue nothing else to thinke on, the other picking fancies out of books, haue little els to meruaile at. Go *Apelles,* take with you your *Campaspe, Alexander* is cloied with looking on that which thou wondrest at.
APELLES. Thankes to your maiestie on bended knee, you haue honoured *Apelles.*
CAMPASPE. Thankes with bowed heart, you haue blessed *Campaspe.*

3. ROBERT GREENE (1558–92)

James IV

Of all the University Wits Greene is perhaps the most interesting figure, largely because of his essential humanity as revealed in the conscience-stricken pages of *A Groatsworth of Wit bought with a Million of Repentance.* It is a strange fact that the man who, by his own confession, had participated in many sins, should in his literary work give us the most delicate and the freshest scenes in all pre-Shakespearian drama. Both in *Friar Bacon* and in *James IV* the idyllic countryside is pictured with a clarity and a romantic glow which we seek in vain elsewhere. Most of the finer passages of the latter play are to

[1] Hephestion has revealed to Alexander the love of Apelles and Campaspe.

be found in the later acts, but it has been thought well to select for quotation here the opening scene, which introduces the fictional "history." This has been done partly because of the appearance there of Oberon and of Bohan, the melancholy Scot, partly because this scene is representative of a dramatic device which is most familiar in *The Taming of the Shrew*. The play opens with a dance of "antiques" or fairies, who are interrupted by the sudden sight of Bohan, only the King, Oberon, remaining.

(*The Scottish Historie of James the fourth, slaine at Flodden. Entermixed with a pleasant Comedie, presented by Oboram, King of Fayeries* seems to have been played originally in 1590 or 1591. It was entered in the Stationers' Register in May 1594, but the only contemporary edition which has come down to us is a quarto dated 1598. On this the following extract is based.)

Bohan tells Oberon of his Pessimism

BOHAN. Ay say, whats thou?

OBERON. Thy friend, *Bohan*.

BOHAN. What wot I or reck I that? whay, guid man, I reck no friend nor ay reck no foe; als ene to me. Git the ganging, and trouble not may whayet,[1] or ays gar the recon me nene of thay friend, by the Mary masse, sall I.

OBERON. Why, angrie Scot, I visit thee for loue; then what mooues thee to wroath?

BOHAN. The deele awhit reck I thy loue. For I knowe too well that true loue tooke her flight twentie winter sence to heauen, whither till ay can, weele I wot, ay sal nere finde loue: an thou lou'st me, leaue me to my selfe. But what were those Puppits that hopt and skipt about me year whayle?[2]

OBERON. My subiects.

BOHAN. Thay subiects! whay, art thou a King?

OBERON. I am.

BOHAN. The deele thou art! whay, thou look'st not so big as the king of Clubs, nor so sharpe as the king of Spades nor so faine as the king a Diamonds:[3] be the masse, ay take thee to bee the king of false harts; therfore I rid thee away, or ayse so curry your Kingdome that youse be glad to runne to saue your life.

OBERON. Why, stoycall Scott, do what thou dar'st to me: heare is my brest, strike.

BOHAN. Thou wilt not threap[4] me, this whiniard[5] has gard[6] many better men to lope then thou! But how now! Gos sayds, what, wilt not out? whay, thou wich, thou deele! Gads fute, may whiniard!

---

[1] quiet; *ay* stands for I.   [2] erewhile.
[3] The quarto reads "A daymonds."   [4] contradict.
[5] sword.   [6] caused.

OBERON. Why, pull, man; but what an 'twear out, how then?

BOHAN. This, then,—thou weart best begon first; for ayl so lop thy lyms that thouse go with half a knaues carkasse to the deele.

OBERON. Draw it out: now strike, foole, canst thou not?

BOHAN. Bread ay gad,[1] what deele is in me? whay, tell mee, thou skipiack, what art thou?

OBERON. Nay, first tell me what thou wast from thy birth, what thou hast past hitherto, why thou dwellest in a Tombe and leauest the world, and then I will release thee of these bonds; before, not.

BOHAN. And not before! then needs must, needs sal. I was borne a gentleman of the best bloud in all *Scotland*, except the King. When time brought me to age, and death tooke my parents, I became a Courtier; where, though ay list not to praise my selfe, ay engraued the memory of *Boughon* on the skin-coate of some of them, and reueld with the proudest.

OBERON. But why, liuing in such reputation, didst thou leaue to be a Courtier?

BOHAN. Because my pride was vanitie, my expence losse, my reward faire words and large promises, and my hopes spilt, for that after many yeares seruice one outran me; and what the deele should I then do there? No, no; flattering knaues, that can cog and prate fastest, speede best in the Court.

OBERON. To what life didst thou then betake thee?

BOHAN. I then chang'd the Court for the Countrey, and the wars for a wife: but I found the craft of swaines more vile then the knauery of courtiers, the charge of children more heauie then seruants, and wiues tongues worse then the warres it selfe; and therefore I gaue ore that, and went to the Citie to dwell; and there I kept a great house with smal cheer, but all was nere the neere.

OBERON. And why?

BOHAN. Because in seeking friends I found table guests to eate me and my meat; my wiues gossops to bewray the secrets of my heart, kindred to betray the effect of my life: which when I noted, the Court ill, the Country worse, and the Citie worst of all, in good time my wife died, ay wood she had died twentie winter sooner, by the masse leauing my two sonnes to the world, and shutting my selfe into this Tombe, where if I dye I am sure I am safe from wilde beasts, but whilest I liue cannot be free from ill companie. Besides now I am sure gif all my friends faile me, I sall haue a graue of mine owne prouiding. This is all. Now, what art thou?

OBERON. Oberon, King of Fayries, that loues thee because thou hatest the world; and to gratulate thee, I brought these Antiques to shew thee some sport in daunsing, which thou haste loued well.

BOHAN. Ha, ha, ha thinkest thou those puppits can please me? whay, I haue two sonnes, that with one Scottish gigge shall breake the necke of thy Antiques.

---

[1] Bread of God.

OBERON. That would I faine see.

BOHAN. Why thou shalt. Howe boyes.

[Enter SLIPPER *and* NANO.
Haud your clacks, lads, trattle not for thy life, but gather vppe
your legges, and daunce me forthwith a gigge worth the sight.

SLIPPER. Why I must talk on I dy for't: wherefore was my
tongue made?

BOHAN. Prattle an thou darst ene word more and ais dab this
whiniard in thy wembe.

OBERON. Be quiet Bohan. Ile strike him dumbe, and his brother
too: their talk shall not hinder our gyg—fall to it; dance, I say, man.

BOHAN. Dance, Humer, dance, ay rid [1] thee.

[The two dance a gig deuised for the nonst.
Now get you to the wide world with more then my father gaue me,
thats learning enough both kindes, knauerie & honestie; and that
I gaue you, spend at pleasure.

OBERON. Nay, for their sport I will giue them this gift: to the
Dwarfe I giue a quicke witte, prettie of body, and a warrant his
preferment to a Princes seruice, where by his wisdome he shall
gaine more loue then common; and to loggerhead your sonne
I giue a wandering life, and promise he shall neuer lacke, and
auow, that if in all distresses he call vpon me, to helpe him.—Now
let them go.   *[Exeunt with curtesies.*

BOHAN. Now, King, if thou bee a King, I will shew thee whay I
hate the world by demonstration. In the year 1520, was in
Scotland a King, ouerruled with parasites, misled by lust, and many
circumstances too long to trattle on now, much like our Court of
Scotland this day. That story haue I set down. Gang with me
to the Gallery, and Ile shew thee the same in action by guid fellowes
of our country men; and then when thou seest that, iudge if any
wise man would not leaue the world if he could.

OBERON. That will I see: lead, and ile follow thee.

4. GEORGE PEELE (*c.* 1557–96)

The Old Wives' Tale

The Old Wiues Tale. A pleasant conceited Comedie exists in
one quarto of the year 1595, and had been performed presumably
a few years previously. Its interest lies in the peculiarly original
handling of the romantic material. Stories of chivalrous adventure, of sorcerers, of spirits who rise amid thunder and lightning,
had been popular on the stage for well over a decade, but such
themes had been treated in a serious manner. Romantic
comedy may have made use of some similar episodes, but, again,
not in any spirit of ridicule. Even the greenwood life of Duke

[1] advise.

Frederick and the domestic troubles of Oberon are dealt with in a straightforward way. Elizabethan drama, however, was nothing if not original and pioneering, and one of its most interesting experiments was this play of Peele's. By the use of a typical romantic colouring the serious treatment of adventurous themes has been blended with burlesque, and real persons meet on the same plane with fictional characters who step out of the story and enact their own parts. It is not too much to say that we have here a kind of strange anticipation of Pirandellesque methods. The passage chosen is from the very beginning of the play; after the introduction of the 'fictional' characters the old wives' tale develops along startling lines with suitable comments from Frolicke and Fantasticke.

(The original quarto has been reprinted by W. W. Greg in the Malone Society publications, and modernized versions have appeared in some collections of representative Elizabethan plays. The following extract is from the quarto.)

THREE TRAVELLERS HEAR AN OLD WIVES' TALE

ANTICKE. How nowe fellowe *Franticke*, what all a mort? Doth this sadnes become thy madnes? What though wee haue lost our way in the woodes, yet neuer hang the head, as though thou hadst no hope to liue till to morrow: for *Fantasticke* and I will warrant thy life to night for twenty in the hundred.

FROLICKE. *Anticke* and *Fantasticke*, as I am frollicke franion, neuer in all my life was I so dead slaine. What? to loose our way in the woode, without either fire or candle so vncomfortable? *O cœlum! O terra! O Maria! O Neptune!*

FANTASTICKE. Why makes thou it so strange, seeing Cupid hath led our yong master to the faire Lady and she is the only Saint that he hath sworne to serue?

FROLICKE. What resteth then but wee commit him to his wench, and each of vs take his stand vp in a Tree, and sing out our ill fortune to the tune of O man in desperation?

ANTICKE. Desperately spoken fellow Frollicke in the darke: but seeing it falles out thus, let vs rehearse the old prouerb.

> Three merrie men, and three merrie men,
> And three merrie men be wee.
> I in the wood, and thou on the ground,
> And Iacke sleepes in the tree.

> *[Enter a* SMITH *with a Lanthorne & Candle.*

FROLICKE. . . . I perceiue the glymring of a Gloworme, a Candle, or a Cats eye, my life for a halfe pennie. In the name of my own father, be thou Oxe or Asse that appearest, tell vs what thou art.

SMITH. What am I? Why I am Clunch the Smith, what are you, what make you in my territories at this time of the night?

ANTICKE. What doe we make dost thou aske? why we make faces for feare. . . .

FROLICKE. And in faith Sir vnlesse your hospitalitie doe releeue vs, wee are like to wander with a sorrowfull hey ho, among the owlets, & Hobgoblins of the Forrest: good *Vulcan*, for Cupids sake that hath cousned vs all: befriend vs as thou maiest, and commaund vs howsoeuer, wheresoeuer, whensoeuer, in whatsoeuer, for euer and euer.

SMITH. Well Masters it seemes to mee you haue lost your waie in the wood: in consideration whereof, if you will goe with Clunch to his Cottage, you shall haue house roome, and a good fire to sit by, althogh we haue no bedding to put you in.

[*They are welcomed by* CLUNCH'S *wife and sing a song.*

ANTICKE. This sport dooes well: but me thinkes Gammer, a merry winters tale would driue away the time trimly, come I am sure you are not without a score.

FANTASTICKE. I faith Gammer a tale of an howre long were as good as an howres sleepe.

FROLICKE. Looke you Gammer, of the Gyant and the Kings Daughter, and I know not what, I haue seene the day when I was a litle one, you might haue drawne mee a mile after you with such a discourse.

OLD WOMAN. Well, since you be so importunate, my good man shall fill the pot and get him to bed, they that ply their worke must keepe good howres, one of you goe lye with him . . . so I am content to driue away the time with an old wiues winters tale. . . .

[ANTICKE *goes off to bed along with the* SMITH.

OLD WOMAN. Nowe this bargaine my Masters must I make with you, that you will say hum & ha to my tale, so shall I know you are awake.

BOTH. Content Gammer that will we doo.

OLD WOMAN. Once vppon a time there was a King or a Lord, or a Duke that had a faire daughter, the fairest that euer was; as white as snowe, and as redd as bloud: and once vppon a time his daughter was stollen away, and hee sent all his men to seeke out his daughter, and hee sent so long, that he sent all his men out of his Land.

FROLICKE. Who drest his dinner then?

OLD WOMAN. Nay . . . heare my tale. . . .

FANTASTICKE. Well sed, on with your tale Gammer.

OLD WOMAN. O Lord, I quite forgot, there was a Coniurer, and this Coniurer could doo any thing, and hee turned himselfe into a great Dragon, and carried the Kinges Daughter away in his mouth to a Castle that hee made of stone, and there he kept hir I know not how long, till at last all the Kinges men went out so long, that hir two Brothers went to seeke hir. O I forget: she (he I would say) turned a proper yong man to a Beare in the night, and a man in the day, and keeps by a crosse that parts three seuerall waies,

F

& he made his Lady run mad: gods me bones who comes
here?   [*Enter the two* BROTHERS.

FROLICKE. Soft Gammer, here some come to tell your tale for you.

FANTASTICKE. Let them alone, let vs heare what they will say.

1 BROTHER. Vpon these chalkie Cliffs of *Albion*
We are ariued now with tedious toile,
And compassing the wide world round about
To seeke our sister, to seeke faire *Delya* forth,
Yet cannot we so much as heare of hir.

2 BROTHER. O fortune cruell, cruell & vnkind,
Vnkind in that we cannot find our sister;
Our sister haples in hir cruell chance:
Soft who haue we here.

                [*Enter* SENEX *at the Crosse, stooping to gather.*

1 BROTHER. Now father God be your speed, what doo you gather
there?

OLD MAN. Hips and Hawes, and stickes and strawes, and thinges
that I gather on the ground my sonne.

1 BROTHER. Hips and Hawes, and stickes and strawes, why is
that all your foode father?

OLD MAN. Yea sonne.

2 BROTHER. Father, here is an Almes pennie for mee, and if
I speede in that I goe for, I will giue thee as good a Gowne of gray
as euer thou diddest wear. . . .

FROLICKE. Why this goes rounde without a fidling stick; but doo
you heare Gammer, was this the man that was a Beare in the night,
and a man in the day?

OLD WOMAN. I this is hee . . . but soft, who comes here?
O these are the haruest men; ten to one they sing a song of mowing.

5. ANTHONY MUNDAY (*c.* 1553–1633)

John a Kent and John a Cumber

The Book of John A Kent & John a Cumber, with the date
"Decembris 1596," is preserved in manuscript (formerly Mostyn
Collection). It has been conjectured that it is the same play as
The Wise Man of West Chester, originally produced by the
Lord Admiral's men on December 3, 1594, and evidently a
popular piece (see W. W. Greg, *Henslowe's Diary*). As the
comedy scenes, some of which are quoted below, seem to suggest
Bottom and his artisans in *A Midsummer Night's Dream* (pro-
bably acted in 1595), it is possible that Shakespeare borrowed
directly from a successful play belonging to a rival company.
It is to be noted that another play of Munday's, *The Two
Italian Gentlemen,* seems to have suggested some of the serious
plot in this same Shakespearian comedy. The Malapropisms
used in the passages quoted recall, too, those of a more famous

82

LATE SIXTEENTH CENTURY

Dogberry and Verges. The drama tells, in a romantic manner, of the adventures of John a Kent, a Welsh magician, who enters into the lives of an Earl of Morton, an Earl of Chester, his son, and the fair Sidanen, daughter of Llwellen. The scenes selected are those which deal with the ' clowns.'

(The original manuscript was edited by J. P. Collier in 1851. In 1912 J. S. Farmer issued a facsimile, and in 1923 Miss M. St C. Byrne re-edited the text.)

TURNOP AND HIS COMPANY COME TO REHEARSE A SHOW

TURNOP. Nay neuer talke of it, Hugh the Sexten stutters, let him read the first lyne, or see if he can say the speeche, that Dawes our Churchwarden made in prayse of his Mill horsse.

HUGH. It makes no matter, I think my selfe the wisest because I am Sexten, and being Sexten, I will say the speeche I made my selfe.

TOM TABRER.[1] Heare ye Hugh, be not so forward, take a little vise of your minstrell.

OMNES. And well sayd Thomas Tabrer, you haue scression,[2] speak on.

TOM. One of the wisest of vs must speak, and either it must be Hugh or Turnop. Now, Hugh is Sexten, an office of retoritie I tell ye.

TURNOP. Yea, thats when he is in the Belfrie, not else.

OMNES. Hugh, Hugh, Hugh shall speak the speache to the Lordes.

TOM. But Turnop beeing my Lordes man, his hogheard, his familiaritie seruaunt, he in my mind is not only fit, but also accessary for the ration making, then Turnop say I.

OMNES. Turnop, Turnop, weele haue none but Turnop.

TURNOP. Well, for your wisedomes, in chusing me, I rest *quoniam dignitatis vestrum primarion*, as the Poet Pediculus sayth, at the next vestrie, bound to deferre ye to seuerall locall places.

SPURLING. How now Hugh? are ye put down in faith?

HUGH. Thats because he has a little more learning, and has borrowed the vshers olde coate to grace him selfe withall.

TOM. O, take heed of learning while ye liue, it is a gandly matter.

TURNOP. *ffrater meum amantissime* Hugo the Belringer, the hebrew *epitheton Barra cans*, as much as to say, no man can barre his chaunce, perswadeth you to remit, or submit or admit your selfe, to the crye of your bretheren. How say ye then fellow mates in armes, in this our showe, who shalbe the speaker?

OMNES. Turnop Turnop, weele haue none but Turnop.

TURNOP. Then let vs set forward, for now it is vppon the Lordes coming. Thomas, firk it with your fiddle. Spurling, you play the Moore, vaunce vp your Tun, and Robert, holde your porrenger right, least you spill the conceit, for heere they come.

---

[1] Tabourer.   [2] *I.e.*, discretion.

[*Enter* PEMBROOK, MOORTON, OSWEN, AMERY, *to them this
crew marching, one drest lik a Moore, wth a Tun painted
with yellow oker, another with a Porrenger full of water
and a pen in it.* TURNOP *speaketh the Oration.*

TURNOP. Lyke to the Cedar in the loftie Sea,
or milke white mast vpon the humble mount:
So hearing that your honors came this way,
Of our rare wittes we came to giue account.
ffor when as princes passe through pettie townes
they must be welcomd, least they tearme vs clownes.
Our presents precious, first the golden Tunne,
borne by that monstrous Murrian black a Moore,
Mortonus Earlus in thy prayse is doone. . . .

OSWEN. My Lordes, my fathers tennants after their homely
guise,
welcome ye with their countrey merriment.
How bad so ere, yet must ye needes accept it.

PEMBROKE. Else Oswen were we very much to blame,
Thankes gentle freendes, heere drinke this for my sake. . . .

TURNOP. Before you goe, in name of all this trayne Turnop
accepts your golde, and thankes you for your payne. Thomas, lead
the vanward with your easement, you with our hiper bolicall
deuises, martche in the middest. And if the Lordes will see vs
make them merry, ere we will want deuise weele make them weary,
marche on. . . .

[*Enter* TURNOP, HUGH, TOM TABRER, WILL *the boy, and*
SPURLING *wth their Consort.*

TOM. Nay either let it be as Mr Turnop will haue, or by my
troth, faire and foul I will goe no further, either let vs haue credit
or no credit.

HUGH. You haue sayd as much as be sayd neighbour Thomas,
and that not learnedly, but loouingly withall. Maister Turnop,
the Lordes were pontiffically pleased with your roration yesterday,
that the Ladyes p[lay to] morrow remayneth altogether at your
disposition.

TURNOP. Why then thus my muse hath magestically, or ministri-
callically written in prayse of fayre *Sydanen*, and she beeing
appoynted to be maryed this day she ought to haue the maydenhead
of my muse, before she loose the *benef[ico] abselutidico*, as much to
say in welsh or english, as her rose mary braunche.

SPURLING. But has Will learnd it perfectly? I tell you, she is
a Lady of some scression, and lookes that the song of *Sydanen* should
be well performd.

TURNOP. Goodman Spurling, though you be spurblinde, and thereby are fauoured for the grosse errours committed in your vocation;
yet I pray ye, commit your selfe to your musique, as for the song, let
it passe vppon my prerogastriue, wth this addition, *He mihi quod
domino, non licet ire tuo.*

Tom. Why then tune all, for it drawes toward day; and if we wake not the Brydes, why then it is woorth nothing.

[They play, the boy sings the welsh song.

Turnop. To add one good morrowe more to your bed sydes, Timothie Turnop bids, Good morrow both the Brydes.
Now to the Brydegroomes, and then my harts look for a largesse.

6. CHRISTOPHER MARLOWE (1564–93)

Doctor Faustus

In recent years Marlowe's fame has witnessed a sudden flourishing. Esteemed in his own day, his plays had sunk to furnishing material for melodrama, farce, and pantomime, until romantic criticism once more recognized his genius. Perhaps Marlowe is more of a poet than a dramatist, but even in the latter sphere he stands forward as the mightiest of the pre-Shakespearians. This power which he possessed is dependent upon several qualities. He brought to tragedy an entirely new conception of the hero and his fate ; from appreciation of Italian *virtù* he was led to conceive of his protagonists as men built beyond the common mould, with thoughts and aspirations which raised them to levels far above those occupied by their companions. By so doing he prepared the way for an Othello and a Macbeth. This new conception of the tragic spirit, however, went alongside an innovation in dramatic media. Before his time blank verse had failed to recognize its own high destiny. It had been treated dully by Norton and Sackville, but never had been used to express passionately those deepest emotions and thoughts to which tragedy must give concrete expression. Marlowe's poetic power, although perhaps it retarded his own development as a playwright, made Shakespeare's plays possible.

(*The tragicall History of D. Faustus* was produced by the Lord Admiral's men in 1589. It was printed in 1604, and frequently reprinted with many variations till 1631. The first quarto has been followed here.)

The Last Hours of Faustus

3rd Scholar. Yet Faustus call on God.

Faustus. On God whome Faustus hath abiurde, on God, whome Faustus hath blasphemed: ah my God, I woulde weepe, but the diuel drawes in my teares. Gush foorth bloud, insteade of teares, yea life and soule. Oh he stayes my tong, I would lift vp my hands, but see, they hold them, they hold them.

All. Who Faustus?

Faustus. *Lucifer* and *Mephastophilis*. Ah Gentlemen! I gaue them my soule for my cunning.

85

ALL. God forbid.

FAUSTUS. God forbade it indeede, but Faustus hath done it: for vaine pleasure of 24 yeares hath Faustus lost eternall ioy and felicitie. I writ them a bill with mine owne bloud, the day is expired, the time wil come, and he wil fetch mee.

1ST SCHOLAR. Why did not Faustus tel vs of this before, that Diuines might haue prayed for thee?

FAUSTUS. Oft haue I thought to haue done so, but the diuell threatned to teare mee in peeces, if I namde God, to fetch both body and soule, if I once gaue eare to diuinitie: and now tis too late: Gentlemen away, lest you perish with me.

2ND SCHOLAR. O what shal we do to [saue] Faustus?

FAUSTUS. Talke not of me, but saue your selues, and depart.

3RD SCHOLAR. God wil strengthen me, I wil stay with Faustus.

1ST SCHOLAR. Tempt not God, sweete friend, but let vs into the next roome, and there pray for him.

FAUSTUS. I, pray for me, pray for me, and what noyse soeuer yee heare, come not vnto me, for nothing can rescue me.

2ND SCHOLAR. Pray thou, and we wil pray that God may haue mercy vpon thee.

FAUSTUS. Gentlemen farewel, if I liue til morning, Ile visite you; if not, Faustus is gone to hel.

ALL. Faustus, farewel. [*Exeunt* SCHOLARS.
[*The clock strikes eleauen.*

FAUSTUS. Ah Faustus,
Now hast thou but one bare hower to liue,
And then thou must be damnd perpetually:
Stand stil you euer moouing spheres of heauen,
That time may cease, and midnight neuer come:
Faire Natures eie, rise, rise againe, and make
Perpetuall day, or let this houre be but
A yeere, a moneth, a weeke, a naturall day,
That Faustus may repent, and saue his soule,
O lente, lente curite noctis equi :
The starres mooue stil, time runs, the clock wil strike,
The diuel wil come, and Faustus must be damnd.
O Ile leape vp to my God: who pulles me downe?
See see where Christs blood streames in the firmament.
One drop would saue my soule, halfe a drop, ah my Christ.
Ah rend not my heart for naming of my Christ,
Yet wil I call on him: oh spare me *Lucifer*!
Where is it now? tis gone: And see where God
Stretcheth out his arme, and bends his irefull browes:
Mountaines and hilles, come come and fall on me
And hide me from the heauy wrath of God.
No, no.
Then wil I headlong runne into the earth:
Earth gape. O no, it wil not harbour me:

86

You starres that raignd at my natiuitie
Whose influence hath alotted death and hel
Now draw vp Faustus like a foggy mist
Into the intrailes of yon labring cloude
That when you vomite foorth into the ayre
My limbes may issue from your smoaky mouthes
So that my soule may but ascend to heauen:
Ah halfe the houre is past,   *[The watch strikes.*
Twil all be past anone.
Oh God
If thou wilt not haue mercy on my soule
Yet for Christs sake whose bloud hath ransomd me
Impose some end to my incessant paine.
Let Faustus liue in hel a thousand yeares
A hundred thousand and at last be sau'd.
O no end is limited to damned soules.
Why wert thou not a creature wanting soule?
Or, why is this immortall that thou hast?
Ah *Pythagoras metemsucossis,* were that true,
This soule should flie from me, and I be changde
Vnto some brutish beast: al beasts are happy
For when they die
Their soules are soone dissolud in elements
But mine must liue still to be plagde in hel:
Curst be the parents that ingendred me:
No Faustus curse thy selfe curse *Lucifer*
That hath depriude thee of the ioyes of heauen:
                         [The clocke striketh twelue.
O it strikes it strikes now body turne to ayre
Or *Lucifer* wil beare thee quicke to hel: *[Thunder and lightning.*
Oh soule be changde into little water drops
And fal into the *Ocean,* nere be found:
My God my God looke not so fierce on me: *[Enter diuels.*
Adders and Serpents let me breathe a while
Vgly hell gape not come not *Lucifer*
Ile burne my bookes ah *Mephastophilis.*   *[Exeunt with him.*

7. THOMAS KYD (1558–94)

The Spanish Tragedy

Of all sixteenth-century plays *The Spanish Tragedy* proved the most popular. Its thrilling theme, with murders galore, ghosts, madness, and love, easily captured the attentions of contemporaries, and even when, in later years, it was ridiculed by literary men with pretensions to taste it kept its hold on the popular imagination. Looking back upon it from the twentieth century, we can readily discern its crudity, yet we can see, too, how skilfully Kyd dealt with his 'melodramatic' theme, and how character emerges from the welter of the bloodstained story. The persons of Bel-imperia, who forgets her love of the dead Andrea in that of the living Horatio, and of Hieronimo, who in his madness avenges the murder of his son, stand out as real figures, while even the more ordinary characters, such as Horatio and Balthazar, are given touches which make them individuals. Besides this, Kyd shows his power by his use of tragic irony, a device in which he was the master for succeeding dramatists. The scenes selected here are those in which Balthazar overhears Bel-imperia's confession of love and in which he, with her brother Lorenzo, murders the unfortunate Horatio.

(*The Spanish Tragedie* was first printed in quarto without date; other contemporary quartos appeared in 1594, 1599, 1602 (*bis*), 1610, 1615, 1618, 1623, and 1633—the number indicating well the popularity of the play. There have been many later reprints, the standard modern text being that edited by F. S. Boas (1901). The tragedy was produced originally about 1589.)

BALTHAZAR PLANS HORATIO'S DEATH

HORATIO. Now, Madame, since by fauour of your loue
Our hidden smoke is turned to open flame,
And that with lookes and words we feed our thoughts
(Two chiefe contents, where more cannot be had);
Thus in the midst of loues faire blandishments,
Why shew you signe of inward languishments?

    [PEDRINGANO *sheweth all to the* PRINCE *and* LORENZO, *placing them in secret.*

BEL-IMPERIA. My hart (sweet freend) is like a ship at sea:
She wisheth port, where riding all at ease
She may repaire what stormie times haue worne,
And leaning on the shore may sing with ioy
That pleasure followes paine, and blisse annoy.
Possession of thy loue is th' onely port,
Wherein my hart, with feares and hopes long tost,
Each howre doth wish and long to make resort,
There to repaire the ioyes that it hath lost,
And, sitting safe, to sing in Cupids Quire
That sweetest blisse is crowne of loues desire.

    [BALTHAZAR *and* LORENZO *above.*[1]

BALTHAZAR. O sleepe, mine eyes, see not my loue prophande;
Be deafe, my eares, heare not my discontent;
Dye, hart: another ioyes what thou deseruest.

LORENZO. Watch still, mine eyes, to see this loue disioynd;
Heare still, mine eares, to heare them both lament;
Liue, hart, to ioy at fond *Horatio's* fall.

    [1] *I.e.*, overhearing their conversation from the gallery.

LATE SIXTEENTH CENTURY

BEL-IMPERIA. Why stands *Horatio* speecheles all this while?
HORATIO. The lesse I speak, the more I meditate.
BEL-IMPERIA. But whereon doost thou chiefly meditate ?
HORATIO. On dangers past, and pleasures to ensue.
BALTHAZAR. On pleasures past, and dangers to ensue.
BEL-IMPERIA. What dangers, and what plesures doost thou mean?
HORATIO. Dangers of warre, and pleasures of our loue.
LORENZO. Dangers of death, but pleasures none at all.
BEL-IMPERIA. Let dangers goe, thy warre shall be with me,
But such a warring as breakes no bond of peace.
Speak thou faire words, ile crosse them with faire words;
Send thou sweet looks, ile meete them with sweet lookes;
Write louing lines, ile answere louing lines;
Giue me a kisse, ile counterchecke thy kisse:
Be this our warring peace, or peace full warre.

THE MURDER OF HORATIO

HORATIO. Now that the night begins with sable wings
To ouer-cloud the brightnes of the Sunne,
And that in darknes pleasures may be done,
Come, *Bel-imperia*, let vs to the bower,
And there in safetie passe a pleasant hower.
BEL-IMPERIA. I follow thee, my loue, and will not backe,
Although my fainting hart controles my soule.
HORATIO. Why, make you doubt of *Pedringanos* faith?
BEL-IMPERIA. No, he is as trustie as my second selfe,
Goe, *Pedringano*, watch without the gate,
And let vs know if any make approch.
PEDRINGANO [*aside*]. In steed of watching, ile deserue more golde
By fetching *Don Lorenzo* to this match.   [*Exit.*
HORATIO. What meanes my loue?
BEL-IMPERIA.   I know not what my selfe:
And yet my hart foretels me some mischaunce.
HORATIO. Sweet, say not so; faire fortune is our freend,
And heauens haue shut vp day to pleasure vs.
The starres, thou seest, hold backe their twinckling shine,
And *Luna* hides her selfe to pleasure vs.
BEL-IMPERIA. Thou hast preuailde; ile conquer my misdoubt,
And in thy loue and councell drowne my feare:
I feare no more ; loue now is all my thoughts.
Why sit we not? for pleasure asketh ease.
HORATIO. The more thou sitst within these leauy bowers,
The more will *Flora* decke it with her flowers.
BEL-IMPERIA. I, but if *Flora* spye *Horatio* heere,
Her iealous eye will thinke I sit too neere.
HORATIO. Harke, Madame, how the birds record by night,
For ioy that *Bel-imperia* sits in sight.

89

BEL-IMPERIA. No, *Cupid* counterfeits the Nightingale,
To frame sweet musick to *Horatios* tale.
HORATIO. If *Cupid* sing, then *Venus* is not farre;
I, thou art *Venus*, or some fairer starre.
BEL-IMPERIA. If I be *Venus*, thou must needs be *Mars*;
And where *Mars* raigneth there must needs be warres.
HORATIO. Then thus begin our wars: put forth thy hand,
That it may combat with my ruder hand.
BEL-IMPERIA. Set forth thy foot to try the push of mine.
HORATIO. But first my lookes shall combat against thine.
BEL-IMPERIA. Then ward thy-selfe: I dart this kisse at thee.
HORATIO. Thus I retort the dart thou threwst at me.
BEL-IMPERIA. Nay then, to gaine the glory of the field,
My twining armes shall yoake and make thee yeeld.
HORATIO. Nay then, my armes are large and strong with
all:
Thus Elmes by vines are compast till they fall.
BEL-IMPERIA. O let me goe, for in my troubled eyes
Now maist thou read that life in passion dies.
HORATIO. O stay a while, and I will die with thee;
So shalt thou yeeld, and yet haue conquered me.
BEL-IMPERIA. Whose there, *Pedringano* ?   We are betraide.
   [*Enter* LORENZO, BALTHAZAR, CERBERINE, PEDRINGANO *dis-
      guised.*
LORENZO. My Lord away with her, take her aside.
O sir, forbeare: your valour is already tride.
Quickly dispatch, my maisters.   [*They hang him in the Arbor.*
HORATIO. What, will you murder me?
LORENZO. I thus, and thus: these are the fruits of loue.
                                          [*They stab him.*
BEL-IMPERIA. O, saue his life, and let me dye for him.
O, saue him, brother; saue him, *Balthazar* :
I loued *Horatio*, but he loued not me.
BALTHAZAR. But *Balthazar* loues *Bel-imperia*.
LORENZO. Although his life were still ambitious proud,
Yet is he at the highest now he is dead.
BEL-IMPERIA. Murder, murder: helpe, *Hieronimo*, helpe.
LORENZO. Come, stop her mouth; away with her.

8. HENRY CHETTLE (*c.* 1560–*c.* 1607)

The Tragedy of Hoffman

The revenge play took a variety of different forms during the sixteenth and seventeenth centuries, but in whatever direction it tended the necessary suspense and thrill as well as the interest in peculiar psychological states kept it popular. One of the best—although one of the most neglected—of the extant early

LATE SIXTEENTH CENTURY

examples of this type was contributed by Henry Chettle, a contemporary of Shakespeare and the University Wits. There is a directness in this play which gives it strength, and the fatal weakness of the hero, Hoffman, is well delineated. That hero is, it is true, a monster of villainy, yet there are motives for his series of crimes, and there is tragic logic in his final overthrow. Compared with the somewhat chaotic adventures of *Antonio and Mellida, Hoffman* possesses an engaging simplicity. The conversation between the avenger and his tool, Lorrique, is fairly representative of the drama as a whole. One may note how Chettle avoids the prevailing weakness of the age—that tendency to lose action in words, to intrude poetic expression into scenes which demand the utmost conciseness in dialogue. One could not claim that his play is a masterpiece, yet it has certain qualities which mark it out as a capable, and, in some respects, an appealing drama.

(*The Tragedy of Hoffman* was produced about 1602. The following extract is taken from the quarto of 1631.)

THE REVENGER DESTROYS HIS INSTRUMENT

HOFFMAN. What? are you gadding sir? what mooues your
    flight?
Coyne not excuses in your crouching; come,
What cause haue you to flie and seeke strange hoords
For your wealth gotten by my liberall gift?
    LORRIQUE. And my desert, my Lord.
    HOFFMAN. Well be it your desert;
But what's the cause you'l flye this country?
    LORRIQUE. As I liue, my Lord, I haue noe such intent;
But with your leaue, I was debating things,
As if it should chaunce thus, and thus, why then
'Twere better be far of, but otherwise
My loue, and life, low at your seruice lye.
    HOFFMAN. You are a villaine damn'd as low as hell;
An hypocrite, a fawning hypocrite:
I know thy heart, come Spaniell vp, arise,
And thinke not with your antickes and your lies
To goe beyond mee, you haue play'd the slaue,
Betrayd me to the Dutchesse, told her all,
Disappoynting all my hopes with your base tongue,
Oreturn'd the height of my intendments,
For which ile hurle thee from my mountaine wracke,
Into the lowest Cauerne of pale death.
    LORRIQUE. Alas my Lord for beare, let me be heard.
    HOFFMAN. Thou hast betrayd me, therefore neuer talke.
    LORRIQUE. By heauen——
    HOFFMAN. O hell! why should'st thou thinke on heauen.

91

LORRIQUE. Stay, and beleeue me, thinke you I am mad,
Soe great a foe to my owne happy chaunce,
When things are sorted to so good an end,
That all is hid, and we held in regard:
After such horrid, and perfidious acts,
Now to betray my selfe; be reasonable,
And thinke how shallow such an act would seeme
In one, chiefe agent in so many ills.

HOFFMAN. Thou hast a tongue as glib and smooth to lyes,
As full of false inuentions, and base fraud,
As prone to circumuent beleeuing soules,
As euer heretique or traytor vsd,
Whose speeches are as hony, their acts gall,
Their words rayse vp, but their hands ruine all.

LORRIQUE. By vertues glorious soule.

HOFFMAN. Blasphemer peace, sweere not by that thou hat'st;
Vertue, and thou haue no more sympathie,
Then day with night, Heauen with Hell.
Thou knowest, I know thy Villanyes excell.

LORRIQUE. Why then by villany, by blood, by sleightes,
By all the horrours tortures can present,
By Hell, and by reuenges purple hand
The Dutchesse had no conference with me,
But onely a desire to see the place
That first receiu'd her son, whom she beleeues
The vnrelenting waues and flinty rocks,
Had seuer'd from sweet life after the wracke.

HOFFMAN. May I beleeue thee?

LORRIQUE. Haue I fayld you yet?
Measure my former acts, and you shall find
My soule allyed to yours, wholly estrang'd
From all I euer lou'd.

HOFFMAN. Noe more, haue done.
Tha'st won me to continue thee my friend;
But I can tell thee somewhat troubles me,
Some dreadfull misaduenture my soule doubts,
And I conceiue it with noe common thought,
But a most potent apprehension;
For it confounds imaginary sence,
Sometimes inflames my blood, another while
'Nums all the Currents that should comfort life,
And I remayne as 'twere a senceles stone.

LORRIQUE. Come, come, I know the cause, you are in loue,
And to be soe, is to be any thing.
Doe you not loue the Dutchesse?

HOFFMAN. Yes, I doe.

LORRIQUE. Why there's the matter, then, be ruld by me,
To morrow morning she desires to see

The shore, that first receiu'd her sea-wrackt son,
And to be vnaccompanied she loues;
Except some one or two, you and I:
Now when you haue her neare your dismall caue,
Force her, I do't man, make no scruple do't,
Else you shall neuer win her to your bed:
Doe a mans part, please her before she goe,
Or if you see, that she turnes violent,
Shut her perpetuall prisoner in that den;
Make her a Philomel, prone Tereus:
Do't, neuer feare it.
    HOFFMAN. Why she will be mist.
    LORRIQUE. By whom? by fooles, grosse, dull, thicke sighted
      fooles,
Whom euery mist can blinde, I'le sway them all,
With exclamation that the grieued Dutchesse
When she beheld the sea that drownd her son,
Stood for a while like weeping *Niobe*,
As if she had bin stone: and when we striu'd
With milde perswasions to make lesse her woe
She madder then the wife of *Athamas*
Leap't suddenly into the troubled sea,
Whose surges greedy of soe rich a prey,
Swallowed her vp, while we in uaine exclaym'd
'Gainst Heauen and hell, 'gainst fortune and her fate.
    HOFFMAN. Oh my good villaine! how I hug thy plots,
This shall be done, shee's mine: run swift slow houres,
Make a short night hasten on day apace,
Rough armes waxe soft soft beauty to embrace.
    LORRIQUE. Why soe, now your feare will quickly end.
    HOFFMAN. Thou wilt not talke of this?
    LORRIQUE. Will I be hang'd?
Nee're take me for a blab, you'l finde me none.
    HOFFMAN. I haue another secret, but——
    LORRIQUE. Come what ist? come, this brest is yours,
My heart's your treasury.
    HOFFMAN. Thou must be secret, 'tis a thing of weight
Concernes thee neere.
    LORRIQUE. Were it as neere as life, come, pray speake.
    HOFFMAN. Hearke in thine eare, I would not haue the ayre
Be priuy to this purpose, wilt thou sweare?
    LORRIQUE. What? to bee secret? if the least iot I tell
Let all my hopes sinke suddenly to hell.
    HOFFMAN [*stabbing him*]. Thou hast thy wish, downe villaine,
keepe this close.
    LORRIQUE. Vnthankefull murtherer, is this my meede?
Oh slaue, tha'st kild thy heart in wounding mine,
This is my day, tomorrow shall be thine.

HOFFMAN. Goe foole; now thou art dead, I neede not feare.
Yet as thou wert my seruant iust and true,
Ile hide thee in the ditch: giue dogs there due,
He that will proue a mercenary slaue
To murder, seldome findes so good a graue,
Hee's gone, I can now spare him, *Lorrique* farewell;
Commend me to our friends thou meet'st in hell:
Next plot for *Mathias* and old *Saxony*,
There ends shall finish our blacke tragedy.

9. GEORGE PEELE (*c.* 1557–96)

The Battle of Alcazar

It would be unfair to historical perspective to omit here a representative passage from one of the more stormy plays of the time. The Elizabethans loved bombast and excitement, and the 'melodramatic' qualities of *The Spanish Tragedy*, of *Doctor Faustus*, and of *Macbeth* appealed quite as much to them as did the poetry and the characterization in these plays. To satisfy this craving many dramatists turned out works which had for their main interest murders, battles, supernatural apparitions, and physical commotions. Of these *The Battle of Alcazar*, now generally ascribed to George Peele, is a not untypical example. The play was probably performed originally in 1589, when Portuguese affairs were being eagerly talked of, but the play seems to have remained popular for many years, the extant 'plot' or manager's scenario being that of a revival of about 1599. The passage chosen here gives a good idea of the dumbshows designed to please the 'groundlings' (and others) as well as of the "alarums" and "noises off" which ever make an appeal in the theatre.

(*The Battell of Alcazar* was printed in 1594, probably after the successful revival of the play as *Muly Mollocco*. W. W. Greg has edited a reprint for the Malone Society. The 'plot' is discussed by the same scholar in a brilliant study, *Alcazar and Orlando*. The extract here follows the original quarto.)

ALARUMS, FIREWORKS, AND NOISES OFF

Enter the PRESENTER *before the last dumbe show, and speaketh.*

PRESENTER. Ill be to him that so much ill bethinkes,
And ill betide this foule ambitious Moore,
Whose wily traines with smoothest course of speech,
Hath tide and tangled in a dangerous warre,
The fierce and manly king of Portugall.
                              [*Lightning and thunder.*
Nowe throwe the heauens foorth their lightning flames,

And thunder ouer Affrickes fatall fields,
Bloud will have bloud, foul murther scape no scourge.

    [*Enter* FAME *like an Angell, and hangs the crownes vpon a tree.*

At last descendeth fame as Iris,
To finish fainting Didoes dying lyfe,
Fame from her stately bowre doth descend,
And on the tree as fruit new ripe to fall,
Placeth the crownes of these vnhappie kings,
That earst she kept in eie of all the world.

                     [*Heere the blazing Starre.*

Now firie starres and streaming comets blaze,
That threat the earth and princes of the same.   [*Fire workes.*
Fire, fire about the axiltres of heauen,
Whoorles round, and from the foot of Casyopa
In fatall houre consumes these fatall crownes,

                  [*One* [*crowne*] *fals.*
Downe fals the diademe of Portugall,   [*The other fals.*
The crownes of Barbary and kingdomes fall,
Ay me, that kingdomes may not stable stand,
And now approching neere the dismall day,
The bloudie daie wherein the battels ioyne,
Mondaie the fourth of August seuentie eight,
The sunne shines wholy on the parched earth,
The brightest planet in the highest heauen,
The heathens eager bent against their foe,
Giue onset with great ordnance to the warre.
The christians with great noise of canon shot,
Send angrie onsets to the enemie.
Geue eare and heare how warre begins his song,
With dreadfull clamors, noise, and trumpets sound.   [*Exit.*

    [*Alarums within, let the chambers be dischargèd, then enter to the battell, and the Moores flie. Skirmish still, then enter* ABDILMELEC *in his chaire,* ZAREO *and their traine.*

ABDILMELEC. Saie on Zareo, tell me all the newes,
Tell me what furie rangeth in our campe,
That hath inforst our Moores to turne their backes.
Zareo saie, what chance did bode this ill,
What ill inforst this dastard cowardise?

    ZAREO. My Lord, such chance as wilfull warre affords,
Such chances and misfortunes as attend
On him, the God of battell and of armes,
My Lord, when with our ordenance fierce we sent
Our Moores with smaller shot as thicke as haile,
Follows apace to charge the Portugall,
The valiant Duke the deuill of Auero,
The bane of Barbary, fraughted full of ire
Breakes through the rankes, and with fiue hundred horsse

All men at armes, forward and full of might,
Assaults the middle wing, and puts to flight
Eight thousand Harquebush that seru'd on foot,
And twentie thousand Moores with speare & sheild:
And therewithall the honour of the day.

    ABDILMELEC. Ah Abdelmelec doost thou liue to heare
This bitter processe of this first attempt?
Labour my Lords to renue our force,
Of fainting Moores, and fight it to the last.
My horsse Zareo, O the goale is lost,
The goale is lost, thou King of Portugall
Thrice happy chance it is for thee and thine
That heauen abates my strength and calles me hence.
My sight doth faile, my soule, my feeble soule
Shall be releaste from prison on this earth:
Farwell vaine world for I haue playd my parte.   *[He dyeth.*
        [A long Skirmidge, and then enter his brother MULY
           MAHOMET SETH.

    MULY. Braue Abdelmelec, thou thrise noble Lord,
Not such a wound was giuen to Barbary,
Had twenty hoasts of men beene put to swoord
As death, pale death with fatall shaft hath giuen.
Loe dead is he, my brother and my King
Whome I might haue reuiu'd with newes I bring.

    ZAREO. His honours and his types he hath resignde
Vnto the world, and of a manly man
Loe, in a twinckling a sencelesse stocke we see.

    MULY. You trustie soldiers of this warlike King,
Be counsailde now by vs in this aduise,
Let not his death be bruted in the campe,
Least with the sodaine sorrowe of the newes,
The armye wholy be discomfited.
My Lord Zareo thus I comforte you,
Our Moores haue brauely borne themselues in fight
Likely to get the honour of the day
If ought may gotten be where losse is such.
Therfore in this apparell as he dyed
My noble brother will we heere aduance
And set him in his chayre with cunning props,
That our Barbarians may beholde their King
And thinke he doth repose him in his Tent.

    ZAREO. Right pollitique and good is your aduice,
Goe then to see it speedily performd.
Braue Lord, if Barbary recouer this,
Thy soule with ioy will sit and see the sight.   *[Exeunt.*
    *[Alarmes. Enter to the battaile, and the christians flye. The
      Duke of Aluero slaine.*

IV. EARLY SEVENTEENTH CENTURY

AFTER Shakespeare drama, while still inventive and capable, tends to decline. The desire for novelty leads toward false effects ; the growing sentimentalism makes pathos take the place of tragic emotion ; declining strength makes for type characterization ; and, above all, loss of true theatrical sense dethrones Shakespeare's nervous and delicately poised style in favour of rhetoric and richness of phrase.

Once more tragi-comedy, but of a different form, is the chief element in the theatre. Again and again we meet with bloody tragedies which yet contain a farcically comic, and often vulgar, under-plot ; again and again we encounter those artificial dramas where through four acts tragedy is suggested, and where in the fifth an unnatural conversion or an unexpected discovery brings all to a happy conclusion. Beaumont and Fletcher are the leaders of this style, which, however, is ultimately derived from the romantic comedy of Shakespeare. Day's *Humour out of Breath* is an early example of the same style. *The Pilgrim* and *The Bondman* illustrate the general type. *The Witch* mingles the "infernall" form with artificialities of all kinds. In *The Jews' Tragedy* and in *The Fool would be a Favourite* there is the mingling of tragic and comic material.

Comedy in this age feels deeply the influence of Ben Jonson. The depicting of 'humours' and the introduction of satire appear in many plays of the time, sometimes mingled with 'realism,' sometimes tending toward sentimental ideas. *Poëtaster* and *Satiromastix* show the satire ; *A New Way to Pay Old Debts* and *A Woman Never Vext* show respectively the realistic 'humours' style and the sentimental. Meanwhile, a new movement is on foot. Life, while decadent, is becoming more refined intellectually, and in *The Witty Fair One* and *The Wild-goose Chase* an approach is being made toward that type of comedy which,

G

in the Restoration period, is named the comedy of manners. Here wit takes the place of character, and the displayal of social manners occupies that position which before had been held by personality. The stress is shifted from the individual to the body social.

Tragedy shows similar movements. The revenge play is an exceedingly popular type, chiefly because of the opportunities it offers for bloody scenes and thrilling emotions. *Antonio and Mellida* follows on from *The Spanish Tragedy* and links itself to *Hamlet*. *The Revenge of Bussy d'Ambois* is a trifle more robust, while *The Maid's Tragedy* plays at least partly with this theme. In general, tragedy is inclined toward blood with ever fresh endeavours made to introduce situations of a frenzied novelty. Ford carries the decadent passion as far as it will reach, while Webster, Massinger, Rowley, and Shirley prove his ready associates. In this section has been included *The Devil's Charter*, a play interesting historically because of its exploitation of the twin forces, both popular, of the " infernall " and of Italian Court intrigue.

Much of the tragic emotion of this time hovers on the verge of the frenziedly insane, but sanity is preserved in that peculiar development of the English theatre, the domestic tragedy. In some ways the dramatic conditions between 1590 and 1630 were similar to those prevailing between 1800 and 1840. Just as lurid drama during the latter period exploited freely the world of contemporary crime, so in the former dramatists eager for success sought in recent murders subjects for their plays. Sometimes these topical plays must have been crude enough—as worthless artistically as the melodramas themselves—but the crudeness of a few—even of many—need not blind us to the fact that out of this exploitation of recent crime sprang that domestic drama which has formed the typical modern expression in the theatre. *A Yorkshire Tragedy* appears here, partly because it illustrates the device of the ' multiple bill,' partly because of the lurid strength shown in the second scene. Heywood's *A Woman Killed with Kindness* is, of course, a much finer work of art, firmly conceived, displaying strong architectural power, and marked by a deep

98

subtlety in the conception of scene. It is the Elizabethan masterpiece in this style.

Finally, there has to be noted the masque. Much of the spectacularism in the plays of 1620–40 is due to the influence of this form of entertainment, which is represented here by *The Temple of Love*, a production interesting not only from the point of view of the masque, but from that of social background. The theories of ' platonic love,' which aided in the building up of the ' love and honour ' tradition, are here the main subject of the poet.

1. JOHN DAY (*c.* 1574–*c.* 1640)

Humour out of Breath

It would seem that John Day has not received from modern criticism the full mede of praise to which he is, by his charm and delicacy, actually entitled. He has something of that fantastic humour which brightens the pages of Lyly and Greene, those too of Shakespeare himself, and he possesses an unquestioned versatility of talent. From *The Blind-Beggar of Bednal-Green* to *The Parliament of Bees* is a far cry, and even within the scenes of a single play of his we find many diverse moods and tendencies. *Humour out of Breath* is a charming comedy of early style, admirably fitted for performance by the " Children of the Kings Reuells." In the framework of a thoroughly romantic plot which tells of conspiracies and of battles there is introduced the delightful pair Florimell and Aspero, moody creatures both, but ultimately destined for each other. My Lady's " pretty tricks," aided by her sprightly page, and Aspero's misfortunes and devices fill out many scenes of the comedy, and the end comes to a bustling stage when a fierce attack on a city is stayed in order that love may wield its power. It seems strange that with so many modern revivals of Elizabethan dramas *Humour out of Breath* should remain untouched. In 1924 it proved its merits in an Elizabethan-set amateur performance at East London College.

(*Humour out of Breath* seems to have been produced in 1607 or 1608. The following extract follows the quarto of the latter year.)

DRY JESTS

PAGE. Sweet hony candy madam, if it be no forefeit to tell tales out of Cupids free schoole, tell what proficient your louer *Aspero* proues.

FLORIMELL. Now so loue helpe me loe, a passing weake one and verye vnready.

PAGE. The better, for women would haue their louers vnreadye to choose.

FLORIMELL. How ready you are to play the knaue? but to *Aspero*.

PAGE. I do not thinke but thers good musick in him, your tongue harps so much vpon his name.

FLORIMELL. I shall neuer forget him.

PAGE. I faith Lady then I know what I know.

FLORIMELL. What do you know I pray?

PAGE. Marry that if you neuer forget him, you shall euer remember him, was he neuer in your chamber?

FLORIMELL. Yes, but he shewed himselfe the strangest foole: And by my troth loe. I am sorry for't to, I had as good an appetite to maintaine discourse; but here a comes, if euer I choose a man by the fulnesse of his Calfe, or a cock by the crowing, looke and the bashfull foole do not blush already.

PAGE. You may do well to kisse him, and make him bold Madam.

[*Enter* ASPERO.

FLORIMELL. Boy, go know what strange gentleman that is.

ASPERO. Slid what a strange Lady's this? madam though I seeme a stranger to you, I lay with one last night that's well acquainted with you.

FLORIMELL. Acquainted with me?

ASPERO. And knowes you, and loues you, and you loue him, & haue bestowed kind fauours on him to.

FLORIMELL. I bestow fauours? what fauours?

ASPERO. Though twere but a trifle he took it as kindly as some would haue done a kisse.

FLORIMELL. Lord what a while this iest has bin a brooding? and it proues but addle too now it is hatched.

ASPERO. Tis a pig of your owne sow madam, and I hope your wit will bestow the nursing of it.

FLORIMELL. So it had need, I thinke 'tis like to haue but a drie nurse of yours.

PAGE. O drie ieast, all the wit in your head will scarce make sippits in't, what a ground? and such a faire landing place? get a shore, or be rankt amongst fooles for euer.

FLORIMELL. And faith ist not pitty such a proper man should keep company with a foole.

ASPERO. I keepe company with none but you Lady.

FLORIMELL. You keepe mine against my will.

ASPERO. So do I the fooles I protest; but take away yours, ile soone shift away the fooles.

PAGE. I haue not seene a foole so handsomely shifted in Venice.

ASPERO. But come, shall the foole and you bee friends?

FLORIMELL. The foole and I? y'are too familiar.

ASPERO. Why, I hope a foole may be a Ladies familiar at all times.

FLORIMELL. Come y'are too saucy.

ASPERO. Indeed tis a fooles part of *Ione* to be in the sauce afore my Lady; otherwise I am neither foole nor saucy.

FLORIMELL. Not, proude sir?

ASPERO. Not, coy Lady; come why should your tongue make so many false fiers that neuer come from your heart: you loue me, I know you loue me, your spirit, your looke, your countenance bewrayes it.

FLORIMELL. You ieast.

ASPERO. In earnest you do, and you shall know't in earnest too, lend me this iewell.

FLORIMELL. Iewell? away you sharking companion.

ASPERO. How?

FLORIMELL. Wandring strauagant, that like a droane flies humming from one land to another.

PAGE. Slight and thou hast any wit, now shew her thy sting.

FLORIMELL. And lightst vpon euery dayry maid and kitchenwench.

ASPERO. And now and then on a Ladies lip as——

FLORIMELL. You did of mine you would say, and I am hart sory you can say it, and when by your buzzing flattery, you haue suckt the smallest fauour from them, you presently make wing for another.

ASPERO. Marry buz.

FLORIMELL. Double the zard and take the whole meaning for your labour.

PAGE. The buzzard wit's not so bald yet I tro.

ASPERO. A word in your eare, madam the buzzard will anger you.

FLORIMELL. With staying you do.

ASPERO. With going I shall.

FLORIMELL. Away.

ASPERO. I away, neuer intreat, tis too late, if you send after me, I wil not come back, if you write to me, I will not answer, drowne your eyes in teares, I will not wipe them, breake your heart with sighes, I will not pitty you: neuer looke, signes cannot moue me, if you speake, 'tis too late, if you intreate, 'tis bootles, if you hang vpon me, 'tis needlesse, I offred loue & you scornd it, my absence will be your death, and I am proud ont. [*Exit.*

FLORIMELL. Is he gon boy?

PAGE. Yes faith Madam.

FLORIMELL. Cleane out of sight?

PAGE. And out of mind to, or els you haue not the mind of a true woman.

FLORIMELL. Thou readst a false comment boy, call him againe; yet doe not, my heart shall breake ere it bend.

PAGE. Or els it holdes not the true temper of woman-hood, but faith tell me Madam, do you loue him?

FLORIMELL. As a Welchman doth toasted cheese, I cannot dine

without him, hee's my pillow I cannot sleep quietly without him; my rest, I cannot liue without him.

PAGE. O that he knew it Lady.

FLORIMELL. He does, he would neuer haue left me els, he does.

2. JOHN FLETCHER (1579-1625)

The Pilgrim

Romantic tragi-comedy gained at once its inventors and greatest exponents in Beaumont and Fletcher. *A King and No King* found many imitations among the works of contemporaries, and its authors, in collaboration or alone, produced many similar works in ensuing decades. Among the more popular of these plays must be accounted *The Pilgrim*, a drama which for its exciting interest, its genuine theatricality, and its strongly marked types held the stage for a couple of centuries. Both the weaknesses and the virtues of the new romantic style are fully apparent in this play. Our sympathies are amply called forth in favour of Alinda, in spite of her many disguises, and the rude Alphonso's blustering temper is well depicted. Tragi-comedy, however, often deals with impossibilities ; indeed, the straining to bring a potentially tragic theme to a happy conclusion almost demands some falsification either of the logic of facts or of character-drawing. This tendency is excellently exemplified in the scene given here. Roderigo, the outlaw, is Pedro's sworn enemy. He has been set upon and bound by some peasants, who are beaten off by Pedro. His unnatural conversion immediately follows, since it was necessary for the plot that he and Pedro should be reconciled.

(*The Pilgrim* was first printed in 1647. The following extract is taken from the folio of 1679.)

AN OUTLAW'S REPENTANCE

PEDRO. You are not much hurt?

RODERIGO.   No Sir;
All I can call a hurt, sticks in my conscience,
That pricks and tortures me.

PEDRO.   Have ye consider'd
The nature of these men, and how they us'd ye?
Was it fair play? did it appear to you handsom?

RODERIGO. I dare not speak: or if I do 'tis nothing
Can bring me off, or justifie me.

PEDRO.   Was it noble
To be o're-laid with odds, and violence?
Manly, or brave in these thus to oppress ye?
Do you blush at this, in such as are meer rudeness,
That have stopt souls, that never knew things gentle?

And dare you glorifie worse in your self Sir?
Ye us'd me with much honour, and I thank ye,
In this I have requited some: ye know me:
Come turn not back, ye must, and ye shall know me;
Had I been over season'd with base anger,
And suited all occasions to my mischiefs,
Bore no respect to honesty, Religion,
No faith, no common tye of man, humanity,
Had I had in me, but given reins, and licence
To a tempestuous will, as wild as winter,
This day, know *Roderigo*, I had set
As small a price upon thy life and fortunes,
As thou didst lately on mine innocence;
But I reserve thee to a nobler service.

   RODERIGO. I thank ye, and I'le study more to honour ye:
You have the nobler soul, I must confess it,
And are the greater Master of your goodness.
Though it be impossible I would now recover,
And my rude will grow handsom in an instant,
Yet touching but the pureness of your metal,
Something shall shew like gold, at least shall glister,
That men may hope, although the mind be rugged,
Stony, and hard to work, yet time, and honour
Shall find and bring forth that, that's rich and worthy.

   PEDRO. I'le trie that: and to th' purpose: ye told me Sir
In noble emulation, so I take it;
I'le put your hatred far off, and forget it,
You had a fair desire to try my valour:
You seem'd to count me to it; you have found a time
A weapon in your hand, an equal enemy,
That, as he puts this off, puts off all injuries,
And only now for honour's sake defies ye:
Now, as you are a man, I know you are valiant,
As you are gentle bred, a Souldier fashioned.

   RODERIGO. His vertue startles me. I dare fight *Pedro*.

   PEDRO. And as you have a Mistris that you honour,
Mark me, a Mistris.

   RODERIGO.   Ha!

   PEDRO.   A handsome Mistris,
As you dare hold your self deserving of her.

   RODERIGO. Deserving? what a word was that to fire me?

   PEDRO. I could compel ye now without this circumstance,
But I'le deal free, and fairly, like a Gentleman:
As ye are worthy of the name ye carry,
A daring man.

   RODERIGO.   O that I durst not suffer:
For all I dare do now, implies but penance.

   PEDRO. Now do me noble right.

RODERIGO.   I'll satisfie ye;
But not by th' sword, pray you hear me, and allow me;
I have been rude; but shall I be a Monster,
And teach my Sword to hurt that that preserv'd me?
Though I be rough by nature, shall my name
Inherit that eternal stain of barbarous?
Give me an enemy, a thing that hates ye,
That never heard of yet, nor felt your goodness,
That is one main antipathy to sweetness;
And set me on, you cannot hold me Coward;
If I have ever err'd, 'thas been in hazard;
The temper of my Sword starts at your Vertue,
And will flye off, nay it will weep to light ye;
Things excellently mingled, and of pure nature,
Hold sacred Love, and peace with one another,
See how it turns.

PEDRO.   This is a strange Conversion:
And can ye fail your Mistriss? can ye grow cold
In such a case?

RODERIGO. Those heats that they add to us,
(O noble *Pedro*) let us feel 'em rightly,
And rightly but consider how they move us.

PEDRO. Is not their honour ours?

RODERIGO.   If they be vertuous,
And then the Sword adds nothing to their lustre,
But rather calls in question what's not doubted;
If they be not, the best Swords, and best valours
Can never fight 'em up to fame again;
No, not a Christian War, and that's held pious.

3. PHILIP MASSINGER (1583–1640)

The Bondman

The Bondman has been chosen for illustration here because of the long-continued popularity of that play, and because it shows well that strain of sentimentalism which was rapidly developing between 1620 and 1642. In many ways the characteristic features of eighteenth-century drama are to be discovered in embryo in the plays of the early seventeenth century. Here are Steele-like attacks on duelling; here are pathetic maidens and noble heroes; here are generous brigands; here are thieves, such as Moll Cutpurse, who will rob from the rich in order to give to the poor. Sentimentalism almost inevitably depends on a certain artificiality of treatment, and the unnaturalness of tragi-comedy permitted its free introduction. In *The Bondman* this sentimentalism appears in a not unpleasant form, the shy and tender love of the disguised Pisander having in it something

104

of nobility. Indeed, we might almost say that it was the presence here of a kind of ' heroic ' note that made *The Bondman* so popular during the Restoration period. In the scene given below Pisander, who has been in Cleora's service as a bondman, heads a rising of the slaves, and now comes to explain to his lady the real objects of his action and the true state of his heart. It will be readily agreed that the language hovers between that of the sentimentalism of 1770 and the heroic declamations of a century previous.

(*The Bond Man : An Antient Story* was printed in 1624. From this quarto the following extract is taken.)

A GENEROUS LOVER

Enter PISANDER *speaking at the doore.*

PISANDER. He that aduances
A foot beyond this, comes vpon my sword
You haue had your wayes, disturbe not mine.
   TIMANDRA. Speake gently,
Her feares may kill her else.
   PISANDER. Now loue inspire me!
Still shall this Canopie of enuious night
Obscure my Suns of comfort? and those dainties
Of purest white and red, which I take in at
My greedy eyes, deny'd my famish'd senses?
The Organs of your hearing yet are open;
And you infringe no vow, though you vouchsafe,
To giue them warrant, to conuey vnto
Your vnderstanding parts the story of
A tortur'd and dispairing Louer, whom
Not Fortune but affection markes your slaue.   [CLEORA *shakes.*
Shake not, best Lady; for (beleeu't) you are
As farre from danger as I am from force.
All violence I'le offer, tendes no farther
Then to relate my suffrings; which I dare not
Presume to doe, till by some gratious signe
You shew, you are pleas'd to heare me.
   TIMANDRA. If you are,
Hold forth your right hand. [CLEORA *holdes forth her right hand.*
   PISANDER. So, 'tis done, and I
With my glad lips seale humbly on your foot,
My soules thankes for the fauour: I forbeare
To tell you who I am, what wealth, what honours
I made exchange of to become your seruant:
And though I knew, worthy *Leosthenes*
(For sure he must be worthy, for whose loue
You haue endur'd so much) to be my riuall,
When rage, and iealousie counsail'd me to kill him,

(Which then I could haue done with much more ease,
Then now, in feare to grieue you, I dare speake it)
Loue seconded with duty boldly told me,
The man I hated, faire *Cleora* fauour'd,
And that was his protection.   [CLEORA *bowes.*

    TIMANDRA. See, she bowes
Her head in signe of thankfulnesse.

    PISANDER. He remou'd,
By th' occasion of the war (my fires increasing
By being clos'd, and stop'd vp) franticke affection
Prompted me to doe something in his absence,
That might deliuer you into my power,
Which you see is effected, and euen now,
When my rebellious passions chide my dulnesse,
And tell me how much I abuse my fortunes;   [CLEORA *starts.*
Now 'tis in my power to beare you hence,
Or take my wishes here, (nay, feare not Madam
True loue's a seruant, brutish lust a Tyrant)
I dare not touch those viands, that ne're taste well,
But when they are freely offred: only thus much,
Be pleas'd I may speake in my owne deare cause,
And thinke it worthy your consideration.
I haue lou'd truly, (cannot say deseru'd
Since duty must not take the name of merit)
That I so farre prise your content, before
All blessings, that my hopes can fashion to mee,
That willingly I entertaine despayre,
And for your sake embrace it.   For I know,
This opportunity lost, by no endeauour
The like can be recouer'd.   To conclude,
Forget not, that I lose my selfe, to saue you.
For what can I expect, but death and torture
The warre being ended? and, what is a taske
Would trouble *Hercules* to vndertake,
I doe deny you to my selfe, to giue you
A pure vnspotted present to my riuall.
I haue said, if it distaste not, best of Virgins,
Reward my temperance with some lawfull fauour,
Though you contemne my person.

      [CLEORA *kneeles, then puls off her Gloue, and offers her hand*
      to PISANDER.

    TIMANDRA. See, she kneeles
And seemes to call vpon the gods to pay
The debt she owes your vertue.   To performe which
As a sure pledge of friendship, she vouchsafes you
Her faire right hand.   [*Makes a lowe curtsie, as she goes off.*

    PISANDER. I am payd for all my suffrings.
Now when you please, passe to your priuate Chamber:

My loue, and dutie, faithfull guards, shall keepe you
From all disturbance; and when you are sated
With thinking of *Leosthenes*, as a fee
Due to my seruice, spare one sigh for me.

4. THOMAS MIDDLETON (*c.* 1570–1627)

The Witch

The chief interest of *The Witch* is the fact that its scenes of supernaturalism reproduce much of the witch matter in *Macbeth*; indeed, the songs of which the first lines only are given in the Shakespeare Folio, appear here in their full form. No one as yet has presented a completely satisfactory solution of the problem thus raised, although the consensus of opinion tends to view Middleton as the imitator. Beyond this, however, *The Witch* is interesting because it furnishes an excellent example of the artificial tragi-comedy of the age. In it a duchess is made by her husband to drink his health out of a cup fashioned of her own father's skull. Naturally offended, this lady seeks to murder the Duke, and, amid scenes of intrigue and supernatural apparitions, apparently achieves her purpose. The scene given below shows her confronted by the Governor, who has learned of her crime. Defending herself successfully against the charge of infidelity, she is about to be executed for murder when suddenly the Duke rises from his supposed deathbed and welcomes her once more to his arms. The unnatural psychology here is self-evident, and however Middleton may clothe the episodes in nervous language we feel the weakness and poverty of the conception of the play. The continual seeking for novelty has brought almost complete disaster to the theatre.

(*The Witch* remained in manuscript till 1778. The following extract follows that of the first edition, published in that year.)

A DUKE RISES FROM THE DEAD

SEBASTIAN. Thancks to heaven
That I am now of age to cleere myself then.
    GOVERNOR. Sebastian!
    SEBASTIAN. The same, much wrong'd, Sir.
    ISABELLA. Am I certaine
Of what mine eie takes joy to looke upon?
    SEBASTIAN. Your service cannot alter me from knowledge:
I am your servant ever.
    GOVERNOR. Wellcom to life (Sir).
Gasper, thou swors't his death.
    GASPER. I did indeed (my Lord)
And have byn since well paid for't: one forsworne mouth
Hath gott me two or three more here.

SEBASTIAN. I was dead (Sir)
Both to my joies, and all men's understanding,
Till this my howre of life; for 'twas my fortune
To make the first of my returne to Urbin
A witnes to that marriage: since which time,
I have walk'd beneath myself, and all my comforts
Like one on earth whose joyes are laid above:
And though it had byn offence small in me
To enjoy mine own, I left her pure and free.
    GOVERNOR. The greater and more sacred is thy blessing.
For where heaven's bountie holly ground-work finds,
'Tis like a sea, encompassing chast minds.   [*Enter* DUCHESS.
    HERMIO. The duchess comes, my lord.
    GOVERNOR. Be you then all witnesses
Of an intent most horrid.
    DUCHESS. One poore night,
Ever Almachildes now.   Better his meaner fortunes wept then
    ours,
That tooke the true height of a princesse spirit
To match unto their greatnes.   Such lifes as his
Were onely made to break the force of fate
Ere it came at us, and receive the venom.
'Tis but a usuall friendship for a mistris
To loose some forty yeares life in hopefull time
And hazard an eternall soule for ever:
As yong as he has don, and more desertfull.
    GOVERNOR. Madam.
    DUCHESS. My Lord.
    GOVERNOR. This is the howre that I have so long desird:
The tumult's full appeaz'd: Now may we both
Exchange embraces with a fortunate arme,
And practice to make love-knotts, thus.   [DUKE *is discovered*.
    DUCHESS. My Lord!
    GOVERNOR. Thus lustfull woman, and bold murdresse, thus.
Blessed powres, to make my loyaltie & truth so happy!
Looke thee, thou shame of greatnes, stayne of honour,
Behold thy worke, and weep before thy death.
If thou bee'st bless'd with sorrow and a conscience,
Which is a guift from heaven, and seldom knocks
At any murderer's breast with sounds of comfort,
See this thy worthie and unequalld piece;
A faire encouragement for another husband!
    DUCHESS. Bestow me upon death, Sir, I am guilty,
And of a cruelty above my cause.
His injury was too low for my revenge.
Performe a justice that may light all others
To noble actions: Life is hatefull to me,
Beholding my dead lord.   Make us an one

In death, whom marriage made one of two living,
Till cursed fury parted us.   My lord,
I covet to be like him.
    GOVERNOR. No, my sword
Shall never stayne the virgin brightnes on't
With blood of an adulteresse.
    DUCHESS. There, my lord,
I dare my accusors, and defy the world.
Death, shame, and torment: Blood I am guilty of,
But not adultery, not the breach of honour.
    GOVERNOR. No! Come forth Almachildes. [*Enter* ALMACHILDES.
    DUCHESS. Almachildes!
Hath time brought him about to save himself
By my distruction?   I am justly doombd.
    GOVERNOR. Doe you know this woman?
    ALMACHILDES. I have knowne her better Sir, then at this time.
    GOVERNOR. But she defies you there.
    ALMACHILDES. That's the common trick of them all.
    DUCHESS. Nay, since I am touch'd so neere, before my death then,
In right of honor's innocence, I am bold
To call heaven and my woman here to witnes.
My lord, let her speak truth, or may she perish! [*Enter* AMORETTA.
    AMORETTA. Then Sir, by all the hopes of a maid's comfort,
Either in faithfull service, or bless'd marriage,
The woman that his blinded folly knew
Was onely a hirde strumpet, a professor
Of lust and impudence, which here is ready
To approve what I have spoken.
    ALMACHILDES. A common strumpet!
This comes of scarffes: I'll never more weare
An habbardashers shop before mine eies agen.
    GOVERNOR. My sword is proud thou art lightend of that syn:
Dye then a murdresse only!
    DUKE [*rising up*]. Live a Duchesse,
Better then ever lov'd, embrac'd and honor'd.
    DUCHESS. My Lord?
    DUKE. Nay, since in honor thou canst justly rise,
Vanish all wrongs, thy former practise dies.
I thanck thee Almachildes, for my life,
This lord for truth, and heaven for such a wife;
Who, though her intent syn'd, yet she makes amends
With greif and honor (vertues noblest ends).
What greivd you then, shall never more offend you;
Your father's skull with honor wee'll inter
And give the peace due to the sepulcher;
And in all times, may this daie ever prove
A daie of triumph, joie, and honest love!

5. WILLIAM HEMINGE (1602–c. 1632)

The Jews' Tragedy

William Heminge was the son of that old actor-friend of Shakespeare's who was one of the editors of the First Folio, and seems himself to have been an eager student of the Shakespearian canon. *The Jews' Tragedy* is full of reminiscences from *Hamlet*, *Much Ado*, *The Merchant of Venice*, and other dramas, some passages indeed being repeated *verbatim*. The tragedy is not untypical of a certain type of contemporary play. Derived from Josephus, it exploits that interest in the East which led so many dramatists to pen Turkish tragedies, and which, later, played an important part in the development of the heroic type. The two following scenes, one of the watch and one in which Zareck the Jew plays a prominent part, indicate fully the general characteristics of the drama which mingles thus comedy and tragedy ; the indebtedness of Heminge both to *Much Ado* and to *King Lear* (not to mention *Macbeth*) is likewise amply apparent.

(*The Jewes Tragedy ; or, their Fatal and Final Overthrow by Vespatian and Titus his Son* was printed in 1662 ; it is not certain when it was first produced. The following extracts are taken from the first and only edition.)

DOGBERRY REDIVIVUS

1 WATCH. Come neighbor, come; 'tis we must stand too't when all's done.

2 WATCH. I neighbour, wee'l stand to our tacklings I warrant ye.

JEHOCHANAN. The Watch, I'le steale aside.

1 WATCH. What was that that went by, neighbour?

2 WATCH. Where, where, neighbour, where?

1 WATCH. Marry there, just there something stole along.

2 WATCH. Was it not a spright, God bless us?

1 WATCH. No, no, no, 'twas nothing but a diffusion. But as I was saying, neighbour; 'tis we must stand too't, because we be not book-learn'd, as they say, they count us but unlitter'd fellows, but let um say what they will, we are the very legs of the Commonwealth; for when we be drunk, the City reels fort I'me sure.

2 WATCH. Mas neighbour, and ye say true.

1 WATCH. I woo'l stand toot, that a Watchman hath more torrity than a Justice a Peace.

2 WATCH. What wool ye neighbour, how prove ye that?

1 WATCH. Marry thus I prove it: Yer watchman (taking him in his office of presermity) may be drunk by torrity of his place, because he watches the City, and no body watches him, so cannot your Justice. Agen, your watchman may issue out, and reprehend any person for any fribolous offence, as murder, or the like, and

110

for a feeling, as they call it, let him go without further excommunication, so cannot your Justice; for when the Benefactor is before him, he must nilli willi reign him according to the vigour of the Law.

2 WATCH. How say by that?

1 WATCH. Nay I heard my neighbour *Timothy* say, that if all your chief officers should dye in a night, your watchman should be a Justice a peace himself: nay I tell ye neighbours, the depth of our places is very high.

3 WATCH. See, see.

1 WATCH. Well, come let us take our stand here, we shall see some vacant fellows rambling this way anon, I warrant you.

2 WATCH. What must we do then neighbour?

1 WATCH. Marry we must remit um to prison, and then ask 'um whither they were going.

3 WATCH. But what if they run away neighbour?

1 WATCH. Why then we must knock um down, and bid 'um stand. Nay I warrant ye neighbour, I have all ye'r points of law Barbatim. This gate neighbour. . . .   [*Thunder.*
What was that, what was that neighbour?

2 WATCH. 'Twas a clap of thunder.

1 WATCH. Mas if this weather hold, we shall have a stormy night on't. Where did I end neighbour, can ye tell?

2 WATCH. At [gate] neighbour *Oliver*:

1 WATCH. Well. Well, this very gate was directed that very night that I was made a watchman, which did pronosticate (as I may say) the good service that I shoo'd do here.   [*Thunders agen.*

2 WATCH. Trust me truly neighbour, if this weather hold, we shall have a foul night on't as you say.

1 WATCH. 'Twas e'ne in such a night as this that my neighbour *Timothy* and I ran away from the Constable; for I tell ye neighbour, we are not to repose our selves to the danger of such seasonable weather.

2 WATCH. Mas neighbour I'me e'ne of your minde for that, let's go get some shelter.

1 WATCH. Content, content.

A STORMY NIGHT

Thunder, and enter ZARECK *with a Rapier, and a wrenching Iron.*

ZARECK. Lye there a while till I have use for thee:
                    [*Layes downe the Iron, and goes soft to the Gate.*
A, as I could wish it, this stormy night hath driven the watch away
Beyond my hopes; why it may now be done
With ease and safety.   [*Thunder.*
Speak lowder, lowder yet thou dreadful sky,
Whose flaming face speaks terror to the world;
The daring Lion now dares not approach
The craggy mountain to devour his prey.

III

The ravening Wolf lies lurking in his den,
And howls to hear this strange combustion.
The fatal bird of night, whose dismal voice
Foretels some ill event, cryes now for fear:
Nor man, nor beast dares budg, yet unto me
Thou art as pleasing as the rosie morn,
Whose lovely cheeks look smiling on the day.
How fit thou comest to give assistance too
My brave exploit? for now no sooner shall
The thunder speak, but I will thunder too
Upon the gates: now, now the sport begins:
                    [*It thunders, and he wrenches the gate.*
The gates unbar'd, and *Edomites* let in,
Ile post immediately to the Synagogue.
And there relate with admiration
The strange effect of the late fearful thunder,
Till I have maz'd the learned fools with wonder:
                    [*Thunder hagen he opens the gates.*
Agen, agen, agen, once more, and then 'tis done
And bravely too, without suspicion.
          [*Enter L.* SKIMEON *with others, with Torches, Rapiers, and*
              a Drum.
  ZARECK. My Lord?
  SKIMEON. Thou art a trusty fellow, I will reward thy pains,
Where is thy Lord?
  ZARECK. Follow me, I will conduct ye to him.
                    [*About to go out.*
          [*Enter* JEHOCHANAN, *and others, with torches and Rapiers.*
  JEHOCHANAN. Welcome, my dearest friend, come wee'l away,
And take our stand within the market-place,
Strike up the Drum, the dreadful noise will fright
The drowsie Prelats in the dead of night.

6. LODOWICK CARLELL (*fl.* 1629–64)

The Fool would be a Favourite

Carlell's *The Fool would be a Favourite* is by no means an
untypical example of tragi-comedy as it developed in Caroline
days. The main plot deals with a series of confused love affairs
cast in a romantic and chivalrous vein, while to this is added
a sub-plot, which tells how Young Gudeon or Gudgen, coming
to Court, is cheated by two rascals into believing that he can
purchase a favourite's place. With this play we are moving
rapidly forward toward the heroic tragi-comedy of the Restoration, where the romantic incidents will be heightened and the
comedy, often as here directed against uncourtly characters,
will be made more refined and delicate.

EARLY SEVENTEENTH CENTURY

(The Fool would be a Favourit; or, The discreet Lover seems to have been acted about 1630. The following extract is taken from the only contemporary edition of 1657, which was reprinted in full in " The Berkshire " series (Golden Cockerel Press, 1926).)

YOUNG GUDGEN BUYS HIS PLACE AT COURT

YOUNG GUDGEN. Passe not beyond this score, I charge thee, Father, upon thy allegiance; we are now within the verge of the Court. Away, make haste, to turn those durty acres into crowns, to buy the place you wote of.

OLD GUDGEN. Well son, e'en god be with thee.

YOUNG GUDGEN. Weep not, I say, but get you home, and remember my blessing to the old woman, your wife; bid her not be proud of me, though she have reason: Many a sweet-fac'd youth, like my selfe, hath miscarried at Court, comming to be a Favourite; but I'le buy 't, and make sure work, I . . . [*To* FIRST COURTIER] But come, how do you like me?

1ST COURTIER. Believe me, Sir, yee'r wondrous well accoutred.

YOUNG GUDGEN. Well accoutred, is that a courtly phrase?

1ST COURTIER. Yes.

YOUNG GUDGEN. I have heard some word neer it in the Country. And how do you like my vassail?

1ST COURTIER. Very proper.   [*Enter a* RAGGED COURTIER.

YOUNG GUDGEN. Is he not well accoutred? What's he, what's he, Sir?

1ST COURTIER. Some poor sleight fellow, you must be surly to such, and look big.

YOUNG GUDGEN. Nay, Sir, I can look big, I learnt that of my father's Bull. He comes towards me.

RAGGED COURTIER. Noble Sir, I shall be wondrous proud of your acquaintance.

YOUNG GUDGEN. Then you shall never have it.

RAGGED COURTIER. Why, Sir?   [*Enter* SECOND COURTIER.

YOUNG GUDGEN. Pride is a deadly vertue, humility a sin, that will better become your clothes. Look I not big? Ha! stay, what's he, what's he.

1ST COURTIER. Some great man, by those that sue to him; you must abase your garb, and with an obsequious look salute him.

YOUNG GUDGEN. Sir, I professe my self the vassail to your Dog; if you keep none, I am a most devout and obsequious servant to your Cat.

GUDGEN'S MAN. I shall desire to have the providing of her Mice.

2ND COURTIER. Sir, I am full of employments, excuse me, I must suddenly give his Grace an account.

YOUNG GUDGEN. A great man certainly, 'tis well if I can come to speak with him this two hours.

1ST COURTIER. Sir, may I intreat to know, what place you hold in

H   113

Court? this Gentleman, I can assure you, is worthy your acquaintance.

YOUNG GUDGEN. No, no, Sir; alas, I'm an ignorant, and know nothing, wondrous simple, believe it; a week hence will be fair, I'le wait your leasure. But what's your place, Sir, I beseech you honour me, Sir.

1ST COURTIER. Pray, Sir, satisfie him.

2ND COURTIER. Sir, I'me a favourite to his Grace.

1ST COURTIER. What luck have you, Sir.

YOUNG GUDGEN. I, is't not good luck? Why, Sir, I come to buy a Favourites place, and think I am as fit for't as another man, and will give as much mony too.

2ND COURTIER. Believe it, Sir, you must pay well for't, 'tis a place of great advantage.

YOUNG GUDGEN. I know't, Sir, but one may ha't for mony, I am assur'd on't.

2ND COURTIER. Yes, you shall have mine on good conditions.

YOUNG GUDGEN. Good or ill conditions, I care not, that's all one, I'll ha't.

2ND COURTIER. Sir, you know not yet the duties, nor the priviledges of the place.

YOUNG GUDGEN. That's true, pray what are they?

2ND COURTIER. First, you may be alwaies next the Duke, and so advance, or else keep back suites, as you favour or dislike the person.

YOUNG GUDGEN. Nay, I'le dislike all suites, that are not like mine own.

GUDGEN'S MAN. Or mine.

YOUNG GUDGEN. I, or thine.

2ND COURTIER. The great men will give thee the first goodmorrow, perhaps shew more respect, they are very courteous in this age: The Ladies, thei'l observe yee too, it may be, more then their husbands.

YOUNG GUDGEN. That's brave ifaith.

1ST COURTIER. Sir, hark yee, you must not seem so desirous of it. Let me alone to talk with him, and make the bargain; let's go to the next Tavern.

YOUNG GUDGEN. Sir, I do not greatly care for this Favourites place of yours, I hear, a man shall never live in peace, my eares will alwaies be glowing; they'l do nothing but talke of me, and they'l be hang'd before they speak any good.

1ST COURTIER. Though you deserve ne're so much. Come, let's go.

2ND COURTIER. Nay, that's certain, they'l misinterpret every action, if it prosper not; their faith in that is like to Turks.

YOUNG GUDGEN. Sir, I would have you know, I care not ij*d*. for your place; but if you'l go to the next Tavern, he shall agree with you for it.

1ST COURTIER. Fie, Sir, you'l spoyle all.

2ND COURTIER. But is there nothing the Duke may except against, in your friend?

YOUNG GUDGEN. Except against me? 'tis impossible, he ne're saw me in's life: why should he except against me then, am not I as fit for a favourite, as another man?

2ND COURTIER. 'Tis but a needfull objection.

YOUNG GUDGEN. Except against me?

2ND COURTIER. Pacifie your selfe.

YOUNG GUDGEN. I tell you Sir, if he should but think of excepting against me, I would return into the Country presently, as wise as I came.

1ST COURTIER. Nay, good Sir, 'tis impossible.

YOUNG GUDGEN. And he were ten Dukes, I'de send him to seek a Favourit, I warrant you. Except against me? what me?

1ST COURTIER. Nay, Sir.

YOUNG GUDGEN. I tell you, Sir, should the Duke use me so,
His Dukeship does not a right *Gudgen* know.

7. BENJAMIN OR BEN JONSON (1572–1637)
Poëtaster

Jonson's art is seen at its finest in *The Alchymist* and *Volpone,* where the bitterness that welled up within the dramatist's breast found its fullest and most poignant utterance. Both these plays, however, depend more upon general impression than upon the brilliance of particular scenes, and, as a consequence, they could be but inadequately represented here. As typical of Jonson's satiric tendency, the scene [where his rival Marston, figured as Crispinus, is made to belch forth his ' monstrous ' words may be taken with greater appropriateness. It reveals at one and the same time Jonson's sense of comedy, his keen satiric touch, and the eminently theatrical nature of his scenes. It is this last quality which most surely distinguishes Jonson's work ; his wit as well as his satire is most appreciated when it is spoken in the playhouse. For an understanding of the following passage it must be remembered that Horace and his friends have previously given Crispinus a literary emetic.

(*Poëtaster ; or, His Arraignement* was acted at Blackfriars in 1601. A quarto appeared in 1602 and a revised text in the folio of 1616. The latter has been followed here.)

CRISPINUS GIVES UP HIS COINED WORDS

HORACE [*to* VIRGIL]. If this be all; faith, I forgiue thee freely.
Enuy me still, so long as *Virgil* loues me,
Gallus, Tibullus, and the best-best *Cæsar,*
My deare *Mecænas*: while these, with many more

(Whose names I wisely slip) shall thinke me worthy
Their honour'd, and ador'd societie,
And reade, and loue, proue, and applaud my *poemes*;
I would not wish but such as you should spight them.

CRISPINUS. O——

TIBULLUS. How now, *Crispinus*?

CRISPINUS. O, I am sicke——

HORACE. A bason, a bason, quickly; our physick works. Faint not, man.

CRISPINUS. O—*retrograde—reciprocall—Incubus*.

CÆSAR. What's that, *Horace*?

HORACE. *Retrograde*, and *reciprocall Incubus* are come vp.

GALLUS. Thankes be to Ivpiter.

CRISPINUS. O—*glibbery—lubricall—defunct*—ô——

HORACE. Well said: here's some store.

VIRGIL. What are they?

HORACE. *Glibbery, lubricall*, and *defunct*.

GALLUS. O, they came vp easie.

CRISPINUS. O—ô——

TIBULLUS. What's that?

HORACE. Nothing, yet.

CRISPINUS. *Magnificate*.

MECŒNAS. *Magnificate*? that came vp somewhat hard.

HORACE. I. What cheere, *Crispinus*?

CRISPINUS. O, I shall cast vp my—*spurious—snotteries*——

HORACE. Good. Againe.

CRISPINUS. *Chilblaind*—ô—ô—*clumsie*——

HORACE. That *clumsie* stucke terribly.

MECŒNAS. What's all that, *Horace*?

HORACE. *Spurious snotteries, chilblain'd, clumsie*.

TIBULLUS. O *Jvpiter*!

GALLUS. Who would haue thought, there should ha' beene such a deale of filth in a *poet*?

CRISPINUS. O—*barmy froth*——

CÆSAR. What's that?

CRISPINUS. —*Puffy—inflate—turgidous—ventositous*.

HORACE. *Barmy froth, puffy, inflate, turgidous,* and *ventositous* are come vp.

TIBULLUS. O, terrible, windie wordes!

GALLUS. A signe of a windie braine.

CRISPINUS. O—*oblatrant—furibund—fatuate—strenuous*——

HORACE. Here's a deale: *oblatrant, furibund, fatuate, strenuous*.

CÆSAR. Now, all's come vp, I trow. What a tumult hee had in his belly!

HORACE. No: there's the often *conscious dampe* behind, still.

CRISPINUS. O—*conscious—dampe*.

HORACE. It's come vp, thankes to *Apollo*, and *Æsculapius*: Yet, there's another; you were best take a pill more?

CRISPINUS. O, no: ô—ô—ô—ô.

HORACE. Force your selfe then, a little with your finger.

CRISPINUS. O—ô—*prorumped*.

TIBULLUS. *Prorumped?* What a noise it made! as if his spirit would haue prorumpt with it.

CRISPINUS. O—ô—ô.

VIRGIL. Helpe him: it stickes strangely, what ever it is.

CRISPINUS. O—*clutcht*.

HORACE. Now it's come: *clutcht*.

CÆSAR. *Clutcht?* It's well, that's come vp! It had but a narrow passage.

CRISPINUS. O——

VIRGIL. Againe, hold him: hold his head there.

CRISPINUS. *Snarling gusts—quaking custard.*

HORACE. How now, *Crispinus?*

CRISPINUS. O—*obstupefact.*

TIBULLUS. Nay: that are all we, I assure you.

HORACE. Hoe doe you feele your selfe?

CRISPINUS. Pretty, and well, I thanke you.

8. THOMAS DEKKER (*c.* 1572–1632)

Satiromastix

The " War of the Theatres," in which a number of the most famous Elizabethan authors were involved, has left us with one or two satirical plays, *Satiromastix* being easily the wittiest and most entertaining. In parts it seems to rise even above the self-assured and downright attack of Ben Jonson in *Poëtaster*. The whole question of the significance of the many contemporary allusions in these plays is a complicated one, and need be no more than referred to here. Sufficient be it to note that Jonson, having depicted himself as Horace in *Poëtaster*, laid himself open to ridicule, and Dekker, eager to have his revenge for the attacks made upon him in that play, where he was depicted as Demetrius Fannius, seized the opportunity of replying. His picture of Horace in a moment of painful composition has undoubtedly a touch of brilliance.

(*Satiro-mastix ; or, The vntrussing of the Humorous Poet* was acted by the Lord Chamberlain's men in 1601. It is preserved in a single quarto, dated 1602.)

THE TROUBLES OF A RIMER

HORACE sitting in a study behinde a Curtaine, a candle by him burning, bookes lying confusedly: to himselfe.

HORACE [*composing a poem*].
To thee whose fore-head swels with Roses,
Whose most haunted bower

Giues life & sent to every flower,
Whose most adored name incloses,
Things abstruse, deep, and diuine,
Whose yellow tresses shine,
Bright as *Eoan* fire.
O me thy Priest inspire.
For I to thee and thine immortall name,
In—in—in golden tunes,
For I to thee and thine immortall name——
In—sacred raptures flowing, flowing, swimming, swimming:
In sacred raptures swimming,
Immortal name, game, dame, tame, lame, lame, lame,
Pax, hath, shame, proclaime, oh——
In Sacred raptures flowing, will proclaime, not——
O me thy Priest inspyre!
For I to thee and thine immortall name,
In flowing numbers fild with spright and flame,
Good, good, in flowing numbers fild with spright & flame.

[*Enter* ASINIUS BUBO.

ASINIUS. *Horace, Horace*, my sweet ningle, is alwayes in labour when I come, the nine Muses be his midwiues, I pray *Iupiter*: Ningle.

HORACE. In flowing numbers fild with sprite and flame,
To thee.

ASINIUS. Tome? I pledge thee sweet Ningle, by *Bacchus* quaffing boule, I thought th'adst drunke to me.

HORACE. It must haue been in the deuine lycour of *Pernassus*, then in which, I know you would scarce haue pledg'd me, but come, sweet roague, sit, sit, sit.

ASINIUS. Ouer head and eares yfaith? I haue a sacke-full of newes for thee, thou shalt plague some of them, if God send vs life and health together.

HORACE. Its no matter. Empty thy sacke anon, but come here, first honest roague, come.

ASINIUS. Ist good, Ist good? pure *Helicon* ha?

HORACE. Dam me ift be not the best that euer came from me, if I haue any iudgement; looke sir, tis an *Epithalamium* for Sir *Walter Terrels* wedding, my braines haue giuen assault to it but this morning.

ASINIUS. Then I hope to see them flye out like gun-powder ere night.

HORACE. Nay good roague marke, for they are the best lynes that euer I drew.

ASINIUS. Heer's the best leafe in England, but on, on, Ile but tune this Pipe.

HORACE. Marke, *To thee whose fore-head swels with Roses.*

ASINIUS. O sweet, but will there be no exceptions taken, because fore-head and swelling comes together?

HORACE. Push, away, away, its proper, besides tis an elegancy to say the fore-head swels.

ASINIUS. Nay an't be proper, let it stand for Gods loue.

118

HORACE. Whose most haunted bower,
Giues life and sent to euery flower,
Whose most adored name incloses,
Things abstruse, deep and diuine.
Whose yellow tresses shine,
Bright as *Eoan* fire.

ASINIUS. O pure, rich, ther's heate in this, on, on.

HORACE. Bright as *Eoan* fire,
O me thy Priest inspire!
For I to thee and thine immortall name——

MARKE THIS.

In flowing numbers fild with spryte and flame.

ASINIUS [*looking at his pipe*]. I, mary, ther's spryte and flame in this.

HORACE. A pox, a this Tobacco.

ASINIUS. Wod this case were my last, if I did not marke, nay all's one, I haue alwayes a consort of Pypes about me, myne Ingle is all fire and water; I markt, by this Candle (which is none of Gods Angels) I remember, you started back at spryte and flame.

HORACE. For I to thee and thine immortall name,
In flowing numbers fild with sprite and flame,
To thee Loues mightiest King,
Himen ô Himen does our chaste Muse sing.

ASINIUS. Ther's musicke in this.

HORACE. Marke now, deare *Asinius*.
Let these virgins quickly see thee,
Leading out the Bride,
Though theyr blushing cheekes they hide,
Yet with kisses will they fee thee,
To vntye theyr Virgin zone,
They grieue to lye alone.

ASINIUS. So doe I by *Venus*.

HORACE. Yet with kisses wil they fee thee, my Muse has marcht (deare roague) no farder yet: but how ist? how ist? nay prethee good *Asinius* deale plainly, doe not flatter me, come, how?——

ASINIUS. If I haue any judgement.

HORACE. Nay look you Sir, and then follow a troope of other rich and labour'd conceipts, oh the end shall be admirable! but how ist sweet *Bubo*, how, how?

ASINIUS. If I haue any Iudgement, tis the best stuffe that euer dropt from thee.

9. PHILIP MASSINGER (1583-1640)

A New Way to Pay Old Debts

After the dramas of Shakespeare and Ben Jonson, this comedy of Massinger's is possibly the best known of all Elizabethan plays. When most of its companions vanished from the theatre it still retained a certain popularity, and there have been important revivals even in our own days. This fame is unquestionably merited, for Massinger, dealing with a subject evidently close to his heart, has shown his power of depicting boldly limned characters and his fine knowledge of stage effect. Sir Giles Over-reach is a perfect masterpiece, drawn with lines which seem to come between those of the 'humours' style of Jonson and the individual style of Shakespeare. He is a man, and yet he is a monstrous type; one who has amassed great wealth, and, careless of the feelings of others, would sacrifice all in order to marry his daughter into a titled family. Surrounding him are the Marralls and the Greedies, figures which form fit foils for his robust nature and which, at the same time, aid in complicating the plot and in imparting life to the scenes. *A New Way to Pay Old Debts* is essentially a theatre play; it acts much better than it reads, although its dialogue has a certain straight and rhetorical beauty of its own. Unfortunately those dramatists of the early nineteenth century who were so enamoured of the Elizabethan stage failed to grasp this fact, and imitated the language of this and kindred dramas without realizing the subtlety of the situations. This note is placed here because Massinger's comedy seems to have been at that time one of the most popular and most eagerly read of plays outside the Shakespeare canon. It is not hard to trace the echoes of Over-reach's style in the dialogue of many dramas written between 1820 and 1840.

(*A New Way to Pay Old Debts* was produced probably in 1625. The following extract is taken from the edition of 1633.)

PREPARATIONS FOR A BANQUET

OUERREACH. Spare for no cost, let my Dressers cracke with the weight
Of curious viands.

GREEDIE. *Store indeed's no sore*, Sir.

OUERREACH. That prouerbe fitts your stomacke Master *Greedie*.
And let no plate be seene, but what's pure gold,
Or such whose workemanship exceeds the matter
That it is made of, let my choicest linnen
Perfume the roome, and when we wash the water
With pretious powders mix'd, so please my Lord,
That he may with enuie wish to bath so euer.

MARRALL. 'Twil be very chargeable.

OUERREACH. Auant you Drudge:
Now all my labour'd ends are at the stake,
Is't a time to thinke of thrift? call in my daughter,

120

And master *Justice*, since you loue choice dishes,
And plenty of 'em.

GREEDIE. As I doe indeed Sir,
Almost as much as to giue thankes for 'em.

OUERREACH. I doe conferre that prouidence, with my power
Of absolute command to haue abundance,
To your best care.

GREEDIE. I'le punctually discharge it
And giue the best directions. Now am I
In mine owne conceite a Monarch, at the least
Arch-president of the boyl'd, the roast, the bak'd,
For which I will eate often, and giue thankes,
When my bellies brac'd vp like a drumme, and that's pure iustice.

OUERREACH. I must bee so: should the foolish girle proue modest,

[*Exit* GREEDIE.

Shee may spoile all, she had it not from me,
But from her mother, I was euer forward,
As she must bee, and therefore I'le prepare her.
Alone, and let your woemen waite without. [*Enter* MARGARET.

MARGARET. Your pleasure Sir?

OUERREACH. Ha, this is a neate dressing!
These orient pearles, and diamonds well plac'd too!
The Gowne affects me not, it should haue beene
Embroider'd o're, and o're with flowers of gold,
But these rich Iewells, and quaint fashion helpe it.
And how below? since oft the wanton eye,
The face obseru'd, descends vnto the foot;
Which being well proportion'd, as yours is,
Inuites as much as perfect white, and red,
Though without art, how like you, your new Woman
The Lady *Downefalne*?

MARGARET. Well for a companion;
Not as a seruant.

OUERREACH. Is she humble *Meg*?
And careful too; her Ladiship forgotten?

MARGARET. I pitty her fortune.

OUERREACH. Pitty her? Trample on her.
I tooke her vp in an old tamin gowne,
(Euen staru'd for want of two penny chopps) to serue thee:
And if I vnderstand, shee but repines
To doe thee any duty, though ne're so seruile,
I'le packe her to her Knight, where I haue lodg'd him,
Into the Counter, and there let 'em howle together.

MARGARET. You know your owne wayes, but for me I blush
When I command her, that was once attended
With persons, not inferior to my selfe
In birth.

OUERREACH. In birth? Why art thou not my daughter?

The blest child of my industrie, and wealth?
Why foolish girle, was't not to make thee great,
That I haue ran, and still pursue those wayes
That hale downe curses on mee, which I minde not,
Part with these humble thoughts, and apt thy selfe
To the noble state I labour to aduance thee,
Or by my hopes to see thee honorable,
I will adopt a stranger to my heyre,
And throw thee from my care, doe not prouoke mee.

    MARGARET. I will not Sir; mould mee which way you please.
    OUERREACH. How interrupted?   *[Enter* GREEDIE.
    GREEDIE. 'Tis matter of importance,
The cooke Sir is selfe-will'd and will not learne
From my experience, there's a fawne brought in Sir,
And for my life I cannot make him rost it,
With a *Norfolke* dumpling in the belly of it.
And Sir, we wisemen know, without the dumpling
'Tis not worth threepence.
    OUERREACH. Would it were whole in thy belly
To stuffe it out; Cooke it any way, prethee leaue me.
    GREEDIE. Without order for the dumpling?
    OUERREACH. Let it be dumpl'd
Which way thou wilt, or tell him I will scall'd him
In his owne Caldron.
    GREEDIE. I had lost my stomake,
Had I lost my mistrisse dumpling, I'le giue thanks for.
    OUERREACH. But to our businesse *Megge*, you haue heard who
        dines here?   *[Exit* GREEDIE.
    MARGARET. I haue Sir.
    OUERREACH. 'Tis an honourable man,
A Lord *Megge*, and commands a regiment
Of Souldiers, and what's rare is one himselfe;
A bold, and vnderstanding one; and to be
A Lord, and a good leader in one volume,
Is granted vnto few, but such as rise vp
The Kingdomes glory.   *[Enter* GREEDIE.
    GREEDIE. I'le resigne my office,
If I be not better obey'd.
    OUERREACH. Slight, art thou franticke?
    GREEDIE. Franticke, 'twould make me a franticke, and stark mad,
Were I not a *Iustice of peace*, and *coram* too,
Which this rebellious Cooke cares not a straw for.
There are a dozen of Woodcockes.
    OUERREACH. Make thy selfe
Thirteene, the bakers dozen.
    GREEDIE. I am contented
So they may be dress'd to my minde, he has found out
A new deuice for sawce, and will not dish 'em

With tosts, and butter; my Father was a Taylor,
And my name though a Iustice, *Greedie Woodcocke*,
And 'ere I'le see my linage so abus'd,
I'le giue vp my commission.

OUERREACH. Cooke, Rogue, obey him.
I haue giuen the word, pray you now remoue your selfe,
To a collar of brawne, and trouble me no farther.

GREEDIE. I will, and meditate what to eate at dinner.

10. WILLIAM ROWLEY (? 1585–? 1642)

A New Wonder, a Woman never Vext

The approach which early seventeenth-century drama made
to the sphere of the sentimental is illustrated clearly enough in
this play of Rowley's. Jonson's satirical treatment of ordinary
London life has here given place to a moralizing strain, in which
white goodness is contrasted with black evil, greed, and in-
humanity. As the title shows, the patient and comforting wife
is the central figure, but the plot tells of hate and imprisonment,
of sympathetic thoughts and release. The passage given below,
in which the principal characters—Old Foster, the father,
Stephen, the uncle, and Robert, the son—plead their causes
before the King, is self-explanatory, and in it the sentimentalizing
reflections are deeply marked. As will be seen, Rowley was
by no means untalented. He has a decided power in the writing
of blank verse, and his characters are well outlined. The sentimental style, however, generally leads toward a certain untruth
to life, so that there is about this domestic comedy something
of the same atmosphere which we discover in the otherwise
totally different sphere of the romantic tragi-comedy. On the
other hand, it was through the sentimental that the modern
drame was reached. There is little to laugh at in *A New Wonder* ;
we can see in the treatment of the play the way in which the
dramatist was striving to secure a dramatic note removed both
from tragedy and from comedy, and yet approaching at times
toward each. The movement is direct from Rowley to Steele,
and from Steele to the modern age we discover many links in a
direct chain of development.

(*A New Wonder, A Woman never Vext* was acted probably about
1625. The following extract is taken from the edition of 1632.)

A SENTIMENTAL CONCLUSION

Enter the one way, STEPHEN'S *wife, the other,* MISTRIS FOSTER,
JANE, OLD FOSTER, ROBERT, *and* KEEPER.

[All kneele.

KING. What are these peticioners?

ROBERT. Each hath a knee for duty, the other for petition.

KING. Rise, your dutie's done, your petitions shall neede
No knees, so your intents be honest, does
None here know them?

STEPHEN. Yes my good Lord, there's now a wonder in your
    sight.

KING. A wonder, Master Sheriffe, you meane for beauty.

STEPHEN. No my Lege, I would not so boast mine
Owne wife, but 'tis a wonder that excels beauty.

KING. A wonder in a woman; what is't I prethee?

STEPHEN. Patience, my Leige, this is a woman that
Was neuer uext.

KING. You may boast it largely; 'tis a subjects happinesse
Above a Queenes; Haue you suites to us?

ROBERT. I am the suppliant plaintiffe, royall *Henry*.
From me their griefes take their originall.

KING. What art thou?

ROBERT. Euen what your Grace shall please to make of me;
I was the son to this distressed father, untill he
Tooke his paternity off, and threw me from his love,
Then I became son to mine Vncle by adoption,
Who likewise that hath tane away againe,
And throwne me backe to pouerty; never was
Son so tost betwixt two fathers, yet knowes
Not one, for still the richest does despise his heire,
And I am backe expulst into despaire.

KING. This may your vices cause.

ROBERT. For that I come to your impartialle censure for
    a doome.

KING. We hear, speake on, we know the parties,
Each one relate his griefe, and if it lye in us,
We'l yeeld reliefe; 'tis first requisite that we
Know of you Sir, the cause of this your Sonnes disinheritance.

OLD FOSTER. Before I understood his uertuous minde,
Or weighed his disposition to be kind,
I did that froward worke; this now great man,
Was an unthrifty wretch, a prodigal then,
And I disdain'd to know his brotherhood,
Denyed reliefe to him; this childe kinde and good
Against my contradiction, did him releive, as his
Distressed Vncle, at this I chide; for bade,
Still he holds on his course,
He growes more kind, and he in wanting worse;
My rage continued as it had begun,
And in that rage I threw away my sonne.

STEPHEN. The like plead I, my Lord: for when my state
Had rais'd it selfe by an uncertaine fate,
I tooke this out-cast childe, made him my oune,
As full and free, as I my selfe had sowne

The seede that brought him forth; for this my loue,
His oblieg'd duty presently did prove
A traytor to my trust, against my will,
Succouring that foe, which I did love so ill,
Only for hating him; my charity being thus
Abus'd, and quit with injurie, what could I then
But as his father erst, so I agen might throw
Him from my loue? for worse is love abus'd
Then new borne hate, and should be soe refus'de:
I did a fathers part, if it were bad
Blame him for both, there I my patterne had.
    KING. You fall betwixt two pillars Sir, is't not so?
    ROBERT. Vnhappy fate, my Lord, yet thus I pleade:
For this my fathers hate I might deserve,
I broke his precepts, and did unchildly swerve
From his commission, I to my Vncle gave
What was my fathers, striuing thereby to save
His falne repute; he rag'd, I did it still,
Yet must confesse as it was well, twas ill,
Well in my love, me thought, ill to my fate:
For I thereby ruin'd my owne estate,
But that mine Vncle throwes me forth of doore
For the same cause he tooke me in before,
Beats sorest 'gainst my bosome; if twere good
To take from a father for an Vncles foode,
In lawes of love and nature, how much rather
Might I abridge an Vncle for a father?
Charitie's, a vertue generally stands,
And shoulde dispersed be through all mens hands.
Then would you keep't alone, for when your heire
I first adopted was, charity was there:
How er'rs your judgement then? seeing you see
What was good in you, makes sin in mee;
You'l say my father did it, oh throw away
That foule excuse; let not discretion stray
So farre a side; if custome lawfull make,
Then sin were lawfull for example sake;
Nor were those wasted goods only your owne,
Since part was mine having adoption;
Then doe him right, my Lord, yet doe no wrong,
For where my duty fai'ld my love was strong.
    KING. With an impartiall eare we have heard your
Louing story, 'tis both fayre and honest.
    STEPHEN. O let me now anticipate your Grace,
And casting off the shadow of a face,
Shew my hearts true figure, how haue I striv'd
To make this forc't counterfeit long liv'd,
And now it bursts; come into my heart,

I haue two iewells here shall never part
From my loves eye watch, two worthy to be fil'd,
On times best record; a woman and a child,
Now Sir, to you I come, we must be friends,
Though envie wils not so, yet love contends
Gainst envy and her forces; my young yeares
Say I must offer first, a peace in tears.

OLD FOSTER. O let my shame my bosomes center breake!
Love is so young it cryes, but cannot speake.

KING. You bless mine eyes with objects that become
The theater of Kings to looke upon.

STEPHEN. The keeper is discharg'd Sir, your debts are paid,
And from the prison yore a new free man made:
Theres not a Creditor can aske you ought,
As your sonne did forme, so haue I bought
Your liberty with mine, and to encrease it more,
Because I know bare liberty is poore
Without assistance: to raise your state agen,
The thirds of mine are yours, say you Amen.

WIFE. No, not to that, you are kind brothers now,
Diuide by halfes that love, and I'l allow.

STEPHEN. Thou art only wise in vertue, as thou setst downe,
So let it be, halfe my estate's your owne.

OLD FOSTER. It whole redownes agen, for I am yours;
Forget this minute my forgetfull houres.

STEPHEN. O, they are all buried Sir.

KING. This union's good, such league should ever be in brotherhood.

STEPHEN. Yet without boast, my Leige, let me relate
One small thing more, remorse of my owne state,
And my deare brothers worse succession;
For that we both haue prisoners been in one
Selfe-same place of woe, and felt those throwes
That *Ludgate* yeelds; my charity bestowes
Some almes of comfort: Keeper you can speake it.

KEEPER. And many hundreds more Sir, you haue reedified
And built it faire, adding more ground to it,
And by pipes of lead from *Paddington*, drawne
Water thither, free for all prisoners, lodgings
Likewise free, and a hundred pounds yearely, to make
Them fires for better comfort: all this is almost finisht.

KING. A worthy work, the better being done in the Founders eie,
Not left unto succession.

STEPHEN. O my good Lord, I ever keep in mind an English
Sentence, which my tutor is, and teaches me to act my
Charity with mine owne hands, so doubtfull is
Performance, when the Benefactor's dead.

KING. What is't I prethee?

126

STEPHEN. This my good Lord, women are forgetfull.
Children unkind, Executors covetous, and take what they find,
If any man aske where the deads goods became,
The Executor swears he dyed a poore man.
  KING. You haue prevented well, so has this good Alderman,
I wish you many Schollers.
  WIFE. You make some doubt of me in this Sir;
Did you not say that women were forgetfull,
  KING. You have vext her now Sir, how doe you answer that?
  STEPHEN. No my Lord, she's exempt from the proverbe.
  WIFE. No my Lord, I'l helpe it better, I doe confesse
That women are forgetfull, yet ne'r the lesse
I am exempt, I know my fate, and finde,
My deare husband must not leave me behind,
But I must goe before him, and 'tis said
The grave's good rest when women go first to bed.
  STEPHEN. Thanks for thy excuse good wife, but not thy love
To fill my grave before me, I would not live to see that day.
  WIFE. Prethee no more, I had rather be angry than flatter'd.
  KING. You have a wonder Master Sheriffe, a prizelesse jewell.
  STEPHEN. Many jewels my good Lord; a brother, wife, and child,
For this I would have strove even with a father,
How e're rough stormes did in my brows appeare,
Within my bosom it was alwaies cleare.

11. JOHN FLETCHER (1579–1625)

The Wild-goose Chase

The Wild-goose Chase has been chosen here to represent the
Fletcher style in comedy, because that play provides a very
interesting parallel with Farquhar's The Inconstant, which is
founded on the earlier work. The Wild-goose Chase shows
Fletcher as a typical precursor of the Restoration 'manners'
style, although it is quite clear how far short he fell of full
achievement of his aims. The comedy of manners depends
ultimately on its wit, and this rare wit the Elizabethans could
never attain. Their very medium prevented the free expression
of that social mood which finds its perfect utterance in the
plays of Congreve. Before we can understand the precise
difference which exists between the earlier courtly comedy and
the later we must gain a full appreciation of the purely stylistic
differences between the dialogue of Fletcher and the dialogue of
Congreve and his companions. At least some of these differences
will be apparent when the extract given here is compared with
Farquhar's treatment of the same episode (see pp. 232–234). It
may be noted how in Fletcher the dialogue is cast in a blank-
verse medium which permits, perhaps demands, just a touch of

emotion, whereas in Farquhar prose has taken the place of verse and the language is the language of the pure intellect.

(*The Wild-Goose Chase* seems to have been acted first about 1621. It was not printed until 1652. The following extract is taken from the folio of 1679.)

THE WAY OF A WORLD THAT WOULD BE POLITE

MIRABEL. Shall I ne'r be at rest? no peace of conscience?
No quiet for these creatures?   Am I ordain'd
To be devour'd quick by these she-Canibals?
Here's another they call handsom, I care not for her,
I ne'r look after her: when I am half tipled
It may be I should turn her, and peruse her,
Or in my want of women, I might call for her;
But to be haunted when I have no fancie,
No maw to th' matter; Now, why do you follow me?
ORIANA. I hope, Sir, 'tis no blemish to my vertue,
Nor need you (out of scruple) ask that question,
If you remember ye, before your Travel
The contract you ty'd to me: 'tis my love, Sir,
That makes me seek ye, to confirm your memory,
And that being fair and good, I cannot suffer:
I come to give ye thanks too.
MIRABEL. For what 'prethee?
ORIANA. For that fair piece of honesty ye shew'd, Sir,
That constant nobleness.
MIRABEL. How? for I am short headed.
ORIANA. I'le tell ye then; for refusing that free offer
Of *Monsieur Natolets*; those handsome Beauties,
Those two prime Ladies, that might well have prest ye;
If not to have broken, yet to have bow'd your promise:
I know it was for my sake, for your faith sake,
You slipt 'em off: your honesty compell'd ye.
And let me tell ye, Sir, it shew'd most handsomly.
MIRABEL. And let me tell thee, there was no such matter:
Nothing intended that way of that nature;
I have more to do with my honesty than to fool it,
Or venture it in such leak barks as women;
I put 'em off, because I lov'd 'em not,
Because they are too queazie for my temper,
And not for thy sake, nor the Contract sake,
Nor vows, nor oaths; I have made a thousand of 'em,
They are things indifferent, whether kept or broken;
Meer venial slips, that grow not near the conscience;
Nothing concerns those tender parts; they are trifles;
For, as I think, there was never man yet hop'd for
Either constancie, or secrecie, from a woman,

Unless it were an Ass ordain'd for sufferance;
Nor to contract with such can be a Tial,[1]
So let them know again; for 'tis a Justice,
And a main point of civil policie,
What e're we say or swear, they being Reprobates,
Out of the state of faith, we are clear of all sides,
And 'tis a curious blindness to believe us.

    ORIANA. You do not mean this sure?

    MIRABEL. Yes sure, and certain,
And hold it positively, as a Principle,
As ye are strange things, and made of strange fires and fluxes,
So we are allow'd as strange wayes to obtain ye,
But not to hold; we are all created Errant.

    ORIANA. You told me other tales.

    MIRABEL. I do not deny it;
I have tales of all sorts for all sorts of women,
And protestations likewise of all sizes,
As they have vanities to make us coxcombs;
If I obtain a good turn, so it is,
I am thankfull for it: if I be made an Ass,
The mends are in mine own hands, or the Surgeons,
And there's an end on't.

    ORIANA. Do not you love me then?

    MIRABEL. As I love others, heartily I love thee,
When I am high and lusty, I love thee cruelly:
After I have made a plenteous meal, and satisfi'd
My senses with all delicates, come to me,
And thou shalt see how I love thee.

    ORIANA. Will not you marry me?

    MIRABEL. No, certain, no, for any thing I know yet;
I must not lose my liberty, dear Lady,
And like a wanton slave cry for more shackles.
What should I marry for?   Do I want any thing?
Am I an inch the farther from my pleasure?
Why should I be at charge to keep a wife of mine own,
When other honest married men will ease me?
And thank me too, and be beholding to me:
Thou thinkst I am mad for a Maiden-head, thou art cozen'd. . . .
        Do'st thou see this book here?
Look over all these ranks; all these are women,
Maids, and pretenders to Maiden-heads; these are my conquests,
All these I swore to marry, as I swore to thee,
With the same reservation, and most righteously,
Which I need not have done neither; for alas they made no scruple,
And I enjoy'd 'em at my will, and left 'em:
Some of 'em are married since, and were as pure maids again,

----

[1] A bond or tie.

Nay o' my conscience better than they were bred for;
The rest fine sober women.

    ORIANA. Are ye not asham'd, Sir?

    MIRABEL. No by my troth, Sir; there's no shame belongs to it;
I hold it as commendable to be wealthy in pleasure,
As others do in rotten sheep, and pasture.

12. JAMES SHIRLEY (1596–1666)

The Witty Fair One

The movement toward the style of the comedy of manners, which has already been marked in Fletcher's *The Wild-goose Chase*, is usually to be discovered during the period before 1642 only in individual scenes. As yet the gaiety, the intellectualism, and the franker relations between men and women had not fully established themselves, and, as a consequence, there is frequently a variety of moods introduced even into those plays of the period which most surely point forward to Congreve. Of these plays *The Witty Fair One* is by no means the least representative. Many portions of the comedy are dull and uninteresting, others are clearly based on the old Jonsonian style; but in the presentation of Fowler and Penelope the dramatist has unquestionably pictured a gallant and his mistress in a way which is 'Restoration' in temper. No more symbolic sentence could be found than that of Fowler's:

> Be not you a Goddesse I know y'are mortall, and had rather make
> you my companion then my Idoll, this is no flattery now.

It shows in its directness and in its frankness how the growing rationalism of the age was battering down the last relics of medieval chivalry and the idealistic visions of the Courts of Love. So long as women were looked on as goddesses the comedy of manners could not come into being; before Congreve could write a Penelope, a Florimel, and a Millamant had to meet their Fowlers, their Celadons, and their Mirabels on equal terms.

(*The Wittie Faire One* was produced in 1628. The following extract is taken from the quarto of 1633.)

RATIONALISM IN LOVE

    FOWLER. Your soft Starres will not let you be so cruell Lady, to giue repulse to a louer.

    CLARE. Do not belieue him, he does but complement,
I ha' knowne him court a hundred, with as much
Formalitie, wooed 'em ith nuptiall cut, made verses
O' their haire, set Lillies and Rosies, a whole
Garden i' their cheekes, cherries i' their lippes, stellifie their
Eyes, and yet in a twinckling——

130

PENELOPE. Sure you doe him wrong sir.

CLARE. Wrong?

FOWLER. He measures my affections by the length of his own. Prethee Satyre chuse another walke, and leaue vs to inioy this, thou knowst not my intent.

CLARE. Thou mayst be honest with one, and that's a miracle and will aske a strong faith to beleeue it, I hope shee has more wit than to trust your voluble courtship, Ile seeke out my friend *Aymwell.*   [VIOLETTA *comes from the Arbor.*

VIOLETTA. Sir, if your engagement requires no hast.

PENELOPE. I doe wonder a Gentleman of your knowledge should so deceive himselfe.

FOWLER. Expresse your selfe Fairest.

PENELOPE. Faire sir, I am not taken with your flatteries, I can see through you.

FOWLER. If you haue so actiue an eye Lady, you may see a throng of Passions flaming at my hart, set a fire by your beauty I protest t'ee; come, shame not your wisdome to beleeue report or opinion ath' world, 'tis a malicious age we liue in, if your eares haue beene abused with any ill noise a me, you shall tell your selfe if you loue me, the world is a shamelesse and miserable detractor, you doe not despise me Lady——

PENELOPE. No, I pitty so handsome a Gentleman, and of so fair a fortune, should want his eyes.

FOWLER. How blind?

PENELOPE. To your owne follies sir.

FOWLER. Shall I sweare I loue you, as I am a Gentleman.

PENELOPE. As you are a Gentleman, I know you can sweare any thing t'is a fashion y' are most constant in, to bee religiously wicked, an oath in your mouth and a reseruation in your heart is a common Courtship, doe not sweare as you are a Gentleman.

FOWLER. As I am an honest man.

PENELOPE. Out vpon't, that's a worse, my Taylor couzened me t'oher day with the same oath, saue your credit and let swearing alone, I dare take your word.

FOWLER. Well sayd.

PENELOPE. For a greater matter, but not for this, you and I ha not eaten a bushell of salt yet, in time I may be conuerted, and thinke your tongue and heart keep house together, for at this time I presume they are very far a sunder.

FOWLER. Would you haue my tongue in my heart Lady?

PENELOPE. No by my troth, I would rather finde your heart in your tongue, but you are valiant, and 'tis onely feare they say, brings a mans heart vp to his mouth.

FOWLER. Why, your wit is a tyrant now, pray tell me doe not you loue me mightily now aboue Potatoes, come I see the little blind Boy in your eyes already.

PENELOPE. Loue you Sir?

FOWLER. Yes, I know by your bitternesses you wish me well and think there is some hope I may be wonne too, you take paines to whip me so handsomely, come Ile be a good child and kisse the rod.

CLARE. You oblige my seruice to you, I am one *Aymwell* called friend, and shall be happy to convay him any knowledge may concerne him.

VIOLETTA. Then briefly thus I vnderstand he loues mee.
Pray you doe him the true office of a friend,
And councell him desist, I am dispos'd of
Already in my fathers thoughts, and must
Shew my obedience, he shall beget
But his owne trouble, if he moue it to
My Vnckle or my Father, and perhaps
Draw their suspition and displeasure
On me too, by so indiscreet proceeding,
I would not haue a Gentleman of his worth
Doe himselfe so great iniury to runne
A course of so much hazard, if you please
To beare the burden of my thankes for his
On my part vndeseru'd opinion,
And make him sensible, in time hee may
Place his affection where he may expect
Better returne, you shall discharge a friendship
To him, and with it make my thoughts your debtor.

CLARE. You haue exprest a noblenesse in this
Were all of your mind Lady,
There would be lesse Willow worne.

FOWLER. You would ha' me praise you now, I could ramble in your commendation.

PENELOPE. I thinke so.

FOWLER. Dee [1] but thinke so, why you shall heare mee, Your hayres are *Cupids* Nets, a Forehead like the fayrest coast of heauen without a cloud, your eybrow is loues bow whiles eyther Eye are arrowes drawne to wound, your lips the Temple or sacred phane of kisses often as they meete exchanging Roses, your tongue Ioues lightning, necke the Milky path or throne where sit the Graces, doe not I know that I haue abused you all this while, or doe you thinke I loue you a thought the better, or with all my Partiall daubings can alter the complection of a hayre now.

PENELOPE. I would not haue you sir.

FOWLER. No dispraise te'e. [2] I haue seene as handsome a woman Ride vpon a sacke to Market, that neuer knew the impulsion of a Coate or the price of a Stammell petticoate, and I ha seene a worse face in a Countesse; what's that? Must ye be proud because men doe call you handsome, and yet though wee are so foolish to tell you so, you might haue more wit then to beeleeue it, your eyes may

---

[1] D'ye = Do ye.   [2] t'ye = to ye.

be matcht I hope, for your nose there be richer in our sexe, t'is true that you haue colour for your hayre wee graunt it, and for your cheekes, but what doe your teeth stand you in Lady, your lips are pretty but you lay 'em too open and men breath too much vpon 'em, for your tongue wee all leaue you ther's no contesting, your hand is fine but your gloues whiter, and for your leg, if the commendation or goodnesse of it bee in the small, there be bad enow in Gentlemens stockings to compare with it; come remember y'are imperfect creatures without a man, be not you a Goddesse I know y'are mortall, and had rather make you my companion then my Idoll, this is no flattery now.

13. JOHN MARSTON (*c.* 1575–1634)

Antonio and Mellida

Toward the end of the sixteenth century revenge plays with thrilling and bloody plots seem to have been especially popular, and among those which have been preserved none is more entertaining than *Antonio and Mellida*, written by the satirist John Marston. The play seems to have been produced in 1599, and may have given Shakespeare hints for the refashioning of *Hamlet* in the early years of the following century. The scene chosen here (taken from two separate portions of the second part of the play) distinctly reminds us of a more famous scene on the battlements of Elsinore. Andrugio has been slain, and like the elder Hamlet returns to bid his son (Antonio) execute revenge. The madness of the hero, too, calls for our special attention.

(*Antonio and Mellida* was printed in two quartos in 1602, and has been edited by W. W. Greg for the Malone Society. The passages given below follow the original.)

ANTONIO CONVERSES WITH HIS FATHER'S GHOST

Enter two pages, the one with two tapers, the other with a chafing dish: a perfume in it. ANTONIO, *in his night gowne, and a night cap, vnbrac't, following after.*

ANTONIO. The black iades of swart night trot foggy rings
Bout heauens browe. 'Tis now starke dead night.
Is this Saint *Markes* Church?
1 PAGE. It is, my Lord.
ANTONIO. Where stands my fathers hearse?
2 PAGE. Those streamers beare his armes. I, that is it.
ANTONIO. Set tapers to the toumbe, & lampe the Church:
Giue me the fire. Now depart and sleepe.   [*Exeunt pages.*
I purifie the ayre with odorous fume.
Graues, valts, and toumbes, groane not to beare my weight.

133

Colde flesh, bleake trunkes, wrapt in your half-rot shrowdes,
I presse you softly, with a tender foote.
Most honour'd sepulchre, vouchsafe a wretch,
Leaue to weepe ore thee.   Toumb, Ile not be long
Ere I creepe in thee, and with bloodlesse lips
Kisse my cold fathers cheeke.   I pree thee, graue,
Prouide soft mould to wrap my carcasse in.
Thou royal spirit of *Andrugio*, where ere thou houerst
(Ayrie intellectt) I heaue vp tapers to thee (viewe thy son)
In celebration of dewe obsequies.
Once euery night, Ile dewe thy funerall hearse
With my religious teares.
O blessed father of a cursed son,
Thou diedst most happie, since thou liuedst not
To see thy sonne most wretched, and thy wife
Pursu'd by him that seekes my guiltlesse blood.
O, in what orbe thy mightie spirit soares.
Stoop and beat downe this rising fog of shame,
That striues to blur thy blood, and girt defame
About my innocent and spotlesse browes.
Non est mori miserum, sed misere mori.
ANDRUGIO. Thy pangs of anguish rip my cerecloth vp:
And loe the ghoast of ould *Andrugio*
Forsakes his coffin.   *Antonio*, reuenge.
I was impoyson'd by *Piero's* hand:
Reuenge my bloode; take spirit gentle boy:
Reuenge my bloode.   Thy *Mellida*, is chaste:
Onely to frustrate thy pursuite in loue,
Is blaz'd vnchaste.   Thy mother yeelds consent
To be his wife, & giue his bloode a sonne,
That made her husbandlesse, and doth complot
To make her sonlesse: but before I touch
The banks of rest, my ghost shall visite her.
Thou vigor of my youth, iuyce of my loue,
Seize on reuenge, graspe the sterne bended front
Of frowning vengeance, with vnpaized clutch.
Alarum *Nemesis*, rouze vp thy blood,
Inuent some stratageme of vengeance:
Which but to thinke on, may like lightning glide,
With horror through thy breast; remember this.
Scelera non vlcisceris, nisi vincis.   [*Exit* ANDRUGIO'S GHOST.

ANDRUGIO'S GHOST PAYS ITS PROMISED VISIT

MARIA. God night *Nutriche*.   Pages, leaue the roome.
The life of night growes short, 'tis almost dead.
                                        [*Exeunt Pages and* NUTRICHE.
O thou cold widdowe bed, sometime thrice blest,

By the warme pressure of my sleeping Lord:
Open thy leaues, and whilst on thee I treade,
Groane out. Alas, my dear *Andrugio's* deade.
    [MARIA *draweth the courtaine: and the ghost of* ANDRUGIO
        is displayed, sitting on the bed.
Amazing terror, what portent is this?
   ANDRUGIO. Disloyal to our Hymniall rites,
What raging heat rains in thy strumpet blood?
Hast thou so soone forgot *Andrugio*?
Are our loue-bands so quickly cancelled?
Where liues thy plighted faith vnto this breast?
O weake *Marya*! Go to, calme thy feares.
I pardon thee, poore soule. O shed no teares,
Thy sex is weake. That black incarnate fiende
May trippe thy faith, that hath orethrowne my life:
I was impoyson'd by *Piero's* hand.
Ioyne with my sonne, to bend vp straind reuenge.
Maintaine a seeming fauour to his suite,
Till time may forme our vengeance absolute.
     [*Enter* ANTONIO, *his armes bloody: a torch and a poniard.*
   ANTONIO. See, vnamaz'd, I will beholde thy face,
Outstare the terror of thy grimme aspect,
Daring the horred'st obiect of the night.
Looke how I smoake in blood, reeking the steame
Of foming vengeance. O my soule's inthroan'd
In the tryumphant chariot of reuenge.
Me thinks I am all ayre, and feele no waight
Of humane dirt clogge. This is *Iulios* bloode.
Rich musique, father; this is *Iulio's* blood.
Why liues that mother?
   ANDRUGIO. Pardon ignorance. Fly deare *Antonio*:
Once more assume disguise, and dog the Court
In fained habit, till *Piero's* blood
May euen ore-flowe the brimme of full reuenge. [*Exit* ANTONIO.
Peace, and all blessed fortunes to you both.
Fly thou from Court, be pearelesse in reuenge:
Sleepe thou in rest, loe here I close thy couch.
     [*Exit* MARIA *in her bed,* ANDRUGIO *drawing the Curtaines.*[1]
And now yee sootie coursers of the night,
Hurrie your chariot into hels black wombe.
Darkenesse, make flight; Graues, eat your dead again:
Let's repossesse our shrowdes. Why lags delay?
Mount sparkling brightnesse, giue the world his day.

---

[1] This simply means that Andrugio draws the curtains round Maria's bed, so that she disappears from the view of the audience; it is thus an 'exit.'

EXTRACTS FROM BRITISH & IRISH PLAYS

14. GEORGE CHAPMAN (c. 1560–1634)

The Revenge of Bussy d'Ambois

In the midst of the motley troop of Elizabethan dramatists George Chapman stands forward as a robust and stalwart figure, lacking the adaptability of many of his companions, yet with a humour of his own, wanting a true sense of the tragic, yet coming close at times to the highest conceptions. In style, Chapman was too heavy to be genuinely effective. He has strength, but his lines have not that grace and ease which we look for in the finest dramatic dialogue. In spite of his fame as a playwright, he succeeds better in that translation of Homer which so fired the enthusiasm of Keats than in his comedies or his tragedies. *The Revenge of Bussy d'Ambois* is as typical as any of his dramatic activities. It is a sequel to the earlier, and apparently popular, *Bussy d'Ambois*, and shows the fate of those whom Bussy, dying, left still on earth.

(*The Revenge of Bussy d'Ambois* was acted at Whitefriars about 1610. The following extract is taken from the quarto of 1613.)

ANOTHER ELIZABETHAN GHOST

Ascendit UMBRA BUSSI.

UMBRA BUSSI. Vp from the Chaos of eternall night,
(To which the whole digestion of the world
Is now returning) once more I ascend,
And bide the cold dampe of this piercing ayre,
To vrge the iustice, whose almightie word
Measures the bloudy acts of impious men,
With equall pennance, who in th'act it selfe
Includes th'infliction, which like chained shot
Batter together still; though (as the thunder
Seemes, by mens duller hearing then their sight,
To breake a great time after lightning forth,
Yet both at one time teare the labouring cloud)
So men thinke pennance of their ils is slow,
Though th'ill and pennance still together goe.
Reforme yee ignorant men, your manlesse liues
Whose lawes yee thinke are nothing but your lusts:
When leauing but for supposition sake,
The body of felicitie (Religion)
Set in the midst of Christendome, and her head
Cleft to her bosome; one halfe one way swaying
Another th'other: all the Christian world
And all her lawes whose obseruation,
Stands vpon faith, aboue the power of reason:
Leauing (I say) all these, this might suffice,
To fray yee from your vicious swindge in ill,

And set you more on fire to doe more good:
That since the world (as which of you denies)
Stands by proportion, all may thence conclude,
That all the ioynts and nerues sustaining nature,
As well may breake, and yet the world abide,
As any one good vnrewarded die,
Or any one ill scape his penaltie.   [*The* GHOST *stands close.*
                                      [*Enter* GUISE, CLERMONT.

  GUISE. Thus (friend) thou seest how all good men would
    thriue,
Did not the good thou prompt'st me with preuent
The iealous ill pursuing them in others.
But now thy dangers are dispatcht, note mine:
Hast thou not heard of that admired voyce,
That at the Barricadoes spake to mee,
(No person seene) Let's leade (my Lord) to Reimes?
  CLERMONT. Nor could you learne the person?
  GUISE.   By no meanes.
  CLERMONT. Twas but your fancie then a waking dreame:
For as in sleepe, which bindes both th'outward senses
And the sense common to, th'imagining power
(Stird vp by formes hid in the memories store,
Or by the vapours of o'er-flowing humours
In bodies full and foule; and mixt with spirits)
Faines many strange, miraculous images,
In which act, it so painfully applyes
It selfe to those formes, that the common sense
It actuates with his motion, and thereby
Those fictions true seeme, and haue reall act:
So, in the strength of our conceits, awake,
The cause alike, doth of like fictions make:
  GUISE. Be what it will, twas a presage of something
Waightie and secret, which th'aduertisements
I haue receiu'd from all parts, both without,
And in this Kingdome, as from Rome and Spaine
Soccaine and Sauoye, giues me cause to thinke,
All writing that our plots Catastrophe,
For propagation of the Catholique cause,
Will bloudy proue, dissoluing all our counsailes.
  CLERMONT. Retyre then from them all.
  GUISE.   I must not doe so.
The Arch-Bishop of Lyons tels me plaine
I shall be said then to abandon France
In so important an occasion;
And that mine enemies (their profit making
Of my faint absence) soone would let that fall,
That all my paines did to this height exhale.
  CLERMONT. Let all fall that would rise vnlawfully:

Make not your forward spirit in vertues right,
A property for vice, by thrusting on
Further then all your powers can fetch you off.
It is enough, your will is infinite
To all things vertuous and religious,
Which within limits kept, may without danger,
Let vertue some good from your Graces gather.
Auarice of all is euer nothings father.

    UMBRA. Danger (the spurre of all great mindes) is euer
The curbe to your tame spirits; you respect not
(With all your holinesse of life and learning)
More then the present, like illiterate vulgars,
Your minde (you say) kept in your fleshes bounds,
Showes that mans will must rul'd be by his power:
When (by true doctrine) you are taught to liue
Rather without the body, then within;
And rather to your God still then your selfe:
To liue to him, is to doe all things fitting
His Image, in which, like himselfe, we liue;
To be his Image, is to doe those things,
That make vs deathlesse, which by death is onely
Doing those deedes that fit eternitie,
And those deedes are the perfecting that Iustice
That makes the world last, which proportion is
Of punishment and wreake for euery wrong,
As well as for right a reward as strong:
Away, then, vse the meanes thou hast to right
The wrong I suffer'd.   What corrupted Law
Leaues vnperform'd in Kings, doe thou supply,
And be aboue them all in dignitie.   [*Exit.*

    GUISE. Why stand'st thou still thus, and applyest thine eares,
And eyes to nothing?

    CLERMONT.   Saw you nothing here?

    GUISE. Thou dream'st, awake now; what was here to see?

    CLERMONT. My Brothers spirit, vrging his reuenge.

15. FRANCIS BEAUMONT (c. 1584–1616) AND JOHN FLETCHER (1579–1625)

The Maid's Tragedy

With Beaumont and Fletcher Elizabethan tragedy, still strong and full of poetic beauty, began to sink into its decadence. Themes of illicit love predominate ; subtle horrors stir a jaded audience ; characterization is governed rather by the desire to startle than by the desire to keep true to life.   Above all, the language begins to lose its earlier strength and tends to become loose and ornamental rather than pulsating and harmoniously

138

EARLY SEVENTEENTH CENTURY

blended with character and plot. Both the beauty and the
latent decadence of this new style are to be traced in *The Maid's
Tragedy*, a drama which tells of the treachery of a king, who,
having deflowered Evadne, marries her to one of his most trusted
courtiers, Amintor. The husband, informed of the trick that
has been played on him, spurns his wife, and she, at last heart-
struck by his words, plans to kill the King. This deed she
accomplishes, but is faced by Amintor's loyalty, and in despair
commits suicide. Particular attention should be paid to the
temper of the blank verse, which seems, in its vague rhythm
and frenzy, premonitory of the dramatic decay to come.

(*The Maides Tragedy* was acted at Blackfriars before 1611 and
printed in 1619. The following extract is from the folio edition
of 1679.)

EVADNE'S FRENZIED CRIME

EVADNE. The night grows horrible, and all about me
Like my black purpose: O the Conscience   [KING *abed.*
Of a lost Virgin; whither wilt thou pull me?
To what things dismal, as the depth of Hell,
Wilt thou provoke me? Let no man dare
From this hour be disloyal: if her heart
Be flesh, if she have blood, and can fear, 'tis a daring
Above that desperate fool that left his peace,
And went to Sea to fight: 'tis so many sins
An age cannot prevent 'em: and so great,
The gods want mercy for: yet I must through 'em.
I have begun a slaughter on my honour,
And I must end it there: he sleeps, good heavens!
Why give you peace to this intemperate beast
That hath so long transgressed you? I must kill him,
And I will do't bravely: the meer joy
Tells me I merit in it: yet I must not
Thus tamely do it as he sleeps: that were
To rock him to another world: my vengeance
Shall take him waking, and then lay before him
The number of his wrongs and punishments.
I'le shake his sins like furies, till I waken
His evil Angel, his sick Conscience:
And then I'le strike him dead: King, by your leave:
        [*Ties his arms to the bed.*
I dare not trust your strength: your Grace and I
Must grapple upon even terms no more:
So, if he rail me not from my resolution,
I shall be strong enough.
My Lord the King, my Lord; he sleeps
As if he meant to wake no more, my Lord;
Is he not dead already? Sir, my Lord.

KING. Who's that?

EVADNE.   O you sleep soundly Sir!

KING.   My dear *Evadne*,
I have been dreaming of thee; come to bed.

EVADNE. I am come at length Sir, but how welcome?

KING. What pretty new device is this *Evadne*?
What do you tie me to you by my love?
This is a quaint one: Come my dear and kiss me;
I'le be thy *Mars* to bed my Queen of Love:
Let us be caught together, that the Gods may see,
And envy our embraces.

EVADNE.   Stay Sir, stay,
You are too hot, and I have brought you Physick
To temper your high veins.

KING. Prethee to bed then; let me take it warm.
There you shall know the state of my body better.

EVADNE. I know you have a surfeited foul body,
And you must bleed.

KING.   Bleed!

EVADNE. I, you shall bleed: lie still, and if the Devil,
Your lust will give you leave, repent: this steel
Comes to redeem the honour that you stole,
King, my fair name, which nothing but thy death
Can answer to the world.

KING.   How's this *Evadne*?

EVADNE. I am not she: nor bear I in this breast
So much cold Spirit to be call'd a Woman:
I am a Tyger: I am any thing
That knows not pity: stir not, if thou dost,
I'le take thee unprepar'd; thy fears upon thee,
That make thy sins look double, and so send thee
(By my revenge I will) to look those torments
Prepar'd for such black souls.

KING. Thou dost not mean this: 'tis impossible:
Thou art too sweet and gentle.

EVADNE.   No, I am not:
I am as foul as thou art, and can number
As many such hells here: I was once fair,
Once I was lovely, not a blowing Rose
More chastly sweet, till thou, thou, thou, foul Canker,
(Stir not) didst poyson me: I was a world of vertue,
Till your curst Court and you (hell bless you for't)
With your temptations on temptations
Made me give up mine honour; for which (King)
I am come to kill thee.

KING.   No.

EVADNE.   I am.

KING.   Thou art not.

I prethee speak not these things; thou art gentle,
And wert not meant thus rugged.

EVADNE.   Peace and hear me.
Stir nothing but your tongue, and that for mercy
To those above us; by whose lights I vow,
Those blessed fires that shot to see our sin,
If thy hot soul had substance with thy blood,
I would kill that too, which being past my steel,
My tongue shall teach: Thou art a shameless Villain,
A thing out of the overchange of Nature;
Sent like a thick cloud to disperse a plague
Upon weak catching women; such a tyrant
That for his Lust would sell away his Subjects,
I, all his heaven hereafter.

KING.   Hear *Evadne,*
Thou soul of sweetness! hear, I am thy King.

EVADNE. Thou art my shame; lie still, there's none about you,
Within your cries; all promises of safety
Are but deluding dreams: thus, thus, thou foul man,
Thus I begin my vengeance. . . .   *[Stabs him.*

KING.   *Evadne,* pity me.

EVADNE. Hell take me then; this for my Lord *Amintor;*
This for my noble brother: and this stroke
For the most wrong'd of women.

16. WILLIAM ROWLEY (? 1585–? 1642)

All's Lost by Lust

    As tragic drama and tragi-comedy developed in the early seventeenth century startling incidents, melodramatic devices, cruder portraiture, and horror came to take the place of that nobler type of emotion which Shakespeare had evolved in his four great tragedies. Sometimes the tendency led toward refinement of horror as in the dramas of Webster, Ford, and Shirley; sometimes it took coarser and less recondite forms as in this play of Rowley's. The main plot here tells of the deflowering of Jacintha by the King Roderigo, or Rodorique, of her father's resultant treachery, and of the insatiate cruelty of the Moor with whom he has allied himself. The scene chosen is designed to show the strength which yet endured in this decaying drama, joined to movements which ultimately lead to the heroic tragedy of the Restoration. The dumbshow anticipates the supernatural elements in that kind of tragedy, and there are moments when Rodorique's words come close to those of characters created by Dryden and Lee.

    (*All's Lost by Lust* was produced by the Lady Elizabeth's men about 1616–19. The edition of 1633 has here been followed.)

EXTRACTS FROM BRITISH & IRISH PLAYS

CONSCIENCE TORMENTS RODORIQUE

RODORIQUE. Some musique.

PIAMENTELLI.   Musique Sir! tis all untunde,
Remember your proud enemies approach,
And your unreadinesse to entertaine um.

RODORIQUE. If all be set upon a carelesse hazard,
What shall care doe there?

PIAMENTELLI.   Rouze you like a Lion,
And fright this heard of Foxes, Wolves, and Beares,
From daring to come neere you: a Kings eye
Has Magicall charmes in't to binde treason down,
They fight like theeves for spoile, you for your owne!

RODORIQUE. O *Piamentelli*, theres within my bosome
An army of Furies mustred, worse than those
Which follow *Iulianus*: Conscience beats
The Drum of horror up.

PIAMENTELLI.   For what! a Maidenhead!
Pray be your selfe, and justifie the act,
Stand on your guard, and royalize the fact
By your owne dispensation.

RODORIQUE. Goe call our friends together, if we have none,
Hire them with double pay, our selfe will search
And breake those dangerous doores which have so long
Kept Spaine in childish ignorance.

PIAMENTELLI.   O good my Lord,
Forbeare, there's fatall prophesies forbid you.

RODORIQUE. There's fatall fooleries; tell me of prophesies!
Shall feare affright me? no; upon my life
Tis hidden treasure kept for needfull houres,
And now tis come; tis gold must purchase soldiers;
Shall I not seeke it then? alone Ile breake
Ope those forbidden doores, goe muster men.

PIAMENTELLI. This I dread more then all our enemies,
If good proceed from this, no Magick Art
Shall fright me.   [*Exit.*

RODORIQUE. Or good, or bad, Ile throw the dice my selfe,
And take the chance that fals; thou art the first,   [*Thunder.*
Hell wakens, yet Ile on, twenty at least
I must passe through before I breake the spell;
If this doore thither lead, Ile enter hell.   [*Exit.*

[*Thunder and Lightning. Enter* RODORIQUE *againe at
another doore.*

RODORIQUE. So now Ime entred to the fatall chamber,
Shew now thy full effects; ha? what sight's this?

[*Enter* IULIANUS, MOORE, IACINTHA, ANTONIO, ALONZO, *one
presenting* RODORIQUE.[1]

[1] *I.e.,* dumbshow apparitions.

142

Tis holliday in hell, the fiends are loose,
I have enfranchiz'd you, thank me Devils.
Was this the fatall incantation
That here was lockt so many fearfull ages,
And was't decreed for me to dislocate?
Fire consume you geomantick Devils,
Where borrowed you those bodies, you damn'd theeves?
In your owne shapes you are not visible,
Or are you yet but fancies imaginarie?
What's he that me presents?   I have not lent
My carcas forth, I am not sleeping now,
And my soule straid forth, I am my reall selfe,
Must I be captiv'd by a traitor so?
Devill, thou playest me false; undiadem'd?
And such a sooty fiend inherit me?
Iacintha, too, that she-curse, must she have part?
Kneeling to them, here's a solemnity
In the Devils name; goe raigne in Sulphur, or in
Some frozen Labyrinth; this Kingdom's mine:
Thou there that me personat'st, draw forth thy sword,
And brandish't against hell, Ile shew thee how.   *[Exeunt show.*
What Magick bindes me? what furies hold mine arme?
Piamentelli, Avilla, none succour me?   *[Enter* PIAMENTELLI.
   PIAMENTELLI. What ayles you Sir?
   RODORIQUE.   My foes are come upon me.
   PIAMENTELLI. Comming they are, but yet a league distant, Sir.
   RODORIQUE. Zounds they are come, and have bin here with me.
Traiterous *Iulianus*, and his ravisht daughter,
An army of Moores, of Turks and infidels.
   PIAMENTELLI. Your fancies trouble you, they are but comming,
Too neere in that; make up to your souldiers,
Full twenty thousand now will follow you and more.
   RODORIQUE. The Moore's a comming, & the devill too that must
Succeed me in my last monarchy, take armes and fight,
The fiends shall know they have not plaid me right.

17. BARNABE BARNES (*c.* 1569–1609)

The Devil's Charter

   The Devil's Charter is a good example of that popular type of
Elizabethan drama to which was given the name of 'infernall.'
Marlowe's *Doctor Faustus* had a numerous progeny, and scenes
of enchantment remained popular for many years, the devils
with their squibs giving as much entertainment to seventeenth-
century spectators as they had done to the *naïve* auditors of
medieval mysteries. Usually the 'infernall' was a 'history'
as well, for it was comforting at least to assume that the enemies

of England or its religious opponents were firmly leagued with the powers of Hades. In this play of Cæsar Borgia and Pope Alexander VI Barnes does not hesitate to show these Italians conversing familiarly with ghosts and nefarious spirits, so that his drama makes a double contemporary appeal—the vicious Court life of Renascence Italy representing one trembling interest of the time and the devils representing another. It is interesting to note how Shakespeare sublimated material such as this, both in comedy (*A Midsummer Night's Dream*) and in tragedy (*Macbeth*).

(*The Divils Charter* was acted about 1606 by the King's men. The following extract follows the quarto of 1607.)

AN INFERNAL SCENE

ALEXANDER *in his studie beholding a Magicall glasse with other obseruations.*

ALEXANDER. Fore-god 'tis *Candie*, 'tis *Candy*, I know 'tis *Candie*,
Where is that traiterous homicide? where is hee?
I cannot see him: hee shall not scape me so.
I must and will finde him, though he went inuisible,
Appeare appeare; not yet; ha and *Candy* murthered too,
Let me looke forth.

        [ALEXANDER *commeth vpon the Stage out of his study with a booke in his hand.*

Oh, oh, very good very good: well I perfectly perceiue.
By this escention of *Arctophilax*,
What time of night it is, sorrow giue place;
Reuenge in blood and fierie sacrafice,
Commaundeth: nature now preuents her current: yeeld,
Let vs adore the second eye of heauen,   [*he boweth his bodie.*
Bright *Armatas* increaseth she, is not combust.
O sacred season for nocturnall Ceremonies.
This ioyeous quarter is in *Casmaran*. ha.   [*he looketh on a watch.*
What hower of night ist? why tis *Salam*, twelue a cloke,
What are our angels of this quarter?
Gargatel Tariel Gauiel.
How goodly these augurize faire auspices of truth,
Now mountes bright *Athaman* in his goulden ascension,
Direct in opposition with our hemispher,   [*he tinketh on a bell.*
And now there hower with them is *Aetalon*:
Bernardo bring hither thy white robes of sanctity,
Hast thou Coles ready burnt bring in my Thurible,
And sence about this sanctified place,
For heere *Festatiui* must haue her honor.
Candie my sonne is murthered, *Candie* my sonne,
Candie my sonne is murthered: I will raise
All the great diuills to shew the murtherer,

144

Euen as thou lou'dst my sonne hast and dispatch,
Hast and dispatch it as thou louest my soule.
Tis not yet *yayne* by three quarters of an hower,
What are our Angels of this night?   *Michael, Dardael, Huratipel.*
In a triumphant carre of burning gold,
Crownd with a circlet of blacke hebeny,
And with a mace of Iet King *Varca* rides.
Attended with his ministers of state, *Andas* and *Cynaball.*
Fit dismall times for our solemnities.   [*Enter* BERNARDO.
Put on my robes giue me my Pentacle,
Cense well *Barnardo*: bring me some fire in an earthen vessell
Now must I laboure like a collyers horse.

> [*After* BERNARDO *had Censed he bringeth in coles, and*
> ALEXANDER *fashioneth out his circle then taketh his rod.*

My pretious best approu'd and trusty seruant,
Hence in all hast be-take thee to thy beads,
Whilst these darke workes of horror are in hand,
Red *Sandall* is my fumigation.

> [*Standing without the circle he waueth his rod to the East.*

And calleth vpon ⎫   ⎧VIONATRABA
  To the West. ⎪   ⎪SVSERATOS.
  To the North. ⎬   ⎨AQUIEL.
  To the South. ⎭   ⎩MACHASAEL.

Coniuro, et confirmo super vos in nomine Eye, eye, ey;
hast vp & ascende *pernomen ya, ya, ya; he, he, he;*
va; hy, hy; ha, ha, ha; va, va, va; an, an, an;

> [*Fiery exhalations lightning thunder ascend a King, with a red*
> *face crowned imperiall riding vpon a Lyon, or dragon:*
> ALEXANDER *putteth on more perfume and saith.*

I coniure thee by these aforesaid names,
That thou receaue no phantasmatike illusions.
  DIUEL. What would great *Alexander* haue with vs,
That from our fiery region millions of leagues,
Beneath the sulphurous bottome of *Abisse,*
Where *Mammon* tells his euer tryed gould,
Thou call'st me from strong busines of high state,
From sure subuersions and mutations
Of mighty Monarches, Emperors, and Kings,
From plotting bloody feilds and massacres,
Triumphant treasons and assassinates?
What's thy demand?
  ALEXANDER. I charge thee by the fower recited names,
And by the dreadfull title of great *Phaa.*
By which all creatures are sure sealed vp,
By which the prince of darknes and all powers,
In earth and hell doe tremble and fall downe,
Shew me the shape of that condemned man,
Which murthered my sonne the duke of *Candy.*

K   145

DIUEL. Keepe a firme station stir not for thy life,
Expect a messenger of trust stand fast,

> [*The* DIUELL *descendeth with thunder and lightning and after more exhalations ascends another all in armor.*

DIUEL. Sent from the foggy lake of fearefull stix,
Am I commaunded by that puissant monarch,
Which rides tryumphing in a charriot,
On misty blacke clouds mixt with quenchles fire,
Through vnquoth corners in darke pathes of death,
To doe what thou demandest.

ALEXANDER. Then by the dreadfull names of *Amioram*,
Titepand Sadai shew me that damned child of reprobation,
Which this night murthered the duke of *Candie*.

DIUEL. Keepe a firme station stir not for thy life.

> [*He goeth to one doore of the stage, from whence he bringeth the ghost of* CANDIE *gastly haunted by* CÆSAR *persuing and stabing it, these vanish in at another doore.*

ALEXANDER. Hold, hold, hold, hold; *per todos santos* now no more,
Cæsar hath kill'd a brother and a father.

DIUEL. What wouldest thou more shall I descend?

ALEXANDER. Shew me the person by whose impious hand,
Gismond Viselli, was done to death?

DIUEL. Keepe a firme station stir not for thy life.

> [*He bringeth from the same doore* GISMUND VISELLI, *his wounds gaping and after him* LUCRECE *vndrest, holding a dagger fix't in his bleeding bosome: they vanish.*

ALEXANDER. Out, out, no more no more, my soule disolues.

DIUEL. Say, say what wouldest thou more? discend,

ALEXANDER. *Beldachiensis, Berolanensis, Helioren, discende, discende, iubeo, mando, impero.*

> [DEUILL *descendeth with thunder, &c.*

18. PHILIP MASSINGER (1583–1640)

The Duke of Milan

Massinger in many ways points out the road toward the rhetoric of Restoration heroic drama. He has an unquestioned sense of the theatre, but his finest scenes are those where his characters can mouth out speeches of oratorical form. He delights in law-court scenes, and in situations of the banquet type when this forensic or after-dinner style can be allowed free play. At the same time, Massinger is no closet dramatist; he aims at and secures theatrical success—sometimes by the bold limning of his characters, sometimes by appeals made to that audience which welcomed Webster and Tourneur. In *The Duke of Milan* he takes for his theme a story of Italian Court-life, and, while he has none of the refinements in horror which graced the plays of some of his contemporaries and successors, he introduces sufficient murder and crime to please the jaded tastes of seventeenth-century spectators. In the scene given below there should be noted the sensual appeal of the language, a characteristic of post-Shakespearian drama, as well as the rhetorical movement of the verse.

(*The Duke of Millaine* was first printed in 1623. The following extract follows that edition.)

THE POWER OF LOVE

1 GENTLEMAN. Quicke quicke for loues sake, let the court put on
Her choicest outside: Cost, and brauerie
Be onely thought of.
2 GENTLEMAN. All that may be had
To please the eye, the eare, taste, touch, or smell,
Are carefully prouided.
3 GENTLEMAN. Ther's a Masque,
Haue you heard what's the inuention?
1 GENTLEMAN. No matter,
It is intended for the *Dutches* honour.
And if it giue her glorious attributes,
As the most faire, most vertuous, and the rest,
'Twill please the *Duke*. They come.
3 GENTLEMAN. All is in order.
[*Enter* TIBERIO, STEPHANO, FRANCISCO, SFORZA, MARCELLIA,
ISABELLA, MARIANA, *and attendants.*
SFORZA. You are the Mistris of the feast, sit heere;
O my soules comfort: And when *Sforza* bowes
Thus low to doe you honour, let none thinke
The meanest seruice they can pay my loue,
But as a fair addition to those tytles,
They stand possest of.   Let me glory in
My happinesse, and mightie Kings looke pale
With enuie, while I triumph in mine own.
O mother looke on her, sister admire her:
And since this present age yeelds not a woman
Worthy to be her second, borrow of
Times past: and let imagination helpe
Of those canoniz'd Ladies *Sparta* boasts of,
And, in her greatnesse, *Rome* was proud to owe
To fashion one; yet still you must confesse,
The *Phœnix* of perfection nere was seene,
But in my fair *Marcelia.*
FRANCISCO. She's indeede
The wonder of all times.
TIBERIO. Your excellence,

(Though I confesse you giue her but her owne)
Enforces her modestie to the defence
Of a sweet blush.

SFORZA. It neede not my *Marcelia*;
When most I striue to praise thee, I appeare
A poor detracter: For thou art indeed
So absolute in bodie, and in minde,
That, but to speake the least part to the height,
Would aske an Angels tongue: and yet then end
In silent admiration!

ISABELLA. You still court her,
As if she were a Mistris, not your wife.

SFORZA. A Mistris mother? she is more to me,
And euery day, deserues more to be su'de too.
Such as are cloyd with those they haue embrac'd,
May thinke their wooing done: No night to mee,
But is a bridall one, where *Himen* lights
His torches fresh, and new: And those delights,
Which are not to be cloth'd in ayrie sounds,
Inioyd, beget desires, as full of heat,
And Iouiall feruor, as when first I tasted
Her virgin fruit; Blest night, and be it numbred
Amongst those happy ones, in which a blessing
Was by the full consent of all the Starrs,
Confer'd vpon mankind.

MARCELIA. My worthiest Lord,
The onely obiect I behold with pleasure:
My pride, my glory, in a word my all;
Beare witnesse *Heauen*, that I esteeme myselfe
In nothing worthy of the meanest praise,
You can bestow, vnlesse it be in this,
That in my heart I loue, and honor you.
And but that it would smell of arrogance,
To speake my strong desire, and zeale to serue you:
I then could say, these eyes yet neuer saw
The rising Sun, but that my vowes, and prayers,
Were sent to Heauen, for the prosperitie
And safety of my Lord; Nor haue I euer
Had other studie, but how to appeare
Worthy your fauour: and that my embraces,
Might yeeld a fruitfull Haruest of content,
For all your noble trauaile, in the purchase,
Of her, that's still your seruant; By these lips,
(Which pardon mee, that I presume to kisse)

SFORZA. O sweare for euer sweare.

MARCELIA. I ne're will seeke
Delight, but in your pleasure: and desire,
When you are sated with all Earthly glories,

And age, and honours make you fit for Heauen,
That one Graue may receiue vs.

SFORZA. 'Tis belieu'd,
Belieu'd, my blest One.

MARIANA. How she winds herselfe
Into his Soule!

SFORZA. Sit all: Let others feed
On those grosse Cates, while *Sforza* banquets with
Immortall Viands, tane in at his Eyes.
I could liue euer thus. Command the Eunuch
To sing the Dittie that I last compos'd,
In prayse of my *Marcelia*.

19. JOHN WEBSTER (*died c.* 1634)

The White Devil

The White Divel ; or, The Tragedy of Paulo Giordano Ursini, Duke of Brachiano, With the Life and Death of Vittoria Corombona the famous Venetian Curtizan has been, since the time of Lamb, one of the best known of Elizabethan tragedies. In Webster Lamb found a quality for which he had been seeking, a gentle tenderness added to a sensitive subtlety which could express itself in the conjuring up both of horror and of pathos. To illustrate these two main elements in Webster's work the scene of Cornelia's madness has been chosen here. Quite clearly Ophelia is in the mind of the dramatist, yet the passage is not merely a slavish imitation. Cornelia has a being of her own apart from that of Hamlet's love, and the exquisite " land-ditty " which Webster has introduced gives a unique and peculiar atmosphere to the whole. Immediately following comes a typical ghostly apparition with a long soliloquy of Flamineo. Webster delights both in the supernatural and in the insane ; so that this consecutive passage from *The White Devil* is a kind of symbol of his work. In both he succeeded, largely because of his fine and delicate language. He ranks with Heywood in being one of the few seventeenth-century writers who attained a style, bold and yet sensitive, akin to the style of Shakespeare, avoiding alike the rhetoric of Massinger, the artificial looseness of Fletcher, and the rich-turned phrases of Ford.

(*The White Devil* was acted by the Queen's men between 1607 and 1612. The following extract follows that of the first edition of 1612.)

ANOTHER OPHELIA AND ANOTHER GHOST

CORNELIA. This rosemarie is wither'd, pray get fresh;
I would haue these herbes grow vp in his graue
When I am dead and rotten. Reach the bayes,

Ile tye a garland heere about his head:
'Twill keepe my boy from lightning.   This sheet
I haue kept this twentie yere, and euerie daie
Hallow'd it with my praiers, I did not thinke
Hee should haue wore it.

    MOORE. Looke you; who are yonder.

    CORNELIA. O reach mee the flowers.

    MOORE. Her Ladyships foolish.

    WOMAN. Alas! her grief
Hath turn'd her child againe.

    CORNELIA [*to* FLAMINEO]. You're very wellcome.
There's Rosemarie for you, and Rue for you,
Hearts-ease for you.   I pray make much of it.
I haue left more for my selfe.

    FRANCISCO. Ladie, who's this?

    CORNELIA. You are, I take it, the graue-maker.

    FLAMINEO. So.

    MOORE. 'Tis *Flamineo*.

    CORNELIA. Will you make mee such a foole? heere's a white hand:
Can bloud so soone bee washt out?   Let mee see,
When scritch-howles croke vpon the chimney tops,
And the strange Cricket ith ouen singes and hoppes,
When yellow spots doe on your handes appeare,
Bee certaine then you of a Course shall heare.
Out vpon't, how 'tis speckled! h'as handled a toad sure.
Couslep-water is good for the memorie: pray buy me
3 ounces of't.

    FLAMINEO. I would I were from hence.

    CORNELIA. Do you heere, sir?   Ile giue you a saying which my grandmother was wont, when she heard the belle tolle, to sing ore vnto her lute.

    FLAMINEO. Doe and you will, doe.

    CORNELIA. Call for the Robin-Red-brest and the wren,

             [CORNELIA *doth this in seuerall formes of distraction.*
Since ore shadie groues they houer,
And with leaues and flowres doe couer
The friendlesse bodies of unburied men.
Call vnto his funerall Dole
The Ante, the field-mouse, and the mole
To reare him hillockes, that shall keepe him warme,
And (when gay tombes are rob'd) sustaine no harme,
But keepe the wolfe far thence: that's foe to men,
For with his nailes hee'l dig them up agen.
They would not bury him 'cause hee died in a quarrell
But I haue an answere for them.
Let holie Church receiue him duly
Since hee payd the Church tithes truly.
His wealth is sum'd, and this is all his store:

This poore men get; and great men get no more.
Now the wares are gone, wee may shut vp shop.
Blesse you all good people.   [*Exeunt* CORNELIA *and Ladies.*
  FLAMINEO. I haue a strange thing in me, to th' which
I cannot giue a name, without it bee
Compassion, I pray leaue mee.   [*Exit* FRANCISCO.
This night Ile know the vtmost of my fate,
Ile bee resolu'd what my rich sister meanes
T'assigne mee for my seruice: I haue liu'd
Riotously ill, like some that liue in Court.
And sometimes, when my face was full of smiles
Haue felt the mase of conscience in my brest.
Oft gay and honour'd robes those tortures trie,
Wee thinke cag'd birds sing, when indeed they crie.
                                [*Enter* BRACHIANO'S GHOST.
Ha! I can stand thee.   Neerer, neerer yet.
What a mockerie hath death made of thee? thou look'st sad.
In what place art thou? in yon starrie gallerie,
Or in the cursed dungeon? No? not speake?
Pray, Sir, resolue me, what religions best
For a man to die in? or is it in your knowledge
To answere mee how long I haue to liue?
That's the most necessarie question.
Not answere?   Are you still like some great men
That onely walke like shadowes vp and downe,
And to no purpose say:
What's that?   O fatall! hee throwes earth vpon mee.
A dead mans scull beneath the rootes of flowers. . . .
Hee's gone; and see, the scull and earth are vanisht.
This is beyond melancholie.   I doe dare my fate
To do its worst.   Now to my sisters lodging,
And summe vp all these horrours ; the disgrace
The Prince threw on mee; next the pitious sight
Of my dead brother; and my Mothers dotage;
And last this terrible vision.   All these
Shall with *Vittoria's* bountie turne to good,
Or I will drowne this weapon in her blood.

20. JOHN FORD (1586–*c.* 1639)

The Broken Heart

That craving for novelty in horror which marks out so much
of later ' Elizabethan ' dramatic effort is excellently shown in
a scene of Ford's *The Broken Heart*. Commonplace stabbings
had been sufficient in the earlier days, but now refinement in
murder was eagerly sought for.   Poison had pleased for a time,
particularly when the poison was not the ordinary dose put

secretly in a bowl of wine, but was some cunning preparation smeared on a picture or on the chapless bones of a skull. Even this, however, seemed to pall, and in his tragedy Ford has seen fit to introduce an even stranger device—a property chair or 'engine' so constructed that one who sits in it is immediately imprisoned and made fast. One wonders whether Ford had heard of that similar throne which, according to legend, once imprisoned Hera; but it is not necessary to seek for its origin in classical sources. It was designed probably out of the brain of the playwright, because the spectators demanded from him themes that were out of the ordinary, situations that should thrill not because of their strength, but because of their novel peculiarity. Ford is one of the finest (albeit one of the most decadent) of the later 'Elizabethans'; the fact that even he saw fit to utilize such devices as these indicates the dramatic tendency of the time.

(*The Broken Heart* was produced at Blackfriars about 1629. The following extract is taken from the quarto of 1633.)

A STRANGE DEVICE OF DEATH

PENTHEA *discovered in a chaire, veiled.*

SERUANT. 'Tis done, that on her right hand.

ORGILUS. Good, begone.

ITHOCLES. Soft peace enrich this roome.

ORGILUS. How fares the Lady?

PHILEMA. Dead.

CHRISTALLA. Dead!

PHILEMA. Staru'd.

CHRISTALLA. Staru'd!

ITHOCLES. Me miserable!

ORGILUS. Tell vs
How parted she from life?

PHILEMA. She call'd for musicke,
And begg'd some gentle voyce to tune a farewell
To life and griefes: *Christalla* touch'd the Lute,
I wept the funerall song.

CHRISTALLA. Which scarce was ended,
But her last breath seal'd vp these hollow sounds,
O cruell *Ithocles*, and iniur'd *Orgilus*!
So downe she drew her vaile, so dy'd.

ITHOCLES. So dy'd!

ORGILUS. Vp; you are messengers of death, goe
from vs;
Here's woe enough to court without a prompter.
Away; and harke ye, till you see vs next,
No sillable that she is dead—Away,

[*Exeunt* PHILEMA & CHRISTALLA.

Keepe a smooth brow.—My Lord.

ITHOCLES. Mine onely sister
Another is not left me.

ORGILUS. Take that chayre,
I'le seat me heare in this: betweene vs sits
The obiect of our sorrowes: some few teares
Wee'll part among vs; I perhaps can mixe
One lamentable story to prepare 'em.
There, there, sit there, my Lord.

ITHOCLES. Yes, as you please.

[ITHOCLES *sits down, and is catcht in the Engine.*
What meanes this treachery?

ORGILUS. Caught, you are caught
Young master! 'tis thy throne of Coronation,
Thou foole of greatnesse: see, I take this vaile off;
Suruey a beauty wither'd by the flames
Of an insulting *Phaeton* her brother.

ITHOCLES. Thou mean'st to kill me basely.

ORGILUS. I foreknow
The last act of her life, and train'd thee hither
To sacrifice a Tyrant to a Turtle.
You dream't of kingdomes, did 'ee? how to bosome
The delicacies of a youngling Princesse,
How with this nod to grace that subtill Courtier,
How with that frowne to make this Noble tremble,
And so forth: whiles Penthea's grones, and tortures,
Her agonies, her miseries, afflictions,
Ne're toucht vpon your thought; as for my iniuries,
Alas they were beneath your royall pitty,
But yet they liu'd, thou proud man, to confound thee:
Behold thy fate, this steele.

ITHOCLES. Strike home, a courage
As keene as thy reuenge shall giue it welcome:
But prethe faint not: if the wound clos vp,
Tent it with double force, and search it deeply.
Thou look'st that I should whine, and beg compassion,
As loath to leaue the vainnesse of my glories;
A statelier resolution armes my confidence,
To cozen thee of honour; neither could I,
With equall tryall of unequall fortune,
By hazard of a duell, 'twere a brauery
Too mighty for a slaue intending murther:
On to the Execution, and inherit
A conflict with thy horrors.

ORGILUS. By *Apollo*,
Thou talk'st a goodly language; for requitall
I will report thee to thy mistresse richly:
And take this peace along; some few short minutes

Determin'd, my resolues shall quickly follow
Thy wrathfull ghost: then if we tug for mastery,
Pentheas sacred eyes shall lend new courage.
Giue my thy hand, be healthfull in thy parting
From lost mortality: thus, thus, I free it.   [*Kils him.*

   ITHOCLES. Yet, yet, I scorne to shrinke.

   ORGILUS. Keep vp thy spirit:
I will be gentle euen in blood: to linger
Paine, which I striue to cure, were to be cruell.

   ITHOCLES. Nimble in vengeance I forgive thee; follow
Safety, with best successe ô may it prosper!
Penthea, by thy side thy brother bleeds:
The earnest of his wrongs to thy forc'd faith,
Thoughts of ambition, or delitious banquet,
With beauty, youth, and loue, together perish
In my last breath, which on the sacred Altar
Of a long look'd-for peace—now—moues—to heauen.   [*moritur.*

   ORGILUS. Farewell, faire spring of manhood; henceforth welcome
Best expectation of a noble suffrance:
I'le locke the bodies safe, till what must follow
Shall be approu'd—Sweet Twins shine stars for euer.

      In vaine they build their hopes, whose life is shame,
      No monument lasts but a happy Name.

21. JAMES SHIRLEY (1596–1666)

The Traitor

Webster, Ford, Shirley, and Tourneur are all associated together
by their experiments in the sphere of horror and revenge tragedy.
All show a deep interest in peculiar psychological states, and
all revel in what may be styled the novelties of terror. The
spectators had clearly become sated with ordinary sights of
cruelty, and expected from the dramatists situations of an
increasingly bizarre kind as well as scenes of a thrillingly spectacular quality. It was partly to meet these demands that
the managers of the theatres introduced the element of the
Court masque into comedy and tragedy (see *supra,* p. 99). *The
Traitor* provides an example of this. In the midst of over-
looming darkness, with murder and horror threatened, the
Duke is regaled by Sciarrha with a masque, in which figure both
Lust and the Furies. The masque is intimately connected with
the theme of the play, and was designed thus to make a double
appeal. Its spectacular qualities pleased the senses, and above
that its grim suggestiveness thrilled with an impression of impending disaster.

(*The Traytor* was produced in 1631. The following extract is
taken from the quarto of 1635.)

154

EARLY SEVENTEENTH CENTURY

A Fateful Masque

Enter DUKE, AMIDEA, LORENZO, SCIARRHA, FLORIO, *&c.*

DUKE. *Sciarrha*, you exceede in entertainment,
Banquet our eyes too.

LORENZO. He will feast all Senses.

SCIARRHA. Onely a toy my Lord, I cannot cal't,
A maske, not worthy of this presence, yet
It speakes freedom of my heart and gratitude
For this great honour.

DUKE. *Amidea* must sit neere us.

SCIARRHA. Lords your places, 'twonot be
Worth halfe this ceremonie, let 'em begin.

            [*Enter* LUST *richly apparreld, the pleasures attending.*

DUKE. Whose the presenter?

SCIARRHA. *Lust* sir, pray observe:

LUST.   Now let *Lust* possesse the throne
Of Loue, and rule in hearts alone:
You sweete tempters to my Sinne,
Beauty, smiles, and kisses winne
Vpon fraile mortals, let them know
There is no happinesse, but you
Shoot us arrowes tip'd with lead
Each shaft have his golden head.
Call no Love, delude men still,
Through the flesh, their spirits kill,
Nor spend all your art to take
Common persons, greatnesse make
By your potent charmes to bee
Subjects unto hell and mee;
Enflame but Kings with loose desire,
Yet soone set all the world on fire.

            [*Enter a young man in rich habit and Crownd.*

DUKE. What's hee?

SCIARRHA. A wild young man that followes lust,
He has too much blood it seemes.

DUKE. Why lookes hee backe?

SCIARRHA. There is a thing cald death that followes
    him
With a large traine of furies, but the Syrens
Of lust make him secure, and now the hagge
Embraces him, and circles him with pleasures,
The harpyes meane to dance too, hang his conscience
It whines too much.   [*Aside.*

LORENZO. This is too plaine.   [*Aside.*

SCIARRHA. Hee does not tremble yet,   [*Aside.*
By and by sir you shall see all his tormentors
Goyne with 'em, ther's the sport on't.

155

LORENZO. Mee thinks they
Should have been first for th'antimaske.
    LORENZO. Oh no!
In hell they doe not stand upon the methode
As wee at Court, the ground maske and the glorie
Begin the revells, Sister you doe ill
To keepe the Duke in talke, he cannot see
The diuell for you, and the whipps: does not
That deaths head look most temptingly? the wormes
Have kist the lips off.

> [*The furies joyne in the dance, and in the end carries the young man away.*]

How does your highnesse like this dance?
    DUKE. My eyes are feasted here, I did not marke it
But I presume 'twas handsome.
    SCIARRHA. Oh the Lethargy
Of Princes! we ha kept you Sir from bed:
More lights!
    DUKE. Good night to all, to you the best:
Sciarrha binde us ever by performance.
    SCIARRHA. We are all yours.
    DUKE. And *Florence* thine, once more—
Brightest of Ladies.
    LORENZO. You are firme.
    SCIARRHA. Suspect not.   [*Exeunt all but* AMIDEA *and* FLORIO.
    FLORIO. I doe not like my brothers Morall Maske,
The Duke himselfe was personated, I
Wonder it did not startle him.
    AMIDEA. I hope
Sciarrha does not meane so ill as that
Did promise, he's return'd: his lookes are full   [*Enter* SCIARRHA.
Of threatning.
    SCIARRHA. *Amidea*, goe not to bed,
And yet no matter, I can doo't alone:
Take both your rest, and in your prayers commend
The Duke to Heaven, tis charity; has made
His will already, and bequeathed his body
To you Sister, pitty his soule for't, 'tis now
Within few minutes of departing.
    AMIDEA. How?
    SCIARRHA. Why this way must I helpe him in his groanes
To bring his flesh a bed.
    AMIDEA. You wonot kill him?
    SCIARRHA. I am not of your minde.
    AMIDEA. I know you cannot.
    SCIARRHA. You are not studied so perfect in
His destiny I hope; I will endeavour——
    AMIDEA. To kill your Prince?

FLORIO. What here?

SCIARRHA. No, in his Chamber.

AMIDEA. Shall it be read in Stories of our *Florence*,
Sciarrha first did staine his family
With such a Treason?

FLORIO. Was he not invited.

SCIARRHA. Yes, by his lust.

FLORIO. And in your crowned tables
And Hospitality will you murder him?

SCIARRHA. Yes, and the reason wherefore he was murderd
Shall justifie the deed to all posterity,
He came to wrong my Sister.

FLORIO. Wanton heate,
Let youthfull blood excuse him.

SCIARRHA. So it must.

FLORIO. Mistake me not, oh thinke but who he is,
The Duke, that word must needs awake your piety.

AMIDEA. How will good men in this remembrance
Abhorre your cruelty, that send to hell
One with the weight of all his sinnes upon him.

SCIARRHA. It is too late to coole with argument
My incensed blood, will you goe dally with him,
And let him bord your pinace: I ha gon
So farre in promise, if you claspe not with him,
It will be dangerous if he out-live
This night.

AMIDEA. I ha thought on't, send him to my bed.

SCIARRHA. Ha?

AMIDEA. Doe not question what I purpose, heaven
Witnesse to my chast thoughts.

SCIARRHA. Wot thou trust him?

AMIDEA. I will doe much sir, to preserve his life,
And your innocence: be not you suspectfull
At the worst, you can but respite your revenge.

SCIARRHA. Dost thou not feare unhappy *Lucresse* chance,
Or wretched *Philomels* dishonour?

AMIDEA. No:
Give me his life, and send your wanton to me;
Ile to my Chamber, feare me not *Sciarrha*,
Have not one thought so bad, I sha' not prosper;
Virgins in heaven will suffer with me.   [*Exit* AMIDEA & FLORIO.

FLORIO. Trust her?

SCIARRHA. Tis but deferring of my justice,
Shee wonot kill him sure; draw on her soule
The guilt shee hates in mine, if shee doe yeeld
To the hot encounter: ha? twill be just,
That both their hearts weep blood, to purge their lust.

22. UNKNOWN AUTHOR

A Yorkshire Tragedy

A Yorkshire Tragedy is one of the most interesting of sixteenth-
or seventeenth-century minor dramas, partly because when
entered in the Stationers' Register on May 2, 1608, and when
printed the same year, it was said to be " Written by W. Shakespeare." This, however, does not constitute its whole interest
for modern readers. It is, in the first place, one of a now lost
set of plays with the generic title *All's One*, a type of drama
developed in the Renascence period and pointing toward the
one-act play of later times. Secondly, it is representative of
that form of contemporary tragedy which chronicled recent
events. The murders it celebrates had actually occurred in
April 1605, and the author, like a nineteenth-century melo-
dramatist, made haste to exploit the grim details in the interests
of the stage. Above all, we trace in this drama an undoubted
strength. The style is not akin to that of Shakespeare in his
maturity, although there are some tricks of phrasing (such as
the repetition of words) which recall *Hamlet* ; yet there is hardly
a playwright of the time to whom we could confidently assign
the first scenes. There is a lurid glow here which illuminates
the darkness of the theme and which shows to us that if we are
not in the presence of Shakespeare we are at least in the
presence of a writer with a strength almost equalling his own.

(*A Yorkshire Tragedy* was performed at the Globe Theatre
presumably between 1605 and 1608. The following extract is
from the quarto of 1608.)

The Misery of Gaming

HUSBAND. Poxe oth Last throw, it made
Fiue hundred Angels vanish from my sight,
Ime damnd, Ime damnd: the Angels haue forsook me
Nay tis certainely true: for he that has no coyne
Is damnd in this world: hee's gon, hee's gon.
WIFE. Deere husband.
HUSBAND. Oh! most punishment of all I haue a wife.
WIFE. I doe intreat you as you loue your soule,
Tell me the cause of this your discontent.
HUSBAND. A vengeance strip thee naked, thou art cause,
Effect, quality, property, thou, thou, thou!   [*Exit.*
WIFE. Bad, turnd to worse?
Both beggery of the soule, as of the bodie.
And so much vnlike him selfe at first,
As if some vexed spirit had got his form vpon him——
             [*Enter* HUSBAND *againe.*

He comes agen:
He saies I am the cause, I never yet
Spoke lesse then wordes of duty, and of loue.

HUSBAND. If mariage be honourable, then Cuckolds are honourable, for they cannot be made without marriage.

Foole: what meant I to marry to get beggars? now must my eldest
sonne be a knaue or nothing, he cannot liue vppot'h foole, for he wil
haue no land to maintaine him: that morgage sits like a snaffle vpon
mine inheritance, and makes me chaw vpon Iron.

My second sonne must be a promooter, and my third a theefe, or
an vnderputter, a slaue pander.

Oh beggery, beggery, to what base vses dost thou put a man.
I think the Deuill scornes to be a bawde.
He beares himselfe more proudly, has more care on's credit.
Base slauish abiect filthie pouertie.

WIFE. Good sir; by all our vowes I doe beseech you,
Show me the true cause of your discontent?

HUSBAND. Mony, mony, mony, and thou must supply me.

WIFE. Alas, I am the lest cause of your discontent,
Yet what is mine, either in rings or Iewels
Vse to your own desire, but I beseech you,
As y'are a gentleman by many bloods,
Though I my selfe be out of your respect,
Thinke on the state of these three louely boies
You haue bin father to.

HUSBAND. Puh Bastards, bastards, bastards; begot in tricks,
  begot in tricks.

WIFE. Heauen knowes how those words wrong me, but I maie
Endure these griefes among a thousand more.
Oh, call to mind your lands already morgadge,
Your selfe woond into debts, your hopefull brother,
At the vniuersitie in bonds for you,
Like to be ceasd vpon. And——

HUSBAND. Ha done thou harlot,
Whome though for fashion sake I married,
I neuer could abide; thinkst thou thy wordes
Shall kill my pleasures, fal of to thy friends, .
Thou and thy bastards begg: I wil not bate
A whit in humor! midnight still I loue you,
And reuel in your Company; Curbd in,
Shall it be said in all societies,
That I broke custome, that I flagd in monie,
No, those thy iewels, I will play as freely
As when my state was fullest.

WIFE. Be it so.

HUSBAND. Nay I protest, and take that for an earnest, [*Spurns her*.
I will for euer hould thee in contempt,
And neuer touch the sheets that couer thee,

But be diuorst in bed till thou consent,
Thy dowry shall be sold to giue new life
Vnto those pleasures which I most affect.

WIFE. Sir doe but turne a gentle eye on me,
And what the law shall giue me leaue to do
You shall command.

HUSBAND. Look it be done, shal I want dust & like a slaue
Weare nothing in my pockets but my hands
To fil them vp with nailes?   [*Holding his hands in his pockets.*
Oh much against my blood, let it be done,
I was neuer made to be a looker on:
A bawde to dice?   Ile shake the drabbs my selfe
And make em yeeld, I saie look it be done.

WIFE. I take my leaue: it shall.   [*Exit.*

HUSBAND. Speedily, speedily, I hate the very howre I chose a
wife: a trouble, trouble, three children like three euils hang vpon
me, fie, fie, fie, strumpet, & bastards, strumpet and bastards.

23. THOMAS HEYWOOD (c. 1570–1641)

A Woman Killed with Kindness

Among the domestic dramas of Elizabethan times Heywood's
A Woman Killed with Kindness is easily the chief.   It secures
what so many of these plays lack—universality of atmosphere;
and contains, both in language and in portraiture, a strength
which comes close to that of Shakespeare himself.   The most
magnificent scene of the play is the discovery by Frankford of
his wife's infidelity, but that has been already quoted in *British
Drama* (p. 202), and, besides, does not represent all the subtleties in the treatment of the theme.   These subtleties are
perhaps better shown in that passage where Wendoll, the faithless
friend, Anne, the frail wife, and Frankford, the already suspicious
husband, play their symbolic game of cards.   Such a scene
displays the infinite resources of Heywood, who, careless crafts-
man as he was at times, possessed a vision and a surety of touch
denied to most of his companions.

(*A Woman Kilde with Kindnesse* seems to have been produced
in 1603.   It was printed in 1607, and reprinted in 1617.   The
former text is followed here.)

THE FATAL CARD GAME

ANNE. Come maister *Frankeford*, who shal take my part?
FRANKFORD. Marry that wil I sweet wife.
WENDOLL. No by my faith sir, when you are togither I sit out,
it must be Mistris Frankeford and I, or els it is no match.
FRANKFORD. I do not like that match.
NICHOLAS [*aside*]. You haue no reason marry knowing al.

FRANKFORD. Tis no great matter neither, come, M. *Cranwel* shal you and I take them vp?

CRANWELL. At your pleasure sir.

FRANKFORD. I must looke to you M. *Wendol*, for you wil be playing false, nay so will my wife too.

NICHOLAS [*aside*]. I, I wil be sworne she wil.

ANNE. Let them that are taken playing false forfet the set.

FRANKFORD. Content; It shall go hard but Ile take you.

CRANWELL. Gentlemen what shal our game be?

WENDOLL. Maister *Frankeford* you play best at Noddy.

FRANKFORD. You shal not find it so : Indeed you shal not.

ANNE. I can play at nothing so well as dubble ruffe.

FRANKFORD. If maister *Wendol* and my wife bee together, theres no playing against them at dubble hand.

NICHOLAS. I can tel you sir the game that master *Wendol* is best at.

WENDOLL. What game is that *Nick*?

NICHOLAS. Marry sir, Knaue out of dores.

WENDOLL. She and I, will take you at Lodam.

ANNE. Husband shall we play at Saint?

FRANKFORD [*aside*]. My Saints turn'd Deuill: no, weele none of Saint, your best at new Cut wife: youle play at that.

WENDOLL. If you play at new Cut, I am soonest hitter of any heere for a wager.

FRANKFORD [*aside*]. Tis me they play on: wel you may draw out For al your cunning: twil be to your shame:
Ile teach you at your new Cut, a new game,
Come, come.

CRANWELL. If you cannot agree vpon the game to post and paire.

WENDOLL. We shal be soonest paires, and my good hoast,
When he comes late home, he must kisse the post.

FRANKFORD. Who euer wins, it shal be to thy cost.

CRANWELL. Faith let it be Vide-ruffe, and lets make honors.

FRANKFORD. If you make honors, one thing let me craue,
Honor the King and Queene: except the knaue.

WENDOLL. Wel as you please for that, lift who shal deale.

ANNE. The least in sight: what are you maister *Wendol*?

WENDOLL. I am a knaue.

NICHOLAS [*aside*].   Ile sweare it.

ANNE.   I a Queene.

FRANKFORD [*aside*]. A queane thou shouldst say: wel the Cards are mine,
They are the grossest paire that ere I felt.

ANNE. Shuffle, Ile cut, would I had neuer dealt!

FRANKFORD. I haue lost my dealing.

WENDOLL.   Sir the faults in me,
This Queene I haue more then my owne you see,
Giue me the stocke.

FRANKFORD.   My minds not on my game,

L

Many a deale I haue lost, the mores your shame,
You have seru'd me a bad tricke maister *Wendol*.

WENDOLL. Sir you must take your lot: to end this strife,
I know I haue dealt better with your wife.

FRANKFORD. Thou hast dealt falsely then.

ANNE. Whats Trumpes?

WENDOLL. Harts, partner, I rub.

FRANKFORD [*aside*]. Thou robst me of my soule, of her chast loue
In thy false dealing, thou hast robd my hart,
Booty you play, I like a looser stand,
Hauing no hart, or here, or in my hand:
I will giue ore the set, I am not well,
Come who wil hold my Cards?

ANNE. Not well sweet Maister Franckford,
Alas, what ayle you: tis some sodaine qualme.

WENDOLL. How long haue you bin so maister Frankford?

FRANKFORD. Sir I was lusty, and I had my health,
But I grew ill when you began to deale.
Take hence this table, gentle maister Cranwell
You are welcome, see your chamber at your pleasure,
I am sorry that this Megrim takes me so
I cannot sit and beare you company,
Ienkin some lights, and shew him to his chamber.

ANNE. A night gowne for my husband quickly there,
It is some rhewme or cold.

WENDOLL. Now in good faith this Ilnesse you haue got
By sitting late without your gowne.

FRANKFORD. I know it maister *Wendol*,
Go, go, to bed, least you complaine like me,
Wife, pretty wife into my bed-chamber,
The night is raw, and cold, and rheumaticke,
Leaue me my gowne and light, Ile walke away my fit.

WENDOLL. Sweet sir good night.

FRANKFORD.   My selfe good night.

24. SIR WILLIAM D'AVENANT (1606–68)

The Temple of Love

In one respect the Court masque is something wholly apart
from the regular development of popular drama, in another it
forms one of the most important influences on the later progress
of the theatre. The masque, in its pure form, is a plaything
for amateurs, a kind of vast elaborated charade, carried out
perhaps with the assistance of professionals, but in essence a
private show conducted by the courtiers. Its rich nature,
however, necessitated the summoning of outside help, and it
was in the sphere of the masque that Inigo Jones attained his

greatest triumphs. It is not to be wondered at that when the Court witnessed such beautiful devices as he and his assistants contrived the ordinary theatres strove, in some way or other, to emulate the brilliance of the private performances. It was through the masque, accordingly, that machines and scenery entered the English stage, for, apart from the scenes introduced into pre-Commonwealth theatres, the first scenic artist of the Restoration was John Webb, who had been the chief colleague of Inigo Jones, and who merely carried over the devices which had been evolved in the earlier years. The masque, too, had an influence on the drama as well as on the theatre. The spectacular features of Shakespeare's latest plays are merely adaptations of the principle of the Court masque to the requirements of comedy and of tragi-comedy. The satyrs in *The Winter's Tale*, the reapers in *The Tempest*, and the visions in *Cymbeline* all attest to the popularity of masque-like scenes and to the endeavour on the part of professional players to imitate the glories of the Court shows. *The Temple of Love*, an extract from which is given here, deals with the then debated question regarding 'platonic love,' a subject popularized by the queen of Charles I, and an important element in the building up of the 'love and honour' tradition which formed the basis of Restoration heroic tragedy.

(*The Temple of Love* was performed at Whitehall in 1635. The extract given here follows that in the D'Avenant folio, 1673.)

PLATONIC LOVE

After this, DIVINE POESIE, *and the* POETS *go forth; then the whole Scæne changeth into Mist and Clouds, through which some glimpse of a Temple is here and there scarcely discern'd.*
The Entry of the MAGICIANS.
Out of Caves from under ground come forth three MAGICIANS, *one more eminent than the rest, their habits of strange fashions, denoting their qualities, and their persons deformed.*

(1). Tell me, thou wise Protector of our Art,
Why dost thou walk with such a hideous brow?
Darkness, and Clouds do hover o're thine eyes;
Thou look'st as thou hadst suck'd the vapor of
A poys'nous Fenne, till it has made thee drunk,
There's venom'd foam about thy lips.
 (2). Is thy belov'd
Old witch, dead and entomb'd? or hast thou heard
Ill news from hell? Does the grand fiend
Chain up thy spirits from thy use? Speak, Art
Thou not within thy Circle still a Soveraign Prince?
When thou dost lift with magick power thy white

Inchanted Scepter thus, do not the thin
Unbodied people bow and obey?

   (3). O the Temple of Love, the mists that hid,
And so reserv'd it from our sinful use,
(Whilst we seduc'd the more voluptuous race
Of Men, to give false worship in our own) must be
Dispell'd! this is the sad ill news; and it
Is come from Heaven! A troublesome Deity
(Whom forsooth they stile *Divine Poesie*)
This morne proclaim'd it from a falling Cloud.

   (2). Who? *Divine Poesie?*

   (3). I know her well.

   (1). But who shall bring this mischief to our Art?

   (3). *Indamora*, the delight of Destiny!
She, and the beauties of her Train; who sure
Though they discover Summer in their looks,
Still carry frozen Winter in their blood.
They raise strange doctrines, and new sects of Love:
Which must not woo or court the Person, but
The Mind; and practice generation not
Of Bodies but of Souls.

   (2). Believe me, my Magical friends,
They must bring bodies with 'em that worship
In our pleasant Temple: I have an odd
Fantastick faith perswades me there will be
Little pastime upon earth without Bodies,
Your Spirit's a cold Companion at midnight.

   (1). Have we so long mis-led and entertain'd
The youthful of the world (I mean their bodies)
And now do they betake themselves unto
The dull imaginary pleasures of
Their soules? This humor cannot last.

   (2). If it should, we may rid our Temple
Of all our Persian Quilts, imbroyder'd Couches,
And our standing Beds; these (I take it) are
Bodily implements; our soules need 'em not.
But where shall this new Sect be planted first?

   (3). In a dull Northern Ile, they call Britaine.

   (2). Indeed 'tis a cold Northerly opinion;
And I'le lay my life begot since their late
Great Frosts; It will be long enough e're it
Shall spread, and prosper in the South! Or if
The Spaniard or Italian ever be
Perswaded out of the use of their bodies,
I'le give mine to a Raven for his Supper.

   (3). The Miracle is more increas'd, in that
It first takes breath and nourishment in Court.

   (2). But my good damn'd friend tell me? Is there not

One Courtier will resent the cause, and give
Some countenance to the affairs of the body?
   (3). Certain young Lords at first disliked the Philosophy
As most uncomfortable, sad, and new;
But soon inclin'd to a superior vote,
And are grown as good Platonical Lovers
As are to be found in an Hermitage, where he
That was born last, reckons above fourscore.

> [*To these come forth in hast another* MAGICIAN, *in shape
> and habit differing from the other, and spake as fol-
> loweth.*

   (1). Here comes a brother of our mistick Tribe!
   (3). He knows th'occasion of our grief, and by
His hast imports discoveries more strange!
   (4). News! news! my sad companions of the shade!
There's lately landed on our fatal shore
Nine Persian youths, their habit and their looks
So smooth, that from the Pleasures i'th'Elisian fields
Each female ghost will come, and enter in
Their flesh again, to make embraces warm.
   (2). I hope these are no Platonical Lovers,
No such Carthusian Poets as do write
Madrigals to the mind? more of thy news!
   (4). The rest infers small joy, and little hope:
For though at first their youth and eager thoughts
Directed them where our gay Altar stood,
And they were ready too for sacrifice,
I cannot tell what luckless light inform'd
Their eyes, but Loves true Temple straight they spy'd
Through the ascending mists, and would have enter'd it
To read grave frosty Homilies,
And antick laws of chastity, but that
(As my swift Spirit brought me word) a voyce
Sent from within bad them with reverence
Desist till *Indamora* did appear, for then
The Gates would open, and the mists dry up:
That thus conceal'd it from the general view,
Which now their expectation doth attend.
   (3). 'Tis time to wake our drowsie Art, and try,
If we have power to hinder Destiny.
Mount! mount! our charmes! fetch me, whilst you aspire,
A Spirit of the Element of fire!
   (2). Me one of Ayre!
   (1). The water me supplies!
   (4). Mine from the center of the earth shall rise!
   (3). These shall infuse their sev'ral qualities
In men; if not t'uphold the faction of
The flesh, yet to infect the queasie age

With blacker Sins: if we (now we have joyn'd
The force of all the Elements t'assist
The horror of our will) shall not prevail
Against this hum'rous vertue of the Time,
Nature, our weakness must be thought thy crime.
 (2). To these I'le add a sect of modern Divels;
Fine precise Fiends, that hear the devout close
At ev'ry vertue but their own, that claim
Chambers and Tenements in heaven, as they
Had purchas'd there, and all the Angels were
Their harbingers. With these I'le vex the world.
 (3). 'Tis well design'd! Thanks to thy courteous Art!
Let's murmure softly in each others ear,
And those we first invok'd, will straight appear!
Enough! they come! to th' woods let's take our flight,
We have more dismal business yet e're night.

The Antimask of the Spirits

1. Entry

The FIERY SPIRITS *all in flames, and their Vizards of a Cholerick Complexion.*

The AIRY SPIRITS *with sanguine vizards, their Garments and Caps all of feathers.*

The WATERY SPIRITS *were all over wrought with scales, and had fishes heads and fins.*

The EARTHY SPIRITS *had their garments wrought all over with leave-less trees and bushes, with Serpents and other little Animals here and there about them, and on their heads barren rocks.*

2. Entry

Brought in by the FIERY SPIRITS, *were debosht and quarrelling men with a loose Wench amongst them.*

3. and 4. Entry

Brought in by the SPIRITS OF AYR, *were of amorous men and women in ridiculous habits and Alchimists.*

5. Entry

Brought in by the SPIRITS OF WATER, *were drunken Dutch skippers.*

6. Entry

Brought in by the SPIRITS OF EARTH, *were Witches, Usurers, and Fools.*

7. Entry

Was of a MODERN DIVEL, *a sworn enemy of Poesie, Musick, and all ingenious Arts, but a great friend to murmuring, libelling, and all seeds of discord, attended by his factious followers; all which was exprest by their Habits and Dance.*

V. RESTORATION

AFTER the eighteen years of only partly broken silence in the theatre the tale is taken up again in 1660, when the King came into his own again. A few years before the Restoration D'Avenant had introduced the Continental operatic type to English audiences, and this operatic type had at least something to do with the development of that characteristic Restoration form, the rimed-couplet 'love and honour' drama. Here Dryden is the chief figure, and *The Conquest of Granada* illustrates at once some of his strength and some of his weakness. Lee's *Sophonisba* shows a spark of emotional poetry amid a bombastic mouthing of extravagant speeches; Settle's *The Empress of Morocco* indicates to what dull depths the rimed tragedy could fall. About 1677 Dryden and others tired of rime, and in *All for Love* the major poet heralded his breakaway toward the older blank-verse medium, with a new search in Shakespeare for inspiration. In *All for Love* the artificial Restoration stage sentiments appear alongside of an atmosphere clearly borrowed from the works of the Elizabethan. The greatest achievement of this new blank-verse school is Otway's *Venice Preserv'd*, although other dramas such as Southerne's *Oroonoko* are certainly deserving of remembrance. As the years passed by new moods developed. Sentimentalism and the freshly acquired patriotism of the last years of the century inspired Banks and Rowe to write their 'she-tragedies,' where English history is depicted through the medium of a heroine instead of a hero. Classicism, too, was growing, and the tones of Philips and Addison are at least suggested in Congreve's *The Mourning Bride*.

The triumph of the Restoration stage lay in the sphere of comedy. At first the 'humours' style, as shown in Howard's *The Committee* and Shadwell's *Epsom Wells*, seemed likely to provide the prevailing form, but Dryden

167

EXTRACTS FROM BRITISH & IRISH PLAYS

early showed a slight break-away from the pure Jonsonian model. In Celadon and Florimel of *The Maiden Queen* he drew two airy, careless lovers, who moved in an atmosphere of gaiety and wit alien to that presented in Jonson's plays. This tentative movement toward the new style was carried on by Etherege, whose *Man of Mode* is one of the best of Restoration comedies, by Wycherley, who is represented here by *The Country Wife*, and, most signally of all, by Congreve, in whose *The Way of the World* the new comedy, the comedy of manners, reaches the acme of fine expression. Here the wit which was dimly aimed at by Fletcher and Shirley has complete domination.

1. SIR WILLIAM D'AVENANT (1606–68)

The Siege of Rhodes

In 1656, when the Puritan domination was growing to a close, D'Avenant brought forward his *Siege of Rhodes* at Rutland House, gaining, by some means or another, permission from the authorities for the performance. No doubt his main argument was that this, being an 'opera,' was not a stage-play, that there was no ordinary spoken dialogue, that everything was sung. The work itself has no great literary value, but its historic significance is literally incalculable. Here D'Avenant fuses together the earlier pre-Commonwealth 'love and honour' drama and the atmosphere of Continental opera. His rimed verse is loose and erratic, but it points forward to the couplet-play of succeeding years. He uses scenery, primitive though it might be, to increase his effects. He makes free use of music. A woman sings the chief feminine part, thus being in reality the first actress on the English stage. In every way *The Siege of Rhodes* is symptomatic of later theatrical and dramatic developments and possesses an interest far beyond its intrinsic worth. Just before the opening of the following piece of dialogue Ianthe, Alphonso's wife, has spent a night in Solyman's camp as his prisoner. She has returned safe to Rhodes, and is narrating her adventures to her husband.

(The following extract is taken from the 1673 folio collected works of D'Avenant.)

JEALOUSY WAKENS IN ALPHONSO'S BREAST

ALPHONSO. *Ianthe* after all this praise
Which Fame so fully to you pays,

168

RESTORATION

For that which all the world beside
Admires you, I alone must chide. . . .
Thy dangers, could I them have seen,
Would not to me have dangers been,
But certain death: Now thou art here
A danger worse than death I fear.
Thou hast, *Ianthe*, honour won,
But mine, alas, will be undone:
For as thou valiant wer't for me,
I shall a Coward grow for thee.

    IANTHE. Take heed *Alphonso*, for this care of me,
      Will to my Fame injurious be;
Your love will brighter by it shine,
      But it eclipses mine.
Since I would here before, or with you fall,
Death needs but beckon when he means to call.

    ALPHONSO. *Ianthe*, even in this you shall command,
      And this my strongest passion guide;
      Your vertue will not be deny'd:
It could even *Solyman* himself withstand;
      To whom it did so beauteous show:
It seem'd to civilize a barb'rous Foe.
      Of this your strange escape, *Ianthe*, say,
      Briefly the motive and the way.

    IANTHE. Did I not tell you how we fought,
How I was taken and how brought
Before great *Solyman*? but there
I think we interrupted were.

    ALPHONSO. Yes, but we will not be so here,
Should *Solyman* himself appear.

    IANTHE. It seems that what the Bassa of me said,
Had some respect and admiration bred
In *Solyman*; and this to me encreast
The jealousies which honour did suggest.
All that of *Turks* and *Tyrants* I had heard
But that I fear'd not Death, I should have fear'd.
I, to excuse my Voyage, urg'd my Love
To your high worth; which did such pity move,
That straight his usage did reclaim my fear.
He seem'd in civil *France*; and Monarch there:
For soon my Person, Gallies, Fraight, were free
By his command.

    ALPHONSO.   O wondrous Enemy!
    IANTHE. These are the smallest gifts his bounty knew.
    ALPHONSO. What could he give you more?
    IANTHE.   He gave me you;
And you may homewards now securely go
Through all his Fleet.

ALPHONSO.   But honour says not so.

IANTHE. If that forbid it, you shall never see
That I and that will disagree.
Honour will speak the same to me.

ALPHONSO. This Generous Turk amazes me, my Dear!
How long, *Ianthe*, stay'd you there?

IANTHE. Two days with *Mustapha*.

ALPHONSO.   How do you say?
Two days, and two whole nights? alas!

IANTHE. That it, my Lord, no longer was,
Is such a mercy, as too long I stay,
E're at the Altar thanks to Heav'n I pay.

ALPHONSO. To Heav'n, Confession should prepare the way.
She is all Harmony, and fair as light,   [*Exit* IANTHE.
But brings me discord, and the Clouds of night.
And *Solyman* does think Heaven's joys to be
In Women not so fair as she.
'Tis strange!   Dismiss so fair an Enemy!
She was his own by right of War,
We are his Dogs, and such as she, his Angels are.
    O wondrous Turkish Chastity!
Her gallies, fraight, and those to send
    Into a Town which he would take!
Are we besieg'd then by a Friend?
    Could Honour such a Present make,
    Then when his Honour is at stake?
Against itself, does Honour booty play?
    We have the liberty to go away!
Strange above miracle!   But who can say
    If in his hands we once should be
What would become of her?   For what of me,
    Though Love is blind, ev'n Love may see.
    Come back my thoughts, you must not rove!
    For sure *Ianthe* does *Alphonso* Love!
Oh *Solyman*, this mistick act of thine,
    Does all my quiet undermine:
    But on thy Troops, if not on Thee,
This Sword my cure, and my revenge shall be.

2. JOHN DRYDEN (1631–1700)

The Conquest of Granada

The heroic tragedy found its mightiest exponent in the person
of John Dryden.   With him, if it did not actually take its rise,
at least it gained most popularity, and with him it sank into
decay.   This is not to say that Dryden's heroic plays are masterpieces.   All of them have strength and a certain rhetorical verse

RESTORATION

beauty, but all show freely those many follies which seemed to be a necessary concomitant of the ruined tragedy. Already in *British Drama* (pp. 228–230) an example has been given of Dryden's lack of power when dealing with passionate themes. This may be supplemented by a typical piece of reasoning in verse, perfectly characteristic of the heroic style, and indeed that particular form in which it achieved its highest flights. Rime as a dramatic medium (unless in the purely artificial pastoral play) is ill calculated to provide the opportunity for a variety of moods and diversity of passions. It inevitably tends toward epigrammatic expression, and hence is seen at its best in passages where argumentation rather than the enunciation of character is the aim of the playwright.

(*The Conquest of Granada by the Spaniards*, otherwise called *Almanzor and Almahide*, was first acted at Drury Lane in 1670. The following extract is taken from the third edition, 1678.)

COURAGE AND LOVE

ALMANZOR. The work is done; now Madam, you are free:
At least, if I can give you Liberty.
But you have Chains which you yourself have chose;
And, oh, that I could free you too from those!
But, you are free from force, and have full pow'r
To go, and kill my hopes and me, this hour.
I see, then, you will go; but yet my toil
May be rewarded with a looking while.
ALMAHIDE. *Almanzor* can from every Subject raise
New matter for our Wonder and his Praise.
You bound and freed me, but the difference is,
That show'd your Valour; but your Vertue this.
ALMANZOR. Madam, you praise a Fun'ral Victory;
At whose sad Pomp the Conqueror must dye.
ALMAHIDE. Conquest attends *Almanzor* every where;
I am too small a Foe for him to fear:
But Heroes still must be oppos'd by some,
Or they would want occasion to o'recome.
ALMANZOR. Madam, I cannot on bare praises live:
Those who abound in praises, seldom give.
ALMAHIDE. While I to all the World your worth make known,
May Heav'n reward the pity you have shown.
ALMANZOR. My Love is languishing and starv'd to death,
And would you give me charity, in breath?
Pray'rs are the Alms of Church-men to the Poor:
They send's to Heaven, but drive us from their door.
ALMAHIDE. Cease, cease a Sute
So vain to you and troublesome to me,

171

If you will have me think that I am free.
If I am yet a Slave, my bonds I'le bear;
But what I cannot grant, I will not hear.

    ALMANZOR. You wonnot hear! you must both Hear, and Grant;
For, Madam, there's an impudence in want.

    ALMAHIDE. Your way is somewhat strange to ask Relief;
You ask with threatning, like a begging Thief.
Once more, *Almanzor*, tell me, am I free?

    ALMANZOR. Madam, you are, from all the World,—but me.
But as a Pyrate, when he frees the Prize
He took from Friends, sees the rich Merchandize,
And after he has freed it, justly buys;
So when I have restor'd your Liberty,——
But, then, alas, I am too poor to buy!

    ALMAHIDE. Nay, now you use me just as Pyrats do:
You free me; but expect a Ransom too.

    ALMANZOR. You'ave all the freedom that a Prince can have:
But Greatness cannot be without a Slave.
A Monarch never can in private move;
But still is haunted with officious Love.
So small an inconvenience you may bear,
'Tis all the Fine Fate sets upon the Fair.

    ALMAHIDE. Yet Princes may retire when e're they please;
And breath free Air from out their Palaces:
They go sometimes unknown, to shun their State;
And then, 'tis manners not to know, or wait.

    ALMANZOR. If not a Subject, then a Ghost I'le be;
And from a Ghost, you know, no place is free.
Asleep, awake, I'le haunt you everywhere,
From my white shrowd, groan Love into your Ear.
When in your Lovers Arms you sleep at night,
I'le glide in cold betwixt, and seize my Right.
And is't not better in your Nuptial Bed,
To have a living Lover than a dead?

    ALMAHIDE. I can no longer bear to be accus'd,
As if what I could grant you I refus'd.
My Fathers choice I never will dispute;
And he has chosen e're you mov'd your Sute,
You know my case, if equal you can be,
Plead for your self, and answer it for me.

    ALMANZOR. Then, Madam, in that hope you bid me live:
I ask no more than you may justly give
But, in strict justice there may favour be:
And may I hope you can have that for me?

    ALMAHIDE. Why do you thus my secret thoughts pursue,
Which known, hurt me, and cannot profit you?
Your knowledge but new troubles does prepare,
Like theirs, who curious in their Fortunes are,

172

To say I could with more content be yours,
Tempts you to hope; but not that hope assures.
For since the King has right,
And favour'd by my Father in his Sute,
'Tis but a blossom which can bear no Fruit.
Yet, if you dare attempt so hard a task,
May you succeed; you have my leave to ask.
    ALMANZOR. I can with courage now my hopes pursue,
Since I no longer have to combat you.
That did the greatest difficulty bring :
The rest are small, a Father, and a King!
    ALMAHIDE. Great Souls discern not when the leap's too wide,
Nor view the passage, but the farther side;
What ever you desire, you think is near:
But, with more reason, the success I fear. . . .
    ALMANZOR. Born, as I am, still to Command, not sue,
Yet you shall see that I can beg for you.
And if your Father will require a Crown,
Let him but name the Kingdom, 'tis his own.
I am, but while I please, a private Man;
I have that Soul which Empires first began.
From the dull crowd which every King does lead,
I will pick out whom I will choose to head:
The best and bravest Souls I can select,
And on their conquer'd Necks my Throne erect.

3. NATHANIEL OR NAT LEE (? 1653–92)

Sophonisba

Nat Lee is always to be associated with Thomas Otway as one
of those authors who, in an age of growing classicism, retained
memories of a period when passion was triumphant. Like Otway
and like Dryden, his career embraced both the rimed-couplet
tragedy and the later blank-verse style ; in both he showed an
emotionalism which, if unrestrained and leading frequently to
bathos, yet marks him out from the Crownes and Settles of his
time. It would be unfair either to Lee or to his age were selection
to be made of a passage of bathos or of a passage of particular
beauty ; and accordingly I have here chosen the scene of Rosalinda's death from the play of *Sophonisba*. There are lines here
which, rhetorically great, must have provided excellent matter
for the robust enunciation of a Mohun—lines, too, which come
near to sheer folly. The occasional splendour and the inherent
weakness of the rimed dialogue is here excellently exemplified.

    (*Sophonisba ; or, Hannibal's Overthrow* was produced at Drury
Lane in 1675. The following extract is taken from the edition
of 1697.)

EXTRACTS FROM BRITISH & IRISH PLAYS

The Death of Rosalinda

ROSALINDA. Heaven thou hast done thy worst, there needs no
    more; }
Bold with my Overthrow, I brave thy Power,
And shake the Glass that holds my latest hour. }
O, *Hannibal*! did I for this design
This Heart, this Youth and Beauty only thine?
Pride and Neglect on every Lover hurl'd,
Scorn'd him that Conquers thee, and all the World?
From me, lost *Hero*, learn, be great and die:
The brave should bleed for loss of Victory.

              [*Enter* HANNIBAL, MAHERBAL, BOMILCAR.

HANNIBAL. *Carthage* is lost, and *Hannibal* o'rethrown;
What is there left that we may call our own?
The bleeding world, *Rome* does by Conquest claim,
And swells the Prize with our revolted Fame:
Yet spight of Fate our Length of Earth we have;
Thus vanquish'd, Glory shrowd thee in a Grave.

BOMILCAR. Hold, General; the Gods your Death forbid;
Vengeance is due; first let false *Hanno* bleed,
Who cut the Wings of Conquest till she fell.

MAHERBAL. By me he shall be headlong sent to Hell;
Where Fiends for Treason kindle double Fire:
Then let the famous *Hannibal* expire.

ROSALINDA. Sure I the Name of *Hannibal* did hear;
Maherbal, tell me, is the General there?

MAHERBAL. Approach, my Lord, view well this wounded fair:
Sure in your *Capuan* Mistress I have seen
The same Majestick Air, and charming meen.

HANNIBAL. Ha! thou hast rows'd a thought that wracks me more,
Than all the losses I in Battel bore.
Either I dream, or in this closing Eye
My dazling senses *Rosalinda* spie.

ROSALINDA. Where do the ambitious rest? O *Hannibal*!

HANNIBAL. What art, that dost upon the wretched call?

ROSALINDA. One that's more wretched, and more rash than thou,
That would to Fate, and not to *Scipio* bow.
Disguis'd, and dying *Rosalinda* see,
Who mourns in Death thy Loss of Victory:
That last Disgrace. . . .

HANNIBAL. O dying fair, look up, revive a while;
With one short joy eternal care beguile:
The setting Sun all curtain'd round with Night,
At his departure gives a larger Light. . . .

ROSALINDA. Dear *Hannibal*, alas! I wish I cou'd: }
But 'twill not be; Life trembling takes the Flood, }
Till well-nigh swallow'd up in Waves of Blood. }

174

RESTORATION

The *Roman* Glory shines too fatal bright;
And with it's gathering lustre dims my sight:
Eternally adieu: My Body take,
Chaste and entire I kept it for your sake:
'Tis the least Present that I now can make.　　　　　　[*Dies.*

HANNIBAL. For ever gone! All her sweet stock of breath
Spent in one Sigh; the Riot of rich Death,
Now by my Arms the Gods too partial are,
Or else they envy'd my full trade of War;
Which cou'd so vast a state of Beauty buy,
As far surpass'd the Mannors of the Sky.
Dead *Rosalinda*——

BOMILCAR.　　　　Raise you from the Ground,
And let not Love your Vertues force confound;
Where is that heat and haughty Courage gone,
Which against Nature's Lets your Troops led on?

MAHERBAL. Think you for naught the Gods such Valour gave?
You should prop Thrones, and falling Kingdoms save.
Buried in thought, and deaf to Honour's call,
Your Soul beneath her mighty pitch does fall.

HANNIBAL. *Maherbal,* no; astonish'd thou shalt be;
We dare be brave in spight of Destiny.
Though rob'd of all the Riches Love could give,
And stript of Glory too, yet we will live:
Courage is form'd of the Etherial mold,
And round it bands of Adamant are roll'd.
To this still haughty breast such Fire is given,
I could the Summons meet of Hell or Heaven:
Cou'd, like the great Eternal Mover, sway
The World in arms, and teach him to obey.
'Twas noble grief that lately chang'd my form,
But I am ruffled now into a storm.

BOMILCAR. Your Mistress body hence we will convey,
And in some hallowed Vault her Relicks lay.

MAHERBAL. Like Pilgrims, once a year we'll Mourning go,
And on her Urn sad Yew with Cypress throw,
And all our stock of Tears and Sighs bestow.

HANNIBAL. For ever, brightest of thy kind, farewel,
Who wert too worthy; therefore early fell.
As the young Phœnix does in sacred Myrrhe,
His Father's Dust to the Sun's Temple bear,
So in Fame's Houses shalt thou Honour'd be,
And every God shall have a grain of thee.

MAHERBAL. Since Glory with her last breath she profest,
May wish'd Dominion widen all your breast.

HANNIBAL. Haste, haste, *Maherbal,* and fresh Levies make;
Honour that did but now calm slumbers take,
Shall like the Ocean in a tempest wake:

We'll pass new *Alpes*, new Consuls overthrow,
To *Rome* with far more dreadful Armies go;
Forcing the *Apian* and *Emilian* way,
To the *Suburra* we'll pursue the Fray;
Nor stop till *Rosalinda's* Statue, Crown'd,
Sits in the Capitol with Gods enthron'd.

4. ELKANAH SETTLE (1648–1724)

The Empress of Morocco

The beauties of the heroic drama are to be seen in the works of Dryden and of Lee, yet even in their plays there are follies, and those follies abound in the many tragedies and tragi-comedies in rime turned out between 1665 and 1679 by the minor brethren of the period. Little thought was taken of verisimilitude. With the type characters, the artificial sentiments of love and honour, and the outlandish scenes chosen for these dramas, the playwrights felt bound by no ties to nature, and indulged in the most wayward scenes, the most impossible incidents. The language took on a similar colouring. Bombast and rant ruled the stage ; possibly the audience grew to like this and regarded it, because out of the ordinary, as majestic and grand. Of the lesser dramatists, Elkanah Settle is not the least important. He had a following in his own day, and the success of one of his plays, *The Empress of Morocco*, is shown by the fact that when it was published in 1673 it was graced with several ' Sculptures ' or engravings, so that it has the distinction of being the first fully illustrated play issued in England. As the title indicates, this is an ' Eastern ' drama. It possesses all the elements that made for contemporary popularity—the 'love and honour' sentiments, a dash of the supernatural, a considerable sprinkling of murders, and a final seasoning of cruelty and horror.

(*The Empress of Morocco* was produced at the Duke's Theatre in 1673. The passage given below is taken from the edition of 1698.)

THE END OF HEROIC STRUGGLING

Enter HAMETALHAZ, *in the Balcony with the Guards, who seize* CRIMALHAZ *and disarm him.*

HAMETALHAZ. Before this Tower does take fire, you'll want a head.

CRIMALHAZ. *Hametalhaz* stand off; am I betray'd !

HAMETALHAZ. I have no time to answer your demands:
Deliver him to *Muly Hamet's* hands.
The highest triumph my weak Arm e're gain'd,
Is to present this Princess to his Hand.

[CRIMALHAZ *is forced down by the Guards.*

RESTORATION

MULY HAMET. Her life preserv'd and he the instrument!
What miracle of Honour has fate sent?
Sure Heaven acts Wonders! Wonders, no 'tis none—
What have the higher powers to do but to take care,
Of so much Vertue and a face so fair?

> [*Enter* CRIMALHAZ *below, lead in by Guards.*

See him convey'd to Execution straight:
He as he rose in blood, in blood shall set.

    CRIMALHAZ. Since I must die, and die condemn'd by you:
Hear Heaven, for I ne'er troubled you till now.
So may my body rot when I am dead,
Till my rank dust has such Contagions bred:
My Grave may dart forth Plagues, as may strike death
Thro' the infected Air where thou drawest breath.
Others may fancy pleasures more divine,
I know not where: this shall in Hell be mine;
To think when dead I yet can death Convey,
And what my Arm can't act my Ashes may.

> [*Exit Guarded with* ABDELCADOR. *Enter* HAMETALHAZ
> *leading* MARIAMNE.

    MULY HAMET. My dear and best Life, welcome: By thy hand,
My Crown, my Happiness and Heaven regain'd.
What mystick blessing does my fate pursue,
To see her sav'd and see her sav'd by you?

    HAMETALHAZ. Oh do not at this mystery admire:
Nothing is strange which Beauty does inspire.
To punish Treason and preserve a Throne
Are due to *Mariamne's* eyes alone.
When to his hand I gave that beauteous prize,
Design'd for his ambitious Sacrifice:
When her hard fate and her bright Charms I saw,
These did my homage, that my pity draw.
Something so kind I to that face did pay,
That to serve her I could my trust betray.
Had I been born a Prince, and, in that name
Like you, erected trophies to her fame:
In all things then I had your Rival proved,
And confidently told her that I Lov'd.
But wanting worth I wanted words, and chose
This way my speechless passion to disclose.
I would defend what I could ne'er enjoy,
And break all bars that did her Peace destroy.
But I too late resolv'd a flight so high:
I cut my wings before I thought to fly:
Too quick to work, too weak to prop her fall.
My penitence could not my sins recal.
Till this blest moment and your influence gave
Her dangers and his insolence a grave.

M

MULY HAMET. Such honour and such Love! I am Conquer'd here,
My deeds and passions are below thy Sphear.
But as your worth, your power shall out-reach mine:
Subjects my Homage pay, but Monarchs thine.   [*Embraces him.*

HAMETALHAZ. Tho' Heaven by me her threaten'd life secures,
And saves her blood to be allay'd to yours.
Despair not, Friendship, yields to that hard task;
I bravely give what I durst never ask.
Hold Heart while I this Treasure do resign,
And Crown her bliss with that which ruins mine.
I perish at her feet whom I adore,
The greatest Wracks are nearest to the shore.

MARIAMNE. Such Language may by chastest ears be heard,
Your Love I admire, and he reward.
A nobler passion Story never writ,
That turn'd a Traytor to a Proselyte.
Thou best of Converts.

MULY HAMET. And of Rivals too.
Sir, as a Tribute to your Vertue due,
All honours merit in a Court, can meet,
And a kind Monarchs Love, Lie at your feet.

HAMETALHAZ. Hold, that great act of mercy must not pass,
Let not your first days Reign a King disgrace.
Of such high bounty I'm unworthy still:
My good Acts have not yet out-weighed my ill.
No—
To some far Country,
I from those Eyes for ever will remove,
I cannot stand the sight of hopeless Love.
Pilgrims, whose Zeal's more blest tho' lest Divine
Go meet their Saints, but I must flie from mine.   [*Offers to go.*

MULY HAMET. Stay I conjure you; stay, you shall, you must:
You've made me great; let me not be unjust.
Speak what command, what power, what Crown you'll choose.

HAMETALHAZ. Crowns, no, such little favours I refuse.
None but the place you hold my wish can bound.
But since I have your free offer to be Crown'd,
It is accepted: I a King will be,
And of my Reign make this my first decree,
This Criminal's Banishment, and to pursue
My state, a Conqueror and a King like you;
To whate'er place my wandring steps incline,
I'll fancy Empires for I'll think her mine.   [*Exit* HAMETALHAZ.
      [*Here the Scene opens, and* CRIMALHAZ *appears cast down on
          the Gaunches, being hung on a Wall set with spikes of
          Iron.   Enter again* ABDELCADOR.

ABDELCADOR. See the reward of Treason; death's the thing

Distinguishes th'usurper from the King.
Kings are immortal, and from life remove,
From their lower Thrones to wear new Crowns above:
But Heaven for him has scarce that bliss in store:
When an usurper dies he reigns no more.
    MULY HAMET. My Justice ended: now I'll meet a Crown:
Crowns are the common Prizes I have won.
Those are entail'd on Courage. No, 'tis you
Can only yield a bliss that's great and new.
The charm of Crowns to Love but dull appears:
Reigning's a whole life's toil, the work of years.
In love a day, an hour, a minute's Bliss,
Is all Flight, Rapture, Flame and Extasies.
Love's livelier Joys so quick and active move;
An Age in Empire's but an hour in Love.   [*Exeunt Omnes.*

5. JOHN DRYDEN (1631–1700)

All for Love

About the year 1677 Dryden, tiring of " his long-loved Mistress—Rhyme," turned to the medium of blank verse, finding in Shakespeare a new strength and a new beauty. He had come to realize that, although the rimed couplet might be used for certain scenes with success, it was ill-fitted for the expression of a variety of moods, that its very regularity demanded a certain uniformity of tone, a mouthing utterance far removed from the nervous lines of earlier dramatists. *All for Love* was his first experiment in the newer style, and for the theme of his play he turned back to Shakespeare's *Antony and Cleopatra*. This is no adaptation, such as the age delighted in, and it is a testimony to Dryden's greatness that, in its own kind, *All for Love* is entitled to hold a place level with that which Shakespeare's tragedy occupies in the field of romantically treated classic themes. It may be that Antony here is too much of a ' hero,' that love and honour are too deeply stressed, that classic decorum is over-strictly observed —but these features cannot take away from a decided greatness in conception and an unquestioned strength of dialogue.

(*All for Love ; or, The World well Lost* was produced at Drury Lane in 1677. The following passage is taken from the *Works* of 1725, edited by William Congreve.)

THE CONFLICT OF LOVE AND HONOUR

    DOLABELLA. Why would you shift it from your self, on me?
Can you not tell her you must part?
    ANTONY. I cannot.
I could pull out an Eye, and bid it go,

179

And t'other should not weep.   Oh, *Dolabella*,
How many Deaths are in this Word *Depart*!
I dare not trust my Tongue to tell her so:
One Look of hers would thaw me into Tears,
And I should melt till I were lost again.

 DOLABELLA. Then let *Ventidius*;
He's rough by Nature.

 ANTONY.   Oh, he'll speak too harshly;
He'll kill her with the News: Thou, only thou.

 DOLABELLA. Nature has cast me in so soft a Mold,
That but to hear a Story feign'd for Pleasure
Of some sad Lover's Death, moistens my Eyes,
And robs me of my Manhood.—I should speak
So faintly; with such Fear to grieve her Heart,
She'd not believe it earnest.

 ANTONY. Therefore; therefore
Thou only, thou art fit: Think thy self me,
And when thou speak'st (but let it first be long)
Take off the Edge from every sharper Sound,
And let our Parting be as gently made
As other Loves begin: Wilt thou do this?

 DOLABELLA. What you have said, so sinks into my Soul,
That, if I must speak, I shall speak just so.

 ANTONY. I leave you then to your sad Task: Farewel.
I sent her word to meet you.   [*Goes to the Door, and comes back.*
I forgot;
Let her be told, I'll make her Peace with mine:
Her Crown and Dignity shall be preserv'd,
If I have Pow'r with *Cæsar*.—O, be sure
To think on that.

 DOLABELLA. Fear not, I will remember.

       [ANTONY *goes again to the Door, and comes back.*
 ANTONY. And tell her, too, how much I was constrain'd;
I did not this, but with extreamest Force:
Desire her not to hate my Memory,
For I still cherish hers;—insist on that.

 DOLABELLA. Trust me, I'll not forget it.

 ANTONY.   Then that's all.

        [*Goes out, and returns again.*
Wilt thou forgive my Fondness this once more?
Tell her, tho' we shall never meet again,
If I should hear she took another Love,
The News would break my Heart.—Now I must go;
For every time I have return'd, I feel
My Soul more tender; and my next command
Would be to bid her stay, and ruin both.   [*Exit.*

 DOLABELLA. Men are but Children of a larger Growth,
Our Appetites as apt to change as theirs,

And full as craving too, and full as vain;
And yet the Soul, shut up in her dark Room,
Viewing so clear abroad, at home sees nothing;
But, like a Mole in Earth, busie and blind,
Works all her Folly up, and casts it outward
To the World's open View: Thus I discover'd,
And blam'd the Love of ruin'd *Antony*;
Yet wish that I were he, to be so ruin'd.   [*Enter* VENTIDIUS *above.*

VENTIDIUS. Alone? and talking to himself? concern'd too?
Perhaps my Guess is right? he lov'd her once,
And may pursue it still.

DOLABELLA. O Friendship! Friendship!
Ill canst thou answer this; and Reason, worse:
Unfaithful in th' Attempt; hopeless to win;
And, if I win, undone: Meer Madness all.
And yet th' Occasion's fair.   What Injury
To him, to wear the Robe which he throws by?

VENTIDIUS. None, none at all.   This happens as I wish,
To ruin her yet more with *Antony*.

> [*Enter* CLEOPATRA, *talking with* ALEXAS; CHARMION, IRAS
> *on the other side.*

DOLABELLA. She comes!   What Charms have Sorrow on that
  Face!
Sorrow seems pleas'd to dwell with so much Sweetness;
Yet, now and then, a melancholy Smile
Breaks loose, like Lightning, in a Winter's Night,
And shows a moments Day.

VENTIDIUS. If she should love him too! her Eunuch there!
That *Porc'pisce* bodes ill Weather.   Draw, draw nearer,
Sweet Devil, that I may hear.

ALEXAS. Believe me; try

> [DOLABELLA *goes over to* CHARMION *and* IRAS; *seems to talk*
> *with them.*

To make him jealous; Jealousie is like
A polisht Glass held to the Lips when Life's in doubt:
If there be Breath, 'twill catch the Damp and show it.

CLEOPATRA. I grant you Jealousie's a Proof of Love,
But 'tis a weak and unavailing Medicine;
It puts out the Disease, and makes it show,
But has no Pow'r to cure. . . .

                    Ah no; my Love's so true,
That I can neither hide it where it is,
Nor show it where it is not.   Nature meant me
A Wife; a silly harmless houshold Dove,
Fond without Art; and kind without Deceit;
But Fortune, that has made a Mistress of me,
Has thrust me out to the wide World, unfurnish'd
Of Falshood to be happy.

6. THOMAS OTWAY (1652–85)

Venice Preserv'd

Despite the passing craze for rimed-couplet dramas, and despite the growing classicism of the age, the Restoration period yet retained many links with the earlier Elizabethan spirit. Dryden shows it in *All for Love*, and there is an emotional fire in the works of Nat Lee which inevitably recalls that of the school of Ford and Shirley. The greatest achievement in this emotional style, however, was reserved for Thomas Otway, whose *Venice Preserv'd* has long been recognized as the finest tragedy produced in England between the downfall of the Caroline stage and the arising of a new drama in the nineteenth century. The prime value of this play rests in its masterly construction and in its fine characterization, but its final impression is added to by the nervous blank verse, essentially theatrical, which Otway, after many experiments in various styles, had taught himself to write. The story tells of a high-souled conspirator, Pierre, who persuades the weak-willed Jaffier to join him in his attempt to overthrow the tyrannical Government of Venice. Like Brutus, Pierre finds companions whose motives are by no means as altruistic as his own, and tragedy results from the clash of temperaments, disaster resulting from Pierre's faith, from Jaffier's vacillation, and from the selfish aims of his pretended friends. The scene selected here is that in which Pierre defends his companion against the accusations of Renault and others of the band.

(*Venice Preserv'd; or, a Plot Discover'd* was produced at Dorset Garden in 1682 and printed the same year. The following extract is from the first quarto.)

PIERRE DEFENDS JAFFIER

RENAULT. Thus happy, thus secure of all we wish for,
Should there my Friends be found amongst us one
False to this glorious Enterprize, what Fate,
What Vengeance were enough for such a Villain?
    ELIOT. Death here without Repentance, Hell hereafter.
    RENAULT. Let that be my lott, if as here I stand,
Lifted by Fate amongst her darling Sons,
Tho' I had one only Brother, dear by all
The strictest Ties of Nature; tho' one hour
Had given us birth, one Fortune fed our wants,
One only love, and that but of each other,
Still fill'd our minds: Could I have such a Friend
Joyn'd in this Cause, and had but ground to fear
Meant fowl play; may this right hand drop from me,
If I'd not hazard all my future peace,

RESTORATION

And stabb him to the heart before you: who
Would not do less?   Wouldst not thou *Pierre* the same?
  PIERRE. You have singl'd me, Sir, out for this hard question,
As if 'twere started only for my sake!
Am I the thing you fear?   Here, here's my bosom,
Search it with all your Swords! am I a Traytor?
  RENAULT. No: but I fear your late commended Friend
Is little less: Come, Sirs, 'tis now no time
To trifle with our safety.   Where's this *Jaffier*?
  SPINOSA. He left the Room just now in strange disorder.
  RENAULT. Nay, there is danger in him: I observ'd him
During the time I took for Explanation,
He was transported from most deep attention
To a confusion which he could not smother.
His looks grew full of sadness and surprize,
All which betray'd a wavering Spirit in him,
That labour'd with reluctancy and sorrow.
What's requisite for safety, must be done
With speedy Execution : he remains
Yet in our Power: I for my own part wear
A Dagger——
  PIERRE. Well.
  RENAULT.   And I could wish it!
  PIERRE.   Where?
  RENAULT. Bury'd in his Heart.
  PIERRE.   Away! w'are yet all friends;
No more of this, 'twill Breed ill blood amongst us.
  SPINOSA. Let us all draw our Swords, and search the
      house,
Pull him from the dark hole where he sits brooding
O're his cold fears, and each man kill his share of him.
  PIERRE. Who talks of killing? who's he'll shed the blood
That's dear to me! is't you? or you? or you Sir?
What, not one speak? how you stand gaping all
On your grave Oracle, your wooden God there;
Yet not a word?   Then Sir, I'l tell you a secret;
Suspition's but at best a Coward's Virtue!   [To RENAULT.
  RENAULT. A Coward——   [*Handles his Sword.*
  PIERRE. Put, put up thy Sword, old Man,
Thy hand shakes at it; come, let's heal this breach,
I am too hot: we yet may live Friends.
  SPINOSA. 'Till we are safe, our Friendship cannot be so,
  PIERRE. Again, who's that?
  SPINOSA.   'Twas I.
  THEODORE.   And I.
  REVELLIDO.   And I.
  ELIOT.   And all.
  RENAULT. Who are on my Side?

Spinosa.   Every honest Sword.
Let's die like men, and not be sold like Slaves.
    Pierre. One such word more, by Heav'n I'l to the Senate,
And hang ye all, like Dogs in Clusters.
Why peep your Coward Swords half out their shells?
Why do you not all brandish them like mine?
You fear to die, and yet dare talk of killing.
    Renault. Go to the Senate and betray us; hasten,
Secure thy wretched Life; we fear to die
Less than thou dar'st be honest.
    Pierre.   That's rank falsehood.
Fear'st not thou death? fy, there's a knavish itch
In that salt blood, an utter foe to smarting.
Had *Jaffeir's* Wife prov'd Kind, he had still been true.
Foh—how that stinks!
Thou dy! thou kill my Friend, or thou, or thou,
Or thou, with that lean, wither'd wretched Face!
Away, disperse all to your several Charges,
And meet to-morrow where your honour calls you;
I'l bring that man, whose blood you so much thirst for,
And you shall see him venture for you fairly—
Hence, hence, I say.   [*Ex.* Renault *angrily.*
    Spinosa.   I fear we've been to blame;
And done too much.
    Theodore. 'Twas too farr urg'd against the man you lov'd.
    Revellido. Here take our Swords, and crush 'em with your feet
    Spinosa. Forgive us gallant Friend.
    Pierre.   Nay, now y'have found
The way to melt and cast me as you will:
I'll fetch this Friend, and give him to your mercy:
Nay he shall dye, if you will take him from me.
For your repose, I'll quit my hearts Jewel;
But would not have him torn away by Villains,
And spiteful villany.
    Spinosa.   No; may you both
For ever live, and fill the world with fame!
    Pierre. Now you are too kind.   Whence rose all this discord?
Oh what a dangerous precipice have we 'scaped!
How near a fall was all we had long been building!
What an eternal blot had stain'd our glories!
If one, the bravest and the best of men,
Had fallen a Sacrifice to rash suspicion!
Butcher'd by those, whose Cause he came to cherish:
Oh could you know him all as I have known him,
How good he is, how true, how brave,
You wou'd not leave this place, 'till you had seen him;
Humbled yourselves before him, kiss'd his feet,
And gain'd remission for the worst of follies.

184

RESTORATION

7. THOMAS SOUTHERNE (1660–1746)

Oroonoko

With Dryden's *All for Love* came the return to Elizabethan models and the readoption of blank verse as a dramatic medium. Heroic standards still endured ; love and honour still lorded it over the depiction of stage passions ; but with this reversion to earlier models there undoubtedly did come some larger attempt to display human nature outside the artificial standards raised by the heroic play. To a certain extent the return to Elizabethan models coalesced with a new mood rising in the later years of the seventeenth century—a mood of sentimentalism and pathos, most familiar perhaps in the pages of Steele, or, for the realm of fiction, in those of Richardson. *Oroonoko* shows this development in the sphere of tragedy. The presentation of the noble-minded but dark-skinned prince and the tracing of his unhappy love owes its very being to the development of that sentimentalism which was later to form the basis of romantic humanitarian fervour. Southerne is a dramatist by no means to be despised, and if at times his blank-verse melody seems a trifle rough and unformed he has as sure a mastery of his material as any dramatist of his time. Perhaps too little attention has been paid by critics to this expression of humane feeling in an age of callous gallantry.

(*Oroonoko* was produced at Drury Lane in 1695. The following extract is taken from the quarto of 1696.)

White Treachery

GOVERNOR. Live, Royal Sir ;
Live, and be happy long on your own Terms:
Only consent to yield, and you shall have
What Terms you can propose, for you, and yours.
    OROONOKO. Consent to yield ! shall I betray my self?
    GOVERNOR. Alas ! we cannot fear, that your small Force,
The Force of two, with a weak Womans Arm,
Shou'd Conquer us. I speak in the regard
And Honour of your Worth, in my desire
And forwardness to serve so great a Man.
I wou'd not have it lie upon my Thoughts,
That I was the occasion of the fall
Of such a Prince, whose Courage carried on
In a more Noble Cause, wou'd well deserve
The Empire of the World.
    OROONOKO. You can speak fair.
    GOVERNOR. Your Undertaking, tho' it would have brought
So great a loss to us, we must all say
Was generous, and noble; and shall be

Regarded only as the Fire of Youth,
That will break out sometimes in Gallant Souls;
We'll think it but the Natural Impulse,
A rash impatience of Liberty:
No otherwise.

OROONOKO. Think it what you will.
I was not born to render an Account
Of what I do, to any but my self.   [BLANDFORD *comes forward.*

BLANDFORD. I'm glad you have proceeded by fair means.
I came to be a Mediator.   [*To the* GOVERNOR.

GOVERNOR. Try what you can work upon him.

OROONOKO. Are you come against me too?

BLANDFORD. Is this to come against you?
   [*Offering his sword to* OROONOKO.
Unarm'd to put my self into your Hands?
I come, I hope, to serve you.

OROONOKO. You have serv'd me;
I thank you for't: and I am pleas'd to think
You were my Friend, while I had need of one:
But now 'tis past; this farewell; and be gone.   [*Embraces him.*

BLANDFORD. It is not past; and I must serve you still.
I wou'd make up these Breaches, which the Sword
Will widen more; and close us all in Love.

OROONOKO. I know what I have done, and I shou'd be
A Child to think they ever can Forgive:
Forgive! were there but that, I wou'd not live
To be Forgiven: is there a Power on Earth,
That I can ever need forgiveness from?

BLANDFORD. You sha' not need it.

OROONOKO. No, I wonnot need it.

BLANDFORD. You see he offers you your own Conditions,
For you and yours.

OROONOKO. I must Capitulate?
Precariously Compound, on stinted Terms,
To save my Life?

BLANDFORD. Sir, he Imposes none.
You make 'em for your own Security.
If your great Heart cannot descend to treat,
In adverse Fortune, with an Enemy:
Yet sure, your Honour's safe, you may accept
Offers of Peace and Safety from a Friend.

GOVERNOR. He will rely on what you say to him: ˙
   [*To* BLANDFORD.
Offer him what you can, I will confirm,
And make all good: be you my Pledge of Trust.

BLANDFORD. I'le answer with my Life for all he says.

GOVERNOR. Ay, do, and pay the Forfeit if you please.   [*Aside.*

BLANDFORD. Consider, Sir, can you consent to throw

That Blessing from you, you so hardly found,
And so much valu'd once?
   OROONOKO. *Imoinda!* Oh!
'Tis She that holds me, on this Argument
Of tedious Life: I cou'd resolve it soon,
Were this curst Being only in Debate.
But *Imoinda* struggles in my Soul;
She makes a Coward of me: I Confess
I am afraid to part with Her in Death:
And more afraid of Life to lose Her here.
   BLANDFORD. This way you must lose her, think upon
The weakness of her Sex, made yet more weak
With her Condition, requiring Rest,
And soft Indulging Ease, to nurse your Hopes,
And make you a glad Father.
   OROONOKO. There I feel
A Father's Fondness, and a Husband's Love.
They seize upon my Hart, strain all its strings,
To pull me to 'em, from my stern resolve.
Husband and Father! all the melting Art
Of Eloquence lives in those softning Names.
Methinks I see the Babe, with Infant Hands,
Pleading for Life, and begging to be born:
Shall I forbid his Birth? deny him Light?
The Heavenly Comforts of all-cheering Light? . . .
His Bleeding Mother his sad Monument?
These are the Calls of Nature, that call loud,
They will be heard, and conquer in their Cause. . . .
No, my *Imoinda*! I will venture all
To save thee, and that little Innocent:
The World may be a better Friend to him,
Than I have found it. Now I yield my self: [*Gives up his sword.*
The Conflict's past, and we are in your Hands.
       [*Several Men get about* OROONOKO *and* ABOAN, *and seize 'em.*
   GOVERNOR. So you shall find you are: Dispose of them
As I commanded you.
   BLANDFORD. Good Heaven forbid! You cannot mean——
   GOVERNOR. This is not your Concern.
               [*To* BLANDFORD *who goes to* OROONOKO.
I must take care of you.   [*To* IMOINDA.
   IMOINDA. I'm at the end
Of all my Care: Here I will die with him.   [*Holding* OROONOKO.
   OROONOKO. You shall not force her from me.   [*He holds her.*
   GOVERNOR. Then I must   [*They force her from him.*
Try other means, and Conquer Force by Force:
Break, cut off his Hold, bring her away.
   IMOINDA. I do not ask to Live, Kill me but here.
   OROONOKO. O Bloody Dogs! Inhumane Murderers.

EXTRACTS FROM BRITISH & IRISH PLAYS

8. WILLIAM CONGREVE (1670-1729)

The Mourning Bride

Few people know that the familiar lines—" Music has charms to soothe a savage Breast "—are the opening words of Congreve's solitary tragedy *The Mourning Bride*. This play, which has a certain beauty, is now never remembered unless when one is reading the life of the author of *Love for Love*. Congreve, it is true, was above all the man of wit ; he possessed little or none of that undercurrent of emotionalism which vivified the dramas of Dryden, Lee, and Otway. His whole outlook upon life was rationalistic, and consequently he, like Addison, could not enter into the world of passions where Tragedy has her throne. Still, in estimating the worth of any period of literature we must endeavour to appreciate the aims of that period, and we have to remember that Congreve and his peers deliberately eschewed emotionalism. We cannot, therefore, read *The Mourning Bride* as we would read *Othello*. In the one passion rules triumphant ; in the other good taste and reasonable sentiment, expressed in the language of formal rhetoric, are the aims of the dramatist. Judged from the standpoint of the age, Congreve's play is by no means negligible. It has form, character, interest, and if we can attune our ears to its music a certain beauty of verse.

(*The Mourning Bride* was produced at Lincoln's Inn Fields in 1697. The following passage is taken from the second edition, 1697.)

THE OPENING OF A CLASSIC TRAGEDY

The Curtain rising slowly to soft Musick, discovers ALMERIA *in Mourning,* LEONORA *waiting in Mourning. After the Musick* ALMERIA *rises from her Chair, and comes forward.*

ALMERIA. Musick has Charms to sooth a savage Breast,
To soften Rocks, or bend a knotted Oak.
I've read, that things inanimate have mov'd,
And as with living Souls, have been inform'd,
By Magick Numbers, and persuasive Sound.
What then am I? Am I more senseless grown
Than Trees, or Flint? O Force of constant Woe!
'Tis not in Harmony to calm my Griefs.
Anselmo sleeps, and is at Peace; last Night,
The silent Tomb receiv'd the good old King;
He and his Sorrows now are safely lodg'd
Within its cold, but hospitable Bosom:
Why am not I at Peace? [*Weeps.*
    LEONORA. For Heaven's sake, dear Madam, moderate
Your Griefs, there is no Cause——
        ALMERIA. Peace—No Cause! yes, there is Eternal Cause,

RESTORATION

And Misery Eternal will succeed.
Thou canst not tell—thou hast indeed no Cause.
   LEONORA. Believe me, Madam, I lament *Anselmo*,
And always did compassionate his Fortune;
Have often wept, to see how cruelly
Your Father kept in Chains, his Fellow-King:
And oft at Night, when all have been retir'd,
Have stoll'n from Bed, and to his Prison crept:
Where, while his Gaoler slept, I thro' the Grate
Have softly whisper'd, and enquir'd his Health;
Sent in my Sighs and Pray'rs for his Deliv'rance;
For Sighs and Pray'rs were all that I could offer.
   ALMERIA. Indeed thou hast a soft and gentle Nature,
That thus couldst melt to see a Stranger's Wrongs :
O *Leonora*, hadst thou known *Anselmo*,
How would thy Heart have bled to see his Suff'rings.
Thou hadst no cause, but general Compassion.
   LEONORA. My Love of you, my Royal Mistress, gave me
     Cause,
My Love of you begot my Greif for him,
For I had heard, that when the Chance of War,
Had bless'd *Anselmo's* Arms with Victory,
And the rich Spoil of all the Field, and you
The Glory of the whole, were made the Prey
Of his Success; that then, in spight of Hate,
Revenge, and that Hereditary Feud
Entail'd between *Valentia's* and *Granada's* Kings;
He did endear himself to your Affection,
By all the worthy and indulgent ways,
His most industrious Goodness cou'd invent;
Proposing by a Match between *Alphonso*
His Son, the brave *Valentia* Prince, and you,
To end the long Dissention, and unite
The Jarring Crowns.
   ALMERIA. O *Alphonso, Alphonso*! thou art too
At Peace; Father and Son are now no more—
Then why am I? O when shall I have Rest?
Why do I live to say you are no more?
Why are all these things thus?—
Is there necessity I must be miserable?
Is it of Moment to the Peace of Heav'n
That I should be afflicted thus?—if not,
Why is it thus contriv'd? Why are all things laid
By some unseen Hand, so, as of consequence
They must to me bring Curses, Grief of Heart,
The last Distress of Life, and sure Despair.
   LEONORA. Alas you search too far, and think too deeply.
   ALMERIA. Why was I carried to *Anselmo's* Court?

189

Or, when there, why was I us'd so tenderly?
Why did he not use me like an Enemy?
For so my Father would have us'd his Child.
O *Alphonso, Alphonso*!
Devouring Seas have wash'd thee from my sight,
But there's no time shall rase thee from my Memory.
No, I will live to be thy Monument;
The cruel Ocean would deprive thee of a Tomb,
But in my Heart thou art inter'd there, there,
Thy dear Resemblance is for ever fixt;
My Love, my Lord, my Husband still, though lost.
    LEONORA. Husband! O Heav'ns!
    ALMERIA. What have I said?
My Grief has hurry'd me beyond all Thought.
I would have kept that secret; though I know
Thy Love and Faith to me, deserve all Confidence.
But 'tis the Wretches Comfort still to have
Some small reserve of near and inward Woe,
Some unsuspected hoard of darling Grief,
Which they unseen, may wail, and weep, and mourn,
And Glutton-like alone devour.
    LEONORA. Indeed I knew not this.
    ALMERIA. O no, thou know'st not half—thou know'st nothing—
—If thou didst!—
    If I should tell thee, wouldst thou pity me?
Tell me? I know thou wouldst, thou art compassionate.
    LEONORA. Witness these Tears——
    ALMERIA. I thank thee—indeed I do—
I thank thee, that thou'lt pity thy sad Mistress;
For 'tis the poor Prerogative of Greatness,
To be wretched and unpitied—
But I did promise I would tell thee—What?
My Griefs? Thou dost already know 'em:
And when I said thou didst know nothing,
It was because thou didst not know *Alphonso*:
For to have known my Loss, thou must have known
His Worth, his Truth, and Tenderness of Love.

9. NICHOLAS ROWE (1674–1718)

Lady Jane Gray

Although Rowe is placed here in the Restoration section, his
work really belongs to the period of Queen Anne. He was, on
the other hand, rather a culminator than a pioneer, and his particular style of historical tragedy is to be traced back to the work
of men such as Bancroft and Banks in the seventeenth century.
The popularity of this type of drama was unquestionably due to

RESTORATION

the reviving patriotism of the times, which sought in the records of English history matter of sympathetic import. In their tragedies, however, Banks and Rowe differed from Shakespeare in dealing with a heroine rather than a hero, and this tendency is to be explained by the developing sentimentalism of the period. The 'she-tragedies' were designed rather to call forth tears on the witnessing of pathetic situations than to summon those higher passions which are the special province of tragic emotion. In this respect they undoubtedly fail, for pathos can never take the place of majesty and terror ; yet Rowe's work is by no means despicable. He has a true sense of blank-verse melody, and at times his lines have a note of real force and strength. In characterization too he was beyond the majority of his companions, so that we can really interest ourselves in the fates of his Lady Jane Gray and his Jane Shore.

(*Lady Jane Gray* was produced at Drury Lane in 1715. The passage given here is based on that in the *Works* of 1792, checked by the first edition.)

A SCENE OF PATHOS

GUILFORD DUDLEY. Ha! seiz'd! shalt thou be seiz'd? and shall I
    stand,
And tamely see thee borne away to death?
Then blasted be my coward name for ever.
No, I will set myself to guard this spot,
To which our narrow empire now is shrunk!
Here will I grow the bulwark of my Queen;
Nor shall the hand of violence profane thee,
Until my breast has borne a thousand wounds,
Till this torn mangled body sink at once
A heap of purple ruin at thy feet.
    LADY JANE GRAY. And could thy rash distracted rage do thus?
Draw thy vain sword against an armed multitude,
Only to have my poor heart split with horror,
To see thee stabb'd and butcher'd here before me?
Oh, call thy better nobler courage to thee,
And let us meet this adverse fate with patience!
Greet our insulting foes with equal tempers,
With even brows, and souls secure of death;
Here stand unmoved; as once the *Roman* senate
Receiv'd fierce *Brennus*, and the conquering *Gauls*,
Till ev'n the rude *Barbarians*, stood amaz'd
At such superior virtue. Be thyself,
For see the trial comes!
            [*Enter* SUSSEX, GARDINER, OFFICERS *and* SOLDIERS.
    SUSSEX. Guards, execute your orders; seize the traitors:
Here my commission ends. To you, my Lord,   [*To* GARDINER.

191

So our great mistress, royal *Mary*, bids,
I leave the full disposal of these pris'ners;
To your wise care the pious Queen commends
Her sacred self, her crown, and what's yet more,
The holy *Roman* church; for whose dear safety,
She wills your utmost diligence be shown,
To bring rebellion to the bar of justice,
Yet farther, to proclaim how much she trusts
In *Winchester's* deep thought, and well-tried faith,
The seal attends to grace those rev'rend hands;
And when I next salute you, I must call you
Chief minister and chancellor of *England*.

GARDINER. Unnumber'd blessings fall upon her head,
My ever-gracious lady! to remember
With such full bounty her old humble beadsman!
For these, her foes, leave me to deal with them.

SUSSEX. The Queen is on her entrance and expects me:
My Lord, farewel.

GARDINER. Farewel, right noble *Sussex*:
Commend me to the Queen's grace; say her bidding
Shall be observ'd by her most lowly creature.   [*Exit* SUSSEX.
Lieutenant of the *Tower*, take hence your pris'ners:
Be it your care to see 'em kept apart,
That they may hold no commerce with each other.

LADY JANE GRAY. That stroke was unexpected.

GUILFORD DUDLEY. Wilt thou part us?

GARDINER. I hold no speech with heretics and traitors.
Lieutenant, see my orders are obey'd.   [*Exit* GARDINER.

GUILFORD DUDLEY. Inhuman, monstrous, unexampl'd cruelty!
Oh, tyrant! but the task becomes thee well;
Thy savage temper joys to do death's office;
To tear the sacred bands of love asunder,
And part those hands which Heav'n itself hath join'd.

DUCHESS OF SUFFOLK. To let us waste the little rest of life
Together, had been merciful.

SUFFOLK. Then it had not
Been done like *Winchester*.

GUILFORD DUDLEY. Thou stand'st unmoved;
Calm temper sits upon thy beauteous brow;
Thy eyes, that flow'd so fast for *Edward's* loss,
Gaze unconcern'd upon the ruin round thee;
As if thou hadst resolv'd to brave thy fate,
And triumph in the midst of desolation.
Ha! see it swells; the liquid crystal rises,
It starts, in spite of thee,—but I will catch it;
Nor let the earth be wet with dew so rich.

LADY JANE GRAY. And dost thou think, my *Guilford*, I can
  see

RESTORATION

My father, mother, and ev'n thee, my husband,
Torn from my side without a pang of sorrow?
How art thou thus unknowing in my heart!
Words cannot tell thee what I feel.   There is
An agonizing softness busy here,
That tugs the strings, that struggles to get loose,
And pour my soul in wailings out before thee.
   GUILFORD DUDLEY. Give way, and let the gushing torrent come;
Behold the tears we bring to swell the deluge,
Till the flood rise upon the guilty world,
And make the ruin common.
   LADY JANE GRAY. *Guilford!* no:
The time for tender thoughts, and soft endearments,
Is fled away and gone: joy has forsaken us;
Our hearts have now another part to play;
They must be steel'd with some uncommon fortitude,
That, fearless, we may tread the paths of horror;
And in despite of fortune and our foes,
Ev'n in the hour of death, be more than conqu'rors.
   GUILFORD DUDLEY. Oh, teach me! say, what energy divine
Inspires thy softer sex, and tender years,
With such unshaken courage?
   LADY JANE GRAY. Truth and innocence;
A conscious knowledge rooted in my heart,
That to have sav'd my country was my duty.
Yes, *England,* yes, my country, I would save thee;
But Heav'n forbids, Heav'n disallows my weakness.
And to some dear selected hero's hand
Reserves the glory of thy great deliverance.
   LIEUTENANT. My Lord, my orders——
   GUILFORD DUDLEY. See we must—must part.
   LADY JANE GRAY. Yet surely we shall meet again.
   GUILFORD DUDLEY. Oh!   Where?
   LADY JANE GRAY. If not on earth, among yon golden stars,
Where other suns arise on other earths,
And happier beings rest on happier seats:
Where, with a reach enlarg'd, our souls shall view
The great Creator's never-ceasing hand
Pour forth new worlds to all eternity,
And people the infinity of space.
   GUILFORD DUDLEY. Fain would I chear my heart with hopes like these;
But my sad thoughts turn ever to the grave,
To that last dwelling, whither now we haste;
Where the black shade shall interpose betwixt us,
And veil thee from these longing eyes for ever.
   LADY JANE GRAY. 'Tis true, by those dark paths our journey leads,

N

And through the vale of death we pass to life,
But what is there in death to blast our hopes?
Behold the universal works of nature,
Where life still springs from death.   To us the sun
Dies ev'ry night, and ev'ry morn revives:
The flow'rs, which Winter's icy hand destroy'd,
Lift their fair heads, and live again in Spring.
Mark with what hopes, upon the furrow'd plain,
The careful ploughman casts the pregnant grain;
There hid, as in a grave a-while it lies,
Till the revolving season bids it rise;
Till nature's genial pow'rs command a birth;
And potent, call it from the teeming earth;
Then large increase the buried treasures yield,
And with full harvest crown the plenteous field.

10. SIR ROBERT HOWARD (1626–98)

The Committee

Hardly any play of the Restoration period had such a contemporary success as *The Committee*, written by Dryden's brother-in-law, Sir Robert Howard.   To a certain extent this success is to be ascribed to the fact that this comedy of satirically presented Puritan manners pleased the new audience of courtiers and their satellites ; but there is in the play as well a genuine comic spirit, which makes it deserve remembrance.   Howard was by no means a mediocre writer.   He has penned some excellent criticism, and his tragedy *The Duke of Lerma* has a certain strength.   In *The Committee*, while he lacks even Dryden's blundering wit, he shows himself as a not unable follower of Ben Jonson, presenting in rude outline his gallery of caricatured types.   Colonels Careless and Blunt are, of course, ordinary gallants, but Mrs Day, the translated kitchen-wench, Day, her husband, Abel, her son, and the clerk Obadiah, have the familiar 'humours' featuring.   The triumph of the comedy, however, was assured by none of these. The character who made the greatest appeal was the faithful but *gauche* Teg or Teague, the first Irish stage servant, who helps to keep the plot in motion, and who provides most of the merriment in the piece.

(*The Committee* was produced at the Theatre Royal about 1662. The extract below is taken from the *Works* of 1722.)

A MESSAGE AND ITS DELIVERY

LIEUTENANT. Hark ye, Colonel; what if you did visit this translated Kitchen-Maid?

TEG. Well, how is that? a Kitchen-maid? where is she now?

BLUNT. The Lieutenant advises well.

RESTORATION

CARELESS. Nay, stay, stay; in the first Place I'll send *Teg* to her, to tell her I have a little Business with her, and desire to know when I may have leave to wait on her.

BLUNT. We shall have *Teg* mistake again.

TEG. How is that now? I will not mistake that Kitchen-maid? Whither must I go now, to mistake that Kitchen-maid?

CARELESS. But d'ye hear, *Teg*? you must take no Notice of that, upon thy Life; but on the contrary, at every Word you must say, Your Ladyship, and Your Honour; as for Example, when you have made a Leg, you must begin you thus; My Master presents his Service to your Ladyship, and having some Business with your Honour, desires to know when he may have Leave to wait upon your Ladyship.

TEG. Well, that I will do. But was she your Father's Kitchen-maid?

CARELESS. Why, what then?

TEG. Upon my Shoul, I shall laugh upon her Face, for all I wou'd not have a Mind to do it.

CARELESS. Not for a hundred Pounds, *Teg*; you must be sure to set your Countenance, and look very soberly, before you begin.

TEG. If I shou'd think then of any Kettles, or Spits, or any thing that will put a Mind into my Head of a Kitchen, I shou'd laugh then, shou'd I not?

CARELESS. Not for a thousand Pounds, *Teg*; thou may'st undo us all.

TEG. Well, I will hope I will not laugh then: I will keep my Mouth if I can, that I will, from running to one Side, and t'other Side. Well now, where does this Mrs *Tay* live?

LIEUTENANT. Come, *Teg*, I'll walk along with thee, and shew thee the House, that thou mayest not mistake that however.

[TEG *goes off and arrives at* MRS DAY'S *House.*

TEG. Well now, who are all you?

ARBELLA. What's here, an *Irish* Elder come to examine us all?

TEG. Well now, what is your Names, every one? . . . Well, cannot some of you all say nothing?

MRS DAY. Why how now Sauce-box? What wou'd you have? What, have you left your Manners without? Go out, and fetch 'em in.

TEG. What shou'd I fetch now?

MRS DAY. D'you know who you speak to, Sirrah?

TEG. Well, what are you then? upon my Shoul, in my own Country they can tell who I am.

ABEL. You must not be so saucy unto her Honour.

TEG. Well, I will knock you, if you be saucy with me then. . . . Is there none of you that I must speak to now?

ARBELLA. Now, Wench, if he shou'd be sent to us.   [*Aside.*

TEG. Well, I wou'd have one Mrs *Tay* speak unto me.

MRS DAY. Well, Sirrah, I am she; what's your Business?

TEG. O so then, are you Mrs *Tay*?—Well,—I will look well first, and I will set my Face in some Worship; yes indeed that I will; and I will tell her then what I will speak to her.   [*Aside*.

RUTH. How the Fellow begins to mould himself!

ARBELLA. And tempers his Chops like a Hound that has lap'd before his Meat was cold enough.

RUTH. He looks as if he had some Gifts to pour forth; those are Mr *Day's* own white Eyes before he begins to say Grace: Now for a Speech ratling in his Kecher, as if his Words stumbled in their Way.

TEG. Well, now I will tell thee, i'faith: My Master the good Colonel *Careless,* bid me ask thy good Ladyship—upon my Soul now the Laugh will come upon me.

                    [*He laughs always when he says Ladyship or Honour.*

MRS DAY. Sirrah, Sirrah; what, were you sent to abuse me? . . .

TEG. I'faith now I do not abuse thy good Honour,—I cannot help my Laugh now, I will try again now; I will not think of a Kitchen then :—My Master wou'd know of your Ladyship——

MRS DAY. Did your Master send you to abuse me, you Rascal? By my Honour, Sirrah——

TEG. Why do'st thou mock thy self now, Joy?

MRS DAY. How, Sirrah, do I mock my self?   This is some *Irish* Traytor.

TEG. I am no Traytor, that I am not; I am an *Irish* Rebel; you are cozen'd now.

MRS DAY. Sirrah, Sirrah, I will make you know who I am.—An impudent *Irish* Rascal!

ABEL. He seemeth a dangerous Fellow, and of a bold seditious Spirit.

MRS DAY. You are a bloody Rascal, I warrant ye.

TEG. You are a foolish brabble bribble Woman, that you are.

ABEL. Sirrah, we that are at the Head of Affairs must punish your Sauciness.

TEG. You shall take a Knock upon your Pate, if you are saucy with me, that I shall; you Son of a Round-head, you.

MRS DAY. Ye Rascally Varlet, get you out of my Doors.

TEG. Will not I give you my Message then?

MRS DAY. Get you out, Rascal.

TEG. I pr'y thee let me tell thee my Message.

MRS DAY. Get you out, I say.

TEG. Well then I care not neither; the Devil take your Ladyship, and Honourship, and Kitchenship too; there now.

11. THOMAS SHADWELL (1640–92)

Epsom Wells

The comedy of manners presents us with the graces, follies, intrigues, and brilliance of the fashionable world of the Restoration.   The life depicted may perhaps be coarse and immoral, but

196

RESTORATION

the fineness of the wit and the polish of the dialogue are superb. In Shadwell we see the other side of the picture. A follower of Ben Jonson, he delights in presenting 'humours' on the stage, and these 'humours' he finds not so much in the world of high life, as among those just below that circle, among those who were denizens of Alsatia, and among country justices and loutish fools. The whole texture of Shadwell's comedies is, therefore, rougher than that of Etherege and Congreve. His plays are always bustling, with much physical action and constantly changing scenes. In language, too, he makes few pretensions to wit, and, if he is not as dull as Dryden would have made us believe, he has none of the refinements of the manners' style. Shadwell, on the other hand, is a dramatist of considerable importance. He has a sense of humour—somewhat solid at times, it must be confessed—and some of his characters are living creations. More vital than all is his atmosphere, for he, perhaps better than any playwright of the time, paints for us the ordinary life of the Restoration period, with all its brutality and with all its crudity. When Sir Walter Scott wanted local colour for a seventeenth-century novel he turned to *The Squire of Alsatia*, recognizing that here as nowhere else he could find naturalistic depiction of the times. *Epsom Wells* is one of the best of Shadwell's productions. Its main theme is the pursuit of Lucia and Carolina by the two gallants Bevil and Rains, but alongside this main plot he introduces many scenes dealing with his beloved 'humours'— Clodpate, the country justice, Kick and Cuff, two "cheating, sharking, cowardly Bullies," Bisket, a comfit-maker, and a whole set of impudent and frail ladies.

(*Epsom Wells* was produced in 1672. The following extract is taken from the edition of 1693.)

COUNTRY LIFE AND TOWN LIFE

LUCIA. Prethee stay with me, that I may be no longer pester'd with this Country Coxcomb.

CAROLINA. Would'st thou have me be so barbarous to interrupt Lovers.

LUCIA. He a Lover! yes, of a clear Title in his next Purchace, his Dapple Mare, a dear year of Corn, or so.

CAROLINA. Come, he has as violent a substantial Country Passion for you, as one would wish; and I will leave you to him.

LUCIA. You mischievous Creature, I'll be reveng'd on you.

[*Exit* CAROLINA.

CLODPATE. If my propositions be not reasonable, I'll ne'er pretend to serve my Country more.

LUCIA. A pretty Country to be serv'd by such Fellows.

CLODPATE. In that noble Brick-house, moted round with Turrets

197

and fine things, that I now spoke of, in the best hunting Country in *Europe*, with a thousand pounds a year will I jointure you.

LUCIA. 'Tis not profit, but honour I respect; and I have vow'd never to Marry one that cannot make me a Lady, and you are no Knight.

CLODPATE. A Knight, no I thank you; why I have known a Fishmonger Knighted: Knighthood's a pretty bawble for a Fellow to play with that is no Gentleman. But what needs he that is a Gentleman desire to be more?

LUCIA. But, methinks, that name of *Clodpate* does not sound well without a title.

CLODPATE. I thank you heartily; my name is now *Hugh Clodpate*; and I should give two or three hundred pounds to add three Letters to it, Sir *Hugh Clodpate*: no, no, I can't make so much on't again.

LUCIA. Oh, a Knight is such a thing!

CLODPATE. Such a thing! has he more hands or legs, or more brains than another man?

LUCIA. But if I could be content without being a Lady, I have vow'd to spend all my life in *London*.

CLODPATE. Pox on her; live in *London* did she say? Death, have you vow'd to live in *London* say you?

LUCIA. Yes, is that so wonderful? why people do really live no where else; they breath, and move, and have a kind of insipid, dull being; but there is no life but in *London*.

CLODPATE. *London*! that sink of Sin.

LUCIA. I believe there is no Village but sins as much, in proportion to the bigness; only your Country Sins are something the more block-headed Sins.

CLODPATE. Madam, give me leave to ask you one question.

LUCIA. You may.

CLODPATE. Do you resolve to live honest?

LUCIA. 'Tis a familiar question; you had need ask my leave first.

CLODPATE. Why you may as reasonably expect to preserve your Health in a Pest-house, as your Chastity in that damn'd lascivious Town.

LUCIA. You are rude, Sir.

CLODPATE. Come, Madam, Plain-dealing is a Jewel. But can you prefer an idle, scandalous *London*-life before a pretty, innocent, huswifely-life in the Country, to look to your Family and visit your Neighbours.

LUCIA. To see my Ducks and Geese fed, and cram my own Chickens.

CLODPATE. Ay.

LUCIA. To have my Closet stink, like a Pothecary's Shop, with Drugs and Medecines, to administer to my sick Neighbours, and spoil the next Quack's Practice with the Receipt-book that belongs to the Family.

CLODPATE. Very well.

LUCIA. And then to have one approved Green-salve, and dress sore Legs with it; and all this to deserve the name of as good a neighbourly Body as ever came into *Sussex*.

CLODPATE. Very good.

LUCIA. Never to hear a Fiddle, but such as sounds worse than the Tongs and Key, or a Gridiron; never to read better Poetry than *John Hopkins* or *Robert Wisdom's* vile Metre; Nor hear better Singing than a Company of Peasants praising God with doleful, untunable, hoarse Voices, that are only fit to be heard under the Gallows.

CLODPATE. However you make bold with the Country, be not prophane. Is not this better than any thing in that stinking Town?

LUCIA. Stinking Town! I had rather be Countess of *Puddle-Duck*, than Queen of *Sussex*.

CLODPATE. Oh foh—but ah, the excellent fresh Air upon the Downs.

LUCIA. So there's fresh Air in a Wilderness, if one could be contented with Bears and Wolves for her Companions. But, Sir, in short, I am resolv'd to live in *London*, and at or very near the Court too.

CLODPATE. 's Death the Court! I shall not only be Cuckolded, but lose all my Country Interest; Madam, I beg your pardon, I shall take my leave; I am not cut out for a *Londoner* or a *Courtier*; fare you well, good Madam, though I like your Person pretty well, I like not your Conditions; I'd not marry a *London* Cherubin.

LUCIA. Farewel, Sir; but I'll not be wholly ungrateful for the Address you have honoured me with: know then my Friend *Carolina* is the most averse to *London*, and most infatuated with the Love of the Country.

CLODPATE. Uds bud, infatuated; pray change that word if you please.

LUCIA. You know my meaning by it: she and I are parting, because she will not with patience hear of returning to *London*; she calls it nothing but vain, obscene, wicked, filthy, Popish place.

CLODPATE. Ha! how's this? I did not think she had so much sense.   [*Aside*.

LUCIA. She often says, she had rather marry a Country Justice of five hundred pounds a year, than a Man of five thousand pounds a year in *London*; nay, than a Duke at Court.

CLODPATE. She's an ingenious Woman, Gad-sooks. [*Aside*] I had rather marry her naked than you with all your Portion, Madam. But a pox on't, I had damn'd ill luck to make my application to you first, as the Devil would have it.

LUCIA. This is a very Country Courtier—— [*aside*] Here she comes, let's withdraw; I will tell you more, and we'll consult about this business.

199

12. JOHN DRYDEN (1631–1700)

Secret Love

The 'humours' style was too coarse in texture to please the gallants of the Restoration for long. They loved wit themselves, and they longed to hear that wit upon the stage. The first movements toward the new style are to be traced in the early works of John Dryden, who, a keen student of pre-Restoration literature, benefited much from Fletcher and those other dramatists who seemed to be striving toward a fresh method of expression and toward a new stress in comedy. Dryden, however, was too robust himself to capture the full secret of Restoration airiness; there is a slight trembling of emotion in his treatment of Celadon and Florimel which distinguishes it from the pure intellectualism of the later comedy of manners. Still, Dryden is an important figure in the development of English comedy, and if we compare his works with those of Congreve on the one hand, and with those of Day,[1] Fletcher, and Shirley on the other, we appreciate the position he held as a link between the new and the old. There may be noted in the two passages given below the emphasis which is laid on dialogue itself. The comedy of humours depends on eccentricity; these scenes are based on fashionable society manners and cultured gaiety.

(*Secret Love; or, The Maiden Queen* was produced at the Theatre Royal in 1667. The following extracts are taken from the *Works* of 1725.)

THE CHARM OF A MASKED WIT

FLORIMEL. A pretty odd kind of Fellow this; he fits my Humour rarely—[*aside*].

FLAVIA. You are as unconstant as the Moon.

FLORIMEL. You wrong him, he's as constant as the Sun; he would see all the World in twenty four Hours.

CELADON. 'Tis very true, Madam; but, like him, I would visit, and away.

FLORIMEL. For what an unreasonable thing it were to stay long, be troublesome, and hinder a Lady of a fresh Lover.

CELADON. A rare Creature this!—Besides, Madam, how like a Fool a Man looks, when, after all his Eagerness of two Minutes before, he shrinks into a faint Kiss, and a cold Compliment. Ladies both, into your Hands I commit my self; share me betwixt you.

FLAVIA. I'll have nothing to do with you, since you cannot be constant to one.

---

[1] A comparison of *Humour out of Breath* (see pp. 99–102) with *Secret Love* may suggest that Dryden was not ignorant of his predecessor's work. It may be noted that the names of the heroines are identical.

RESTORATION

CELADON. Nay, rather than lose either of you, I'll do more; I'll be constant to an hundred of you: Or, (if you will needs fetter me to one), agree the Matter between yourselves; and the most handsome take me.

FLORIMEL. Tho' I am not she, yet since my Mask's down, and you cannot convince me, have a good Faith of my Beauty, and for once I take you for my Servant.

CELADON. And for once I'll make a blind Bargain with you: Strike Hands; is't a Match, Mistress?

FLORIMEL. Done, Servant.

CELADON. Now I am sure I have the worst on't: For you see the worst of me, and that I do not of you, 'till you shew your Face —Yet, now I think on't, you must be handsome——

FLORIMEL. What kind of Beauty do you like?

CELADON. Just such a one as yours.

FLORIMEL. What's that?

CELADON. Such an oval Face, clear Skin, hazel Eyes, thick brown Eye-brows, and Hair as you have for all the World.

FLAVIA. But I can assure you she has nothing of all this.

CELADON. Hold thy Peace, Envy; nay, I can be constant an I set on't.

FLORIMEL. 'Tis true she tells you.

CELADON. Ay, ay, you may Slander your self as you please; then you have—let me see.

FLORIMEL. I'll swear you sha'not see.

CELADON. A turn'd up Nose, that gives an Air to your Face: Oh, I find I am more and more in love with you! a full neather Lip, an Out-mouth, that makes mine water at it: The bottom of your Cheeks a little blub, and two Dimples when you smile; for your Stature 'tis well, and for your Wit, 'twas given you by one that knew it had been thrown away upon an ill Face; come, you are handsome, there's no denying it.

FLORIMEL. Can you settle your Spirits to see an ugly Face, and not be frighted? I could find in my Heart to lift up my Mask and disabuse you.

CELADON. I defie your Mask, would you would try the Experiment.

FLORIMEL. No, I won't; for your Ignorance is the Mother of your Devotion to me.

CELADON. Since you will not take the Pains to convert me, I'll make bold to keep my Faith: A miserable Man I am sure you have made me.

FLAVIA. This is pleasant.

CELADON. It may be so to you, but it is not to me; for ought I see, I am going to be the most constant *Maudlin*——

FLORIMEL. 'Tis very well, *Celadon*, you can be constant to one you have never seen; and have forsaken all you have seen.

CELADON. It seems you know me then: Well, if thou should'st

prove one of my cast Mistresses, I would use thee most damnably, for offering to make me love thee twice.

FLORIMEL. You are i' th' right: An old Mistress or Servant is an old Tune, the Pleasure on't is past, when we have once learn'd it.

FLAVIA. But what Woman in the World would you wish her like?

CELADON. I have heard of one *Florimel*, the Queen's Ward, would she were as like her for Beauty, as she is for Humour.

FLAVIA. Do you hear that, Cousin?   [*To* FLORIMEL *aside.*

FLORIMEL. *Florimel's* not handsome: Besides, she's unconstant; and only loves for some few Days.

CELADON. If she loves for shorter time than I, she must love by Winter Days and Summer Nights i'faith.

FLORIMEL. When you see us together you shall judge: In the mean time, adieu sweet Servant.

CELADON. Why, you won't be so inhuman to carry away my Heart, and not so much as tell me where I may hear News on't?

FLORIMEL. I mean to keep it safe for you; for if you had it, you would bestow it worse: Farewel, I must see a Lady.

CELADON. So must I too, if I can pull off your Mask.

FLORIMEL. You will not be so rude, I hope.

CELADON. By this Light, but I will.

FLORIMEL. By this Leg, but you shan't.

[*Exeunt* FLORIMEL *and* FLAVIA *running.*

RESTORATION CHIVALRY

CELADON. Nay, i'faith I am got betwixt you and home, you are my Pris'ner, Lady Bright, till you resolve me one Question. [*She makes signs she is dumb.*] Pox; I think she's dumb: What a Vengeance dost thou at Court, with such a rare face, without a Tongue to answer to a kind Question? Art thou dumb indeed? then thou canst tell no tales.   [*Goes to kiss her.*

FLORIMEL. Hold, hold, you are not mad!

CELADON. Oh, my Miss in a Mask! have you found your Tongue?

FLORIMEL. 'Twas time, I think; what had become of me if I had not?

CELADON. Methinks your Lips had done as well.

FLORIMEL. Ay, if my Mask had been over'em, as it was when you met me in the Walks.

CELADON. Well; will you believe me another time? Did not I say you were infinitely handsome: They may talk of *Florimel* if they will, but i'faith she must come short of you.

FLORIMEL. Have you seen her, then?

CELADON. I look'd a little that way, but I had soon enough of her, she is not to be seen twice without a Surfeit.

FLORIMEL. However you are beholden to her, they say she loves you.

RESTORATION

CELADON. By Fate she shan't love me: I have told her a piece of my Mind already: Pox o' these coming Women: They set a Man to Dinner before he has an Appetite. [FLAVIA *at the Door*.

FLAVIA. *Florimel*, you are call'd within. [*Exit*.

CELADON. I hope in the Lord you are not *Florimel*.

FLORIMEL. Ev'n she, at your Service; the same kind and coming *Florimel*, you have describ'd.

CELADON. Why then we are agreed already: I am as kind and coming as you for the Heart of you: I knew at first we two were _____ e another.

_____ out Railery, are you in Love?

_____ ly much, that contrary to my own Maxims, _____ ence I could marry you.

_____ o, 'tis not come to that yet: But if you are really _____ done me the greatest Pleasure in the World.

_____ t Pleasure, and a better too I have in store for you. _____ is Animal, call'd a Lover, I have long'd to see these

_____ ure you walk'd with your Mask on all the while; for if _____ en seen, you could not have been without your Wish.

_____ L. I warrant you mean an ordinary whining Lover; but _____ ve other proofs of Love ere I believe it.

_____ ON. You shall have the best that I can give you.

_____ MEL. I would have a Lover, that if need be, should hang _____ drown himself, break his Neck, poison himself, for very _____ : He that will scruple this, is an impudent Fellow, if he says _____ love.

_____ DON. Pray, Madam, which of these four things would you _____ ur Lover to do? For a Man's but a Man, he cannot hang, _____ own, and break his Neck, and poison himself, all together.

_____ ORIMEL. Well then, because you are but a Beginner, and I _____ uld not discourage you, any of these shall serve your turn in a fair way.

CELADON. I am much deceiv'd in those Eyes of yours, if a Treat, a Song, and the Fiddles, be not a more acceptable Proof of Love to you, than any of those Tragical ones you have mentioned.

FLORIMEL. However, you will grant it is but decent you should be pale, and lean, and melancholick, to shew you are in Love: And that I shall require of you when I see you next.

CELADON. When you see me next? Why you do not make a Rabbet of me, to be lean at twenty four Hours warning? In the meanwhile, we burn Day-light, lose Time and Love. . . .

FLORIMEL. Shall I make a Proposition to you? I will give you a whole year of Probation to love me in; to grow reserv'd, discreet, sober and faithful, and to pay me all the Services of a Lover——

CELADON. And at the end of it you'll marry me?

FLORIMEL. If neither of us alter our Minds before——

CELADON. By this Light a necessary Clause—But if I pay in all

203

the foresaid Services before the Day, you shall be obliged to take me sooner into Mercy.

FLORIMEL. Provided if you prove unfaithful, then your time of a Twelve-month to be prolong'd; so many Services, I will bate you so many Days or Weeks; so many Faults, I will add to your 'Prentiship so much more: And of all this, I only to be Judge.

13. SIR GEORGE ETHEREGE (1635-91)

The Man of Mode

The gay Sir George Etherege, courtier, ambassador, and wit, is a representative figure of the Restoration period. Adorned with grace of manner, he captured many hearts; brilliant and fascinating, he endeared himself to the King; talented with parts, he flung off an idle song or two in addition to three plays which mark the beginning of the manners style. Characteristically, for he was no professional such as Dryden was proud to be, his work is not voluminous. Many years elapsed between the productions of his three plays. The atmosphere is that of aristocratic carelessness, conscious that success will add lustre to the already distinguished name, but that the impression of too great application will savour a trifle of the "mechanick." Etherege's plays are not uniformly good. *Love in a Tub* is an unequal first attempt; *She Wou'd if she Cou'd* comes near to painting the artificiality of contemporary society; in *The Man of Mode* at last Etherege captures the secret of the new style, creating in Sir Fopling Flutter a brilliantly conceived portrait of the Frenchi-fied gallant. Etherege, it is true, lacks the fine balance and polish of his follower, Congreve; but his dialogue shows that appreciation for wit, that endeavour at one and the same time to reproduce and to ridicule the language of high society, which, brought to perfection, makes the glory of Congreve's dramas. A comparison with Dryden will show in what direction the spirit of comedy is moving in this age.

(*The Man of Mode; or, Sr Fopling Flutter* was produced in 1676. The following extract is taken from the edition of the same year.)

FRENCH AIRS AND ENGLISH WIT

Enter SIR FOPLING *and others in Masques.*

DORIMANT. What's here, Masquerades?

HARRIET. I thought that foppery had been left off, and people might have been in private with a Fiddle.

DORIMANT. 'Tis endeavour'd to be kept on foot still by some who find themselves the more acceptable, the less they are known.

204

YOUNG BELLAIR. This must be Sir *Fopling*.

MEDLEY. That extraordinary habit shews it.

YOUNG BELLAIR. What are the rest?

MEDLEY. A company of French rascals whom he pick'd up in *Paris* and has brought over to be his dancing Equipage on these occasions! Make him own himself; a Fool is very troublesome when he presumes he is Incognito.

SIR FOPLING. Do you know me?   [*To* HARRIET.

HARRIET. Ten to one but I guess at you!

SIR FOPLING. Are you women as fond of a Vizard as we men are?

HARRIET. I am very fond of a Vizard that covers a face I do not like, Sir.

YOUNG BELLAIR. Here are no Masques, you see, Sir, but those which came with you; this was intended a private meeting, but because you look like a Gentleman, if you will discover your self and we know you to be such, you shall be welcome.

SIR FOPLING. Dear *Bellair*.   [*Pulling off his Mask.*

MEDLEY. Sir *Fopling*! how came you hither?

SIR FOPLING. Faith, as I was coming late from *White-Hall*, after the *Kings* Couchée, one of my people told me he had heard Fiddles at my Lady *Townleys*, and——

DORIMANT. You need not say any more, Sir.

SIR FOPLING. *Dorimant*, let me kiss thee.

DORIMANT. Hark you, Sir *Fopling*!   [*Whispers.*

SIR FOPLING. Enough, enough, Courtage. A pretty kind of young Woman that, *Medley*, I observ'd her in the Mail more Eveliè than our English Women commonly are, prithee what is she?

MEDLEY. The most noted Coquetté in Town; beware of her.

SIR FOPLING. Let her be what she will, I know how to take my Measures, in *Paris* the Mode is to flatter the Prudè, laugh at the Faux-proudè, make serious love to the Demi-proudè, and only railly with the Coquetté. *Medley*, what think you?

MEDLEY. That for all this smattering of the Mathematicks, you may be out in your Judgment at Tennis.

SIR FOPLING. What a Coque a Lasne is this? I talk of Women and thou answer'st Tennis.

MEDLEY. Mistakes will be for want of apprehension.

SIR FOPLING. I am very glad of the acquaintance I have with this Family.

MEDLEY. My Lady truly is a good Woman.

SIR FOPLING. Ah! *Dorimant*, Courtage I would say, would thou hadst spent the last Winter in *Paris* with me. When thou wer't there La corneùs and Sallyes were the only habitudes we had, a Comedian would have been a boné fortune. No stranger ever pass'd his time so well as I did some months before I came over. I was well receiv'd in a dozen families, where all the Women of quality us'd to visit; I have intrigues to tell thee, more pleasant, than ever thou read'st in a Novel.

HARRIET. Write 'em, Sir, and oblige us Women! our Language wants such little stories.

SIR FOPLING. Writing Madam's a Mechanick part of Witt! A Gentleman should never go beyond a Song or a Billèt.

HARRIET. *Bussiè* was a Gentleman.

SIR FOPLING. Who, *D'Ambois*?

MEDLEY. Was there ever such a brisk blockhead?

HARRIET. Not *D'Ambois*, Sir but *Rubutin*. He who writ the Loves of *France*.

SIR FOPLING. That may be, Madam! many Gentlemen do things that are below 'em. Damn your Authors, Courtage, Women are the prettiest things we can fool away our time with.

HARRIET. I hope ye have weari'd your self to night at Court, Sir, and will not think of fooling with any body here.

SIR FOPLING. I cannot complain of my Fortune there, Madam —Dorimant——

DORIMANT. Again!

SIR FOPLING. Courtage, a pox on't! I have something to tell thee. When I had made my Court within, I came out and flung my self upon the Matt under the state i' th' outward room, i' th' midst of half a dozen Beauties who were withdrawn to jeer among themselves, as they call'd it.

DORIMANT. Did you know 'em?

SIR FOPLING. Not one of 'em, by Heav'ns! not I. But they were all your friends.

DORIMANT. How are you sure of that?

SIR FOPLING. Why, we laugh'd at all the Town; spar'd no body but yourself; they found me a man for their purpose.

DORIMANT. I know you are malitious to your power.

SIR FOPLING. And faith! I had occasion to show it, for I never saw more gaping fools at a Ball or on a Birth-day.

DORIMANT. You learn'd who the women were?

SIR FOPLING. No matter! they frequent the Drawing Room.

DORIMANT. And entertain themselves pleasantly at the expence of all the Fops who come there.

SIR FOPLING. That's their bus'ness; faith, I sifted 'em, and find they have a sort of wit among them—— Ah filthy.

[Pinches a Tallow Candle.

DORIMANT. Look, he has been pinching the Tallow Candle.

SIR FOPLING. How can you breathe in a Room where there's Grease frying! *Dorimant*, thou art intimate with my Lady, advise her for her own sake and the good Company that comes hither to burn Wax lights.

HARRIET. What are these Masquerades who stand so obsequiously at a distance?

SIR FOPLING. A set of Balladins, whom I pickt out of the best in *France* and brought over, with a Flutes deux or two, my Servants; they shall entertain you.

RESTORATION

HARRIET. I had rather see you dance your self, Sir *Fopling*.

SIR FOPLING. And I had rather do it—all the company knows it —but Madam——

MEDLEY. Come, come! no excuses, Sir *Fopling*.

SIR FOPLING. By Heav'ns, *Medley*——

MEDLEY. Like a woman I find you must be struggl'd with before one brings you to what you desire.

HARRIET. Can he dance?   [*Aside.*

EMILIA. And fence and sing too, if you'l believe him.

DORIMANT. He has no more excellence in his heels than in his head. He went to *Paris* a plain bashful English Blockhead, and is return'd a fine undertaking *French Fopp*.

MEDLEY. I cannot prevail.

SIR FOPLING. Do not think it want of Complaisance, Madam.

HARRIET. You are too well bred to want that, Sir *Fopling*. I believe it want of power.

SIR FOPLING. By Heav'ns and so it is. I have sat up so damn'd late and drunk so curs'd hard since I came to this lewd Town, that I am fit for nothing but low dancing now, a Corant, a Boreè, or a Minnuét; but St *Andrè* tells me, if I will but be regular in one Month I shall rise agen. Pox on this Debauchery. [*Endeavours at a Caper.*

EMILIA. I have heard your dancing much commended.

SIR FOPLING. It had the good Fortune to please in *Paris*, I was judg'd to rise within an inch as high as the Basqué, in an Entry I danc'd there.

HARRIET. I am mightily taken with this Fool, let us sit: here's a seat, Sir *Fopling*.

SIR FOPLING. At your feet, Madam; I can be no where so much at ease: by your leave, Gown.

HARRIET *and* EMILIA. Ah! you'll spoil it.

SIR FOPLING. No matter, my Cloaths are my Creatures. I make 'em to make my Court to you Ladies. Hey—[*dance*] Quon Comencè—to an English Dancer English motions! I was forc'd to entertain this Fellow, one of my set miscarrying—Oh horrid! leave your damn'd manner of dancing, and put on the French Air: have you not a pattern before you—pretty well! imitation in time may bring him to something.

14. WILLIAM WYCHERLEY (1640–1715)

The Country Wife

In *The Country Wife* the Restoration comedy of manners reached the acme of impropriety, yet this play contains some of the most brilliant scenes produced in an age when wit was sharpened upon wit and lightness of touch descended even upon dullards and dunces. In the Restoration wit can hardly be separated from gallantry, for intrigue ruled the life of the day, and men and women filled their hours with the excitement of the chase. This life the comedy of manners sets itself out to depict. It deals joyously with the affairs of the courtiers and throws its ridicule on those who, like Pinchwife, adopt a standard of existence which is foreign to the easy standards of contemporary society. In *The Country Wife* the morose and jealous husband thinks to restrain his country bride from the temptations of fashion, but, by his very insistence, serves to drive her into them. The scene selected here is that in which Pinchwife, learning that Horner, the universal gallant, is pursuing his wife, bids her write to her lover. The humour of the scene is excellently obtained by the clever contrast of the simple slyness of the girl and the confident folly of the husband, expressed in that language, lucid and precise, which was developed by the masters of the manners style.

(*The Country-Wife* was produced at Drury Lane in 1675. The extract below follows the first quarto of 1675.)

THE WAY OF A WIFE

MRS PINCHWIFE. Indeed and indeed, but I won't, so I won't.

PINCHWIFE. Why?

MRS PINCHWIFE. Because he's in Town; you may send for him if you will.

PINCHWIFE. Very well, you wou'd have him brought to you; is it come to this? I say, take the pen and write, or you'll provoke me.

MRS PINCHWIFE. Lord, what d'ye make a fool of me for? Don't I know that Letters are never writ but from the Countrey to London, and from London into the Countrey? Now he's in Town, and I am in Town too; therefore I can't write to him, you know.

PINCHWIFE [*aside*]. So, I am glad it is no worse; she is innocent enough yet.—Yes, you may, when your Husband bids you, write Letters to people that are in Town.

MRS PINCHWIFE. O, may I so? then I'm satisfied.

PINCHWIFE. Come, begin :—[*Dictates.*] " Sir——"

MRS PINCHWIFE. Shan't I say, " Dear Sir "?—You know one says always something more than bare " Sir."

PINCHWIFE. Write as I bid you, or I will write . . . with this Penknife in your Face.

MRS PINCHWIFE. Nay, good bud—" Sir——"   [*She writes.*

PINCHWIFE. " Though I suffer'd last night your nauseous, loath'd Kisses and Embraces——" Write!

MRS PINCHWIFE. Nay, why shou'd I say so? You know I told you he had a sweet breath.

PINCHWIFE. Write!

MRS PINCHWIFE. Let me but put out *loath'd*.

PINCHWIFE. Write, I say!

MRS PINCHWIFE. Well then.   [*Writes.*

PINCHWIFE. Let's see, what have you writ?—[*Takes the paper and reads.*] "Though I suffer'd last night your kisses and embraces"—Thou impudent creature! where is "nauseous" and "loath'd"?

MRS PINCHWIFE. I can't abide to write such filthy words.

PINCHWIFE. Once more write as I'd have you, and question it not, or I will spoil thy writing with this. I will stab out those eyes that cause my mischief.   [*Holds up the penknife.*

MRS PINCHWIFE. O Lord! I will.

PINCHWIFE. So—so—let's see now.—[*Reads.*] "Though I suffer'd last night your nauseous, loath'd kisses and embraces"—go on—"yet I would not have you presume you shall ever repeat them"—so——   [*She writes.*

MRS PINCHWIFE. I have writ it.

PINCHWIFE. On, then—"I then conceal'd my self from your knowledge, to avoid your insolencies——"   [*She writes.*

MRS PINCHWIFE. So——

PINCHWIFE. "The same reason, now I am out of your hands,——"
                                    [*She writes.*

MRS PINCHWIFE. So——

PINCHWIFE. "Makes me own to you my unfortunate, though innocent frolick, of being in man's cloths——"   [*She writes.*

MRS PINCHWIFE. So——

PINCHWIFE. "That you may for ever more cease to pursue her, who hates and detests you——"   [*She writes on.*

MRS PINCHWIFE. So—h——   [*Sighs.*

PINCHWIFE. What, do you sigh?—"detests you—as much as she loves her Husband and her Honour——"

MRS PINCHWIFE. I vow, Husband, he'll ne'er believe I shou'd write such a Letter.

PINCHWIFE. What, he'd expect a kinder from you? Come, now your name only.

MRS PINCHWIFE. What, shan't I say "Your most faithful, humble Servant till death"?

PINCHWIFE. No, tormenting Fiend!—[*Aside*] Her stile, I find, wou'd be very soft.—Come, wrap it up now, whilest I go fetch wax and a candle; and write on the back side, "For Mr Horner."
                                    [*Exit PINCHWIFE.*

MRS PINCHWIFE. "For Mr Horner."—So, I am glad he has told me his name. Dear Mr Horner! but why should I send thee such a letter, that will vex thee, and make thee angry with me?—Well, I will not send it.—Ay, but then my husband will kill me—for I see plainly, he won't let me love Mr Horner—but what care I for my Husband?—I won't, so I won't, send poor Mr Horner such a Letter—But then my Husband—but oh—what if I writ at bottom, my Husband made me write it?—Ay, but then my Husband wou'd see't—Can one have no shift? ah, a London woman wou'd have had a

O   209

hundred presently. Stay—what if I shou'd write a Letter, and wrap it up like this, and write upon't too? Ay, but then my Husband wou'd see't—I don't know what to do.—But yet y vads I'll try, so I will—for I will not send this letter to poor Mr Horner, come what will on't.

"Dear, sweet Mr Horner—" [*She writes and repeats what she hath writ.*]—so—"my Husband wou'd have me send you a base, rude, unmannerly Letter; but I won't"—so—"and wou'd have me forbid you loving me; but I wont"—so—"and wou'd have me say to you, I hate you, poor Mr Horner; but I won't tell a lye for him"—there—"for I'm sure if you and I were in the Countrey at cards together"—so—"I cou'd not help treading on your Toe under the Table"—so—"or rubbing knees with you, and staring in your face, 'till you saw me"—very well—"and then looking down, and blushing for an hour together"—so—"but I must make haste before my Husband come; and now he has taught me to write Letters, you shall have longer ones from me, who am, dear, dear, poor, dear Mr Horner, your most Humble Friend and Servant to command 'till death, Margery Pinchwife." Stay, I must give him a hint at bottom—so—now wrap it up just like t'other—so—now write "For Mr Horner"—— But oh now, what shall I do with it? for here comes my Husband. [*Enter* PINCHWIFE.

PINCHWIFE [*aside*]. I have been detained by a Sparkish Coxcomb, who pretended a visit to me; but I fear 'twas to my Wife—— What, have you done?

MRS PINCHWIFE. Ay, ay, bud, just now.

PINCHWIFE. Let's see't: what d'ye tremble for? what, you wou'd not have it go?

MRS PINCHWIFE. Here—— [*Aside*] No, I must not give him that: so I had been served if I had given him this.

[*He opens and reads the first letter.*

PINCHWIFE. Come, where's the Wax and Seal?

MRS PINCHWIFE [*aside*]. Lord, what shall I do now? Nay, then, I have it—Pray let me see't. Lord, you think me so errand a fool, I cannot seal a Letter; I will do't, so I will.

[*Snatches the letter from him, changes it for the other, seals it, and delivers it to him.*

PINCHWIFE. Nay, I believe you will learn that, and other things too, which I wou'd not have you.

MRS PINCHWIFE. So, han't I done it curiously?— [*Aside*] I think I have; there's my Letter going to Mr Horner, since he'll needs have me send Letters to Folks.

PINCHWIFE. 'Tis very well; but I warrant, you wou'd not have it go now?

MRS PINCHWIFE. Yes, indeed, but I wou'd, bud, now.

RESTORATION

15. WILLIAM CONGREVE (1670–1729)

The Way of the World

The Way of the World, Congreve's last comedy, is in many ways too fine for the stage. The theatre, as a place of practical art, always demands something that shall have a certain robustness of texture ; there must be an element of melodrama in every successful tragedy and a strain of farce in every successful comedy. Congreve is the perfect stylist, but he is by no means perfect in his plot-construction or in his truth to character. For a *bon mot* he will sacrifice both the one and the other. It is largely because of this that The Way of the World, brilliant in dialogue as it is, has rarely been a great popular success in the theatre. The scene chosen here is from Act IV, when the fascinating Millamant is finally captured by her lover Mirabell. The precision and balance of the prose is exquisite, and might well be compared with the polished and yet less exquisite prose of earlier writers in the same style.

(The Way of the World appeared at Lincoln's Inn Fields in 1700, and was printed the same year. The following extract is taken from the 1710 definitive edition.)

MIRABELL'S PROVISOS

MIRABELL. *Like* Daphne *she, as Lovely and as Coy.* Do you lock your self up from me, to make my Search more curious? Or is this pretty Artifice Contriv'd, to signifie that here the Chace must end, and my Pursuit be crown'd, for you can fly no further?

MILLAMANT. Vanity! No I'll fly and be follow'd to the last Moment, tho' I am upon the very Verge of Matrimony, I expect you should sollicit me as much as if I were wavering at the Grate of a Monastery, with one Foot over the Threshold. I'll be sollicited to the very last, nay and afterwards.

MIRABELL. What, after the last?

MILLAMANT. O, I should think I was poor and had nothing to bestow, if I were reduc'd to an inglorious Ease; and freed from the agreeable Fatigues of Sollicitation.

MIRABELL. But do not you know, that when Favours are conferr'd upon instant and tedious Sollicitation, that they diminish in their Value, and that both the Giver loses the Grace, and the Receiver lessens his Pleasure?

MILLAMANT. It may be in Things of common Application; but never sure in Love. O, I hate a Lover, that can dare to think he draws a Moment's Air, independent on the Bounty of his Mistress. There is not so impudent a Thing in Nature, as the sawcy Look of an assured Man, confident of Success. The Pedantick Arrogance of a very Husband, has not so Pragmatical an Air. Ah! I'll never marry, unless I am first made sure of my Will and Pleasure.

EXTRACTS FROM BRITISH & IRISH PLAYS

MIRABELL. Would you have 'em both before Marriage? Or will you be contented with the first now, and stay for the other 'till after Grace?

MILLAMANT. Ah don't be impertinent. My dear Liberty, shall I leave thee? My faithful Solitude, my darling Contemplation, must I bid you then Adieu? Ay–h adieu—My Morning Thoughts, agreeable Wakings, indolent Slumbers, all ye *douceurs*, ye *Someils du Matin*, adieu—I can't do't, 'tis more than impossible—Positively *Mirabell*, I'll lye a-bed in a Morning as long as I please.

MIRABELL. Then I'll get up in a Morning as early as I please.

MILLAMANT. Ah! Idle Creature, get up when you will—And d'ye hear, I won't be call'd Names after I'm Marry'd; positively I won't be call'd Names.

MIRABELL. Names!

MILLAMANT. Ay, as Wife, Spouse, my Dear, Joy, Jewel, Love, Sweet-heart, and the rest of that nauseous Cant, in which Men and their Wives are so fulsomly familiar,—I shall never bear that— Good *Mirabell* don't let us be familiar or fond, nor kiss before Folks, like my Lady *Fadler* and Sir *Francis*: Nor go to *Hide-Park* together the first *Sunday* in a new Chariot, to provoke Eyes and Whispers; And then never be seen there together again; as if we were proud of one another the first Week, and asham'd of one another ever after. Let us never Visit together, nor go to a Play together, but let us be very strange and well bred: Let us be as strange as if we had been marry'd a great while; and as well bred as if we were not marry'd at all.

MIRABELL. Have you any more Conditions to offer? Hitherto your Demands are pretty reasonable.

MILLAMANT. Trifles—As Liberty to pay and receive Visits to and from whom I please; to write and receive Letters, without Interrogatories or wry Faces on your Part; to wear what I please; and chuse Conversation with regard only to my own Taste; to have no Obligation upon me to converse with Wits that I don't like, because they are your Acquaintance; or to be intimate with Fools, because they may be your Relations. Come to Dinner when I please, dine in my Dressing-Room when I'm out of Humour, without giving a Reason. To have my Closet inviolate; to be sole Empress of my Tea-Table, which you must never presume to approach without first asking leave. And lastly where-ever I am, you shall always knock at the Door before you come in. These Articles subscrib'd, if I continue to endure you a little longer, I may by degrees dwindle into a Wife.

MIRABELL. Your Bill of Fare is something advanc'd in this latter Account. Well, have I Liberty to offer Conditions—That when you are dwindled into a Wife, I may not be beyond measure enlarg'd into a Husband.

MILLAMANT. You have free leave, propose your utmost, speak and spare not.

212

RESTORATION

MIRABELL. I thank you. *Imprimis* then, I covenant that your Acquaintance be general; that you admit no sworn Confident, or Intimate of your own Sex; no she Friend to skreen her Affairs under your Countenance, and tempt you to make Trial of a mutual Secresie. No Decoy-Duck to wheadle you a *Fop—scrambling* to the Play in a Mask—Then bring you home in a pretended Fright, when you think you shall be found out—And rail at me for missing the Play, and disappointing the Frolick which you had to pick me up and prove my Constancy.

MILLAMANT. Detestable *Imprimis*! I go to the Play in a Mask!

MIRABELL. *Item*, I Article that you continue to like your own Face, as long as I shall: And while it passes currant with me, that you endeavour not to new Coin it. To which End, together with all Vizards for the Day, I prohibit all Masks for the Night, made of Oil'd-skins and I know not what—Hog's Bones, Hare's Gall, Pig Water, and the Marrow of a roasted Cat. In short, I forbid all Commerce with the Gentlewoman in *what-d'ye-call-it* Court. *Item*, I shut my Doors against all Bauds with Baskets, and penny-worths of *Muslin, China, Fans, Atlasses,* &c. . . . Lastly, to the Dominion of the *Tea-Table* I submit.—But with *proviso*, that you exceed not in your Province; but restrain your self to native and simple *Tea-Table* Drinks, as *Tea, Chocolate,* and *Coffee*. As likewise to Genuine and Authoriz'd *Tea-Table* Talk—Such as mending of Fashions, spoiling Reputations, railing at absent Friends, and so forth—But that on no Account you encroach upon the Mens Prerogative, and presume to drink Healths, or toast Fellows; for prevention of which, I banish all *Foreign Forces,* all Auxiliaries of the *Tea-Table,* as *Orange-Brandy,* all *Anniseed, Cinamon, Citron* and *Barbado's-waters,* together with *Ratafia* and the most noble Spirit of *Clary.*—But for *Couslip-Wine, Poppy-Water,* and all *Dormitives,* those I allow.—These *Proviso's* admitted, in other things I may prove a tractable and complying Husband.

MILLAMANT. O horrid *Proviso's*! filthy strong Waters! I toast Fellows, Odious Men! I hate your odious *Proviso's*.

VI. EIGHTEENTH CENTURY

AFTER Otway truly great tragedy vanished. For some years neo-classic restraint ruled in the realms of Melpomene, with results disastrous and absurd. Addison's *Cato*, because of his adoption of a non-emotional theme, is readable, and Ambrose Philips' *The Distrest Mother* has certain passages of moderate strength, but beside these there is a sorry rout of dull and tedious dramas. At one time it seemed as if the domestic tragedy were to bear fruit. Lillo's *The London Merchant* created a furore, but few of his imitators, save Moore in *The Gamester*, succeeded in achieving even qualified success. At another time it seemed as if romanticism were to bring new life-blood to the tragic stage ; but Home's *Douglas* has only historical value and romanticism brought nothing that could be truly called great. Chill decay laid a dead hand on all forms of serious drama.

In comedy there is more life. Congreve was not the last of the comic-writers of the manners style. He was followed by Vanbrugh and Farquhar, who, although their wit is not so fine and their situations rougher, yet retained that flamboyant gaiety and carelessness which marked the Restoration plays. This pure comedy was continued by many hands till near the close of the century—Fielding, Colman, Murphy, Goldsmith, and Sheridan all proving that, if tragedy were dying, comedy could still laugh in this strange world. The strange world, however, seemed to have a propensity for weeping, and sentimental tears, tentatively called upon by Steele and Cibber in the earlier years, flowed copiously when Kelly, Cumberland, and Holcroft came to write. A little smile, a little gaiety, might enter in ; but pathetic situations and serious humanitarian thoughts dominated the stage. Worse than all, individuality became lost in type-characterization. The passage from Holcroft's *The Road to Ruin* shows how the older wit had given place

214

to a kind of verbal horse-play which was only intensified and exaggerated in after-years. The sentimental comedy, it is true, aided later in the development of the problem-drama, but in itself it gave few works of worth to the theatre and many ridiculous pieces which read almost like burlesque.

Burlesque itself flourished, for the age was not unaware of its own follies. Two of the finest skits in the language, Fielding's *Tom Thumb* and Sheridan's *The Critic*, come from these years. Ridicule, however, could not stay the general movement; tragedy and comedy went on their weary ways. With them travelled opera. The Italian type had been made popular in the age of Queen Anne—*Clotilda* is here taken as an example—and this Italian type soon gave rise to imitations in English. Furthermore, the opera came to be joined to the ever-popular pantomime, as in Theobald's *The Rape of Proserpine*, in which form it drew much money to the box-keepers. The only operatic type which is deserving of much notice from the literary point of view is the ballad, and the later comic, opera. With *The Beggar's Opera* in 1728 Gay achieved a tremendous triumph, and this was rivalled half a century later when Sheridan produced *The Duenna*. Most comic operas make but dull reading, yet here and there are to be discovered many sprightly scenes and catching lyrics which, even in our own days, have not entirely lost their appeal.

1. JOSEPH ADDISON (1672–1719)

Cato

Of all the better-known English tragedies, the *Cato* of Addison is probably the most difficult to represent by a single scene. Addison's style is the triumph of familiarity; he rises to no grand heights of eloquence and he seldom descends to poverty of expression. The merit of *The Spectator* rests in its sustained effort rather than in particular beauties or sudden strength. In the same way, *Cato*, a play for long held to be the supreme example of pseudo-classic tragedy, secures what effect it possesses by means of steady, even conception. There are no surprises in it; the whole drama is as logical as a treatise on philosophy. Inevitably, therefore, a single scene but ill suggests the entire spirit of the play. The passage chosen here presents Cato's soliloquy when disaster is approaching him and those he loves. This soliloquy is interrupted by the entry of his son, Portius. In spite of the strength which Addison undoubtedly possessed, there should be noted here the weaknesses of the pseudo-classic style in drama. Rhetoric tends to replace action, and vague philosophical dicta tend to take the place of true expression of character.

(*Cato* first appeared in 1713. It was frequently played up to the nineteenth century, and there were many reprints of the printed text. The following scene is taken from the seventh edition, 1713.)

CATO CONTEMPLATES A ROMAN DEATH

CATO *solus, sitting in a thoughtful Posture : In his Hand* PLATO'S *Book on the Immortality of the Soul. A drawn Sword on the Table by him.*

CATO. It must be so—*Plato*, thou reason'st well!—
Else whence this pleasing Hope, this fond Desire,
This Longing after Immortality?
Or whence this secret Dread, and inward Horror,
Of falling into Nought? Why shrinks the Soul
Back on her self, and startles at Destruction?
'Tis the Divinity that stirs within us;
'Tis Heav'n it self, that points out an Hereafter,
And intimates Eternity to Man.
Eternity! thou pleasing, dreadful Thought!
Through what Variety of untry'd Being,
Through what new Scenes and Changes must we pass!
The wide, th'unbounded Prospect, lies before me;
But Shadows, Clouds, and Darkness, rest upon it.
Here will I hold. If there's a Pow'r above us,
(And that there is all Nature cries aloud
Through all her Works) He must delight in Virtue;
And that which he delights in, must be happy.
But when! or where!—This World was made for *Cæsar*.
I'm weary of Conjectures—This must end 'em.
                    [*Laying his Hand on his Sword.*
Thus am I doubly arm'd: my Death and Life,
My Bane and Antidote are both before me;
This in a Moment brings me to an End;
But this informs me I shall never die.
The Soul, secur'd in her Existence, smiles
At the drawn Dagger, and defies its Point.
The Stars shall fade away, the Sun himself
Grow dim with Age, and Nature sink in Years;

216

But thou shalt flourish in immortal Youth,
Unhurt amidst the War of Elements,
The Wrecks of Matter, and the Crush of Worlds.
What means this Heaviness that hangs upon me?
This Lethargy that creeps through all my Senses?
Nature oppress'd, and harras'd out with Care,
Sinks down to Rest. This once I'll favour her.
That my awaken'd Soul may take her Flight,
Renew'd in all her Strength, and fresh with Life,
An Off'ring fit for Heav'n. Let Guilt or Fear
Disturb Man's Rest: *Cato* knows neither of 'em,
Indiff'rent in his Choice to sleep or die. [*Enter* PORTIUS.
But hah! how's this, my Son? Why this Intrusion?
Were not my Orders that I would be private?
Why am I disobey'd?

PORTIUS. Alas, my Father!
What means this Sword? this Instrument of Death?
Let me convey it hence!

CATO. Rash Youth, forbear!

PORTIUS. O let the Pray'rs, th'Entreaties of your Friends,
Their Tears, their common Danger, wrest it from you.

CATO. Would'st thou betray me? Would'st thou give me up
A Slave, a Captive, into *Cæsar's* Hands?
Retire, and learn Obedience to a Father,
Or know, young Man!——

PORTIUS. Look not thus sternly on me;
You know I'd rather die than disobey you.

CATO. 'Tis well! again I'm Master of my self.
Now, *Cæsar*, let thy Troops beset our Gates,
And Barr each Avenue, thy gath'ring Fleets
O'er-spread the Sea, and stop up ev'ry Port;
Cato shall open to himself a Passage,
And mock Thy Hopes——

PORTIUS. O Sir, forgive your Son,
Whose Grief hangs heavy on him! O my Father!
How am I sure it is not the last Time
I e'er shall call you so! Be not displeased,
O be not angry with me whilst I weep,
And, in the Anguish of my Heart, beseech you
To quit the dreadful Purpose of your Soul!

CATO. Thou hast been ever good and dutiful. [*Embracing him.*
Weep not, my Son. All will be well again.
The righteous Gods, whom I have sought to please,
Will succour *Cato*, and preserve his Children.

PORTIUS. Your Words give Comfort to my drooping Heart.

CATO. *Portius*, thou may'st rely upon my Conduct.
Thy Father will not act what misbecomes him.
But go, my Son, and see if aught be wanting

Among thy Father's Friends; see them embarked;
And tell me if the Winds and Seas befriend them.
My Soul is quite weigh'd down with Care, and asks
The soft Refreshment of a Moment's Sleep.

2. AMBROSE PHILIPS (? 1675–1749)

The Distrest Mother

The classical style, which has already been exemplified in Addison's *Cato*, found many exponents in the eighteenth century. Most of these had but an ephemeral success ; among the few whose works became stock-pieces Ambrose Philips is the most important. *The Distrest Mother* stood with *Cato* as one of the prime representations of pseudo-classicism in the theatre, and indeed is the nearest approach the English stage made to the atmosphere of French classical tragedy. The theme is that of Andromache and Pyrrhus, and is dealt with in the rhetorical fashion which then ruled. Philips, however, is more of a poet than Addison, and his lines, written in the grand style, have a sonorousness and majesty to which his contemporary could not rise. The failure of pseudo-classical tragedy lies partly in the use of this rhetorical grand style, partly too in the attempt to display passion through an intellectual medium. Emotion is conceived largely in terms of thought.

(*The Distrest Mother* was produced with success at Drury Lane in 1712. The following passage is based on the fourth edition, 1718.)

ANDROMACHE AND PYRRHUS

ANDROMACHE. How can *Andromache*, a Captive Queen,
O'er-whelm'd with Grief, a Burden to her self,
Harbour a Thought of Love? Alas! what Charms
Have these unhappy Eyes, by you condemn'd
To weep for ever?—Talk of it no more,—
To reverence the Misfortunes of a Foe;
To succour the Distrest; to give the Son
To an afflicted Mother; to repel
Confederate Nations, leagued against his Life;
Unbribed by Love, unterrify'd by Threats,
To pity, to protect him: These are Cares,
These are Exploits worthy *Achilles'* Son.
  PYRRHUS. Will your Resentments, then, endure for ever?
Must *Pyrrhus* never be forgiven?—'Tis true,
My Sword has often reek'd in *Phrygian* Blood,
And carry'd Havock through your Royal Kindred:
But you, fair Princess, amply have avenged

218

Old *Priam's* vanquish'd House: And all the Woes,
I brought on them, fall short of what I suffer.
We both have suffer'd in our Turns: And now
Our common Foes should teach us to unite.

    ANDROMACHE. Where does the Captive not behold a Foe?

    PYRRHUS. Forget that Term of Hatred; and behold
A Friend in *Pyrrhus*! Give me but to hope,
I'll free your Son; I'll be a Father to him:
Myself will teach him to avenge the *Trojans*.
I'll go in Person to chastise the *Greeks*,
Both for your Wrongs and mine. Inspired by you,
What would I not atchieve? Again shall *Troy*
Rise from its Ashes: This right Arm shall fix
Her Seat of Empire; and your Son shall reign.

    ANDROMACHE. Such Dreams of Greatness suit not my Condition:
His Hopes of Empire perish'd with his Father.
No; thou imperial City, ancient *Troy*,
Thou Pride of *Asia*, founded by the Gods;
Never, oh never! must we hope to see
Those Bulwarks rise, which *Hector* could not guard!—
Sir, all I wish for, is some quiet Exile;
Where far from *Greece* remov'd, and far from you,
I may conceal my Son, and mourn my Husband.
Your Love creates my Envy. Oh, return!
Return to your betroth'd *Hermione*.

    PYRRHUS. Why do you mock me thus? you know, I cannot.
You know my Heart is yours: My Soul hangs on you:
You take up every Wish: My waking Thoughts,
And nightly Dreams are all employ'd on you.
'Tis true, *Hermione* was sent to share
My Throne and Bed; and would with Transport hear
The Vows, which you neglect.

    ANDROMACHE.   She has no *Troy*,
No *Hector* to lament: She has not lost
A Husband by your Conquests: Such a Husband!
(Tormenting Thought!) whose Death alone has made
Your Sire immortal: *Pyrrhus* and *Achilles*
Are both grown great by my Calamities.

    PYRRHUS. Madam, 'tis well! 'Tis very well! I find,
Your Will must be obey'd: Imperious Captive,
It shall. Henceforth I blot you from my Mind:
You teach me to forget your Charms; to hate you.
For know, inhuman Beauty, I have loved
Too well to treat you with Indifference.
Think well upon it: My disorder'd Soul
Wavers between th' Extreams of Love and Rage.
I've been too tame! I will awake to Vengeance!
The Son shall answer for the Mother's Scorn.

The *Greeks* demand him: Nor will I endanger
My Realms, to pleasure an ungrateful Woman.
ANDROMACHE. Then he must die! alas, my Son must die!
He has no Friend, no Succour left, beside
His Mother's Tears, and his own Innocence.
PYRRHUS. Go, Madam; visit this unhappy Son.
The Sight of him may bend your stubborn Heart;
And turn to Softness your unjust Disdain.
I shall once more expect your Answer.   Go;
And think, while you embrace the Captive Boy,
Think, that his Life depends on your Resolves.   [*Exit* PYRRHUS.
ANDROMACHE. I'll go; and, in the Anguish of my Heart,
Weep o'er my Child—If he must dye, my Life
Is wrapt in his; I shall not long survive.
'Tis for his sake, that I have suffer'd Life;
Groan'd in Captivity; and out-liv'd *Hector*.
Yes, my *Astyanax*; we'll go together!
Together to the Realms of Night we'll go!
There to thy ravish'd Eyes thy Sire I'll show,
And point him out among the Shades below.

3. GEORGE LILLO (1693–1739)

The London Merchant

The London Merchant, in an early Victorian setting, has been revived in our own times by Mr Nigel Playfair, but the scheme of the revival was such that modern audiences could hardly judge of the merits or the demerits of the play.   Vincent Crummles was the centre of attraction, and part at least of Lillo's drama was acted in a spirit of frank burlesque.   That this burlesque treatment, considering the heights to which domestic tragedy has soared in recent years, was justified is certainly true ; but in order to appreciate *The London Merchant* one must endeavour to gain some historical perspective.   In 1731 it was unique, and fluttered a society which had seen nothing in its kind, which had been fed for years on the remnants of heroic drama and the chill periods of the classical style.   It is easy to show the faults of Lillo's work.   The moral is too deeply stressed ; the characters are types rather than individuals ; the merchant's office is treated too sentimentally ; the language, aiming as it does at naturalism, falls only too frequently into the cadences of a rough blank verse. These are its errors, but against those one must place many things which mark the play out as an epoch-making experiment.   The vague suggestion of fate, more deeply stressed in Lillo's later drama, *Fatal Curiosity*, is something which the classical playwrights had neglected.   The language may not be naturalistic,

220

but at least it points the way toward a dialogue more truly dramatic than the constant rhetoric of classical tragedies. The treatment of the subject may be sentimental, but it has in it more of potentiality than the contemporary treatment of fictional kings and long-forgotten empires. It must ever be remembered that it was this play which was taken by eighteenth-century Continental dramatists as their prime model, that it inspired a Lessing and a Diderot, and with them that whole school of *bourgeois* playwrights who led the way toward Ibsen and Strindberg.

(*The London Merchant ; or, the History of George Barnwell* was produced at Drury Lane in June 1731. The following extract is taken from the first edition of that year.)

BARNWELL MURDERS HIS UNCLE

UNCLE. If I was superstitious, I shou'd fear some Danger lurk'd unseen, or Death were nigh:—A heavy Melancholy clouds my Spirits; my Imagination is fill'd with gashly Forms of dreary Graves, and Bodies chang'd by Death,—when the pale lengthen'd Visage attracks each weeping Eye,—and fills the musing Soul, at once, with Grief and Horror, Pity and Aversion,—I will indulge the Thought. The wise Man prepares himself for Death, by making it familiar to his Mind.—When strong Reflections hold the Mirror near,—and the Living in the Dead behold their future selves, how does each inordinate Passion and Desire cease or sicken at the View?—The Mind scarce moves;—The Blood, curdling, and chill'd, creeps slowly thro' the Veins,—fix'd, still, and motionless, like the solemn Object of our Thoughts.—We are almost at present—what we must be herafter, 'till Curiosity awakes the Soul, and sets it on Inquiry.— [GEORGE BARNWELL *enters at a distance.*

O Death, thou strange mysterious Power,—seen every Day, yet never understood—but by the incommunicative Dead, What art thou? The extensive Mind of Man, that with a Thought circles the Earth's vast Globe,—sinks to the Centre, or ascends above the Stars; that World's exotick finds, or thinks it finds,—thy thick Clouds attempts to pass in vain, lost and bewilder'd in the horrid Gloom,—defeated she returns more doubtful than before; of nothing certain, but of Labour lost.

[*During this Speech,* BARNWELL *sometimes presents the Pistol, and draws it back again; at last he drops it,— at which his Uncle starts, and draws his Sword.*

BARNWELL. Oh, 'tis impossible.

UNCLE. A Man so near me, arm'd and masqu'd!

BARNWELL. Nay, then there's no Retreat.

[*Plucks a Poniard from his Bosom, and stabs him.*

UNCLE. Oh! I am slain! All gracious Heaven regard the Prayer

221

of thy dying Servant. Bless, with thy choicest Blessings, my dearest Nephew; forgive my Murderer, and take my fleeting Soul to endless Mercy.

[BARNWELL *throws off his Mask, runs to him, and, kneeling by him, raises and chafes him.*

BARNWELL. Expiring Saint ! Oh, murder'd, martyr'd Uncle! Lift up your dying Eyes, and view your Nephew in your Murderer. —O do not look so tenderly upon me.—Let Indignation lighten from your Eyes, and blast me ere you die.—By Heaven, he weeps in Pity of my Woes.—Tears,—Tears, for Blood.—The Murder'd, in the Agonies of Death, weeps for his Murderer.—O, speak your pious Purpose,—pronounce my Pardon then,—and take me with you.—He wou'd, but cannot.—O why, with such fond Affection do you press my murdering Hand!—What! will you kiss me!

[*Kisses him.*

UNCLE. *Groans and dies.*

BARNWELL. He's gone for ever,—and oh! I follow.—[*Swoons away upon his* UNCLE'S *dead Body.*] Do I still live to press the suffering Bosom of the Earth?—Do I still breath, and taint with my infectious Breath the wholesome Air!—Let Heaven, from its high Throne, in Justice or in Mercy, now look down on that dear murder'd Saint, and me the Murderer.—And, if his Vengeance spares,—let Pity strike and end my wretched Being.—Murder the worst of Crimes, and Parricide the worst of Murders, and this the worst of Parricides. *Cain,* who stands on Record from the Birth of Time, and must to its last final Period, as accurs'd, slew a Brother, favour'd above him.—Detested *Nero,* by another's Hand, dispatch'd a Mother, that he fear'd and hated.—But I, with my own Hand, have murder'd a Brother, Mother, Father, and a Friend; most loving and belov'd.—This execrable Act of mine's without a Parallel.—O may it ever stand alone,—the last of Murders, as it is the worst.—

> The rich Man thus, in Torment and Despair,
> Prefer'd his vain, but charitable Prayer.
> The Fool, his own Soul lost, wou'd fain be wise
> For others Good; but Heaven his Suit denies.
> By Laws and Means well known we stand or fall,
> And one eternal Rule remains for all.

4. EDWARD MOORE (1712–57)

The Gamester

The *bourgeois* tragedy, which had risen to such heights with Heywood, and had sunk again only to show fresh signs of promise in Lillo's plays, failed to capture fully the attentions of eighteenth-century dramatists. While sporadic efforts were made by

EIGHTEENTH CENTURY

individual writers to revive or popularize the prose style both
classicism and the newer mood of flamboyant romantic sentiment
forbade the development of real strength in this kind.   Almost
the only drama of even moderate worth penned in this form
during the period was Moore's once-famous *Gamester*.   This play
deserves particular notice because of its powerful characterization
and its excellent construction, even while we note in it the prevalent weaknesses of the age—a prose that often trembles on the
verge of blank verse and a tendency, in any moments of emotion,
to fall back on the enunciation of moral platitudes.   The hero of
The Gamester is Beverley, led to destruction by his pretended
friend Stukely.   In the scenes given below he is presented in
prison after a last desperate fit of gaming ; although he does not
know it, the death of a relation has made him a rich man.

(*The Gamester* was produced at Drury Lane in 1753.   The
passages given below are taken from the second edition, 1753.)

THE IRONY OF FATE

BEVERLEY [*in prison*]. Why, there's an End then.   I have judg'd
deliberately, and the Result is Death.   How the Self-Murderer's
Account may stand, I know not.   But this I know—the Load of
hateful Life oppresses me too much—The Horrors of my Soul are
more than I can bear—[*Offers to kneel.*] Father of Mercy!—I cannot
pray—Despair has laid his iron Hand upon me, and seal'd me for
Perdition—Conscience! Conscience! thy Clamours are too loud
—Here's that shall silence thee. [*Takes a Vial out of his Pocket,
and looks at it.*] Thou art most friendly to the Miserable.   Come
then, thou Cordial for sick Minds—come to my Heart. [*Drinks.*]
O, that the Grave wou'd bury Memory as well as Body!   For if the
Soul sees and feels the Sufferings of those dear Ones it leaves behind,
the Everlasting has no Vengeance to torment it deeper—I'll think
no more on't—Reflection comes too late—Once there was a Time
for't—but now 'tis past.—Who's there? [*Enter* JARVIS.

JARVIS. One that hop'd to see you with better Looks—Why
d'you turn so from me?   I have brought Comfort with me—And
see who comes to give it welcome.

BEVERLEY. My Wife and Sister! Why, 'tis but one Pang more
then, and farewel World. [*Aside.*
[*Enter* MRS BEVERLEY *and* CHARLOTTE.

MRS BEVERLEY. Where is he? [*Runs and embraces him.*] O I have
him! I have him! And now they shall never part us more—I have
News, Love, to make you happy for ever.—But don't look coldly
on me.

CHARLOTTE. How is it, Brother?

MRS BEVERLEY. Alas! he hears us not—Speak to me, Love.   I
have no Heart to see you thus.

223

BEVERLEY. Nor I to bear the Sense of so much Shame—This is a sad Place.

MRS BEVERLEY. We come to take you from it. To tell you that the World goes well again. That Providence has seen our Sorrows, and sent the Means to heal 'em—Your Uncle dy'd Yesterday.

BEVERLEY. My Uncle!—No, do not say so—O! I am sick at Heart!

MRS BEVERLEY. Indeed!—I meant to bring you Comfort.

BEVERLEY. Tell me he lives then—If you wou'd give me Comfort, tell me he lives.

MRS BEVERLEY. And if I did—I have no Power to raise the Dead. He dy'd Yesterday.

BEVERLEY. And I am Heir to him?

JARVIS. To his whole Estate, Sir. But bear it patiently—pray bear it patiently.

BEVERLEY. Well, well—— [*pausing*] Why, Fame says I am rich then?

MRS BEVERLEY. And truly so—Why do you look so wildly?

BEVERLEY. Do I? The News was unexpected. But has he left me all?

JARVIS. All, all, Sir—He cou'd not leave it from you.

BEVERLEY. I'm sorry for it.

CHARLOTTE. Sorry? Why sorry?

BEVERLEY. Your Uncle's dead, *Charlotte*.

CHARLOTTE. Peace be with his Soul then—Is it so terrible that an old Man should die?

BEVERLEY. He shou'd have been immortal.

MRS BEVERLEY. Heaven knows I wish'd not for his Death. 'Twas the Will of Providence that he shou'd die—Why are you disturbed so?

BEVERLEY. Has Death no Terrors in it?

MRS BEVERLEY. Not an old Man's Death. Yet if it troubles you, I wish him living.

BEVERLEY. And I, with all my Heart.

CHARLOTTE. Why, what's the Matter?

BEVERLEY. Nothing—How heard you of his Death?

MRS BEVERLEY. His Steward came Express. Wou'd I had never known it!

BEVERLEY. Or had heard it one Day sooner—For I have a Tale to tell, shall turn you into Stone; or if the Power of Speech remain, you shall kneel down and curse me.

MRS BEVERLEY. Alas! What Tale is this? And why are we to curse you?—I'll bless you for ever.

BEVERLEY. No; I have deserv'd no Blessings. The World holds not such another Wretch. All this large Fortune, this second Bounty of Heaven, that might have heal'd our Sorrows, and satisfy'd our utmost Hopes, in a curs'd Hour I sold last Night.

CHARLOTTE. Sold! How sold!

MRS BEVERLEY. Impossible!—It cannot be!

BEVERLEY. That Devil *Stukely*, with all Hell to aid him, tempted me to the Deed. To pay false Debts of Honour, and to redeem past Errors, I sold the Reversion—Sold it for a scanty Sum, and lost it among Villains. . . .

THE GAMESTER'S DEATH

MRS BEVERLEY. Restore him, Heaven! Stretch forth thy Arm omnipotent, and snatch him from the Grave!—O save him! save him!

BEVERLEY. Alas! that Prayer is fruitless. Already Death has seiz'd me—Yet Heaven is gracious—I ask'd for Hope, as the bright Presage of Forgiveness, and like a Light, blazing thro' Darkness, it came and chear'd me—'Twas all I lived for, and now I die.

MRS BEVERLEY. Not yet!—Not yet!—Stay but a little, and I'll die too.

BEVERLEY. No; live I charge you.—We have a little One. Tho' I have left him, You will not leave him.—To *Lewson's* Kindness I bequeath him—Is not this *Charlotte*? We have liv'd in Love, tho' I have wrong'd you—Can you forgive me, *Charlotte*?

CHARLOTTE. Forgive you!—O my poor Brother!

BEVERLEY. Lend me your Hand, Love—so—raise me—No—'twill not be—My Life is finish'd—O! for a few short Moments! to tell you how my Heart bleeds for you—That even now, thus dying as I am, dubious and fearful of Hereafter, my Bosom Pang is for Your Miseries. Support her Heaven!—And now I go—O, Mercy! Mercy!

5. JOHN HOME (1722–1808)

Douglas

" My name is Norval " was the beginning of a passage once famous both on the stage and in the schoolroom, at a time when *Douglas* was regarded, not only by perfervid Scots, as a master-piece second only to the tragedies of Shakespeare. The fame of this play has now sadly decayed, yet perhaps one can still trace those qualities in it which made their appeal to an age when the liberal tendencies of romanticism were striving to burst the strong classic fetters forged in the age of Queen Anne. Home's tendency was decidedly oriented toward romance, and his choice of theme is, to a certain extent, harmonious with Percy's interest in the old ballads and with Chatterton's 'medieval' revivals. On the other hand, *Douglas* is by no means a completely romantic play. The language, albeit a trifle richer, is the language of rhetoric, and, being so, it shows how the dramatic activities of the eighteenth century were being thwarted. In poetry the writers of the new age were soon to find fitting media of expression, but

P

in serious drama they knew of nothing save this rhetorical pseudo-classic utterance and—later—the blank verse of the Elizabethan era. So long as a Home had to write in the style of *Cato* no progress could be hoped for in the realm of tragedy.

(*Douglas* was first acted at Edinburgh in 1756, and was later produced at Covent Garden in 1757. The passage below is taken from the first edition, 1757.)

THE STRANGER'S TALE

LADY RANDOLPH. What means this clamour? stranger, speak secure;
Hast thou been wrong'd? have these rude men presum'd
To vex the weary traveller on his way?

FIRST SERVANT. By us no stranger ever suffer'd wrong:
This man with outcry wild has call'd us forth;
So sore afraid he cannot speak his fears.

[*Enter* LORD RANDOLPH *and young man, with their swords drawn and bloody.*

LADY RANDOLPH. Not vain the stranger's fears! how fares my lord?

LORD RANDOLPH. That it fares well, thanks to this gallant youth,
Whose valour sav'd me from a wretched death!
As down the winding dale I walk'd alone,
At the cross way four armed men attack'd me:
Rovers, I judge, from the licentious camp,
Who would have quickly laid Lord *Randolph* low,
Had not this brave and generous stranger come,
Like my good angel in the hour of fate,
And, mocking danger, made my foes his own.
They turn'd upon him: but his active arm
Struck to the ground, from whence they rose no more,
The fiercest two; the others fled amain,
And left him master of the bloody field.
Speak, Lady *Randolph*: upon Beauty's tongue
Dwell accents pleasing to the brave and bold.
Speak, noble dame, and thank him for thy lord.

LADY RANDOLPH. My lord, I cannot speak what now I feel.
My heart o'erflows with gratitude to heav'n,
And to this noble youth, who all unknown
To you and yours, deliberated not,
Nor paus'd at peril, but humanely brave
Fought on your side, against such fearful odds.
Have you yet learn'd of him whom we should thank?
Whom call the saviour of Lord *Randolph's* life?

LORD RANDOLPH. I ask'd that question, and he answer'd not:
But I must know who my deliverer is.   [*To the* STRANGER.

STRANGER. A low born man, of parentage obscure,
Who nought can boast but his desire to be
A soldier, and to gain a name in arms.
  LORD RANDOLPH. Whoe'er thou art, thy spirit is ennobled
By the great King of Kings! thou art ordain'd
And stampt a hero by the sovereign hand
Of nature! blush not, flower of modesty
As well as valour, to declare thy birth.
  STRANGER. My name is *Norval*: on the Grampian hills
My father feeds his flocks; a frugal swain,
Whose constant cares were to encrease his store,
And keep his only son, myself, at home.
For I had heard of battles, and I long'd
To follow to the field some warlike lord;
And heaven soon granted what my sire denied.
This moon which rose last night, round as my shield,
Had not yet fill'd her horns, when, by her light,
A band of fierce barbarians, from the hills,
Rush'd like a torrent down upon the vale,
Sweeping our flocks and herds.   The shepherds fled
For safety, and for succour.   I alone,
With bended bow, and quiver full of arrows,
Hover'd about the enemy, and mark'd
The road he took, then hasted to my friends;
Whom with a troop of fifty chosen men,
I met advancing.   The pursuit I led,
Till we o'ertook the spoil-encumber'd foe.
We fought and conquer'd.   E're a sword was drawn,
An arrow from my bow had pierc'd their chief,
Who wore that day the arms which now I wear.
Returning home in triumph, I disdain'd
The shepherd's slothful life; and having heard
That our good king had summon'd his bold peers
To lead their warriours to the Carron side,
I left my fathers house, and took with me
A chosen servant to conduct my steps:—
Yon trembling coward who forsook his master.
Journeying with this intent, I past these towers,
And, heaven-directed, came this day to do
The happy deed that gilds my humble name.
  LORD RANDOLPH. He is as wise as brave.   Was ever tale
With such a gallant modesty rehears'd?
My brave deliverer! thou shalt enter now
A nobler list, and in a monarch's sight
Contend with princes for the prize of fame.
I will present thee to our Scottish king,
Whose valiant spirit ever valour lov'd.
Ha! my *Matilda*! wherefore starts that tear?

EXTRACTS FROM BRITISH & IRISH PLAYS

LADY RANDOLPH. I cannot say: for various affections,
And strangely mingled, in my bosom swell;
Yet each of them may well command a tear.
I joy that thou art safe; and admire
Him and his fortunes who hath wrought thy safety.
Obscure and friendless, he the army fought,
Bent upon peril, in the range of death
Resolv'd to hunt for fame, and with his sword
To gain distinction which his birth denied.
In this attempt unknown he might have perish'd,
And gain'd, with all his valour, but oblivion.
Now grac'd by thee, his virtue serves no more
Beneath despair. The soldier now of hope
He stands conspicuous; fame and great renown
Are brought within the compass of his sword.
On this my mind reflected, whilst you spoke,
And bless'd the wonder-working Lord of heaven.

6. SIR JOHN VANBRUGH (1664–1726) AND COLLEY CIBBER (1671–1757)

The Provoked Husband

The author-heading to this extract is not precisely correct, for apparently the portion of *The Provoked Husband* quoted here is entirely of Cibber's creation. The inception of the play, however, was due to Vanbrugh, who left behind at his death a fragment entitled *A Journey to London* ; this was incorporated by the laureate into the later, completed drama. *The Provoked Husband* is a good example of early sentimental comedy, mingled with relics of the old style of wit. The aim of the play, according to Cibber, was " to expose, and reform the licentious Irregularities that too often break in upon the Peace and Happiness of the married State," and this aim he proceeds to put into effect by showing us the gay, honest but pleasure-loving Lady Townly, who gives infinite amusement to her friends, but who offends mightily her rather serious husband and his slightly prudish sister, Lady Grace. Manly, Lady Grace's suitor, advises his prospective brother-in-law to threaten a divorce, and by this means tranquillity is restored in the Townly mansion. As can be seen even in the short passage given here, Cibber tells the story with a certain *verve*. He was, after all, a contemporary of Congreve's, and could not entirely forget the gaiety of *The Way of the World*. The time of duller sentimental sententiousness had not yet come.

(*The Provok'd Husband ; or, A Journey to London* was produced at Drury Lane in 1728. The following extract is taken from the edition of 1735.)

EIGHTEENTH CENTURY

A Gay Wife causes Domestic Friction

LADY TOWNLY. Well! look you, my Lord; I can bear it no longer! nothing still but about my Faults, my Faults! an agreeable Subject truly!

LORD TOWNLY. Why, Madam, if you won't hear of them; how can I ever hope to see you mend them?

LADY TOWNLY. Why, I don't intend to mend them—I can't mend them—you know I have try'd to do it an hundred times, and—it hurts me so—I can't bear it!

LORD TOWNLY. And I, Madam, can't bear this daily licentious abuse of your Time and Character.

LADY TOWNLY. Abuse! Astonishing! when the Universe knows, I am never better Company, than when I am doing what I have a mind to! But to see this World! that Men can never get over that silly Spirit of Contradiction—why but last Thursday now—there you wisely amended one of my Faults as you call them—you insisted upon my not going to the Masquerade—and pray, what was the Consequence! was not I as cross as the Devil, all the Night after? was not I forc'd to get Company at home? and was not it almost three o'Clock in the Morning, before I was able to come to my self again? and then the Fault is not mended neither—for next time, I shall only have twice the Inclination to go: so that all this mending, and mending, you see, is but dearning an old Ruffle, to make it worse than it was before.

LORD TOWNLY. Well, the Manner of Women's living, of late, is insupportable; and one way or other——

LADY TOWNLY. It's to be mended, I suppose! why, so it may; but then, my dear Lord, you must give one Time—and when Things are at worst, you know, they mend themselves! ha! ha!

LORD TOWNLY. Madam, I am not in a Humour, now, to trifle.

LADY TOWNLY. Why then, my Lord, one Word of fair Argument —to talk with you, your own way now—You complain of my late Hours, and I of your early ones—so far are we even, you'll allow —but pray which gives us the best Figure, in the Eye of the Polite World? my active, spirited Three in the Morning, or your dull, drowsy Eleven at Night? Now, I think, one has the Air of a Woman of Quality, and t'other of a plodding Mechanick, that goes to Bed betimes, that he may rise early, to open his Shop!—Faugh!

LORD TOWNLY. Fy, fy, Madam! is this your way of Reasoning? 'tis time to wake you then—'tis not your ill Hours alone, that disturb me, but as often the ill Company, that occasion those ill Hours.

LADY TOWNLY. Sure I don't understand you now, my Lord; what ill Company do I keep?

LORD TOWNLY. Why, at best, Women that lose their Money, and Men that win it! Or, perhaps, Men that are voluntary Bubbles at one Game, in hopes a Lady will give them fair play at another.

Then that unavoidable mixture with known Rakes, conceal'd Thieves, and Sharpers in Embroidery—or what, to me, is still more shocking, that Herd of familiar chattering cropear'd Coxcombs, who are so often like Monkeys, there would be no knowing them asunder, but that their Tails hang from their Head, and the Monkey's grows where it should do.

LADY TOWNLY. And a Husband must give eminent Proof of his Sense, that thinks their Powder-puffs dangerous.

LORD TOWNLY. Their being Fools, Madam, is not always the Husband's Security: Or if it were, Fortune, sometimes, gives them Advantages might make a thinking Woman tremble.

LADY TOWNLY. What do you mean?

LORD TOWNLY. That Women, sometimes, lose more than they are able to pay; and if a Creditor be a little pressing, the Lady may be reduc'd, to try if instead of Gold, the Gentleman will accept of a Trinket.

LADY TOWNLY. My Lord, you grow scurrilous; you'll make me hate you. I'll have you to know, I keep Company with the politest People in Town, and the Assemblies I frequent are full of such.

LORD TOWNLY. So are the Churches—now and then.

LADY TOWNLY. My Friends frequent them too, as well as the Assemblies.

LORD TOWNLY. Yes, and would do it oftner, if a Groom of the Chambers there were allow'd to furnish Cards to the Company.

LADY TOWNLY. I see what you drive at all this while; you would lay an Imputation on my Fame, to cover your own Avarice! I might take any Pleasures, I find that were not expensive.

LORD TOWNLY. Have a Care, Madam; don't let me think you only value your Chastity, to make me reproachable for not indulging you in every thing else, that's vicious—I, Madam, have a Reputation too, to guard, that's dear to me, as yours—The Follies of an un-govern'd Wife may make the wisest Man uneasy; but 'tis his own Fault, if ever they make him contemptible.

LADY TOWNLY. My Lord—you would make a Woman mad!

LORD TOWNLY. You'd make a Man a Fool.

LADY TOWNLY. If Heav'n has made you otherwise, that won't be in my Power.

LORD TOWNLY. Whatever may be in your Inclination, Madam; I'll prevent your making me a Beggar, at least.

LADY TOWNLY. A Beggar! *Crœsus*? I'm out of Patience! I won't come home 'till four to-morrow Morning.

LORD TOWNLY. That may be, Madam; but I'll order the Doors to be lock'd at twelve.

LADY TOWNLY. Then I won't come home 'till to-morrow Night.

LORD TOWNLY. Then, Madam;—you shall never come home again. [*Exit* LORD TOWNLY.

LADY TOWNLY. What does he mean! I never heard such a word from him in my Life before! the Man always us'd to have Manners
230

in his worst Humours! there's something, that I don't see, at the Bottom of all this—but his Head's always upon some impracticable Scheme or other, so I won't trouble mine any longer about him. Mr *Manly*, your Servant.   *[Enter* MANLY.

MANLY. I ask Pardon for my intrusion, Madam; but I hope my Business with my Lord will excuse it.

LADY TOWNLY. I believe you'll find him in the next Room, Sir.

MANLY. Will you give me leave, Madam?

LADY TOWNLEY. Sir—you have my leave, tho' you were a Lady.

MANLY [*aside*]. What a well-bred Age do we live in!

                      [Exit MANLY.
                      [Enter LADY GRACE.

LADY TOWNLY. O! my dear Lady *Grace*! how could you leave me so unmercifully alone all this while?

LADY GRACE. I thought my Lord had been with you.

LADY TOWNLY. Why yes—and therefore I wanted your Relief; for he has been in such a fluster here——

LADY GRACE. Bless me! for what?

LADY TOWNLY. Only our usual Breakfast; we have each of us had our Dish of Matrimonial Comfort, this Morning! we have been charming Company!

LADY GRACE. I am mighty glad of it! sure it must be a vast happiness, when a Man and a Wife can give themselves the same Turn of Conversation!

LADY TOWNLY. O! the prettiest thing in the World!

LADY GRACE. Now I should be afraid, that where two People are every Day together so, they must often be in want of something to talk upon.

LADY TOWNLY. O my Dear, you are the most mistaken in the World! married People have things to talk of, Child, that never enter into the Imagination of others—why, here's my Lord and I now, we have not been married above two short Years, you know, and we have already eight or ten Things constantly in Bank, that whenever we want Company, we can take up any one of them for two Hours together, and the Subject never the flatter: nay, if we have occasion for it, it will be as fresh next Day too, as it was the first Hour it entertained us.

LADY GRACE. Certainly, that must be vastly pretty!

LADY TOWNLY. O! there's no Life like it! Why t'other Day for Example, when you din'd abroad; my Lord and I, after a pretty cheerful *tête à tête* Meal, sat us down by the Fire-side, in an easy, indolent, pick-tooth Way, for about a Quarter of an Hour, as if we had not thought of one another's being in the Room—at last, stretching himself, and yawning—My Dear, says he—aw—you come home very late, last Night—'Twas but just turn'd of Two says I —I was a-bed—aw—by Eleven, says he; so you are every Night, says I—Well, says he, I am amaz'd you can sit up so late—How can you be amaz'd, says I, at a Thing that happens so often?—upon which we enter'd into a Conversation—and tho' this is a Point has entertained us above fifty times already, we always find so many pretty new Things to say upon it, that I believe, in my Soul, it will last as long as we live!

7. GEORGE FARQUHAR (1678–1707)

The Inconstant

The Restoration comedy of manners ultimately takes its rise from that type of comedy which was popularized in the early seventeenth century by Fletcher and his companions. The general indebtedness in regard to style, characterization, and choice of plot is everywhere apparent, while the continued success of some of the older plays proves the constant appeal which they made to succeeding generations. Occasionally, too, the 'Restoration' dramatists turned directly back to their predecessors, seeking in those works for themes and suggestions. Thus Farquhar for *The Inconstant* borrowed the main plot of Fletcher's *The Wild-goose Chase*, a passage from which has been given (see pp. 128–130). He has altered, it is true, not only the main lines of the plot, but the whole atmosphere of the play as well; but his alterations cannot conceal the fact that Fletcher's play, although rougher in texture than his, belongs to the same dramatic *genre*. The points of contact as well as the points of difference are at least suggested by a comparison of the two short scenes quoted in this book. Particular attention should be paid to the utilization of a prose medium by Farquhar in place of Fletcher's blank verse.

(*The Inconstant; or, The Way to Win Him* was produced at Drury Lane in 1702. It was frequently revived and printed during the eighteenth century. The following passage is taken from the collected *Comedies* of 1718.)

The Way of the Polite World

MIRABEL. Well, Madam, why d'ye follow me?

ORIANA. Well, Sir, why do you shun me?

MIRABEL. 'Tis my Humour, Madam, and I'm naturally sway'd by Inclination.

ORIANA. Have you forgot our Contract, Sir?

MIRABEL. All I remember of that Contract is, that it was made some three Years ago, and that's enough in Conscience to forget the rest on't.

ORIANA. 'Tis sufficient, Sir, to recollect the passing of it, for in that Circumstance, I presume, lies the force of the Obligation.

MIRABEL. Obligations, Madam, that are forc'd upon the Will are no tye upon the Conscience; I was a Slave to my Passion when I pass'd the Instrument, but the Recovery of my Freedom makes the Contract void.

ORIANA. Sir, you can't make that a Compulsion which was your own Choice; besides, Sir, a Subjection to your own Desires has not the Virtue of a forcible Constraint: And you will find, Sir, that to plead your Passion for the killing of a Man will hardly exempt you from the Justice of the Punishment.

MIRABEL. And so, Madam, you make the Sin of Murther and the Crime of a Contract the very same, because Hanging and Matrimony are so much alike.

ORIANA. Come, Mr *Mirabel*, these Expressions I expected from the Raillery of your Humour, but I hope for very different Sentiments from your Honour and Generosity.

MIRABEL. Look'e, Madam, as for my Generosity, 'tis at your Service, with all my Heart: I'll keep you a Coach and six Horses, if you please, only permit me to keep my Honour to my self, for I can assure you, Madam, that the thing call'd Honour is a Circumstance absolutely unnecessary in a natural Correspondence between Male and Female, and he's a Mad-man that lays it out, considering its Scarcity, upon any such trivial Occasions. There's Honour requir'd of us by our Friends, and Honour due to our Enemies, and they return it to us again; but I never heard of a Man that left but an Inch of his Honour in a Woman's keeping, that cou'd ever get the least account on't.—Consider, Madam, you have no such thing among ye, and 'tis a main Point of Policy to keep no Faith with Reprobates—thou art a pretty little Reprobate, and so get thee about thy Business.

ORIANA. Well, Sir, even all this I will allow to the gayety of your Temper; your Travels have improv'd your Talent of Talking, but they are not of Force, I hope, to impair your Morals.

MIRABEL. Morals! Why there 'tis again now—I tell thee, Child there is not the Least Occasion for Morals in any Business between you and I—Don't you know that of all Commerce in the World there is no such Cozenage and Deceit as in the Traffick between Man and Woman; we study all our Lives long how to put Tricks upon one another—What is your Business now, from the time you throw away your Artificial Babies, but how to get Natural Ones with the most Advantage?—No Fowler lays abroad more Nets for his Game, nor a Hunter for his Prey, than you do to catch poor innocent Men—Why do you sit three or four Hours at your Toylet in a Morning? only with a villanous Design to make some poor Fellow a Fool before Night. What are your languishing Looks, your study'd Airs and Affectations, but so many Baits and Devices to delude Men out of their dear Liberty and Freedom?—What d'ye sigh for? What d'ye weep for? What d'ye pray for? Why for a Husband: That is, you implore Providence to assist you in

EXTRACTS FROM BRITISH & IRISH PLAYS

the just and pious Design of making the wisest of his Creatures a
Fool, and the Head of the Creation a Slave.

ORIANA. Sir, I am proud of my Power, and am resolv'd to use it.

MIRABEL. Hold, hold, Madam, not so fast—As you have Variety
of Vanities to make Coxcombs of us; so we have Vows, Oaths, and
Protestations, of all sorts and sizes to make Fools of you.   As you
are very strange and whimsical Creatures, so we are allow'd as
unaccountable ways of managing you.   And this, in short, my
dear Creature, is our present Condition, I have sworn and ly'd
briskly to gain my Ends of you; your Ladyship has patch'd and
painted violently, to gain your Ends of me—But, since we are both
disappointed, let us make a drawn Battel, and part clear on both
sides. . . .

ORIANA. Pshaw, I despise thee,—Monster.

MIRABEL. Kiss and be Friends then—Don't cry, Child, and you
shall have your Sugar-plumb—Come, Madam, d'ye think I could
be so unreasonable as to make you fast all your Life long?   No,
I did but jest, you shall have your Liberty; here, take your Contract,
and give me mine.

ORIANA. No, I won't.

MIRABEL. Eh!   What is the Girl a Fool?

ORIANA. No, Sir, you shall find me cunning enough to do my
self Justice; and since I must not depend upon your Love, I'll be
reveng'd, and force you to marry me out of spight.

MIRABEL. Then I'll beat thee out of spight; make a most confounded Husband.

ORIANA. O Sir, I shall match ye; A good Husband makes a good
Wife at any time.

MIRABEL. I'll rattle down your China about your Ears.

ORIANA. And I'll rattle about the City to run you in Debt for
more.

MIRABEL. Your Face-mending Toylet shall fly out of the Window.

ORIANA. And your Face-mending Perriwig shall fly after it.

MIRABEL. I'll tear the Furbelow off your Cloaths, and when you
swoon for Vexation, you sha'n't have a Penny to buy a Bottle of
Hart's-horn.

ORIANA. And you, Sir, shall have Hart's-horn in Abundance. . . .

MIRABEL. But, sweet Madam, there is such a thing as a Divorce.

ORIANA. But, sweet Sir, there is such a thing as Alimony, so
divorce on, and spare not.

8. SIR RICHARD STEELE (1672–1729)

The Funeral

Dick Steele is a typical representative of the Restoration
gallant smitten by conscience.   His own gaiety and his own
delinquencies link him with the Ethereges and the Sedleys, and

234

in some moods he would have been eagerly welcomed to their drinking-bouts. One of Steele's earliest works, however, was *The Christian Hero*, one of his latest, *The Conscious Lovers* ; and these two works indicate surely enough the serious element in his nature and the working in him of that sentimental mood which was to take such a hold of the eighteenth-century stage. Between the one mood of gaiety and the other of reflection, *The Funeral* was written. The devotion of Lord Hardy for Lady Sharlot and that of Campley for Lady Harriot savour little of Restoration intrigue ; yet Steele could still laugh, and in the scene of the undertakers he makes capital dramatic use of the satirically conceived undertakers and their companions. This scene is not imbued with wit, for the characters are ' low,' but the laughter is genuine and, save for a phrase or two suggestive of sentimental satire, is unmixed with conscience-stricken thoughts.

(*The Funeral ; or, Grief à la Mode* was produced at Drury Lane in 1701. The following extract is taken from the edition of 1721.)

UNDERTAKERS' WIT

CABINET. I burst into laughter, I can't bear to see writ over an Undertaker's door, Dresses for the Dead, and Necessaries for Funerals; Ha, ha, ha!

SABLE. Well, Gentlemen, 'tis very well; I know you are of the Laughers, the Wits that take the liberty to deride all things that are Magnificent and Solemn.

CAMPLEY. Nay, but after all, I can't but admire *Sable's* nice discerning on the superfluous cares of Mankind, that could lead him to the thought of raising an Estate by providing Horses, Equipage, and Furniture, for those that no longer need 'em.

CABINET. But is it not strangely contradictory, that Men can come to so open, so apparent an hypocrisy, as in the face of all the World, to hire profess'd Mourners to grieve, lament, and follow in their stead, their nearest Relations; and suborn others to do by Art, what they themselves should be prompted to by Nature?

SABLE. That's reasonably enough said: but they regard themselves only in all they act for the Deceas'd; and the poor Dead are deliver'd to my custody, to be embalm'd, slash'd, cut, and drag'd about; not to do them honour, but to satisfy the vanity or interest of their Survivors.

CAMPLEY [*aside to* CABINET]. This Fellow's every way an undertaker: How well and luckily he talks! His prating so aptly, has methinks something more ridiculous in it, than if he were absurd.

CABINET. But, as Mr *Campley* says, how could you dream of making a Fortune from so chimerical a foundation, as the provision of things wholly needless and insignificant?

SABLE. Alas Gentlemen, the value of all things under the Sun is

merely fantastick: We run, we strive, and purchase things with our
blood and money, quite foreign to our intrinsick real happiness,
and which have a being in imagination only; as you may see by
the pudder that is made about Precedence, Titles, Court-favour,
Maidenheads, and China-ware.

CAMPLEY. Ay, Mr *Sable*, but all those are objects that promote
our joy, are bright to the eye, or stamp upon our minds pleasure,
and self-satisfaction.

SABLE. You are extremely mistaken Sir; for one would wonder
to consider that after all our outcrys against self-interested Men,
there are few, very few in the whole World that live to themselves,
but sacrifice their bosom bliss to enjoy a vain show and appearance
of prosperity in the eyes of others. And there is often nothing
more inwardly distress'd than a young Bride in her glittering retinue,
or deeply joyful, than a young Widow in her weeds and black train;
of both which, the Lady of this house may be an instance; for she
has been the one, and is, I'll be sworn, the other.

CABINET. You talk, Mr *Sable*, most learnedly.

SABLE. I have the deepest learning, Sir, Experience. Remember
your Widow-cousin that married last month.

CABINET. Ay, but how cou'd you imagine she was in all that
grief a Hipocrite? Could all those shreiks, those swoonings, that
rising falling bosom be constrain'd? You're uncharitable, *Sable*,
to believe it. What colour, what reason had you for it?

SABLE. First, Sir, her carriage in her concerns with me; for I
never yet could meet with sorrowful Relict, but was her self enough
to make a hard bargain with me: Yet I must confess they have
frequent interruptions of grief and sorrow when they read my Bill.
But as for her, nothing she resolv'd that look'd bright or joyous,
should after her Love's death approach her. All her Servants that
were not coal-black must turn out. A fair complexion made her
eyes and heart ake, she'd none but downright jet: and to exceed
all example she hir'd mourning-furniture by the year, and in case
of my mortality ty'd my Son to the same article; so in six weeks
time ran away with a young Fellow. Prithee push on briskly,
Mr *Cabinet*, now is your time to have this Widow, for *Tattleaid* tells
me she always said she'd never marry.

CABINET. As you say that's generally the most hopeful sign.

SABLE. I tell you Sir, 'tis an infallible one. You know those
professions are only to introduce discourse of matrimony and young
Fellows.

CABINET. But I swear I could not have confidence, ev'n after
all our long acquaintance, and the mutual Love which his Lordship
(who indeed has now been so kind as to leave us) has so long interrupted, to mention a thing of such a nature so unseasonably.

SABLE. Unseasonably! Why I tell you 'tis the only season,
granting her sorrow unfeigned. When you speak of passion, but
in the midst of passions? There's a what de' call, a Crisis. The

lucky minute that's so talk'd of, is a moment between joy and grief, which you must take hold of, and push your fortune. But get you in, and you'll best read your fate in the reception Mrs *Tattleaid* gives you. All she says and all she does, nay her very love and hatred are mere repetition of her Ladyship's passions. I'll say that for her, she's a true Lady's Woman; and is her self as much a second hand thing as her cloaths. But I must beg your pardon Gentlemen, my People are come I see.   [*Exeunt* CABINET *and* CAMPLEY.

[*Enter* SABLE'S MEN.

Where in the name of goodness have you all been? have you brought the saw-dust and tar for embalming? Have you the hangings and the six-penny nails, and my Lord's coat of Arms?

SERVANT. Yes Sir, and had come sooner, but I went to the Herald's for a Coat for Alderman *Gathergrease* that dy'd last night; he has promised to invent one against to-morrow.

SABLE. Ah! Pox take some of our Cits; the first thing after their death is to take care of their birth. Pox! let him bear a pair of stockings, he's the first of his family that ever wore one. Well, come you that are to be Mourners in this house, put on your sad looks, and walk by me that I may sort you. Ha you! a little more upon the dismal; [*forming their countenances*] this Fellow has a good mortal look, place him near the Corps. That wanscot face must be o'top of the Stairs; that Fellow almost in a fright, that looks as if he were full of some strange misery, at the entrance of the Hall. So—but I'll fix you all my self. Let's have no laughing now on any provocation: [*makes faces*] Look yonder, that hale well looking puppy: You ungrateful Scoundrel; did I not pity you, take you out of a great Man's service, and show you the pleasure of receiving wages? Did I not give you ten, then fifteen, now twenty shillings a week, to be sorrowful; and the more I give you, I think, the gladder you are.   [*Enter a* BOY.

BOY. Sir, the Grave-digger of St *Timothy's* in the fields would speak with you.

SABLE. Let him come in.   [*Enter* GRAVE-DIGGER.

GRAVE-DIGGER. I carry'd home to your house the Shrowd the Gentleman was buried in last night; I could not get his ring off very easily, therefore I brought the finger and all; and Sir, the Sexton gives his Service to you, and desires to know whether you'd have any Bodies remov'd or not: if not, he'll let' em lie in their graves a week longer.

SABLE. Give him my service; I can't tell readily, but tell him our Friend, Dr *Passeport* with the powder, has promised me six or seven funerals this week. I'll send to our country-farm at *Kensington-Gravel-Pits*, and our City house in *Warwick-lane* for news; you shall know time enough. Hark'e, be sure there's care taken to give my Lady *Languishe's* Woman a Fee, to keep out that young Fellow came last from *Oxford*; He'll ruine us all.   [*Enter* GOODY TRASH.
I wonder Goody Trash you could not be more punctual; when I

told you, I wanted you and your two Daughters to be three Virgins
to-night, to stand in white about my Lady *Katherine Grissel's* body;
and you know you were privately to bring her home from the
Man-Mid-Wife's, where she dy'd in Childbirth, to be buried like a
Maid; But there is nothing minded. Well I have put off that till
to-morrow: go and get your bagg of brickdust and your whiting.
Go and sell to the Cook-maids; know who has surfeited about
Town: bring me no bad news, none of your recoverys again. And
you Mr Blockhead, I warrant you have not call'd at Mr *Pestles* the
Apothecary: Will that fellow never pay me? I stand bound for
all the Poison in that starving Murderer's shop: He serves me just
as Dr *Quibus* did, who promis'd to write a Treatise against Water-
gruel, a damn'd healthy slop, that has done me more injury than
all the Faculty. Look you now, you're all upon the sneer; let me
have none but downright stupid countenances. I've a good mind
to turn you all off, and take people out of the Play-house: but
hang' em they are as ignorant of their parts as you are of yours;
they never act but when they speak: when the chief indication of
the mind is in the gesture, or indeed in case of sorrow in no gesture,
except you were to act a Widow, or so. But yours you Dolts, is
all in dumb show; Dumb show! I mean expressive eloquent show:
as who can see such an horrid ugly Phiz as that Fellow's, and not
be shock'd, offended, and kill'd of all joy while he beholds it? But
we must not loiter . . . ye stupid rogues whom I have pick'd
out of all the rubbish of Mankind, and fed for your eminent worth-
lessness, attend and know, that I speak you this moment stiff and
immutable to all sense of noise, mirth or laughter: So they are
pretty well . . . pretty well. . . .

[*Makes mouths at 'em as they pass by him, to bring 'em to a
constant countenance.*]

9. ROBERT DODSLEY (1703-64)

The King and the Miller of Mansfield

With the lengthy entertainments which the theatres of the
eighteenth and nineteenth centuries provided for their *clientèle*,
the afterpiece became one of the commonest types of drama in
the age. This might, of course, take a variety of forms, from
pantomimic ballet to operatic farce. As might be imagined, the
majority of the pieces in this kind are of absolutely no real worth,
although there are some excellent farces and a few operatic performances worthy of remembrance. *The King and the Miller of
Mansfield*, which is presented here, was among the more popular
of these afterpieces, and it has an interest denied to many in its
'philosophically' sentimental tone. The story tells how a king,
going to hunt at Mansfield, is separated from his companions and

238

EIGHTEENTH CENTURY

is taken by the honest miller to his house. The influence of the French sentimental spirit is strong on the little playlet, so that Dodsley's drama forms a fitting prelude to the humanitarianism of a Cumberland and a Holcroft.

(*The King and the Miller of Mansfield* was produced at Drury Lane in 1737. The following extract is from the *Trifles* of 1745.)

THE KING AND THE COMMONERS
MARGERY *and* KATE *knitting.*

KATE. O dear, I would not see a spirit for all the world; but I love dearly to hear stories of them.—Well, and what then?

MARGERY. And so, at last, in a dismal, hollow tone it cry'd——

[*A knocking at the door frights them both; they scream out, and throw down their Knitting.*

BOTH. Lord bless us! what's that?

KATE. O dear, mother, it's some judgment upon us, I'm afraid. They say, talk of the devil and he'll appear.

MARGERY. Kate, go and see who's at the door.

KATE. I durst not go, mother; do you go.

MARGERY. Come let's both go.

KATE. Now don't speak as if you was afraid.

MARGERY. No, I won't if I can help it.—Who's there?

DICK [*without*]. What won't you let me in?

KATE. O Gemini! it's like our Dick, I think: He's certainly dead, and it's his spirit.

MARGERY. Heav'n forbid! I think in my heart it's he himself. Open the door, Kate.

KATE. Nay, do you.

MARGERY. Come, we'll both open it.   [*They open the door.*
                                           [*Enter* DICK.

DICK. Dear mother, how do you do? I thought you would not have let me in.

MARGERY. Dear child, I'm overjoy'd to see thee; but I was so frighted, I did not know what to do.

KATE. Dear brother, I'm glad to see you; how have [you] done this long while?

DICK. Very well, Kate. But where's my father?

MARGERY. He heard a gun go off just now, and he's gone to see who 'tis. . . .

MILLER [*without*]. Hoa! Madge! Kate! bring a light here.

MARGERY. Yonder he is.

KATE. Has he catch'd the rogue, I wonder?

                          [*Enter the* KING *and the* MILLER.

MARGERY. Who have you got?

MILLER. I have brought thee a stranger, Madge; thou must give him a supper, and a lodging if thou canst.

239

MARGERY. You have got a better stranger of your own, I can tell you: Dick's come.

MILLER. Dick! Where is he? Why Dick! how is't my lad?

DICK. Very well, I thank you, father.

KING. A little more, and you had push'd me down.

MILLER. Faith, sir, you must excuse me; I was over-joy'd to see my boy. He has been at London, and I have not seen him these four years.

KING. Well, I shall once in my life have the happiness of being treated as a common man; and of seeing human nature without disguise.   [*Aside.*

MILLER. What has brought thee home so unexpected?

DICK. You will know that presently.

MILLER. Of that by-and-by then. We have got the king down in the forest a-hunting this season, and this honest gentleman, who came down with his majesty from London, has been with 'em to day, it seems, and has lost his way. Come, Madge, see what thou can'st get for supper. Kill a couple of the best fowls; and go you, Kate, and draw a pitcher of ale.——We are famous, sir, at Mansfield, for good ale, and for honest fellows that know how to drink it.

KING. Good ale will be acceptable, at present, for I am very dry. But pray, how came your son to leave you, and go to London?

MILLER. Why, that's a story which Dick, perhaps, won't like to be told.

KING. Then I don't desire to hear it.

          [*Enter* KATE *with an earthen pitcher of ale and a horn.*

MILLER. So, now do you go help your mother.——Sir, my hearty service to you.

KING. Thank ye, sir.——This plain sincerity and freedom is a happiness unknown to kings.   [*Aside.*

MILLER. Come, sir.

KING. Richard, my service to you.

DICK. Thank you, sir.

MILLER. Well, Dick, and how dost thou like London? Come, tell us what thou hast seen?

DICK. Seen! I have seen the land of promise.

MILLER. The land of promise! What dost thou mean?

DICK. The court, father.

MILLER. Thou wilt never leave joking.

DICK. To be serious then, I have seen the disappointment of all my hopes and expectations; and that's more than one would wish to see.

MILLER. What! would the great man, thou wast recommended to, do nothing at all for thee at last?

DICK. Why, yes; he would promise me to the last.

MILLER. Zoons! do the courtiers think their dependents can eat promises?

DICK. No, no; they never trouble their heads to think, whether we eat at all or not. I have now dangled after his lordship several years, tantaliz'd with hopes and expectations; this year promis'd one place, the next another, and the third in sure and certain hope of—a disappointment. One falls, and it was promised before; another, and I am just half an hour too late; a third, and it stops the mouth of a creditor; a fourth, and it pays the hire of a flatterer; a fifth, and it bribes a vote; and, the sixth, I am promis'd still. But having thus slept away some years, I awoke from my dream: My lord, I found, was so far from having it in his power to get a place for me, that he had been all this while seeking after one for himself.

MILLER. Poor Dick! And is plain honesty then a recommendation to no place at court?

DICK. It may recommend you to be a footman, perhaps, but nothing farther, nothing farther, indeed. If you look higher, you must furnish yourself with other qualifications: You must learn to say ay, or no; to run, or stand; to fetch, or carry, or leap over a stick at command. You must be master of the arts of flattery, insinuation, dissimulation, application and [*pointing to his palm*] right application too, if you hope to succeed.

KING. You don't consider I am a courtier, methinks.

DICK. Not I, indeed; 'tis no concern of mine what you are. If in general my character of the court is true, 'tis not my fault if it's disagreeable to your worship. There are particular exceptions I own, and I hope you may be one.

KING. Nay, I don't want to be flatter'd, so let that pass. Here's better success to you the next time you come to London.

DICK. I thank ye; but I don't design to see it again in haste.

MILLER. No, no, Dick; instead of depending upon lords promises, depend upon the labour of thine own hands; expect nothing but what thou can'st earn, and then thou wilt not be disappointed. But come, I want a description of London; thou hast told us nothing thou hast seen yet.

DICK. O! 'tis a fine place! I have seen large houses with small hospitality; great men do little actions; and fine ladies do nothing at all. I have seen the honest lawyers of Westminster-Hall, and the virtuous inhabitants of Change-Alley. The politick madmen of coffee-houses, and the wise statesmen of Bedlam. I have seen merry tragedies, and sad comedies; devotion at an opera, and mirth at a sermon; I have seen fine cloaths at St James's, and long bills at Ludgate-hill. I have seen poor grandeur, and rich poverty; high honours, and low flattery; great pride, and no merit. In short, I have seen a fool with a title, a knave with a pension, and an honest man with a thread-bare coat. Pray how do you like London?

MILLER. And is this the best description thou can'st give of it?

DICK. Yes.

KING. Why, Richard, you are a satirist, I find.

Q

241

DICK. I love to speak truth, sir; if that happens to be satire, I can't help it.

MILLER. Well, if this be London, give me my country cottage; which, tho' it is not a great house, nor a fine house, is my own house, and I can shew a receipt for the building on't.—But come, sir, our supper, I believe, is ready for us by this time; and to such as I have, you're as welcome as a prince.

KING. I thank you.

10. HUGH KELLY (1739–77)

A Word to the Wise

Kelly and Cumberland are nearly always associated together, but this linking of their names, justified as it is by the authority of Goldsmith's *Retaliation*, does not precisely accord with the facts. It is true that both were sentimentalists, that both used that elaborated and 'genteel' diction which marred so much eighteenth-century comedy, but these points of similarity are countered by others of difference. Kelly is the less didactic of the two. He may write to show up a folly, but he never produced anything quite on the lines of *The Jew*. His aim is rather to present a sentimentalized picture of the manners of his age, and in this respect he follows much more closely than does Cumberland the main lines of dramatic development laid down by the Restoration masters. He is far off from them, certainly, but there are in his plays many touches which indicate that he had at least read their works. The scene chosen here is that in which Miss Dormer reveals the sentiments of her heart to her paternally selected *fiancé*, and in which she discusses her action with her friend Miss Montagu.

(*A Word to the Wise* was produced at Drury Lane in 1770. The passage given below is taken from the first edition of 1770.)

A MAIDEN'S FRANKNESS

MISS DORMER. O, Sir George, to the greatness of your humanity let me appeal against the prepossession of your heart.—You see before you a distressed young creature, whose affection is already engaged;—and who, tho' she thinks herself highly honoured by your sentiments, is wholly unable to return them.

SIR GEORGE. I am extremely sorry, madam,—to have been— I say, madam,—that—really I am so exceedingly disconcerted, that I don't know what to say.——

MISS DORMER. O, Sir George, you have no occasion for apologies, tho' I have unhappily too much;—but I know the nicety of your honour, and I depend upon it with security.—Let me then entreat an additional act of goodness at your hands, which is absolutely

242

necessary, as well for my peace, as for my father's :—this is to contrive such a method of withdrawing your addresses, as will not expose me to his displeasure.—Let the discontinuance of them appear, not to be the result of my request, but the consequence of your own determination; he is a zealous advocate for you, and I shou'd incur his severest resentment, if he was to be acquainted with the real impediment to the match.—You are distressed, Sir George, and I am sinking with confusion;—I shall therefore only add that I trust you with more than life, and that I conjure you to compassionate my situation.—By this conduct you will engage my eternal esteem, and merit that happiness with a much more deserving woman, which it is impossible for you ever to enjoy with me.   [*Exit.*

SIR GEORGE. What is all this!—a dream!—No, 'tis no dream, and I feel myself awake but too sensibly.—What then, am I rejected, despis'd, where I suppos'd myself certain of success and approbation. —This is too much;—neither my pride nor my tenderness can support the indignity,—and I shall—what shall I do? Shall I meanly betray the poor girl who has generously thrown herself upon my humanity, and convince the world by such a conduct that she was right in refusing me :—no, damn it—I scorn a littleness of that nature, and I must shew myself worthy of her affection, tho' her unfortunate pre-engagement wou'd not suffer me to obtain it. But how in the name of perplexity shall I manage the matter?—A refusal on my side necessarily incurs the general resentment of the family, and the censure of the world into the bargain;—so that in all probability I shall not only have the honour of risquing my life but my reputation, and this for the happiness of giving the woman I admire to the arms of my rival.—Really the prospect is a very comfortable one.   [*Exit.*

[*Enter* MISS MONTAGU *and* MISS DORMER.

MISS MONTAGU. Upon my word, Caroline, you have acted a very heroic part;—but this unaccountable love is able to carry the most timid of the romantic ladies thro' the greatest difficulties.— Now had I been in your situation, I cou'd no more have ask'd the man to take my fault upon himself, than I cou'd have made down-right love to him.

MISS DORMER. Ah, Harriot, you little know to what extremities a strong prepossession is capable of driving a woman, even where there is the most evident impossibility of ever obtaining the object of her inclinations.

MISS MONTAGU. O, my dear, I see very plainly that it is capable of driving a woman to very great extremities.

MISS DORMER. Well I am convinc'd that if any thing was to prevent your marriage with my brother, you wou'd, notwithstanding this seeming insensibility, look upon the rest of his sex with the utmost aversion.

MISS MONTAGU. I wonder, Caroline, after my repeated declarations of indifference with regard to your brother, that you can imagine I consider him with the smallest partiality.—There was indeed a time when I might have been prevailed upon to endure the creature,—but his negligence quickly alarmed my pride, and prevented me from squandering a single sentiment of tenderness, upon a man who seem'd so little inclin'd to deserve it.

MISS DORMER. Well, my dear, I am in hopes that you will have but little reason to blame his negligence for the future,—because I know he intends this very day to solicit your approbation.

MISS MONTAGU. O he does me infinite honour, and I suppose you imagine he is entitled to one of my best curtsies for so extraordinary an instance of his condescension;—but, Caroline, I am not altogether so critically situated as to be glad of a husband at any rate.—nor have I such a meanness of disposition as to favour any addresses which are made to me with a visible reluctance. . . .

MISS DORMER. Well, well, Jack must solicit for himself, and I am sure, notwithstanding this pretended want of feeling, you are no way destitute of good-nature and sensibility.

MISS MONTAGU. Good-nature and sensibility, Caroline;—ay, 'tis this good-nature and sensibility that makes the men so intolerably vain, and renders us so frequently contemptible.—If a fellow treats us with ever so much insolence, he has only to burst into a passionate rant, and tell a gross lie with a prodigious agitation;—in proportion as he whines we become softened; till at last, bursting into tears, we bid the sweet creature rise,—tell him that our fortune is entirely at his service, and beg that he will immediately assume the power of making us compleatly miserable.

MISS DORMER. What a picture!

MISS MONTAGU. While he, scarcely able to stifle his laughter, retires to divert his dissolute companions with our weakness, and breaking into a yawn of insolent affectation, cries, " poor fool she's doatingly fond of me."

11. RICHARD CUMBERLAND (1732–1811)

The Jew

Sentimentalism, starting vaguely as a mere moral reaction to the frankness of Restoration society, moved steadily in the eighteenth century toward humanitarianism. In the sphere of drama the development can be clearly traced in the plays of Cibber, Steele, Kelly, and Cumberland. While humanitarianism in this last-mentioned author has not yet become strong, it at least points forward to the future. There is, in his dramas, evident thinking about life, evident sympathy with those distressed. Of this tendency no clearer example could be found than *The Jew*, in which the author, taking a figure which had been for centuries a laughing-stock or the victim of bitter contumely, creates the generous-minded character of Sheva. It is Sheva who rescues the son of Sir Stephen Bertram when he is in distress; it is he who is, as it were, the *deus ex machina*—not only in the last act of the play, but throughout its entirety. One cannot claim that in *The Jew* there is high art; but in a play such as this there is infinite promise. We are approaching nearer to Galsworthy.

(*The Jew* was first acted at Drury Lane in 1794. The passage quoted below is taken from the fifth edition of 1795.)

A GENTILE SHAMED

SHEVA. Aha! I am very much fatigued: there is great throng and press in the offices at the bank, and I am aged and feeble.

SIR STEPHEN. Hold, Sir;—Before I welcome you within these doors, or suffer you to sit down in my presence, I demand to know explicitly, and without prevarication, if you have furnish'd my son with money secretly, and without my leave?

SHEVA. If I do lend, ought I not to lend it in secret? If I do not ask your leave, Sir Stephen, may I not dispose of my own monies according to my own liking? But if it is a crime, I do wish to ask you who is my accuser? that, I believe, is justice everywhere, and in your happy country I do think it is law likewise.

SIR STEPHEN. Very well, Sir, you shall have both law and justice. The information comes from your own servant Jabal. Can you controvert it?

SHEVA. I do presume to say my servant ought not to report his master's secrets; but I will not say he has not spoken the truth.

SIR STEPHEN. Then you confess the fact——

SHEVA. I Humbly think there is no call for that: you have the information from my foot-boy—I do not deny it.

SIR STEPHEN. And the sum——

SHEVA. I do not talk of the sum, Sir Stephen, that is not my practice; neither, under favor, is my foot-boy my cashier. If he be a knave, and listen at my key-hole, the more shame his; I am not in the fault.

SIR STEPHEN. Not in the fault! Wretch, miser, usurer! you never yet let loose a single guinea from your gripe, but with a view to doubling it at the return. I know you what you are.

SHEVA Indeed! 'tis more than I will say of myself.—I pray you, goot sir Stephen, take a little time to know my heart, before you rob me of my reputation. I am a Jew, a poor defenceless Jew; that is enough to make me miser, usurer—— Alas! I cannot help it.

SIR STEPHEN. No matter: you are caught in your own trap: I tell you now my son is ruin'd, disinherited, undone. One consolation is, that you have lost your money.

SHEVA. If that be a consolation, you are very welcome to it. If my monies are lost, my motives are not.

SIR STEPHEN. I'll never pay one farthing of his debts; he has offended me for life; refus'd a lady with ten thousand pounds, and married a poor miss without a doit.

SHEVA. Yes, I do understand your son is married.

SIR STEPHEN. Do you so? By the same token I do understand you to be a villain.

SHEVA. Aha! that is a very bad word—villain. I did never think to hear that word from one, who says he knows me. . . . How can I be a villain?

SIR STEPHEN. Do you not uphold the son against the father?

SHEVA. I do uphold the son, but not against the fader; it is not natural to suppose the oppressor and the fader one and the same person. I did see your son struck down to the ground with sorrow, cut to the heart: I did not stop to ask whose hand had laid him low: I gave him mine, and rais'd him up.

SIR STEPHEN. You! you to talk of charity!

SHEVA. I do not talk of it: I feel it.

SIR STEPHEN. What claim have you to generosity, humanity, or any manly virtue? Which of your money-making tribe ever had sense of pity? Shew me the terms, on which you have lent this money, if you dare! Exhibit the dark deed, by which you have mesh'd your victim in the snares of usury; but be assured I'll drag you to the light, and publish your base dealings in the world.

[Catches him by the sleeve.

SHEVA. Take your hand from my coat—my coat and I are very old, and pretty well worn out together—There, there! be patient—moderate your passions and you shall see my terms: they are in little compass: fair dealings may be comprised in few words.

SIR STEPHEN. If they are fair, produce them.

SHEVA. Let me see, let me see!—Ah, poor Sheva!—I do so tremble, I can hardly hold my papers—So, so! Now I am right—Aha! here it is.

SIR STEPHEN. Let me see it.

SHEVA. Take it—Do you not see it now? Have you cast your eye over it? Is it not right? I am no more than broker, look you: If there is a mistake, point it out, and I will correct it.

SIR STEPHEN. Ten thousand pounds invested in the three per cents., money of Eliza, late Ratcliffe, now Bertram!

SHEVA. Even so! a pretty tolerable fortune for a poor disinherited son not worth a penny.

SIR STEPHEN. I'm thunderstruck!

SHEVA. Are you so? I was struck too, but not by thunder. And what has Sheva done to be call'd villain?—I am a Jew, what then? Is that a reason none of my tribe shou'd have a sense of pity? You have no great deal of pity yourself, but I do know many many noble British merchants that abound in pity, therefore I do not abuse your tribe.

SIR STEPHEN. I am confounded and asham'd; I see my fault, and most sincerely ask your pardon.

SHEVA. Goot lack, goot lack! that is too much. I pray you, goot Sir Stephen, say no more ; you'll bring the blush upon my cheek, if you demean yourself so far to a poor Jew, who is your very humble servant to command.

12. THOMAS HOLCROFT (1745–1809)

The Road to Ruin

Of the many sentimental comedies of the late eighteenth century *The Road to Ruin* (it is difficult to say for what reason) has retained a certain fame. Its title is known to many, and I believe it may yet be seen occasionally in small provincial theatres. Holcroft, its author, was a man of undoubtedly interesting personality. A humanitarian and revolutionist, he incurred odium during those years when the Rights of Man were being upheld or condemned, practically in France and philosophically in England. His dramatic works are numerous, and nearly all are coloured by the sentimental tints already made popular by Kelly and Cumberland, although he does, in general, keep more clearly to the delineation of contemporary life than their artificialities would allow. The weaknesses of the style, however, are also apparent in his work, and these at once destroy any claims he might otherwise have to artistry. His dialogue is often unnatural and his types, ultimately copied though they may be from London society, are exaggerated and frequently dull. The scene chosen from *The Road to Ruin* has been selected in order to show, first, the element of melodramatic villainy nearly always introduced into these plays, and, secondly, the over-emphasized type characteristics (intended to be comic), here represented by Goldfinch with his *staccato* utterance.

(The following extract is taken from the first edition (1792).)

THE WIDOW CONFESSES TO HER LOVE OF THE HERO

Silky has, by chance, come into possession of a will left by Alderman Warren, by the terms of which he cuts his Widow off with a pittance (£600 a year) should she marry again. He refuses to part with it unless at his own price.

SILKY. Why, Madam, I have a proposal—You know the power of your own charms!

WIDOW. Which I believe is more than you do, Mr Silky——

SILKY. Hah! Don't say so, madam! Don't say so!—Would I

were a handsome, rich and well-born youth!—But you know Mr Goldfinch?—Ah, ha, ha, ha! I could tell you a secret!

WIDOW. What, that he is dying for me, I suppose?

SILKY. Ah!—So smitten!—Talks of nothing else!

WIDOW. And is that any secret, think you?

SILKY. The alderman I find died worth more than a plum and a half——

WIDOW. Well?

SILKY. I have talked the matter over with my friend, Mr Goldfinch, and he thinks it but reasonable, that for a secret of so much importance, which would almost sweep the whole away, I should receive one third.

WIDOW. Fifty thousand pounds, Mr Silky?

SILKY. I can't take less.

WIDOW. Why you are a greater rogue than even I thought you!

SILKY. Lord, madam, it's no roguery! It's only a knowledge of the world! A young husband with a hundred thousand pounds, or poor six hundred a year without any husband!

WIDOW. You are a very shocking old miser, Mr Silky! A very repulsive sort of a person! What heart you had is turned to stone! You are insensible of the power of a pair of fine eyes! But I have made a conquest that places me beyond your reach—I mean to marry Mr Dornton!

SILKY [surprised]. What! Old Mr Dornton, madam?

WIDOW. Old Mr Dornton, man?—I never saw the figure in my life! No! the gay and gallant young Mr Dornton! The pride of the city, and the lawful monarch of my bleeding heart!

SILKY. Ha, ha, ha! Young Mr Dornton!

WIDOW. So you may take your will and light your fires with it! You will not make a penny of it in any other way. Mr Sulky, the executor, is Mr Dornton's partner, and when I marry Mr Dornton he will never inflict the absurd penalty.

SILKY. Ha, ha, ha! No, madam! When you marry Mr Dornton, that he certainly never will! But if any accident should happen to prevent the match, you will then let me hear from you? . . . Only remember, ha, ha, ha! If you should want me, I live at Number 40. My name is on the door. Ha, ha, ha! Mr Dornton! Good morning, madam! Mr Dornton! Ha, ha, ha! You'll send if you should want me? [Exit laughing.

WIDOW. Jenny! [Calling.

[Enter JENNY.

JENNY. Ma'am!

WIDOW. As I was saying, Jenny, pray how did it happen that Mr Dornton went away without seeing me?

JENNY. Indeed, ma'am, I don't know.

WIDOW. Cruel youth!

JENNY. I'm sure, ma'am, I wonder how you can like him better than Mr Goldfinch!

248

WIDOW. Mr Goldfinch is very well, Jenny—But Mr Dornton! Oh incomparable!

JENNY. I am sure, ma'am, if I was a rich lady, and a handsome lady, and a fine lady, like you, I should say Mr Goldfinch for my money!

WIDOW. Should you, Jenny?—Well, I don't know——

[*Languishing.*

GOLDFINCH [*without*]. Tellee I must see her.

WIDOW. As I live, here he comes!—He is such a boisterous person! [*Goes to the glass.*] How do I look, Jenny? I protest my face is of all colours!

JENNY [*significantly after examining*]. You had better go up to your toilette for a minute.

WIDOW. The smooth-tongued old extortioner has put me into such a fluster—— Don't let him go, Jenny.

JENNY. Never fear, ma'am.

WIDOW. I'll not stay too long.   [*Exit.*

[*Enter* GOLDFINCH, *his Clothes, Hat, and Boots dirtied by a Fall.*

GOLDFINCH. Here I am——All alive.

JENNY. Dear! What's the matter?

GOLDFINCH. Safe and sound! Fine kick up!

JENNY. Have you been thrown?

GOLDFINCH. Pitched five-and-twenty feet into a ditch—Souse!

JENNY. Dear me!

GOLDFINCH. Pretty commence!—No matter—Limbs whole—Heart sound—That's your sort!

JENNY. Where did it happen?

GOLDFINCH. Bye road—Back of Islington—Had them tight in hand too—Came to a short turn and a narrow lane—Up flew a damned dancing-master's umbrella—Bounce—Off they went—Road repairing—Wheelbarrow in the way—Crash—Out flew I—Whiz—Fire flashed—Lay stunned—Got up—Looked foolish—Shafts broke—Snarler and Blackguard both down—Black-and-all-black paying away, pannels smashed, traces cut, Snarler lamed.

JENNY. Terrible!

GOLDFINCH. Damned mad!—Cursed a few, cut up Black-and-all-black, horsewhipped Tom, took coach and drove here like a devil in a whirlwind!

JENNY. 'Tis very well your neck's not broke!

GOLDFINCH. Little stiff—No matter—Damn all dancing-masters and their umbrellas!

JENNY. You had better have been here, Mr Goldfinch. You stand so long, shilly shally, that you'll be cut out at last. If you had but a licence now in your pocket, I'd undertake to have you married in half an hour!

GOLDFINCH. Do you think so?

JENNY. Think? I'm sure on't.

GOLDFINCH. Dammee, I'll post away and get one—Must not lose

her; the games up if I do!—Must have her! Be true to me, and
I'll secure you the hundred! I'll be back from the Commons in a
smack!

13. GEORGE COLMAN THE ELDER (1732–94)

Polly Honeycombe

Among the many writers of comedy in the Garrick period
George Colman the Elder deserves an honoured place. His
talent, definitely anti-sentimental, led him to depict the manners
of his age in a way more natural than could Cumberland, and his
intimate association with the theatre gave his works a genuine
dramatic quality. Most famous for *The Jealous Wife* and *The
Clandestine Marriage*, he yet deserves remembrance not only for
these, but also for the many lesser pieces with which he provided
his theatres. One of his earliest efforts was "A Dramatick
Novel" entitled *Polly Honeycombe* (produced at Drury Lane on
December 5, 1760), in which he endeavoured to ridicule the
affected tastes of young ladies whose heads were filled with
amorous chimeras culled from the circulating library. The scene
selected here shows Polly, the fiction-mad heroine, locked into her
room by her father, who is ignorant of the fact that Scribble, her
lover, has concealed himself in a closet. The style has not the
polish of a Sheridan play, but there is an ease which comes close
to that and which was later to be developed and improved by its
author.

(The following passage is taken from *The Dramatick Works of
George Colman* (1777), vol. iv.)

SCRIBBLE ESCAPES FROM AN EMBARRASSING SITUATION

POLLY. And so I will have Mr Scribble too, do what you can, old
Squaretoes! I am provided with pen, ink, and paper, in spite of
their teeth. I remember that Clarissa had cunning drawers made
on purpose to secure those things, in case of an accident: I am very
glad I have had caution enough to provide myself with the same
implements of intrigue, tho' with a little more ingenuity. Indeed,
now they make standishes, and tea-chests, and dressing-boxes, in all
sorts of shapes and figures; But mine are of my own invention.
Here I've got an excellent ink-horn in my pincushion; and a case
of pens, and some paper, in my fan. [*Produces them.*] I will write
to Mr Scribble immediately. I shall certainly see him eaves-dropping
about our door the first opportunity and then I'll toss it to him out
of the window. [*Sits down to write.*

[SCRIBBLE, *putting his head out of the door of the closet.*

SCRIBBLE. A clear coast, I find. The old codger's gone, and has
lock'd me up with his daughter. So much the better!—Pretty soul!

250

what is she about? writing? A letter to me, I'll bet ten to one. I'll go and answer it in *propria persona.*

> [*Comes forward, and stands behind* POLLY, *looking over her writing.*

POLLY [*writing*]. " Me—in—your—arms." Let me see; what have I written? [*Reading*] " My dearest, dear Mr Scribble."

SCRIBBLE. I thought so!

POLLY [*reading*]. " I am now writing in the most cruel confinement. Fly then, oh, fly to me on the wings of love, release me from this horrid gaol, and imprison me in your arms."

SCRIBBLE. That I will with all my heart.   [*Embracing her.*

POLLY. Oh!   [*Screaming.*

SCRIBBLE. Oh, the devil! why do you scream so? I shall be discovered, in spite of fortune.   [*Running about.*

POLLY. Bless me! is it you? Hush! [*Running to the door*] here's my father coming upstairs, I protest.

SCRIBBLE. What the deuce shall I do? I'll run into the closet again.

POLLY. Oh, no! he'll search the closet. Jump out of the window!

SCRIBBLE. I beg to be excus'd.

POLLY. Lord! here's no time to—he's here! get under the table! [SCRIBBLE *hides.*] Lie still. What shall I say?

> [*Sits down by the table.*
> [*Enter* HONEYCOMBE.

HONEYCOMBE. How now, hussy? What's all this noise?

POLLY. Sir!   [*Affecting surprise.*

HONEYCOMBE. What made you scream so violently?

POLLY. Scream, papa?

HONEYCOMBE. Scream, papa? Ay, scream, hussy! What made you scream, I say?

POLLY. Lord, papa, I have never opened my lips, but have been in a philosophical resverie ever since you left me.

HONEYCOMBE. I am sure I thought I heard—— But, how now, hussy? what's here? Pens, ink, and paper! Hark ye, hussy! how came you by these? So, so! fine contrivances! [*Examining them*] And a letter begun too: " Cruel confinement—wings of love—your arms" [*reading*]. Ah, you forward slut! But I am glad I have discovered this: I'll seize these moveables. So, so! now write, if you can. Nobody shall come near you: Send to him, if you can. Now, see how Mr Scribble will get at you: Now I have you safe, mistress! and now—ha! ha!—now you may make love to the table. Hey-day! what's here? a man! [*Seeing* SCRIBBLE] There was a noise then. Have I caught you, madam? Come, Sir, come out of your hole! [SCRIBBLE *comes from under the table.*] A footman! who the devil are you, Sir? where did you come from? what d'ye want? how came you here? eh, sirrah!

SCRIBBLE. Sir—I—I—what the deuce shall I say to him?

HONEYCOMBE. Speak, rascal!

SCRIBBLE. Sir—I—I—I came about a little business to Miss Honeycombe.

HONEYCOMBE. Business! Ay, you look like a man of business, indeed. What! you were to carry this scrawl of a love-letter, I suppose. Eh, sirrah!

SCRIBBLE. A lucky mistake! I'll humour it.   [*Aside.*

HONEYCOMBE. What's that you mutter?—Whose livery is this? who do you belong to, fellow?

SCRIBBLE. My master.

HONEYCOMBE. And who is your master, Sir?

SCRIBBLE. A gentleman.

POLLY. Papa don't suspect who he is. I must speak for him [*aside*]. This honest young man belongs to the gentleman I told you I was devoted to; Mr Scribble, papa!

HONEYCOMBE. To Mr Scribble, does he? Very fine!

SCRIBBLE. Yes, Sir! to Mr Scribble; a person of fortune and character; a man of fashion, Sir! Miss Polly need not blush to own her passion for him: I don't know a finer gentleman about town than Mr Scribble.

POLLY. Lord, how well he behaves! We shall certainly bam the old gentleman.   [*Aside.*

HONEYCOMBE. Hark ye, sirrah! Get out of my house this instant. I've a good mind to have you tossed in a blanket, or dragged thro' a horse-pond, or tied neck and heels, and—I've a good mind to carry you before the sitting alderman, you dog you!

SCRIBBLE. I won't give you that trouble, Sir! Miss Honeycombe, I kiss your hands. You have no further commands to my master, at present, ma'am? your compliments, I suppose?

POLLY. Compliments! my best love to my dear Mr Scribble!

SCRIBBLE. Pretty soul!

HONEYCOMBE. This is beyond all patience. Out of my house, sirrah! Where are all my fellows? I'll have you thrown out of the window! you shall be trundled down stairs headlong! you shall——

SCRIBBLE. Patience, old gentleman! I shall go out of the house the same way I came into it, I promise you! And let me tell you, Sir, by way of a kind word at parting, that scold Miss Polly ever so much, watch her ever so narrowly, or confine her ever so closely, Mr Scribble will have her, whether you will or no, you old cuff you!

14. ARTHUR MURPHY (1727-1805)

Know Your Own Mind

Arthur Murphy and George Colman were the two most stalwart companions of Goldsmith and Sheridan in the attempt to preserve the spirit of pure, as distinct from sentimental, comedy in the late eighteenth century. Murphy's work, it is true, is varied in character—from 'Augustan' tragedies to veriest farce ; but in the non-tragic sphere he nearly always endeavoured to imitate not the serious *drames*, which had been imported from France, but the older style, which ultimately is to be traced back to the Restoration. *The Way to Keep Him* (1760) is probably his best comedy, but as that play is now readily obtainable in an Oxford University Press reprint (1927), it has been considered advisable to make a selection from another play. *Know Your Own Mind* does not possess the sustained interest of the other, but it has the same general atmosphere, while the opposition of the gay Lady Bell and the staid Lady Jane is happily conceived.

(The play was first acted and printed in 1777. The following extract is taken from *The Works of Arthur Murphy, Esq.* (1786), vol. iv, which seems to give the author's finally considered dialogue.)

LADY BELL ANNOYS HER SISTER, LADY JANE, BY HER LEVITY

LADY JANE. Miss Neville, I am very angry with you. What is the matter? Has any thing made you uneasy?

MISS NEVILLE. No; I am not remarkable for high spirits, you know.

LADY JANE. Why would not you give us your company? How can you be so cross? That sister of mine is the verriest madcap!

MISS NEVILLE. Lady Bell is rather lively to be sure.

LADY JANE. But when she once begins, she hazards every thing, and talks sometimes like a very libertine.

MISS NEVILLE. The overflowing of gaiety, and good humour.

LADY JANE. I wish she would restrain herself a little. Madam La Rouge is with her: she has the sweetest Point eyes ever beheld. I was endeavouring to cheapen it, but Lady Bell was so troublesome; she called me a thousand prudes, and will have it that nothing runs in my head, but a lover.

MISS NEVILLE. I don't know but she may be right. We are apt to deceive ourselves. We talk of vapours, and fidgets, and retirement, but it is often artful, sly, insinuating man, that lurks at the bottom.

LADY JANE. Well, I vow you'll make me hate you.

MISS NEVILLE. Has Captain Bygrove made no disturbance in your heart?

LADY JANE. How can you? You are as great a plague as my sister. As I live and breathe, the giddy romp is coming. You must take my part.   [*Enter* LADY BELL.

LADY BELL [*repeating*].

> Yes, I'm in love, I own it now,
> And Cœlia has undone me;
> And yet, I swear, I can't tell how,
> The pleasing plague stole on me.

What would I give to have some miserable swain talk in that style of me? "Belinda has undone me"; charming!

MISS NEVILLE. A lively imagination is a blessing, and you are happy, Lady Bell.

LADY BELL. I am so: but then I am not talked of: I am losing all my time.

LADY JANE. Why, you bold creature! I hate to hear you talk with so much intrepidity.

LADY BELL. Prudery! my dear sister, downright prudery! I am not for making mysteries of what all the world knows.

LADY JANE. And how do I make mysteries pray?

LADY BELL. Why, you confident thing, I'll prove it against you.

LADY JANE. But what? what? what will you prove?

LADY BELL. That you are ready to jump out of your little wits for a husband, my demure, sober sister. Miss Neville, a poet is not more eager for the success of a new comedy, nor one of his brother poets more desirous to see it fail, than that girl is to throw herself into the arms of a man.

LADY JANE. All scandal, sister.

LADY BELL. Miss Neville shall be judge.

LADY JANE. Your story is mere invention.

LADY BELL. Was there ever such a wrangler?

LADY JANE. You'll not make good your words.

LADY BELL [pats her hand]. Hold your tongue, Miss, will you?

LADY JANE. Very well, go on.

LADY BELL. Will you have done? Now mind, Miss Neville. She does not want to be married, she says. The other night, my young madam, whose thoughts are always composed and even, went to sleep as soon as we got to bed, and then her busy imagination went to work with all the vivacity of an intriguing chambermaid.

LADY JANE. And how can you tell that, pray?

LADY BELL. Out of your own mouth you shall be judged. Miss Neville, she talked in her sleep, like a beauty in a side box, and then fell a singing:

> No, no; he is true, and I believe;
> He look'd, he sigh'd, he can't deceive;
> No, no; I have conquer'd; he is mine;
> My heart is touch'd, and I resign.

LADY JANE. Oh! you scurrilous creature.

MISS NEVILLE. Fairly caught, Lady Jane.

LADY JANE. All odious slander; you judge of me by yourself.

LADY BELL. I do so. I mean to be married, and am frank enough to own it. But you may let "concealment feed on your damask cheek." My damask cheek, I hope, was made for other purposes.

LADY JANE. Gracious! there is no bearing this. What a mad girl you are!

LADY BELL. Not in the least. A natural character. One would not, to be sure, tell a hideous man that one loves him: but when one has encouraged him by degrees, and drawn him on, like a new glove, and perhaps done him a mischief in the doing it, why then one would draw him off again, and may be ask a pretty fellow to help a body; and then the wretch looks so piteous, and kneels at your feet; then rises in a jealous fit. "I take my everlasting farewell; never to return; no, never; what to her? who encouraged me? encouraged him? who promised? broke her promise? the treacherous, faithless, dear, deluding"—then returns in an instant; hands dangling; eyes imploring; tongue faultering; "Lady Bell,—Lady Bell—when you know that I adore you"—And I burst out into a fit of laughter in his face: oh! that's my joy, my triumph, my supreme delight.

LADY JANE. And is there not a kind of cruelty in all this?

LADY BELL. Oh! your very humble servant, my sweet Lady Graveairs. Cruelty! The difference between you and me, sister, is this; you deny your love to your female friends, and own it to the man; now I deny it to him, but among ourselves, I fairly own that Miss Neville is not more impatient to be married to Sir Harry, than I to——

MISS NEVILLE. Who, I? Spare me, I beg of you. Why Sir Harry?

LADY JANE. Now, now, your turn is come. Never spare her, sister.

MISS NEVILLE. You must excuse me, I am not in spirits for all this raillery.

15. OLIVER GOLDSMITH (1728–74)

She Stoops to Conquer

Of all eighteenth-century comedies this is the best known, so well known that, did this volume not essay to present examples of the various dramatic styles, it might well have been omitted here. Goldsmith, however, obviously has to take his place among the major English playwrights, and the scene of "equi-vogue," when Marlow and Hastings come to Hardcastle's house, mistaking it for an inn, has such a genuine comic force that it may well be represented here. Goldsmith shines hardly at all in the wit beloved by his contemporary Sheridan, but he atones for his lack of this quality by an all-pervading humour. His very situations are humorous, and all his characters are conceived in the light of this mood. There will be noted here in particular not only the contrast between the idea (the inn) and the real (the country mansion), but the additional contrast afforded by the reminiscence-loving Hardcastle and the two travellers with their genteel airs.

EXTRACTS FROM BRITISH & IRISH PLAYS

(*She Stoops to Conquer; or, The Mistakes of a Night* was produced at Covent Garden in 1773. The passage below is taken from the fourth edition, 1773.)

A SCENE OF EQUIVOQUE

HARDCASTLE. Gentlemen, once more you are heartily welcome. Which is Mr Marlow? Sir, you're heartily welcome. It's not my way, you see, to receive my friends with my back to the fire. I like to give them a hearty reception in the old stile at my gate. I like to see their horses and trunks taken care of.

MARLOW [*aside*]. He has got our names from the servants already. [*To him*] We approve your caution and hospitality, Sir. [*To* HASTINGS] I have been thinking, George, of changing our travelling dresses in the morning. I am grown confoundedly ashamed of mine.

HARDCASTLE. I beg, Mr Marlow, you'll use no ceremony in this house.

HASTINGS. I fancy, George, you're right: the first blow is half the battle. I intend opening the campaign with the white and gold.

HARDCASTLE. Mr Marlow—Mr Hastings—gentlemen—pray be under no constraint in this house. This is Liberty-hall, gentlemen. You may do just as you please here.

MARLOW. Yet, George, if we open the campaign too fiercely at first, we may want ammunition before it is over. I think to reserve the embroidery to secure a retreat.

HARDCASTLE. Your talking of a retreat, Mr Marlow, puts me in mind of the Duke of Marlborough, when we went to besiege Denain. He first summoned the garrison.

MARLOW. Don't you think the *ventre dor* waistcoat will do with the plain brown?

HARDCASTLE. He first summoned the garrison, which might consist of about five thousand men——

HASTINGS. I think not: Brown and yellow mix but very poorly.

HARDCASTLE. I say, gentlemen, as I was telling you, he summoned the garrison, which might consist of about five thousand men——

MARLOW. The girls like finery.

HARDCASTLE. Which might consist of about five thousand men, well appointed with stores, ammunition, and other implements of war. Now, says the Duke of Marlborough, to George Brooks, that stood next to him—You must have heard of George Brooks; I'll pawn my Dukedom, says he, but I take that garrison without spilling a drop of blood. So——

MARLOW. What, my good friend, if you gave us a glass of punch in the mean time, it would help us to carry on the siege with vigour.

HARDCASTLE. Punch, Sir! [*Aside*] This is the most unaccountable kind of modesty I ever met with.

MARLOW. Yes, Sir, Punch. A glass of warm punch, after our journey, will be comfortable. This is Liberty-hall, you know.

HARDCASTLE. Here's Cup, Sir.

MARLOW [*aside*]. So this fellow, in his Liberty-hall, will only let us have just what he pleases.

HARDCASTLE [*taking the Cup*]. I hope you'll find it to your mind. I have prepared it with my own hands, and I believe you'll own the ingredients are tolerable. Will you be so good as to pledge me, Sir? Here, Mr Marlow, here is to our better acquaintance. [*Drinks.*

MARLOW [*aside*]. A very impudent fellow this! but he's a character, and I'll humour him a little. Sir, my service to you. [*Drinks.*

HASTINGS [*aside*]. I see this fellow wants to give us his company, and forgets that he's an innkeeper, before he has learned to be a gentleman.

MARLOW. From the excellence of your cup, my old friend, I suppose you have a good deal of business in this part of the country. Warm work, now and then, at elections, I suppose.

HARDCASTLE. No, Sir, I have long given that work over. Since our betters have hit upon the expedient of electing each other, there's no business *for us that sell ale*.

HASTINGS. So, then you have no turn for politics I find.

HARDCASTLE. Not in the least. There was a time, indeed, I fretted myself about the mistakes of government, like other people; but finding myself every day grow more angry, and the government growing no better, I left it to mend itself. Since that, I no more trouble my head about *Heyder Ally*, or *Ally Cawn*, than about *Ally Croaker*. Sir, my service to you. . . . Your Generalship puts me in mind of Prince Eugene, when he fought the Turks at the battle of Belgrade. You shall hear.

MARLOW. Instead of the battle of Belgrade, I believe it's almost time to talk about supper. What has your philosophy got in the house for supper?

HARDCASTLE. For Supper, Sir! [*Aside*] Was ever such a request to a man in his own house?

MARLOW. Yes, Sir, supper, Sir; I begin to feel an appetite. I shall make devilish work to-night in the larder, I promise you.

HARDCASTLE [*aside*]. Such a brazen dog sure never my eyes beheld. [*To him*] Why really, Sir, as for supper I can't well tell. My Dorothy, and the cook maid, settle these things between them. I leave these kind of things entirely to them. . . .

HASTINGS. Let's see your list of the larder then. I ask it as a favour. I always match my appetite to my bill of fare.

MARLOW [*to* HARDCASTLE, *who looks at them with surprise*]. Sir, he's very right, and it's my way too.

HARDCASTLE. Sir, you have a right to command here. Here, Roger, bring us the bill of fare for to night's supper. I believe it's drawn out. Your manner, Mr Hastings, puts me in mind of my uncle, Colonel Wallop. It was a saying of his, that no man was sure of his supper till he had eaten it.

HASTINGS [*aside*]. All upon the high ropes! His uncle a Colonel!

We shall soon hear of his mother being a justice of peace. But let's hear the bill of fare.

MARLOW [*perusing*]. What's here? For the first course; for the second course; for the desert. The devil, Sir, do you think we have brought down the whole Joiners Company, or the Corporation of Bedford, to eat up such a supper? Two or three little things, clean and comfortable, will do.

HASTINGS. But, let's hear it.

MARLOW [*reading*]. For the first course at the top, a pig, and pruin sauce.

HASTINGS. Damn your pig, I say!

MARLOW. And damn your pruin sauce, say I.

HARDCASTLE. And yet, gentlemen, to men that are hungry, pig, with pruin sauce, is very good eating.

MARLOW. At the bottom, a calve's tongue and brains.

HASTINGS. Let your brains be knock'd out, my good Sir; I don't like them.

MARLOW. Or you may clap them on a plate by themselves. I do.

HARDCASTLE [*aside*]. Their impudence confounds me. [*To them*] Gentlemen, you are my guests, make what alterations you please.

16. UNKNOWN AUTHOR

Clotilda

The Italian opera played no mean part in the fortunes of the English stage during the eighteenth and nineteenth centuries. Not only did it prove a fashionable diversion responsible for not a few of the troubles of other theatres, but it had its influence upon the development both of serious drama in English and of scenic art. The pure Italian style did not become popular until the age of Queen Anne, and its early fortunes are to be traced in the pages of Addison's *Spectator*. Starting with translated efforts, the managers soon saw the advantage of engaging foreign singers, and in *Clotilda* we reach a form of opera in which some of the parts are in English, some in Italian. Valentino, Grimaldi, and Margarita sang (in Italian) the parts of Fernando, Alphonso, and Clotilda, while Ramondon, Lawrence, Mrs Tofts, and Mrs Lindsay sang (in English) those of Sancho, Roderigo, Isabella, and Leonora. "The King or Hero of the Play," says Addison, "generally spoke in *Italian*, and his Slaves answered him in *English*: The Lover frequently made his Court, and gained the Heart of his Princess in a Language which she did not understand." Obviously this passage from *Clotilda* is given for its historical interest alone.

(*Clotilda* was first acted in England in 1709. The text of 1709

258

is here followed, save that in the original the Italian and English
are given on opposite pages.)

BILINGUAL LOVE-MAKING

ISABELLA. Has he then seen th' Imperial Beauty?
LEONORA. He has not only seen her,
But with a ready Care appointed
The welcome Stranger's Coronation.
ISABELLA. Where are his Vows? O why did I believe him?
LEONORA. Whilst on his Throne she sits forsaken,
You in his Love may reign unrival'd.
ISABELLA. The Soul of Love is Power,
And Love without it is an airy Phantome.
I ne'er had left *Alphonso,*
But for the sake of Empire.
Why for my Beauty do Men praise me,
If to a Throne he will not raise me?
LEONORA. Madam, the King's at hand.
ISABELLA. I will withdraw a Moment:
Thou Know'st my Thoughts, prepare him to my Wishes.

Fortune, bright Queen o' the Skies,
From Cupid's wanton Eyes
Do thou secure me:
To Empire let me rise,
And Love's deluding Smiles
Shall ne'er allure me.

Fortune, &c.   [*Exit.*

LEONORA. The King by Love is guided,
And *Isabella* by Ambition:
Which will prevail, as yet I know not,
But now begins the Trial.   [*Enter* FERNANDO.
FERNANDO. *Le gran cure de Regnanti*
Son tal hor un grave incarco
Sol amor può sollerarlo
Dou e l'Idolo mio.
LEONORA. Retir'd to Pray.
FERNANDO. *Pregar perche?*
LEONORA. For Blessings on the fair *Clotilda,*
Whose Coronation Day approaches.
FERNANDO. *O lascia idee cosi funeste*
E condum mi alla bella
Tu lo sai il Ciel lo sa
Quanto l'adoro.   [*Enter* ISABELLA.[1]
ISABELLA. *Al mio ossequio e sorpresa*
La tua Real presenza.
FERNANDO. *E che non m'ami Isabella?*

[1] Who here sings partly in Italian, partly in English.

259

ISABELLA. *Fan fede del mio amor gli occhi stillanti.*
FERNANDO. *Perche tepido amante in sen m'accogli?*
ISABELLA. *Perche Clotilde offesa ti rinfaccia:*
E del Cielo all' aspetto
L'infedel cor le desti.
FERNANDO. *Non potiamo esse beati*
Senza il sacro Imenco?
Di Giove averti
E di Giunon sprezzata;
Non fu benche consorte
Felice al par di Leda.
ISABELLA. *Tenta in van amor legarmi,*
Se l'honor sciolta mi rende.

> Honour is a Virgin's Treasure,
>   Which unlawful Love destroys.
> She who wou'd be Happy ever,
> Let her fly, with her best Endeavour,
>   Wanton Wishes, guilty Joys.
>   Honour, &c.

FERNANDO. *T'acquieta, hô trovo*
Agli ostacol riparo
Devi esser mia:
Voglio ascoltar del Dio d'Amor le mosse
Esser felice
Della grandezza ad onta. . . .   [*Exeunt.*
LEONORA. Tho' both with Hearts united seem concurring,
With different Inclinations are they guided:
The King for Love of her forgets his State,
And she foregoes her Lover to be Great.

> Wou'd you, free and easie,
> A sweet Contentment find?
> From Love your Heart defending,
> Let no vain Hopes or Fears
> Your soft Repose molest.
> The Wretch t'Ambition bending,
> Or Love's Delights inclin'd,
> A thousand Torments bears
> Within his troubled Breast:
>   Wou'd you, &c.

17. JOHN GAY (1685–1732)

The Beggar's Opera

One of the most complete and permanent successes that the
English theatre has witnessed is that of *The Beggar's Opera*. Not
only did it furnish a record on its first production, but it remained

EIGHTEENTH CENTURY

a stock favourite during the eighteenth and nineteenth centuries and contributed another 'record' to our own age. This success is largely due to the grace and delicacy of the author's style. Taking the well-known airs of his time, he gave to them new words of a harmony and exactitude which none of his many imitators could excel. There is, too, in this, the first of the ballad operas, a peculiar atmosphere which we may call the fantasy of rationalism. In Shakespeare's *Midsummer Night's Dream* we get the fantasy of emotion, with a dim-wood setting, an ancient Athenian atmosphere, a mingling of fairies, lovers, and artisans. In *The Beggar's Opera* the time is that of 1728, the characters are the rogues and vagabonds of the day, and the setting is almost sordid. By treating this material, however, almost in a spirit of romance, by artificializing, by jesting, by exaggerating, Gay has been able to create a new world of his own. His Macheath is a creature of his amused imagination, and the quarrels of Lucy and Polly have the colouring not of reality, but of the fantastic. It should be noted how cleverly the dialogues and the airs are welded together, and how carefully, by the exercise of wit and laughter, Gay keeps his characters without the bounds of the emotional.

(*The Beggar's Opera* was produced at Lincoln's Inn Fields in 1728. The following extract is taken from the second edition of that year.)

"HOW HAPPY COULD I BE WITH EITHER"

POLLY. Where is my dear Husband?—Was a Rope ever intended for his Neck!—O let me throw my Arms about it, and throttle thee with Love!—Why dost thou turn away from me?—'Tis thy *Polly* —'Tis thy Wife.

MACHEATH. Was there ever such an unfortunate Rascal as I am!

LUCY. Was there ever such another Villain!

POLLY. O *Macheath*! was it for this we parted? Taken! Imprison'd! Try'd! Hang'd!—cruel Reflection! I'll stay with thee 'till death—no Force shall tear thy dear Wife from thee now.— What means my Love?—Not one kind Word! not one kind Look! think what thy *Polly* suffers to see thee in this Condition.

(*Air XXXIV*—"All in the Downs," &c.)

Thus when the Swallow, seeking Prey,
Within the Sash is closely pent,
His Consort, with bemoaning Lay,
Without sits pining for th'Event,
Her chatt'ring Lovers all around her skim;
She heeds them not (poor Bird!) her Soul's with him.

MACHEATH. I must disown her. [*Aside*] The Wench is distracted.

LUCY. Am I then bilk'd of my Virtue? Can I have no Repara-

261

tion? Sure Men were born to lye, and Women to believe them! O Villain! Villain!

POLLY. Am I not thy Wife?—Thy Neglect of me, thy Aversion to me too severely proves it.—Look on me.—Tell me, am I not thy Wife?

LUCY. Perfidious Wretch!

POLLY. Barbarous Husband!

LUCY. Hadst thou been hang'd five Months ago, I had been happy.

POLLY. And I too—If you had been kind to me 'till Death, it would not have vex'd me—And that's no very unreasonable Request, (though from a Wife) to a Man who hath not above seven or eight Days to Live.

LUCY. Art thou then married to another? Hast thou two Wives, Monster?

MACHEATH. If Women's Tongues can cease for an Answer—hear me.

LUCY. I won't—Flesh and Blood can't bear my Usage.

POLLY. Shall I not claim my own? Justice bids me speak.

(*Air XXXV*—"Have you heard of a frolicksome ditty," &c.)
MACHEATH.

> How happy could I be with either,
> Were t'other dear Charmer away!
> But while you thus teaze me together,
>   To neither a Word will I say;
>   But tol de rol, &c.

POLLY. Sure, my Dear, there ought to be some Preference shown to a Wife! At least she may claim the Appearance of it. He must be distracted with his Misfortunes, or he could not use me thus!

LUCY. O Villain, Villain! thou hast deceiv'd me—I could even inform against thee with Pleasure. Not a Prude wishes more heartily to have Facts against her intimate Acquaintance, than I now wish to have Facts against thee. I would have her Satisfaction, and they should all out.

(*Air XXXVI*—"Irish Trot")
POLLY. I'm bubbled.

LUCY. —I'm bubbled.

POLLY. Oh how I am troubled!

LUCY. Bambouzled, and bit!

POLLY. —My Distresses are doubled.

LUCY. When you come to the Tree, should the Hangman refuse, These Fingers with Pleasure, could fasten the Noose.

POLLY. I'm bubbled, *etc*.

MACHEATH. Be pacified, my dear *Lucy*—This is all a Fetch of *Polly's*, to make me desperate with you in case I get off. If I am hang'd, she would fain have the Credit of being thought my Widow

262

—Really, *Polly*, this is no time for a Dispute of this sort; for whenever you are talking of Marriage, I am thinking of Hanging.

POLLY. And hast thou the Heart to persist in disowning me?

MACHEATH. And hast thou the heart to persist in persuading me that I am married? Why, *Polly*, dost thou seek to aggravate my Misfortune?

LUCY. Really, Miss *Peachum*, you but expose yourself. Besides, 'tis barbarous in you to worry a Gentleman in his Circumstances.

(*Air XXXVII*)

POLLY.
Cease your Funning;
Force, or Cunning
Never shall my Heart trepan.
All these Sallies
Are but Malice
To seduce my constant Man.
'Tis most certain,
By their flirting
Women oft' have Envy shown;
Pleas'd, to ruin
Others wooing;
Never happy in their own!

LUCY. Decency, Madam, methinks might teach you to behave yourself with some Reserve with the Husband, while his Wife is present.

MACHEATH. But seriously, *Polly*, this is carrying the Joke a little too far.

LUCY. If you are determined, Madam, to raise a disturbance in the Prison, I shall be oblig'd to send for the Turnkey to shew you the Door. I am sorry, Madam, you force me to be so ill-bred.

POLLY. Give me leave to tell you, Madam; These forward Airs don't become you in the least, Madam. And my Duty, Madam, obliges me to stay with my Husband, Madam.

(*Air XXXVIII*—" Good-morrow, Gossip Joan.")

LUCY.
Why, how now, Madam Flirt?
If you thus must chatter;
And are for flinging Dirt,
Let's try who best can spatter;
Madam Flirt!

POLLY.
Why how now, saucy Jade;
Sure the Wench is Tipsy!
How can you see me made
The Scoff of such a Gipsy?
Saucy Jade!

18. RICHARD BRINSLEY SHERIDAN (1751–1816)

The Duenna

After *The Beggar's Opera*, *The Duenna* proved by far the most popular comic opera of the eighteenth century, and, as it is sprightlier than the majority of the contemporary works in this kind, it has been thought well to select it for quotation here rather than the better-known *Rivals* or *School for Scandal*. Sheridan possessed a pretty wit, a delicate hand for verse-making, and a sense of theatrical effect. The actual stage picture formed by the nervous little Isaac, full of expectations, and the Duenna, full of desire to get a husband, and disguised as the beautiful Louisa, is one conceived by a man who is intimately aware of the value of purely theatrical effect.

(*The Duenna* was produced at Covent Garden in 1775. The Moore text (1820) has here been followed.)

ISAAC AND THE DUENNA

MAID. Sir, my mistress will wait on you presently.

[Goes to the door.

ISAAC. When she's at leisure—don't hurry her. [*Exit* MAID.] I wish I had ever practised a love scene—no doubt I shall make a poor figure—I couldn't be more afraid, if I was going before the Inquisition—so! the door opens—yes, she's coming—the very rustling of her silk has a disdainful sound.

[Enter DUENNA, *dressed as* LOUISA.

Now dar'n't I look round for the soul of me—her beauty will certainly strike me dumb if I do. I wish she'd speak first.

DUENNA. Sir, I attend your pleasure.

ISAAC. So! the ice is broke, and a pretty civil beginning too! hem! madam—miss—I'm all attention.

DUENNA. Nay, sir, 'tis I who should listen, and you propose.

ISAAC. Egad, this isn't so disdainful neither—I believe I may venture to look—no—I dar'n't—one glance of those roguish sparklers would fix me again.

DUENNA. You seem thoughtful, sir—let me persuade you to sit down.

ISAAC. So, so; she mollifies apace—she's struck with my figure! this attitude has had its effect.

DUENNA. Come, sir, here's a chair.

ISAAC. Madam, the greatness of your goodness overpowers me —that a lady so lovely should deign to turn her beauteous eyes on me so.   [*She takes his hand, he turns and sees her.*

DUENNA. You seem surprised at my condescension.

ISAAC. Why, yes, madam, I am a little surprised at it.—Zounds! this can never be Louisa—she's as old as my mother!   [*Aside.*

DUENNA. But former prepossessions give way to my father's commands.

ISAAC [aside]. Her father! Yes, 'tis she then—Lord, Lord; how blind some parents are!

DUENNA. Signor Isaac.

ISAAC. Truly, the little damsel was right—she has rather a matronly air indeed! ah! 'tis well my affections are fixed on her fortune, and not on her person.

DUENNA. Signor, won't you sit? [She sits.

ISAAC. Pardon me, madam, I have scarce recovered my astonishment at—your condescension, madam—she has the devil's own dimples to be sure! [Aside.

DUENNA. I do not wonder, sir, that you are surprised at my affability—I own, signor, that I was vastly prepossessed against you, and being teased by my father, I did give some encouragment to Antonio; but then, sir, you were described to me as a quite different person.

ISAAC. Ay, and so were you to me, upon my soul, madam.

DUENNA. But when I saw you, I was never more struck in my life.

ISAAC. That was just my case too, madam: I was struck all on a heap, for my part.

DUENNA. Well, sir, I see our misapprehension has been mutual—you expected to find me haughty and averse, and I was taught to believe you a little, black, snub-nosed fellow, without person, manners, or address.

ISAAC. Egad, I wish she had answer'd her picture as well.

DUENNA. But, sir, your air is noble—something so liberal in your carriage, with so penetrating an eye, and so bewitching a smile!

ISAAC. Egad, now I look at her again, I don't think she is so ugly.

DUENNA. So little like a Jew, and so much like a gentleman!

ISAAC. Well, certainly there is something pleasing in the tone of her voice.

DUENNA. You will pardon this breach of decorum in praising you thus, but my joy at being so agreeably deceived has given me such a flow of spirits!

ISAAC. O, dear lady, may I thank those dear lips for this goodness. [Kisses her.] Why, she has a pretty sort of velvet down, that's the truth on't! [Aside.

DUENNA. O, sir, you have the most insinuating manner, but indeed you should get rid of that odious beard—one might as well kiss an hedgehog.

ISAAC. Yes, ma'am, the razor wouldn't be amiss—for either of us [aside]. Could you favour me with a song?

DUENNA. Willingly, sir, though I am rather hoarse—ahem ! [Begins to sing.

ISAAC. Very like a Virginia nightingale!—ma'am, I perceive you're hoarse—I beg you will not distress——

DUENNA. Oh, not in the least distressed;—now, sir.

EXTRACTS FROM BRITISH & IRISH PLAYS

SONG

When a tender maid
Is first essay'd
By some admiring swain,
How her blushes rise
If she meets his eyes,
While he unfolds his pain!
If he takes her hand—she trembles quite!
Touch her lips—and she swoons outright!
While a pit-a-pat, &c.
Her heart avows her fright.

But in time appear
Fewer signs of fear;
The youth she boldly views:
If her hand he grasp,
Or her bosom clasp,
No mantling blush ensues!
Then to church well pleased the lovers move,
While her smiles her contentment prove;
And a pit-a-pat, &c.
Her heart avows her love.

ISAAC. Charming, ma'am! enchanting! and truly, your notes put me in mind of one that's very dear to me; a lady, indeed, whom you greatly resemble!

DUENNA. How! is there, then, another so dear to you!

ISAAC. O, no, ma'am, you mistake; it was my mother I meant.

19. LEWIS THEOBALD (1688–1744)

The Rape of Proserpine

A short extract from Lewis Theobald's *The Rape of Proserpine* is given here in order to illustrate one type of popular eighteenth-century afterpiece, the 'operatic pantomime.' The pure opera had become a fashionable success since the introduction of the Italian type in the reign of Queen Anne, and the pantomime, encouraged by the skill of Harlequin Rich, was a popular diversion. A union of the two seemed to many managers to be a wholesome recipe for playhouse receipts. Not many of these pieces found their way into print, but we possess a few from the pen of Lewis Theobald, the one-time hero of Pope's *Dunciad*. In *The Rape of Proserpine* only the serious portion is given; the "Grotesque Part" and "The Actions of Harlequin" having to be filled in by the reader's imagination.

(*The Rape of Proserpine* was produced at Lincoln's Inn Fields in 1727. The following passage is taken from the first edition of that year.)

266

DIVINE AND INFERNAL MACHINES

SCENE. *An open Country with Cornfields.*
Enter PLUTO, *attended by Infernals.*

PLUTO. My Soul's on fire—Flames, hot as those
Which scorch the Daemons in my Realms below,
Burn up my Breast, and rob me of Repose.
O *Proserpine*! I bend beneath thy Power;
Oft to these Vales the Charmer steals,
And, pleas'd to weave the Chaplet for her Brow,
With rosy Fingers plucks the breathing Flowers,
Less fragrant than her self.

       Flights of Cupids hover round me,
       Spread your little subtle Snares;

       Beauty found the Force to wound me,
       Beauty must relieve my Cares.
             Flights of, *&c.* [*A Dance of Daemons.*
But see, she comes.
Instant be gone;—I'll too retire;   [*Exeunt Infernals*
And watch a Moment may assist my Joy.
           [PLUTO *shades himself behind a Tree.*
           [*Enter* PROSERPINE *and Nymphs.*
PROSERPINE. Content and Bliss serene dwell here,
Safe from the Pains the Wretches feel,
Who pine with Love's fantastick Chains.
Haste, see the Flowers luxuriant rise;
And court your Hands to crop their swelling Odours.
      [*All the Nymphs but* CYANA *disperse themselves.*
         [PLUTO *advancing, seizes* PROSERPINE.
Protect me, Heaven!
  PLUTO. You pray in vain.
The Heavens consenting doom you mine.
  PROSERPINE. Is there no Aid?
  PLUTO. None.
  PROSERPINE. O my Fears!
  PLUTO. Be gone, bold Nymph; if you give Breath
To what you here behold,
Eternal Dumbness is your Curse.
  PROSERPINE. I'm lost; protect me, Heaven!
    [*The Earth opens, and* PLUTO'S *Chariot rises; he forces*
      PROSERPINE *into it*: *All but* CYANA *sink.* CERES
      descends in her Chariot.
CERES. The *Phrygian* Soil, as *Jove* enjoin'd,
Reaps the full Blessings of my Power,
And Plenty-giving Hand. Each Altar smokes
To *Ceres'* Name, and gladden'd Crowds
Send up their Vows to *Jove* and Me,

In grateful Sacrifice of Praise.
For this my Bosom glows with Joy,
But more for my Return to Thee,
O much-lov'd *Proserpine*!—My Nymphs,—

[CYANA *and Nymphs enter.*

Ha! wherefore shun you thus my Eyes?
Where is my *Proserpine*?   In Tears!
O my foreboding Heart!—*Cyana*, quick,
Resolve my doubting Soul.

CYANA. O *Ceres*—— [*Offering to speak, is turn'd into a Brook.*
CERES. Ha! surprising Change!
What mean the envious Gods?
Must I my darling Offspring lose,
Yet be deny'd to know what Fate
Has robb'd me of so dear a Prize?
Have I for this Reward, O *Jove*,
Enrich'd the lean and barren Earth,
And with my Harvests bought thee Praise?
But I'll resume the Gifts conferr'd;
Rage on the Wings of Fire shall ride,
And flaming Ruin cover every Plain.

> Rise, ye Flames, and blaze around me,
> Haste, and arm each deadly Hand:
> Lift up the consuming Brand,
> And the guilty World destroy.
> Rise ye Flames, *&c.*

[*The Gods of the Woods enter and take the Part of* CERES, *and break the Trees; the People of Sicily enter and oppose 'em.*

SICILIANS. O, sacred CERES, spare the Land,
Nor thy own Gifts in Rage destroy.
CERES. Pity, nor Remorse shall wound me,
> Vengeance now is all my Joy.
> Pity nor, *&c.*
[CERES *here snatches flaming Branches from her Train, and sets the Corn, &c. on fire.*

> SCENE, *The Side of a Wood.*
> *The Actions of* HARLEQUIN *continued.*

20. HENRY FIELDING (1707–54)

Tom Thumb

As a playwright, Fielding is now no longer remembered; only *Tom Thumb*, and that but faintly, keeps alive the memory of his early activities in the theatre.   It is true that the majority of these are but flimsy pieces, for Fielding lacked a fineness of touch which makes for great drama, and perhaps was a trifle careless in his efforts ; but he had a certain gift for the writing of somewhat rough farcical scenes, and had a decided talent in the sphere of burlesque. *The Tragedy of Tragedies; or, The Life and Death of Tom Thumb the Great*, acted originally in 1730 as *Tom Thumb*, is decidedly his happiest work, and in the expanded form " With the Annotations of H. Scriblerus Secundus " gave enjoyment to many who never saw it on the stage. Fielding's satire is fairly general, and is directed at the follies of tragedy-writing from the time of Shakespeare to his own day. The ghost scene here may be compared with some would-be serious ghost scenes also given in this book (*cf.* pp. 133 and 136) and *British Drama* (pp. 228–230).

(*Tom Thumb* was first published in 1730. The extract given below is taken from the third edition, 1737.)

GHOSTLY SIMILES

SCENE, KING ARTHUR'S *Palace.*
GHOST *solus.*

GHOST. Hail ! ye black Horrors of Midnight's Midnoon !
Ye Fairies, Goblins, Bats and Screech-Owls, Hail !
And Oh ! ye mortal Watchmen, whose hoarse Throats
Th' immortal Ghosts dead Croakings counterfeit,
All Hail !—Ye dancing Fantoms, who by Day,
Are some condemn'd to fast, some feast in Fire;
Now play in Churchyards, skipping o'er the Graves,
To the loud Musick of the silent Bell,
All Hail !   [*Enter the* KING.
  KING. What Noise is this—What Villain dares,
At this dread Hour, with Feet and Voice prophane,
Disturb our Royal Walls?
  GHOST. One who defies
Thy empty Power to hurt him; one who dares
Walk in thy Bed-Chamber.
  KING. Presumptuous Slave!
Thou diest!
  GHOST. Threaten others with that Word,
I am a Ghost, and am already dead.
  KING. Ye Stars! 'tis well; were thy last Hour to come
This Moment had been it; yet by thy Shrowd
I'll pull thee backward, squeeze thee to a Bladder,
'Till thou dost grone thy Nothingness away.
Thou fly'st ! 'Tis well.   [GHOST *retires.*
I thought what was the Courage of a Ghost !
Yet, dare not, on thy Life—Why say I that,
Since Life thou hast not !—Dare not walk again
Within these Walls, on pain of the *Red-Sea.*

For, if hence forth I ever find thee here,
As sure, sure as a Gun, I'll have thee laid—— [GHOST *re-enters.*
GHOST. Were the *Red-Sea* a Sea of *Holland's* Gin,
The Liquor (when alive) whose very Smell
I did detest, did loath—yet, for the Sake
Of *Thomas Thumb*, I would be laid therein.
KING. Ha! said you?
GHOST. Yes, my Liege, I said *Tom Thumb*,
Whose Father's Ghost I am—once not unknown
To mighty *Arthur*. But, I see, 'tis true,
The dearest Friend, when dead, we will forget.
KING. 'Tis he, it is the honest Gaffer *Thumb*.
Oh! let me press thee in my eager Arms,
Thou best of Ghosts! Thou something more than Ghost!
GHOST. Would I were Something more, that we again
Might feel each other in the warm Embrace.
But now I have th' Advantage of my King,
For I feel thee, whilst thou dost not feel me.
KING. But say, thou dearest Air, Oh! say, what Dread,
Important Business sends thee back to Earth?
GHOST. Oh! then prepare to hear—which, but to hear,
Is full enough to send thy Spirit hence.
Thy Subjects up in Arms, by *Grizzle* led,
Will, ere the rosy-finger'd Morn shall ope
The Shutters of the Sky, before the Gate
Of this thy Royal Palace, swarming spread:
So have I seen the Bees in Clusters swarm,
So have I seen the Stars in frosty Nights,
So have I seen the Sand in windy Days,
So have I seen the Ghosts on *Pluto's* Shore,
So have I seen the Flowers in Spring arise,
So have I seen the Leaves in *Autumn* fall,
So have I seen the Fruits in Summer smile,
So have I seen the Snow in Winter frown——
KING. D—n all thou'st seen!——Dost thou, beneath
the Shape
Of Gaffer *Thumb*, come hither to abuse me
With Similes to keep me on the Rack?
Hence—or, by all the Torments of thy Hell,
I'll run thee thro' the Body, tho' thou'st none.
GHOST. *Arthur*, beware; I must this Moment hence,
Not frighted by your Voice, but by the Cocks;
Arthur beware, beware, beware, beware!
Strive to avert thy yet impending Fate;
For if thou'rt kill'd To-day,
To-morrow all thy Care will come too late.

VII. NINETEENTH CENTURY (to 1870)

IF the eighteenth century was dull, the nineteenth was duller, yet there is some good fun to be obtained still from its dullness. It was [in this period that there grew up that distinction between the 'legitimate' and the 'illegitimate' drama, which had such an influence upon the work of playwrights. Primarily legitimate drama was poetic or seriously conceived drama produced at, or written to be produced at, Drury Lane or Covent Garden; illegitimate drama was drama written to be produced at the various minor theatres. This distinction, of course, did not hold good for long, and when the two major theatres sank to elephants and clownery legitimate came to mean 'literary' drama and illegitimate purely 'theatrical' drama. The great field of illegitimacy was the melodrama, a form of play which ultimately sprang from native romantic sentiment, aided originally by German example and later by that of France. Scott's version of Goethe's *Götz von Berlichingen* is placed among the illegitimates not because it is itself an illegitimate drama, but because German sentimentalism, spectacularism, and supernaturalism laid such an impress upon the minor English stage. "Monk" Lewis' *Adelmorn* is taken as a semi-literary specimen and Fitzball's *The Flying Dutchman* as a good example of the 'spirity' show in which audiences of the time delighted.[1]

At the opposite pole from the melodramatic is the poetic. Nearly all the lyric-writers of the Romantic Revival had their say in the attempt to found a new national dramatic output which should rival the Elizabethan. All failed because this attempt was entirely imitative, the plays produced being full of unassimilated phrases and devices culled

---

[1] It is obviously impossible here to discuss the various forms of melodrama and the implications of the word 'illegitimate.' The subject is dealt with in *British Drama* and, at greater length, in my forthcoming *History of Early Nineteenth-century Drama.*

from Shakespeare and his fellows. A few typical examples are represented here. Coleridge in *Remorse* shows the prevalent failing of dealing with an abstract theme. Baillie's *Ethwald* is dully 'Elizabethan' in tone; Knowles' *Virginius* is as dully pedestrian; while Talfourd's *Ion* mingles memories of Shakespeare with memories of Addison. Only two poets succeeded in giving something of strength to the theatre—Byron and Shelley; yet of these the former declared most of his plays mere closet pieces, while the latter wrote only one drama, and that a piece in which may be traced the prevalent imitative failings of his companions.

In the sphere of comedy the nineteenth century produced little. Most of the so-called comedies of the time are the crudest of farces. Three plays only have been taken as representative here. Colman's *John Bull* shows the miserable relics of the earlier eighteenth-century style as cultivated by his father, George Colman the Elder. Tobin's *The Honeymoon* is a slightly skilful, but hopelessly imitative, replica of Shakespeare and the Elizabethans. Lytton's *Money* alone suggests something of worth to come. In *Money* we see at least a faint premonition of *Caste*, but the time was not yet ripe for the creation of a truly natural comedy and a sincere domestic drama. Up to 1870 there seemed but little hope for the English theatre.[1]

1. SIR WALTER SCOTT (1771–1832) (GOETHE)

Goetz of Berlichingen

Götz von Berlichingen, one of Goethe's earlier efforts, was published in 1773, and exercised a wide-spread influence both on German and non-German dramatists. Its medieval setting and the introduction in it of thrilling episodes culled from history at once attracted the age, so that critics of romantic literature can designate an entire movement in early nineteenth-century art by the term "Götzism." *Götz* was translated twice before 1800; the present version was one of the first literary works of the young

[1] The above rapid review of the nineteenth-century stage is necessarily (because so brief) one-sided. In the sphere of the illegitimate play there is much of great historical value; some farces of the period are jolly enough and some melodramas are genuinely thrilling. Considered from the point of view of dramatic literature, however, hardly any plays of the time deserve praise.

Walter Scott, later to become famous as the Wizard of the North. One cannot claim that his rendering is among those greater translations of which Rossetti's *Early Italian Poets* stands as a prime example, but the play was so important as a guiding force in the realm of medievalism generally, and particularly in that of the melodrama, that it cannot be neglected. The passage chosen will indicate the type of scene which thrilled contemporaries and urged them to imitation.

(The following extract is taken from the first and only edition —*Goetz of Berlichingen, with the Iron Hand : A Tragedy. Translated from the German of Goethé . . . by Walter Scott, Esq., Advocate, Edinburgh* (1799).)

THE MEETING OF THE SECRET TRIBUNAL

SCENE : *A narrow vault dimly illuminated. The judges of the Secret Tribunal discovered seated, all muffled in black cloaks, and silent.*

ELDEST JUDGE. Judges of the Secret Tribunal, sworn by the cord and the steel to be unpitying in justice, to judge in secret, and to avenge in secret, like the Deity! Are your hands clean and hearts pure?—Raise them to heaven, and cry, Woe upon misdoers!

ALL. Woe! woe!

ELDEST JUDGE. Cryer, begin the diet of judgment.

CRYER. I cry for accusation against misdoers!—Whose heart is pure, whose hand is clean, let him accuse, and call upon the steel and the cord for Vengeance! vengeance! vengeance!

ACCUSER [*comes forward*]. My heart is pure from misdeed, and my hand clean from innocent blood:—God pardon my sins of ignorance, and frame my steps to his way!—I raise my hand aloft, and cry, Vengeance! vengeance! vengeance!

ELDEST JUDGE. Vengeance upon whom?

ACCUSER. I call upon the cord and upon the steel for vengeance against Adela von Weislingen.—She has committed adultery and murder—She has poisoned her husband by the hands of his servant —the servant hath slain himself—the husband is dead.

ELDEST JUDGE. Swearest thou by the God of truth, that thy accusation is true?

ACCUSER. I swear!

ELDEST JUDGE. Dost thou take upon thy own head the punishment of murder and adultery, should it be found false?

ACCUSER. I take it.

ELDEST JUDGE. Your voices?

[*They converse a minute in low whispers.*

ACCUSER. Judges of the Secret Tribunal, what is your doom upon Adela von Weislingen, accused of murder and adultery?

ELDEST JUDGE. She shall die!—shall die a bitter and double

S

death!—By the double doom of the steel and the cord shall she expiate the double misdeed. Raise your hands to heaven, and cry, Woe unto her!—Be she given to the hand of the avenger.

ALL. Woe! woe!

ELDEST JUDGE. Come forth, avenger!   [*A man advances.* There hast thou the cord and the steel!—Within eight days must thou take her from before the face of heaven: wherever thou findest her, let her no longer cumber the ground.—Judges, ye that judge in secret and avenge in secret like the Deity, God keep your hearts from wickedness, and your hands from innocent blood!

[*The scene closes.*

2. MATTHEW GREGORY LEWIS (1775–1818)

Adelmorn, the Outlaw

A close friend and collaborator of Scott, M. G. Lewis—better known as " Monk" Lewis, from the title of his notorious novel—is a not unimportant literary figure.   Destitute of true abilities, he yet had a *flair* for the understanding of popular tastes, and he flung himself wholeheartedly into all the *diablerie* of the German school of romance.   His best-known drama is *The Castle Spectre*, produced at Drury Lane in 1797, but this was followed by a whole series of similar works in the early years of the nineteenth century. These ‘romantic’ plays anticipate and share the characteristics of the later melodrama.   To be noted in the following passage, taken from the last scene of *Adelmorn*, are (1) the evident desire to subordinate good style to ‘ effect,’ (2) the sentimental colouring, and (3) the melodramatic stock types—villain, hero, comic friend. Ulric is the villain about to slay the innocent Adelmorn ; Lodowick is the comic honest man, companioned by Hugo, a minstrel, and Innogen, the distressed heroine.

(*Adelmorn, the Outlaw* was produced at Drury Lane on May 4, 1801.   The extracts given below are taken from the second edition, 1801.)

ULRIC PREPARES TO EXECUTE ADELMORN

A magnificent Gothic Hall.—The Windows of painted Glass are lighted by the rising Sun.

Enter ULRIC, much agitated.

ULRIC. The body is concealed—no search can find it. Even should Lodowick possess my secret—want of proofs—the improbability of his tale—Calm, calm, my bosom! Yet, to make all secure, Adelmorn's fate shall be hastened. The scaffold is prepared —'tis already morning—the death-bell shall be sounded instantly —[*going*].

BRENNO [*without*]. This way, traitor!

HUGO [*without*]. *Piano*, good master Brenno! *Pianissimo*, if you please.   [*Enter* BRENNO, *dragging in* HUGO.

BRENNO. This way, I say. Nay, no struggling! Good my Lord, hasten to the Duke's apartment. Adelmorn's wife is no other than the Princess Innogen, long believed dead. At this moment she kneels at Sigismond's feet, and pleads for her husband.

ULRIC. Hell and furies! How got she entrance?

BRENNO. Hugo having the key of a private door——

ULRIC [*seizing* HUGO]. You too, wretch!—you leagued against me!

HUGO [*kneeling*]. Mercy, my Lord! mercy!

[*Singing*]   See me kneeling!
                     Tear drops stealing . . .

ULRIC [*throwing him from him*]. Silence, old Brawler!

HUGO [*aside*]. Brawler?—What taste!

BRENNO. Nay, my Lord, waste not your time with this driveller. The Duke's fortitude is shaken; his daughter weeps on his neck; the domestics kneel; the groans of your vassals pierce to his chamber!

ULRIC. I need but name his oath, and their efforts must prove vain. But I hasten to him.—You, Brenno, speed to Adelmorn's prison: to the block with him this moment! . . .

THE PRAYERS OF INNOGEN

Enter SIGISMOND, *followed by* INNOGEN, ULRIC, MAURICE, *and attendants.*

SIGISMOND. Oh! leave me, cruel girl! Why still solicit what I cannot grant?

INNOGEN. Leave you? Never!—Still will I thus hang round you! still thus shriek in tones of despair!—"Mercy, my father! mercy, mercy!"—

SIGISMOND. Take her from me, Ulric; she tortures me!

ULRIC. Lady, the Duke's oath. . . .

INNOGEN. Oh! peace, peace! That oath was suggested by his darker angel! 'tis registered in the catalogue of his offences: to break it will be virtue!

ULRIC. Most impious! Hear her not, my Lord. . . .

INNOGEN. How? Not hear me? He bids the father not listen to his child! Now, when he pleads to thee for mercy, hear him not, Heaven! But my father will not heed this cruel one! He cannot with a heart unmoved see that his child's is breaking!—cannot, when thus I throw me at his feet, and bathe them thus with tears of anguish. . . . [*The Bell tolls: she starts from the ground with a dreadful shriek.*]—Hark!—God! 'tis the knell of death!—

          [*She sinks upon* SIGISMOND'S *bosom: the Bell continues to toll.—Solemn Music.—A procession of Guards, Friars, and Nuns with lighted tapers, Choristers, &c., enter, conducting* ADELMORN *in deep mourning.*

275

CHORUS

Hark! the bell tolls! the sinner's course is ending!
Sad swells the hymn, and tears obscure the sight!
Rise, pious pray'rs! pure sighs to Heav'n ascending
Waft the repentant soul to realms of light.

ADELMORN [*to* INNOGEN, *who hangs weeping on his bosom*]. Be calm, my beloved! While thus you rest on my bosom, let its fortitude spread to thine.—Look on me, Innogen! Does my cheek lose its colour when I speak of the grave? Does my hand tremble while I say that Death's soon must clasp it?

INNOGEN. Oh! no, nor need it! You feel not for yourself what I feel for you—And you leave me, Adelmorn; you leave me and can be calm!

ADELMORN. I leave you for a moment; when next we meet our union will be eternal. Innogen, last night I heard not my uncle's spirit shriek for vengeance! I saw him in my dreams, and he smiled on me forgiveness. Think on this, my only-one! and for *my* sake, for your own. . . . [*The Bell tolls*.]—Hark! I am summoned—Sweet, farewell!—[*embracing her*].

INNOGEN. Friend!—Husband!—All!—Oh! yet one moment. . . .

ADELMORN. Farewell!—Duke Sigismond, receive from me a daughter, who never erred, but in her love for me—and who, for that single error, woe is me! has suffered most severely! Be her friend, her comforter! and, should ever the memory of her fault call to your lips reproaches, repress them, when you look on this—[*giving him a ring*].

SIGISMOND. Ha!—Merciful Heavens! 'Tis the same!—[*clasping his hands in agony*]—'Tis he! 'Tis the man to whom I owed my life but yesterday, and my orders doom him to the block!

ADELMORN [*to* INNOGEN, *who is absorbed in grief*]. Nay, sweet Innogen!—Speak, noble Sigismond! Shall my request be granted?

SIGISMOND. Granted?—Oh! that my life could purchase—that my heart's best blood—— Vain, vain wishes!—Sovereigns, be warned by what I suffer, how ye make laws which exclude mercy!

ADELMORN. Receive then your daughter, and with her the gratitude of a dying man! Now to you, Ulric!—We have long been foes; be in my grave, our enmity forgotten!—Your hand—[*extending his hand*—ULRIC *motions to take it, but starts back in horror, and hides his face in his cloak*.]—You will not? You know not how to pardon?—Heaven, amidst all my sufferings I thank thee that my heart never felt like Ulric's!—I am ready—Guards, lead on!

ULRIC IS DISTURBED BY CONSCIENCE AND A GHOST

LODOWICK. You have heard me assert your guilt: Dare you as solemnly assert your innocence?

ULRIC. I dare, but . . .

276

LODOWICK. Swear then.

ULRIC. To need such a test, is . . .

LODOWICK. Swear, I say! . . .

SIGISMOND. Count, if you refuse . . .

ULRIC [*taking the Cross*]. Refuse?—Be patient! I obey.

ALL [*except* ULRIC]. Silence!—   [*A dead pause.*

ULRIC. As I have hopes of happiness hereafter, by all that is holy in Heaven, by all that is fearful in Hell, I swear that . . .

    [*As he proceeds, the Ghost rises slowly with a flaming dagger in his hand, and stands opposite to* ULRIC, *who stops and remains gazing upon him for some time without motion.*

SIGISMOND. Why stop you?

ULRIC [*motionless*]. My Lord!

SIGISMOND. What gaze you at?

ULRIC. My Lord!

SIGISMOND. Proceed.

ULRIC. He cannot be a witness in his own cause.

SIGISMOND. Who?

ULRIC. He!—He!—My uncle—See you not my dagger?—Flames curl round it!—Lo! how he points to his bleeding bosom!—But 'tis false—'tis false!—The wound I gave him was not half so deep!—

    [*All utter a cry of mingled joy and horror.*

INNOGEN [*wild with joy*]. Heard ye that, heard ye that?—Oh! father, heard ye that?   [*Embracing* SIGISMOND.

ADELMORN. They are Ulric's lips, but the voice is Heaven's!

ULRIC. Look off me! I cannot bear thy glance!—Flames shoot from thine eye-balls, and fire my brain!—Oh! look off me!

SIGISMOND. Mark, how passion shakes him.

ULRIC [*frantic*]. Thy grave was deep: why hast thou left it? To save thy darling? To drag me to the block prepared for him? This prevents it!—[*Drawing his dagger, and rushing toward the Ghost, who till now has remained fixed like a statue, but on his approach raises his arm with a terrible look, and motions to stab him.* ULRIC *utters a cry of horror.*] Mercy!—I am guilty, but not fit to die.

    [*He falls on the ground, while the Ghost sinks.*

3. EDWARD FITZBALL (1792–1873)

The Flying Dutchman

In the early nineteenth century melodrama, introduced in its most fully developed form by Holcroft, developed along several main lines, of which the 'nautical' and the 'supernatural' were the chief. *The Flying Dutchman* by Fitzball, one of the most prolific writers of the age, combines these two types. Quite clearly such works as this have no great value as literature—indeed even dialogue often succumbs to the excitements of a stage direction full of action. On the other hand, it must be remembered that this and other kindred dramas were popular on the stage, and that the drama in the nineteenth century was largely divided into the theatrical melodramatic works of a Fitzball and the untheatrical poetic plays of a Wordsworth and a Browning. Here at least is the expression of a crude romanticism which must not be lost sight of in our study of dramatic history. The passage chosen for quotation is from the last scene of the play. The supernatural attributes of Vanderdecken, the distress of the heroine Lestelle, the bravery of the hero Mowdrey, the faithfulness of the honest tar Varnish—all these will be noted ; together with the tendency to replace dialogue by action and to arouse the imaginations of the audience by means of music.

(*The Flying Dutchman ; or, The Phantom Ship* was first performed at the Adelphi in 1826. The passage given below is taken from Cumberland's edition.)

The Ghastly End of Vanderdecken

*Interior of the Devil's Cave—an overhanging Rock, L.S.E., leading into the Cave—a grotesque Rock in the centre, resembling an antique table, and massy book, closed. Music.—*Lestelle *discovered, supporting herself against the rock, L.S.E., in an attitude of distress.—*Vanderdecken, R., *comes down, with a torch in his hand—he gazes at* Lestelle, *puts down the torch, and points to the magic book.*

Lestelle. Thine, earthly or unearthly ! never ! Terrible being, thou mayst indeed trample on my mortal frame, but the soul of Lestelle is far above thy malice.

[*Music.—He is angry—he takes her hand, and, approaching the book, it flies open and displays hieroglyphics—* Lestelle *screams, and sinks at the base of the rock— footsteps heard without—*Vanderdecken *listens.*

[*Enter* Mowdrey, *from the rock, L.S.E.*

Mowdrey [*calling*]. Lestelle ! I am here—you are safe ! Lestelle ! [*He descends, and sees* Vanderdecken.] Ah, wretch, is it you ? Tremble !

[*Music.—*Vanderdecken *laughs, then draws a sword—a terrific fight—*Mowdrey, *after repeatedly stabbing his opponent in vain, is taken up by* Vanderdecken, *and furiously thrown down.*

Vanderdecken. Mortal, die ! [*Thunder.*] Ah, what have I done ! [*He displays bodily agony.*] I have spoken ! [*Music.*] The spell which admits my stay on earth is destroyed with my silence. I must begone to my phantom ship again, to the deep and howling waters ; but ye, the victims of my love and fury, yours is a dreadful fate —a hundred years here, in torpid life, to lie entombed till my return. Behold !   [*Points to the book—A Chord.*

278

[*Enter* VARNISH, *L.S.E.—he runs across, and hides behind the magic book.*

MOWDREY. Is there no hope?

VANDERDECKEN. None! Seest thou this magic book: its mystic pages, consumed by the hand of a sailor's son, on ocean born, would set ye free; but never can that be accomplished, for in Vanderdecken's absence 'tis denied that human footstep e'er seek this cavern, or pierce those flinty walls.

[VARNISH *comes cautiously forward and snatches up the torch, which* VANDERDECKEN *has inserted in the ground —he sets fire to the mystic book, and advancing triumphantly to* L., *with the torch in his hand, exclaims,* "'Tis done! 'Tis done!"

VARNISH [*to* VANDERDECKEN]. What d'ye think of that? I've burnt the writings, old one. I'm a sailor's son! I was born at sea, too; my father was a stout-hearted British tar, and so was my mother! [VARNISH *joins the hands of* MOWDREY *and* LESTELLE.

VANDERDECKEN [*after covering his face with his hands*]. Malediction! malediction! you triumph. But I go to my revenge. Tremble, tremble! the rushing waves which rise to welcome the return of Vanderdecken, shall bury ye deep, deep in their unfathomed darkness. Burst, stormy clouds, and overwhelm them; rise, ye many waters of ocean, cover them up for ever. [*Thunder.*] Rockalda! I come.

[*Music.*—VANDERDECKEN *goes behind the rock-table, whereon the magic-book was placed, and sinks with the altar, amidst thunder and flames of red fire.—Exit* VARNISH, *with the torch, R.S.E.*

VARNISH [*with a torch, on a projecting rock, R.U.E.*]. Master, dear master, the rock, the rock—follow me; this way—I hear voices.

MOWDREY. 'Tis the voice of Varnish; he has found an outlet to liberty. Come, love, come!

[*Exeunt* MOWDREY *and* LESTELLE, *hastily, R.S.E.; and they all appear on an eminence of the rock, R.U.E.*

MOWDREY. Alas, there is no hope!—Hark! hark! the torrent is rushing down upon us. See! see! Assistance is at hand—help! help! help! [*Waves handkerchief.*

[*Music.*—VARNISH *continues waving his torch, and the agitated waters rush furiously into the cave, entirely covering the stage to the orchestra—the sound of the gong, and loud peals of thunder heard—a pilot,* PETER VON BUMMELL, *with a torch,* CAPTAIN PEPPERCOAL, *&c., appear in a sloop from the very back—they come under the rock, R.U.E., and receive* LESTELLE, MOWDREY, *and* VARNISH *aboard—sails are hoisted, with British flag, and as the cutter turns round to return, shout,* "Huzza!"—*incessant noise, as on board a vessel, with crash, gong, and thunder, until the Curtain falls.*

EXTRACTS FROM BRITISH & IRISH PLAYS

4. THOMAS GREENWOOD (*fl.* 1820–40)

Jack Sheppard

Melodrama of the infernal type has been exemplified in *The Flying Dutchman*, but the melodramatic movement, particularly after 1830, tended rapidly toward a domestic note, and possibly this had some effect upon the naturalistic drama of later years. Contemporary (and earlier) crime was much sought after for plot-material, and the appearance of Harrison Ainsworth's novels was veritable treasure-trove for the minor playwrights. In *Jack Sheppard* Greenwood, following his model, makes Jack an unfortunate victim of circumstance, pursued by an implacable villain in Jonathan Wild. Sentimentalism rules, obviously, in the sphere of character-drawing, yet there is more " truth to reality " here than was possible in Fitzball's experiments in *diablerie*. There may be noted here the popular gibbet scene, treated in pure action. One of the chief weaknesses of the melodrama lay in its sacrifice of dialogue to movement on the stage and to the gestures of the actors.

(*Jack Sheppard ; or, The House-Breaker of the Last Century* appeared in 1839. The following extract is taken from Cumberland's edition (*c.* 1840).)

AN EXECUTION SCENE

On the road to Tyburn . . . JACK SHEPPARD *discovered in a cart, R.C.*—MARVEL, *the Executioner, seated on a coffin, smoking his pipe—the Landlord, R., with a bowl of punch, which he hands to* SHEPPARD—*Mob, C.—Soldiery ranged R. and L.—* JONATHAN WILD, *R.*

JACK [*to* WILD]. I leave this bowl for you.

WILD. Your father once said so, yet it has tarried long.

JACK. Monster! listen to my parting words: you'll call for this bowl before six months are passed!

WILD. Peace, drivelling fool!—My fate you've yet to learn; yours I've rendered certain. Whether your prophecy be true or false, thanks to the gibbet, you cannot live to know. [*Exultantly*] Ha! ha! ha! Over father and son, my triumph is complete!

JACK. By you have both been murdered. [*To the Driver*] I am prepared! On—quick to Tyburn!

[*The Procession moves on, and as it gains the centre,* MR WOOD *is seen in the balcony, R., waving his hand, and the cart stops.*

JACK. My kind old friend!

WOOD. Heaven bless you, poor unhappy boy!

WILD. No lingering here: on—on, I say!

[*All move forward, and the scene closes.*

NINETEENTH CENTURY

[*Enter* BAPTISTE KETTLEBY, *L.*, *heading Minters and Mob, armed with staves and stones.*

BAPTISTE. Now, my lads, up with your arms, and down with your cudgels! I've got the ready, and you've got the needful. [*The Mob shout.*] We've all come from the Mint; and if we don't pay the red jackets, and old Jonathan Wild at their head, in their own coin, say my name isn't Baptiste Kettleby.

MOB. Hurrah!

BAPTISTE. When you hear Blueskin's signal, be as full of fire as a washerwoman's ironing stove.

MOB. We will! we will!

BAPTISTE. Lay the rascals as flat as a smoothing iron, or as a barrel of ale after a double allowance of thunder.

MOB. Hurrah!

BAPTISTE [*looking off*]. Hollo! who have we here? Blueskin himself, or I'm no true gentleman.

[*Enter* BLUESKIN, *L.*, *followed by* THAMES DARRELL, *masked.*

BLUESKIN. That's right, my lads; we've gained the start upon our men, and we must keep it. Hurry on to Tyburn—secure your places near the gibbet, and when I fire, [*flourishing a pistol*] rush to the rescue of our noble captain. On, Baptiste, with your men!

[*Exeunt* BAPTISTE, MINTERS, *and* MOB, *R.*, *shouting.*

DARRELL [*L.*]. Poor Jack! I would sacrifice all my fortune—all my hopes, to save him from this wretched end!

BLUESKIN. All hope is not yet lost, thanks to the gold you gave me! I've bribed with it some daring lads, who'll die to save him. But I've no time to lose: you'll meet me at Tyburn, and, in case of need, you'll lend a helping hand.

DARRELL. I will, I swear it!

BLUESKIN. Enough. Now, then, for Tyburn!

[*Exeunt, R.—Shouts and groans without, L.*
[*Enter* WINIFRED, *leading on* MR WOOD, *L.*

WOOD. The people hurry this way. Poor lad! some strong inducement leads me to the fatal spot. Doubtless by this time he has reached the gibbet. Unhappy Jack! your fate may teach all youths a useful lesson: with your talent, wealth and honour were within your grasp; but, lured from the paths of virtue, your lot is infamy and shame! [*A bell tolls without.*] Ah! that bell!—Then all is over! [*A pistol and shouting heard without.*] On—on, my child! 'tis an attempt at rescue!   [*Exeunt, R.*

[*Tyburn—the Gibbet, L.C.—a Gentleman's Carriage waiting, L.*

Soldiers and Mob discovered ranged R. and L.—
BLUESKIN, *amidst the shouts of the Mob and the firing of the Soldiers, is seen descending from the gallows, with* JACK *on his shoulder—he throws him hastily into the arms of the Minters, who hurry off with the body, L.—The Soldiers fire on the people, who return a volley of stones, and*

281

charge them furiously with sticks—JONATHAN WILD *is
shot by* BLUESKIN, *and falls wounded, R.C.*—BLUESKIN
is shot by a Police Officer, and drops dead, C.—*a Picture
is formed, and the curtain descends amidst firing, uproar, and confusion.*

5. SAMUEL TAYLOR COLERIDGE (1772–1834)

Remorse

Coleridge's *Remorse* is a fairly typical example of the type of
poetic play which in the early nineteenth century found its way
to the stage.   When such plays as this could be accepted by the
playhouses, truly the literary dramatists of the age had not much
of which they could complain.   As the following extract shows
plainly enough, the language is rather rhetorical than dramatic ;
long soliloquies continually arrest the action ; and that action
itself has little that could make the play have a powerful appeal
in its time.   Obviously Coleridge is deeply under the influence
of the German school.   *Die Räuber* probably suggested the theme
of the two brothers, and the mark of Kotzebue is to be traced in
more than one scene.   The Elizabethans, too, play their part ;
the unnatural dialogue must to a certain extent be credited to a
blinded imitation of Shakespeare's style.   One feels, in reading
Remorse, that the author has no great necessity for writing drama.
He admires the Elizabethans and he admires the Germans.
Both of these groups of authors had produced plays ; and there
is thus raised in his mind the vague desire to follow in their footsteps.   Of dominant, all-embracing purpose there is none, nor
is there even the slightest spark of originality.   A few lines in
the drama may be singled out as beautiful, but fundamentally
neither Coleridge nor any of his poetic contemporaries gave anything fresh to the world of the theatre.

(*Remorse*, originally drafted in 1797, was produced in an altered
version at Drury Lane in 1813.   The following extract is taken
from the second edition, 1813.)

THE INEVITABLE DUNGEON SCENE

ALVAR, *alone, rises slowly from a bed of reeds.*

ALVAR. And this place my forefathers made for Man!
This is the process of our Love and Wisdom
To each poor brother who offends against us—
Most innocent, perhaps—and what if guilty?
Is this the only cure?   Merciful God!
Each pore and natural outlet shrivell'd up
By Ignorance and parching Poverty,
His energies roll back upon his heart,

And stagnate and corrupt, 'till chang'd to poison,
They break out on him, like a loathsome plague-spot!
Then we call in our pamper'd mountebanks;
And this is their best cure! uncomforted
And friendless Solitude, Groaning and Tears,
And savage Faces, at the clanking hour,
Seen through the steam and vapours of his dungeon
By the lamp's dismal twilight! So he lies
Circled with evil 'till his very soul
Unmoulds its essence, hopelessly deformed
By sights of evermore deformity!

With other ministrations thou, O Nature!
Healest thy wand'ring and distemper'd child;
Thou pourest on him thy soft influences,
Thy sunny hues, fair forms, and breathing sweets;
Thy melodies of woods, and winds, and waters!
Till he relent, and can no more endure
To be a jarring and a dissonant thing
Amid this general dance and minstrelsy;
But, bursting into tears, wins back his way,
His angry spirit heal'd and harmoniz'd
By the benignant touch of love and beauty.

I am chill and weary! Yon rude bench of stone,
In that dark angle, the sole resting-place!
But the self-approving mind is its own light,
And light's best warmth still radiates from the heart,
Where love sits brooding, and an honest purpose.
                                    [*Retires out of sight.*
                          [*Enter* TERESA *with a Taper.*
    TERESA. It has chill'd my very life—my own voice scares me;
Yet when I hear it not, I seem to lose
The substance of my being—my strongest grasp
Sends inwards but weak witness that I am.
I seek to cheat the echo—How the half sounds
Blend with this strangled light! Is he not here? [*Looking round.*
O for one human face here—but to see
One human face here to sustain me.—Courage!
It is but my own fear!—The life within me,
It sinks and wavers like this cone of flame,
Beyond which I scarce dare look onward! Oh,   [*Shuddering.*
If I faint? If this inhuman den should be
At once my death-bed and my burial vault?
                [*Faintly screams as* ALVAR *emerges from the recess.*
    ALVAR [*rushes towards her, and catches her as she is falling*]. O
        gracious heaven! it is, it is Teresa!
Shall I reveal myself? The sudden shock

Of rapture will blow out this spark of life,
And Joy compleat what Terror has begun.
O ye impetuous beatings here, be still!
Teresa, best belov'd! pale, pale, and cold!
Her pulse doth flutter! Teresa! my Teresa!

TERESA [*recovering, looks round wildly*]. I heard a voice; but often
    in my dreams
I hear that voice! and wake, and try—and try—
To hear it waking! but I never could—
And 'tis so now—even so! Well! he is dead—
Murder'd perhaps! And I am faint, and feel
As if it were no painful thing to die!

ALVAR [*eagerly*]. Believe it not, sweet maid! Believe it not,
Beloved woman! 'Twas a low imposture,
Fram'd by a guilty wretch.

TERESA [*retires from him, and feebly supports herself against a pillar
    of the dungeon*]. Ha! Who art thou?

ALVAR [*exceedingly affected*]. Suborned by his brother——

TERESA. Did'st *thou* murder him?
And dost thou now repent? Poor wretched man,
I do forgive thee, and may Heaven forgive thee!

ALVAR. Ordonio—he——

TERESA.   If thou didst murder him—
His spirit ever at the throne of God
Asks mercy for thee: prays for mercy for thee,
With tears in Heaven!

ALVAR.   Alvar was not murder'd.
Be calm! Be calm, sweet maid!

TERESA [*wildly*]. Nay, nay, but tell me!

                [*A pause, then presses her forehead.*
                    O 'tis lost again!
This dull confused pain——   [*A pause, she gazes at* ALVAR.
             Mysterious man!
Methinks I cannot fear thee: for thine eye
Doth swim with love and pity—Well! Ordonio—
Oh my foreboding heart! And *he* suborn'd thee,
And thou did'st spare his life? Blessings shower on thee,
As many as the drops twice counted o'er
In the fond faithful heart of his Teresa!

ALVAR. I can endure no more. The Moorish sorcerer
Exists but in the stain upon his face.
That picture——

TERESA [*advances towards him*]. Ha! speak on!

ALVAR.   Belov'd Teresa!
It told but half the truth. O let this portrait
Tell all—that Alvar lives—that he is here!
Thy much deceived but ever faithful Alvar.

          [*Takes her portrait from his neck, and gives it her.*

TERESA [*receiving the portrait*]. The same—it is the same. Ah!
Who art thou?
Nay I will call thee, ALVAR!   [*She falls on his neck.*
ALVAR.   O joy unutterable!
But hark! a sound as of removing bars
At the dungeon's outer door.   A brief, brief while
Conceal thyself, my love!   It is Ordonio,
For the honour of our race, for our dear father,
O for himself too (he is still my brother)]
Let me recall him to his nobler nature,
That he may wake as from a dream of murder!
O let me reconcile him to himself,
Open the sacred source of penitent tears,
And be once more his own beloved Alvar.
    TERESA. O my all-virtuous Love!   I fear to leave thee
With that obdurate man.
    ALVAR.   Thou dost not leave me!
But a brief while retire into the darkness:
O that my joy could spread it's sunshine round thee!
    TERESA. The sound of thy voice shall be my music!
        [*Retiring, she returns hastily and embraces* ALVAR.
Alvar! my Alvar! am I sure I hold thee?
Is it no dream? thee in my arms, my Alvar!

6. JOANNA BAILLIE (1762–1851)

Ethwald

Among the poetic dramatists of the early nineteenth century,
Joanna Baillie was probably the most energetic and the most
resolute in her efforts.   Her various prefaces indicate that she
had a lofty aim in the writing of tragedy, while some of her plays
come very close to real success.   In spite of this, however, she
failed, largely because the impress of her age was laid upon her
too strongly.   The dialogue in her plays is artificially ' Shake-
sperian' ; her characters are all subordinated to a fixed, abstract
' passion' ; and her scenes are far removed from the life of her
day.   It would be possible to choose from *Plays on the Passions*
many individual scenes of high merit ; but such scenes would,
in reality, be untrue to her work.   The passage selected here from
Ethwald (first published 1811) is thoroughly typical.   Note
should be taken of several features making for dramatic weakness : (1) the division of action and of dialogue ; (2) the false
language, blindly following Elizabethan blank verse with the
ridiculous protracted simile toward the close ; (3) the disastrously
named characters ; and (4) the wholly artificial questionings and
answers.   This scene is from the last act of the first part of the
tragedy, just after Ethwald, ambitious and selfish, has deserted

EXTRACTS FROM BRITISH & IRISH PLAYS

his Bertha, and, becoming King of Mercia, has married Elburga, daughter of the former monarch.

(The extract given below is taken from *A Series of Plays*, 1821, vol. ii.)

THE WARRIORS LEARN OF THE FATE OF MERCIA

An arched passage from a gateway in the royal castle. The sound of warlike music without. Enter ETHELBERT *and* SELRED *with their Followers, as if just come from a long march : enter, by the opposite side,* ALWY, *upon which they halt, the foremost of the Followers but just appearing under the gateway.*

ALWY. Welcome, most valiant chieftains ! Fame reports
That crown'd with full success ye are return'd.

ETHELBERT. Good sooth we boast but little of our arms !
Tho' Woggarwolfe, our base ignoble spoiler,
Wounded and sorely shent, we've left behind,
Again in cloister'd walls with ghostly men,
Winding his soul, with many a heavy groan,
Into a saintly frame ! God speed the work !
We are but just in time to save our halls.

SELRED. It is a shame that such a ruffian thief
Should thus employ the arms of warlike Thanes.

ALWY. In truth it is, but now there reigns in Mercia
A warlike king, who better knows to deal
With valiant men. The messenger inform'd you?

SELRED. He did; yet, be it own'd, to call him king
Sounds strangely in our ears. How died King Oswal?

ETHELBERT [*to* SELRED]. Patience, my friend! good time will
shew thee all.
Yet pray inform us, Alwy, ere we part.
Where is young Edward? In these late commotions
What part had he?

ALWY. Would to the holy saints I could inform you !
Reports there are, incongruous and absurd—
Some say, in hunting from his followers stray'd,
Passing at dusk of eve a high-swoln stream,
Therein he perish'd; others do maintain
That, loathing greatness, he conceals himself
In some lone cave: but, as I bear a heart
True to King Ethwald and the public weal,
I know of him no more.

SELRED. Thou liest !

ETHELBERT [*pulling back* SELRED]. Peace, art thou mad?

ALWY [*pretending not to hear*]. What said brave Selred?

ETHELBERT. A hasty exclamation of no meaning.

ALWY. I must away, and bear the welcome tidings
Of your arrival to the royal ear.

286

ETHELBERT. But stop, before thou go'st I fain would know
How far'd Elburga in the passing storm?
Where has she refuge found?

ALWY. Within these walls; she is the Queen of Mercia.

ETHELBERT. I am indebted to thee.   [*Exit* ALWY.

SELRED [*staring with surprise upon* ETHELBERT]. What dost
   thou think of this?   Did we hear truly?
To the usurper of her father's crown,
And if our fears be true, his murd'rer too!
To him!   O most unnatural!

ETHELBERT. Ay, so it is.   As one who ventures forth
After an earthquake's awful visitation,
The country round in strange unwonted guise
Beholds; here swelling heights and herby knolls,
Where smok'd the cottage and the white flocks browz'd,
Sunk into turbid pools; there rifted rocks,
With all their shaggy woods upon their sides,
In the low bosom of the flowery vale
Resting uncouthly—even so does he,
Who looks abroad after the storms of state,
Strange changes see; unnatural and strange.

SELRED. It makes my spirit boil—the gentle Edward!
So gently brave!

ETHELBERT. Yes, there is cause of grief
And indignation too: but Ethwald reigns,
Howe'er he gain'd his height, and he possesses
The qualities that suit his lofty station.
With them I fear he has his passions also,
Hostile to public good: be it our part
To use the influence we still retain
O'er his ambitious mind for Mercia's weal!
This is our duty now.

SELRED. I'll take thy counsel. [*To the* SOLDIERS] Follow,
   weary comrades.

7. LORD BYRON (1788–1824)

Sardanapalus

Sardanapalus, A Tragedy was first published, along with *The
Two Foscari* and *Cain*, in 1821. It is characteristic of his age
that Byron prefaces these with the remark that "they were not
composed with the most remote view to the stage." In spite of
this, and in spite of Byron's leanings toward the 'rules' of neo-
classic theory (he "has in one instance attempted to preserve,
and in the other to approach the 'unities'"), *Sardanapalus* is
one of the few poetic tragedies of this time which can be truly

styled dramatic. It is not a great masterpiece, but the action is interwoven with character, and the character itself has an interest often denied to the heroes of romantic drama. The tragedy deals mainly with the fate of Sardanapalus, King of Nineveh, and Myrrha, a Greek slave, his favourite. Myrrha loves him passionately in spite of the fact that he has allowed himself to sink into a state of luxurious effeminacy. A rebellion stirs the latent heroism of his soul to action, and in the end, defeated by his enemies, yet master of himself, he dies gloriously on a funeral pile made of his own treasure-filled palace. A genuine attempt here is made to present conflicting emotions, and Byron has been able to capture a tragic note denied to most of his contemporaries.

(The following passage is taken from the first (1821) edition.)

SARDANAPALUS IS ROUSED TO ACTION

SARDANAPALUS [*after* PANIA *has announced that* SALEMENES *is sore beset*]. What, ho!
My armour there.
    MYRRHA. And wilt thou?
    SARDANAPALUS. Will I not?
Ho, there!—But seek not for the buckler; 'tis
Too heavy:—a light cuirass and my sword.
Where are the rebels?
    PANIA. Scarce a furlong's length
From the outward wall, the fiercest conflict rages.
    SARDANAPALUS. Then I may charge on horseback. Sfero, ho!
Order my horse out.—There is space enough
Even in our courts, and by the outer gate,
To martial half the horsemen of Arabia.
                [*Exit* SFERO *for the armour.*
    MYRRHA. How I do love thee!
    SARDANAPALUS. I ne'er doubted it.
    MYRRHA. But now I know thee.
    SARDANAPALUS [*to his Attendant*]. Bring down my spear, too.—
Where's Salemenes?
    PANIA. Where a soldier should be,
In the thick of the fight.
    SARDANAPALUS. Then hasten to him—Is
The path still open, and communication
Left 'twixt the palace and the phalanx?
    PANIA. 'Twas
When I late left him, and I have no fear:
Our troops were steady, and the phalanx form'd.
    SARDANAPALUS. Tell him to spare his person for the present,
And that I will not spare my own—and say,
I come.
288

PANIA. There's victory in the very word.   [*Exit* PANIA.
          [*Enter* SFERO *and others with the King's Arms, &c.*
     SFERO.   King! your armour.
     SARDANAPALUS [*arming himself*]. Give me the cuirass—so: my
     baldric; now
My sword: I had forgot the helm, where is it?
That's well—no, 'tis too heavy: you mistake, too—
It was not this I meant, but that which bears
A diadem around it.
     SFERO.   Sire, I deem'd
That too conspicuous from the precious stones
To risk your sacred brow beneath—and, trust me,
This is of better metal though less rich.
     SARDANAPALUS. You deem'd! Are you too turn'd a rebel?
     Fellow!
Your part is to obey: return, and—no—
It is too late—I will go forth without it.
     SFERO. At least wear this.
     SARDANAPALUS.   Wear Caucasus! why, 'tis
A mountain on my temples.
     SFERO.   Sire, the meanest
Soldier goes not forth thus exposed to battle.
All men will recognise you—for the storm
Has ceased, and the moon breaks forth in her brightness.
     SARDANAPALUS. I go forth to be recognised, and thus
Shall be so sooner. Now—my spear! I'm arm'd.
                    [*In going stops short, and turns to* SFERO.
Sfero—I had forgotten—bring the mirror.
     SFERO. The mirror, sire?
     SARDANAPALUS.   Yes, sir, of polish'd brass,
Brought from the spoils of India—but be speedy.   [*Exit* SFERO.
Myrrha, retire unto a place of safety.
Why went you not forth with the other damsels?
     MYRRHA. Because my place is here.
     SARDANAPALUS.   And when I am gone——
     MYRRHA. I follow.
     SARDANAPALUS.   *You!* to battle?
     MYRRHA.   If it were so,
'Twere not the first Greek girl had trod the path.
I will await here your *return.*
     SARDANAPALUS.   The place
Is spacious, and the first to be sought out,
If they prevail; and, if it should be so,
And I return not——
     MYRRHA.   Still, we meet again.
     SARDANAPALUS. How?
     MYRRHA.   In the spot where all must meet at last—
In Hades! if there be, as I believe,

T   289

A shore beyond the Styx; and if there be not,
In ashes.

    SARDANAPALUS. Dar'st thou so much?

    MYRRHA.   I dare all things
Except survive what I have loved, to be
A rebel's booty: forth, and do your bravest.

                          [*Re-enter* SFERO *with the mirror.*

    SARDANAPALUS [*looking at himself*]. This cuirass fits me well, the
    baldric better,
And the helm not at all.   Methinks, I seem

                [*Flings away the helmet after trying it again.*

Passing well in these toys; and now to prove them.
Altada!   Where's Altada?

    SFERO.   Waiting, sire,
Without: he has your shield in readiness.

    SARDANAPALUS. True; I forgot he is my shield-bearer
By right of blood, derived from age to age.
Myrrha, embrace me; yet once more—once more—
Love me. whate'er betide.   My chiefest glory
Shall be to make me worthier of your love.

    MYRRHA. Go forth, and conquer!

                 [*Exit* SARDANAPALUS *and* SFERO.
                 Now, I am alone.
All are gone forth, and of that all how few
Perhaps return.   Let him but vanquish, and
Me perish!   If he vanquish not, I perish;
For I will not outlive him. . . . If it should be so,
This cunning Colchian poison, which my father
Learn'd to compound on Euxine shores, and taught me
How to preserve, shall free me!   It had freed me
Long ere this hour, but that I loved, until
I half forgot I was a slave.

8. JAMES SHERIDAN KNOWLES (1784–1862)

Virginius

    In his own day Knowles was famous ; now he is barely remem-
bered, his name being merely a name in text-books.   This neglect
is merited, if we think of the purely intrinsic worth of his plays,
yet no playwright of the period shows so well the vitiating
tendencies at work on nineteenth-century drama.   Knowles
battled hard for success, but to secure that success he saw only
one way—the writing of a type of play which should be 'poetic'
and yet contain a dash of melodrama.   Sometimes the melodramatic dash, as in *Alfred the Great*, nearly filled the tumbler;
sometimes, as in *Virginius*, decorous 'poetry' predominated.

NINETEENTH CENTURY

Always, however, the result was stilted, full of unassimilated imitations of Shakespeare, vapid, lacking in any sort of novelty or direct appeal. The language for the most part is Victorian Elizabethan; the characters, be they kilted as in *Glencoe*, or togaed as in *Virginius*, are cast in a mould wherein we see the main features of nineteenth-century life sentimentalized and mawkish. This is as much as to say that Knowles never succeeded in coming to grips with life. His plays, however popular some may have been in that age of misapplied dramatic talent, could never have a real theatrical interest for any age. A comparison of *Virginius* with a play by Tom Robertson will show clearly enough what was needed to convert the stagnation of the early nineteenth century into the flowing vitality of the modern period.

(*Virginius* was produced at Covent Garden in 1820. The following passage is taken from the *Dramatic Works* of 1859.)

A Roman Family Party

VIRGINIUS. Welcome, Icilius! Welcome, friends! Icilius,
I hoped to speak with you, to-day, of feasting
And merriment, but war is now the word;
One that unlovingly keeps time with mirth,
Unless war's own—when the fierce fight is won,
And safe carousing, comrades drink to victory!
ICILIUS. Virginius! have you changed your mind?
VIRGINIUS. My mind?
What mind? How now! Are you that boy, Icilius,
You set your heart so earnestly upon
A dish of poor confections, that to balk you
Makes you look blank! I did design to feast you
Together with your friends. The times are changed—
The march, the tent, the fight becomes us now!
ICILIUS. Virginius!
VIRGINIUS. Well!
ICILIUS. Virginius!
VIRGINIUS. How the boy
Reiterates my name!
ICILIUS. There's not a hope
I have but is the client of Virginius!
VIRGINIUS. Well, well! I only meant to put it off!
We'll have the revel yet! the board shall smoke!
The cup shall sparkle, and the jest shall soar
And mock us from the roof! Will that content you?
Not till the war be done, though—Yet, ere then,
Some tongue, that now needs only wag to make
The table ring, may have a tale to tell
So petrifying, that it cannot utter it!
I'll make all sure, that you may be my guest

At any rate—although you should be forced
To play the host for me and feast yourself.
Look here, [*shows a parchment to* ICILIUS].
How think you?—Will it meet the charge?
Will it not do?   We want a witness, though!
I'll bring one; of whom if you approve, I'll sign
The bond.   I'll wait upon you instantly.   [*Goes out.*

 LUCIUS. How feel you now, Icilius?

 ICILIUS. Like a man
Whom the next moment makes or quite unmakes.
With the intensity of exquisite
Suspense, my breathing thickens, and my heart
Beats heavily, and with remittent throb,
As like to lose its action—See! my hope
Is bless'd!   I live!   I live!

  [*Enter* VIRGINIUS, *conducting* VIRGINIA, *with* NUMITORIUS.

 VIRGINIUS. You are my witnesses
That this young creature I present to you,
I boast of, as my profitably cherish'd,
And most deservedly belovèd child;
My daughter truly filial—both in word
And act—yet even more in act than word;
And—for the man who hopes to win her hand—
A virgin, from whose lips a soul as pure
Exhales, as e'er responded to the blessing
Breathed in a parent's kiss.   [*Kissing her*] Icilius!

  [ICILIUS *rushes towards* VIRGINIUS, *and kneels.*
             Since

You are upon your knee, young man, look up;
And lift your hand to heaven—you will be all
Her father has been—added unto all
A lover would be!

 ICILIUS. All that man should be
To woman, I will be to her!

 VIRGINIUS. The oath
Is register'd!   Didst thou but know, young man,
How fondly I have watch'd her, since the day
Her mother died, and left me to a charge
Of double duty bound—how she hath been
My ponder'd thought by day, my dream by night,
My prayer, my vow, my offering, my praise,
My sweet companion, pupil, tutor, child!—
Thou wouldst not wonder that my drowning eye,
And choking utterance, upbraid my tongue
That tells thee, she is thine!—Icilius,
I now betroth her to thee!   When the war
Is done—you shall espouse her.   Friends, a word!

       [VIRGINIUS *and the rest retire.*

ICILIUS. Virginia! my Virginia!   I am all
Dissolved—o'erpower'd with the munificence
Of this auspicious hour—and thou, nor movest—
Nor look'st—nor speak'st—to bless me with a sign—
Of sweet according joy!—I love thee, but
To make thee happy!   If to make thee so
Be bliss denied to me—lo, I release
The gifted hand—that I would faster hold,
Than wretches, bound for death, would cling to life.
If thou wouldst take it back—then take it back.
   VIRGINIA. I take it back—to give it thee again!
   ICILIUS. O help me to a word to speak my bliss,
Or I am beggar'd—No!   There's no such word!
There cannot be; for never man had bliss
Like mine to name!
   VIRGINIA. Thou dost but beggar me,
Icilius, when thou makest thyself a bankrupt;
Placing a value on me far above
My real little worth.—I'd help thee to
A hundred words; each one of which would far
O'er-rate thy gain, and yet no single one
Rate over high!
   ICILIUS. Thou couldst not do it!   No;
Thou couldst not do it!   Every term of worth
Writ down and doubled, then the whole summ'd up,
Would leave with thee a rich remainder still!—
Pick from each rarer pattern of thy sex
Her rarest charm, till thou hast every charm
Of soul and body that can blend in woman,
I would out-paragon the paragon
With thee!
   VIRGINIA. And if thou wouldst, I'd find thee, for
Thy paragon a mate—if that can be
A mate which beats the thing 'tis ta'en to match—
One that would make thy paragon look poor—
And I would call that so o'ermatching mate
"Icilius."
   ICILIUS. No!   I will not let thee win
On such a theme as this!
   VIRGINIA. Nor will I drop
The controversy, that the richer makes me
The more I lose!
   ICILIUS. My sweet Virginia,
We do but lose and lose, and win and win;
Playing for nothing but to lose and win.
Then let us drop the game—and thus I stop it.   [*Kisses her.*

293

EXTRACTS FROM BRITISH & IRISH PLAYS

9. SIR THOMAS NOON TALFOURD (1795–1854)
Ion

Ion, by Serjeant T. N. Talfourd, is thoroughly typical of the nineteenth-century poetic drama. Talfourd himself was a man of no mean abilities. A friend of Wordsworth and Lamb, he was esteemed no less in literary circles than at the Bar, and many of his critical essays have an ease and acumen which speak highly of his talent. Like the others, however, when he turned to the theatre he grew cold; his fire vanished, and we can barely discern even glowing embers of true spirit. In theme *Ion* seems capable of romantic treatment; but the hardness of the portraiture and the solemnity of the dialogue alike bring the play nearer to *Cato* than to the passionate poetry of the epoch. The following scene from the second act of the play shows well the artificial language which contemporaries hailed as dramatic verse, as well as the general stolidity of the characters.

(*Ion* was first printed for private circulation in 1835; a 'second edition,' from which the extract below is taken, appeared the same year. It was subsequently acted at Covent Garden in 1836.)

Frigid Sentiments

ABRA. Look, dearest lady!—the thin smoke aspires
In the calm air, as when in happier times
It show'd the gods propitious; wilt thou seek
Thy chamber, lest thy father and his friends,
Returning, find us hinderers of their council?
She answers not—she hearkens not—with joy
Could I believe her, for the first time, sullen!—
Still she is rapt.   [*Enter* AGENOR.
                    O, speak to my sweet mistress,
Haply thy voice may rouse her.
    AGENOR.   Dear Clemanthe,
Hope dawns in every omen; we shall hail
Our tranquil hours again.
                    [*Enter* MEDON, CLEON, TIMOCLES, *and others.*
    MEDON.   Clemanthe here!
How sad! how pale!
    ABRA.   Her eye is kindling—hush!
    CLEMANTHE. Hark! hear ye not a distant footstep?
    MEDON.   No.
Look round, my fairest child; thy friends are near thee.
    CLEMANTHE. Yes!—now 'tis lost—'tis on that endless
        stair—
Nearer and more distinct—'tis his—'tis his—
He lives! he comes!

294

[CLEMANTHE *rises and rushes to the back of the stage, at
which* ION *appears, and returns with him.*
                    Here is your messenger,
Whom Heaven has rescued from the tyrant's rage
Ye sent him forth to brave.   Rejoice, old men,
That ye are guiltless of his blood!—why pause ye,
Why shout ye not his welcome?
    MEDON.   Dearest girl,
This is no scene for thee; go to thy chamber,
I'll come to thee ere long.   [*Exeunt* CLEMANTHE *and* ABRA.
                    She is o'erwrought
By fear and joy for one whose infant hopes
Were mingled with her own, even as a brother's.
    TIMOCLES.   Ion!
How shall we do thee honour?
    ION.   None is due
Save to the gods whose gracious influence sways
The king ye deem'd relentless;—he consents
To meet ye presently in council: speed;
This may be nature's latest rally in him,
In fitful strength, ere it be quench'd for ever!
    MEDON. Haste to your seats; I will but speak a word
With our brave friend, and follow; though convened
In speed, let our assembly lack no forms
Of due observance, which to furious power
Plead with the silent emphasis of years.
                    [*Exeunt all but* MEDON *and* ION.
Ion, draw near me; this eventful day
Hath shown thy nature's graces circled round
With firmness which accomplishes the hero;—
And it would bring to me but one proud thought
That virtues which required not culture's aid
Shed their first fragrance 'neath my roof, and there
Found shelter;—but it also hath reveal'd
What I may not hide from thee, that my child,
My blithe and innocent girl—more fair in soul,
More delicate in fancy than in mould—
Loves thee with other than a sister's love.
I should have cared for this: I vainly deem'd
A fellowship in childhood's thousand joys
And household memories had nurtured friendship
Which might hold blameless empire in the soul;
But in that guise the traitor hath stolen in,
And the fair citadel is thine.
    ION.   'Tis true.
I did not think the nurseling of thy house
Could thus disturb its holiest inmate's duty
With tale of selfish passion;—but we met

295

As playmates who might never meet again,
And then the hidden truth flash'd forth, and show'd
To each the image in the other's soul
In one bright instant.

MEDON.   Be that instant blest
Which made thee truly ours.   My son! my son!
'Tis we should feel uplifted, for the seal
Of greatness is upon thee; yet I know
That when the gods, won by thy virtues, draw
The veil which now conceals their lofty birthplace,
Thou wilt not spurn the maid who prized them lowly.

ION. Spurn her!   My father!   [*Enter* CTESIPHON.
MEDON.   Ctesiphon!—and breathless—
Art come to chide me to the council?

CTESIPHON.   No;
To bring unwonted joy; thy son approaches.

MEDON. Thank Heaven!   Hast spoken with him?   Is he well?

CTESIPHON. I strove in vain to reach him, for the crowd,
Roused from the untended couch and dismal hearth
By the strange visiting of hope, press'd round him;
But, by his head erect and fiery glance,
I know that he is well, and that he bears
A message which shall shake the tyrant. [*Shouts.*]   See!
The throng is tending this way—now it parts,
And yields him to thy arms.

10. PERCY BYSSHE SHELLEY (1792–1822)

The Cenci

The Cenci is usually acclaimed as the greatest tragedy written
in England between the time when *Venice Preserv'd* made its
appearance and modern days.   This, to a certain extent, is true,
but it has to be confessed that as a complete work of dramatic
art it has its serious failings.   Its greatest qualities are poetic
and not definitely theatrical.   There is much mechanical borrow-
ing from the Elizabethans, particularly Shakespeare, and many
of the speeches seem ill-calculated for successful enunciation in
a playhouse.   For presentation here I have chosen one of the
finer scenes from the drama—the great banquet scene in the first
act, although this must not be taken as typical of the tragedy as
a whole.   It is, indeed, of especial importance to consider the
totality of impression when studying the poetic plays of the nineteenth century.   Many of the poets of the time could produce
individually striking scenes, but even a Shelley failed in the most
difficult of all dramatic tasks—the creation of an impression,
united and clear, borne out not by separate scenes, but by a consideration of the play as a whole.

NINETEENTH CENTURY

(*The Cenci* was printed in 1820. It was first performed by the Shelley Society in 1886, and has seen some revivals in recent times under the direction of Miss Sybil Thorndike.)

THE GROWTH OF A TERRIBLE THOUGHT

CENCI [*filling a bowl of wine and lifting it up*].
Oh, thou bright wine whose purple splendour leaps
And bubbles gaily in this golden bowl
Under the lamplight, as my spirits do,
To hear the death of my accursed sons!
Could I believe thou wert their mingled blood,
Then would I taste thee like a sacrament,
And pledge with thee the mighty Devil in Hell,
Who, if a father's curses, as men say,
Climb with swift wings after their children's souls,
And drag them from the very throne of Heaven,
Now triumphs in my triumph!—But thou art
Superfluous; I have drunken deep of joy,
And I will taste no other wine to-night.
Here, Andrea! Bear the the bowl around.

    A GUEST [*rising*].   Thou wretch!
Will none among this noble company
Check the abandoned villain?

    CAMILLO.   For God's sake
Let me dismiss the guests! You are insane.
Some ill will come of this.

    SECOND GUEST.   Seize, silence him!
    FIRST GUEST. I will!
    THIRD GUEST.   And I!
    CENCI [*addressing those who rise with a threatening gesture*].
Who moves? Who speaks? [*turning to the company*] 'tis nothing,
Enjoy yourselves.—Beware! For my revenge
Is as the sealed commission of a king
That kills, and none dare name the murderer.

       [*The Banquet is broken up; several of the Guests are departing.*
    BEATRICE. I do entreat you, go not, noble guests;
What, although tyranny and impious hate
Stand sheltered by a father's hoary hair?
What, if 'tis he who cloathed us in these limbs
Who tortures them, and triumphs? What, if we,
The desolate and the dead, were his own flesh,
His children and his wife, whom he is bound
To love and shelter? Shall we therefore find
No refuge in this merciless wide world?
O think what deep wrongs must have blotted out
First love, then reverence, in a child's prone mind,
Till it thus vanquish shame and fear! O think!

I have borne much, and kissed the sacred hand
Which crushed us to the earth, and thought its stroke
Was perhaps some paternal chastisement!
Have excused much, doubted; and when no doubt
Remained, have sought by patience, love, and tears
To soften him, and when this could not be
I have knelt down through the long sleepless nights,
And lifted up to God, the Father of all,
Passionate prayers; and when these were not heard
I have still borne,—until I meet you here,
Princes and kinsmen, at this hideous feast
Given at my brothers' deaths. Two yet remain;
His wife remains and I, whom if ye save not,
Ye may soon share such merriment again
As fathers make over their children's graves.
O Prince Colonna, thou art our near kinsman;
Cardinal, thou art the Pope's chamberlain;
Camillo, thou art chief justiciary; .
Take us away!

 CENCI. [*He has been conversing with* CAMILLO *during the first
  part of* BEATRICE'S *speech; he hears the conclusion, and now
  advances.*] I hope my good friends here
Will think of their own daughters—or perhaps
Of their own throats—before they lend an ear
To this wild girl.

 BEATRICE [*not noticing the words of* CENCI]. Dare no one look
  on me?
None answer? Can one tyrant overbear
The sense of many best and wisest men?
Or is it that I sue not in some form
Of scrupulous law, that ye deny my suit?
O God! That I were buried with my brothers!
And that the flowers of this departed spring
Were fading on my grave! And that my father
Were celebrating now one feast for all!

 CAMILLO. A bitter wish for one so young and gentle;
Can we do nothing?

 COLONNA.   Nothing that I see.
Count Cenci were a dangerous enemy;
Yet I would second anyone.

 A CARDINAL.   And I.

 CENCI. Retire to your chamber, insolent girl!

 BEATRICE. Retire thou, impious man! Ay, hide thyself
Where never eye can look upon thee more!
Wouldst thou have honour and obedience,
Who art a torturer? Father, never dream
Though thou mayst overbear this company,
But ill must come of ill. Frown not on me!

Haste, hide thyself, lest with avenging looks
My brothers' ghosts should hunt thee from thy seat!
Cover thy face from every living eye,
And start if thou but hear a human step;
Seek out some dark and silent corner, there,
Bow thy white head before offended God,
And we will kneel around, and fervently
Pray that he pity both ourselves and thee.
   CENCI. My friends, I do lament this insane girl
Has spoilt the mirth of our festivity.
Good night, farewell; I will not make you longer
Spectators of our dull domestic quarrels.
Another time.—   [*Exeunt all but* CENCI *and* BEATRICE.
            My brain is swimming round;
Give me a bowl of wine!   [*To* BEATRICE.
           Thou painted viper!
Beast that thou art! Fair and yet terrible!
I know a charm shall make thee meek and tame,
Now get thee from my sight!   [*Exit* BEATRICE.
           Here, Andrea,
Fill up this goblet with Greek wine. I said
I would not drink this evening; but I must;
For, strange to say, I feel my spirits fail
With thinking what I have decreed to do. [*Drinking the wine.*
Be thou the resolution of quick youth
Within my veins, and manhood's purpose stern,
And age's firm, cold, subtle villainy;
As if thou wert indeed my children's blood
Which I did thirst to drink! The charm works well;
It must be done; it shall be done, I swear!

11. GEORGE COLMAN THE YOUNGER (1762–1836)

John Bull

One of the most brilliant theatrical successes of the early nineteenth century was attained by *John Bull*, a comedy that for long remained on the acting list. A study of this play will indicate how easily the public of the time was satisfied and what slight wit served to secure contemporary popularity. *John Bull* is a *mélange* of rude farce and dull sentimentality. Its characters are nothing but types, and its language is poverty-stricken. There is a story in it, certainly, but it is told in a manner entirely unnaturalistic, with facts and episodes warped from reality in order to make a false theatrical appeal. Yet this play succeeded. It succeeded precisely because of its broad effects and of its type characterization. It is a comedy fitted for production in a huge theatre, where all the little niceties of wit would be lost and the finer shades in characterization pass unnoticed. The rudely pictured Dennis, the farcical Dan, their companion Mrs Brulgruddery, and the sentimental Peregrine could make an appeal where a Millamant and a Mirabel might jest in vain. There are much worse plays than *John Bull*, for Colman had at least a slight dash of talent, but out of a style of drama such as is represented by this play no real good could arise. We have here the last remnants of the decaying eighteenth-century manner ; to attain a new standard a start had to be made afresh.

(*John Bull* was produced at Covent Garden in 1803. The following passage follows Mrs Inchbald's corrected edition.)

THE IRISH LANDLORD

MRS BRULGRUDDERY. And what do you want, now, with Mrs Brulgruddery? What's to become of us? tell me that. How are we going on, I shou'd like to know?

DENNIS. Mighty like a mile-stone—standing still, at this present writing.

MRS BRULGRUDDERY. A pretty situation we are in truly!

DENNIS. Yes;—upon Muckslush Heath, and be damn'd to it.

MRS BRULGRUDDERY. And, where is the fortune I brought you?

DENNIS. All swallow'd up by the Red Cow.

MRS BRULGRUDDERY. Ah! had you follow'd my advice, we shou'd never have been in such a quandary.

DENNIS. Tunder and turf! didn't yourself advise me to take this public house?

MRS BRULGRUDDERY. No matter for that. I had a relation who always kept it. But, who advised you to drink out all the brandy?

DENNIS. No matter for that—I had a relation who always drank it.

MRS BRULGRUDDERY. Ah! my poor dear Mr Skinnygauge never brought tears into my eyes, as you do!   [*Crying.*

DENNIS. I know that—I saw you at his funeral.

MRS BRULGRUDDERY. You're a monster!

DENNIS. Am I?—Keep it to yourself, then, my lambkin.

MRS BRULGRUDDERY. You'll be the death of me; you know you will.

DENNIS. Look up, my sweet Mrs Brulgruddery! while I give you a small mörsel of consolation.

MRS BRULGRUDDERY. Consolation indeed!

DENNIS. Yes—There's a customer coming.

MRS BRULGRUDDERY [*brightening*]. What!

DENNIS. A customer. Turn your neat jolly face over the heath, yonder. Look at Dan, towing him along, as snug as a cock salmon into a fish basket.

MRS BRULGRUDDERY. Jimminy, and so there is! Oh, my dear Dennis! But I knew how it would be, if you had but a little patience. Remember, it was all by my advice you took the Red Cow.

DENNIS. Och ho! it was, was it?

MRS BRULGRUDDERY. I'll run, and spruce myself up a bit. Aye, aye, I hav'nt prophesied a customer to-day, for nothing.

[*Goes into the House.*

DENNIS. Troth, and it's prophesying on the sure side, to foretel a thing when it has happen'd.

[*Enter* DAN, *conducting* PEREGRINE—PEREGRINE *carrying a small Trunk under his Arm.*

PEREGRINE. I am indifferent about accomodation.

DAN. Our'n be a comfortable parlour, zur: you'll find it clean; for I wash'd un down mysen, wringing wet, five minutes ago.

PEREGRINE. You have told me so, twenty times.

DAN. This be the Red Cow, zur, as ye may see by the pictur; and here be measter—he'll treat ye in an hospital manner, zur, and show you a deal o' contention.

DENNIS. I'll be bound, sir, you'll get good entertainment whether you are a man or a horse.

PEREGRINE. You may lodge me as either, friend. I can sleep as well in a stable as a bedchamber; for travel has season'd me.— Since I have preserved this [*half aside, and pointing to the Trunk under his Arm*], I can lay my head upon it with tranquillity, and repose any where.

DENNIS. Faith, it seems a mighty decent, hard bolster. What is it stuff'd with, I wonder?

PEREGRINE. That which keeps the miser awake—money.

DAN. Wauns! all that money!

DENNIS. I'd be proud, sir, to know your upholsterer—he should make me a feather bed gratis of the same pretty materials. If that was all my own, I'd sleep like a pig, though I'm married to Mrs Brulgruddery.

PEREGRINE. I shall sleep better, because it is not my own.

DENNIS. Your own's in a snugger place, then? safe from the sharks of this dirty world, and be hang'd to 'em!

PEREGRINE. Except the purse in my pocket, 'tis, now, I fancy, in a place most frequented by the sharks of this world.

DENNIS. London, I suppose?

PEREGRINE. The bottom of the sea.

DENNIS. By my soul, that's a watering place—and you'll find sharks there, sure enough, in all conscience.

[*Enter* MRS BRULGRUDDERY.

MRS BRULGRUDDERY. What would you chuse to take, sir, after your walk this raw morning? We have anything you desire.

DENNIS. Yes, sir, we have any thing. Any thing's nothing, they say.

[*Aside.*

MRS BRULGRUDDERY. Dan, bustle about; and see the room ready, and all tidy; do you hear?

DAN. I wull.

MRS BRULGRUDDERY. What would you like to drink, sir?

PEREGRINE. O, mine is an accomodating palate, hostess. I have swallowed burgundy with the French, holland with the Dutch, sherbet with a Turk, sloe juice with an Englishman, and water with a simple Gentoo.

DAN [going]. Dang me, but he's a rum customer! It's my opinion, he'll take a fancy to our sour beer. [Exit into the House.

PEREGRINE. Is your house far from the sea shore?

MRS BRULGRUDDERY. About three miles, sir.

PEREGRINE. So!—And I have wander'd upon the heath four hours, before day break.

MRS BRULGRUDDERY. Lackaday! Has any thing happen'd to you, sir?

PEREGRINE. Shipwreck—that's all.

MRS BRULGRUDDERY. Mercy on us! cast away!

PEREGRINE. On your coast, here.

DENNIS. Then, compliment apart, sir, you take a ducking as if you had been used to it.

PEREGRINE. Life's a lottery, friend; and man should make up his mind to the blanks. On what part of Cornwall am I thrown?

MRS BRULGRUDDERY. We are two miles from Penzance, sir.

PEREGRINE. Ha!—from Penzance!—that's lucky!

MRS BRULGRUDDERY [aside to DENNIS]. Lucky!—Then he'll go on, without drinking at our house.

DENNIS. A hem! Sir, there has been a great big thunder storm at Penzance, and all the beer in the town's as thick as mustard.

PEREGRINE. I feel chill'd—get me a glass of brandy.

DENNIS. Oh, the devil [aside]. Bring the brandy bottle for the jontleman, my jewel. [Aloud to his Wife.

MRS BRULGRUDDERY [apart]. Don't you know you've emptied it, you sot you!

DENNIS [apart]. Draw a mug of beer—I'll palaver him.

MRS BRULGRUDDERY [apart and going]. Ah! if you would but follow my advice ! [Exit into the House.

DENNIS. You see that woman that's gone, sir—she's my wife, poor soul! She has but one misfortune, and that's a wapper.

PEREGRINE. What's that?

DENNIS. We had as neat a big bottle of brandy, a week ago—and damn the drop's left. But I say nothing—she's my wife, poor creature! and she can tell who drank it. Wouldn't you like a sup of sour—I mean, of our strong beer?

PEREGRINE. Pshaw! no matter what. Tell me, is a person of the name of Thornberry still living in Penzance.

DENNIS. Is it one Mr Thornberry you are asking after.

PEREGRINE. Yes. When I first saw him (indeed, it was the first time and the last), he had just begun to adventure humbly in trade. His stock was very slender, but his neighbours accounted him a kindly man—and I know they spoke the truth. Thirty years ago, after half an hour's intercourse, which proved to me his benevolent nature, I squeezed his hand, and parted.

DENNIS. Thirty years! Faith, after half an hour's dish of talk, that's a reasonable long time to remember!

PEREGRINE. Not at all; for he did me a genuine service; and gratitude writes her records in the heart, that, till it ceases to beat, they may live in the memory.

12. JOHN TOBIN (1770–1804)

The Honeymoon

It has been often urged against the dramatic taste of the early nineteenth century that poor John Tobin was allowed to die unrecognized. That his plays have some poetic merit may be immediately acknowledged, but that they are either original or truly dramatic may perhaps be questioned ; and perhaps, too, one may be prepared to sympathize with the managers who first rejected his work. Tobin's plays show well the fatal influence of Shakespeare. He writes 'comedies,' but in his dignified endeavour to recapture the romantic spirit of *As You Like It* he forgets that the prime mission of comedy is to laugh or smile. Barely a curving of the lips or the dimmest sparkle of an eye is to be traced in Tobin's serious visage. As a concrete example, at once of Tobin's style and of his imitative tendencies, I have chosen here the opening of the third act of *The Honeymoon*. The main plot of the play distinctly recalls *The Taming of the Shrew*, while no one can overlook the palpable appropriation here of a famous scene in *Twelfth Night*. Rolando (Shakespeare's Duke) is conversing with Zamora, dressed as a page, Eugenio (who is Shakespeare's Viola).

(*The Honey Moon* was produced at Drury Lane in 1805. The extract given below is taken from the first edition, published the same year.)

ZAMORA TELLS OF HER LOVE

ROLANDO. 'Sdeath, that a reasonable thinking man
Should leave his friend and bottle for a woman!—
Here is the Count, now, who, in other matters,
Has a true judgment, only seeth his blood
With a full glass beyond his usual stint;
And woman, like a wildfire, runs throughout him.
Immortal man is but a shuttlecock,

TRACTSFROMBRITISH & IRISH PLAYS

And wine and women are the battledores
That keep him going!—What!   Eugenio!

[*Enter* EUGENIO *alias* ZAMORA.

ZAMORA. Your pleasure, sir?
ROLANDO.   I am alone, and wish
One of your songs to bear me company.
ZAMORA. A merry or a sad one, sir?
ROLANDO.   No matter.
ZAMORA. I have but one that you have never heard.
ROLANDO. Let it be that.
ZAMORA.   I shall obey you, sir.
Now, woman's wit, assist me!   [*Sings.*

Song—ZAMORA

In vain the tears of anguish flow,
    In vain I mourn, in vain I sigh;
For he, alas! will never know
    That I must live for him, or die.

Ah! could I dare myself reveal!—
    Would not my tale his pity move?—
And sighs of pity seldom fail,
    In noble hearts, to waken love.

But should he view, without a tear,
    My altering form, my waning bloom,
Then, what is left me but despair!
    What refuge, but the silent tomb!

ROLANDO. It is a mournful ditty, yet 'tis pleasing!
ZAMORA. It was, indeed, a melancholy tale
From which I learnt it.
ROLANDO.   Lives it with you still?
ZAMORA. Faintly, as would an ill-remember'd dream, Sir:
Yet so far I remember—Now my heart—[*aside*]
'Twas of a gentleman—a soldier, sir,
Of a brave spirit; and his outward form
A frame to set a soul in.   He had a page,
Just such a boy as I, a faithful stripling,
Who, out of pure affection, and true love,
Follow'd his fortune to the wars.
ROLANDO.   Why this
Is our own history.[1]
ZAMORA.   So far, indeed,
But not beyond, it bore resemblance, sir.
For in the sequel (if I well remember)
This loving boy—(so, sir, the story ran)—
Turn'd out to be a woman.
ROLANDO.   How! a woman?

[1] The reader is invited to note Rolando's becoming modesty.

ZAMORA. Yes, sir, a woman.

ROLANDO.   Live with him a twelvemonth,
And he not find the secret out!

ZAMORA.   'Twas strange.

ROLANDO. Strange! 'twas impossible! At the first blush,
A palpable and most transparent lie!
Why, if the soldier had been such an ass,
She had herself betray'd it!—

ZAMORA.   Yet, 'tis said,
She kept it to her death;—that, oft as Love
Would heave the struggling passion to her lips,
Shame set a seal upon them;—thus long time
She nourish'd, in this strife of love and modesty,
An inward slow-consuming martyrdom,
Till in the sight of him her soul most cherish'd,—
Like flow'rs that on a river's margin, fading
Thro' lack of moisture, drop into the stream,—
So, sinking in his arms, her parting breath
Reveal'd her story.

13. LORD LYTTON (1803–73)

Money

After the thirties of the nineteenth century there is to be traced
a gradual movement away from the rude type of farce and the
boisterous comedy which had flourished in the hands of the
younger Colman and of Reynolds. It is true that these types of
drama still formed the principal fare of the theatres, but at the
same time there came a slight change in favour of more realistic
methods. Both the styles of acting and the settings of plays
became more naturalistic, and with this there developed a comedy
form which, not yet divorced from the artificialities of the earlier
types, endeavoured to keep more closely to life and to depict the
true manners of the age. The most famous exponent of this new
style was Tom Robertson (see pp. 311–315), but Robertson was by
no means the first to point the way toward modern drama. He may
have applied the new methods with more deliberate purpose; he
may have had a greater skill and talent than the others; but his
work was as much that of a culminator as of a pioneer. Among
his predecessors Lord Lytton is probably the most important.
With a determination to gain immediate success, he combined
a greater literary conscience than the ordinary 'theatrical
writers' of the age possessed with a frank acceptance of many of
the conventions popular in his time. *The Lady of Lyons*, his
most famous play, is a kind of superior melodrama with a happy
ending, and *Money*, which is chosen for representation here,

a U

mingles something of the older and still popular manner with the more modern aims.   Particular notice should be taken of Lytton's style, which is, judged by comparison with that of other comedy-writers of the time, simple and lifelike.   He strains after no wit, but prefers to rely for comic effect upon situations and the contrast of characters.   The scene given below is that in which the will of a certain Mr Mordaunt of Calcutta is read to his fondly expectant relatives.   Evelyn, the tormented and downtrodden secretary of the vulgar Sir John Vesey, is in love with his cousin Clara.   This is probably the first of modern ' will scenes,' a popular type in present-day drama.

(*Money* was produced at the Haymarket in 1840.   The following extract is taken from the edition of that year.)

Polite Mourning and Natural Greed

Sir John. How d'ye do!—Ah!   How d'ye do, gentlemen?   Ah, Stout!   This is a most melancholy meeting!   The poor deceased! —what a man he was!

Blount. I was chwistened Fwedewick after him!   He was my first cousin.

Sir John. And Georgina his own niece—next of kin!—an excellent man, though odd—a kind heart, but no liver!   I sent him twice a-year thirty dozen of the Cheltenham waters.   It's a comfort to reflect on these little attentions at such a time.

Stout. And I, too, sent him the Parliamentary Debates regularly, bound in calf.   He was my second cousin—sensible man— and a follower of Malthus ; never married to increase the surplus population, and fritter away his money on his own children.   And now——

Evelyn [*at table seated*]. He reaps the benefit of celibacy in the prospective gratitude of every cousin he had in the world!

Lady Franklin. Ha! ha! ha!

Sir John. Hush! hush! decency, Lady Franklin, decency!

[*Enter* Servant.

Servant. Mr Graves—Mr Sharp.

Sir John. Oh, here's Mr Graves; that's Sharp, the lawyer, who brought the will from Calcutta.

[*Enter* Graves, *and* Sharp.   *Directly* Sharp *enters, he goes to the sofa and prepares his papers.*

Ah, sir—Ah, Mr Graves!

[Georgina *holds her handkerchief to her eyes.*

Sir John. A sad occasion!

Graves. But everything in life is sad.

[*Enter two* Servants *with wine, &c., which they hand round, beginning with* Lady Franklin.

Be comforted, Miss Vesey.   True, you have lost an uncle; but I —I have lost a wife—such a wife!—the first of her sex—and the

306

second cousin of the defunct! Excuse me, Sir John; at sight of your mourning my wounds bleed afresh.

[SERVANTS *hand round wine and sandwiches.*

SIR JOHN. Take some refreshment—a glass of wine.

GRAVES. Thank you!—(very fine sherry!)—Ah! my poor sainted Maria! Sherry was *her* wine; everything reminds me of Maria! [*Goes up to* LADY FRANKLIN, *who is seated at table.*] Ah, Lady Franklin! *you* knew her. Nothing in life can charm me now. [*Aside*] A monstrous fine woman that! [*Crosses back.*

SIR JOHN. And now to business. [*All sit.* SERVANTS *exeunt.* Evelyn, you may retire [*He rises to go.*

SHARP [*looking at his notes*]. Evelyn—any relation to Alfred Evelyn?

EVELYN. The same.

SHARP. Cousin to the deceased, seven times removed. Be seated, sir; there may be some legacy, though trifling: all the relations, however distant, should be present. [EVELYN *sits again.*

LADY FRANKLIN. Then Clara is related—I will go for her. [*Exit.*

GEORGINA. Ah, Mr Evelyn; I hope you will come in for something —a few hundreds, or even more.

SIR JOHN. Silence! Hush! Whugh! ugh! Attention.

[*While the lawyer opens the will, re-enter* LADY FRANKLIN *and* CLARA.

SHARP. The will is very short, being all personal property. He was a man that always came to the point.

SIR JOHN. I wish there were more like him!—

[*Groans and shakes his head. Chorus groan and shake their heads.*

SHARP [*reading*]. " I, Frederick James Mordaunt, of Calcutta, being, at the present date, of sound mind, though infirm body, do hereby give, will, and bequeath—*imprimis* to my second cousin, Benjamin Stout, Esq., of Pall-Mall, London—

[STOUT *places his handkerchief to his eyes. Chorus exhibit lively emotion.*

Being the value of the Parliamentary Debates with which he has been pleased to trouble me for some time past—deducting the carriage thereof, which he always forgot to pay—the sum of £14. 2s. 4d."

[STOUT *takes away handkerchief. Chorus breathe more freely.*

STOUT. Eh, what!—£14? Oh, hang the old miser!

SIR JOHN. Decency—decency! Proceed, sir. Go on, go on.

SHARP. " Item.—To Sir Frederick Blount, Baronet, my nearest male relative—" [*Chorus exhibit lively emotion.*

BLOUNT. Poor old boy!

[GEORGINA *puts her arm over* BLOUNT'S *chair.*

SHARP. " Being, as I am informed, the best-dressed young gentleman in London, and in testimony to the only merit I ever heard he possessed, the sum of £500, to buy a dressing-case."

EXTRACTS FROM BRITISH & IRISH PLAYS

[Chorus breathe more freely; GEORGINA *catches her father's eye and removes her arm.*

BLOUNT [*laughing confusedly*]. Ha! Ha! Ha! Vewy poor wit—low!—vewy—vewy low!

SIR JOHN. Silence, now, will you?

SHARP. " Item.—To Charles Lord Glossmore—who asserts that he is my relation—my collection of dried butterflies, and the pedigree of the Mordaunts from the reign of King John." [*Chorus as before.*

GLOSSMORE. Butterflies!—Pedigree!—I disown the plebeian!

SIR JOHN [*angrily*]. Upon my word, this is too revolting! Decency—go on.

SHARP. " Item.—To Sir John Vesey, Baronet, Knight of the Guelph, F.R.S., F.S.A., &c." [*Chorus as before.*

SIR JOHN. Hush! *Now* it is really interesting!

SHARP. " Who married my sister, and who sends me, every year, the Cheltenham waters, which nearly gave me my death—I bequeath —the empty bottles."

SIR JOHN. Why, the ungrateful, rascally old——

LADY FRANKLIN. Decency, Sir John—decency!

OMNES. Decency, Sir John—decency!

SHARP. " Item.—To Henry Graves, Esq., of the Albany—"
[*Chorus as before.*

GRAVES. Pooh, Gentlemen!—my usual luck—not even a ring, I dare swear!

SHARP. " The sum of £5,000 in the Three per Cents."

LADY FRANKLIN. I wish you joy!

GRAVES. Joy—pooh! Three per Cents!—Funds sure to go! Had it been *land*, now—though only an acre!—just like my luck.

SHARP. " Item.—To my niece, Georgina Vesey—"
[*Chorus as before.*

SIR JOHN. Ah, now it comes!

SHARP. " The sum of £10,000 India stock, being, with her father's reputed savings, as much as a single woman ought to possess."

SIR JOHN. And what the devil, then, does the old fool do with all his money?

LADY FRANKLIN. Really, Sir John, this is too revolting! Decency! Hush!

SHARP. " And, with the aforesaid legacies and exceptions, I do will and bequeath the whole of my fortune, in India stock, Bonds, Exchequer bills, Three per Cent. Consols, and in the Bank of Calcutta (constituting him hereby sole residuary legatee and joint executor with the aforesaid Henry Graves, Esq.) to Alfred Evelyn [*pause—a movement on the part of everybody but* SHARP], now or formerly of Trinity College, Cambridge [*universal excitement*], being, I am told, an oddity, like myself—the only one of my relations who never fawned on me; and who, having known privation, may the better employ wealth."—And now, sir, I have only to wish you joy, and give you this letter from the deceased. I believe it is important.

308

[All rise.

EVELYN [*looking over to* CLARA]. Ah, Clara, if you had but loved me!

CLARA [*turning away*]. And his wealth, even more than poverty, separates us for ever!

LADY FRANKLIN. I wish you joy.

OMNES [*crowding round to congratulate* EVELYN]. I wish you joy.

SIR JOHN [*to* GEORGINA]. Go, child—put a good face on it—he's an immense match! My dear fellow, I wish you joy; you are a great man now—a very great man! I wish you joy.

EVELYN [*aside*]. And *her* voice alone is silent!

GLOSSMORE. If I can be of any use to you——

STOUT. Or I, sir——

BLOUNT. Or I? Shall I put you up at the clubs?

SHARP. You will want a man of business. I transacted all Mr Mordaunt's affairs.

SIR JOHN [*rushing to centre of crowd, and pushing them aside*]. Tush, tush! Mr Evelyn is at home *here*—always looked on him as a son! Nothing in the world we would not do for him!

EVELYN. Lend me £10 for my old nurse!

OMNES. Certainly! Certainly!

[*Chorus put their hands into their pockets, producing purses, and offering them eagerly.*

VIII. THE MODERN PERIOD

IT is well known that in the sphere of drama the modern period is heralded by Tom Robertson, whose comedies have a serious note that almost creates them into problem plays. It is fitting, therefore, to open this section with an example from what is probably his most famous production, *Caste*. In the last decades of the nineteenth century Sir Arthur Pinero and Mr Henry Arthur Jones boldly forged ahead in the endeavour to give to the stage something that should do more than copy past models. The influence of Ibsen is on their works, and in such a play as *Mrs Dane's Defence* there is a genuinely serious treatment and discussion of a definite 'problem,' handled with sure theatric craft. This type of problem drama has been one of the most characteristic of modern developments in the playhouse. In diverse forms it appears in Mr Galsworthy's *Strife*, in Mr Granville-Barker's *The Voysey Inheritance*, in Miss Baker's *Chains*, in Stanley Houghton's *Hindle Wakes*, in Mr St John Ervine's *Mixed Marriage*, in Mr Murray's *Maurice Harte*, and in Mr Colum's *The Land*. All these plays deal with real life, and—now with a smile, now with tears—treat some aspect of that real life which involves a conflict or a clash of forces. Meanwhile other types have formed themselves. Mr Robinson in *The Lost Leader* is no less realistic, but his theme is not a problem in the same sense ; it is a study in character with historic questionings. The poetic play has taken on a new lease of life, both in prose and verse. Synge's *Deirdre*, Sir J. M. Barrie's romantic *A Kiss for Cinderella*, Lord Dunsany's *The Gods of the Mountain*, and Miss Dane's *Will Shakespeare* suggest different approaches made toward what may be styled the non-realistic theatre. These approaches are amplified in various directions. Mr Drinkwater's revived 'chronicle-history' play (illustrated here by *Mary Stuart*), Professor Abercrombie's almost Crabbelike verse treatment of real life (illustrated by *Deborah*),

310

and Mr Bottomley's fanciful treatment of the background for Shakespeare's tragedies (illustrated by *King Lear's Wife*) all indicate the inventiveness and the wideness of scope in this sphere of modern drama.

In comedy there is equal vitality. This section has been prefaced (wrongly from the strictly chronological point of view) by a passage from Planché's *The Camp at the Olympic*. This has been done because the 'extravaganza' which Planché so prolifically cultivated seems to be the natural parent of Gilbert's new comic-opera style, while that in turn links itself on to that cultivation of wit which has marked out the modern period. Oscar Wilde, Mr Bernard Shaw, and Mr Henry Arthur Jones were the early leaders of this movement, which has developed during more recent years in the hands of Mr Somerset Maugham and others. A revival of the comedy of manners, however, is only one aspect of the modern theatre. Many of the comedies treat gaily problems similar to those treated more seriously by other dramatists. Calderon's *The Fountain* is of this type, as is St John Hankin's *The Cassilis Engagement*. National comedy, after Synge, has been cultivated by Lady Gregory, while a grim and bitter humour peers through the darkness of Mr O'Casey's scenes.

1. TOM ROBERTSON (1829–71)

Caste

In many respects the modern realistic movement is to be traced back to the work of Robertson ; even if his plays seem artificial and crude when compared with those of Ibsen or of Ibsen's successors, we must recognize the immense gulf between such a play as *Caste* and the artificial comedies that preceded it. Robertson still retains the old trick of exaggeration of types. No marchioness would utter quite the phrases that his marchioness uses ; no marchioness would so glibly quote Froissart in Elizabethan spelling. On the other hand, he does strive to present a problem of a kind, and, in presenting it, he endeavours to keep more close to reality than his predecessors had done. If he fails to see the problem in the way that St John Hankin sees it (see pp. 425–428) that simply means that he lived in the second half of the nineteenth and not in the twentieth century. Important, too, is Robertson's influence on the methods of acting. In the earlier period the style had been always 'typical.' The players secured their effects by means of stock tricks, and had their regular gestures for certain passions, their regular exaggerated costumes for certain types, their formal semicircular groupings at the end of the acts. A slight change had come with the Mathews-Vestris managements in the forties of the century, but it seems to have been Robertson who most potently influenced the stage in a new and naturalistic direction. The last stage direction in the passage given below indicates the fact that in his own comedies he sought for such grouping in the theatre as would accord with the situation had that occurred in real life. It was this naturalistic and individual method that prepared the way for modern comedy; so long as the type standards held no approach could be made toward realistic situations and more natural dialogue. The scene here explains itself. George has married Esther, the daughter of the low-class and drunken Eccles. The latter are discovered in the rich house of his parents to the manifest discomfort of the Froissart-loving Marchioness.

(*Caste* was produced in 1867. The extract given below follows the edition of 1889.)

MÉSALLIANCE

MARCHIONESS. When my boy fights—and you will fight—he is sure to distinguish himself. It is his nature to—[*toys with his hair*] —he cannot forget his birth. And when you meet these Asiatic ruffians, who have dared to revolt, and to outrage humanity, you will strike as your ancestor Sir Galtier of Chevrault struck at Poictiers. [*Changing tone of voice as if remembering*] Froissart mentions it thus—"Sir Galtier, with his four squires, was in the front of that battell, and there did marvels in arms. And Sir Galtier rode up to the Prince, and sayd to him—'Sir, take your horse and ryde forth, this journey is yours. God is this day in your hands. Gette us to the French Kynge's batayle. I think verily by his valyantesse he woll not fly. Advance banner in the name of God and of Saynt George!' And Sir Galtier galloped forward to see his Kynge's victory, and meet his own death."

GEORGE [*aside*]. If Esther hears all this!

MARCHIONESS. There is another subject about which I should have spoken to you before this; but an absurd prudery forbade me. I may never see you more. I am old—and you—are going into battle—[*kissing his forehead with emotion*]—and this may be our last meeting. [*A noise heard within folding-doors.*] What's that?

GEORGE. Nothing—my man Dixon in there.

MARCHIONESS. We may not meet again on this earth. I do not fear your conduct, my George, with men; but I know the temptations that beset a youth who is well born. But a true soldier, a true gentleman, should not only be without fear, but without reproach. It is easier to fight a furious man than to forego the conquest of a love-sick girl. A thousand Sepoys slain in battle

312

cannot redeem the honour of a man who has betrayed the confidence of a trusting woman. Think, George, what dishonour—what stain upon your manhood—to hurl a girl to shame and degradation! And what excuse for it? That she is plebeian? A man of real honour will spare the woman who has confessed her love for him, as he would give quarter to an enemy he had disarmed. [*Taking his hands*] Let my boy avoid the snares so artfully spread; and when he asks his mother to welcome the woman he has chosen for his wife, let me take her to my arms and plant a motherly kiss upon the white brow of a lady. [*Noise of a fall heard within folding-doors; rising*] What's that?

GEORGE. Nothing. [*Rising.*

MARCHIONESS. I heard a cry.

[*Folding-doors open, discovering* ESTHER *with* POLLY, *staggering in, fainting.*

POLLY. George! George!

[GEORGE *goes up and* ESTHER *falls in his arms.* POLLY *stands R.C.* GEORGE *places* ESTHER *on sofa.* GEORGE *on her R.,* POLLY *on her L.*

MARCHIONESS [*coming down R.*]. Who are these *women*?

POLLY. Women!

MARCHIONESS. George D'Alroy, these persons should have been sent away. How could you dare to risk your mother meeting women of their stamp?

POLLY [*violently*]. What does she mean? How dare she call me a woman? What's she, I'd like to know?

GEORGE [*R. of sofa*]. Silence, Polly! You mustn't insult my mother.

MARCHIONESS. The insult is from you. I leave you, and I hope that time may induce me to forget this scene of degradation.

[*Turning to go.*

GEORGE. Stay, mother. [MARCHIONESS *turns slightly away.*] Before you go [GEORGE *has raised* ESTHER *from sofa in both arms*] let me present to you Mrs George D'Alroy. *My wife!*

MARCHIONESS. Married!

GEORGE. Married.

[*The* MARCHIONESS *sinks into easy-chair R.H.* GEORGE *replaces* ESTHER *on sofa up L., but still retains her hand. Three hesitating taps at door are heard.* GEORGE *crosses to door, R.H., opens it, discovers* ECCLES *who enters.* GEORGE *drops down back of* MARCHIONESS' *chair.*

ECCLES [*C.*]. They told us to come up. When your man came Polly was out; so I thought I should do instead. [*Calling at door*] Come up, Sam.

[*Enter* SAM *in his Sunday clothes, with short cane and smoking a cheroot. He nods and grins—*POLLY *points to* MARCHIONESS—SAM *takes cheroot from his mouth and quickly removes his hat.*

Sam had just called; so we three—Sam and I, and your man, all came in the 'ansom cab together. Didn't we, Sam?

[ECCLES *and* SAM *go over to the girls, L.H., and* ECCLES
   drops down to front of table—smilingly.

MARCHIONESS [*with glasses up, to* GEORGE]. Who is this?

GEORGE [*coming L. of* MARCHIONESS]. My wife's father.

MARCHIONESS. What is he?

GEORGE. A—nothing.

ECCLES. I am one of nature's noblemen. Happy to see you, my lady—[*turning to her*]—now, my daughters have told me who you are—[GEORGE *turns his back in an agony as* ECCLES *crosses to* MARCHIONESS]—we old folks, fathers and mothers of the young couples, ought to make friends. [*Holding out his dirty hand.*

MARCHIONESS [*shrinking back*]. Go away! [ECCLES *goes back to table again, disgusted, L.H.*] What's his name?

GEORGE. Eccles.

MARCHIONESS. Eccles! Eccles! There never was an Eccles. He don't exist.

ECCLES [*L.*]. Don't he, though! What d'ye call this?

[*Goes up again L., to back of table as* SAM *drops down. He
   is just going to take a decanter, when* SAM *stops him.*

MARCHIONESS. No Eccles was ever born!

GEORGE. He takes the liberty of breathing notwithstanding. [*Aside*] And I wish he wouldn't!

MARCHIONESS. And who is the little man? Is he also Eccles?

[SAM *looks round.* POLLY *gets close up to him, and looks
   with defiant glance at the* MARCHIONESS.

GEORGE. No.

MARCHIONESS. Thank goodness! What then?

GEORGE. His name is Gerridge.

MARCHIONESS. Gerridge! It breaks one's teeth. Why is he here?

GEORGE. He is making love to Polly, my wife's sister.

MARCHIONESS. And what is he?

GEORGE. A gasman.

MARCHIONESS. He looks it. [GEORGE *goes up to* ESTHER, *L.*] And what is she—the—the—the sister?

[ECCLES, *who has been casting longing eyes at the decanter
   on table, edges towards it, and when he thinks no one is
   noticing, fills wine-glass.*

POLLY [*asserting herself indignantly*]. I'm in the ballet at the Theatre Royal, Lambeth. So was Esther. We're not ashamed of what we are! We have no cause to be.

SAM [*back, L.C.*]. That's right, Polly! pitch into them swells! —who are they?

[ECCLES *by this time has seized wine-glass, and, turning his
   back, is about to drink, when* HAWTREE *enters door, R.
   flat.* ECCLES *hides glass under his coat, and pretends
   to be looking up at picture.*

HAWTREE [*entering*]. George! [*Stops suddenly, looking round.*] So, all's known!

MARCHIONESS [*rising*]. Captain Hawtree, see me to my carriage; I am broken-hearted! [*Takes* HAWTREE'S *arm, and is going up.*

ECCLES [*who has tasted the claret, spits it out with a grimace, exclaiming*]. Rot!

> [POLLY *goes to piano, sits on stool*—SAM *back to audience, leaning on piano*—ECCLES *exits through folding-doors.*

GEORGE [*L., to* MARCHIONESS]. Don't go in anger. You may not see me again.

> [ESTHER *rises in nervous excitement, clutching* GEORGE's *hand.* MARCHIONESS *stops, R.* ESTHER *brings* GEORGE *down C.*

ESTHER [*L.C., with arm round his neck*]. Oh, George! Must you go? [*They come L. to front of table.*

GEORGE [*R.C.*]. Yes.

ESTHER. I can't leave you! I'll go with you!

GEORGE. Impossible! The country is too unsettled.

ESTHER. May I come after you?

GEORGE. Yes.

ESTHER [*with her head on his shoulder*]. I may.

MARCHIONESS [*coming down, R.,* HAWTREE *at door R.H.*]. It is his duty to go. His honour calls him. The honour of his family— *our* honour!

ESTHER. But I love him so! Pray don't be angry with me!

HAWTREE [*looking at watch, and coming down C.*]. George!

GEORGE. I must go, love! [HAWTREE *goes up to door again.*

MARCHIONESS [*advancing*]. Let me arm you, George—let your mother, as in the days of old. There is blood—and blood, my son. See, your wife cries when she should be proud of you!

GEORGE. My Esther is all that is good and noble. No lady born to a coronet could be gentler or more true. Esther, my wife, fetch me my sword, and buckle my belt around me.

ESTHER [*clinging to him*]. No, no; I can't!

GEORGE. Try. [*Whispers to* ESTHER] To please my mother. [*To* MARCHIONESS] You shall see. [ESTHER *totters up stage,* POLLY *assisting her L., and brings down his sword. As* ESTHER *is trying to buckle his belt, he whispers.*] I've left money for you, my darling. My lawyer will call on you to-morrow. Forgive me! I tried hard to tell you we were ordered for India; but when the time came, my heart failed me, and I——

> [ESTHER, *before she can succeed in fastening his sword-belt, reels, and falls fainting in his arms.* POLLY *hurries to her.* SAM, *standing at piano, looking frightened;* HAWTREE *with hand upon handle of door, R.F.;* MARCHIONESS *looking on, R. of* GEORGE.

EXTRACTS FROM BRITISH & IRISH PLAYS

2. SIR ARTHUR WING PINERO (*born* 1855)

Sweet Lavender

Modern drama owes a tremendous debt to the work of Sir
Arthur Wing Pinero and of Mr Henry Arthur Jones. These
playwrights are the *doyens* of the present-day theatre. They
bring to fulfilment that which was prophesied by Robertson, and
show in their progressive developments the broad tendencies of
dramatic art from the eighties of the last century to the present
day. *Sweet Lavender* has been selected for quotation here
because it shows the new style at an early period in its career.
With a sure sense of the theatre the author has told a story which
may seem sentimental to the twentieth century, but which nevertheless proved popular in its own and did much to accustom
audiences to a better dramatic technique. The crude world of
the melodrama disappears in face of the spirit of this play, and
the excitements which had of old been raised by the former are
exploited in the interests of the newer style. In *Sweet Lavender*
the story is told of Clement Hale, the adopted son of Geoffrey
Wedderburn, who falls in love with Lavender, the daughter of
the laundress, Ruth. He is about to be disinherited when
Wedderburn discovers in Ruth the sweetheart of his early years,
and in Lavender his own daughter. Needless to say, this discovery brings the plot to an emotional and happy conclusion.

(*Sweet Lavender* was produced at Terry's Theatre in 1888, and
witnessed many revivals. The following passage is taken from
the edition of 1895, by kind permission of the author and of the
publishers, Messrs William Heinemann, Ltd., London, and the
Walter H. Baker Company, Boston, U.S.A.)

A HAPPY DISCOVERY

CLEMENT. Dad, you know——

WEDDERBURN. Know! All the world knows when a terrible chap
like you is in love.

CLEMENT [*embarrassed*]. I was going to write to you to-night.

WEDDERBURN. Don't you trouble yourself, Clem. [*Taking a
bundle of letters and papers from his pocket*] Your Aunt Clara's
telegram gives a few interesting particulars.

CLEMENT. Mrs Gilfillian's telegram!

WEDDERBURN. Why, what dy'e think has brought me from Paris
in such a deuce of a hurry—eh?

CLEMENT. And you're not angry, father?

WEDDERBURN. Angry. Now, have I ever been angry with you,
my boy?

CLEMENT. No, dad—never.

WEDDERBURN. No, and a plague of a child you've been, too.

CLEMENT [*laughing*]. Ha, ha!

316

THE MODERN PERIOD

WEDDERBURN [*taking* CLEMENT'S *hand and looking into his face*]. But the only time you really hurt me, Clem, was when you had the fever years ago, and I sat by your bedside through some dreadful nights and—you didn't know me when I spoke to you. Ah, Clem!

CLEMENT [*putting his hand on* WEDDERBURN'S *shoulder*]. Ah, dad!

WEDDERBURN. However, confound that! [*Selecting a telegram from among his letters and looking at it through a gold-rimmed eye-glass*] And so she's the daughter of the laundress of these new chambers of yours, is she, Clement?

CLEMENT [*biting his lip*]. Yes, father, but——

WEDDERBURN. But she's very beautiful, hey?

CLEMENT. She's very sweet, very good——

WEDDERBURN [*reading the telegram*]. Oh, I know, my dear lad—I know.

CLEMENT. Father, would you like to see her—this evening?

[WEDDERBURN *returns his papers to his pocket and rises, putting his arm round* CLEMENT'S *shoulder.*

WEDDERBURN. Now, my dear Clement, why on earth should I see her?

CLEMENT [*under his breath*]. Father!

WEDDERBURN. Come, come, we'll have a bit of a jaunt together, you and I. They don't want me at the bank—I'm only a name there nowadays; but for form's sake we'll run down to Barnchester in the morning, and then we'll cut away North and be lazy and happy. Look sharp; tell your man to throw a few things into a portmanteau, and come back with me to the hotel to-night.

[*Taking up his hat and coat.*

CLEMENT. Dad! You—you don't understand. I can never leave here until—— Father, Lavender is to be my wife!

[WEDDERBURN *stands for a moment thoughtfully, then throws down his hat and coat and crosses to the fireplace, taking a cigar from his cigar-case, while* CLEMENT *watches him.*

WEDDERBURN. Clement, my dear boy, my son, when I was a young man—old enough to know better, but a young man—I fell in love with a woman just as enchanting, I dare swear, as this Miss—Lavender, as you call her.

CLEMENT. Well, father?

WEDDERBURN. She was a woman in humble life but I loved her—dearly. But just as I was on the point of marrying her, Clem, my hard, old-fashioned common sense pulled me back.

CLEMENT. Ah, sir!—why?

WEDDERBURN. Why? Why, my lady would have been all elbows, as we say, among the starched gentlefolks of Barnchester. She would have been mercilessly cut by the whole county, Clement.

CLEMENT. Then confound the whole county, sir.

WEDDERBURN. Oh, by all means. But the neglect would have soured her and made me cross, and it would have been a damned wretched marriage. That's all, my boy. [*Taking* CLEMENT'S *hand*]

317

But, Clem, it nearly broke me up at that time, and to find some corner to hide my love in, I made a son of the child of a dear dead schoolfellow of mine.

CLEMENT. Sir, I can't ever repay you.

WEDDERBURN. Yes, you can—all the payment I want you can make me to-night. What I did for common sense years ago you must do for me at this moment. So put on your hat and come along.

                         [Goes to the sofa and takes up his coat and hat.

CLEMENT. I—I can't, father.

WEDDERBURN [*sharply*]. You—you won't, you mean?

CLEMENT. Father!

WEDDERBURN. She or I—which is it?

CLEMENT. God bless you for all your goodness to me, sir; but she is to be my wife.

DICK [*calling from his room*]. Clemen', my boy! Clemen'!

WEDDERBURN. What's that?

CLEMENT [*going towards the door of* DICK's *room*]. Hush, Dick!

        [*The door opens, and* DICK *staggers on, flourishing the tele-*
            gram which MAW *has given him.*

DICK. Clemen'! Look here! This telegram to my s'licitor! Look!

CLEMENT [*trying to silence him*]. Be quiet, Dick! Mr Wedderburn!

DICK. Wedderburn!

WEDDERBURN. May I ask the name of your friend?

CLEMENT. Richard Phenyl. We share these rooms together.

WEDDERBURN [*angrily, to* DICK]. Then, sir, I congratulate you on acquiring the undivided companionship of Mr Clement Hale, who can now accompany you to the gutter with all possible speed.

DICK [*indignantly*]. The gurr'er!

WEDDERBURN. The gutter, sir—which I take to be your destination.

DICK. The gurr'er! [*Handing him the telegram*] Then we can give you a lift, Mr Wedderburn.

CLEMENT. Dick, be silent.

WEDDERBURN. What's this mean?   *[Taking the telegram.*

DICK. It means that Wedderburn, Green, and Hoskett, bankers, of Barnchester, have s'spended paymen'! Broke, sir, to atoms!

        [*There is a knocking at the outer door.* DICK *staggers up to*
           it. CLEMENT *goes to* WEDDERBURN, *who stands gazing*
           steadily at the telegram.

CLEMENT. Father! You know better than to believe this. [*The knock is repeated.* WEDDERBURN *is silent.*] Father!

        [*DICK opens the door and admits* MRS GILFILLIAN, MINNIE,
           and HORACE. *The two former, seeing* WEDDERBURN,
           go to him, while HORACE *speaks rapidly to* CLEMENT.
           DICK, *leaving the door open, joins them.*

MRS GILFILLIAN. Geoffrey!

MINNIE. Uncle! Uncle! [*Putting her arm round his neck*] There's some dreadful news in the paper—about the bank, Uncle Geoffrey.

WEDDERBURN. The paper—send for it; let me see it.

MRS GILFILLIAN. Geoffrey, it isn't true.

WEDDERBURN [*with an effort*]. Show me—the paper. [*Hearing a movement, he turns sharply and sees* CLEMENT *reading from a newspaper which* HORACE *holds.*] You have it there—give it me. [MRS GILFILLIAN *sits weeping on the sofa;* MINNIE *stands bending over her consolingly.* CLEMENT *gives* WEDDERBURN *the newspaper. After looking at the paper for a moment,* WEDDERBURN, *with a groan, bows his head upon the mantelpiece. In a smothered voice*] The villains! Dishonour! Dishonour!

RUTH [*calling softly outside*]. Lavender! Lavender! [*She enters hurriedly.*] Lavender! [*To* CLEMENT, *seeing all but* WEDDERBURN] Where is she? I want—my daughter.

> [CLEMENT *disappears through the curtains.* WEDDERBURN, *hearing* RUTH'S *voice, turns, and he and* RUTH *come face to face.*

WEDDERBURN [*in a whisper*]. Ruth!

> [*They stand staring at each other.* LAVENDER *comes through the curtains. With an effort* RUTH *seizes her and goes out with her quickly. As they disappear* WEDDERBURN *puts his hand to his eyes and staggers, and* CLEMENT, *re-entering at that moment, catches him as he drops into the armchair fainting.*

CLEMENT. Father! Father!

3. HENRY ARTHUR JONES (*born* 1851)

Mrs Dane's Defence

In the development of the domestic *drame* in England Mr Henry Arthur Jones has played one of the most important parts. His eminence consists in his ability to write dialogue which is at once naturalistic and precise, and in his keen appreciation of theatrical situation. The effect of his comedy of manners, *The Liars*, depends on these two qualities, which, applied in a different way, make of *Mrs Dane's Defence* a drama of manners which has more than a temporary significance. Parts of the latter play may 'date,' for one of the weaknesses of realism is that the concrete facts of life which it reflects are frequently destroyed in a succeeding age, either by the operation of law or by that of the social conscience. The greater artist, however, usually succeeds in portraying these facts in a way which makes them of universal significance, or in stressing, instead of the external facts of life, the emotions and the thoughts of the characters. Elizabethan society has vanished, yet we can read with pleasure and with understanding Heywood's *A Woman Killed with Kindness*, and in a similar manner, although the precise surroundings of *Mrs Dane's Defence* carry us back to a period already ancient (the year 1900), the attention of the author has been so concentrated upon his characters and upon his situations that the play is of permanent interest. Its most brilliant scene is that in which Sir Daniel examines Mrs Dane, who, engaged to Sir Daniel's adopted son Lionel, has been accused of being none other than a certain Felicia Hindemarsh with a somewhat shady past. It will be noted how, in spite of the retention of a 'naturalistic' atmosphere, the dialogue takes on a precision and a logical exactitude which would rarely be found in real life, for the domestic *drame* at its best uses that same refining and selecting process which is to be more clearly traced in the comedy of manners.

(*Mrs Dane's Defence* was produced in October 1900 at Wyndham's Theatre. The passage below is taken, by kind permission of the author and of the publishers, Messrs Macmillan and Co., Ltd., from the edition of 1905.)

THE TRACKING OF TRUTH

SIR DANIEL. Then we'll consider that episode closed, and we'll make a fresh start.

MRS DANE. Yes, ask me anything you please. I'm only too anxious to help you in getting at the truth.

SIR DANIEL. That ought not to be very difficult. [*Seats himself in revolving chair at writing-table, takes a pen and occasionally makes notes of her answers.*] Now, Felicia Hindemarsh was your cousin?

MRS DANE. Yes.

SIR DANIEL. Her father was the vicar of Tawhampton?

MRS DANE. Yes.

SIR DANIEL. And your other cousin—Annie Allen?

MRS DANE. I had no other cousin. When you asked what my cousin's name was I couldn't say " Felicia Hindemarsh," so I gave the first name I could think of.

SIR DANIEL. Had you any other relatives in or near Tawhampton?

MRS DANE. No.

SIR DANIEL. You were the only child of—[*consulting foolscap sheets*] of Robert and Sophia Allen?

MRS DANE. Yes, my mother and her mother were sisters.

SIR DANIEL [*reading from foolscap*]. Robert Allen, woollen manufacturer, Tawhampton. In eighty-seven, being in difficulties, he sold his business and went to Montreal. You, his only child, went with him, and five years later you married Charles Lewis Dane, surgeon, Montreal. You lived there till two years ago, when your husband died, and a year ago you came back to England, and took up your residence at Winchester.

MRS DANE. Yes.

SIR DANIEL. There are, of course, people in Montreal who knew you intimately as Mrs Dane, and can identify you?

MRS DANE. Oh, yes, of course.

SIR DANIEL. Will you please make me out a list of their names and addresses?

MRS DANE. Yes, certainly. Shall I do it now? [*Half rising to go.*

SIR DANIEL. No, by and by will do. Now to go back to your cousin, Felicia Hindemarsh. You have no idea where she is now?

MRS DANE. Not the least.

SIR DANIEL. When was the last time you saw her?

MRS DANE. When I left Tawhampton.

SIR DANIEL. You haven't seen her since?

MRS DANE. No. Sir Daniel, I feel I could collect my thoughts much better if I were alone and had time to remember. I feel so confused——

SIR DANIEL. I'll try not to tax you, if you'll answer one or two simple questions.

MRS DANE. Very well. You won't think I'm trying to deceive you if I don't remember every little fact?

SIR DANIEL. You will remember all that I require to know. Felicia Hindemarsh was younger or older than you?

MRS DANE. A year younger.

SIR DANIEL. Have you any portrait of her?

MRS DANE. No.

SIR DANIEL. You kept up a correspondence with her when you left England?

MRS DANE [*after a little pause*]. Yes.

SIR DANIEL. For how long?

MRS DANE. For some years, I think.

SIR DANIEL. Have you any letter of hers?

MRS DANE. No. After the dreadful affair in Vienna I destroyed everything.

SIR DANIEL. There would doubtless be persons in Tawhampton who would remember her, as well as you?

MRS DANE. Oh, yes, I should think. We only lived there as girls, and perhaps people might not recollect sufficiently to be sure——

SIR DANIEL. When Felicia Hindemarsh left Tawhampton, where did she go?

MRS DANE. I don't quite know.

SIR DANIEL. But you had letters from her. Where did they come from?

MRS DANE. Let me think—it was some seaside place I think.
[*Pause.*

SIR DANIEL. You don't remember?

MRS DANE. No. I'm getting so terribly muddled, I don't know what I'm saying. I—I—you frighten me!

SIR DANIEL. I frighten you?

[*His manner throughout has been calm and kind but very firm.*

MRS DANE. Yes. I know you're very kind, and that I've nothing

X

to fear, but I feel—I feel as if I were being thumb-screwed, and if you ask me one more question I must shriek out for help. [*A little pause.*] I'm sure it would be better for me to go and write it all out when I'm alone [*making a movement to go*]. Don't you think so?

SIR DANIEL [*arresting her with a gesture*]. No.

MRS DANE. I'm in such a state that I can't be sure I'm giving the right answers.

SIR DANIEL [*calm, stern*]. You must be sure you are giving me the right answers. Come, now, sit down, and [*very kindly*] remember that I have not a single interest at stake except what is yours and Lionel's. Remember that I have no hope or desire in this matter, except to clear you triumphantly in the eyes of the world, and give you to Lionel for his wife. Now don't get anxious or excited. We'll soon get this tiresome business over!

MRS DANE. Oh, I know I'm foolish, and you have been so patient and kind.

SIR DANIEL. This seaside place that Felicia Hindemarsh wrote from? Was it north, south, east, or west?

MRS DANE. South, I think.

SIR DANIEL. Portsmouth, Brighton, Hastings, Eastbourne?

MRS DANE. Brighton, I think.

SIR DANIEL. What was she doing there? [*No reply.*] You said your cousin was a governess?

MRS DANE. I think she was pupil teacher at a school.

SIR DANIEL [*making a note*]. Good. That's a clue.

MRS DANE [*showing great fright as he turns from her*]. A clue to what?

SIR DANIEL. If Felicia Hindemarsh was a pupil teacher at a school on the south coast, we shall doubtless be able to find out where it was, and some one who remembers her.

MRS DANE. Yes. Yes. But I hope I shall find somebody at Tawhampton to-morrow——

SIR DANIEL. Yes. By the way, I'm free to-morrow, I think I'll run down to Tawhampton with you?

MRS DANE [*feigning delight*]. Will you? That will be such a help to me. You can tell me exactly what kind of evidence you want, and you can be sure whether people are telling the truth.

SIR DANIEL. Can I? [*Looking at her.*

MRS DANE [*looking at him with the utmost frankness*]. I know that I shouldn't like to tell you what was false. I should feel sure that you would very soon drag the truth out of me. See how quickly you forced me to tell you that Felicia Hindemarsh was my cousin. And I'm glad you did! I should never have been happy or comfortable till I had told you and Lionel. Then you will go down to Tawhampton with me?

SIR DANIEL [*has been keenly watching her*]. If you don't mind.

MRS DANE I shall be delighted. I hope my head will be better, and that I shall be well enough to go.

SIR DANIEL. I hope so. If not, I'll take a little journey there by myself.

MRS DANE. Ye—es——

SIR DANIEL. Was your cousin anything like you?

MRS DANE. I think there was a likeness. I dare-say it was that which made Mr Risby mistake me for her.

SIR DANIEL. Possibly. But Mr Fendick said the other day that you were not in the least like Felicia Hindemarsh.

MRS DANE. Did he? But one person often sees a likeness where another sees none. What time shall we start for Tawhampton to-morrow?

SIR DANIEL. I'll look out the trains by and by. . . . Then you never saw your cousin after childhood?

MRS DANE. No—I—I——[*suddenly breaks down*]. I can't bear it! I can't bear it!

SIR DANIEL. What?

MRS DANE. Your questioning me as if I was guilty! I feel you suspect me still. Tell me, do you trust me thoroughly? [*He does not reply.*] Ah, you see you do not answer! So be it. Make me out a list of the questions you want answered and I'll answer them. But I can endure this torture no longer. [*Going to door.*

SIR DANIEL. Come, my dear Lucy, this won't do. [*Takes her gently back.*] We are here to get at the truth, aren't we?

MRS DANE. Yes, and you must see how ready and willing I am to answer your questions—I'm very faint——

SIR DANIEL. I'll only keep you a moment. Now I am going to ask you one question. Think well before you reply, because all your happiness and Lionel's depend upon my receiving a correct answer.

MRS DANE. Well?!

SIR DANIEL. When was the last time you saw your cousin Felicia Hindemarsh? [*A long pause.*

MRS DANE. I'll tell you everything.

SIR DANIEL. Go on.

MRS DANE. I don't know what you'll think of me. I don't care. I'd almost rather everybody believed me guilty than suffer what I have done the last few weeks. It's horrible!

SIR DANIEL. When was the last time you saw Felicia Hindemarsh?

MRS DANE. After the fearful scandal in Vienna she wrote to me in Montreal. She was desperate and begged us to shelter her. We had been like sisters, and I wrote to her to come out to us, and we would give her a home.

SIR DANIEL. And you did?

MRS DANE. Yes, till her death.

SIR DANIEL. When was that?

MRS DANE. About a year ago.

SIR DANIEL. Where? [*Pause.*

MRS DANE. At Montreal.

SIR DANIEL. She lived with you in Montreal—as Felicia Hindemarsh?

MRS DANE. No; we called her Mrs Allen.

SIR DANIEL. Give me the names and addresses of those people who knew you in Montreal as Mrs Dane, and her as Mrs Allen.

MRS DANE. I'll write them out. Let me bring it to you this evening. What are you going to do with it?

SIR DANIEL. I'm going to prove that you are Lucy Dane—*if you are Lucy Dane.* [*She looks at him.*

SIR DANIEL. Does Risby know who you are?

MRS DANE. What do you mean?

SIR DANIEL. Does Risby know who you are?

MRS DANE. Yes—he knows that I am Mrs Dane.

SIR DANIEL. The cousin of Felicia Hindemarsh.

MRS DANE [*after a pause*]. Yes.

SIR DANIEL. You told Risby, a mere acquaintance, that Felicia Hindemarsh was your cousin, and you didn't tell Lionel, you didn't tell me?

MRS DANE. I—I—[*she looks at him*] I—oh—I'll answer you no more. Believe what you please of me! I want no more of your help! Let me go!

SIR DANIEL [*stopping her*]. How much does Risby know?

MRS DANE. Don't I tell you he knows I am Mrs Dane?

SIR DANIEL. Woman, you're lying!

MRS DANE [*flashes out on him*]. How dare you? How dare you?
[*Stands confronting him.*

SIR DANIEL [*looking straight at her*]. I say you're lying! You are Felicia Hindemarsh!

4. JOHN GALSWORTHY (*born* 1867)

Strife

The naturalistic style, coupled with a fine sense of what may be called the Fate in human society, has found no more powerful an exponent than Mr Galsworthy. He is interested in society and he is interested in men, and out of the two he calls forth the spirit of tragedy. He does not satirize and he does not argue for this side or for that ; there is rather in his pages a divine pity as of one who, half god and half man, looks upon the petty, baffling, miserable ways of the world in which he himself plays a part. *Justice* and *Strife* are probably the two strongest and most representative of his plays, in that they show more clearly than the others this drama of individual men face to face with society, some, enwrapped in its folds, aiding it in its tasks, some, often for no fault of their own, opposed to it and suffering from its vengeance. The vague yet firmly felt presence of this society

THE MODERN PERIOD

raises Mr Galsworthy's dramas to a plane which otherwise they could not have reached, brings them to the level of tragedy, and provides them at one and the same time with a poignant conflict and a sense of universality. In order the better to show the effect of a Galsworthy play, there has been chosen for selection here the last scene of *Strife*, where the men and the strikers come together once more after the bitter struggle which has caused misery untold on both sides, and which has led to the death of at least one innocent woman. The divine pity is evident here, as is also the impression that each of those individuals, fighting for what he deems to be his own, is in reality beaten and baffled by a Fate which is none the less awful for remaining unseen and unpersonified.

(*Strife* [1] was produced at the Duke of York's theatre in March 1909. The following extract is taken, by kind permission of the author and of the publishers, Messrs Gerald Duckworth and Co., Ltd., from the edition of 1913.)

A Sense of Waste

ROBERTS. Mr Anthony, I am afraid I am a little late, I would have been here in time but for something that—has happened. [*To the men*] Has anything been said?

THOMAS. No! But, man, what made ye come?

ROBERTS. Ye told us this morning, gentlemen, to go away and reconsider our position. We have reconsidered it; we are here to bring you the men's answer. [*To* ANTHONY] Go ye back to London. We have nothing for you. By no jot or tittle do we abate our demands, nor will we until the whole of those demands are yielded.

> [ANTHONY *looks at him, but does not speak. There is a movement amongst the men as though they were bewildered.*

HARNESS. Roberts!

ROBERTS [*glancing fiercely at him, and back to* ANTHONY]. Is that clear enough for ye? Is it short enough and to the point? Ye made a mistake to think that we would come to heel. Ye may break the body, but ye cannot break the spirit. Get back to London, the men have nothing for ye.

> [*Pausing uneasily, he takes a step towards the unmoving* ANTHONY.

EDGAR. We're all sorry for you, Roberts, but——

ROBERTS. Keep your sorrow, young man. Let your father speak!

HARNESS [*with the sheet of paper in his hand, speaking from behind the little table*]. Roberts!

ROBERTS [*to* ANTHONY, *with passionate intensity*]. Why don't ye answer?

HARNESS. Roberts!

[1] Copyright 1909 in U.S.A. by Messrs Charles Scribner's Sons, New York.

325

ROBERTS [*turning sharply*]. What is it?

HARNESS [*gravely*]. You're talking without the book; things have travelled past you.

> [*He makes a sign to* TENCH, *who beckons the Directors. They quickly sign his copy of the terms.*

Look at this, man! [*Holding up his sheet of paper*] " Demands conceded, *with the exception of those relating to the engineers and furnace-men.* Double wages for Saturday's overtime. Night-shifts as they are." These terms have been agreed. The men go back to work again to-morrow. The strike is at an end.

ROBERTS [*reading the paper, and turning on the men. They shrink back from him, all but* ROUS, *who stands his ground. With deadly stillness*] Ye have gone back on me? I stood by ye to the death; ye waited for *that* to throw me over!

> [*The men answer, all speaking together.*

ROUS. It's a lie!

THOMAS. Ye were past endurance, man.

GREEN. If ye'd listen to me——

BULGIN [*under his breath*]. Hold your jaw!

ROBERTS. Ye waited for *that*!

HARNESS [*taking the Directors' copy of the terms, and handing his own to* TENCH]. That's enough, men. You had better go.

> [*The men shuffle slowly, awkwardly away.*

WILDER [*in a low, nervous voice*]. There's nothing to stay for now, I suppose. [*He follows to the door.*] I shall have a try for that train! Coming, Scantlebury?

SCANTLEBURY [*following with* WANKLIN]. Yes, yes; wait for me.

> [*He stops as* ROBERTS *speaks.*

ROBERTS [*to* ANTHONY]. But *ye* have not signed them terms! They can't make terms without their Chairman! Ye would never sign them terms! [ANTHONY *looks at him without speaking.* Don't tell me ye have! for the love o' God! [*With passionate appeal*] I reckoned on ye!

HARNESS [*holding out the Directors' copy of the terms*]. The Board has signed!

> [ROBERTS *looks dully at the signatures—dashes the paper from him, and covers up his eyes.*

SCANTLEBURY [*behind his hand to* TENCH]. Look after the Chairman! He's not well; he's not well—he had no lunch. If there's any fund started for the women and children, put me down for—for twenty pounds.

> [*He goes out into the hall, in cumbrous haste; and* WANKLIN, *who has been staring at* ROBERTS *and* ANTHONY *with twitchings of his face, follows.* EDGAR *remains seated on the sofa, looking at the ground;* TENCH, *returning to the bureau, writes in his minute-book.* HARNESS *stands by the little table, gravely watching* ROBERTS.

ROBERTS. Then you're no longer Chairman of this Company!

THE MODERN PERIOD

[*Breaking into half-mad laughter*] Ah, ha—ah, ha, ha! They've thrown ye over—thrown over their Chairman: Ah—ha—ha! [*With a sudden dreadful calm*] So—they've done us both down, Mr Anthony?

[ENID, *hurrying through the double doors, comes quickly to her father and bends over him.*

HARNESS [*coming down and laying his hands on* ROBERTS' *sleeve*]. For shame, Roberts! Go home quietly, man; go home!

ROBERTS [*tearing his arm away*]. Home? [*Shrinking together—in a whisper*] Home!

ENID [*quietly to her father*]. Come away, dear! Come to your room!

[ANTHONY *rises with an effort. He turns to* ROBERTS, *who looks at him. They stand several seconds, gazing at each other fixedly;* ANTHONY *lifts his hand, as though to salute, but lets it fall. The expression of* ROBERTS' *face changes from hostility to wonder. They bend their heads in token of respect.* ANTHONY *turns, and slowly walks towards the curtained door. Suddenly he sways as though about to fall, recovers himself, and is assisted out by* ENID *and* EDGAR, *who has hurried across the room.* ROBERTS *remains motionless for several seconds, staring intently after* ANTHONY, *then goes out into the hall.*

TENCH [*approaching* HARNESS]. It's a great weight off my mind, Mr Harness! But what a painful scene, sir! [*He wipes his brow.*

[HARNESS, *pale and resolute, regards with a grim half-smile the quavering* TENCH.

It's all been so violent! What did he mean by: "Done us both down"? If he has lost his wife, poor fellow, he oughtn't to have spoken to the Chairman like that!

HARNESS. A woman dead; and the two best men both broken!

[UNDERWOOD *enters suddenly.*

TENCH [*staring at* HARNESS—*suddenly excited*]. D'you know, Sir —these terms, they're the *very same* we drew up together, you and I, and put to both sides before the fight began? All this—all this—and—and what for?

HARNESS [*in a slow grim voice*]. That's where the fun comes in!

[UNDERWOOD *without turning from the door makes a gesture of assent.*

5. HARLEY GRANVILLE-BARKER (*born* 1877)

The Voysey Inheritance

Mr Granville-Barker's strength comes from his unflinching acceptance of things as they are, his supreme knowledge of the stage, and his ability to depict and contrast characters who, although not cast in any heroic mould, have an enduring interest and attraction of their own. Rarely does he attempt wit in his

327

EXTRACTS FROM BRITISH & IRISH PLAYS

dialogue, for his figures are ordinary figures, and their language the language of ordinary life. He aims rather at presenting the essential being of those figures and of the atmosphere which surrounds them. This he does with an entirely unprejudiced mind, for he is the observer and the spectator, rather than the enthusiast and the propagandist. In *The Voysey Inheritance*, for example, Edward, who at first condemns his father's misappropriation of money entrusted to him, shows up in a slightly priggish manner, and the father himself is presented with a not unsympathetic pen. If to anyone in the play, Mr Granville-Barker's feelings seem to go forth to Alice, who, clear-sighted and sane, is prepared to take the way of reason and social convention.

(*The Voysey Inheritance* was produced at the Court Theatre in November 1905. The following extract is taken from the edition of 1909, by kind permission of the author and of the publishers, Messrs Sidgwick and Jackson, Ltd., London, and Messrs Little, Brown and Company, Boston, U.S.A.

EDWARD'S ACQUIESCENCE

ALICE. Edward, I'm afraid you're feeling heroic.

EDWARD. I!

ALICE. Don't be so proud of your misfortune. You looked quite like Booth for the moment. [*This effectually removes the starch.*] It will be very stupid to send you to prison and you must do your best to keep out. [*She goes on very practically.*] We were discussing if anything could be done for these one or two people who'll be beggared.

EDWARD. Yes, Alice. I'm sorry nothing can be done for them.

ALICE. It's a pity.

EDWARD. I suppose I was feeling heroic. I didn't mean to.

[*He has become a little like a child with her.*

ALICE. That's the worst of acting on principle . . . one begins thinking of one's attitude instead of the use of what one is doing.

EDWARD. I'm exposing this fraud on principle.

ALICE. Perhaps that's what's wrong.

EDWARD. Wrong!

ALICE. My dear Edward, if people are to be ruined . . .!

EDWARD. What else is there to be done?

ALICE. Well . . . have you thought?

EDWARD. There's nothing else to be done.

ALICE. On principle.

[*He looks at her, she is smiling, it is true, but smiling quite gravely.* EDWARD *is puzzled. Then the yeast of her suggestion begins to work in his mind slowly, perversely at first.*

EDWARD. It had occurred to Booth . . .

ALICE. Oh, anything may occur to Booth.

EDWARD.⌉ . . . In his grave concern for the family honour that I might quietly cheat the firm back into credit again.

ALICE. How stupid of Booth!

EDWARD. Well . . . like my father . . . Booth believes in himself.

ALICE. Yes, he's rather a credulous man.

EDWARD [*ignoring her little joke*]. He might have been lucky and have done some good. I'm a weak sort of creature, just a collection of principles as you say. Look, all I've been able to do in this business . . . at the cost of my whole life perhaps . . . has been to sit senselessly by my father's side and prevent things going from bad to worse.

ALICE. That was worth doing. The cost is your own affair.

> [*She is watching him, stilly and closely. Suddenly his face lights a little and he turns to her.*

EDWARD. Alice . . . there's something else I could do.

ALICE. What?

EDWARD. It's illegal.

ALICE. So much the better perhaps. Oh, I'm lawless by birthright, being a woman.

EDWARD. I could take the money that's in my father's name and use it only to put right the smaller accounts. It'd take a few months to do it well . . . and cover the tracks. That'd be necessary.

ALICE. Then you'd give yourself up as you'd meant to do now?

EDWARD. Yes . . . practically.

LICE. It'd be worse for you then at the trial?

EDWARD [*with a touch of another sort of pride*]. You said that was my affair.

ALICE [*pain in her voice and eyes*]. Oh, Edward!

EDWARD. Shall I do this?

ALICE [*turning away*]. Why must you ask me?

EDWARD. You mocked at my principles, didn't you? You've taken them from me. The least you can do is to give me advice in exchange.

ALICE [*after a moment*]. No . . . decide for yourself.

> [*He jumps up and begins to pace about, doubtful, distressed.*

EDWARD. Good Lord . . . it means lying and shuffling!

ALICE [*a little trembling*]. In a good cause.

EDWARD. Ah . . . but lying and shuffling takes the fine edge off one's soul.

ALICE [*laughing at the quaintness of her own little epigram*]. Edward, are you one of God's dandies?

EDWARD. And . . . Alice, it wouldn't be easy work. It wants qualities I haven't got. I should fail.

ALICE. Would you? [*He catches a look from her.*

EDWARD. Well, I might not.

ALICE. And you don't need success for a lure. That's like a common man.

EDWARD. You want me to try to do this?

[For answer, she dares only put out her hand, and he takes it.
ALICE. Oh, my dear . . . cousin!

EDWARD *[excitedly]*. My people will have to hold their tongues.
I needn't have told them all this to-day.

ALICE. Don't tell them the rest . . . they won't understand.
I shall be jealous if you tell them.

EDWARD *[looking at her as she at him]*. Well, you've the right to
be. This deed . . . it's not done yet . . . is your property.

ALICE. Thank you. I've always wanted to have something useful
to my credit . . . and I'd almost given up hoping.

*[Then suddenly his face changes, his voice changes and he
grips the hand he is holding so tightly as to hurt her.*

EDWARD. Alice, if my father's story were true . . . he must have
begun like this. Trying to do the right thing in the wrong way . . .
then doing the wrong thing . . . then bringing himself to what he
was . . . and so to this. *[He flings away from her.]* No, Alice, I
won't do it. I daren't take that first step down. It's a worse risk
than any failure. Think . . . I might succeed.

[ALICE stands very still, looking at him.
ALICE. It's a big risk. Well . . . I'll take it.

[He turns to her, in wonder.
EDWARD. You?

ALICE. I'll risk your becoming a bad man. That's a big risk
for me. *[He understands, and is calmed and made happy.*

EDWARD. Then there is no more to be said, is there?

ALICE. Not now. *[As she drops this gentle hint she hears something
—the hall door opening.]* Here's Booth back again.

EDWARD *[with a really mischievous grin]*. He'll be so glad he's
convinced me.

ALICE. I must go back to Honor, poor girl. I wonder she has a
tear left.

*[She leaves him, briskly, brightly; leaves her cousin with his
mouth set and a light in his eyes.*

6. ELIZABETH BAKER (*born* 1879)

Chains

That which, above all other things, the drama of the first decade
of the twentieth century succeeded in capturing was the tragedy
and the pathos inherent in that 'common life' which had before
been either neglected in the theatre or else treated comically or
melodramatically. There is a connexion between such a melodrama as *Luke the Labourer* and *Chains*, but the connexion is
possibly less than the difference. In the one the tragedy in the
life of the poor, while appreciated, is treated as a minor incident
in a typical villain-hero-heroine play, and at that is given by

330

THE MODERN PERIOD

narration only. In such a drama as *Chains* this tragic or pathetic essence is laid bare, slowly, gradually, not by narration, but by the depiction of character upon the stage. The whole atmosphere of the play is quiet, but there is a persistent building up of dark emotion. Charley Wilson is a clerk, fretting at the stiffness and the rigour of his life. His lodger, Tennant, is about to go to Australia, and this sets the pent-up yet vague aspirations in Charley's heart aflame. Hour by hour his determination grows, until finally his wife, Lily, tells him she is to have a child. It is a situation which must happen in more homes than 55 Acacia Avenue, but, precisely because of that, it rises to greatness. The play is realistic, in the sense that Charley and Lily and Tennant are individuals, speaking the language of ordinary life ; yet these figures are symbols, representative of thousands of other men and women. By the simplicity of the theme, *Chains* secures unquestioned universality. The scene given below has been selected because it illustrates the manner in which the playwright has built up her atmosphere of littleness and triviality to form a grey, sombre background for the figure of the restless and fettered clerk.

(*Chains* was produced in 1909. The following passage is taken from the edition of 1911, by kind permission of the publishers, Messrs Sidgwick and Jackson, Ltd., London, and Messrs John W. Luce and Company, Boston, U.S.A.

THE FETTERED SOUL

LILY. We ought to have *Auld Lang Syne——*

TENNANT. Please don't.

LILY. It would be so nice for you to remember. [*Going up L.*] Yes, we must. Come. [*She puts out her hands and makes them all form a ring, with hands crossed and all round table.*]

[TENNANT *and* CHARLEY *join most reluctantly, and are not seen to sing a note.*

There! That's better.

SYBIL. Now I must go, Mrs Wilson.

LILY. Must you really? Come and get your things. [*They go out.*

[*A tapping is heard at the window in the near room—*MAGGIE *runs and opens it.*

VOICE. Is my husband there, Mrs Wilson?

LESLIE. Y—es. I'm here. Coming, darling.

[SYBIL *and* LILY *re-enter R.*

LESLIE. My wife has sent for me home, Mrs Wilson.

MAGGIE. Are you going over the wall?

SYBIL. Oh, do, Mr Leslie—I should love to see you.

LESLIE. If it will give you any pleasure it shall be done, though I am not at my best on the fence.

331

[They all crowd round—he shakes hands, smiling profusely, and disappears through the window.

VOICE. Mind the flower-pot. No—not there—that's the dustbin. Not the steps. *[There is a great shout to announce his safe arrival.*

LESLIE. Safe!

SYBIL. I do think he is so funny!

LILY. Yes, isn't he? Are you going by 'bus?

PERCY. I'm going Miss Frost's way.

SYBIL [*much surprised*]. Are you really?

MAGGIE. How extraordinary!

[Much kissing between SYBIL, LILY *and* MAGGIE. SYBIL *and* PERCY *go out.*

LILY. She's so sweet, isn't she? And Percy's so awfully gone.

MAGGIE [*as they start clearing away the dishes*]. Very. So he was over Daisy Mallock and Ruby Denis—and who's the other girl with the hair?

LILY. The hair? What do you mean?

MAGGIE. The one with the hair all over her eyes—nice hair, too.

LILY. Gladys Vancouver? Poor Percy—I'm afraid he is a little bit of a flirt.

MAGGIE. He's got nothing else to do with his evenings.

LILY. And then people like Mr Tennant think it's a dull life.

MAGGIE. Well, good night, all. No, don't come out, Mr Tennant —I'm quite a capable person.

TENNANT. Oh, but I shall—if you'll allow me.

MAGGIE. I'd rather you didn't—still, if you will.

[They go out with LILY.

*[*CHARLEY *looks round and sighs with relief—he walks round, looks out of the window, then at the garden—he takes up the paper, but after trying in vain to settle to it, throws it on the floor—he refills his pipe and lights it. Re-enter* TENNANT.

TENNANT. Well. [*He pauses, but* CHARLEY *does not stir.*] I say, Wilson, I never thought you'd take it like this.

*[*CHARLEY *does not answer, but only shifts restlessly.* I thought you'd think I was a fool too. In fact I was half ashamed to say anything about it. It wouldn't do for most people, you know. I'm in an exceptional position, and even in spite of that they call me an ass. I've got a little cash, too.

CHARLEY [*quickly*]. So have I.

TENNANT. Yes, but the cases are different. I can rough it.

CHARLEY. Let me have the chance to rough it.

TENNANT. You're married. [CHARLEY *does not reply.* You're settled. Your friends are here. I've got nothing and no-body to worry about. [*They both smoke in silence.* I say, don't sit up and think. Go to bed.

CHARLEY. I'm going soon. Don't stay up, old chap.

TENNANT. You'll get over it. *[He goes out.*

332

THE MODERN PERIOD

[Enter LILY—*she pulls down blind and fastens catch of window.*

LILY. I'm going up now. Don't be long. You look so tired.

CHARLEY *[irritably]*. Oh, don't fret about me. I'm a little worried, that's all.

LILY *[timidly]*. Did Mr Fenwick bring bad news? He looked miserable enough.

CHARLEY *[looking at her steadily]*. Yes, I'm not going to have that rise.

LILY. Oh, dear—what a shame! Why?

CHARLEY. Lots of reasons—but that's all.

LILY. Of course, you're worried. Still—it might have been worse. You might have been sent away.

CHARLEY. Yes.

LILY. It's very disheartening—after all we'd planned to do with it. You won't be able to have the greenhouse, now, will you, dear?

CHARLEY *[with a short laugh]*. What's the good of a greenhouse in that yard? It isn't that.

LILY *[a little timidly]*. But we can manage very well, dear. We—you remember what I said this morning—about the other lodger.

CHARLEY. Oh, don't for heaven's sake. It isn't losing the cash I mind; it's having to give in like this. I want to go to them and tell them to do their worst and get somebody else.

LILY. But, dear, you might lose your place.

CHARLEY. I should.

LILY. But that—we couldn't afford that, could we? Why, we can manage quite well as we are. I can be very careful still——

CHARLEY. I'm tired of going on as we've been going.

LILY. What do you want to do?

CHARLEY. I—I want to go away. *[Pause.*

LILY. And leave me?

CHARLEY *[suddenly remembering]*. Oh—er——

LILY. It's just that horrid Mr Tennant——

CHARLEY. It's nothing to do with him—at least . . .

LILY. I said it was. He wants you to go with him—and you want to go—you're tired of me——

CHARLEY *[going up to her and trying to speak gently, but being very irritated—his voice is sharp]*. Oh, don't cry . . . you don't understand. Look, Lil, supposing I went and you came out afterwards.

LILY. You want to go without me.

CHARLEY. I couldn't take you, dear, but I would soon send for you; it wouldn't be long.

LILY. You want to go without me. You're tired of me.

CHARLEY. Oh, don't cry, Lil. I didn't say I was going. Of course I don't want to leave you, dear. You mustn't take any notice *[attempting to take her in his arms]*.

LILY *[turning away from him, sobs]*. But you do . . .

CHARLEY. I don't want to go because I want to leave you . . .

333

LILY. But you said . . .

CHARLEY. Never mind what I said. [*He kisses her and pets her like a child.*] Come, go to bed. It's the news—and the excitement about Tennant—and all that. Come, go back to bed and I'll be up in a few minutes.

> [CHARLEY *leads her to the door and coaxes her outside and stands at the door a few seconds, then he comes back into the room, stands still, looking round. He goes to the front parlour and hunts over the chairs and the piano as if in search of something. Finally he picks up a paper off the floor and brings it to table—it is the map of Australia. He opens it on the table and leans over it, his pipe unnoticed burning out in his left hand.*]

7. STANLEY HOUGHTON (1881–1913)

Hindle Wakes

Hindle Wakes, like so many plays of the period immediately preceding 1914, is the result of the 'Repertory' movement. Encouraged by the success of Irish drama, Mr Houghton has created a play born out of Lancashire soil, with Lancashire people and Lancashire dialect. It is a 'drama' in the sense that it aims at presenting, within a setting of real life, a certain problem which is shown not merely in theory, but in action. Alan Jeffcote, the son of a well-to-do mill-owner, has spent a gay week-end with Fanny Hawthorn, the daughter of a slasher at Jeffcote's mill. The affair, when known, naturally causes some commotion, and Jeffcote, with his Puritanical tendencies, threatens to cut his son off with a shilling unless he makes Fanny an 'honest woman' by marrying her. At first Alan is inclined to resist, but when he is rejected by his *fiancée*, Beatrice Farrar, he decides to do as his father wills. Fanny, however, shows she is a girl of spirit, and at the same time of logic. "You choose to be a girl who's lost her reputation," complains her mother, "instead of letting Alan make you an honest woman." "How can he do that?" asks Fanny. "By wedding you, of course," is the mother's reply, to which comes the daughter's retort, "You called him a blackguard this morning. . . . I don't see how marrying a blackguard is going to turn me into an honest woman!" In *Hindle Wakes*, therefore, there are evident the two forces predominant in early twentieth-century drama—the desire to secure what may be called local reality, and the desire to battle with romantic pre-occupations in the cause of rationalism and logic.

(*Hindle Wakes* was produced at the Gaiety Theatre, Manchester, and later appeared in London (in 1912), presented by the Stage Society. The extract given below is taken from the ninth

334

impression, 1923, by kind permission of the publishers, Messrs Sidgwick and Jackson, Ltd., London, and Messrs John W. Luce and Company, Boston, U.S.A.

THE LOGIC OF MODERN YOUTH

ALAN. No. You know I like you, Fanny—I'm fond of you.

FANNY. You didn't give up Beatrice Farrar because of me, but because of the money.

ALAN. If it comes to that, I didn't really give her up at all. I may as well be straight with you. It was she that gave me up.

FANNY. What did she do that for? Her father's plenty of money, and she can get round *him*, I'll bet, if you can't get round *yours*.

ALAN. She gave me up because she thought it was her duty to.

FANNY. You mean because she didn't fancy my leavings.

ALAN. No. Because she thought you had the right to marry me.

FANNY. Glory! She must be queer!

ALAN. It was jolly fine of her. You ought to be the first to see that.

FANNY. Fine to give you up? [*She shrugs her shoulders, and then admits grudgingly*] Well, I reckon it was a sacrifice of a sort. That is, if she loves you. If I loved a chap I wouldn't do that.

ALAN. You would. You're doing it now.

FANNY. Eh?

ALAN. Women are more unselfish than men and no mistake!

FANNY. What are you getting at?

ALAN. I know why you won't marry me.

FANNY. Do you? [*She smiles.*] Well, spit it out, lad!

ALAN. You're doing it for my sake.

FANNY. How do you make that out?

ALAN. You don't want to spoil my life.

FANNY. Thanks! Much obliged for the compliment.

ALAN. I'm not intending to say anything unkind, but of course it's as clear as daylight that you'd damage my prospects, and all that sort of thing. You can see that, can't you?

FANNY. Ay! I can see it now you point it out. I hadn't thought of it before.

ALAN. Then, that isn't why you refused me?

FANNY. Sorry to disappoint you, but it's not.

ALAN. I didn't see what else it could be.

FANNY. Don't you kid yourself, my lad! It isn't because I'm afraid of spoiling *your* life that I'm refusing you, but because I'm afraid of spoiling *mine*! That didn't occur to you?

ALAN. It didn't.

FANNY. You never thought that anybody else could be as selfish as yourself.

ALAN. I may be very conceited, but I don't see how you can hurt yourself by wedding me. You'd come in for plenty of brass, anyhow.

335

FANNY I don't know as money's much to go by when it comes to a job of this sort. It's more important to get the right chap.

ALAN. You like me well enough?

FANNY. Suppose it didn't last? Weddings brought about this road have a knack of turning out badly. Would you ever forget it was your father bade you marry me? No fear! You'd bear me a grudge all my life for that.

ALAN. Hang it! I'm not such a cad as you make out.

FANNY. You wouldn't be able to help it. It mostly happens that road. Look at old Mrs Eastwood—hers was a case like ours. Old Joe Eastwood's father made them wed. And she's been separated from him these thirty years, living all alone in that big house at Valley Edge. Got any amount of brass, she has, but she's so lonesome-like she does her own housework for the sake of something to occupy her time. The tradesfolk catch her washing the front steps. You don't find me making a mess of my life like that.

ALAN. Look here, Fanny, I promise you I'll treat you fair all the time. You don't need to fear that folk'll look down on you. We shall have too much money for that.

FANNY. I can manage all right on twenty-five bob a week.

ALAN. Happen you can. It's not the brass altogether. You do like me, as well, don't you?

FANNY. Have you only just thought of that part of the bargain?

ALAN. Don't be silly. I thought of it long ago. You *do* like me? You wouldn't have gone to Llandudno with me if you hadn't liked me?

FANNY. Oh! yes, I liked you.

ALAN. And don't you like me now?

FANNY. You're a nice, clean, well-made lad. Oh, ay! I like you right enough.

ALAN. Then, Fanny, for God's sake, marry me, and let's get this job settled.

FANNY. Not me!

ALAN. But you must. Don't you see it's your duty to?

FANNY. Oh! come now, *you* aren't going to start preaching to me?

ALAN. No. I don't mean duty in the way Beatrice did. I mean your duty to me. You've got me into a hole, and it's only fair you should get me out.

FANNY. I like your cheek!

ALAN. But just look here. I'm going to fall between two stools. It's all up with Beatrice, of course. And if you won't have me I shall have parted from her to no purpose; besides getting kicked out of the house by my father, more than likely!

FANNY. Nay, nay! He'll not punish you for this. He doesn't know it's your fault I'm not willing to wed you.

ALAN. He may. It's not fair, but it would be father all over to do that.

FANNY. He'll be only too pleased to get shut of me without eating his own words. He'll forgive you on the spot, and you can make it up with Beatrice to-morrow.

ALAN. I can never make it up with Bee!

FANNY. Get away!

ALAN. You won't understand a girl like Bee. I couldn't think of even trying for months, and then it may be too late. I'm not the only pebble on the beach. And I'm a damaged one, at that!

FANNY. She's fond of you, you said?

ALAN. Yes. I think she's very fond of me.

FANNY. Then she'll make it up in a fortnight.

ALAN [*moodily*]. You said *you* were fond of me once, but it hasn't taken you long to alter.

FANNY. All women aren't built alike. Beatrice is religious. She'll be sorry for you. I was fond of you in a way.

ALAN. But you didn't ever really love me?

FANNY. Love you? Good heavens, of course not! Why on earth should I love you? You were just some one to have a bit of fun with. You were an amusement—a lark.

ALAN [*shocked*]. Fanny! Is that all you cared for me?

FANNY. How much more did you care for me?

ALAN. But it's not the same. I'm a man.

FANNY. You're a man, and I was your little fancy. Well, I'm a woman, and *you* were *my* little fancy. You wouldn't prevent a woman enjoying herself as well as a man, if she takes it into her head?

ALAN. But do you mean to say that you didn't care any more for me than a fellow cares for any girl he happens to pick up?

FANNY. Yes. Are you shocked?

ALAN. It's a bit thick; it is really!

FANNY. You're a beauty to talk!

ALAN. It sounds so jolly immoral. I never thought of a girl looking on a chap just like that! I made sure you wanted to marry me if you got the chance.

8. GEORGE CALDERON (1868–1915)

The Fountain

The Fountain is the fountain of charity, which, seemingly philanthropic, is more often than not merely a throwing out of money which has ultimately come from the source into which it flows again. The scene quoted here is perhaps not the best of Calderon's work, but it illustrates that movement in modern drama which endeavours to make theatrical use of the shams of present-day society. In *The Fountain* Calderon is as anti-romantic as Mr Shaw. Chenda's sentimental gifts to the poor are revealed as having come from rack-rented tenants of her own ;

all that her "slapdash" good has done is to reveal the apparent impossibility of ridding society of the evils accumulated during the passing of generations. *The Fountain* is didactic, but it is not merely a sermon or an economic lecture in acts and scenes. The strength of modern drama lies in the fact that the playwrights of to-day, however deeply moved they may be by such evils as they see around them, recognize that in writing for the theatre they must think of the theatre first and last. The characters are, therefore, living creations and the situations such as are likely to have an immediate playhouse appeal.

(*The Fountain* was produced in 1909. The following extract is taken, by kind permission of Mrs Calderon and of the publishers, the Richards Press, Ltd., from the edition of 1912.)

The Irony of Social Conditions

CHENDA. Oh, Jimbo, Jimbo! I see it all. You mean that *I* am the owner of this horrible place, that it is *I* who live at ease because these poor creatures live in misery. Oh, where can I hide myself? Where can I hide myself? [*Hiding her face on* WREN's *bosom.*

PONTIFEX [*grasping it at last*]. Well, dammy, if that isn't the finest thing that ever I heard! After all the talking at I've had, and been obliged to resign my post as rent-collector and all, for oppressin' the innocent pore. And all the time it was Mr Oliver that's been raisin' the rents and creatin' all this hullabaloo. [*Laughing*] Ho, I must go and tell the boys. . . . [*Exit.*

CHENDA. Oh, Jimbo, Jimbo! What a nightmare it all is! Oh, why didn't I listen to you when you said it was no good doing anything?

WREN. My poor, poor darling! You've done your best.

CHENDA. I've done nothing but harm.

KATE. It was all done for the sake of charity.

WREN. Charity! Now you see what charity means. All the money you were spending on Oliver's parishioners was being pumped up into your horn of plenty out of Oliver's parishioners' pockets all the time. There they were, the poor tenants, Pontifex, Mr Palmer, Davenil, Nix, and Oliver; and at the top of all, yourself, like a nymph on a fountain, pouring the water back into the basin. That's charity! That's why we erect fountains at street corners to philanthropical gentlemen. It's an allegory, a satire. Why, every time I . . .

KATE. I think we've had enough speech-making, James.

WREN. So we have! So we have! [*To* CHENDA] My darling pet! Chennie my angel, you'll break my heart if you cry so.

CHENDA. I'm better now. How I detest myself! I'll never be charitable again. There was a picture I always loved all my childhood, of a tall lady in white giving money out of a purse to the poor; you know, Jimbo, the one that hangs over my burry; I

338

THE MODERN PERIOD

always wanted to be like that. But now I know how the purse is filled. . . . Oh, I'll smash that beastly picture when I get back!

[*She goes and gets her hat from its peg.*

KATE. Where are you going?

CHENDA. I'm going home with Jimbo.

[JIMBO *wears a pensive, doubtful air.*

OLIVER. You mustn't be selfish, Chenda; you've undertaken certain obligations to my parish.

CHENDA. What obligations?

OLIVER. There's the Settlement to begin with, for which you've signed the lease, you know. [*Holding out the lease.*

CHENDA [*taking it melodramatically, tearing it up, and throwing it on the floor*]. There's your lease then! You and I are not fit stewards for such a trust. [*A pause, a thrill.*

NIX [*prosaic, disillusioning*]. What's the good of that? . . . Tearing up the counterpart of an indenture don't make the indenture void. You're bound to pay rent to the Trust Estate.

CHENDA. My own?

NIX. You're only a life tenant.

CHENDA. The Trust Estate is at an end.

NIX. Nonsense. Nobody can put an end to a Trust Estate.

PALMER. Come along, Mr Nix, we'd better be going.

[*Exeunt* NIX, PALMER, *and* DAVENIL.

OLIVER. I may as well be going too. [*Exit* OLIVER.

CHENDA [*to* KATE]. Good-bye.

KATE. What about your luggage?

CHENDA. Send it on by Carter Pat.

KATE. Good-bye, darling. I'll go and put your things in.

[*Exit to bedroom.* JIM CROW *remains asleep on the sofa at the back.*

CHENDA. Come along, Jimbo.

WREN. Wait a bit.

CHENDA. *You're* not going to make difficulties now!

WREN. Come and sit here. [*A pause.*] I'm a selfish beggar, Chen, and I've been longing to get you back home at any price, but you've opened my eyes.

CHENDA. Whatever do you mean?

WREN. I think you ought to stay down here.

CHENDA. Me stay here?

WREN. For a time, I mean.

CHENDA. No, I can't do without you now. I must have you by me.

WREN. I'll stay too.

CHENDA. You? . . . Oh, Jimbo, I can't face this place after my ghastly failure.

WREN. I tell you what, Chen, you're wrong about the failure.

CHENDA. Wrong about the failure?

WREN. If it's a failure it's succeeded in a way that nothing else

339

could have succeeded. Things are in an awful mess, that's true; you're grabbing with one hand and doling out with the other. But it isn't you that made the mess. It's society that made the mess, and you, you've been fumbling round to clear it up. Nobody would have discovered what a mess it was if you hadn't gone fumbling round; and the discovery is the first step to the remedy.

CHENDA. Oh, Jimbo! And what's the remedy?

WREN. I don't know.

CHENDA. You don't know?

WREN. Nobody does.

CHENDA. Then what can we do?

WREN [*impressively, as if it were a policy and a solution*]. Fumble on! . . . You remember what you said about Jack Smiley's method of hunting? "Blundering through the hedges and floundering in the ponds." . . . Well, that's the way to tackle social questions.

CHENDA [*seeing a humorous side to it*]. But I can't imagine you down here, my Jimbo.

WREN. Hm! It certainly isn't much in my line.

CHENDA. Going about arm in arm with Tom, doing good works.

WREN. No, that isn't quite the idea. No. I've suddenly realised how valuable your slapdash methods are for *theory*, how illuminating. *That's* the object of action. Action does no good. In fact it always does harm; but theory, lovely theory, rises from the ruins. I've learnt more political economy this last week than I did in ten years before. I want to stay here and watch you all at it and penetrate the full irony of the situation. Then I think we might see if we can't give your tenants better value for their money, don't you think? And if we can spare any time from mending our own ways, we'll spend it in harassing employers, landlords, insanitary people, brewers, publicans, every one who battens on the poor. . . .

CHENDA. All the other Chendas in fact.

WREN. Yes, all the other Chendas. What fun it'll be!

CHENDA. You duck! [*A long kiss.*

[JIM CROW *stirs on the sofa, coughs and stretches.*

WREN [*rising*]. Hullo, are you still there, old friend?

JIM [*sitting up*]. Wish I was back in Raparoa wid de ole wife and little chillun.

9. A. A. MILNE (*born* 1882)

Success

Mr A. A. Milne has lately proved himself a master of comedy, but his work has included much that is of a serious quality. In *Success* he deals with a theme (which has been dealt with more than once in recent years) of ambition. His interest rests mainly on the psychology of his hero, Mannock, and he strives to delineate

340

THE MODERN PERIOD

the conflicting movements of his mind. In the scene given below there is shown, subtly, the despondency, the hope, the regret, and the pride of a man who, crossing his Rubicon, sees the goal in sight, yet perhaps looks back with a wistful glance to the past. The conclusion of this passage may be noted. After a period when dramatists wrote for the theatre alone there has come a time when once more tragedies and comedies are read as well as witnessed. For the new reading public the playwrights introduce stage directions which, avoiding the old-fashioned symbols, *L.* and *R.C.* and *C.*, give intimate descriptions not only of the ideal setting, but of the thoughts and passions experienced by their characters. Literally the conclusion to this scene of *Success* is not a speech or a portion of dialogue, but a series of reflections and feelings which can be written down in ' stage direction,' but which must remain unexpressed upon the stage itself.

(*Success* was produced in 1923. The passage below is taken, by kind permission of the author, from the edition published by Messrs Chatto and Windus, London, and Messrs G. P. Putnam's Sons, New York.)

The Dregs of the Cup

LADY JANE [*in suppressed excitement*]. Richard! Bertie says . . . Why, what's that? [*She is looking at the letter.*] But that's— why don't you open it? That's the letter. Open it! Open it!

MANNOCK [*dully*]. This is just acknowledging and accepting my resignation.

LADY JANE. But have you opened it yet? [*She snatches it from him, looks at it, and gives it back to him.*] But you haven't opened it yet! Open it! Bertie says——

BERTIE. The omens are distinctly favourable. But—well, now we shall know.

MANNOCK [*opening it*]. It's only just to accept my resignation.
[*He reads. You can see at once that it is not that.*

LADY JANE [*watching his face*]. It is! [MANNOCK *looks in front of him, seeing visions.*] May I—— [*She takes the letter from him.*] I must. [*She reads.*] Oh, well done, Richard!
[MANNOCK *stands there, breathing heavily. To be Chancellor of the Exchequer!*

BERTIE. He has? [*She nods.*] By Jove! Congratulations!

LADY JANE. I never thought——

BERTIE. Well, I don't know. Mowbray has a good deal against him one way and another.

LADY JANE. Yes. But I was almost afraid to hope.

BERTIE [*proudly*]. Didn't I tell you to leave it to him?
[*He nods towards* MANNOCK.

LADY JANE. Yes, you were quite right, Bertie.

[*She looks admiringly at her husband.*

BERTIE. Of course, I know all about the resignation stunt—it's as old as the hills. But if you can do it with conviction, you can still pull it off sometimes.

LADY JANE. Yes, yes.

BERTIE. Mannock carried conviction—that's where he's such an artist. The P.M. really thought he was going. Didn't dare to lose him. Prepared to offer anything to keep him.

LADY JANE. Yes.

BERTIE. I've always said that, in the matter of political strategy, Mannock can give them all points. Even the P.M. I knew he'd pull it off.

LADY JANE. Richard!   [*She means " Come and talk to us."*

MANNOCK [*his control suddenly giving way*]. So you knew I'd pull it off?   [*He is almost shouting.*

BERTIE. Rather!

MANNOCK. I can give 'em all points in political strategy?

BERTIE. I've always said so.

MANNOCK. And I carry conviction—eh?—that's where I'm such an artist.

BERTIE. Exactly. [MANNOCK *gives a loud, bitter laugh.*] Well, I mean——

MANNOCK [*half hysterically*]. An artist! That's what I am. Carry conviction! I carried conviction all right. I pulled *your* leg pretty well, Bertie. [*To* LADY JANE] *And* yours. You thought I meant to resign—yes, you did, both of you—you thought I meant it—you were frightened to death, yes, you were. You thought I really meant to give it all up. So did Arthur. I had Arthur in here just now—frightened to death—thought I meant to give it all up—talked about *his* career—his career!—my God!—frightened to death he was, just like you two. Ha! I pulled your legs pretty well. Resign? Why the devil should I resign? Haven't I got what I always wanted? You ask Reader—he'll tell you—the supreme goal for any man to reach. Chancellor of the Exchequer —*that* gives you power. Me! I've done it! Just pure strategy. Pretending I wanted to give up politics. Why should I? Success —it closes in on you! My God, there's nothing I can't do! Nothing!

[*His voice rises almost to a shriek, as he drops into a chair, and sits there, his hands over his face, his shoulders shaking with long, tearless sobs.*

BERTIE [*soothingly*]. I say, old fellow——

LADY JANE [*quietly*]. No. Go, Bertie.

BERTIE. Oh, right. [*Going*] I'll come in this evening if I can. He'll be all right? [*She nods.*] Right.   [*He goes out.*

LADY JANE [*putting an arm calmly on* MANNOCK'S *shoulders*]. It's all right now, Richard. I know how you must feel. It has been a

342

very anxious time for both of us. But it's all over now. You've got what you wanted. I'm proud of you, very proud of you.

MANNOCK [*pulling himself together*]. I'm sorry. I——

LADY JANE [*calmly*]. It's all right. I understand perfectly. The strain—naturally.

MANNOCK. Yes.

LADY JANE. I'll leave you now. You'll want to be alone. But come and talk to me afterwards.

MANNOCK [*nodding*]. Yes.

LADY JANE [*giving him the letter*]. You'll want to answer this.

MANNOCK. Yes. Thank you.

LADY JANE [*looking at him admiringly*]. I'm very proud of you, Richard. [*She goes out.*

  [*Alone,* MANNOCK *walks slowly to his desk, a tired man.*
   There he sees EVERSLEY'S *card, picks it up, looks at it,*
   puts it down, and takes up the telephone.

MANNOCK [*at the telephone*]. Hullo! Come in, will you? [*He goes back to his chair and waits.* READER *comes in, notebook in hand.*] I want a telegram sent at once. To Mr Eversley. You'll find a card on my desk. [READER *goes there.*] Got it? With an address in Porchester Terrace.

READER. Yes, sir.

  [*He writes down the name and address, and waits.*

MANNOCK. "Afraid cannot dine to-night."

READER [*writing*]. "Afraid cannot dine to-night."

MANNOCK. That's all.

READER. Signed?

MANNOCK. Yes, "Dick." . . . [*An end to this weakness. He corrects himself firmly.*] No—"Mannock."

READER. "Afraid cannot dine to-night. Mannock." . . . Anything else, sir?

MANNOCK. No. . . . Yes. . . . Yes. . . . [READER *waits.*] Another telegram.

READER [*waiting*]. Yes?

MANNOCK. Lady Carchester, Enderways, Riley, Yorkshire.

READER [*murmuring to himself*]. Enderways, Riley, R–I–L–E–Y?

MANNOCK. Yes.

READER. Yorkshire. [*He waits.*

MANNOCK [*after a long pause*]. "I beg your pardon." [READER *says nothing.* MANNOCK *looks up.*] That's all.

READER. Oh, I beg—I see—I didn't understand. [*Writing*] "I beg your pardon."

MANNOCK. We had a—a discussion. I—I was wrong. I have found out since that I was wrong. This is—— [*He shrugs.*

READER [*pleasantly*]. A very graceful way of saying so, if I may be allowed——

MANNOCK [*to himself*]. Graceful!

READER [*after waiting*]. Signed? Or will she understand?

343

EXTRACTS FROM BRITISH & IRISH PLAYS

MANNOCK. She will understand. [*To himself, ashamed*] I think she
will understand. . . . All right, Reader. [READER *goes out*.
> [MANNOCK *walks slowly to his desk. For a little while he
> sits there, holding the letter in his hand.* . . .
>
> SALLY *is dead. He has killed her. No good explain-
> ing, apologising, whining, to a person whom you have
> killed. Let him be man enough to spare her that last insult.
> No, there's nothing to say. It was* EVERSLEY *and that
> damned tune that got into a man's head, and made him
> dream.* . . . *The sweetness of her in his dream! But
> that was twenty-five years ago. They're dead now; both
> dead.* . . . *But—Chancellor of the Exchequer! It will
> be in all the papers to-morrow. Chancellor of the
> Exchequer! What will the papers say? What will
> people say? Everybody will see it.* . . . SALLY *will see
> it. Will know, will understand. No, there's nothing
> to be said. That damned tune, that damned dream.
> O Sally, Sally, Sally! Don't! Don't come into my
> dreams again.* . . .
>
> *So for a little he sits, thinking. Then, with a bitter,
> contemptuous laugh, he tosses away his thoughts and
> comes back to the letter. Chancellor of the Exchequer!
> Briskly he dips his pen into the ink, and writes to the
> Prime Minister.*

10. MILES MALLESON (*born* 1888)

A Man of Ideas

Mr Miles Malleson is among the more powerful of our younger
dramatists, and he has one quality which places him above the
majority—he has, as an actor, a complete and intimate knowledge of the theatre. All his dramas and his comedies show his
skill in devising effective situations. In the little one-act play
A Man of Ideas the darkened room provides a fitting atmosphere
for the theme developed later, and there is 'theatre' of the best
in the snatching of the revolver toward the close. Mr Malleson
is, as most of the moderns, a man of ideas himself, one with clear-
cut convictions and the desire of expressing those convictions.
The treatment of the burglar in this play is not sentimental,
because it is based on reflections upon society and its conventions.
Sentimentalism is vague; here is truth to life and a firm humanitarian feeling. The scene given here follows upon a conversation
of Cartwright and Frank. A masked figure has been seen
wandering about the house. Fear has made it into a monster.
As this scene opens the figure has just been confronted by the two
watchers.

344

THE MODERN PERIOD

(*A Man of Ideas* was produced at the Court Theatre in 1913. The following passage is taken, by kind permission of the author and of the publishers, Messrs George Allen and Unwin, Ltd., from the edition of 1918.)

A STORY OF LIFE

CARTWRIGHT [*covering him with the pistol*]. Now just take that thing off your face, and put your hands up. [*He repeats his command.*] Take that thing off your face, and put your hands up—unless you want a hole in you! [THE FIGURE *seems to pull itself together—it stands up straight, facing* FRANK; *and then deliberately puts its hands behind its back.*] Come along! No nonsense! If you don't do what I tell you, I shall shoot. [THE FIGURE *remains perfectly still.*] I shall count three, and then I shall shoot! One . . . Two . . . Three! . . .

> [FRANK *never had any intention of shooting, and the sound of the " Three! " dies away, and still they are standing there. Unable to frighten the visitor into surrender,* FRANK *is nonplussed. Suddenly the newcomer speaks. The voice of an educated man, but low, with intense feeling.*

THE MAN. Shoot, go on! Shoot!

BILLY [*really rather frightened—his first burglar*]. I say, why don't you do what you're told?

THE MAN. Why don't you shoot . . . I want you to. But I'm damned if I can stand waiting like this . . . it . . . it gets on your nerves.

BILLY. What are you?

> [THE MAN *takes off his mask. He is about thirty years old. He has revealed the face of one who has suffered cruelly at the hands of the world, but all the suffering can't hide its refinement. He speaks perfectly good English in a voice that all the bitterness in it cannot make unmusical.*

THE MAN. What am I? A thief—a common thief—that's what I am. Why didn't you shoot? . . . I wanted you to. It would have been a way out. I'd have thanked you for it.

CARTWRIGHT [*cold, practical, and strong*]. Stay quite still where you are. . . . Billy, bolt the windows, will you? [*Billy does so.*] You'd better lock the door, too. [BILLY *locks the door.*] Put on the light. [*The electric switch is by the door, and* BILLY *does that too.*]

THE MAN [*when this has been done and after a considerable pause, in quite a different tone; there is an unexpected twinkle in his voice—like a star on a stormy night*]. Well? . . . *Now* what are you going to do? Send for the police, I suppose? . . . It's a mile's walk to the police-station, isn't it? . . . Are you on the telephone?

CARTWRIGHT [*shortly*]. No.

THE MAN. That's rather a nuisance. [*He talks half humorously, but one feels the man is utterly beaten and hopeless*]. I say, I'm afraid I'm an awful bother. . . . It's only just half-past one, isn't it?

345

Such an awkward time. [CARTWRIGHT *is silent. He really doesn't quite know what to do.* THE MAN *continues.*] It's lucky there are two of you. One of you'll have to stop with me here while the other goes into the town. [*As if it were a brilliant idea.*] Unless we all three stop here together?

CARTWRIGHT [*drily*]. Suppose you let *us* make the arrangements.

THE MAN. That's all right. I'm only talking for the sake of not keeping quiet. . . . Oh!

[*A sudden exclamation of pain. He passes a hand across his eyes, and has to support himself by a chair to prevent himself from falling. The other two watch him, half curiously, half suspiciously—he is not quite the sort of person they expected to catch. He has a struggle to pull himself together, and when he has done so he seems to have forgotten that he is not alone. All the half-impudent, half-humorous manner has dropped from him—he looks utterly broken. His eyes wander dully round the room. They light on the decanter and biscuits on the side-table.*

THE MAN. I say, d'you mind if I had some of those things? I haven't had anything since . . . some time the day before yesterday.

CARTWRIGHT [*his revolver still in his hand*]. Stay where you are. Billy, you might give him some.

[BILLY *puts some biscuits on a table before him.*

THE MAN. Thanks. [*He eats—badly in need of the food.*] . . . Could I have some whisky?

CARTWRIGHT. If you'd let us know you were coming, we'd have got some champagne up for you—and a decent meal.

THE MAN [*unconsciously sensible to the rebuff—rather as if he had been refused a second cup of tea at a party*]. I beg your pardon . . . I suppose it *is* rather rum—my asking for things. . . . I'm a thief. It's difficult to realise, somehow [*as if by way of explanation*]. This is the first time I've been caught. [CARTWRIGHT *motions* BILLY *to put the whisky before him—which he does.*] Thanks, it's kind of you. [*He pours out and drinks some.*] I assure you—I wanted it.

[*Then some more.*

CARTWRIGHT [*to* BILLY]. Look here—what *are* we going to do? I'd better go down into the town and fetch somebody up—or the other way on, if you like.

BILLY. I don't mind. I'll stay if you like.

THE MAN [*having drained his glass*]. I'll keep quite quiet.

CARTWRIGHT. I wish you would.

[THE MAN *chuckles appreciatively—strong whisky, on an empty stomach and a tired weak body, works quickly.*

BILLY. Which is the quickest way? Across the fields, or the road?

CARTWRIGHT. The fields—only you might miss your way. Perhaps I'd better go?

BILLY. I know the way quite well.

CARTWRIGHT. Sure?

BILLY. Quite.

CARTWRIGHT. Well, I ask you as your host. Will you go—or stay here?

THE MAN. Why don't you toss for it? [*His remark is thrown in so suddenly that they both turn to him.*] I'll lend you some money. [*He takes a coin from his pocket and throws it on the table.*] There it is! A halfpenny—the only one I've got in the world! So let me have it back, won't you?

> [CARTWRIGHT *and* BILLY *look at one another—a sort of "Well, I never!" look between them, and then by a sort of wireless message, they agree to carry out the little comedy.*

CARTWRIGHT. You're a man of ideas. [*He takes up the coin.*] Now, Billy. . . . Heads you stop—tails you go.

BILLY. Right.

> [BILLY *is on the left of the little table in the centre of the room.* CARTWRIGHT *on the right*, THE MAN *behind it, swaying gently.* CARTWRIGHT *spins the coin into the air.*

THE MAN. Stop! I've got another idea. I'm in form. I think it's the whisky. [*A very slight slurring of his words lends colour to the suggestion.*] Let's all three go down together. You won't be left alone with me, and you'll be able to keep one another company on the way home when—when our ways have parted.

CARTWRIGHT. By jove! you're right.

THE MAN. My ideas generally are. That's why I'm like this. . . . This stuff's getting into my head. . . . It's on an empty stomach, and I'm a wreck. . . . I say, would you mind if I sat in a comfortable chair and smoked a cigarette for a few minutes before we start? I haven't done it for months. . . . You can't think what a difference it would make.

CARTWRIGHT. Well, I'm damned!

BILLY. You're rather a rum 'un.

THE MAN [*a tired hopelessness in his voice*]. Am I?

CARTWRIGHT. You don't seem to realise what you are?

THE MAN. Does anyone? . . . What are *you*? [*With a little groan he sinks into an armchair. He looks up.*] I'm afraid I'm keeping you up; but, in a way, it's your own fault—you shouldn't have sat up for me. [*In the chair there is something so pathetic about him that the good-natured* BILLY *feels he wants to do something for him. Fetching a box of cigarettes, he takes them over to* THE MAN, *who takes one, smiling up into* BILLY'S *face rather like a grateful child.*] Thank you.

> [BILLY *fetches a match and lights* THE MAN'S *cigarette for him. Their eyes meet for a moment.* THE MAN *drops his—but* BILLY *stands watching him.*

CARTWRIGHT [*appreciating the boy's kindness, while laughing at him*]. Anything else you can do for him?

BILLY [*in a low voice*]. Poor devil! It's like a bad dream.

EXTRACTS FROM BRITISH & IRISH PLAYS

THE MAN. Why should *you* say that? . . . and it's not. [*He gives himself up gratefully to the luxury of the cigarette and the armchair. He leans back, stretches, and crosses his legs—but his knee makes its appearance through a great tear in his trousers, so he alters his position.*] It's like a beautiful dream; and I've dreamed it often—until I forgot what it was like. . . . To be in a decent room again. [*Without getting out of the chair he sits up in it so that he can see round the room.*] God! Decent pictures and a carpet. [*His eye is caught by a particular picture—he looks at it, critically.*] I like that one. It's good. I dare say it doesn't look so well in the daytime, but the light suits it. . . . It's Maeterlinck like that. [*His eyes drop again and travel slowly back across the rich carpet to his own torn trousers.*] It's taken me ten years to get like this. This stuff *is* getting into my head. . . . What a baby I am.

11. J. R. ACKERLEY (*born* 1897)

The Prisoners of War

The drama of the past decade has been tending more and more toward a static impression. The playwrights have been paying greater and greater attention to the subtler shades of character or to abstract movements which for true expression require the deepest care and the finest delicacy in treatment. *The Prisoners of War* is of this nature. The scene remains one from beginning to end. There is hardly any violent movement, and the close of the play is practically silent. This is a study in psychology, not in external action. It presents the mood of several prisoners of war, rendered nervous and irritable by their enforced leisure, despondent by their thoughts of the work they might have been doing. The central figure is Conrad, the most intellectual of all, and the play with profound effect shows us his gradual descent—his irritation at trifles, his feeling of isolation, and, finally, the complete breaking of his mind. The scene given below marks the height of the mental 'conflict.' Grayle has been Conrad's companion, has deserted him for the sake of others, and has thereby deepened Conrad's sense of loneliness. *The Prisoners of War* is undoubtedly one of the most effective plays which have been produced within the last few years.

(The passage given below is taken, by kind permission of the author, from the edition of 1925, published by Messrs Chatto and Windus.)

THE BREAKING-POINT

CONRAD [*ignoring her, taking off his mackintosh*]. What have I done to deserve this, Allan?

GRAYLE. What?

CONRAD [*now completely controlled*]. Your presence here.

GRAYLE [*flushing*]. I don't understand. I'm always here.

CONRAD [*hanging his coat behind the door*]. On the contrary, you haven't been near me for two days.

GRAYLE. Haven't I?

MADAME LOUIS. Ah, Allan has been looking after me.

CONRAD [*to* GRAYLE]. You don't mean to say you didn't realise it?   [*There is a mocking note in his voice.*

GRAYLE. Do you mind my being here?

CONRAD. Not a bit. [*He takes off his tunic.*] I only wondered why. You haven't come to forgive me, have you?

GRAYLE. Don't be silly.

CONRAD. Well, then—perhaps to ask forgiveness? [GRAYLE *is silent.*] I haven't got any money to lend, if that's what you want. [*Pause. He buttons his blazer on.*] Have you run out of cigarettes?

GRAYLE [*angrily*]. I suppose you've been talking to Tetford.

CONRAD [*surprised*]. Tetford?

GRAYLE. He said he was going to report [*he sneers on this*] me to you for "stealing" your fags.

CONRAD. So you *did* come up for cigarettes? I haven't heard a word from Tetford about it, as a matter of fact.

GRAYLE [*disbelieving*]. Then why did you mention it?

CONRAD [*breezily, hanging up his tunic*]. My dear fellow, I was only trying to think of different reasons for your presence here. I felt sure it couldn't be for the pleasure of seeing me. And apparently I was right. You say it was my cigarettes.

GRAYLE [*uncomprehensive as usual*]. Well, don't make a fuss, anyway. [*With a meaning glance at* MADAME LOUIS] I told Tetford that I'd let you know what I'd done. I'll put them back.
                                        [*He does so.*

CONRAD [*transferring pipe, etc., from his tunic to his blazer*]. Not at all. Keep them, by all means. They're there for visitors. The room too. I never look upon it as *really* mine.

GRAYLE. I suppose you're trying to be funny?

CONRAD. No, no. Only curiosity. I like trying to follow the workings of your brain. I suppose I had no right to ask really.

GRAYLE [*crossing to him*]. I say. For God's sake keep that for afterwards! Don't make a scene!

MADAME LOUIS. It is not with me you are angry, is it, Captain Conrad?

CONRAD. I'm not angry. Who said I was angry?

MADAME LOUIS. I thought you did not like me to be here, perhaps. You see, I have heard you do not like much the fair sex.
                            [*She gives him a ravishing smile.*

CONRAD. The fair sex? Which sex is that?

GRAYLE [*getting off the arm of his chair*]. He's not very well to-day, madame. Let's go downstairs. Tea must be ready.

MADAME LOUIS. I must go first to my room to prepare myself.

GRAYLE. Right-oh. [*He opens the door for her.*] I'll be downstairs waiting for you.

MADAME LOUIS. I shall not be long. *Au revoir, Monsieur le Capitaine.*

> [CONRAD *does not answer. He is looking at* GRAYLE. *She goes out.*

GRAYLE. I suppose you think the way you behaved was rather funny? It wasn't.

CONRAD [*his back to the window*]. No, it wasn't.

GRAYLE. I don't mind for myself, of course, but you might have waited until she was out of the room.

CONRAD [*like an echo*]. I suppose I might have.

GRAYLE. Of course you should. It was very rude. I don't know what she'll think of me now. [*Finding* CONRAD *so amenable, he has decided to let him off this time.*] Look here. I want to know where I stand.

CONRAD [*who appears to speak with difficulty*]. Where you stand . . .

GRAYLE. There's no need to go on repeating what I say. What did you mean about being surprised to see me?

CONRAD. I thought you weren't going to speak to me again?

GRAYLE. I didn't intend to. Every time we meet you grouse at something. I'm rather tired of it.

CONRAD. Then why did you come up?

GRAYLE. I thought we might come to some arrangement.

CONRAD. Why didn't you come alone?

GRAYLE [*evading*]. I'm having tea with Madame Louis.

CONRAD [*after a pause—passing a hand over his forehead*]. Oh, yes. Er—what were we talking about?

GRAYLE. Can't we come to some arrangement?

CONRAD. Some arrangement?

GRAYLE. Well, do you want me to continue coming to this room? You never treat me as if you do.

CONRAD. Does it matter much what I want?

GRAYLE. Of course it does. It's your room. I propose that if we are to share this room we share expenses too. [*Pause.*] Do you hear?

CONRAD [*as though waking up*]. What was that?

GRAYLE. I wish you'd listen. I say that if you don't want me to come here any longer I'll stay away; but if you *do* want me to go on sharing this room with you I must share expenses too. That's fair, I think.

CONRAD. How do you mean?

GRAYLE [*patiently*]. Why, that I pay for half the room, of course. Then I shan't be under any obligation to you as I am at present.

CONRAD. I see. And then you can bring up whomsoever you like?

GRAYLE. Yes.

CONRAD. And if we quarrel you can still use the room—conscientiously.

GRAYLE [*detecting a note he doesn't like*]. Now, don't start that.

CONRAD. And in course of time you'll probably look upon it as entirely yours and just let me use it on sufferance, or not at all. Is that it? [*He is trembling.*

GRAYLE. I shan't talk to you if you're going to start that sort of thing.

CONRAD [*controlling himself*]. I'm sorry. I suppose I'm not well. About the room. . . . You find it comfortable?

GRAYLE. It's better than the lounge downstairs.

CONRAD. Er . . . which half would you like? [*He laughs oddly.*

GRAYLE. Be sensible. [*There is a pause.*

CONRAD. Aren't you keeping Madame Louis waiting?

GRAYLE. I shouldn't be if you'd make up your mind.

CONRAD [*rapping on the window behind him*]. I'm not very good at riddles to-day.

GRAYLE [*turning away*]. Well, think it over, anyway.

CONRAD [*suddenly*]. Come here a moment.

GRAYLE [*turning*]. What is it?

CONRAD. I want to know something.

[GRAYLE *moves rather impatiently over to the chair by the table* (C.). CONRAD *comes down the room, his hands behind him, his eyes fixed on the carpet.*

GRAYLE. Well?

CONRAD [*looking at him from under his brows*]. Why did you apologise for me to Madame Louis?

GRAYLE. I didn't.

CONRAD. You said I was ill. Why?

GRAYLE. Well, you are, aren't you? You've just said so.

CONRAD. Come, come! That wasn't it. You were rather ashamed of me, weren't you?

GRAYLE. Well, yes, I was, if you want to know the truth. I couldn't let her go away with the idea that you meant to be rude.

CONRAD. So you apologised for me to that woman?

GRAYLE. You ought to be jolly grateful.

CONRAD [*his voice rising*]. You dared to apologise for me! You dared!

GRAYLE. Oh, for God's sake don't start that game!
[*He is about to go away.*

CONRAD [*seizing him by the wrists, his face livid*]. You were ashamed of me, and apologised—and then you want to come to some arrangement—some arrangement—about the room . . . only the room . . . just the room . . .

GRAYLE [*wrenching his left hand free*]. What the Hell! You and your bloody temper! Let go, will you?
[*He tries to push him away with his free hand.*

CONRAD. You apologised . . .

351

EXTRACTS FROM BRITISH & IRISH PLAYS

[GRAYLE *wrenches his other hand free and staggers back a pace*. CONRAD *hits him heavily in the mouth. He falls and lies there, lies there long enough for* CONRAD *to become suddenly frightened.* GRAYLE *gets up slowly, his mouth bleeding.*

GRAYLE. You swine!

CONRAD. I'm sorry.   [*He makes as though to help him.*

GRAYLE. Leave me alone, you beast! It was a foul blow!

CONRAD. I didn't mean . . .

GRAYLE [*hitting at him*]. Go to Hell! [*He staggers towards the door.*

CONRAD. I didn't mean it, Allan. I'm sorry I . . .

[GRAYLE *goes out, holding his mouth.* CONRAD *is suddenly overcome by a feeling of faintness, his face pales, and the muscles round his mouth twitch. He staggers, almost falls, but saves himself by clutching the back of the chair beside him.*

12. C. K. MUNRO (*born* 1889)

The Rumour

Mr C. K. Munro has made a name for himself among modern dramatists through his comedy *At Mrs Beam's*, but possibly his serious plays form his greatest contribution to the world of the theatre, for they are written in a new style, and have a different aim from the majority of the ordinary contributions to the theatre. The style may almost be called impressionistic, and the aim is to reveal not merely the story of a limited circle, but the international complications following on the activities of a group of men. In *The Rumour* a circle of small financiers decide to start gossip moving with a tale of intended attacks by the Lorians upon their neighbours, the Przimians. Step by step we follow the progress of this tale. It arouses the Lorians living in Przimia ; it agitates the Przimians themselves ; it engages the attentions of the major Governments; it leads to a world war ; and the result, save for the loss of millions of men, is very much as it was at the beginning. To convey this story over the foot-lights requires more than an ordinary degree of skill, and it is to Mr Munro's credit that he has been able by his impressionistic method to make the whole plot real and interesting, both in the theatre and in the study. In the scene given below appear Lennard, the Przimian representative of the Imperial Armament Association, Moodie, the British Attaché in Przimiprzak, and La Rubia, the representative of the Przimian Government.

(*The Rumour* was produced in 1922. The following extract is taken, by kind permission of the author, from the stage version published by Messrs W. Collins, Sons and Co., Ltd., in 1927.)

352

THE MODERN PERIOD

The First Result of Rumour

LENNARD [*dictating to his* SECRETARY]. " . . . In the event of a clash, I have no doubt that the Przimians will win, because it is to the interest of several of the Great Powers not only that they should not be destroyed, but that their territory should be extended at the expense of the Lorians. I am prepared, therefore, to supply them, on my own authority, with anything they may require. If they can't pay for it, some one else will. But the Lorians are another matter, and before accepting their contract, I should be glad of definite instructions from headquarters." Thank you.

> [*The* SECRETARY *rises and goes out, but returns a moment later and announces that* MR MOODIE *has arrived. He is shown in.* LENNARD *rises and they shake hands.*

MOODIE [*very spruce and cheerful*]. Ha, good morning, Lennard! How are you?

LENNARD. Very well, thanks. And you? You look brown.

MOODIE. Yes, rather. Last week-end I was up fishing in the Majadalla Lake. I needed a rest, I'd just come back from England, I've been having a pretty warm time just lately. . . . Anyhow, you see we brought that hasty little devil, La Rubia, round all right after all?

LENNARD [*vaguely*]. Yes. . . . So I understand.

MOODIE. Not such a bad bit of work. Poor old La Rubia, after all his talk we managed to make him toe the line pretty quick! . . . Yes, we can't have any tampering with British prestige. That's one thing we won't have. It's not, you'll understand, Lennard, that we want to coerce anyone. We don't; I don't. The British Empire has never stood for that sort of thing. It stands for self-determination and the freedom of small nations. But here it's a matter of *vital prestige*. We're acting on their behalf really. You see, we simply can't afford to let the prestige of the Simian people drop to the level they'd let it. But, do you know, even now, if you please, La Rubia's doing his best to hush up the fact that these orders have been placed, or any steps taken by way of preparation. Think of it! Trying to hide from the Lorians the fact that they'll get a damned good hiding if they try any of their games on! Well, I tell you I've seen to it that the Lorians know all right!

LENNARD. Yes, I expect they know all right, by now. . . .

MOODIE [*struck by his tone*]. Oh, why?

LENNARD. Well, if murders and massacres and shootings can tell them anything.

MOODIE. Yes, I know. I've been away, of course, but I heard something about that. . . . Yes—well, of course [*sinking his voice*]— I don't agree with that sort of thing, but between ourselves I don't mind telling you that I'm not sure it isn't one of the best things that could have happened. It'll show the Lorians that the Simians have some spirit left—even if their Government haven't. . . . Well,

I only hope I've been in time. I risked my soul in the bluff I used, about things being ready when they weren't. But I think—I say, I think it will be discovered that I've saved the situation, or rather it will *not* be discovered, because things never are in this world. People never get what they deserve!

[*The* SECRETARY *enters and announces the arrival of* MR LA RUBIA, *and a moment later he enters in a state of excitement.*

LA RUBIA. Good morning, gentlemen. I'm sorry to be so abrupt, but the situation demands it. Well, now, Mr Lennard, what d'you think of this! Of course I suppose you're a business man, and I suppose that's what you do in business, but really I think the British Government might be above such a thing.

LENNARD. But what—what is the——

LA RUBIA. We've been tricked, sir. The representatives of the British Government have tricked us, lied to us. That information about the Lorians was completely unfounded—not a word of truth in it. I've discovered the source of the report, so I know. The Lorians were as quiet as they've ever been. At a moment like that, the British Government must needs threaten to withdraw certain facilities that are vital to us if we don't strengthen our munitions supply and defences—all because some financiers are absurdly nervous.

MOODIE. La Rubia, I'm sorry to cut you short, but you're merely wasting time. I am no longer willing to argue with you as to the reasons which make us require you to take this action. I merely tell you that if you don't, we shall withdraw those facilities to which you have referred. You can choose which course you like.

LA RUBIA [*more slowly*]. Mr Moodie, let me put a question to you. If I can prove to you, on evidence that you cannot ignore, that the Lorians are not contemplating any attack, will you agree to withdraw your pressure?

MOODIE. If you could do such a thing, La Rubia, I might be willing to consider it. But unfortunately there is no possibility that you can.

LA RUBIA. Wait a minute, sir, wait a minute. I am contemplating a step which perhaps has not occurred to you. You are going to force us to load ourselves with a lot of stuff not only that we've no use for, but that it's highly dangerous for us to possess. Look at the brawls and killings there have been, that we've been unable to restrain, simply arising out of this foolish rumour. Already they've made the position very much more difficult. Your British firms set the example by making preparations as though there was going to be a siege, and some of ours take fright and do the same. All this makes things terribly difficult. And then on the top of this, suppose it gets known that we're placing large orders, there's no knowing what the effect may be. The situation is most delicate. For years now we've managed it with the greatest tact, and that is beginning to bear fruit. But suppose we do this and it gets known. That would be a first-class blunder. A very great deal is involved; and in the circumstances I have no course but one left, and that I am going to take. Here you and I, Mr Moodie, are quarrelling about what the Lorians are going to do. [*Suddenly pointing at* MR LENNARD] There, Mr Moodie, sits the man who can tell us! I ask you, Mr Lennard, in order to settle a matter which may involve the lives and happiness of thousands, to tell us what orders the Lorian Government has been placing with you recently!

[*The other two sit surprised,* LENNARD *looking very stern.*

LENNARD [*after a moment*]. I don't quite follow you, Mr La Rubia.

LA RUBIA. I ask you, Mr Lennard, in order to settle a matter in which a very great deal is involved, to tell Mr Moodie and myself what orders the Lorian Government has recently placed with you.

LENNARD [*shocked, in a remonstrative tone*]. But, Mr La Rubia, you don't really imagine, do you, that I can tell anyone—even my own Government—what contracts I have, across a table at an informal conference? Of course I can't. . . . Would you like me to disclose to the Lorians the contracts you are contemplating having to place with us? . . . Of course you wouldn't; and of course you know very well that I won't.

LA RUBIA [*excited*]. You mean to say you won't tell me? When, by a word now, you might save a dreadful catastrophe. You hold us both in the hollow of your hands and you play us against each other like pawns!

LENNARD. I do nothing of the sort. I am a mere man of business. I sell a certain kind of article, called munitions of war, for which the world appears to have a great need. I have no policy in these matters, except to maintain the reserve usual in business, though apparently not always usual in politics.

LA RUBIA. In politics, sir, we have to do with human beings, beings of flesh and blood, lit with the divine fire. To you a human being is nothing but an object to be destroyed by your munitions. You are a monster, sir; your company is a monster, stalking about the world like a Black Death, killing where it goes. You possess information which might save the lives of thousands, of tens of thousands of human beings, the happiness of a thousand homes. And you will not reveal it, because your *business* interests lie in another direction.

LENNARD [*perfectly calm*]. You are completely mistaken. As I have told you, in these matters I have no policy, except to keep faith with my clients and maintain the reserve as to their commitments, which every one of them—including *yourself*—desires. And do you suppose that such honesty pays? Do you suppose that if I threw honesty to the winds, and entered on a policy of juggling with your fears and hopes, I could not exact from you, and from all the rest of the powers of the world, an amount vastly greater than that which you now rush to give me? I'm afraid, La Rubia, that

355

while you may know all about politics, you don't know anything about business. And I begin to doubt your boasted acquaintance with human nature. . . .

LA RUBIA. Then you refuse to tell me?

LENNARD. Most certainly I do.

LA RUBIA. Very well, sir. Then my answer is this. . . . I refuse to act at the dictation of anyone in this matter, no matter what threats they may hold over my head. I will place no orders with you, and the British Government—and their representative—may swallow that as best they can. I bid you good-day, gentlemen.

[*He turns with a grand defiant gesture and walks rapidly towards the door.*

[*Enter* SECRETARY.

SECRETARY. Mr La Rubia, this is an urgent paper from your secretary. The messenger asked me to give it to you at once.

[LA RUBIA *takes the paper, and opens it. As he reads his attitude changes. The telephone meanwhile has rung.*

LENNARD. Yes. . . . Yes! . . . That's a strategic position, isn't it? . . . Yes. [*He puts down the receiver. To* LA RUBIA] Well? . . . The Lorian light troops have occupied the Zarina triangle, I'm told.

[*Slight pause.*

MOODIE [*leaping up*]. What? . . . [*After a moment, sinking down again*] Then I was too late! Too late after all. . . . Well, La Rubia? You see! You brought it on yourself. I told you so. I warned you. . . . Well, I did my best—that's one thing.

13. ST JOHN G. ERVINE (*born* 1883)

Mixed Marriage

Mr St John Ervine writes a propaganda play, " with a difference." His dramatic material is firmly embedded in the soil of life ; his theories and his aims are always kept subordinate to the matter of the theatre, to situation effect, and to characterization. In *Mixed Marriage* he writes a realistic play ; the figures in it are typical of actual persons who might have lived in Belfast, yet each of these figures is given just that touch of generalization which raises the play from the level of the sordidly naturalistic. The language is true to life, and at the same time has the turn of phrase which stamps it as the creation of its author. *Mixed Marriage*, in its sense of waste, secures genuine tragic impression. Michael, the Catholic, and old Rainey, the Orangeman, have agreed to do what they can to stamp out bigotry. Rainey has arranged to address a meeting at his Orange Lodge, when suddenly he finds that his son Hugh is engaged to Nora, a Catholic girl. His latent prejudices burst forth, and he goes to the Lodge not to utter words of peace, but to decry the " Papists." A riot ensues ;

356

soldiers are called out, and in their fire Nora, pitiful plaything of Fate, falls mortally wounded.

(*Mixed Marriage* was produced in 1911. The passage given below is taken, by kind permission of the author, from the play as published by Messrs George Allen and Unwin, Ltd., in 1914.)

THE CURSE OF RELIGION

MICHAEL. It's not enough fur a man an' a wumman til join han's. A want til see the whole wurl' at peace.

MRS RAINEY. Ye'll on'y git that be men an' weemen bein' at peace. Him an' her, Mickie, are bigger than the wurl', if ye on'y knew it. That man o' mine can't see fardher nor churches an' Or'nge Lodges, an' all the time there's men an' wimmen stan'in' about, waitin' fur somethin' til bring them thegither.

MICHAEL. Aw, but selfishness is the curse o' the wurl . An' it's the curse o' Irelan' more nor anny other country. They wur alwis thinkin' o' their selves, the men an' weemen that might ha' saved Irelan'. Whinivir a man's come near deliverin' Irelan', a wumman's stepp'd in an' destroyed him. It's alwis bin the way since the beginnin'. Alwis, alwis, alwis! There'll be no salvation fur Irelan' til a man is born that dussen care a God's curse for weemen. They're hangin' about the neck o' the lan', draggin' her down.

MRS RAINEY. Ye're blamin' us fur the follies o' men. Is Nora to blame acause my man's a fool?

RAINEY. A'm no fool. A must stick til the right. It's onnacherl fur a man an' a wumman til live in the same house an' worship in a differ'nt church.

MRS RAINEY. Sure, if they can live in the same lan' they can live in the same house. It's ony igner'nce an' wickedness an' men wi' foul tongues that makes it hard. John, ye'll be a good man, an' go til the Or'nge Hall the night, an' do yer best t' keep the peace.

RAINEY. A can't go.

HUGH. A'll go meself. A won't belave that the men o' Irelan' will let bigotry destroy them fur ivir.

MICHAEL. Ye can't go. Ye're not an Or'ngeman.

HUGH. A'll git in somehow. If A've spoiled the work, A can mend it again. . . .

MRS RAINEY. Now, jus' sit down, the whole o' ye. Dear-a-dear, it's the quare hard work fur a wumman, keepin' men at peace. If there wussen the like o' us in the wurl' ye'd be kickin' wan another iv'ry five minits. Now, what are ye goin' t' do about it all? Are ye goin' t' the Lodge, John?

RAINEY. A'm not.

MRS RAINEY. Is that yer last answer?

RAINEY. Ay, it is.

MRS RAINEY. It's a quare pity o' ye. Ye'll be sorry fur this, A tell ye.

RAINEY. A can't help that.

MRS RAINEY. Well, Mickie, an' what are you goin' t' do?

MICHAEL. A don't know. A'll have til think o' somethin'. A'm all throughover. What wi' the slap on the head an' this suddent trouble, A don't know what A'm doin'. A'm near broke wi' grief. A'm the one feels it most. A've dreamt o' this since A wus born, an' now it's near done, this comes an' destroys it. My God, Mrs Rainey, what a wurl'.

MRS RAINEY [*patting him on the back*]. Aw, keep yer heart up, Mickie. Mebbe, it'll be all right. A wish there wus Or'ngeweemen. A'd go meself in his place.

HUGH [*jumping up*]. A'm not an Or'ngeman, but A'll go. Hart issen nayther, an' if they'll let him in, they'll let me. A'll spake til them, an' put a stop til Hart's nonsense. A'm the one'll do it. A'll not let it be said the peace o' Irelan' was destroyed be the Raineys.

RAINEY. Ay, ye'll do a quare lot. Ye can't spake?

HUGH. A can spake as good as you.

MRS RAINEY. Aw, can't ye control yer tongues. Ye do too much spakin' atween ye. Ye're consated about yer spakin'.

HUGH. A've nivir spoke afore, but A'll spake the night. A will, A declare til God. A'll put a stap til bigotry.

RAINEY. Will ye tell them why A've refused til have anythin' more til do wi' it?

MRS RAINEY. What wud he be doin' that fur?

RAINEY. Naw, iv coorse not. Ye'll desave them as ye desaved me. D'ye think anny good'll come out o' that?

HUGH. It's noan o' their business who A marry.

NORA. A can't ondherstan' why a man an' a wumman can't git married wi'out iv'ry wan goin' out o' their wits?

MRS RAINEY. Och, they alwis do, dear. Sure, it's the way the wurl's made. Ye have t' put up wi' it.

TOM. It's a funny soart o' wurl' then.

HUGH. A don't belave the Or'ngemen are such fools as ye make out. They're brave sensible men, a lot o' them, if they wur on'y let alone be them that's supposed t' be their betters.

RAINEY. Will ye tell them why?

HUGH. It's not necessary. It's nathing t' do wi' it.

RAINEY. Then A'll go meself an' tell them. We'll see who can spake the best then.

MRS RAINEY. Aw, ye cudden go out on a night like this. Sure, ye're gettin' ould.

RAINEY. Lave me alone, will ye. Ye're all conspirin' agin me, but A'll bate ye yit. Gimme me coat, an' let me git out o' this.

MICHAEL. Ye'll have blood on yer han's, Mr Rainey, if ye do that.

RAINEY. A don't care, A tell ye. A'll put a stap t' this.

MRS RAINEY. Aw, give him his coat, an' let him go, the headstrong oul' man.

HUGH. A'll be left whin he comes back.

TOM. Ay, an' so will I.

RAINEY [to MRS RAINEY]. A suppose you'll be gone too?

MRS RAINEY. Naw, A think A'll be here. God help ye, ye'll need some one t' luk after ye.

RAINEY. Nathin'll stap me. A've made up me min'. Goodnight t' ye. [To NORA] Mebbe ye're satisfied, now, me fine girl?

MRS RAINEY. Lave her alone. Aren't ye content wi' the bad work ye've done wi'out proddin' her wi' a knife? G'long wi' ye, an' do yer dirty work, an' don't stan' there hurtin' a girl that nivir done you no harm.

RAINEY. She tuk me son thrum me.

MRS RAINEY. G'long wi' ye, an' make yer spache.

14. LENNOX ROBINSON (born 1886)

The Lost Leader

The art of Mr Lennox Robinson may be said to consist in the romantic—or wondering—treatment of the real. He does not pass, like Lord Dunsany, to unknown realms of the Orient, but, keeping close to his own native soil, enwraps the figures he sees there with a thin cloak of mystery. This tendency is excellently exemplified in *The Lost Leader*. The theme of this play has a peculiar interest. Into an ordinary, 'naturalistic' Irish setting there suddenly steps the person of Lucius Lenihan, an old man, at first seemingly the same as other old men. Gradually, however, it is hinted that this Lucius is none other than Parnell, not come to life again, but never dead, having lived in seclusion, unknown, for long years. And at the end we are left wondering, romance shedding a strange half-light on the Standing Stones of Knockpatrick. Mr Robinson's style well harmonizes with his theme and its treatment. His language is realistic, yet at times it takes on that shy, dreaming utterance which the Irish dialect is so well fitted to express, and which suggests the mystery in daily life. The passage chosen for representation here is that in which members of various parties meet to consult with the supposed Parnell.

(*The Lost Leader* was first produced at the Abbey Theatre, Dublin, in February 1918. It was published by Thomas Kiersey at the Eigeas Press, Dublin, the passage presented here being given with the kind permission of Mr Robinson.)

THE LIVING DEAD

PETER. Come in, Michael, come in. Now, Mr Smith, you have before you representatives of the three great parties. Of course you won't be so ignorant as to think that they represent all Ireland.

359

We're still wanting an O'Brienite, and a Southern Unionist, and a Labour man, and a Protestant Home Ruler, and a genuine die-hard Ulsterman, and a Devolutionist, and, and—oh, representatives of the other twenty or thirty parties. But this will do for a beginning.

SMITH. Yes. Three parties are as much as I can get hold of at once. [*To* MICHAEL] I think I heard you speaking at the meeting to-day?

MICHAEL. I was.

PETER. And did you win your match, Michael?

MICHAEL. We did to be sure.

PETER. And now you've dropped in to see Mr Parnell?

MICHAEL. I don't believe he's Parnell.

PETER. Sure none of us believe he is, that's why we're all here.

SMITH. Suppose he is. How will it affect you Sinn Feiners?

MICHAEL [*coolly*]. 'Twon't make any difference to us.

PETER. Now, now, Michael; even the English gentleman will hardly believe that.

MICHAEL. He can join us if he wants to.

PETER. 'Tis kind of you to say that, Michael.

SMITH. Won't he be a little apt to—to queer your pitch?

MICHAEL. What do you mean?

PETER. He means he'll be apt to play puck with you. What's your opinion, Major?

MAJOR. I'm not going to say anything to Mr O'Connor and his party.

PETER. Bedad, you're cutting yourself off from a lot of Ireland, Major. You're likely to feel lonely one of these days.

MAJOR. I—oh!   [*He breaks off for* LUCIUS *and* MARY *appear.*

ALL. Good evening, Sir, *or* Good evening, Mr Lucius.

LUCIUS [*coldly*]. Evening.

> [*There is a moment of embarrassed silence, the* MAJOR *is as uneasy as the rest.*

LUCIUS. Well, what do you all want? What do you want, Clancy?

CLANCY [*hastily*]. Oh—oh—nothing, sir.

LUCIUS [*to* MICHAEL]. Who are you, I don't know you?

MICHAEL. Michael O'Connor, sir.

PETER. We—we just dropped in to see you, Mr Lucius. I believe the Major here has—has a paper, some questions——

MAJOR [*quickly*]. No, no, I haven't, I—I mean I've lost it.

LUCIUS. I'm tired, I'm going to rest now for a couple of hours. I'll meet you at the Standing Stones on Knockpatrick in two hours' time.

MAJOR. What an absurd place. Why should we go there?

LUCIUS. Because I wish it.

MAJOR. No, but really—why not now, here——

LUCIUS [*turning away from him*]. Mind you are all there.

CLANCY [*submissively*]. I'll be there, sir, on the minute.

PETER. I'll be there too.

MICHAEL. And I.

MAJOR. I suppose I'll—I'll manage to come. But I must say——

LUCIUS. Very well. I shall expect you all. You needn't wait now. [*The men go towards the door.*

A VOICE OUTSIDE. Where is he? Bring me to him.

KATE'S VOICE. He's inside in the room. The door's just opposite you.

THE VOICE. Where is the man says he is Parnell?

PETER. Bedad, here's Tomas Houlihan.

SMITH. Tomas Houlihan! [*To* POWELL-HARPER] That's the blind man I was telling you about, the man who has always believed Parnell to be alive.

POWELL-HARPER. This is getting exciting.

[TOMAS HOULIHAN *comes in feeling his way with his stick. An elderly man but vigorous.*

HOULIHAN. Where is he? Where is he?

LUCIUS. Are you looking for me?

HOULIHAN. Are you the man that calls himself Parnell?

LUCIUS. I am Parnell. [*A pause. The blind man trembles.*

HOULIHAN. 'Tis twenty long years since I heard your voice, how do I know you are speaking the truth? It was in Carlow I heard you.

LUCIUS. I was a sick man that day.

HOULIHAN. You were, you were, but sick and all you had the power still. . . . You have power now, whoever you are. I feel it, I feel it. Oh, Almighty God, give me my sight for one minute only till I'll know are you the man I'm looking for.

LUCIUS. I'm old now, I'm white.

HOULIHAN. White or black I'd know you among a million. There was never your like or equal in the whole wide world. Let me feel your face, let me know are you my heart's darling come back to me at last or are you a liar and a cheat.

LUCIUS. Here is my hand.

HOULIHAN [*taking it*]. That's a firm hand, a strong hand, a ruling hand like the hand of a king.

LUCIUS. Touch my face.

HOULIHAN. I'm in dread.

LUCIUS. Do as I bid you.

HOULIHAN. If you're not Parnell—oh, my heart would break.

LUCIUS [*lifting* HOULIHAN'S *hand to his face*]. Feel it.

[HOULIHAN *passes his hand over his face.*

HOULIHAN [*in a whisper*]. The same noble brow, the eyebrows, the—oh! [*He staggers.*

LUCIUS. Sit here. [*He helps him to a chair.*

HOULIHAN [*kneeling before him and clasping his knees*]. Don't leave me, don't go from me. Twenty years and more I've been looking for you and I've found you at last. You've come back to me, you've come back to Ireland, oh, 'tis we were lonesome and lost without you, wandering and lost we were like strayed lambs. I've looked for you on the mountains and in the fairs till the eyes went from me looking for you, many a time I'd be in a crowd and I'd hear a voice and think 'twas you, many a night I'd be lying under a rick of hay and I'd stop awake all night in dread you'd pass by me and I asleep. Soon or late I knew you'd come back to me, I knew I'd find you, when I touched you just now 'twas like something going through me. Didn't I know well you weren't in that coffin! Ha! you fooled them all but you couldn't fool me. I knew better. Tomas the Omadhaun they called me, 'tis they were the omadhauns, the dirty cowards that betrayed you, but you came back to me at last, my heart's darling, you came back to me at last.

> [*The blind man is murmuring words of endearment half in English, half in Gaelic. The others begin to steal quietly out.*

MARY [*stopping* POWELL-HARPER]. Dr Harper, 'tisn't for us to interfere.

POWELL-HARPER. You believe? [*Pointing to the kneeling figure*] *That* has convinced you?

MARY. 'Tisn't for us to be interfering. We must leave it to God. And may He have mercy on—on Charles Stuart Parnell.

> [*They go out, the blind man is still kneeling at* LUCIUS' *feet.*

15. T. C. MURRAY (*born* 1873)

Maurice Harte

The Irish drama has taken many directions, but always it has based its strength upon the soil of Ireland. The characters, the situations, the language, the tragedy, and the humour of that land have provided infinite scope for a score of dramatists, each one of whom approaches his material in an individual way. Mr T. C. Murray, in *Maurice Harte*, has dealt with a problem of peasant tradition and personal conscience. Maurice Harte has been destined from his boyhood for the Church ; his mother, with the obstinacy of the peasant mind, has determined that, and every sacrifice has been made to further his studies. Suddenly, however, Maurice discovers he has no vocation ; he is determined not to become a priest ; and only severe external pressure forces him back to the seminary. The result is that he has a severe breakdown and dies ; only the keening is left for those who, in all love and affection, have caused his death. There is a certain starkness and simple grandeur in Mr Murray's treatment of this theme which immediately grips our attention. The characters stand out in bold outlines and the story has a strong primitive majesty. Part of the soul of peasant Ireland has been incorporated into his work.

(The passage given below is taken, by kind permission of the author, from the edition of the play published in 1912 by Messrs Maunsel and Co., Dublin.)

THE MODERN PERIOD

A Conflict of Custom and Conscience

MRS HARTE [*vaguely uneasy*]. Is there anything wrong with Maurice, Father?

FATHER MANGAN. Wrong?

MRS HARTE. For the love o' God, if there is, tell us!

FATHER MANGAN. The two of you must promise me first——

MICHAEL. What bad news have you, Father?

MRS HARTE [*trembling*]. Father, Father, don't keep me in this state! What's wrong with Maurice?

FATHER MANGAN [*after a slight pause*]. I'm sorry to tell you he's not returning to Maynooth. He has asked me to break it to you. He has no vocation.

> [*They look at him in stupefied amazement. There is a painful pause.*]

MRS HARTE [*hoarsely*]. 'Tis not true, Father.

FATHER MANGAN. It is, indeed, poor woman—only too true.

MRS HARTE [*crushed*]. A Mhuire! Mhuire! Mhuire!

FATHER MANGAN [*deeply moved*]. God help ye, poor people, I'm sorry in my soul for this!

MRS HARTE [*in a high note of despair*]. A Mhuire! Mhuire! Mhuire!

FATHER MANGAN. Don't, Mrs Harte, don't.. You must try to be more patient. . . . Think of Mary and her Seven Sorrows.

MRS HARTE [*wildly*]. Don't give me any of that talk, Father, and my heart breaking! What did we ever do to God that He should give us this blow?

MICHAEL [*gently*]. Whisht, Ellen, whisht.

MRS HARTE. The curse o' the Lord is on this house this day! . . . [*In sudden desperation*] You must make him go back, Father! For the love of Christ you'll do it. Won't you? Won't you?

FATHER MANGAN. I have already done all that any man could do.

MICHAEL [*piteously*]. Talk to him again, Father?

FATHER MANGAN. There is no use, Michael. His mind is finally made up. There is no moving him. You might as well try to move that mountain beyond.

MRS HARTE [*in a strained, unfamiliar voice*]. Do you know what it is you're saying at all, Father? Would you kill us dead this day?

FATHER MANGAN [*raising his hand as if to reason with her*]. Mrs Harte——

MRS HARTE [*hysterically*]. No! No! I won't believe it! I won't, till I hear it from his own two lips.

FATHER MANGAN [*persuasively*]. Mrs Harte——

MRS HARTE. I won't. I won't! I won't! He couldn't do it— he couldn't! You don't know him as we do. He couldn't—— No! No! No!

FATHER MANGAN. Don't blind yourself with false hopes. 'Tis very hard, I know, but God has His own wise ends in everything.

363

. . . Take the poor fellow gently. 'Tis wrong, remember, to interfere in such a matter. God comfort you both this day.

[*He goes out slowly. They sit in dreary silence. There is a long pause.*

MRS HARTE [*with a sob*]. Oh, Michael, Michael, isn't it terrible, terrible, altogether! . . . The Lord in Heaven pity us, 'tis the cruellest blow He ever sent on any man or woman since the beginning o' the world!   [*There is another pause. OWEN returns.*

OWEN [*entering*]. Upon my word I thought he'd never go. [*Seating himself at table.*] I'm dead out with the hunger.

[*They return no answer.*

OWEN. What's the matter at all?

[MRS HARTE *gives a broken sob.*

OWEN [*wonderingly*]. In the name o' God what's wrong with ye? What is it, father?

MICHAEL. Your brother that says he won't go back to Maynooth any more.

OWEN. Good God!

MICHAEL. He sent the priest to tell us.

OWEN. And, in God's name, why? Why, father? What happened him at all?

MICHAEL. Nothing. He says something about not having a vocation.

OWEN. Upon my soul, that's the strangest thing I ever heard in all my life! 'Tis mad he must be. Sure no man in his right senses would think o' doing the like o' that. Here he is himself.

[MAURICE *comes in deadly pale.* MICHAEL *remains with his back turned to him.* MRS HARTE *sits with drooped head, her apron to her eyes. She gives a stifled sob.*

MAURICE [*quiveringly*]. Mother? . . . Father?

[*They give no answer.*

[*Distressfully*] For God's sake don't let me see you like that. I can't bear it. 'Twill set me mad.

MICHAEL [*after a short pause*]. 'Tisn't true, Maurice?

MAURICE. It is, father. I would to God it weren't so.

MRS HARTE [*rising with the air of one who has formed a desperate resolution and going to him*]. And with the help o' God it won't be so either, Maurice. [*Persuasively*] You'll go back again? You will, Maurice? You will, boy?

MAURICE [*bracing himself*]. There is no use. I cannot.

MRS HARTE. But why? Why, Maurice?

MAURICE. There is no use explaining. You would not understand. It is a matter of conscience.

MRS HARTE [*striving to subdue her feelings*]. Look here, Maurice. I don't understand that kind o' talk at all.

MICHAEL [*with affected incredulity*]. Yeh, Ellen, 'tis only a passing notion he's got, you'll find. 'Twill be gone out of his mind like a bad dream to-morrow morning.

THE MODERN PERIOD

MAURICE. God help me this hour! I thought he made everything plain for you. He promised he would. . . . [*With impressive deliberation*] Listen to me. I can never go back. *Never*. It's impossible. . . . [*They look at him imploringly.*] Don't ask me. Don't, don't, I beg of you.

MICHAEL [*gravely*]. Maurice, would you break our hearts?

MAURICE. Father, would you have your son live a life of sacrilege? Would you, father? Would you?

MRS HARTE. That's only foolish talk. Aren't you every bit as good as the next?

MAURICE. I may be, but I haven't a vocation. . . . God has spoken to me in my soul.

MRS HARTE. In the name o' the Lord, boy, what kind o' talk at all is that? Aren't you that was ever and always so good and graceful as likely to make as good a priest as Father Kelly over any day? And wouldn't one like you, with all the wonders you did at the learning, make a better priest than many another of them?

MAURICE. That's only a mother's opinion. . . . My mind is finally made up.

MRS HARTE. Maurice, listen to me—listen to me!

OWEN [*restrainingly*]. Ah, let him alone, mother; let him alone. What's the use?

MRS HARTE [*passionately*]. What's the use, Owen? What's the use? Is it out o' your mind you are to ask? If it went out about him this day isn't it destroyed for ever we'd be? Look! the story wouldn't be east in Macroom when we'd have the bailiffs walking in at that door. The whole world knows he's to be priested next June, and only for the great respect they have for us through the means o' that, 'tisn't James M'Carthy alone, but every other one o' them would come down on us straight for their money. In one week there wouldn't be a cow left by us, nor a horse, nor a lamb, nor anything at all!

OWEN [*incredulously*]. Yeh, not at all, not at all. . . . Leave him alone.

MRS HARTE. Leave him alone, is it? If I will 'tis you'll have the good cause to regret it! . . . Look at them books [*producing the two account books from drawer*]. 'Tis about time you should know how we stand here.

OWEN [*staggered*]. Is—is this the way 'tis with us?

MRS HARTE. 'Tis so, and if your brother is going to bring the bailiffs to this house, tell me who's the girl would be willing to walk in here ever after with a fortune? Not Bride Burke, anyway—much as she thinks of you. [*To MAURICE*] God knows, I wouldn't be hard on you at all, but look at the great load o' money that's on us this day, and mostly all on your account.

MAURICE. Mother, don't make my cross harder to bear.

MRS HARTE. An' would you be seeing a heavier cross put on them that did all that mortal man and woman could do for you?

365

MAURICE. Look! I'll wear the flesh off my bones but in pity spare me!

MRS HARTE [*bitterly*]. And will you have no pity at all on us and on Owen here, that have slaved for you all our lives? And will you have no pity either on your three brothers who sent home, for your sake, the money that they earned in sweat and hard labour in the city of Boston? And, Maurice——

MAURICE. Don't, mother, don't, I beseech you.

MRS HARTE. Will you be talking wild, frightening, foolish talk about your conscience, and not think at all of them, nor of us, and all we done for you?

MAURICE [*distressfully*]. Mother! Mother!

MRS HARTE. You'll go back? 'Tis only a mistake?

MAURICE. Great God of Heaven! . . . you'll kill me.

MICHAEL. You'll go back, Maurice? The vocation will come to you in time with the help o' God. It will, surely.

MAURICE. Don't ask me! Don't ask me!

OWEN. 'Twould be better for you, Maurice. 'Twould surely.

MRS HARTE [*passionately*]. If you don't know how can I ever face outside this door or lift up my head again?

MAURICE [*piteously*]. Mother!

MRS HARTE. How could I listen to the neighbours making pity for me, and many a one o' them only glad in their hearts? How could I ever face again into the town o' Macroom?

MAURICE. Oh, don't!

MRS HARTE. I tell you, Maurice, I'd rather be lying dead a thousand times in the graveyard over at Killnamartyra——

MAURICE [*with a sudden cry*]. Stop, mother, stop! . . . [*There is a tense pause.*] I'll—I'll go back—as—as you all wish it.

[*He sinks into a seat with an air of hopeless dejection.*

MICHAEL [*drawing a long, deep breath*]. God bless you, boy, for that! I knew you would.

OWEN. 'Tis the best thing, surely.

MRS HARTE [*kneeling*]. Oh, thanks be to the Almighty God and His Blessed Mother this day!

16. PADRAIC COLUM (*born* 1881)

The Fiddler's House

The Irish world is treated by Mr Padraic Colum in no spirit of melodrama, hilarious mirth, or flamboyant excitement. Throughout his work there runs a note of quietness, almost of resignation, and in this respect perhaps the Maire of *The Fiddler's House* is his most representative creation. Maire has struggled to keep her home together—to prevent her artistically vagrant father, Conn, from falling back on his evil drinking habits, and

366

THE MODERN PERIOD

to provide shelter for her younger sister, Anne. After years of control old Conn starts dreaming once more of his famous battles with other minstrels. The conflict begins again, but it is a subdued, an almost static, conflict, and (in the scene given here) Maire, half questioning her own motives, bows to her father's desire and brings him with her own hands the fiddle he longs for. The subtle study of Maire's character, hardened by struggle, but gaining a deeper sympathy as years pass by, gives to *The Fiddler's House* an unquestioned beauty and grandeur.

(*The Fiddler's House*,[1] a revised play taken from *Broken Soil* (1903), was produced in 1907. The following extract is taken, by kind permission of the author, from the edition published by Messrs Maunsel and Co., Dublin.)

THE OLD FIDDLER'S DREAMS

CONN [*passionately, starting up*]. I'll go out of the house.

MAIRE. Let you stay here.

CONN [*going towards entrance*]. I'll go out of the house, I tell you.

MAIRE. No.   [CONN *goes over to the fire.*

CONN. God help me that ever came into this country at all. [*He sits down on the armchair, his hands resting on his stick.*] I had friends once, and was well thought of ; I can tell you that, my daughter.

MAIRE. I know that.

CONN. Well, you can have your own way with me now.

MAIRE. Why can't you stay here? There's lots to be done here. Our fields are a laughing-stock to the neighbours, they're that poor and wasted. Let us put all our minds into working, and have a good place of our own.

CONN. Ay, and the grabbers and informers of this place would think well of you then.

MAIRE. Who do you call grabbers and informers?

CONN. The people of this place. The people *you* want to shine before.

MAIRE. I don't want to shine before the people.

CONN. I'm not saying against you, Maire.

MAIRE. You're wrong in thinking I want to shine at all.

CONN. Sure you go to every dance and ceilidh; and to every house where you can show off your face, and dancing and conversation.

MAIRE. Do I ? Maybe I do. Every girl does the like.

CONN. I'm not saying against it.   [*Pause.*

MAIRE. You think I'm like yourself, wanting the praise of the people.

CONN. And what's the harm if you do?

[1] Copyright 1916 in U.S.A. by the Macmillan Company, New York.

367

MAIRE. No harm at all. But I don't go to houses to show myself off.

CONN. Troth and you do, Maire.

[*He rises and goes towards the entrance, and remains looking out.*

MAIRE. I won't believe it.

[*She goes to the settle.* ANNE *comes in.* ANNE *goes to the glass to fix her hair.*

CONN. Had you a good night at Moynihan's, Anne ?

ANNE. A sort of a good night.

CONN. I was going to tell you about a man I met last night. He had a song about your grandmother.

ANNE. Was grandmother a great beauty, father?

CONN. Honor Gilroy had good looks, and indeed she made the most of them.

MAIRE. It's likely there was some to tell her that she was showing off.

CONN. No one was to her liking unless they praised her.

ANNE. Ah, well, a fiddler ought to forgive that to a woman.

MAIRE. Fiddlers and women are all alike, but don't say that to him.　　　　　[ANNE *goes to* MAIRE *and sits beside her.*

CONN [*speaking to both*]. Well, Honor Gilroy wasn't the worst maybe.

MAIRE. And fiddlers and women oughtn't be hard on each other.

CONN. Do you say that, Maire?

MAIRE [*rising and going to him*]. I say it, father.

CONN. God forgive me if I vexed you, Maire.

ANNE. It's clearing up now, father, and you ought to go out to James. [CONN *turns to the door. He remains in the doorway.* ANNE *rises and goes to* MAIRE.] What did you say to him?

MAIRE [*looking at* CONN]. He doesn't feel it at all. Father will always be the fiddler, no matter what we say.

ANNE. Maire. Come and talk to me. [*They sit at fire.*] I was talking to James. He'll never be happy until we're under the one roof.　　　　　[MAIRE *clasps* ANNE'S *hands passionately.*

MAIRE [*with cry*]. Anne, daughter, I'll be very lonesome for you.

ANNE. But sure I won't be far off, Maire.

MAIRE. Ay, but it's terrible to face things alone.

[JAMES *has come to the door.* CONN *and* JAMES *have been talking. They turn in.*

CONN. But I'll be glad enough to have the scythe in my hands after it all, James.

JAMES. Anne was telling me how you took the victory from Connaught.

CONN. Still I'm sorry for him! That poor Heffernan! He'll never hold up his head again.

JAMES. Sure I'd have it in a ballad that would be sung in his own town. It would be well worth putting into a ballad.

CONN. Well indeed, it would make a right good ballad, James.

JAMES. I'd like to make a ballad about it, that would be sung all over Connaught.

CONN. And why wouldn't you do it, James Moynihan? Sure it would be the making of you. It would be sung all over Ireland, and your name to it. Do you hear that, Maire? Do you hear that, Anne?

JAMES. I'm saying that I'd like to do a ballad about your father's victory.

CONN. Maybe you could have it this night week, James?

ANNE. Will it be a poem or a ballad, James?   [ANNE *goes to him.*

CONN. If you had it this night week, we could bring the boys to the place. What do you say to that, Maire? We'll bring the boys here this night week to hear James Moynihan's ballad.

MAIRE. I was thinking of the Feis at Ardagh.

CONN. The Feis at Ardagh?

MAIRE. Maybe you'll be going to it this night week.

CONN. Sure you're not joking with me, Maire?

MAIRE. No.   [*She rises.*

CONN. God forgive me, Maire, if I vexed you.

[MAIRE *goes up to* CONN'S *room.*

CONN. Anne, jewel, had Maire anything to say about Ardagh?

ANNE. We weren't talking about that at all.

JAMES. Play me a rouse on the fiddle, and maybe the ballad will come into my head.   [MAIRE *comes down, a fiddle in her hands.*

MAIRE. Here's the fiddle that was your favourite, the Granard fiddle.

CONN. And this is the fiddle I'll bring with me to Ardagh.

ANNE. And is he going to Ardagh?

JAMES. And what about the ballad, Mister Hourican?

CONN. I leave it all to Maire now. How well she bethought of the Granard fiddle.

MAIRE. Father, we were always together.

[*She hands him the fiddle.* CONN, MAIRE, JAMES, ANNE, *are at table.*

17. SEAN O'CASEY (*born* 1885 (?))

The Plough and the Stars

That vitality is still springing forth in the sphere of Irish drama, and that there are still independent avenues of approach to the life of Ireland, has been nowhere more strikingly proved than by the plays of Mr Sean O'Casey. With a startling realism he has done for the poor in Dublin what others have done for the peasantry, and his strength, like that of so many of his compatriots, develops out of his intimate knowledge of the material with which he is dealing and out of his determination to keep true to the facts he observes. There is a rougher note in Mr O'Casey's work than is to be observed in the plays written by the followers of Synge, but that rougher note is made necessary by the characters whom he places on the stage. Clearly his whole creative production is dominated by the fatal days of Easter week 1916, and it is largely the reflection of this struggle upon ordinary existence to which he strives to give dramatic form. In the scene given below Jack Clitheroe is a commandant in the Irish Citizen Army, Nora is his wife, and Captain Brennan is of the Irish Citizen Army.

(*The Plough and the Stars*[1] was produced at the Abbey Theatre in 1926. The following passage is taken, by kind permission of the author and of the publishers, Messrs Macmillan and Co., Ltd., from the edition of that year.)

THE ETERNAL STRIFE

NORA. You haven't sung me a song since our honeymoon. Sing me one now, do . . . please, Jack!

CLITHEROE. What song? *Since Maggie Went Away?*

NORA. Ah, no, Jack, not that; it's too sad. *When You Said You Loved Me.*

[*Clearing his throat,* CLITHEROE *thinks for a moment, and then begins to sing.* NORA, *putting an arm around him, nestles her head on his breast and listens delightedly.*

CLITHEROE [*singing verses following to the air of " When You and I were Young, Maggie "*].

> Th' violets were scenting th' woods, Nora,
>   Displaying their charm to th' bee,
> When I first said I lov'd only you, Nora,
>   An' you said you lov'd only me!
>
> Th' chestnut blooms gleam'd through th' glade, Nora,
>   A robin sang loud from a tree,
> When I first said I lov'd only you, Nora,
>   An' you said you lov'd only me!
>
> Th' golden-rob'd daffodils shone, Nora,
>   An' danc'd in th' breeze on th' lea;
> When I first said I lov'd only you, Nora,
>   An' you said you lov'd only me!
>
> Th' trees, birds an' bees sang a song, Nora,
>   Of happier transports to be,
> When I first said I lov'd only you, Nora,
>   An' you said you lov'd only me!

[NORA *kisses him.*

[1] Copyright 1926 in U.S.A. by the Macmillan Company, New York.

THE MODERN PERIOD

[*A knock is heard at the door, right; a pause as they listen.* NORA *clings closely to* CLITHEROE. *Another knock, more imperative than the first.*

CLITHEROE. I wonder who can that be, now?

NORA [*a little nervous*]. Take no notice of it, Jack; they'll go away in a minute.   [*Another knock, followed by a voice.*

VOICE. Commandant Clitheroe, Commandant Clitheroe, are you there? A message from General Jim Connolly.

CLITHEROE. Damn it, it's Captain Brennan.

NORA [*anxiously*]. Don't mind him, don't mind, Jack. Don't break our happiness. . . . Pretend we're not in. . . . Let us forget everything to-night but our two selves!

CLITHEROE [*reassuringly*]. Don't be alarmed, darling; I'll just see what he wants, an' send him about his business.

NORA [*tremulously*]. No, no. Please, Jack; don't open it. Please, for your own little Nora's sake!

CLITHEROE [*rising to open the door*]. Now don't be silly, Nora.

[CLITHEROE *opens door, and admits a young man in the full uniform of the Irish Citizen Army—green suit; slouch green hat caught up at one side by a small Red Hand badge; Sam Brown belt, with a revolver in the holster. He carries a letter in his hand. When he comes in he smartly salutes* CLITHEROE. *The young man is* CAPTAIN BRENNAN.

CAPTAIN BRENNAN [*giving the letter to* CLITHEROE]. A dispatch from General Connolly.

CLITHEROE [*reading. While he is doing so,* BRENNAN'S *eyes are fixed on* NORA, *who droops as she sits on the lounge*]. "Commandant Clitheroe is to take command of the eighth battalion of the I.C.A., which will assemble to proceed to the meeting at nine o'clock. He is to see that all units are provided with full equipment: two days' rations and fifty rounds of ammunition. At two o'clock A.M. the army will leave Liberty Hall for a reconnaissance attack on Dublin Castle.—Com.-Gen. Connolly."

CLITHEROE. I don't understand this. Why does General Connolly call me Commandant?

CAPTAIN BRENNAN. Th' Staff appointed you Commandant, and th' General agreed with their selection.

CLITHEROE. When did this happen?

CAPTAIN BRENNAN. A fortnight ago.

CLITHEROE. How is it word was never sent to me?

CAPTAIN BRENNAN. Word was sent to you. . . . I meself brought it.

CLITHEROE. Who did you give it to, then?

CAPTAIN BRENNAN [*after a pause*]. I think I gave it to Mrs Clitheroe, there.

CLITHEROE. Nora, d'ye hear that?   [NORA *makes no answer.*

CLITHEROE [*there is a note of hardness in his voice*]. Nora . . .

371

Captain Brennan says he brought a letter to me from General Connolly, and that he gave it to you. . . . Where is it? What did you do with it?

NORA [*running over to him, and pleadingly putting her arms around him*]. Jack, please Jack, don't go out to-night an' I'll tell you; I'll explain everything. . . . Send him away, an' stay with your own little red-lipp'd Nora.

CLITHEROE [*removing her arms from around him*]. None o' that nonsense, now; I want to know what you did with th' letter?

[NORA *goes slowly to the lounge and sits down.*

CLITHEROE [*angrily*]. Why didn't you give me th' letter? What did you do with it? . . . [*He shakes her by the shoulder.*] What did you do with th' letter?

NORA [*flaming up*]. I burned it, I burned it! That's what I did with it! Is General Connolly an' th' Citizen Army goin' to be your only care? Is your home goin' to be only a place to rest in? Am I goin' to be only somethin' to provide merry-makin' at night for you? Your vanity'll be th' ruin of you an' me yet. . . . That's what's movin' you: because they've made an officer of you, you'll make a glorious cause of what you're doin', while your little red-lipp'd Nora can go on sittin' here, makin' a companion of th' loneliness of th' night!

CLITHEROE [*fiercely*]. You burned it, did you? [*He grips her arm.*] Well, me good lady——

NORA. Let go—you're hurtin' me!

CLITHEROE. You deserve to be hurt. . . . Any letther that comes to me for th' future, take care that I get it. . . . D'ye hear—take care that I get it!

[*He goes to the chest of drawers and takes out a Sam Brown belt, which he puts on, and then puts a revolver in the holster. He puts on his hat, and looks towards NORA.*

CLITHEROE [*at door, about to go out*]. You needn't wait up for me; if I'm in at all, it won't be before six in th' morning.

NORA [*bitterly*]. I don't care if you never come back!

CLITHEROE [*to* CAPTAIN BRENNAN]. Come along, Ned.

[*They go out ; there is a pause. . . . There is a gentle knock at door, right, which opens, and* MOLLSER *comes into the room. She is about fifteen, but looks to be only about ten, for the ravages of consumption have shrivelled her up. She is pitifully worn, walks feebly, and frequently coughs. She goes over to* NORA.

MOLLSER [*to* NORA]. Mother's gone to th' meetin' an' I was feelin' terrible lonely, so I come down to see if you'd let me sit with you, thinkin' you mightn't be goin' yourself. . . . I do be terrible afraid I'll die sometime when I'm be meself. . . . I often envy you, Mrs Clitheroe, seein' th' health you have, an' th' lovely place you have here, an' wondherin' if I'll ever be sthrong enough to be keepin' a home together for a man. Oh, this must be some more o' the Dublin Fusiliers flyin' off to the front.

> [*Just before* MOLLSER *ceases to speak, there is heard in the distance the music of a brass band playing a regiment to the boat on the way to the front. The tune that is being played is " It's a Long Way to Tipperary" ; as the band comes to the chorus the regiment is swinging into the street by* NORA'S *house, and the voices of the soldiers can be heard lustily singing the chorus of the song.*

" It's a long way to Tipperary, it's a long way to go;
It's a long way to Tipperary, to th' sweetest girl I know!
Good-bye Piccadilly, farewell Leicester Square.
It's a long way to Tipperary, but my heart's right there!"

> [NORA *and* MOLLSER *remain silently listening. As the chorus ends, and the music is faint in the distance again,* BESSIE BURGESS *appears at door, right, which* MOLLSER *has left open.*

BESSIE [*speaking in towards the room*]. There's th' men marchin' out into th' dhread dimness o' danger, while th' lice is crawlin' about feedin' on th' fatness o' the land! But yous'll not escape from th' arrow that flieth be night, or th' sickness that wasteth be day. . . . An' ladyship an' all, as some o' them may be, they'll be scatthered abroad, like th' dust in th' darkness!

> [BESSIE *goes away ;* NORA *steals over and quietly shuts the door. She comes back to the lounge and wearily throws herself on it beside* MOLLSER.

MOLLSER [*after a pause and a cough*]. Is there anybody goin', Mrs Clitheroe, with a titther o' sense?

18. SIR JAMES M. BARRIE (*born* 1860)

A Kiss for Cinderella

Sir James Barrie aims at charm and fancy and whimsicalness. He comes as near as any modern dramatist to that atmosphere out of which was created the Elizabethan romantic comedy. Just as Puck and Oberon are at home with Bottom and his companions, Lob and his midsummer forest seem real things in *Dear Brutus*. Part of this atmosphere Sir James Barrie secures by making concrete the fancies of the mind, by mingling together the dream and the reality. In *A Kiss for Cinderella* there are two Cinderellas—the little waif who struggles to keep herself alive and the Lady Cinderella who confidently awaits the coming of the flunkey with his great ' invite.' The fairy-tale has entered into the common London world, or that London world has taken on the fashion of an old wives' tale. A dingy street may bear the aura of romance and elves sport in the silent glades of

Kensington Gardens after the prams and their attendants have moved homeward. A slight touch of sentimentalism seems to mar some of Sir James Barrie's best work, but his humour is perfect and his skill in weaving the two worlds thus together has enabled him to establish in modern English dramatic literature an almost unique type of expression.

(*A Kiss for Cinderella*[1] was produced in 1916. The following passage is taken, by kind permission of the author, from the edition of 1920, published by Messrs Hodder and Stoughton, Ltd.)

THE POLICEMAN AND CINDERELLA

POLICEMAN [*in his winding-sheet*]. I've all run to beard.

CINDERELLA [*the ever-ready*]. I have a ointment for the hair; it is my own invention. The price is a penny.

POLICEMAN [*gruffly*]. Beard, please.

CINDERELLA. I've got some voice drops.

POLICEMAN. Beard, please.

CINDERELLA [*as she prepares the lather*]. Is the streets quiet?

POLICEMAN [*cunningly*]. Hereabouts they are; but there's great doings in the fashionable quarters. A ball, I'm told.

CINDERELLA [*gasping*]. You didn't see no peculiar person about in this street?

POLICEMAN. How peculiar?

CINDERELLA. Like a—a flunkey?

POLICEMAN. Did I now—or did I not?

CINDERELLA [*eagerly*]. He would be carrying an invite maybe; it's a big card.

POLICEMAN. I can't say I saw him.

[*Here an astonishing thing happens. The head of a child rises from one of the boxes. She is unseen by either of the mortals.*]

CINDERELLA [*considering the beard*]. How do I start with the like of this?

POLICEMAN. First you saws. . . .

[*She attempts to saw. The beard comes off in her hand.*]

CINDERELLA [*recognising his face*]. You!

POLICEMAN [*stepping triumphantly out of his disguise*]. Me!

[*As sometimes happens, however, the one who means to give the surprise gets a greater. At sight of his dreaded uniform the child screams, whereat two other children in other boxes bob up and scream also. It is some time before the policeman can speak.*]

So that's what the boxes was for!

CINDERELLA [*feebly*]. Yes.

POLICEMAN [*portentously*]. Who and what are these phenomenons?

CINDERELLA [*protectingly*]. Don't be frightened, children. Down!

[1] Copyright 1920 in U.S.A. by Messrs Charles Scribner's Sons, New York.

374

THE MODERN PERIOD

[*They disappear obediently.*

There's no wrong in it. They're just me trying to do my bit. It's said all should do their bit in wartime. It was into a hospital I wanted to go to nurse the wounded soldiers. I offered myself at every hospital door, but none would have me, so this was all I could do.

POLICEMAN. You're taking care of them? [*She nods.*] Sounds all right. Neighbours' children?

CINDERELLA. The brown box is. She's half of an orphan, her father's a blue-jacket, so, of course, I said I would.

POLICEMAN. You need say no more. I pass little blue-jacket.

CINDERELLA. Those other two is allies. She's French—and her's a Belgy. [*Calls.*] Marie-Therese! [*The* FRENCH CHILD *sits up.* Speak your language to the gentleman, Marie-Therese.

MARIE. *Bon soir, monsieur—comment portez-vous ? Je t'aime.*
[*She curtsies charmingly to him from the box.*

POLICEMAN. Well, I'm ——d !

CINDERELLA. Delphine. [*The* BELGIAN *looks up.* Make *votre* bow.

Gladys. [*The* ENGLISH CHILD *bobs up.*

A friend, Gladys. [GLADYS *and the* POLICEMAN *grin to each other.*

GLADYS. What cheer!

CINDERELLA. Monsieur is a Britain's defender.

MARIE. *Oh, là, là ! Parlez-vous français, monsieur ? Non !* I blow you two kisses, monsieur—the one is to you [*kisses hand*] to keep, the other you will give—[*kisses hand*] to Kitch.

POLICEMAN [*writing*]. Sends kiss to Lord Kitchener.

CINDERELLA. She's the one that does most of the talking.

POLICEMAN [*who is getting friendly*]. I suppose that other box is an empty. [CINDERELLA'S *mouth closes.* Is that box empty?

CINDERELLA. It's not exactly empty.

POLICEMAN. What's inside?

CINDERELLA. She's the littlest.
[*The* CHILDREN *exchange glances and she is severe.*

Couchy. [*They disappear.*

POLICEMAN. An ally?

CINDERELLA. She's—she's—Swiss.

POLICEMAN [*lowering*]. Now then!

CINDERELLA. She's not exactly Swiss. You can guess now what she is.

POLICEMAN [*grave*]. This puts me in a very difficult position.

CINDERELLA [*beginning to cry*]. Nobody would take her. She was left over. I tried not to take her. I'm a patriot, I am. But there she was—left over—and her so terrible little—I couldn't help taking her.

POLICEMAN. I dunno. [*Quite unfairly*] If her folk had been in your place and you in hers, they would have shown neither mercy nor pity for you.

375

CINDERELLA [*stoutly*]. That makes no difference.

POLICEMAN [*was this the great moment?*]. I think there's something uncommon about you.

CINDERELLA [*pleased*]. About *me*?

POLICEMAN. I suppose she's sleeping?

CINDERELLA. Not her!

POLICEMAN. What's she doing?

CINDERELLA. She's strafing!

POLICEMAN. Who's she strafing?

CINDERELLA. Very likely you. She misses nobody. You see I've put some barb-wire round her box.

POLICEMAN. I see now.

CINDERELLA. It's not really barb-wire. It's worsted. I was feared the wire would hurt her. But it just makes a difference.

POLICEMAN. How do the others get on with her?

CINDERELLA. I makes them get on with her. Of course there's tongues out, and little things like that.

POLICEMAN. Were the foreign children shy of you at first?

CINDERELLA. Not as soon as they heard my name. " Oh, are you Cinderella? " they said, in their various languages—and " When's the ball? " they said.

POLICEMAN. Somebody must have telled them about you.

CINDERELLA [*happy*]. Not here. They had heard about me in their foreign lands. Everybody knows Cinderella: it's fine. Even her—[*indicating* GERMAN] the moment I mentioned my name— " Where's your ugly sisters? " says she, looking round.

POLICEMAN. Sisters? It's new to me, your having sisters.

[*He produces his notebook.*

CINDERELLA [*uneasily*]. It's kind of staggering to me, too. I haven't been able to manage them yet, but they'll be at the ball.

POLICEMAN. It's queer.

CINDERELLA. It *is* queer.

POLICEMAN [*sitting down with her*]. How do you know this ball's to-night?

CINDERELLA. It had to be some night. You see, after I closes my business I have chats with the children about things, and naturally it's mostly about the ball. I put it off as long as I could, but it had to be some night—and this is the night.

POLICEMAN. You mean it's make-believe?

CINDERELLA [*almost fiercely*]. None of that!

POLICEMAN [*shaking his head*]. I don't like it.

CINDERELLA [*shining*]. You wouldn't say that if you heard the blasts on the trumpet and loud roars of " Make way for the Lady Cinderella! " [*Three heads pop up again.*

POLICEMAN. Lady?

CINDERELLA [*in a tremble of exultation*]. That's me. That's what you're called at royal balls. Then loud huzzas is heard outside from the excited popu-lace, for by this time the fame of my beauty has

THE MODERN PERIOD

spread like wildfire through the streets, and folks is hanging out at windows and climbing lamp-posts to catch a sight of me

[Delight of the CHILDREN.

POLICEMAN. My sakes, you see the whole thing clear!

CINDERELLA. I see it from beginning to end—like as if I could touch it—the gold walls and the throne, and the lamp-posts and the horses.

POLICEMAN. The horses?

CINDERELLA. . . . Well, the competitors. The speeches—everything. If only I had my invite! That wasn't a knock at the door, was it?

POLICEMAN [*so carried away that he goes to see*]. No.

CINDERELLA [*vindictively*]. I dare say that flunkey's sitting drinking in some public-house.

> [*Here* MARIE-THERESE *and* GLADYS, *who have been communicating across their boxes, politely invite the* POLICEMAN *to go away.*

MARIE. *Bonne nuit, monsieur.*

GLADYS. Did you say you was going, mister?

POLICEMAN. They're wonderful polite.

CINDERELLA. I doubt that's not politeness. The naughties—they're asking you to go away.

POLICEMAN. Oh!

[He rises with hauteur.

CINDERELLA. You see we're to have a bite of supper before I start—to celebrate the night.

POLICEMAN. Supper with the kids! When I was a kid in the country at Badgery—— You've done it again!

CINDERELLA. Done what?

POLICEMAN [*with that strange feeling of being at home*]. I suppose I would be in the way?

CINDERELLA. There's not very much to eat. There's just one for each.

POLICEMAN. I've had my supper.

CINDERELLA [*seeing her way*]. Have you? Then I would be very pleased if you would stay.

POLICEMAN. Thank you kindly.

> [*She prepares the table for the feast. Eyes sparkle from the boxes.*

CINDERELLA [*shining*]. This is the first party we've ever had. Please keep an eye on the door in case there's a knock.

> [*She darts into her bedroom, and her charges are more at their ease.*

MARIE [*sitting up, the better to display her nightgown*]. *Monsieur, monsieur, voilà!*

GLADYS. Cinderella made it out of watching a shop window.

POLICEMAN [*like one who has known his hostess from infancy*]. Just like her.

MARIE [*holding up a finger that is adorned with a ring*]. Monsieur!

GLADYS [*more practical*]. The fire's going out.

POLICEMAN [*recklessly*]. In with another penny. [*He feeds the fire with that noble coin.*] Fellow-allies, I'm going to take a peep into the German trench! Hah!

19. J. M. SYNGE (1871–1909)

Deirdre of the Sorrows

Synge is undoubtedly better known for his tragic *Riders to the Sea* and for his comic *Playboy of the Western World* than for *Deirdre of the Sorrows*, yet in many respects his is the most powerful of all the many efforts made to dramatize that most poignant of all Irish legends. He has been able to see Deirdre and Naisi neither as mythical visions, nor as people of our own times; his strength lies in the fact that these two ill-starred lovers with those who surround them are viewed half realistically, half through the spectacles of romance. To a certain extent Synge here follows the line taken by Shakespeare in *King Lear*. The legend is a legend; there are many situations which constantly emphasize the mythical quality of the original story; the characters are conceived partly as men and women of Shakespeare's day, partly in terms of the heroic. In Synge's play it will be noted what aid he received from his peculiar Irish prose. The words are English, but the Erse background of thought and feeling peers through those words to give a strange poetic atmosphere to the whole.

(*Deirdre of the Sorrows* was produced at the Abbey Theatre in 1910. The extract given below is taken from the edition published by the Cuala Industries, by kind permission of Miss Elizabeth C. Yeats and Messrs John W. Luce and Company, Boston, U.S.A.)

DEIRDRE'S END

DEIRDRE [*startled*]. Let us throw down clay on my three comrades. Let us cover up Naisi along with Ainnle and Ardan, they that were the pride of Emain. [*Throwing in clay*] There is Naisi was the best of three, the choicest of the choice of many. It was a clean death was your share, Naisi; and it is not I will quit your head, when it's many a dark night among the snipe and plover that you and I were whispering together. It is not I will quit your head, Naisi, when it's many a night we saw the stars among the clear trees of Glen da Ruadh, or the moon pausing to rest her on the edges of the hills.

OLD WOMAN. Conchubor is coming, surely. I see the glare of flames throwing a light upon his cloak.

LAVARCHAM [*eagerly*]. Rise up, Deirdre, and come to Fergus, or be the High King's slave for ever!

DEIRDRE [*imperiously*]. I will not leave Naisi, who has left the whole world scorched and desolate. I will not go away when there is no light in the heavens, and no flower in the earth under them, but is saying to me that it is Naisi who is gone for ever.

CONCHUBOR [*behind*]. She is here. Stay a little back. [LAVARCHAM *and* OLD WOMAN *go into the shadow on left as* CONCHUBOR *comes in. With excitement, to* DEIRDRE] Come forward and leave Naisi the way I've left charred timber and a smell of burning in Emain Macha, and a heap of rubbish in the storehouse of many crowns.

DEIRDRE [*more awake to what is round her*]. What are crowns and Emain Macha, when the head that gave them glory is this place, Conchubor, and it stretched upon the gravel will be my bed to-night?

CONCHUBOR. Make an end with talk of Naisi, for I've come to bring you to Dundalgan since Emain is destroyed.

[CONCHUBOR *makes a movement towards her.*

DEIRDRE [*with a tone that stops him*]. Draw a little back from Naisi, who is young for ever. Draw a little back from the white bodies I am putting under a mound of clay and grasses that are withered; a mound will have a nook for my own self when the end is come.

CONCHUBOR [*roughly*]. Let you rise up and come along with me in place of growing crazy with your wailings here.

DEIRDRE. It's yourself has made a crazy story, and let you go back to your arms, Conchubor, and to councils where your name is great, for in this place you are an old man and a fool only.

CONCHUBOR. If I've folly I've sense left not to lose the thing I've bought with sorrow and the deaths of many.

[*He moves towards her.*

DEIRDRE. Do not raise a hand to touch me.

CONCHUBOR. There are other hands to touch you. My fighters are set round in among the trees.

DEIRDRE. Who'll fight the grave, Conchubor, and it opened on a dark night?

LAVARCHAM [*eagerly*]. There are steps in the wood. I hear the call of Fergus and his men.

CONCHUBOR [*furiously*]. Fergus cannot stop me. I am more powerful than he is, though I am defeated and old.

FERGUS [*comes in to* DEIRDRE; *a red glow is seen behind the grave*]. I have destroyed Emain, and I'll guard you all times, Deirdre, though it was I, without knowledge, brought Naisi to his grave.

CONCHUBOR. It's not you will guard her, for my whole armies are gathering. Rise up, Deirdre, for you are mine surely.

FERGUS [*coming between them*]. I am come between you.

CONCHUBOR [*wildly*]. When I've killed Naisi and his brothers, is there any man that I will spare? And is it you will stand against

379

me, Fergus, when it's seven years you've seen me getting my death with rage in Emain?

FERGUS. It's I, surely, will stand against a thief and traitor.

DEIRDRE [*stands up and sees the light from Emain*]. Draw a little back with the squabbling of fools when I am broken up with misery. [*She turns round.*] I see the flames of Emain starting upward in the dark night; and because of me there will be weazels and wild cats crying on a lonely wall where there were queens and armies and red gold, the way there will be a story told of a ruined city and a raving king and a woman will be young for ever. [*She looks round.*] I see the trees naked and bare, and the moon shining. Little moon, little moon of Alban, it's lonesome you'll be this night, and to-morrow night, and long nights after, and you pacing the woods beyond Glen Laoi, looking every place for Deirdre and Naisi, the two lovers who slept so sweetly with each other!

FERGUS [*going to* CONCHUBOR's *right and whispering*]. Keep back, or you will have the shame of pushing a bolt on a queen who is out of her wits.

CONCHUBOR. It is I who am out of my wits with Emain in flames, and Deirdre raving, and my own heart gone within me.

DEIRDRE [*in a high and quiet tone*]. I have put away sorrow like a shoe that is worn out and muddy, for it is I have had a life that will be envied by great companies. It was not by a low birth I made kings uneasy, and they sitting in the halls of Emain. It was not a low thing to be chosen by Conchubor, who was wise, and Naisi had no match for bravery. It is not a small thing to be rid of grey hairs, and the loosening of the teeth. [*With a sort of triumph*] It was the choice of lives we had in the clear woods, and in the grave we're safe, surely.

CONCHUBOR. She will do herself harm.

DEIRDRE [*showing* NAISI's *knife*]. I have a little key to unlock the prison of Naisi you'd shut upon his youth for ever. Keep back, Conchubor; for the High King who is your master has put his hands between us. [*She half turns to the grave.*] It was sorrows were foretold, but great joys were my share always; yet it is a cold place I must go to be with you, Naisi; and it's cold your arms will be this night that were warm about my neck so often. . . . It's a pitiful thing to be talking out when your ears are shut to me. It's a pitiful thing, Conchubor, you have done this night in Emain; yet a thing will be a joy and triumph to the ends of life and time.

[*She presses the knife into her heart and sinks into the grave.*
CONCHUBOR *and* FERGUS *go forward. The red glow fades, leaving the stage very dark.*

FERGUS. Four white bodies are laid down together, four clear lights are quenched in Ireland. [*He throws his sword into the grave.*] There is my sword that could not shield you—my four friends that were the dearest always. The flames of Emain have gone out: Deirdre is dead and there is none to keen her. That is the fate of

Deirdre and the Children of Usna, and for this night, Conchubor, our war is ended.   [*He goes out.*

LAVARCHAM. I have a little hut where you can rest, Conchubor; there is a great dew falling.

CONCHUBOR [*with the voice of an old man*]. Take me with you. I'm hard set to see the way before me.

OLD WOMAN. This way, Conchubor.   [*They go out.*

LAVARCHAM [*beside the grave*]. Deirdre is dead, and Naisi is dead; and if the oaks and stars could die for sorrow, it's a dark sky and a hard and naked earth we'd have this night in Emain.

20. LORD DUNSANY (*born* 1878)

The Gods of the Mountain

The stirring of fear and the arousing of what may almost be styled a mood of mystic cynicism are the two qualities which most clearly characterize the dramas of Lord Dunsany. Dead burglars prize open the gates of heaven—to find only illimitable space and the laughter of unseen voices; a king sacrifices his crown to the stars—and it is trundled away by a little child. These are the themes of *The Glittering Gates* and of *The Golden Doom*. In *The Gods of the Mountain* the atmosphere is the same. Some beggars impose on an ignorant village community by pretending that they are the incarnations of seven stone gods who sit silent on the mountain slopes. For a time they are treated reverently and then, doubt entering into the minds of the people, messengers are sent to see whether the stone gods have really left their places. The men return and report that the green idols are no longer there. As we reach the passage quoted below, the beggars are fondly awaiting a sumptuous banquet and sunset revelry.

(Produced at the Haymarket Theatre in 1911, *The Gods of the Mountain* was printed in *Five Plays* in 1914. The following extract is given by kind permission of the author and of the publishers, Messrs G. P. Putnam's Sons, London and New York.)

THE COMING OF DOOM

Enter a frightened MAN. *He kneels before* AGMAR *and abases his forehead.*

MAN. Master, we implore you, the people beseech you.

        [AGMAR *and the beggars, in the attitude of gods, sit silent.*

MAN. Master, it is terrible. [*The beggars maintain silence.*] It is terrible when you wander in the evening. It is terrible on the edge of the desert in the evening. Children die when they see you.

AGMAR. In the desert? When did you see us?

MAN. Last night, master. You were terrible last night. You

381

were terrible in the gloaming. When your hands were stretched out and groping. You were feeling for the city.

AGMAR. Last night do you say?

MAN. You were terrible in the gloaming!

AGMAR. You yourself saw us?

MAN. Yes, master, you were terrible. Children too saw you and they died.

AGMAR. You say you saw us?

MAN. Yes, master. Not as you are now, but otherwise. We implore you, master, not to wander at evening. You are terrible in the gloaming. You are . . .

AGMAR. You say we appeared not as we are now. How did we appear to you?

MAN. Otherwise, master, otherwise.

AGMAR. But how *did* we appear to you?

MAN. You were all green, master, all green in the gloaming, all of rock again as you used to be in the mountains. Master, we can bear to see you in flesh like men, but when we see rock walking it is terrible, it is terrible.

AGMAR. That is how we appeared to you?

MAN. Yes, master. Rock should not walk. When children see it they do not understand. Rock should not walk in the evening.

AGMAR. There have been doubters of late. Are they satisfied?

MAN. Master, they are terrified. Spare us, master.

AGMAR. It is wrong to doubt. Go, and be faithful. [*Exit* MAN.

SLAG. What have they seen, master?

AGMAR. They have seen their own fears dancing in the desert. They have seen something green after the light was gone, and some child has told them a tale that it was us. I do not know what they have seen. What should they have seen?

ULF. Something was coming this way from the desert he said.

SLAG. What should come from the desert?

AGMAR. They are a foolish people.

ULF. That man's white face has seen some frightful thing.

SLAG. A frightful thing?

ULF. That man's face has been near to some frightful thing.

AGMAR. It is only we that have frightened them and their fears have made them foolish.

[*Enter an attendant with a torch or lantern which he places
in a receptacle. Exit.*

THAHN. Now we shall see the faces of the girls when they come to the banquet.

MLAN. Never had beggars such a time.

AGMAR. Hark! They are coming. I hear footsteps.

THAHN. The dancing-girls. They are coming.

THIEF. There is no sound of flutes; they said they would come with music.

OOGNO. What heavy boots they have, they sound like feet of stone.

THE MODERN PERIOD

THAHN. I do not like to hear their heavy tread; those that would dance to *us* must be light of foot.

AGMAR. I shall not smile at them if they are not airy.

MLAN. They are coming very slowly. They should come nimbly to us.

THAHN. They should dance as they come. But the footfall is like the footfall of heavy crabs.

ULF [*in a loud voice, almost chanting*]. I have a fear, an old fear and a boding! We have done ill in the sight of the seven gods; beggars we were and beggars we should have remained; we have given up our calling and come in sight of our doom; I will no longer let my fear be silent: it shall run about and cry: it shall go from me crying, like a dog from out of a doomed city; for my fear has seen calamity and has known an evil thing.

SLAG [*hoarsely*]. Master!

AGMAR [*rising*]. Come, come!

> [*They listen. No one speaks. The stony boots come on. Enter in a single file a procession of seven green men, even hands and faces are green; they wear green-stone sandals; they walk with knees extremely wide apart, as having sat cross-legged for centuries; their right arms and right forefingers point upwards, right elbows resting on left hands; they stoop grotesquely. They pass in front of the seven beggars, now in terrified attitudes, and six of them sit down in the attitude described, with their backs to the audience. The leader stands, still stooping. As they come, OOGNO cries out:*

OOGNO. The gods of the mountain!

AGMAR [*hoarsely*]. Be still. They are dazzled by the light. They may not see us.

> [*The leading green thing points his forefinger at the lantern—the flame turns green. When the six are seated the leader points one by one at each of the seven beggars, shooting out his forefinger at them. As he does this each beggar in his turn gathers himself back on to his throne and crosses his legs, his right arm goes stiffly upwards with forefinger erect, and a staring look of horror comes into his eyes. In this attitude the beggars sit motionless while a green light falls upon their faces. The gods go out. Presently enter the citizens, and dancing-girls with victuals and fruit. One touches a beggar's arm and then another's.*

CITIZEN. They are cold; they have turned to stone.

> [*All abase themselves foreheads to the floor.*

ONE. We have doubted them. We have doubted them. They have turned to stone because we have doubted them.

ANOTHER. They were the true gods.

ALL. They were the true gods.

383

21. WILLIAM BUTLER YEATS (*born* 1865)

At the Hawk's Well

" Perhaps in the end," writes Mr Yeats in his preface to *Four Plays for Dancers*, " one would write plays for certain masks. If some fine sculptor should create for my *Calvary*, for instance, the masks of Judas, of Lazarus, and of Christ, would not this suggest other plays now, or many generations from now, and possess one cannot tell what philosophical virility ? The mask, apart from its beauty, may suggest new situations at a moment when the old ones seem exhausted." These words go far to explain the spirit in which *At the Hawk's Well* was written. Its model is admittedly the "Nō" plays of Japan, and in it an attempt is made to secure an atmosphere which may be fittingly expressed through rhythmic dancing and beautiful masks. This is decidedly the utmost reach of the *théâtre intime*; the first performance of the play took place " in a friend's drawing-room," and the dancing which Mr Yeats desires is not " any existing form of stage dancing, but something with a smaller gamut of expression, something more reserved, more self-controlled, as befits performers within arm's reach of their audience." How far this form of drama is capable of development it is impossible to say, but here is one more of those experiments in the search for methods of expression which mark out the inventiveness and the questing of the modern theatre ; here is something " stiffly and gravely " beautiful in a style which, like all great art, is both new and old.

(*At the Hawk's Well*[1] was first performed privately in April 1916, with masks and costumes designed by Mr Dulac. The following extract is taken, by kind permission of the author and of Messrs Macmillan and Co., Ltd., from *Four Plays for Dancers* (1921).)

THE COMING OF CUCHULAIN

The OLD MAN *stands for a moment motionless by the side of the stage with bowed head. He lifts his head at the sound of a drum-tap. He goes towards the front of the stage moving to the taps of the drum. He crouches and moves his hands as if making a fire. His movements, like those of the other persons of the play, suggest a marionette.*

FIRST MUSICIAN [*speaking*]. He has made a little heap of leaves ;
He lays the dry sticks on the leaves
And, shivering with cold, he has taken up
The fire-stick and socket from its hole.
He whirls it round to get a flame;
And now the dry sticks take the fire

[1] Copyright 1921 in U.S.A. by the Macmillan Company, New York.

And now the fire leaps up and shines
Upon the hazels and the empty well.
    MUSICIANS [*singing*]. "O wind, O salt wind, O sea wind!"
Cries the heart, " it is time to sleep;
Why wander and nothing to find?
Better grow old and sleep."
    OLD MAN [*speaking*]. Why don't you speak to me? Why don't
      you say
" Are you not weary gathering those sticks?
Are not your fingers cold?" You have not one word,
While yesterday you spoke three times. You said:
" The well is full of hazel leaves." You said:
" The wind is from the west." And after that:
" If there is rain it's likely there'll be mud."
To-day you are as stupid as a fish,
No, worse, worse, being less lively and as dumb. [*He goes nearer.*
Your eyes are dazed and heavy. If the Sidhe
Must have a guardian to clean out the well
And drive the cattle off, they might choose somebody
That can be pleasant and companionable
Once in the day. Why do you stare like that?
You had that glassy look about the eyes
Last time it happened. Do you know anything?
It is enough to drive an old man crazy
To look all day upon these broken rocks,
And ragged thorns, and that one stupid face,
And speak and get no answer.
    YOUNG MAN [*who has entered through the audience during the last
      speech*].   Then speak to me,
For youth is not more patient than old age;
And though I have trod the rocks for half a day
I cannot find what I am looking for.
    OLD MAN.   Who speaks?
Who comes so suddenly into this place
Where nothing thrives? If I may judge by the gold
On head and feet and glittering in your coat,
You are not of those who hate the living world.
    YOUNG MAN. I am named Cuchulain, I am Sualtam's son.
    OLD MAN. I have never heard that name.
    CUCHULAIN.   It is not unknown.
I have an ancient house beyond the sea.
    OLD MAN. What mischief brings you hither, you are like
      those
Who are crazy for the shedding of men's blood,
And for the love of women?
    YOUNG MAN.   A rumour has led me,
A story told over the wine towards dawn.
I rose from table, found a boat, spread sail

a 2 B

And with a lucky wind under the sail
Crossed waves that have seemed charmed, and found this shore.

    OLD MAN. There is no house to sack among these hills,
Nor beautiful woman to be carried off.

    YOUNG MAN. You should be native here, for that rough tongue
Matches the barbarous spot. You can, it may be,
Lead me to what I seek, a well wherein
Three hazels drop their nuts and withered leaves,
And where a solitary girl keeps watch
Among grey boulders. He who drinks, they say,
Of that miraculous water lives for ever.

    OLD MAN. And are there not before your eyes at the instant
Grey boulders and a solitary girl
And three stripped hazels?

    YOUNG MAN.   But there is no well.

    OLD MAN. Can you see nothing yonder?

    YOUNG MAN.   I but see
A hollow among stones half full of leaves.

    OLD MAN. And do you think so great a gift is found
By no more toil than spreading out a sail,
And climbing a steep hill? Oh, folly of youth,
Why should that hollow place fill up for you,
That will not fill for me? I have lain in wait
For more than fifty years to find it empty,
Or but to find the stupid wind of the sea
Drive round the perishable leaves.

    YOUNG MAN.   So it seems
There is some moment when the water fills it.

    OLD MAN. A secret moment that the holy shades
That dance upon the desolate mountain know,
And not a living man, and when it comes
The water has scarce plashed before it is gone.

    YOUNG MAN. I will stand here and wait. Why should the luck
Of Sualtam's son desert him now? For never
Have I had long to wait for anything.

    OLD MAN. No! Go from this accursed place, this place
Belongs to me, that girl there and those others,
Deceivers of men.

    YOUNG MAN.   And who are you who rail
Upon those dancers that all others bless?

    OLD MAN. One whom the dancers cheat. I came like you
When young in body and in mind, and blown
By what had seemed to me a lucky sail.
The well was dry, I sat upon its edge,
I waited the miraculous flood, I waited
While the years passed and withered me away.
I have snared the birds for food and eaten grass
And drunk the rain, and neither in dark nor shine

386

Wandered too far away to have heard the plash,
And yet the dancers have deceived me.   Thrice
I have awakened from a sudden sleep
To find the stones were wet.
    YOUNG MAN.   My luck is strong,
It will not leave me waiting, nor will they
That dance among the stones put me asleep;
If I grow drowsy I can pierce my foot.
    OLD MAN. No, do not pierce it, for the foot is tender,
It feels pain much.   But find your sail again
And leave the well to me, for it belongs
To all that's old and withered.
    YOUNG MAN.   No, I stay.
            [*The* GIRL *gives the cry of the hawk.*
There is that bird again.
    OLD MAN.   . There is no bird.
    YOUNG MAN. It sounded like the sudden cry of a hawk,
But there's no wing in sight.   As I came hither
A great grey hawk swept down out of the sky,
And though I have good hawks, the best in the world
I had fancied, I have not seen its like.   It flew
As though it would have torn me with its beak,
Or blinded me, smiting with that great wing.
I had to draw my sword to drive it off,
And after that it flew from rock to rock.
I pelted it with stones a good half-hour,
And just before I had turned the big rock there
And seen this place, it seemed to vanish away.
Could I but find a means to bring it down
I'd hood it.

22. JOHN DRINKWATER (*born* 1882)

Mary Stuart

    The chronicle history, or biographical chronicle, which had
proved so popular in Elizabethan times, has recently been revived
with considerable success by Mr John Drinkwater, whose *Abraham
Lincoln* had recently a long run in London.   Mr Drinkwater has
the unquestioned ability of grasping the essentials of an historical
situation and of an historical character.   He has, too, the power
of seeing those situations and characters in the light of an abstract
idea or principle, so that his history plays differ from those of
the Elizabethans in being, to a certain extent at least, problem
dramas.   Mr Drinkwater's effect is often largely secured by means
of his style, which exhibits what may be called a heightened
or concentrated realism.   His dialogue is such as might have

*a 2 B

been spoken by the originals of his stage figures, but he has always striven to make each speech bear its weight in the impression which he is building up, so that non-essentials are eliminated and there is, in the scenes, a species of condensation which adds to the strength and interest of the whole. *Mary Stuart* provides as good an example as any of these qualities. When the play is taken from one point of view it becomes a thesis drama; when taken from another it is merely a study in historical character.

(*Mary Stuart* was produced in 1921, and followed by a revised version in the following year. The passage given below is reprinted by kind permission of the author and the Houghton Mifflin Company.)

MARY AND BOTHWELL

MARY. Did you find my Lord Bothwell?

BEATON. He waits your word.

MARY. Ask him to come. First draw the curtains and light the candle.

[BEATON *does so, while* MARY *reads again the same passage aloud.*

"And in the evening they will return: grin like a dog, and will go about the city. . . . Unto thee, O my strength, will I sing: for thou, O God, art my refuge, and my merciful God."

[BEATON *goes, and* MARY *closes the book. She stands at the desk, her back to the door.* BOTHWELL *appears.*

BOTHWELL. Madam.

MARY [*half turning*]. My lord.

BOTHWELL. You sent for me.

MARY. You were not seen to come?

BOTHWELL. No. Not that I care for all their eyes.

MARY. But you must. I have small reason to cherish security I know; that is past. But this would confuse things too much. They will destroy me, but I will not help them too generously. So this must not be known.

BOTHWELL. I understand.

MARY. Will you help me?

BOTHWELL. Madam, I have no interest but to please myself. To please you is that.

MARY. Darnley threatens Riccio.

BOTHWELL. Shall I trip Darnley? But why should one be concerned for Riccio? There should be better ambitions.

MARY. They think he's my lover. Or Darnley occupies his mind in a pretence that he thinks it. Let him think it—it is no matter.

BOTHWELL. Surely not Riccio?

MARY. No. But I did not send for you to question me. Riccio

has served me well enough in his kind. I remember these things. He is in danger, and he must be saved. That is all.

BOTHWELL. What can I do?

MARY. He must leave Scotland, secretly, and at once. Can you contrive that?

BOTHWELL. It could be done. There is a Dane in port now. I will give word to the captain. I have his service. Tell Riccio to meet me at midnight, by Frobisher's Croft. I will have a fellow to take him out from shore. When they are clear they can carry a light, and the Dane shall take him up. He can make his own way from Copenhagen?

MARY. Surely. Riccio shall be there at midnight. And my thanks.   *[She offers her hand.*

BOTHWELL [*taking it*]. No more?

MARY. It must not be. No—not yet.

BOTHWELL. Woman, why do you waste yourself among crowns and peddlers? Who is Elizabeth—who Darnley? What is Scotland, a black country, barren, that it should consume this beauty? You were born to love, to mate strongly, to challenge passion —this passion, I tell you, this. They come to you, and plead as peevish boys, or watch round corners—winds that cannot stir one tress of that hair. You are not aware of them, you are unmoved. But I am not as these—do you think I will wait and wait? I do not plead. I bid your love to me. Mary. Mary. You know it, you know.

MARY. Don't. Think.

BOTHWELL. But I have thought, and it is enough. You may desert all, but not this.

MARY. Listen. You woo well—boldly at least. Better than Darnley ever did, and Riccio has no more than a little elegance. And he whines. So did Darnley. But you have courage. You are aflame, and I kindle—yes, I tell you so much. What then? Should we leave Scotland? No. Queens are limed. And here, what is there for us but stealthy moments, fugitive? I should burn to them, but they would but add more smother to my life. I do not know what may come—I love you, yes, if you will—but no hope is in it, none. For I must tell you. I am of those who must be loved always, for all things, for there to be any peace in love. If you, or any man, could fathom that—ah, then. You love me now, you love my beauty. It needs love, it cherishes your love, it sings back to your hot words. But my beauty is not all. It will pass, and I should be unsatisfied. For you could not love me always, for all things. There is nothing between us but the minute. You could give me that, but you have nothing else to give.

BOTHWELL. And then? Shall the minute be denied?

MARY. That's good. You make no pretence, even. But remember, there is no hope in it, there can be none. Even were Darnley less husband than he is, and I free to take you to the throne, there would still be but the minute between us. You are not the man. He will not come.

BOTHWELL. I am no schemer in my love. Policy's a game—there I'm all wits. But love comes, and is now. You are beautiful, Mary. You betray no one. What remorse can there be?

MARY. Remorse? No; love is remorseless. But frustration always, always.

BOTHWELL. Not of our minute—not of that, I say.

MARY. No, then, not of that.

[BOTHWELL *takes her in his arms, she giving herself passionately. After a moment they part, as* MARY BEATON'S *voice is heard.*

BEATON [*calling from without*]. Madam—madam.

MARY. Yes, what is it?

BEATON. Madam.

MARY. Yes, yes—come in.

BEATON [*entering*]. Madam, the King is crossing the yard—he may be coming here.

MARY [*to* BOTHWELL]. You must go.

BOTHWELL. Why should we slink about for any king?

MARY. No—you must. There are confusions enough.

[*She looks out from the window.*

Yes, he is coming. Go through the Close—quickly. At midnight, remember. [BOTHWELL *kisses her hand and goes.*

BEATON. You play very dangerously, madam.

MARY. Beaton, love should be lucky for you. I think it will. But for me . . . He took me in his arms—a moment's fury—fire to slake fire, and that is all. That is my most of love. Why should I not be dangerous?

BEATON. Do you love my Lord Bothwell?

MARY. A little of me—a moment. There is so much else to deny myself, after all. But he means so little more than the others. Still, a little—it is something.

23. LASCELLES ABERCROMBIE (*born* 1881)

Deborah

The poetic style in drama may, as is obvious, be used either for the expression of themes romantic, or for that of themes realistic. Still further, in the latter sphere there may be either the imaginative picture of the real, or else the attempt to reproduce through the poetic form something that remains close to ordinary phenomena. In pure poetry this last form is most successfully attained by Crabbe, where, in spite of the impression

390

made by the poet upon his material, that material remains more 'naturalistic' than, say, does that of a poem by Shelley. In other words, a poet of the type of Crabbe will select from life those things which suit his imaginative purpose, whereas a Shelley will prefer to embroider reality with his own visions and his own dreams. The modern poetic drama has unquestionably tended toward the more freely imaginative. Old legends and bygone tales have been for the most part preferred to contemporary life, and even when contemporary types are dealt with there are frequently brought in alongside of these figures others of a super-natural significance. Almost the only playwright who has attempted to create for the drama a world similar to that created by Crabbe is Professor Lascelles Abercrombie, whose *Deborah* is set in "a fishing and pilot village on a great estuary," peopled with characters of ordinary familiarity. The dialogue necessarily agrees with the choice of subject-matter and the treatment of the theme. Instead of the richness of Yeats there is an endeavour on the part of the writer (not dissimilar from that of Crabbe) to leave the poetic form as near in spirit and in expression to peasant language as can possibly be attained.

(The following passage is taken from the edition of 1913, by kind permission of the author and of the publishers, Messrs John Lane The Bodley Head, Ltd., London, and Messrs Dodd, Mead and Company, Inc., New York.)

AND WOMEN MUST WEEP

BARNABY. Well; you will have it then?—It's not my fault;
Nor yours, Miriam. It just had to be.

DEBORAH. What is it? What is it?

BARNABY.   I'ld liever have gone off
Without coming to this——

MIRIAM.   What have I done?

BARNABY. Why, nothing.—It's a troublesome thing to say,
A troublesome thing to know rightly the work
My mind's been making in me.—But I know this,
Miriam: I must clean go from you to-night;
And from to-night on,—you must be done with me.

MIRIAM. You're going for a good while?

BARNABY.   For good and all.

MIRIAM. What does he say, Deborah? Sure I have
Some faintness on me, and it hurts my hearing.

DEBORAH. You will get used to this. 'Tis how things go
Here in the world. You trusted in your life,
Did you not? Ay, you trusted there was joy
To carry you through life. This is what falls
To those who trust so.—But it cannot be;

391

The old despair cannot be coming down
On me again. Now, not for the love of me,
Barnaby, but for the love of God, say out
What it is truly we two women must
Look for at your hands now.

BARNABY.   Have I not said it?—
[*With sudden impatience*] It's all too small for me here: it's all
    crampt,
A misery of little drudging work,
With now and then some fair risk of a danger
Out on the river; and that's the one fine thing
In this half-smothered life. And what comes then,
When we are through the danger, with a breath
That's all sharp tingling from it? Back we come,
A penny or two in our pockets maybe, back
To this—what shall I call it? ay, a kennel,
A kennel made of mud, this penn'd village,
This knab of dirt between river and marsh.
But I'll fling free. I'll not keep stifling here.
Out in the world there's China and the Indies,
Lands they speak of wonderfully, and capes
That ask a month of storming to get round;
All the great life of sailors, as I've heard
The pilots tell of, they who bring to dock
And through our shoals the ships that trade in the East.
And what's the best for me if I stay here?
Grow to a pilot's wisdom, maybe; climb
In the half-light the sides of vessels, stained
With pushing through the salty weather of seas
Where the sun makes the waters burn like stone
That floors a furnace; and have some snatch of talk
With them who live what I must dream, as men
Visit a cripple bedrid in a room.

DEBORAH. I know all this; I have long seen it growing,
And there's no harm in it. And is this all
The reason for your cruelty,—your want
To go a-vagabonding with the sailors?

BARNABY. No, 'tis not all; but it is all my words
Can fashion of the mind in me. That life
Which leaps so keen awake within my brain
When, like a hatred that has been in hiding,
Danger blows on the fishing fleet, and we
Must fight to win ashore, that power of life
Is what has taken a strong hold on me.
I must go out and let it spend itself
Somewhere—somehow—I don't know rightly; yet
This is plain as a candle-flame in darkness—
I'm to have done with being hampered here.

DEBORAH. And this girl—why should you not come back to her,
When you have seen the world?

BARNABY.   Well, I've myself
To please about that first. I'll not be made
A mammet for you women to play games with.

DEBORAH. I understand your meaning now. You've done
The wicked thing by her.

BARNABY.   And what did she
But please her own mind in it?

MIRIAM.   O God! God!

DEBORAH. Why, you should smile when you drink gall, Miriam,
For there's nought else your soul will drink of life.

BARNABY. O, but it's not so easy for me to leave her!
A deal of comfort calls me here; and she
Keeps all of it,—she's all the little close
Sweetness of comfortable wonted life
Which would grip firm about me; and it's that—
That is the thing I must be cruel with,
And to myself, too, I must be cruel.

DEBORAH. And you care nought for what may happen to her?

BARNABY. And what should happen to her?—what should
     happen?   [DEBORAH *looks steadily at* BARNABY.

BARNABY. Deborah, leave us for a moment.

                            [DEBORAH *goes into the inner room.*
                                      I suppose
That you've let on about our foolishness?

MIRIAM. Foolishness! It was sacred to me.

BARNABY.   Leave that,
And tell me. Is there aught like to come of it?

MIRIAM. And if there was, what would it mean to you?

BARNABY. Why—why, I think—I should come back to you.

MIRIAM. You may go with an easy mind then. No,
There's nothing like to come of it—nothing.

BARNABY. Well, the boat's waiting at the jetty now
To row me and my traps up to the dock——

     [He hesitates a moment, then suddenly picks up his box,
       shoulders it, and makes off through the door into the
       lane.

DEBORAH [*coming in from the bedroom*]. He's gone?

MIRIAM. Gone.

DEBORAH. And I thought my ears surely lied to me, when
They heard the door latch. And he's gone!

MIRIAM. Deborah! He has left me, Deborah!

DEBORAH. And David loved her so, she but a bairn!—
Saul and Barnaby; David and his sister!

MIRIAM. Deborah!—I am with child.

EXTRACTS FROM BRITISH & IRISH PLAYS

24. GORDON BOTTOMLEY (*born* 1874)

King Lear's Wife

It was a happy thought that led Mr Bottomley back to Shakespeare. His two plays, *King Lear's Wife* and *Gruach*, show more plainly than any others the power of modern drama and the inherent weaknesses of the nineteenth-century romantic poets. The latter could think of nothing but imitations of Shakespeare, conspiracies, jealousies, romantic-comedy scenes with plentiful reminiscences of earlier phrase and imagery. Mr Bottomley looks back also to Shakespeare, but not for the purpose of filching language and sentiment. He takes *King Lear*, and endeavours to reconstruct such a royal household as might form a fitting habitation for the Elizabethan tragic theme. Lear is cruel and faithless. Goneril has been despised in girlhood. Cordelia (or Cordeil) is a little spoilt brat. It is obvious that, in order to accept Shakespeare's postulate, we must admit some such preliminary reconstruction, and it is Mr Bottomley's merit that he has been able effectively to put this story down in dramatic form and to make his characters live through the situations he devises. His task is a difficult one, for our minds are full of Shakespeare ; but Mr Bottomley's mature Lear and girlish Goneril have no less of an appealing and firm existence than his new-created Hygd and Gormflaith.

(*King Lear's Wife* was produced in 1915. The extract given below is taken, by kind permission of the author and of the publishers, Messrs Constable and Co., Ltd., from the edition of that year.)

THE CHILDHOOD OF CORDELIA

HYGD. The hour comes for you to turn to a man
And give yourself with the high heart of youth
More lavishly than a queen gives anything.
But when a woman gives herself
She must give herself for ever and have faith;
For woman is a thing of a season of years,
She is an early fruit that will not keep,
She can be drained and as a husk survive
To hope for reverence for what has been;
While man renews himself into old age,
And gives himself according to his need,
And women more unborn than his next child
May take him yet with youth
And lose him with their potence.
　　GONERIL. But women need not wed these men.
　　HYGD. We are good human currency, like gold,
For men to pass among them when they choose.

394

THE MODERN PERIOD

[*A* CHILD'S *hands beat on the outside of the door beyond the bed.*

CORDEIL'S VOICE [*a* CHILD'S *voice, outside*]. Father. . . . Father.
   . . . Father. . . . Are you here?
Merryn, ugly Merryn, let me in. . . .
I know my father is here. . . . I want him. . . . Now. . . .
Mother, chide Merryn, she is old and slow. . . .

HYGD. My little curse. Send her away—away. . . .   [*Softly.*

CORDEIL'S VOICE. Father. . . . O, father, father. . . . I want my
   father.

GONERIL [*opening the door a little way*]. Hush; hush—you hurt
   your mother with your voice.
You cannot come in, Cordeil; you must go away:
Your father is not here. . . .

CORDEIL'S VOICE. He must be here:
He is not in his chamber or the hall,
He is not in the stable or with Gormflaith:
He promised I should ride with him at dawn
And sit before his saddle and hold his hawk,
And ride with him and ride to the heron-marsh;
He said that he would give me the first heron,
And hang the longest feathers in my hair.

GONERIL. Then you must haste to find him;
He may be riding now. . . .

CORDEIL'S VOICE. But Gerda said she saw him enter here.

GONERIL. Indeed, he is not here. . . .

CORDEIL'S VOICE. Let me look. . . .

GONERIL. You are too noisy. Must I make you go?

CORDEIL'S VOICE. Mother, Goneril is unkind to me.

HYGD [*raising herself in bed excitedly, and speaking so vehemently
   that her utterance strangles itself*]. Go, go, thou evil child, thou
   ill-comer.

      [GONERIL, *with a sudden strong movement, shuts the resisting
         door and holds it rigidly. The little hands beat on it
         madly for a moment, then the* CHILD'S VOICE *is heard
         in a retreating wail.*

GONERIL. Though she is wilful, obeying only the King,
She is a very little child, mother,
To be so bitterly thought of.

HYGD. Because a woman gives herself for ever
Cordeil the useless had to be conceived
(Like an afterthought that deceives nobody)
To keep her father from another woman.
And I lie here.

GONERIL [*after a silence*]. Hard and unjust my father has been
   to me;
Yet that has knitted up within my mind
A love of coldness and a love of him

Who makes me firm, wary, swift and secret,
Until I feel if I become a mother
I shall at need be cruel to my children,
And ever cold, to string their natures harder
And make them able to endure men's deeds;
But now I wonder if injustice
Keeps house with baseness, taught by kinship—
I never thought a king could be untrue,
I never thought my father was unclean. . . .
O mother, mother, what is it?   Is this dying?
   Hygd. I think I am only faint. . . .
Give me the cup of whey. . . .

       [Goneril *takes the cup and, supporting* Hygd, *lets her*
         drink.

   Goneril. There is too little here.   When was it made?
   Hygd. Yester-eve. . . . Yester-morn. . . .
   Goneril.   Unhappy mother,
You have no daughter to take thought for you—
No servant's love to shame a daughter with,
Though I am shamed—you must have other food,
Straightway I bring you meat. . . .
   Hygd.   It is no use. . . .
Plenish the cup for me. . . . Not now, not now,
But in a while; for I am heavy now. . . .
Old Wynoc's potions loiter in my veins,
And tides of heaviness pour over me
Each time I wake and think.   I could sleep now.
   Goneril. Then I shall lull you, as you once lulled me.

                 [*Seating herself on the bed, she sings.*

         The owlets in roof-holes
         Can sing for themselves;
         The smallest brown squirrel
         Both scampers and delves;
         But a baby does nothing—
         She never knows how—
         She must hark to her mother
         Who sings to her now.
         Sleep then, ladykin, peeping so;
         Hide your handies and ley lei lo.

   [*She bends over* Hygd *and kisses her; they laugh softly*
     together.
   [Lear *parts the curtains of the door at the back, stands there*
     a moment, then goes away noiselessly.

         The lish baby otter
         Is sleeky and streaming,
         With catching bright fishes,
         Ere babies learn dreaming;

THE MODERN PERIOD

> But no wet little otter
> Is ever so warm
> As the fleecy-wrapt baby
> 'Twixt me and my arm.
> Sleep big mousie. . . .

HYGD [*suddenly irritable*]. Be quiet. . . . I cannot bear it.

25. CLEMENCE DANE (*born* 1888)

Will Shakespeare

Will Shakespeare could not have been written in 1928, for we now know at least some of the details concerning that fascinating biographic puzzle, Marlowe's death. But creative art is not defaced by the discoveries of science or research. We know more of Henry IV than Shakespeare did; yet *Henry IV* survives. In the same way, we must not judge Miss Dane's drama *Will Shakespeare* by reference to the documents of the time. We must treat it as if Will Shakespeare were Will Smith and as if Kit Marlowe were Kit Morton. In other words, we have to judge the play as a play and not as a piece of history or biography. Considered in this way, *Will Shakespeare* is a very effective poetic drama, with well-outlined characters and situations of a genuine theatrical cast. It is interesting to compare the drama with any of the early nineteenth-century poetic experiments. In the latter, as we have seen, the language is hopelessly imitative, falsely 'redolent' of the Elizabethans; Miss Dane, writing of the Elizabethans themselves, and expressing the greater part of the action through the medium of blank verse, develops a style of her own. She is not imitating as Tobin imitated; she is striving to give to the modern world her imaginative picture of a certain sphere of life. Instead of imitation, she aims at creation; and it is precisely by these qualities of creativeness, of independence, that modern drama is to be distinguished from the old.

(*Will Shakespeare* [1] was produced in 1921. The passage below is taken, by kind permission of the authoress, from the edition published by Messrs William Heinemann, Ltd., in 1922.)

MARLOWE'S DEATH

MARY. He's married?
MARLOWE. I do not tell you so.
MARY. Married! He shall pay me. Married! I guessed it—but he shall pay me. A country girl?
MARLOWE. If you must know! He has not seen her these ten years. She sent for him the night of *Juliet*.
MARY. Why now all's plain.

[1] Copyright 1921 in U.S.A. by the Macmillan Company, New York.

So she's the canker that hath drooped our rose!
If I had loved him—I do not love him, Marlowe—
This would have fanned a flame. Well, we're all cheats!
But now I cheat with better conscience. Married!
Lord, I could laugh! He must not know I know it.

MARLOWE. I shan't boast I told you. O Mary, when I first came
to you, it was he sent me. He came like a child and asked me to
see you, to say what good of him I could,
Because I was his friend. And now, see, see,
How I have friended him!

MARY.   I love you for it.
He shall not know. Why talk of him? Forget him!

MARLOWE. Can you?

MARY. Why, that I cannot makes me mad——

MARLOWE.   Forget him?
As soon forget myself! I am his courage,
His worldly wisdom—Mary, I think I am
The youth he lost in Stratford. Yet we're one age,
And now we write one play. If I died of a sudden,
It seems he'd breathe me as I left my body,
And I should live in him as sunshine lies
Forgotten in a forest, and be found
In slants and pools and patterns, golden still
In all he writes.

MARY. O dull Kit! have I adventured here to hear you talk of
    dying?

MARLOWE. You borrowed Archer's name.

MARY. I wanted one that would startle you out to me, and you
told me the tale of him once, how young he died.

MARLOWE. And how unwilling! You've set him running in my
head like a spider in a skull,
Spinning across the hollows of mine eyes
A web of dusty thought. Sweet, brush him off!
Death's a vile dreg in this intoxicant,
This liquor of the gods, this seven-hued life.
Sometimes I pinch myself, say—"Can you die?
Is it possible? Will you be winter-nipped
One day like other flies?" I'm glad you came.
Stay with me, stay, till the last minute of life!
Let the Court go, the world go, stay with me!

MARY [her arms round him]. So—quiet till the dawn comes, quiet!
    Hark!
Who called? Did you hear it?

MARLOWE.   Birds in the ivy.

MARY.   No.
Twice in the road I stopped and turned about
Because I heard my name called. There was nothing;
Yet I heard it—Mary—Mary—Mary!

398

MARLOWE. You heard your own heart pound from riding.

MARY.   Again!
Open the window!   [MARLOWE *rises and goes to the window.*
                    Do you see anything?

MARLOWE. All's sinister. The moon fled out of the sky
Long since, and the black trees of midnight quake.

MARY. And the wind! What a wind! It tugs at the window-
    frame
Like jealousy, mad to break in and part us.
Could you be jealous?

MARLOWE.   If I were a fool
I'd let you guess it.

MARY.   Wise, you're wise, but—jealous?
Too many men in the world! I'd lift no finger
To beckon back the fool that tired of me,
Would you? But he, he glooms and says no word,
But follows with his eyes whene'er I stir.
I hate those asking eyes. Look thus at me
But once and—ended, Marlowe! I'll not give
But when I choose.   [*He sits beside her.*

MARLOWE.   But when *I* choose.
              [*Behind them the blur of the window is darkened.*

MARY [*in his arms*].   Why yes!
Had he your key-word—— Sometimes I like him yet,
When anger comes in a white lightning-flash,
Then he's the man of men still, then with shut eyes
I think him you and shiver and I like him,
Held roughly in his arms, thinking of you.
The Warwick burr is like an afterwards
Of thunder when he's angry, in his speech.

MARLOWE. What does he say?

MARY.   He says he is not jealous!
He would not wrong me so, nor wrong himself.
Then the sky lightens and we kiss—or kiss not!
Who cares?
Then in come you. It's well he thinks you his
In friendship——

MARLOWE. So I was.
              [SHAKESPEARE *swings himself noiselessly over the sill.*

MARY.   And so you are,
And have all things in common as friends should.
Eh, friend?
Oh, stir not! Frowning? If you were a fool—
(How did it run?) you'd let me guess you—jealous!
But you're no fool.

MARLOWE.   Let's have no more! You know
I loved—I love the man.

MARY.   Why, so do I!

MARLOWE. You shall not!

MARY.   Then I will not.   Not to-night.

SHAKESPEARE [*standing by the window*]. Why not to-night, my
  lover and my friend?

                    [*He comes down into the room as they start up.*

Will you not give me wine and welcome me?
Sit down, sit down—we three have much to say!
But tell me first, what does that hand of yours
Upon her neck, as there were custom in it?
Part! Part, I say! Part! lest I couple you
Once and for all!

MARY.   He's armed!

MARLOWE.   He shall not touch you!

SHAKESPEARE. You, Marlowe! You!

MARLOWE.   Stand out of her way!

SHAKESPEARE.   You! You!

MARLOWE. Why then——

          [MARLOWE *darts at* SHAKESPEARE *and is thrown off. He
          staggers against the table, knocking over a candle. As
          he strikes the second time his arm is knocked up, striking
          his own forehead. He falls across the bed. There is
          an instant's pause, then* SHAKESPEARE *rushes to him,
          slipping an arm under his shoulder.*

MARY.   Dead? Is he dead? Oh, what an end!
I never saw a dead man. Will—to me!

SHAKESPEARE. Get help!

MARY.   I dare not.

MARLOWE.   Oh!

SHAKESPEARE.   What is it?

MARLOWE.   Oh!
My life, my lovely life, and cast away
Untasted, wasted—
Death, let me go!   [*He dies*

26. J. R. PLANCHÉ (1796–1880)

The Camp at the Olympic

J. R. Planché, like so many other playwrights of the nineteenth
century, was a prolific writer, his dramatic works being numbered
in the hundreds. Gifted with the contemporary ability of
making puns, a decided talent for writing light verse, and an
observant eye, he readily took over the style of the original
French *revue*, where current theatrical activities were presented,
criticized, or burlesqued. *The Camp at the Olympic*, produced
at the Olympic Theatre under the Wigans on October 17,
1853, is a typical *pièce d'occasion*. Wigan and his wife have just

taken over their theatre; properties and costumes are few, and they know not what to do, when Fancy rises to aid them. The passage quoted explains itself.

(The extract is taken from *The Extravaganzas of J. R. Planché* (1879), vol. iv.)

FANCY COMES TO THE AID OF THE WIGANS

MR WIGAN. Ah, if we could bring Fancy to our aid!

[FANCY *rises from trap, in a jester's costume.*

FANCY. Fancy you can. It's done as soon as said.

MR WIGAN. "Angels and ministers of grace defend us!"
What does this novel stage effect portend us?

MRS WIGAN. "Be thou a spirit of health or goblin"——

FANCY. Hum!

MR WIGAN. "Bring with thee airs from heaven or blasts from "——

FANCY. Mum!
I'm Fancy.

MRS WIGAN. Only fancy that!

MR WIGAN. Who'd guess,
In such a habit——

FANCY. It's a fancy dress.

MRS WIGAN. A fool's—saving your presence.

FANCY. You forget
That Fancy plays the fool with sense, and yet
Without some Fancy Sense would be a frump,
While without sense Fancy's not worth a dump!
Their happy union makes for youth and age
The choicest entertainments of the stage,
(For which I have the greatest partiality)
And give to every scene I touch reality.

MR WIGAN. Then pray touch some of mine up, and I'd name
This tent for one. [*Indicating a canvas tent on the stage.*

FANCY. With that *intent* I came. . . .

[*Scene changes to the Camp of the Combined British Dramatic Forces; on one side are the characteristic tents of* TRAGEDY, MELODRAMA, *and* OPERA; *on the other those of* COMEDY, FARCE, *and* PANTOMIME—*In the centre is the large and splendid pavilion of* SPECTACLE. . . . *Enter* TRAGEDY *from her tent in the costume of* LADY MACBETH, 1753, *a letter in her hand.*

FANCY. First in the field, old English Tragedy
In stately hoop and train "comes sweeping by!"
As in the British Drama's palmy day,
When people took an interest in the play!

MR WIGAN. A letter in her hand! why then the dame is——

FANCY. The wife of the ambitious Thane of Glamis!

2 C

MRS WIGAN. Lady Macbeth! In Dollalolla's dress!

TRAGEDY [*reading the letter*]. "They met me in the day of my success."

MR WIGAN. That must have been a hundred years ago,
To judge from a costume so rococo!

TRAGEDY [*indignantly*]. In my day, sir, judgment, and power, and feeling,
With confidence to public taste appealing,
Received the crown—no matter what its fashion,
It *was* the crown!

MR WIGAN.   Well, don't be in a passion.

TRAGEDY. Not in a passion! when I see the State
Of Denmark rotten! When I hear the fate
Which hath befallen both the classic domes,[1]
'Neath which my votaries once found their homes!
Where Garrick, monarch of the mimic scene,
His sceptre passed from Kemble down to Kean;
Where Cibber's silver tones the heart would steal,
And Siddons left her mantle to O'Neil!
The Drama banished from her highest places
By *débardeurs* and "fools with varnished faces,"
Sees foreign foes her sacred ruins spurning,
Fiddling like Neros while her Rome is burning!

FANCY. The times have changed; but there is still a stage,
And one on which Macbeth has been the rage! . . .

[*The pavilion opens and discovers "The Blasted Heath,"
same as at the Princess's Theatre, with the Three Witches
—*MACBETH *and* BANQUO *in the costume worn at that
theatre.*[2]

TRAGEDY. "My countryman—and yet I know him not!"

MR WIGAN. More like an antique *Rum'un* than a Scot!

TRAGEDY. A Scotchman, and no kilt?

MRS WIGAN.   Don't Macbeth say,
"We've *scotch'd* the snake, not *kilt* it!"

MR WIGAN.   Oh, don't, pray! . . .

[*Enter* COMEDY *from her tent, in the costume of* LADY
TEAZLE.

FANCY. But see, where brilliant Comedy appears,
Blooming as brightly as in former years,
Invincible, with powder, paint, and patches,
Loaded and primed—her eyes the lighted matches—
Ready to play upon a yawning pit,
She brings up the artillery of wit!

COMEDY. Wit! oh, my dear, don't mention such a thing!

---

[1] Drury Lane and Covent Garden.
[2] During the greater part of the eighteenth century Macbeth was habited in a contemporary military costume; in 1853 he was clad 'historically'—that is, as an ancient Scot was supposed to dress.

THE MODERN PERIOD

Wit on the stage what wit away would fling?
There are so few who know it when they hear it,
And half of those don't like so much as fear it.
Wit! If to theatres for wit they'd come,
Would Farquhar, Congreve, Wycherley be dumb?
Or even the poor devils nowadays,
Who can't help scribbling, hawk their hapless plays
From house to house, to hear the sentence chilling,
" Your piece is clever, but won't draw a shilling."
   Mr Wigan. Then, what will draw?
   Comedy.   O mercy! Tell me, pray,
What horse will win the Derby, sir? You may,
I'm sure, as easily as I tell you
What the dear British public will come to!
Just what they like—whatever that may be—
Not much to hear, and something strange to see. . . .
            My only consolation
Is that all sorts of folks are now so funny,
My dulness will be soon worth any money.
E'en Tragedy—my sister there—sad soul,
Has recently become so very droll,
That the judicious few her acts who see,
Laugh at her more than at poor Comedy!
   Tragedy [advancing on her]. Madam! This irony!——
   Comedy.   Oh, Lud! she'll bite!
   Mr Wigan. Part them! they are incensed!
   Fancy.   A jest so light
Should not to any serious censure doom her;
Like Mr Sulky—she " will have her humour."
   Tragedy. Will she, indeed? Then I'll forgive her gladly,
For lately she has wanted humour sadly.
   Comedy. Now who's ironical, dear sister, pray?
" Oh, sister, sister! sister ev'ry way!"

27. SIR W. S. GILBERT (1836–1911)

Patience

   The 'extravaganza' style, which had flourished in the hands
of J. R. Planché, took on a new lease of life in those of W. S.
Gilbert. It would seem as if the popularity of the " Savoy
operas " would never pass away. Part of this popularity, of
course, comes from the happy collaboration of the author and
the composer, Sir Arthur Sullivan, but there is in Gilbert's work
an enduring literary charm and a wit which is in itself symptomatic of the change coming over English theatrical literature.
In some respects—particularly in the sphere of the pun—Gilbert

403

is the successor of Planché ; in others he points forward toward the new comedy of manners. It would almost seem as if in the eighties of the nineteenth century the minds of dramatists were freeing themselves ; as if the flat drabness of earlier Victorian days were vanishing before a new clarity and refinement of line. It is peculiar that two of the men who most aided this movement should have been Gilbert and Wilde, for the two are intimately associated (not in terms of collaboration) in *Patience*. This opera is one long good-natured but severely critical attack upon that atmosphere which Wilde, the author of the *Poems*, strove to establish in London. It is the answer of wit to that outworn romanticism which is called the æsthetic movement. The passage quoted here explains itself ; and must, in any case, be familiar to many who have never had a volume of the Savoy operas in their hands.

(*Patience ; or, Bunthorne's Bride* was produced at the Opéra-Comique in 1881. The extract given below is taken, by kind permission of the publishers, Messrs Macmillan and Co., Ltd., from *The Savoy Operas* (1926).)

ÆSTHETIC LOVE

Enter BUNTHORNE, *who changes his manner and becomes intensely melodramatic.*

Recit. and Song—BUNTHORNE

Am I alone,
 And unobserved? I am!
Then let me own
 I'm an æsthetic sham!
This air severe
 Is but a mere
     Veneer!
This cynic smile
 Is but a wile
     Of guile!
This costume chaste
 Is but good taste
     Misplaced!
Let me confess!

A languid love for lilies does *not* blight me!
Lank limbs and haggard cheeks do *not* delight me!
 I do *not* care for dirty greens
 By any means.
 I do *not* long for all one sees
 That's Japanese.

THE MODERN PERIOD

I am *not* fond of uttering platitudes
    In stained-glass attitudes.
In short, my mediævalism's affectation,
    Born of a morbid love of admiration!

Song

If you're anxious for to shine in the high æsthetic line as a man of
    culture rare,
You must get up all the germs of the transcendental terms, and
    plant them everywhere.
You lie upon the daisies and discourse in novel phrases of your
    complicated state of mind,
The meaning doesn't matter if it's only idle chatter of a tran-
    scendental kind.
        And every one will say,
        As you walk your mystic way,
"If this young man expresses himself in terms too deep for *me*,
Why, what a very singularly deep young man this deep young man
    must be!"

Be eloquent in praise of the very dull old days which have long
    since passed away,
And convince 'em, if you can, that the reign of good Queen Anne
    was Culture's palmiest day.
Of course you will pooh-pooh whatever's fresh and new, and declare
    it's crude and mean,
For Art stopped short in the cultivated Court of the Empress
    Josephine.
        And every one will say,
        As you walk your mystic way,
"If that's not good enough for him which is good enough for *me*,
Why, what a very cultivated kind of youth this kind of youth
    must be!"

Then a sentimental passion of a vegetable fashion must excite your
    languid spleen,
An attachment *à la* Plato for a bashful young potato, or a not-too-
    French French bean!
Though the Philistines may jostle, you will rank as an apostle in
    the high æsthetic band,
If you walk down Piccadilly with a poppy or a lily in your mediæval
    hand.
        And every one will say,
        As you walk your flowery way,
"If he's content with vegetable love which would certainly not
    suit *me*,
Why, what a particularly pure young man this pure young man
    must be!"

[*At the end of his song* PATIENCE *enters. He sees her.*

BUNTHORNE. Ah! Patience, come hither. I am pleased with thee. The bitter-hearted one, who finds all else hollow, is pleased with thee. For you are not hollow. *Are* you?

PATIENCE. No, thanks, I have dined; but—I beg your pardon—I interrupt you.

BUNTHORNE. Life is made up of interruptions. The tortured soul, yearning for solitude, writhes under them. Oh, but my heart is a-weary! Oh, I am a cursed thing! Don't go.

PATIENCE. Really, I'm very sorry——

BUNTHORNE. Tell me, girl, do you ever yearn?

PATIENCE [*misunderstanding him*]. I earn my living.

BUNTHORNE [*impatiently*]. No, no! Do you know what it is to be heart-hungry? Do you know what it is to yearn for the Indefinable, and yet to be brought face to face, daily, with the Multiplication Table? Do you know what it is to seek oceans and find puddles?—to long for whirlwinds and yet to have to do the best you can with the bellows? That's my case. Oh, I am a cursed thing! Don't go.

PATIENCE. If you please, I don't understand you—you frighten me!

BUNTHORNE. Don't be frightened—it's only poetry.

PATIENCE. Well, if that's poetry, I don't like poetry.

BUNTHORNE [*eagerly*]. Don't you? [*Aside*] Can I trust her? [*Aloud*] Patience, you don't like poetry—well, between you and me, *I* don't like poetry. It's hollow, unsubstantial—unsatisfactory. What's the use of yearning for Elysian Fields when you know you can't get 'em, and would only let 'em out on building leases if you had 'em?

PATIENCE. Sir, I——

BUNTHORNE. Patience, I have long loved you. Let me tell you a secret. I am not as bilious as I look. If you like, I will cut my hair. There is more innocent fun within me than a casual spectator would imagine. You have never seen me frolicsome. Be a good girl—a very good girl—and one day you shall. If you are fond of touch-and-go jocularity—this is the shop for it.

PATIENCE. Sir, I will speak plainly. In the matter of love I am untaught. I have never loved but my great-aunt. But I am quite certain that, under the circumstances, I couldn't possibly love *you*.

BUNTHORNE. Oh, you think not?

PATIENCE. I'm quite sure of it. Quite sure. Quite.

BUNTHORNE. Very good. Life is henceforth a blank. I don't care what becomes of me. I have only to ask that you will not abuse my confidence; though *you* despise me, I am extremely popular with the other young ladies.

PATIENCE. I only ask that you will leave me and never renew the subject.

BUNTHORNE. Certainly. Broken-hearted and desolate, I go.

[*Recites.*

> Oh, to be wafted away
>   From this black Aceldama of sorrow,
> Where the dust of an earthy to-day
>   Is the earth of a dusty to-morrow!

It is a little thing of my own. I call it *Heart Foam*. I shall not publish it. Farewell! Patience, Patience, farewell!

28. SIR ARTHUR WING PINERO (*born* 1855)

Trelawny of the "Wells"

Trelawny of the "Wells" contains one of the most delightful pictures we possess of the life of a provincial company. Perhaps the picture is tinged with the hues of sentiment, but Sir Arthur Pinero's powers of observation and his sense of humour will not let him depart overfar from life. He might, it is true, have painted in darker colours, but for his purpose the lighter and the brighter colours are the more harmonious. As in all the work of Sir Arthur Pinero, the theatrical effect is skilful. On the stage the first act (the conclusion of which is given here) works up to the climax of Rose's speech, and on the stage the hilarity and the gaiety, mingled with almost happy tears, provide a magnificent atmosphere on which the rest of the plot can be built up. The scene presented below is self-explanatory. Rose Trelawny has become engaged to Arthur Gower, and in her honour a party is being held in the lodgings of Mr and Mrs Telfer, principals in the theatre of the "Wells." As the author notes in his directions to the stage manager, this play should be read in the light of the sixties of the nineteenth century, not in that either of the nineties or of the present day.

(*Trelawny of the "Wells"* was produced at the Court Theatre in 1898. The following passage is taken, by kind permission of the author, from the play as published by Messrs William Heinemann, Ltd., in 1898.)

THE COMPANY OF THE "WELLS"

TELFER [*filling his glass*]. I give you The Queen, coupling with that toast the name of Miss Violet Sylvester—Mrs Telfer—formerly, as you are aware, of the Theatre Royal, Drury Lane. Miss Sylvester has so frequently and, if I may say so, so nobly impersonated the various queens of tragedy that I cannot but feel she is a fitting person to acknowledge our expression of loyalty. [*Raising his glass*] The Queen! And Miss Violet Sylvester!

> [*All rise, except* MRS TELFER, *and drink the toast. After drinking* MRS MOSSOP *passes her tumbler to* ABLETT.

ABLETT. The Queen! Miss Vi'lent Sylvester!

> [*He drinks and returns the glass to* MRS MOSSOP. *The*

407

company being reseated, MRS TELFER *rises. Her reception is a polite one.*

MRS TELFER [*heavily*]. Ladies and gentlemen, I have played fourteen or fifteen queens in my time——

TELFER. Thirteen, my love, to be exact; I was calculating this morning.

MRS TELFER. Very well, I have played thirteen of 'em. And, as parts, they are not worth a tinker's oath. I thank you for the favour with which you have received me.

> [*She sits; the applause is heartier. During the demonstration* SARAH *appears in the doorway, with a kitchen chair.*

ABLETT [*to Sarah*]. Wot's all this?

SARAH [*to* ABLETT]. Is the speeches on?

ABLETT. H'on! yes, and you be h'off!

> [*She places the chair against the open door and sits, full of determination. At intervals* ABLETT *vainly represents to her the impropriety of her proceeding.*

TELFER [*again rising*]. Ladies and gentlemen. Bumpers, I charge ye! The toast I 'ad next intended to propose was Our Immortal Bard, Shakespeare, and I had meant, myself, to 'ave offered a few remarks in response——

GADD [*to* IMOGEN, *bitterly*]. Ha!

TELFER. But with our friend's horses champing their bits, I am compelled—nay, forced—to postpone this toast to a later period of the day, and to give you now what we may justly designate the toast of the afternoon. Ladies and gentlemen, we are about to lose, to part with, one of our companions, a young comrade who came amongst us many months ago, who in fact joined the company of the "Wells" last February twelvemonth, after a considerable experience in the provinces of this great country.

COLPOYS. Hear, hear!

AVONIA [*tearfully*]. Hear, hear! [*With a sob*] I detested her at first.

COLPOYS. Order!

IMOGEN. Be quiet, 'Vonia!

TELFER. Her late mother an actress, herself made familiar with the stage from childhood if not from infancy, Miss Rose Trelawny —for I will no longer conceal from you that it is to Miss Trelawny I refer—[*loud applause*] Miss Trelawny is the stuff of which great actresses are made.

ALL. Hear, hear!

ABLETT [*softly*]. 'Ear, 'ear!

TELFER. So much for the actress. Now for the young lady— nay, the woman, the gyirl. Rose is a good girl—[*Loud applause, to which* ABLETT *and* SARAH *contribute largely.* AVONIA *rises and impulsively embraces* ROSE. *She is recalled to her seat by a general remonstrance.*] A good girl——

MRS TELFER [*clutching a knife*]. Yes, and I should like to hear anybody, man or woman——!

THE MODERN PERIOD

TELFER. She is a good girl, and will be long remembered by us as much for her private virtues as for the commanding authority of her genius. [*More applause, during which there is a sharp altercation between* ABLETT *and* SARAH.] And now, what has happened to "the expectancy and Rose of the fair state"?

IMOGEN. Good, Telfer! good!

GADD [*to* IMOGEN]. Tsch, tsch! forced! forced!

TELFER. I will tell you—[*impressively*]—a man has crossed her path.

ABLETT [*in a low voice*]. Shame!

MRS MOSSOP [*turning to him*]. Mr Ablett!

TELFER. A man—ah, but also a gentle-man. [*Applause.*] A gentleman of probity, a gentleman of honour, and a gentleman of wealth and station. That gentleman, with the modesty of youth,—for I may tell you at once that 'e is not an old man,—comes to us and asks us to give him this gyirl to wife. And, friends, we have done so. A few preliminaries 'ave, I believe, still to be concluded between Mr Gower and his family, and then the bond will be signed, the compact entered upon, the mutual trust accepted. Riches this youthful pair will possess—but what is gold? May they be rich in each other's society, in each other's love! May they—I can wish them no greater joy—be as happy in their married life as my—my—as Miss Sylvester and I 'ave been in ours! [*Raising his glass*] Miss Rose Trelawny—Mr Arthur Gower! [*The toast is drunk by the company, upstanding. Three cheers are called for by* COLPOYS, *and given. Those who have risen then sit.*] Miss Trelawny.

ROSE [*weeping*]. No, no, Mr Telfer.

MRS TELFER [*to* TELFER, *softly*]. Let her be for a minute, James.

TELFER. Mr Gower. [ARTHUR *rises and is well received.*]

ARTHUR. Ladies and gentlemen, I—I would I were endowed with Mr Telfer's flow of—of—of splendid eloquence. But I am no orator, no speaker, and therefore cannot tell you how highly—how deeply I appreciate the—the compliment——

ABLETT. You deserve it, Mr Glover!

MRS MOSSOP. Hush!

ARTHUR. All I can say is that I regard Miss Trelawny in the light of a—a solemn charge, and I—I trust that if ever I have the pleasure of —of meeting any of you again, I shall be able to render a good—a a—satisfactory—satisfactory——

TOM [*in an audible whisper*]. Account.

ARTHUR. Account of the way—of the way—in which I—in which—— [*Loud applause.*] Before I bring these observations to a conclusion, let me assure you that it has been a great privilege to me to meet—to have been thrown with—a band of artists—whose talents—whose striking talents—whose talents——

TOM [*kindly, behind his hand*]. Sit down.

ARTHUR [*helplessly*]. Whose talents not only interest and instruct the—the more refined residents of this district, but whose talents——

409

IMOGEN [*quietly to* COLPOYS]. Get him to sit down.

ARTHUR. The fame of whose talents, I should say——

COLPOYS [*quietly to* MRS MOSSOP]. He's to sit down. Tell Mother Telfer.

ARTHUR. The fame of whose talents has spread to—to regions——

MRS MOSSOP [*quietly to* MRS TELFER]. They say he's to sit down.

ARTHUR. To—to quarters of the town—to quarters——

MRS TELFER [*to* ARTHUR]. Sit down!

ARTHUR. Eh?

MRS TELFER. You finished long ago. Sit down.

ARTHUR. Thank you. I'm exceedingly sorry. Great heavens, how wretchedly I've done it!

> [*He sits, burying his head in his hands. More applause.*

TELFER. Rose, my child.

> [ROSE *starts to her feet. The rest rise with her, and cheer again, and wave handkerchiefs. She goes from one to the other, round the table, embracing and kissing and crying over them all excitedly.* SARAH *is kissed, but upon* ABLETT *is bestowed only a handshake, to his evident dissatisfaction.* IMOGEN *runs to the piano and strikes up the air of "Ever of Thee." When* ROSE *gets back to the place she mounts her chair, with the aid of* TOM *and* TELFER, *and faces them with flashing eyes. They pull the flowers out of the vases and throw them at her.*

ROSE. Mr Telfer, Mrs Telfer! My friends! Boys! Ladies and gentlemen! No, don't stop, Jenny! go on! [*Singing, her arms stretched out to them*] "Ever of thee I'm fondly dreaming, Thy gentle voice——" You remember! the song I sang in *The Peddler of Marseilles*—which made Arthur fall in love with me! Well, I know I shall dream of *you*, of all of you, very often, as the song says. Don't believe [*wiping away her tears*], oh, don't believe that, because I shall have married a swell, you and the old "Wells"—the dear old "Wells"!—— [*Cheers.* You and the old "Wells" will have become nothing to me! No, many and many a night you will see me in the house, looking down at you from the Circle—me and my husband——

ARTHUR. Yes, yes, certainly!

ROSE. And if you send for me I'll come behind the curtain to you, and sit with you and talk of bygone times, these times that end to-day. And shall I tell you the moments which will be the happiest to me in my life, however happy I may be with Arthur? Why, whenever I find that I am recognised by people, and pointed out—people in the pit of a theatre, in the street, no matter where; and when I can fancy they're saying to each other, "Look! that was Miss Trelawny! you remember—Trelawny! Trelawny of the 'Wells'!"——

> [*They cry "Trelawny!" and "Trelawny of the 'Wells'!" and again "Trelawny!" wildly.*

THE MODERN PERIOD

29. HENRY ARTHUR JONES (*born* 1851)

The Liars

From the time of Robertson the new comedy of manners, depending upon characterization and dialogue rather than upon plot, developed slowly but certainly. Wilde cultivated the wit which had been a distinguishing feature of the earlier manners style, while others, such as Mr Henry Arthur Jones in *The Liars*, leant more toward the depiction of contemporary types and contemporary society. In many ways *The Liars* forms a landmark in the history of modern drama, for, brilliant as it is in itself, it does not indicate the end but the beginning of a period. Vastly different as Mr Somerset Maugham's comedies may be from those of Mr Henry Arthur Jones, they belong to that same movement to which the latter contributed so much from the nineties of the last century to the present time. The true comedy of manners is realistic in aim, but from the very fact that its main objective is the displaying of the manners of society it is artificial; it aims at the realistic depiction of artificial life, and frequently the success of the picture depends upon the subtle contrast instituted by the dramatist between the external veneer of society manners and the evidences of natural man (and woman) peeping through the veil. This quality appears often in the present play and contributes much to its permanent interest. Since a comedy of manners rarely uses a plot for a greater purpose than as an excuse to display society, it is unnecessary to say anything here by way of introduction to the passage quoted below. The reader needs to understand only that the story depends on an unfortunate flirtation of a married lady and on its complications.

(*The Liars* was produced at the Criterion Theatre in October 1897. The passage presented here is taken, by kind permission of the author and of the publishers, Messrs Macmillan and Co., Ltd., from the edition of 1904.)

SOCIETY CONVERSATION IN THE NINETIES

SIR CHRISTOPHER. Oh, nonsense, Nepean; you're mistaken!

GEORGE NEPEAN. You'd better say a word to Falkner——

SIR CHRISTOPHER [*with a warning look*]. Shush!

GEORGE. If you don't, I shall drop a very strong hint to my brother.

SIR CHRISTOPHER [*more peremptorily*]. Shush, shush!

FREDDIE. What's the matter?

SIR CHRISTOPHER. Nothing, Freddie, nothing! Our friend here [*trying to link his arm in* GEORGE'S—GEORGE *stands off*]. He is a little old-fashioned. He doesn't understand that in all really innocent flirtations ladies allow themselves a very large latitude

411

indeed. In fact, from my very modest experience of the sex—take it for what it's worth—I should say the more innocent the flirtation, the larger the latitude the lady allows herself, eh, Mrs Crespin?

MRS CRESPIN. Oh, we are all latitudinarians at heart.

SIR CHRISTOPHER. Yes; but a lady who practises extensively as a latitudinarian rarely becomes a—a—a—longitudinarian, eh?

MRS CRESPIN. Oh, I wouldn't answer for her! It's a horrid, wicked world; and if once a woman allows one of you wretches to teach her the moral geography of it, it's ten to one she gets her latitude and longitude mixed up before she has had time to look at the map. *[Goes up to opening, and looks off.*

FREDDIE [*to* SIR CHRISTOPHER]. I say, I'm awfully sorry about this. You know I told Rosamund how it would be if we had Falkner here——.

SIR CHRISTOPHER [*draws* FREDDIE *aside*]. Shush! Tell Lady Rosamund to caution Lady Jessica——

FREDDIE. I will. But Rosamund generally does just the opposite of what I tell her. Don't be surprised, old fellow, if you hear some of these days that I've—well, don't be surprised.

SIR CHRISTOPHER. At what?

FREDDIE. Well, I shall—now, candidly, old fellow—we're tiled in, quite between ourselves—if you found yourself landed as I am, what would you do?

SIR CHRISTOPHER. You mean if I found myself married?

FREDDIE. Yes.

SIR CHRISTOPHER. I should make the best of it.

[GEORGE *comes up to them.* MRS CRESPIN *comes from back of tent.*

GEORGE [*to* SIR CHRISTOPHER]. Then its understood that you'll give Falkner a hint?

SIR CHRISTOPHER. My dear fellow, surely your brother is the best judge——

GEORGE. Of what he doesn't see?

SIR CHRISTOPHER. He's here.

GEORGE. He's leaving for Devonshire to-night—unless I stop him. Will that be necessary?

SIR CHRISTOPHER. No. Falkner is my friend. I introduced him to Lady Jessica. If you insist, I'll speak to him. But I'm sure you're wrong. He's the very soul of honour. I didn't live with him out there those three awful years without knowing him.

GEORGE. I don't see what your living three years in Africa with him has got to do with it.

MRS CRESPIN. Let's see how it works out. Falkner behaves most gallantly in Africa. Falkner rescues Mrs Ebernoe. Falkner splendidly avenges Colonel Ebernoe's death, and strikes terror into every slave-dealer's heart. Falkner returns to England covered with glory. A grateful nation goes into a panic of admiration, and makes itself slightly ridiculous over Falkner. Falkner is the

THE MODERN PERIOD

lion of the season. Therefore we may be quite sure that Falkner won't make love to any pretty woman who comes in his way. It doesn't seem to work out right.

SIR CHRISTOPHER. But Falkner is not an ordinary man, not even an ordinary hero.

MRS CRESPIN. My dear Sir Christopher, the one cruel fact about heroes is that they are made of flesh and blood! Oh, if only they were made of waxwork, or Crown Derby ware, or Britannia metal; but, alas and alas! they're always made of flesh and blood.

COKE. Where did Falkner come from? What were his people?

SIR CHRISTOPHER. His grandfather was what Nonconformists call an eminent divine, his father was a rich city merchant; his mother was a farmer's daughter. Falkner himself is a—well, he's a Puritan Don Quixote, mounted on Pegasus.

MRS CRESPIN. Put a Puritan Don Quixote on horseback, and he'll ride to the—Lady Jessica, eh?

SIR CHRISTOPHER. Hush! He'll love and he'll ride away.

MRS CRESPIN [significantly]. I sincerely hope so.

COKE. I must say that Falkner is less objectionable than Dissenters generally are. I have an unconquerable aversion to Dissenters.

SIR CHRISTOPHER. Oh, I hate 'em! But they saved England, hang 'em! And I'm not sure whether they're not the soundest part of the nation to-day.

MRS CRESPIN. Oh, pray don't tell them so, just as they're getting harmless and sensible—and a little artistic.

[A piano is played very softly and beautifully at a distance of some twenty yards. They all listen.

MRS CRESPIN. Is that Mrs Ebernoe?

SIR CHRISTOPHER. Yes.

MRS CRESPIN. What a beautiful touch she has?

SIR CHRISTOPHER. She has a beautiful nature.

MRS CRESPIN. Indeed! I thought she was a little stiff and unsociable. But perhaps we are too frivolous.

SIR CHRISTOPHER. Perhaps. And she hasn't quite recovered from poor Ebernoe's death.

[Enter LADY ROSAMUND and DOLLY COKE in evening dress. DOLLY is without any wrap on her shoulders.

MRS CRESPIN. But that's nearly two years ago. Is it possible we still have women amongst us who can mourn two years for a man? It gives me hopes again for my sex.

FREDDIE [his back to LADY ROSAMUND]. I know jolly well Rosamund won't mourn two years for me.

LADY ROSAMUND [a clear-cut, bright, pretty woman]. You're quite right, Freddie, I shan't. But if you behave very prettily meantime, I promise you a decent six weeks. So be satisfied, and don't make a disturbance down there [with a little gesture pointing down] and create the impression that I wasn't a model wife.

EXTRACTS FROM BRITISH & IRISH PLAYS

[FREDDIE *makes an appealing gesture for sympathy to* SIR CHRISTOPHER.

COKE [*in a very querulous, pedantic tone to* DOLLY]. No wrap again! Really, my dear, I do wish you would take more precautions against the night air. If you should take influenza again——

DOLLY [*a pretty, empty-headed little woman*]. Oh, my dear Archie, if I do, it is I who will have to cough and sneeze!

COKE. Yes; but it is I who will be compelled to listen to you. I do wish you would remember how very inconvenient it is for me when you have influenza.

DOLLY. My dear, you can't expect me to remember *all* the things that are inconvenient to you. Besides, other people don't wrap up. Jessica is out on the river with absolutely nothing on her shoulders.

MRS CRESPIN. Is it not a physiological fact that when our hearts reach a certain temperature our shoulders may be, and often are, safely left bare?

[GEORGE NEPEAN *has been listening. He suddenly rises, comes some steps towards them as if about to speak, stops, then turns and exit with great determination.*

SIR CHRISTOPHER. Mrs Crespin, you saw that?

MRS CRESPIN. Yes. Where has he gone?

SIR CHRISTOPHER. I suppose to tell his brother his suspicions. I'm sure you meant nothing just now, but—[*glancing round*]—we are all friends of Lady Jessica's, aren't we?

MRS CRESPIN. Oh, certainly. But don't you think you ought to get Mr Falkner away?

SIR CHRISTOPHER. He'll be leaving England soon. These fresh outbreaks amongst the slave-traders will give us no end of trouble, and the Government will have to send Falkner out. Meantime——

MRS CRESPIN. Meantime, doesn't Mrs Ebernoe play divinely?

[*Going off.*

SIR CHRISTOPHER [*politely intercepting her*]. Meantime it's understood that nothing more is to be said of this?

MRS CRESPIN. Oh, my dear Sir Christopher, what more can be said?

30. GEORGE BERNARD SHAW (*born* 1856)

How He Lied to Her Husband

One of the chief motives in the work of Mr Shaw is the desire to ridicule romanticism, and in so far he is one of the leading figures in the modern classical school. Romanticism is inclined to argue from the ideal; to assume a theory and overlook facts that will not fit in with that theory; to base a conception of life on a series of polite assumptions. Mr Shaw has the eye of the frank and observant classicist. For him the facts will not square

414

THE MODERN PERIOD

with the assumptions, and in his plays he endeavours to laugh those assumptions out of court. It is this that makes the playlet *How He Lied to Her Husband*—which would otherwise be only a bright dramatic joke—a kind of symbol of Mr Shaw's aims and purpose. The romantic convention is that a poet should be pale and anæmic ; Henry (or He) is a prize-fighter. The romantic convention is that husbands should be jealous of admirers of their wives ; Mr Bompas gets really annoyed only when Henry mendaciously pretends that he has no real passion for Mrs Bompas. The whole playlet shows the theme of the romantic triangle topsy-turvy. Preconceptions are crushed down by the author's delightful wit and by his hold on reality. Mr Shaw has dealt with these subjects both seriously and in a laughing strain, but always there is the same quality of mood and the same quizzical and good-natured satire of hypocrisy, whether that be conscious or unconscious, and of the artificial standards of romanticism.

(*How He Lied to Her Husband* was written in 1904. Characteristically Mr Shaw has written to me that I " have a statutory privilege of reasonable quotation to which " he does " not demur in the least." The following extract, I trust of reasonable proportions, is taken from the edition of 1907, published by Messrs Constable and Company, Ltd., and Brentano's, New York.)

THE ETERNAL TRIANGLE

HER HUSBAND [*shaken*]. Apjohn: play fair. Don't abuse your intellectual gifts. Do you really mean that I am making a fool of myself?

HE [*earnestly*]. Believe me, you are. I assure you, on my honor as a gentleman, that I have never had the slightest feeling for Mrs Bompas beyond the ordinary esteem and regard of a pleasant acquaintance.

HER HUSBAND [*shortly, showing ill humor for the first time*]. Oh, indeed.

[*He leaves his hearth and begins to approach* HENRY *slowly, looking him up and down with growing resentment.*

HE [*hastening to improve the impression made by his mendacity*]. I should never have dreamt of writing poems to her. The thing is absurd.

HER HUSBAND [*reddening ominously*]. Why is it absurd?

HE [*shrugging his shoulders*]. Well, it happens that I do not admire Mrs Bompas—in that way.

HER HUSBAND [*breaking out in* HENRY'S *face*]. Let me tell you that Mrs Bompas has been admired by better men than you, you soapy headed little puppy, you.

HE [*much taken aback*]. There is no need to insult me like this. I assure you, on my honor as a——

415

HER HUSBAND [*too angry to tolerate a reply, and boring* HENRY *more and more towards the piano*]. You dont admire Mrs Bompas! You would never dream of writing poems to Mrs Bompas! My wife's not good enough for you, isnt she? [*Fiercely*] Who are you, pray, that you should be so jolly superior?

HE. Mr Bompas: I can make allowances for your jealousy——

HER HUSBAND. Jealousy! do you suppose I'm jealous of *you*? No, nor of ten like you. But if you think I'll stand here and let you insult my wife in her own house, youre mistaken.

HE [*very uncomfortable with his back against the piano and* TEDDY *standing over him threateningly*]. How can I convince you? Be reasonable. I tell you my relations with Mrs Bompas are relations of perfect coldness—of indifference——

HER HUSBAND [*scornfully*]. Say it again: say it again. You're proud of it, arnt you? Yah! youre not worth kicking.

> [HENRY *suddenly executes the feat known to pugilists as slipping, and changes sides with* TEDDY, *who is now between* HENRY *and the piano*.

HE. Look here: I'm not going to stand this.

HER HUSBAND. Oh, you have some blood in your body after all! Good job!

HE. This is ridiculous. I assure you Mrs Bompas is quite——

HER HUSBAND. What is Mrs Bompas to you, I'd like to know. I'll tell you what Mrs Bompas is. Shes the smartest woman in the smartest set in South Kensington, and the handsomest, and the cleverest, and the most fetching to experienced men who know a good thing when they see it, whatever she may be to conceited penny-a-lining puppies who think nothing good enough for them. It's admitted by the best people; and not to know it argues yourself unknown. Three of our first actor-managers have offered her a hundred a week if she'll go on the stage when they start a repertory theatre; and I think they know what theyre about as well as you. The only member of the present Cabinet that you might call a handsome man has neglected the business of the country to dance with her, though he dont belong to our set as a regular thing. One of the first professional poets in Bedford Park wrote a sonnet to her, worth all your amateur trash. At Ascot last season the eldest son of a duke excused himself from calling on me on the grounds that his feelings for Mrs Bompas were not consistent with his duty to me as host; and it did him honour and me too. But [*with gathering fury*] she isnt good enough for *you*, it seems. You regard her with coldness, with indifference; and you have the cool cheek to tell me so to my face. For two pins I'd flatten your nose in to teach you manners. Introducing a fine woman to you is casting pearls before swine [*yelling at him*] before SWINE! d'ye hear?

HE [*with a deplorable lack of polish*]. You call me a swine again and I'll land you one on the chin thatll make your head sing for a week

HER HUSBAND [*exploding*]. What——!

THE MODERN PERIOD

> [*He charges at* HENRY *with bull-like fury.* HENRY *places
> himself on guard in the manner of a well taught boxer,
> and gets away smartly, but unfortunately forgets the
> stool which is just behind him. He falls backwards
> over it, unintentionally pushing it against the shins
> of* BOMPAS, *who falls forward over it.* MRS BOMPAS,
> *with a scream, rushes into the room between the sprawling
> champions, and sits down on the floor in order to get her
> right arm round her husband's neck.*

SHE. You shant, Teddy: you shant. You will be killed: he is
a prizefighter.

31. ARNOLD BENNETT (*born* 1867)

The Great Adventure

The theme of pretended death is by no means a new one; it
appears as a comic theme at least as early as the eighteenth
century; but Mr Arnold Bennett in *The Great Adventure* has
used it with unquestioned freshness and novelty. The characterization of his famous painter, Ilam Carve, was precisely that
which was required to make his theme seem probable. The first
act, indeed, is a masterpiece considered from this point of view.
From the time when the curtain rises to reveal the great but
practically useless artist and his pneumonia-stricken valet in the
hall of the empty house to the time when the doctor calls and
assumes the valet to be the master we have an excellent example
of successful foundation-building. The characters are well harmonized with the theme, and, although parts of the dialogue
are witty, the wit is never allowed to break unduly into the
probability of the story. Indeed, *The Great Adventure* provides
an excellent example of the blending of naturalistic dialogue and
of that literary refinement which is an inheritance of the manners
style. On the stage part of the interest we take in the play
comes from the action, but our chief enjoyment is derived from
the neat, attractive, and always characteristic dialogue itself.

(*The Great Adventure*[1] was first produced at the Kingsway
Theatre in March 1913. The passage given below is taken, by kind
permission of the author and of the publishers, Messrs Methuen
and Co., Ltd., from the edition published in 1913.)

THE GREAT PAINTER IS TAKEN FOR HIS VALET

CARVE. What's this about a nurse?

PASCOE [*busy with syringe, water, and syringe-case*]. I'm sending
one in. [*Ironically*] Do you see any objection?

[1] Copyright 1913 in U.S.A. by Messrs Doubleday, Doran and Company,
Inc., Garden City, New York.

2 D

417

CARVE. On the contrary, I should like him to be treated with every care. He's invaluable to me.

PASCOE [*staggered*]. Invaluable to *you*! Of course in my line of business I get used to meeting odd people——

CARVE [*recovering from his mistake*]. But you think I carry oddness rather far?

PASCOE. The idea did pass through my mind.

CARVE. Nervousness—nothing but nervousness. I'm very nervous. And then—you know the saying—like master, like man.

PASCOE [*indicating back room with a gesture ; in a slightly more confidential tone as* CARVE's *personal attractiveness gains on him*]. Mr Carve odd?

CARVE. Oh, very. Always was. Ever since I've known him. You remember his first picture at the Academy?

PASCOE. No, not exactly.

CARVE. Either you remember it exactly or you don't remember it at all. Life-size picture of a policeman blowing his whistle.

PASCOE. Yes; it must have been odd, that must.

CARVE. Not a bit. The oddness of the fellow——

PASCOE. What "fellow"—your governor?

CARVE [*nods*]. His oddness came out in this way—although the thing had been really a great success, from that day to this he's never painted another life-size picture of a policeman blowing his whistle.

PASCOE. I don't see anything very odd there——

CARVE. Don't you? Well, perhaps you don't go in for art much. If you did, you'd know that the usual and correct thing for a painter who has made a great success with a life-size picture of a policeman blowing his whistle, is to keep on doing life-size pictures of a policeman blowing his whistle for ever and ever, so that the public can always count on getting from him a life-size picture of a policeman blowing his whistle.

PASCOE. I observe you are one of those comic valets. Nervousness again, no doubt.

CARVE [*smiling and continuing*]. Seeing the way he invariably flouted the public, it's always been a mystery to me how he managed to make a name, to say nothing of money.

PASCOE. Money! He must make pots. You say I don't go in for art much, but I always read the big sales at Christie's. Why, wasn't it that policeman picture that Lord Leonard Alcar bought for 2000 guineas last year?

CARVE. No, not Alcar. I think the bobby was last bought by Texel.

PASCOE. Texel? Who's Texel?

CARVE. Collector—United States—one of their kings, I'm told.

PASCOE. Oh, him! Controls all the ink in the United States.

CARVE. Really! That's what I should call influence. No. It was the *Pelicans feeding their Young* that Alcar bought. Four thousand. You're getting mixed up.

418

THE MODERN PERIOD

PASCOE. Perhaps I am. I know I'm constantly seeing Mr Carve's name in connection with Lord Leonard Alcar's. It's a nice question which is the best known of the two.

CARVE. Then the—governor really is famous in England? You see we never come to England.

PASCOE. Famous—I should think he was. Aren't they always saying he's the finest colourist since Titian? And look at his prices!

CARVE. Yes. I've looked at his prices. Titian's prices are higher, but Titian isn't what you'd call famous with the general public, is he? What I want to know is—is the governor famous among the general public?

PASCOE. Yes.

CARVE. About how famous should you say he is?

PASCOE [hesitating]. Well—[abruptly] that's a silly question.

CARVE. No, it isn't. Is he as famous as—er—Harry Lauder?

PASCOE [shakes his head]. You mustn't go to extremes.

CARVE. Is he as famous as Harry Vardon?

PASCOE. Never heard of him.

CARVE. I only see these names in the papers. Is he as famous as Bernard Shaw?

PASCOE. Yes, I should say he was.

CARVE. Oh, well that's not so bad. Better than I thought! It's so difficult to judge where one is—er—personally concerned. Especially if you're never on the spot.

PASCOE. So it's true Mr Carve never comes to England?

CARVE. Why should he come to England? He isn't a portrait-painter. It's true he owns this house, but surely that isn't sufficient excuse for living in a place like England?

PASCOE. Of course, if you look at it like that, there's no particular attractiveness in England that I've ever seen. But that answer wouldn't satisfy Redcliffe Gardens. Redcliffe Gardens is persuaded that there must be a special reason.

CARVE. Well, there is.

PASCOE [interested in spite of himself]. Indeed!

CARVE [confidentially]. Have a cigarette? [Offering case.

PASCOE [staggered anew, but accepting]. That's a swagger case.

CARVE. Oh! [Calmly] He gave it me.

PASCOE. Really?

CARVE. Well, you see we're more like brothers—been together so long. He gives me his best suits too. Look at this waistcoat.

[Motions the hypnotised PASCOE to take a chair. They light their cigarettes.

[Enter HORNING.

PASCOE [somewhat impatient]. He's not worse already?

HORNING. Where's that brandy and water?

PASCOE. Be careful. He's had about enough of that.

HORNING. Seeing I've had no dinner yet—I thought it might suit me. [Exit with tumbler.

PASCOE [*to* CARVE *with renewed eagerness*]. So there is a special reason why you keep out of England.

CARVE. Yes—shyness.

PASCOE. How—shyness?

CARVE. Just simple shyness. Shyness is a disease with the governor, a perfect disease.

PASCOE. But every one's shy. The more experience I get the more convinced I am that we're all shy. Why, you were shy when you came to fetch me!

CARVE. Did you notice it?

PASCOE. Of course. And I was shy when I came in here. I was thinking to myself, "Now I'm going to see the great Ilam Carve actually in the flesh," and I was shy. You'd think my profession would have cured me of being shy, but not a bit. Nervous disease, of course! Ought to be treated as such. Almost universal. Besides, even if he is shy, your governor—even if he's a hundred-fold shy, that's no reason for keeping out of England. Shyness is not one of those diseases you can cure by change of climate.

CARVE. Pardon me. My esteemed employer's shyness is a special shyness. He's only shy when he has to play the celebrity. So long as people take him for no one in particular he's quite all right. For instance, he's never shy with me. But instantly people approach him as the celebrity, instantly he sees in the eye of the beholder any consciousness of being in the presence of a toff—then he gets desperately shy, and his one desire is to be alone at sea or to be buried somewhere deep in the bosom of the earth. [PASCOE *laughs*. What are you laughing at? [CARVE *also laughs*.

PASCOE. Go on, go on. I'm enjoying it.

CARVE. No, but seriously! It's true what I tell you. It amounts almost to a tragedy in the brilliant career of my esteemed. You see now that England would be impossible for him as a residence. You see, don't you?

PASCOE. Quite.

CARVE. Why, even on the Continent, in the big towns and the big hotels, we often travel *incognito* for safety. It's only in the country districts that he goes about under his own name.

PASCOE. So that he's really got no friends?

CARVE. None, except a few Italian and Spanish peasants—and me.

PASCOE. Well, well! It's an absolute mania then, this shyness.

CARVE [*slightly hurt*]. Oh, not so bad as that! And then it's only fair to say he has his moments of great daring—you may say rashness.

PASCOE. All timid people are like that.

CARVE. Are they? [*Musing*] We're here now owing to one of his moments of rashness.

PASCOE. Indeed!

CARVE. Yes. We met an English lady in a village in Andalusia,

420

and—well, of course, I can't tell you everything—but she flirted with him and he flirted with her.

PASCOE. Under his own name?

CARVE. Yes. And then he proposed to her. I knew all along it was a blunder.

PASCOE [*ironic*]. Did you?

CARVE. Yes. She belonged to the aristocracy, and she was one of those amateur painters that wander about the Continent by themselves—you know.

PASCOE. And did she accept?

CARVE. Oh, yes. They got as far as Madrid together, and then all of a sudden my esteemed saw that he had made a mistake.

PASCOE. And what then?

CARVE. We fled the country. We hooked it. The idea of coming to London struck him—just the caprice of a man who's lost his head—and here we are.

PASCOE [*after a pause*]. He doesn't seem to me from the look of him to be a man who'd — shall we say? — strictly avoided women.

CARVE [*startled, with a gesture towards back*]. Him? [PASCOE *nods*.] Really! Confound him! Now, I've always suspected that; though he manages to keep his goings-on devilish quiet.

PASCOE [*rising*]. It occurs to me, my friend, that I'm listening to too much. But you're so persuasive.

CARVE. It's such a pleasure to talk freely—for once in a way.

PASCOE. Freely—is the word.

CARVE. Oh! He won't mind!

PASCOE [*in a peculiar tone*]. It's quite possible!

32. W. SOMERSET MAUGHAM (*born* 1874)

Our Betters

In the last decade of last century one of the signs of revival in comic drama was the return made by several playwrights to the style of the Restoration comedy of manners. Those comedies which, in the mid-nineteenth century, aimed at depicting real life generally dealt with middle-class existence in an artificial way ; the true comedy of manners delineates the artificial conventions of upper-class society in a realistic way. It loves the intrigues of that society, its jealousies, its envies, its cynical hardness ; it delights in contrasting the outer conventions of society and the natural passions of the men and women composing that society. *Our Betters* is as near an approach to the spirit of Wycherley as we can find in our own days. The wit is not so apparent, for these modern fashionables are not so brilliant as the lords and ladies of Charles' Court, but the treatment of their lives is the same, the dramatic devices are the same. Pearl is a true denizen of the world of intrigue, and Fenwick is such a character as might have provided amusement for a Sedley or a Rochester.

(*Our Betters* was originally produced at the Globe Theatre in September 1923. The following extract is taken from the edition of 1924, by kind permission of the author and of the publishers, Messrs William Heinemann, Ltd., London, and Messrs Doubleday, Doran and Company, Inc., Garden City, New York.)

RESTORATION MANNERS IN MODERN LONDON

FENWICK. You've got a great heart, girlie. The world just thinks you're a smart, fashionable woman, clever, brilliant, beautiful, a leader of fashion, but I know different. I know you've got a heart of gold.

PEARL. You're a romantic old thing, Arthur.

FENWICK. My love for you is the most precious thing I have in the world. You're my guiding star, you're my ideal. You stand to me for all that's pure and noble and clean in womanhood. God bless you, girlie. I don't know what I should do if you failed me. I don't believe I could live if I ever found out that you weren't what I think you.

PEARL [*with her tongue in her cheek*]. You shan't, if I can help it.

FENWICK. You do care for me a little, girlie?

PEARL. Of course I do.

FENWICK. I'm an old man, girlie.

PEARL. What nonsense! I look upon you as a mere boy.

FENWICK [*flattered*]. Well, I expect a good many young men would be glad to have my physique. I can work fourteen hours on end and feel as fresh as a daisy at the end of it.

PEARL. Your vitality is wonderful.

FENWICK. I sometimes wonder what it is that first drew you to me, girlie.

PEARL. I don't know. I suppose it was the impression of strength you gave.

FENWICK. Yes, I've often been told that. It's very difficult for people to be with me long without realising that—well, that I'm not just the man in the street.

PEARL. I always feel I can rely on you.

FENWICK. You couldn't have said anything to please me better. I want you to rely on me. I know you. I'm the only man who's ever understood you. I know that, deep down in that big, beating, human heart of yours, you're a timid, helpless little thing, with the innocence of a child, and you want a man like me to stand between you and the world. My God, how I love you, girlie!

PEARL. Take care, there's the butler.

FENWICK. Oh, damn it, there's always the butler.

[POLE *comes in with a telegram and a parcel of books.*

PEARL. What's that, Pole?

POLE. They're books, my lady. They've just come from Hatchard's.

PEARL. Oh, I know. Undo them, will you? [POLE *cuts open the parcel and takes out a bundle of four or five books.* PEARL *opens the telegram.*] Oh, bother! There's no answer, Pole.

POLE. Very good, my lady. [*Exit.*

FENWICK. Is anything the matter?

PEARL. That fool Sturrey was dining here to-night, and he's just wired to say he can't come. I do hate having my parties upset. I'd asked ten people to meet him.

FENWICK. That's too bad.

PEARL. Pompous owl. He's refused invitation after invitation. I asked him six weeks ago this time, and he hadn't the face to say he was engaged.

FENWICK. Well, I'm afraid you must give him up. I daresay you can do without him.

PEARL. Don't be a fool, Arthur. I'll get hold of him somehow. He may be Prime Minister one of these days. [*She reflects a moment.*] I wonder what his telephone number is. [*She gets up and looks in a book, then sits down at the telephone.*] Gerrard 7035. If he comes once because I force him to he'll come again because he likes it. This house is like the kingdom of heaven: I have to compel them to come in. . . . Is Lord Sturrey in? Lady George Grayston. I'll hold the line. [*Making her voice sweet and charming*] Is that you, Lord Sturrey? It's Pearl Grayston speaking. I just rang up to say it doesn't matter a bit about to-night. Of course, I'm disappointed you can't come. But you must come another day, will you? That's very nice of you. How about this day week? Oh, I'm sorry. Would Thursday suit you? Oh! Well, how about Friday? You're engaged every evening next week? You are in demand. Well, I'll tell you what, get your book and tell me what day you are free.

FENWICK. You're the goods, girlie. You'll get there.

PEARL. Tuesday fortnight. Yes, that'll suit me beautifully. 8.30. I'm so glad you chose that day, because I'm having Kreisler in to play. I shall look forward to seeing you. Good-bye. [*She puts down the receiver.*] This time I've got him. The ape thinks he understands music.

FENWICK. Have you got Kreisler for Tuesday fortnight?

PEARL. No.

FENWICK. Are you sure you can get him?

PEARL. No, but I'm sure you can.

FENWICK. You shall have him, girlie. [*She takes the books that* POLE *brought in and puts them about the room. One she places face downwards, open.*] What are you doing that for?

PEARL. They're Richard Twining's books. He's coming to dinner to-night.

FENWICK. Why d'you trouble about authors, girlie?

PEARL. London isn't like New York, you know. People like to meet them over here.

FENWICK. I should have thought your position was quite strong enough to do without them.

PEARL. We live in a democratic age. They take the place in society of the fools whom kings kept about their Courts in the Middle Ages. They have the advantage that they don't presume on their position to tell one home truths. They're cheap. A dinner and a little flattery is all they want. And they provide their own clothes.

FENWICK. You litter up your house with their rotten books.

PEARL. Oh, but I don't keep them. These are on approval. I shall send them all back to the bookseller to-morrow morning.

FENWICK. Pearl, you're a little wonder. When you want to go into business you come to me and I'll take you into partnership.

PEARL. How is business?

FENWICK. Fine! I'm opening two new branches next week. They laughed at me when I first came over here. They said I'd go bankrupt. I've turned their silly old methods upside down. He laughs longest who laughs last.

PEARL [*reflectively*]. Ah, I can't help thinking that's what my dressmaker said when she sent me in my bill.

[*He gives a slight start and looks at her shrewdly. He sees her blandly smiling.*

FENWICK. Girlie, you promised me you wouldn't run up any more bills.

PEARL. That's like promising to love, honour, and obey one's husband, the kind of undertaking no one is really expected to carry out.

FENWICK. You naughty little thing.

PEARL. It's Suzanne—you know, the dressmaker in the Place Vendôme. The War has dislocated her business and she wants to get her money in. It isn't very convenient for me to pay just at present. It's rather a large sum.

[*She gives him a sheaf of typewritten documents.*

FENWICK. This looks more like a five-act play than a bill.

PEARL. Clothes are expensive, aren't they? I wish I could dress in fig-leaves. It would be cheap, and I believe it would suit me.

FENWICK [*putting the bill in his pocket*]. Well, I'll see what I can do about it.

PEARL. You are a duck, Arthur. . . . Would you like me to come and lunch with you to-morrow?

FENWICK. Why, sure.

PEARL. All right. Now you must go, as I want to lie down before I dress for dinner.

FENWICK. That's right. Take care of yourself, girlie, you're very precious to me.

PEARL. Good-bye, dear old thing.

FENWICK. Good-bye, girlie.

> [*He goes out. As he goes to the door the telephone rings.*
> PEARL *takes up the receiver.*

PEARL. You're speaking to Lady George Grayston. Tony! Of course I knew your voice. Well, what is it? I'm not at all stern. I'm making my voice as pleasant as I can. I'm sorry you find it disagreeable. [*She gives a chuckle.*] No, I'm afraid I couldn't come to tea to-morrow. I shall be engaged all the afternoon. What is the day after to-morrow? [*Smiling*] Well, I must ask Bessie. I don't know if she is free. Of course I'm not coming alone. It would be most compromising. A nice-looking young man like you. What would Minnie say? Oh, I know all about that. . . . I didn't promise anything. I merely said the future was every-body's property. A sleepless night. Fancy! Well, good-bye. . . . Tony, do you know the most enchanting word in the English language? Perhaps.

> [*She puts down the telephone quickly and the curtain falls.*

33. ST JOHN HANKIN (1869–1909)

The Cassilis Engagement

Likewise a 'repertory' and a problem play, *The Cassilis Engagement* deals with a theme not dissimilar to that of Robertson's *Caste*, although a comparison of the earlier with the later comedy will show how far the theatre had travelled in the first decade of this century from the eighties of the last. The problem here is that of the engagement of a youth belonging to a rich family, Geoffrey Cassilis, to a girl, Ethel Borridge, who is the daughter of a defunct bookmaker, and who owns a mother not calculated to harmonize with the polite manners of the county family at Deynham Abbey. Instead, however, of sending Geoffrey into the arms of Ethel, Mrs Cassilis invites the Borridges down to her estate. The result is that, instead of looking with envious eyes at the social world around her, Ethel becomes horrified at the thought that in this atmosphere she may have to spend the rest of her life. She breaks off the engagement and holds to her decision in spite of all her mother's protestations. Once more, in this comedy, reality (or reason) comes to grips with romance. The romantic convention is that the poor adventuress endeavours to ensnare the rich youth; reason, in the guise of comedy, would point out that there are two sides to every question, particularly to a question which romance has put. In *The Cassilis Engagement* St John Hankin does not so much aim at wit as at the depicting of situations amusing because based on the clash of incongruous forces. Topsy-turvyism always leads us to the door of laughter.

EXTRACTS FROM BRITISH & IRISH PLAYS

(*The Cassilis Engagement* was produced by the Stage Society in 1907. The passage below is given by kind permission of the publishers, Messrs Martin Secker, Ltd.)

THE ADVENTURESS IS THREATENED WITH BOREDOM

WARRINGTON. What does Mrs Borridge do?

ETHEL. Lady Marchmont looks after her. I believe she gets a kind of pleasure in leading her on and watching her make a fool of herself. Old cat! And mother sees nothing. She's as pleased with herself as possible. She's actually made Lady Marchmont promise to come and stay with us in London!

WARRINGTON. Bravo, Mrs Borridge!

ETHEL. So I sit here in the drawing-room with a book or the newspaper and I'm bored! bored!

WARRINGTON. And Geoffrey?

ETHEL. He doesn't seem to notice. If I say anything to him about it he just says I'm not *well*! He's very kind and tries to find things to amuse me, but it's a strain. And so it goes on day after day. Heigho!   [*A short silence.*

WARRINGTON. Well, my dear, I admire your courage.

ETHEL [*surprised*]. What do you mean?

WARRINGTON. A lifetime of this! Year in year out. Till you can yawn yourself decently into your grave.

ETHEL [*alarmed*]. But it won't always be like this. We shan't *live* here, Geoff and I.

WARRINGTON. Oh, yes, you will. Mrs Cassilis was talking only at dinner of the little house she was going to furnish for you both down here, just on the edge of the Park. So that you could always be near her.

ETHEL. But Geoff has his profession.

WARRINGTON. His profession is only a name. He makes nothing at it. And never will. Geoffrey's profession is to be a country gentleman and shoot pheasants.

ETHEL. But we shall have a house in London as well.

WARRINGTON [*shaking his head*]. Not you. As long as his mother lives Geoffrey will be dependent on her, you know. He has nothing worth calling an income of his own. And he's proud. He won't accept more from her than he's obliged even if her trustees would allow her to hand over anything substantial to him on his marriage —which they wouldn't.

ETHEL [*defiantly*]. I shall refuse to live down here.

WARRINGTON. My dear, you won't be asked. You'll have to live where Mrs Cassilis provides a house for you. Besides, Geoff will prefer it. He likes the country, and he's devoted to his mother.

ETHEL. Phew!

426

WARRINGTON. Happily, it won't last for ever. I dare say you'll have killed poor Mrs Cassilis off in a dozen years or so. Though you never know how long people will last nowadays, by the way. These modern doctors are the devil.

ETHEL. Kill her off? What do you mean? I don't want to kill Mrs Cassilis. I like her.

WARRINGTON [*looking at her in genuine astonishment*]. My dear young lady, you don't suppose you'll be able to *stand* this sort of thing, do you? Oh, no. You'll kick over the traces, and there'll be no end of a scandal, and Geoff'll blow his brains out— if he's got any—and she'll break her heart, and that'll be the end of it.

ETHEL [*fiercely*]. It won't.

WARRINGTON. Oh, yes, it will. You don't know what County Society is. The dulness of it! How it eats into your bones. I do.

ETHEL. Does it bore *you*, too?

WARRINGTON. Bore? It bores me to *tears*! I'm not a bad lot, really. At least no worse than most middle-aged bachelors. But Julia thinks me an utterly abandoned character, and I take care not to undeceive her. Why? Because I find Milverton so intolerable. I used to come down every Christmas. One of those ghastly family reunions. A sort of wake without the corpse. At last I couldn't stand it, and did something perfectly outrageous. I forget what. But I know the servants all gave warning. So now I'm supposed to be thoroughly disreputable, and that ass Remenham won't have me asked to the house. Thank heaven for that!

ETHEL. But Geoff likes the country.

WARRINGTON. I dare say. But Geoffrey and I are different. So are Geoffrey and you. You and I are town birds. He's a country bumpkin. *I* know the breed!

ETHEL [*in horror*]. And I shall have to stand this all my life! All my life! [*Savagely*] I won't! I won't!

WARRINGTON [*calmly*]. You will!

ETHEL. I won't, I tell you! [WARRINGTON *shrugs.*] It's too sickening. [*Pause. She seems to think for a moment, then grasps him by the arm, and speaks eagerly, dropping her voice, and looking cautiously over towards the others.*] I say, let's go off to Paris, you and I, and leave all this. It'd be awful fun.

WARRINGTON [*appalled, rising*]. Hush! Hush! For God's sake. Julia'll hear.

ETHEL [*almost in a whisper*]. Never mind. What does it matter? Let's go. You'd enjoy it like anything. We'd have no end of a good time.

WARRINGTON [*shaking himself free, desperately*]. My dear young lady, haven't I just told you that I'm not that sort at all? I'm a perfectly respectable person, of rather austere morality than otherwise.

EXTRACTS FROM BRITISH & IRISH PLAYS

ETHEL. Rot! You'll come? *[Grasping his arm again.*

WARRINGTON. No, I won't. I decline. I can't go off with the girl my host is going to marry. It wouldn't be decent. Besides, I don't want to go off with anybody.

ETHEL [*her spirits dropping to zero*]. You won't?

WARRINGTON [*testily*]. No, I won't. And, for goodness' sake, speak lower. Julia's listening with all her ears.

ETHEL [*with a bitter little laugh*]. Poor Major Warrington! How I scared you!

WARRINGTON. I should say you did. I'm not so young as I was. A few years ago, a little thing like that never made me turn a hair. Now I can't stand it.

[*Subsiding into chair, and wiping the perspiration from his brow.*

ETHEL. You've gone through it before, then?

WARRINGTON. More than once, my dear.

ETHEL [*dismally*]. And now *you'll* look down on me, too.

WARRINGTON [*trying to cheer her up*]. On the contrary, I admire you immensely. In fact, I don't know which I admire more, your pluck or your truly marvellous self-control. To ask me to go off with you without letting Julia hear! [*Looking anxiously towards her*] It was masterly.

ETHEL [*sighs*]. Well, I suppose I shall have to marry Geoff after all.

WARRINGTON. I suppose so. Unless you could go off with the Rector.

[*She laughs shrilly. The two ladies turn sharply and glare.*

ETHEL. Now I've shocked your sister again.

WARRINGTON. You have. She thinks I'm flirting with you. That means I shan't be asked down to Milverton for another five years. Thank heaven for that!

34. ASHLEY DUKES (*born* 1885)

The Man with a Load of Mischief

The intrigue loved in olden comedy and the atmosphere of those times have come to have a special appeal to twentieth-century authors, readers, and audiences. Restoration comedies are revived; the eighteenth-century drama is not entirely forgotten; and many novelists take the period from 1660 to the introduction of railways as their happy hunting-ground. Something of this new taste is reflected in Mr Ashley Dukes' cynically romantic comedy *The Man with a Load of Mischief*. His scene is a room in a wayside inn; his time is any time when men used horses only to convey them from one place to another, when a prince's coach might be conveniently misdirected on the road to

428

THE MODERN PERIOD

Oxford, when manners were polite and intrigue was in the air. The characters themselves are nameless. It is sufficient here to say that the Lady, pursued by the Nobleman, ends by galloping off over the crest of the downs with the Man—for whom in her heart love has awakened.

(*The Man with a Load of Mischief* was produced in 1924. The passage quoted is taken from the edition of the same year, by kind permission of the author and of the publishers, Messrs Ernest Benn, Ltd., London, and Messrs Doubleday, Doran and Company, Inc., Garden City, New York.)

THE MEETING

MAN. There are highwaymen in these parts. One of them swung on the gibbet across your road.

LADY. That was the unhappy occasion of our meeting. I shall not forget it—this skeleton haunts me still. That men can be so barbarous!

MAN. If my lady fears that she may be followed from Bath, I can tell her that the danger is past.

LADY [*with spirit*]. *You* can tell me?

MAN. The Prince's coach has been directed by the highroad to Oxford.

LADY. Misdirected?

MAN. As my lady pleases.

LADY. Who has done this? Who are you, sir?

MAN. I am a friend.

LADY. Have I a friend? I must take it on trust, for plainly you know me.

MAN. I know you better than I know myself.

LADY. Here are deep waters indeed. I do not remember your face.

MAN. It is five years since my lady was a singer at Covent Garden Playhouse.

LADY. And you were—— ?

MAN. I was one of the gallery.

LADY. The gallery to whom I sang. [*With a smile*] So I meet with an unknown admirer?

MAN. Those are empty words.

LADY. True. Those are empty words. I think, sir, you are not an admirer.

MAN. I am a friend.

LADY. Only five years, can it be? It seems half a lifetime. I have travelled far since then. The music has run out of my horses' hoofs.

MAN. It is in the earth, where nothing is lost.

LADY. You speak my thoughts. [*Rising*] Who are you, sir? What is this place?

MAN. It is a simple alehouse called " The Man with a Load of Mischief."

LADY. Another man. God save us, I am weary of them. O, I will not play the weak woman with you. The pretence of weakness is our hypocrisy. Frailty is a pretty word to please our masters. [*A silence.*] So the Prince takes the wrong turning—outriders, coach and all?

MAN. He will pass in the night.

LADY. Outriders, coach and all. There's a chapter closed. Put not your trust in princes. [*A silence.*] You know that I was his mistress?

MAN. So much every one knows.

LADY. Ask me why I chose that trade of all trades.

MAN. My lady has seen the world.

LADY. A sort of world. Too many fops and their tailors, too few men. Too many wits and too little honesty. Too many bottles and too little entertainment. A lackey's paradise.

MAN. My lady speaks to a lackey.

LADY. Then I ask your pardon. A nobleman's paradise. A dunghill sprouting sword-grass, a hedgerow rank with lords and ladies. No fruitful earth.

MAN. The world is as we make it.

LADY. Have we made that? I think that you and I are in league against our betters.

MAN. My lady must speak for herself.

LADY. O, my friend, no more of my lady! and no more talk of what is dead and done with. Our wits were given us to hide our hearts. [*A silence.*] Now I have spoken too freely. Your Man with a Load of Mischief carries a gun on his shoulder.

MAN. It will not go off unless you fear him.

LADY. I fear nothing, but I have more pride than you suppose.

MAN. I understand. Your ladyship forgot for a moment that you were speaking with a servant.

LADY. Believe me, I trust you.

MAN. Good servants are made to be trusted. Trust is less than I ask.

LADY. You are proud too. I should have known it. Listen——

MAN. My lord is coming.

LADY. That man!

> [*Re-enter the* NOBLEMAN, *and from the other side the* INN-
> KEEPER *and his* WIFE, *bringing their bowl of roses.
> The* MAN *assists them at the table. The* NOBLEMAN
> *crosses over to where the* LADY *is seated.*

NOBLEMAN. So, madam, you will sup with me. This is an honour indeed.

LADY. Call it rather the payment of a debt, my lord.

NOBLEMAN. To a man whose debts are unpaid, your integrity is overwhelming. Such obligations are made to be forgotten.

430

LADY. Always excepting debts of honour?

NOBLEMAN. We pay those from necessity. The bailiffs are on the spot.

LADY. And our supper on the table. Well, hunger spells necessity. I am famished.

> [*During the foregoing the* MAID *has descended.*

NOBLEMAN. Is all ready, Charles?

MAN. My lord and my lady, supper is served.

> [*The* NOBLEMAN *and the* LADY *seat themselves at the table, the* MAN *and the* MAID *taking post behind their chairs*.

LADY. It was thoughtful of you, my lord, to choose these flowers.

NOBLEMAN [*indifferently*]. The roses? Ah, to be sure. They are in season.

LADY. By your leave, I will take one of them.

35. W. A. DARLINGTON (*born* 1890)

Alf's Button

Farce, along with tragedy and comedy, seems to have gained new life in the modern period. It is, of course, difficult to make a strict line of demarcation between certain forms of comedy and certain forms of farce, but in general one may define a farce as a type of comedy in which an impossibility is postulated at the beginning and is followed out logically to the end. In that hilarious farce *It Pays to Advertise* a youth establishes a gigantic soap-manufacturing firm in a few weeks by aid of a recipe in a cookery-book and a thousand pounds for advertisements. This we might call the impossibility of the real. In Mr Darlington's farce we have the impossibility of the unreal. A soldier in the trenches rubs one of his buttons and a *djinn* appears to fulfil his wishes, howsoever ridiculous or extravagant these may be. This introduction of the impossibility of the unreal corresponds with the general tendency in the latest modern drama to escape from pure naturalism. It is a tendency seen on all sides, manifesting itself in all forms of dramatic art from poetic tragedy to comedy and farce, for the mingling of mortal and supermundane forces may be used either for the creation of a majestic atmosphere or, as here, for the simpler purposes of fun. In tragedy the supermundane is harmonized with the real, so that, in a mood of idealism, we see the two fused into one; in *Alf's Button* laughter is raised by the separation of the two, by the contrast instituted between Alf and Bill on the one hand and the Djinn with his attendants on the other.

(*Alf's Button* was produced in 1924. The passage here quoted is taken, by kind permission of the author and of the publishers, Messrs Herbert Jenkins, Ltd., from the edition of 1925.)

ALF IS STRUCK PINK

BILL. Think they'll ever make me an officer, Alf?

ALF [*comfortably*]. I shouldn't worry if I was you.

[*Here the unaccustomed Burgundy begins to take effect on
       BILL. He eyes his cigarette with an air of disillusion.*

BILL. Tastes funny!

ALF. I like 'em all right.   [*Pause.*

BILL. Smells funny!

ALF. I like 'em all right.

[BILL *has another puff, and throws his cigarette away.*

BILL. I'd like to find the bloke as made 'em.

ALF [*resuming his polishing operations*]. I like 'em all right.

BILL [*rising with solemnity*]. Excuse me, Alf.

[ALF *rises and bows with equal solemnity. BILL lurches
       unsteadily into the billet.*

ALF [*sitting down, and transferring his button-stick to the second
button of his tunic*]. Good thing Bill didn't join the Navy. . . .
Lord, I wish something would 'appen!

[*He begins to polish—and gets his wish. There is a rumble
       and a flash, and a moment's darkness, after which
       you can see a large green DJINN standing behind ALF,
       who is still polishing, unaware that he is no longer
       alone. He takes the cigarette from his lips and eyes it
       curiously.*

ALF. Bill was right—they *do* smell funny!

[*He turns round and sees the DJINN. He utters a yell of
       terror, and shrinks away. His hand encounters the
       Burgundy bottle, and he mutters to himself, "Lumme,
       I mustn't have any more of this."*

DJINN [*bowing and speaking in a sepulchral voice*]. What wouldst
thou have? I am ready to obey thee as thy slave, and the slave
of any who have that Button in their possession. I, and the other
slaves of that Button.

ALF [*appalled*]. Well, strike me pink!

DJINN. Strike thee pink? Verily, my lord's command is strange!
Nevertheless, I hear and obey.

[*He makes a gesture towards* ALF, *who immediately turns
       a brilliant pink colour. The* DJINN *vanishes.*

[BILL *enters from the billet.*

BILL. I feels a bit better now. I . . . [*He sees* ALF *and staggers
back.*] Lor' lumme!

ALF [*startled*]. What's the matter, Bill?

BILL. Matter? Look at yourself!

ALF [*looking at his hands, and realising his plight for the first time*].
What's 'appened?

BILL. Why, you must 'ave got measles an' scarlet fever an'
smallpox an'—an' nettle-rash all mixed up! D'yer *feel* bad?

432

ALF. No. No more'n usual. [*Terrified*] Bill, what's the matter with me?

BILL. That's for the doctor to say, if I can find him. You wait 'ere.

> [*He dashes off in quest of the M.O. ALF left alone, gets a bit of glass from his pack and examines his face despondently. He feels his pulse, looks at his tongue, and shakes his head. Then he notices his tunic still lying on the ground and picks it up. He finds the buttonstick still in position. He looks at this with a dawning idea that it may have something to do with his adventure. He sits down and scratches his head thoughtfully.*]

ALF [*aloud*]. I *wonder*! That spook said something about a button!

> [*He picks up his toothbrush and makes as if to rub the button, but hesitates. After a struggle with himself, however, he rubs it. The DJINN immediately reappears.*]

DJINN. What wouldst thou have?

ALF. It *is* the button.

DJINN. I am ready to obey thee as thy slave, and the slave of any that have that Button in their possession. I, and the other slaves of the Button.

ALF. Look 'ere, was it *you* turned me this ruddy colour?

DJINN. Indeed, master, with thine own lips thou didst command me to strike thee pink.

ALF. Oh! . . . Well, if that's your idea of a joke, it ain't mine, that's all. You can just blinkin' well think again, if you want to make *me* laugh. See?

DJINN [*not understanding*]. Thy wish is my command. What wouldst thou have? I am ready to obey thee as thy slave. . . .

ALF. Oh, stop it. I didn't *want* yer to turn me pink. 'Tain't likely I should ask yer to do a silly thing like that. Put me right for the Lord's sake!

> [*The DJINN waves his arms. ALF turns his normal colour, to his great joy.*]

DJINN. Has the great master any further commands for his servant?

ALF. N-no. . . . 'Ere, tell me. 'Ow do you come to be my servant?

DJINN. Lord, I am chief of the slaves of the Button that was aforetime the Lamp. Whosoever may be Lord of the Button, him do I serve and perform all his will—I, and the other slaves of the Button.

ALF. And 'ave I got to be your master? [DJINN *bows*.] Well, I dunno 'ow we shall get on, but if I must, I s'pose I must. Where was your last place?

DJINN [*puzzled*]. Master?

ALF [*trying to translate it into the Oriental idiom*]. 'Oo didst you— thou—servedst before you comest to me?

2 E

DJINN. The great prince, 'Ala-ad-deen.

ALF. Never 'eard of 'im. Prince 'oo?

DJINN. 'Ala-ad-deen.

ALF. Oh! I see! You mean Aladdin—the pantomime feller. 'E 'ad a lamp, I remember. Lumme you must be gettin' on in years.

DJINN. Many centuries was I the slave of the Lamp, great master; until men came that melted the Lamp to a boiling liquid, and made of it thy Button. Now, therefore, am I the slave of that Button.

ALF. And what's yer name, cocky?

DJINN. 'Abdulkindeelil'ajeeb was I aforetime, O master, but now I am called 'Abdulzirril'ajeeb.

ALF. Gorblimey, I can never remember that. I shall call you Eustace.

EUSTACE [pleased]. In truth, it is a beautiful name from a beautiful master.

ALF. Beautiful! That's good—I must tell Bill that! . . . 'Op it now, there's somebody coming.

[EUSTACE vanishes, as BILL enters with SERGEANT LEES.

SERGEANT. Well! Now what's the matter? Are you ill?

ALF. Er . . . er. . . .

SERGEANT. Stand to attention when you talk to me. Put your tunic on! Go on!

[He stands over ALF to superintend this operation; then he stands back and surveys him.

You're all right. [He turns to BILL.] He ain't ill.

BILL [on the defensive]. I tell yer 'e was all pink, with eyes like a guinea-pig.

SERGEANT [with a dark suspicion that he is having his lordly leg pulled]. I've 'ad enough of you two. Any more of this an' I'll stop yer bloomin' leave!

36. LADY GREGORY (born 1852)

The Full Moon

Infinite have been the approaches made to Irish life and character, the peculiar atmosphere of Irish life and the misery of the country having provided many dramatists with opportunities for the presentation both of comedy and of tragedy. This dramatic exploitation of national themes has, of course, flourished with the Abbey Theatre of Dublin, and no one has been more deeply identified with the particular experiment, or with the larger movement to which it is so closely linked, than Lady Gregory. Lady Gregory can see both the humour and the sadness in the life of her native land. A kind of folk-history play

434

has developed under her hands, and the poignancy lying in the lives of the poor has been profoundly expressed in some of her writings. Possibly, however, it is in the sphere of comedy, particularly in the range of that mood which we call humour, that Lady Gregory's art has most felicitously found utterance. She loves her characters, yet can see in them all their foibles and all their follies. The strange mixture of shrewdness and simplicity which appears to dwell in the Irish nature has hardly been better displayed than in her pages. The language she uses is a modification of that literary dialect which owed its invention to Synge. Her sentences are a trifle more peculiar than his, yet there is an attempt made to keep even closer to reality. *The Full Moon*, which is represented here, resembles, like so much of her work, an old interlude. It has practically no action, but depends upon the character of the persons as revealed in their conversation. There is a talk of a mad dog, and of the dangers of hydrophobia, but the main interest of the piece comes from the *naïve* reflections of the group gathered in the little railway-shed, and in their gossiping discussions.

(The passage given below is taken from *New Comedies* (1913), by kind permission of Messrs G. P. Putnam's Sons, London and New York.)

The Fear of the Dog

BARTLEY FALLON *gives a deep groan.*

SHAWN EARLY. What is on you, Bartley?

BARTLEY FALLON. I'm in dread it is I myself has got the venom into my blood.

HYACINTH HALVEY. What makes you think that?

BARTLEY FALLON. It's a sort of a thing would be apt to happen me, and any malice to fall within the town at all.

MRS BRODERICK. Give heed to him, Hyacinth Halvey; you are the most man we have to baffle any wrong thing coming in our midst!

HYACINTH HALVEY. Is it that you are feeling any pain as of a wound or a sore?

BARTLEY FALLON. Some sort of a little catch I'm thinking there is in under my knee. I would feel no pain unless I would turn it contrary.

HYACINTH HALVEY. What class of feeling would you say you are feeling?

BARTLEY FALLON. I am feeling as if the five fingers of my hand to be lessening from me, the same as five farthing dips the heat of the sun would be sweating the tallow from.

HYACINTH HALVEY. That is a strange account.

BARTLEY FALLON. And a sort of a megrim in my head, the same as a sheep would get a fit of staggers in a field.

435

EXTRACTS FROM BRITISH & IRISH PLAYS

HYACINTH HALVEY. That is what I would look for. Is there some sort of a roaring in your ear?

BARTLEY FALLON. There is, there is, as if I would hear voices would be talking.

HYACINTH HALVEY. Would you feel any wish to go tearing and destroying?

BARTLEY FALLON. I would indeed, and there is to be an enemy upon my path. Would you say now, Widow Broderick, am I getting anyway flushy in the face?

MRS BRODERICK. Don' leave your eye off him for pity's sake. He is reddening as red as a rose.

BARTLEY FALLON. I could as if walk on the wind with lightness. Something that is rising in my veins the same as froth would be rising on a pint.

HYACINTH HALVEY. It is the doctor I'd best call for—and maybe the sergeant and the priest.

BARTLEY FALLON. There are three thoughts going through my mind—to hang myself or to drown myself, or to cut my neck with a reaping-hook.

MRS BRODERICK. It is the doctor will serve him best, where it is the mad blood that should be bled away. To break up eggs, the white of them, in a tin can, will put new blood in him, and whiskey, and to taste no food through twenty-one days.

BARTLEY FALLON. I'm thinking so long a fast wouldn't serve me. I wouldn't wish the lads will bear my body to the grave, to lay down there was nothing within but a grasshopper or a wisp of dry grass.

SHAWN EARLY. No, but to cut a piece out of his leg the doctor will, the way the poison will get no leave to work.

PETER TANNIAN. Or to burn it with red-hot irons, the way it will not scatter itself and grow. There does a doctor do that out in foreign.

MRS BRODERICK. It would be more natural to cut the leg off him in some sort of a Christian way.

SHAWN EARLY. If it was a pig was bit, or a sow or a bonav, it to show the signs, it would be shot, if it was a whole fleet of them was in it.

MRS BRODERICK. I knew of a man that was butler in a big house was bit, and they tied him first and smothered him after, and his master shot the dog. A splendid shot he was ; the thing he'd not see he'd hit it the same as the thing he'd see. I heard that from an outside neighbour of my own, a woman that told no lies.

SHAWN EARLY. Sure, they did the same thing to a high-up lady over in England, and she after being bit by her own little spaniel and it having a ring around its neck.

PETER TANNIAN. That is the only best thing to do. Whether the bite is from a dog, or a cat, or whatever it may be, to put the quilt and the blankets on the person and smother him in the bed. To smother them out-and-out you should, before the madness will work.

436

HYACINTH HALVEY. I'd be loth he to be shot or smothered. I'd sooner give him a chance in the asylum.

MRS BRODERICK. To keep him there and to try him through three changes of the moon. It's well for you, Bartley, Mr Halvey being in charge of you, that is known to be a tender man.

PETER TANNIAN. He to have got a bite and to go biting others, he would put in them the same malice. It is the old people used to tell that down, and they must have had some reason doing that.

SHAWN EARLY. To get a bite of a dog you must chance your life. There is no doubt at all about that. It might work till the time of the new moon or the full moon, and then they must be shot or smothered.

HYACINTH HALVEY. It is a pity there to be no cure found for it in the world.

SHAWN EARLY. There never came out from the Almighty any cure for a mad dog.

[BARTLEY FALLON *has been edging towards door.*

SHAWN EARLY. Oh! stop him and keep a hold of him, Mr Halvey!

HYACINTH HALVEY. Stop where you are.

BARTLEY FALLON. Isn't it enough to have madness before me, that you will not let me go fall in my own choice place?

HYACINTH HALVEY. The neighbours would think it bad of me to let a raving man out into their midst.

BARTLEY FALLON. Is it to shoot me you are going?

HYACINTH HALVEY. I will call to the doctor to say is the padded room at the workhouse the most place where you will be safe, till such time as it will be known did the poison wear away.

BARTLEY FALLON. I will not go in it! It is likely I might be forgot in it, or the nurses to be in dread to bring me nourishment, and they to hear me barking within the door. I'm thinking it was allotted by nature I never would die an easy death.

HYACINTH HALVEY. I will keep a watch over you myself.

BARTLEY FALLON. Where's the use of that the time the breath will be gone out of me, and you may be playing cards on my coffin, and I having nothing around or about me but the shroud, and the habit, and the little board?

37. OSCAR WILDE (1856–1900)

The Importance of Being Earnest

Wilde's plays have been both over- and under-rated. No one can justifiably claim that they are masterpieces of dramatic art, but, if it is impossible thus to place them in the front rank, it is equally impossible to suggest, as has been done, that they have hardly any real or historic significance. Looking back with true perspective, we can see that they form an interesting link between the new and the old, and that, antiquated though they may seem to be, they are among the first of wholly 'modern' comedies.

EXTRACTS FROM BRITISH & IRISH PLAYS

Wilde had in him many characters, and these characters for the most part he kept distinct. There is the Wilde who wrote the decadent poetry, and there is the Wilde who wrote the sentimentally realistic *Ballad of Reading Gaol*; there is also the Wilde who, reverting back for inspiration to the style of the comedy of manners, strove to establish on the modern stage a type of drama which should provide, through the medium of an epigrammatic prose, an idealized picture of the society life of his day. It is certainly true that Wilde's comedies are dated; it is equally true that, viewed alongside some more recent productions in a similar style, they may seem unduly sentimental and artificial. These facts, however, cannot take from the one cardinal fact that in Wilde's plays we see clearly outlined both the medium and the atmosphere of the modern comedy of manners, itself, as is plainly evident, a descendant—or rather a reborn form—of the comedy of the Restoration.

(*The Importance of Being Earnest* was produced in 1895. The extract given below is published by kind permission of Messrs Methuen and Co., Ltd.)

A QUESTION OF NAMES

Enter MERRIMAN.

MERRIMAN. Miss Fairfax.

[*Enter* GWENDOLYN. *Exit* MERRIMAN.

CECILY. Pray let me introduce myself. My name is Cecily Cardew.

GWENDOLYN [*moving to her and shaking hands*]. Cecily Cardew! What a very sweet name! Something tells me we are going to be great friends. I like you already more than I can say.

CECILY. How nice of you to like me so much after we have known each other such a comparatively short time! Pray sit down.

GWENDOLYN [*still standing up*]. I may call you Cecily, may I not?

CECILY. With pleasure.

GWENDOLYN. And you will always call me Gwendolyn, won't you?

CECILY. If you wish.

GWENDOLYN. Then that is all quite settled, is it not?

CECILY. I hope so. [*They both sit down together.*

GWENDOLYN. Perhaps this might be a favourable opportunity for my mentioning who I am. My father is Lord Bracknell. You are here on a short visit, I suppose.

CECILY. Oh, no, I live here. I am Mr Worthing's ward.

GWENDOLYN. Oh! It is strange that he never mentioned to me that he had a ward. I am very fond of you, Cecily. But I am bound to state that now that I know that you are Mr Worthing's ward, I cannot help expressing a wish you were—well, just a little older

438

than you seem to be—and not quite so very alluring in appearance. Ernest has a strong, upright nature. But even men of the noblest possible moral character are extremely susceptible to the influence of the physical charms of others.

CECILY. I beg your pardon, Gwendolyn, did you say Ernest?

GWENDOLYN. Yes.

CECILY. Oh, but it is not Mr Ernest Worthing who is my guardian. It is his brother—his elder brother.

GWENDOLYN. Ernest never mentioned to me that he had a brother. You are quite sure that it is not Mr Ernest Worthing who is your guardian?

CECILY. Quite sure. [*A pause.*] In fact, I am going to be his——

GWENDOLYN. I beg your pardon?

CECILY. Dearest Gwendolyn, Mr Ernest Worthing and I are engaged to be married.

GWENDOLYN [*quite politely, rising*]. My darling Cecily, I think there must be some slight error. Mr Ernest Worthing is engaged to me.

CECILY [*very politely, rising*]. I am afraid you must be under some misconception. Ernest proposed to me exactly ten minutes ago.

GWENDOLYN. It is certainly very curious, for he asked me to be his wife yesterday afternoon at five-thirty.

CECILY. It would distress me more than I can tell you, dear Gwendolyn, if it caused you any mental or physical anguish, but I feel bound to point out that since Ernest proposed to you he clearly has changed his mind.

GWENDOLYN [*meditatively*]. If the poor fellow has been entrapped into any foolish promise I shall consider it my duty to rescue him at once, and with a firm hand.

CECILY [*thoughtfully and sadly*]. Whatever unfortunate entanglement my dear boy may have got into, I will never reproach him with it after we are married.

GWENDOLYN. Do you allude to me, Miss Cardew, as an entanglement? You are presumptuous. On an occasion of this kind it becomes more than a moral duty to speak one's mind. It becomes a pleasure.

CECILY. Do you suggest, Miss Fairfax, that I entrapped Ernest into an engagement? How dare you? This is no time for wearing the hollow mask of manners. When I see a spade I call it a spade.

GWENDOLYN. I am glad to say that I have never seen a spade.

[*Enter* MERRIMAN, *to lay tea.*

MERRIMAN. Shall I lay tea here as usual, miss?

CECILY [*sternly, in a calm voice*]. Yes, as usual.

[*He does so.* CECILY *and* GWENDOLYN *glare at each other.*

CECILY. May I offer you some tea, Miss Fairfax?

GWENDOLYN [*with elaborate politeness*]. Thank you. [*Aside*] Detestable girl! But I require tea!

439

CECILY. Sugar?

GWENDOLYN. No, thank you.   Sugar is not fashionable any more.
[CECILY *puts in four lumps.*

CECILY. Cake or bread and butter ?

GWENDOLYN. Bread and butter, please.   Cake is rarely seen in the best houses nowadays.

CECILY [*cutting a very large slice of cake and putting it on a plate*]. Hand that to Miss Fairfax.

[MERRIMAN *does so and goes out.* GWENDOLYN *drinks the tea, and makes a grimace.   Puts down cup, reaches out for her bread and butter, and finds it is cake.   Rises in indignation.*

GWENDOLYN. You have filled my tea with lumps of sugar, and though I asked most distinctly for bread and butter, you have given me cake.   I warn you, Miss Cardew, you may go too far.   From the first moment I saw you I distrusted you.   [*Enter* JACK.

GWENDOLYN. Ernest!   My own Ernest!

JACK. Gwendolyn!   Darling!   [*Offers to kiss her.*

GWENDOLYN. A moment! May I ask if you are engaged to be married to this young lady?

JACK. To dear little Cecily?   Of course not !

GWENDOLYN. Thank you.   You may !
[*Offers her cheek, and* JACK *kisses her.*

CECILY. I knew there must be some misunderstanding, Miss Fairfax. That is Mr John Worthing, my guardian. [*Enter* ALGERNON.]   Here is Ernest.

ALGERNON [*going straight to* CECILY *without noticing anyone else*]. My own love!   [*Offers to kiss her.*

CECILY. A moment, Ernest !   May I ask you—are you engaged to be married to this young lady?

ALGERNON [*looking round*]. To what young lady? Gwendolyn! Of course not!

CECILY. Thank you.   You may.
[*Offers her cheek, and* ALGERNON *kisses her.*

GWENDOLYN. I felt there was some slight error, Miss Cardew. That is my cousin, Mr Algernon Moncrieff.

CECILY. Oh! [*Breaking away.*]   Are you called Algernon?

ALGERNON. I cannot deny it.   [*The two girls go to each other.*

GWENDOLYN. Is your name really John?

JACK. I could deny it if I liked.   I could deny anything if I liked. But my name certainly is John.   It has been John for years.

CECILY [*to* GWENDOLYN]. A gross deception has been practised on both of us.

INDEX

441

443

INDEX

INDEX

445

INDEX